OUR WORLD HISTORY

By C. E. BLACK

Professor of History, Princeton University

Based on *World History* by SMITH, MUZZEY, LLOYD

GINN AND COMPANY

BOSTON · NEW YORK · CHICAGO · ATLANTA · DALLAS · PALO ALTO · TORONTO · LONDON

Acknowledgments: This book is in the direct line of descent and is derived from *World History* by Smith, Muzzey, Lloyd, as adapted from *Our World Today and Yesterday* by James Harvey Robinson, Emma Peters Smith, and James Henry Breasted, to whom appreciation is acknowledged herewith.

Meet the People Who Made Our World History
This is how they dressed. In the fascinating story which follows we shall learn much more about them. And in the process we may better understand ourselves—for they are our ancestors.

Table of Contents

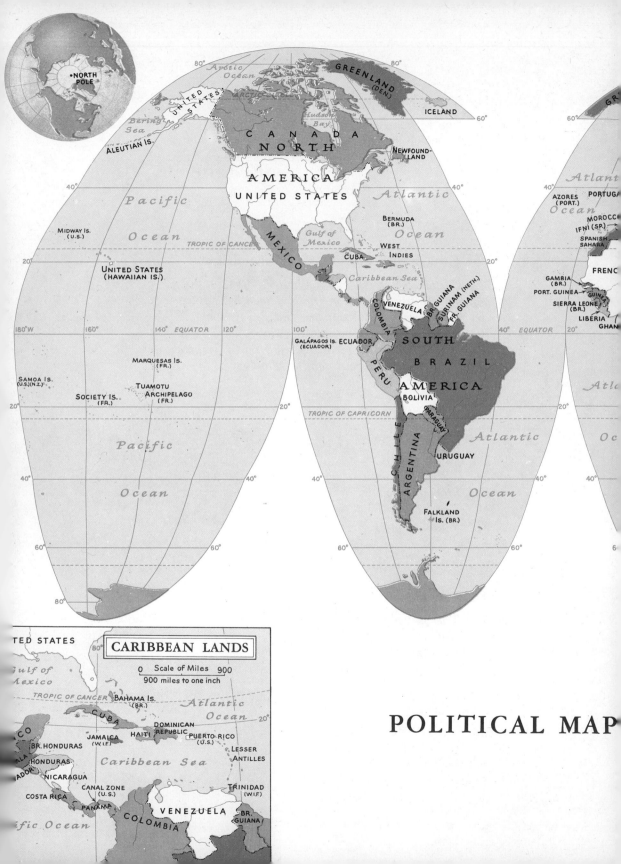

NORTH POLE

Arctic Ocean

GREENLAND (DEN.)

ICELAND

UNITED STATES

Bering Sea

ALEUTIAN IS.

ARCTIC CIRCLE

Hudson Bay

CANADA

NORTH

AMERICA

UNITED STATES

Newfound-land

Atlantic

Ocean

BERMUDA (BR.)

Pacific

Ocean

MIDWAY IS. (U.S.)

TROPIC OF CANCER

Gulf of Mexico

WEST INDIES

CUBA

Caribbean Sea

MEXICO

UNITED STATES (HAWAIIAN IS.)

VENEZUELA

BR. GUIANA
SUR INAM (NETH.)
FR. GUIANA

COLOMBIA

GALÁPAGOS IS. ECUADOR
(ECUADOR)

ECUADOR

180°W   160°   140°   EQUATOR   120°   100°   40°   EQUATOR   20°

SOUTH

BRAZIL

AMERICA

PERU

BOLIVIA

MARQUESAS IS. (FR.)

SAMOA IS. (U.S.)(N.Z.)

TUAMOTU ARCHIPELAGO (FR.)

SOCIETY IS. (FR.)

TROPIC OF CAPRICORN

PARAGUAY

Pacific

CHILE

ARGENTINA

URUGUAY

Atlantic

Ocean

Ocean

FALKLAND IS. (BR.)

80°

AZORES (PORT.)   PORTUGAL

Atlant

Ocean

MOROCCO
IFNI (SP.)
SPANISH SAHARA

GAMBIA (BR.)
PORT. GUINEA
SIERRA LEONE (BR.)
LIBERIA

FRENC

GUINEA
GHAN

Atla

Oc

POLITICAL MAP

TED STATES

Gulf of Mexico

TROPIC OF CANCER   BAHAMA IS. (BR.)

Atlantic Ocean

CUBA

DOMINICAN REPUBLIC

HAITI   PUERTO RICO (U.S.)

JAMAICA (W.I.F.)

LESSER ANTILLES

BR. HONDURAS

HONDURAS

NICARAGUA

Caribbean Sea

COSTA RICA

CANAL ZONE (U.S.)

PANAMA

TRINIDAD (W.I.F.)

VENEZUELA

BR. GUIANA

COLOMBIA

ific Ocean

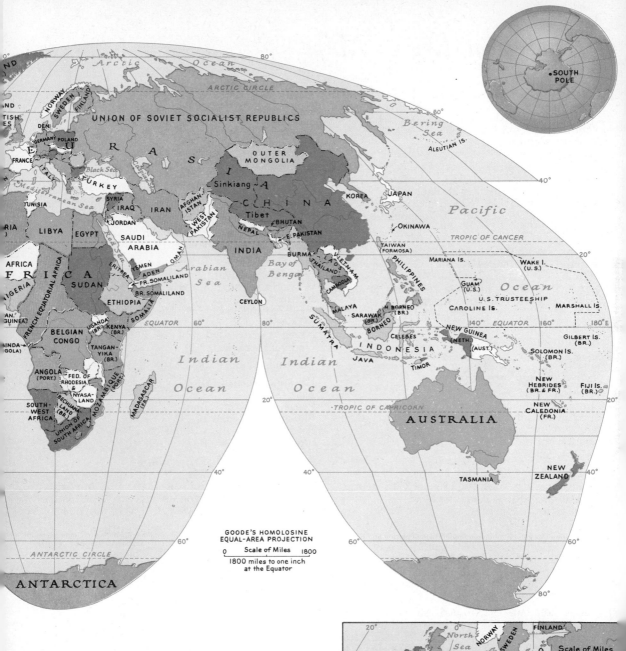

Alphabetical Key to Maps

Why Every Student Should Study

WORLD HISTORY

1. To understand how the present came to be.
2. To develop a sense of time and place.
3. To enjoy the drama of history as it unfolds.
4. To meet the heroic men and women who shaped our heritage.
5. To find causes for the rise and fall of nations.
6. To be able to apply historic principles to present problems.
7. To gain perspective for American history.
8. To appreciate the progress man has made.
9. To benefit from the experiences of the past.
10. To help make this a better world.

"The supreme purpose of history is a better world. Yesterday's records can keep us from repeating yesterday's mistakes."

—HERBERT HOOVER

Teacher-Pupil Aids

Each chapter contains an introduction, outline, key words and dates, timeline, reading guide questions, activities, and an annotated bibliography. The *Chapter Exercises* are by Leola M. Stewart, Chairman of Social Studies Department, Lakewood, Ohio, High School. Available also are a *Workbook for Pupils* by Minnie Lloyd, formerly head of history department, Shortridge, Indianapolis, High School; *Manual for Teachers* by Geraldine Workman, television teacher, Kansas City, Missouri, Public Schools; *Unit and Final Tests* by William R. Spears, Supervisor, Denver, Colorado, Public Schools.

The Ancient World

4000 B.C.   500 A.D.

B.C.   A.D.

4000   2000

THOUSANDS OF YEARS AGO primitive people lived without language, tools, or fire. They gathered their food where they found it. They were at the mercy of the cold, the rain, and the wind. Gradually they developed speech, tools, and weapons. They domesticated animals and grains, and learned to live together in settled communities. Here is the cornerstone of our civilization.

In four fertile river valleys (the Nile, Tigris-Euphrates, Indus, and Hwang Ho) especially great progress was made. The Stone Age Egyptians built settled communities on the banks of the Nile. They erected majestic buildings and monuments. Beautiful objects of art were created. Beginnings were made in science and mathematics. A means of writing was devised. Religion and well-organized governments were begun.

Along the banks of the Tigris and Euphrates rivers other people were learning and creating. Much that they produced in this Fertile Crescent is part of our world today: the wheel, the use of iron, the alphabet, the idea of one God, and the first written code of laws.

Traders carried the ideas from Egypt and the Fertile Crescent to the islands of the Aegean Sea, and thence to the European mainland. Then Greek barbarians, moving down from the north, conquered the civilized Aegean peoples. Borrowing freely from all the civilizations which had gone before, the Greeks developed the most glorious civilization the world had known. They were the first people to be concerned with democracy. The beautiful simplicity of their art and architecture is still an inspiration. Their stirring literature is part of our tradition. Our debt to these creative thinkers is great indeed.

While Greece was flourishing, a small republic was growing on the Italian peninsula. In time it became the mighty Roman Empire. The Romans were a practical people, with great skills for organization. They made contributions to civilization in the fields of law, government, engineering, and language. They spread civilization throughout their far-flung empire. It was under Roman rule that Christianity became a world religion.

Greece and then Rome ruled the ancient world for more than 1500 years and left a rich legacy in almost every area of our lives, from art to government, from philosophy to road building, from medicine to drama.

The imagination and efforts of men in Egypt, western Asia, Greece, and Rome helped to create the world in which we live. In this unit we shall read about these daring peoples, their interesting ways of living, and their enduring achievements.

Our Prehistoric Ancestors

KEY WORDS AND DATES

prehistoric
artifacts
archaeologists
geologists
anthropologists
carbon-dating
Ice Age
fossils
survival advantages
Stone Ages
tools and weapons
climatic influences
agricultural discoveries
division of labor
Swiss Lake dwellers
"time"
continuity
heritage

GEOLOGISTS estimate the age of the planet Earth to be about five billion years. Man has been around about one million. Over 99 per cent of these years slipped away before man learned to write. We call this long period *prehistory*. The written record of man's activities, covering the last five thousand years, we label *history*.

Most of the pages which follow tell the story of the *historic* period, for this is a history book. But we devote the first chapter to an account of our *pre*historic ancestors for a very significant reason. They made the great adaptations and discoveries upon which our civilization is founded. Language, fire, agriculture, and group life we owe to them. They discovered and used in their tools the basic principles of the lever, the wedge, the wheel, and the inclined plane, without which our machine technology would be quite helpless today.

Our growing knowledge of prehistoric man is the result of endless research by scientists from many fields. As bits of evidence are pieced together the fascinating story of man's long struggle for existence unfolds. We note the tools, weapons, art, and magic of the cave dwellers and the effects of climate on their ways of living. And we acknowledge the basic contributions made by our nameless ancestors to the heritage we call our history.

1. How We Know about Prehistoric Man

The Search for Artifacts · The story of our early ancestors has had to be interpreted from artifacts (products of human workmanship) found in caves, graves, peatbogs, and other places in which they have survived. Among these remains are (1) tools, weapons, and pottery; (2) buildings, paintings, and carvings; plus (3) the bones of people and the animals they killed.

Archaeologists are scholars who search for clues from which they can reconstruct the culture of our dim and distant past. Digging at Ternefine near Mascara, Algeria, they recently found two human jawbones dating back several hundred thousand years. Remains in a camp found at Tule Springs, Nevada, gave evidence of camel hunters cooking game there 23,800 years ago.

Geologists are able to determine the age and climate in which early people lived by studying the fossilized remains of plants and animals found in certain strata or layers of the earth. Thus at Makapansgat, South Africa, stone tools were recently found in the same stratum with bones of Australopithecus man-apes. *Anthropologists* reconstruct the physical, social, and cultural development of primitive man by studying aborigines still living in parts of Asia, Africa, Australia, and South America today.

Science Aids Discovery · Scientific sleuths from many specialized fields are called upon for analysis, interpretation, and dating of each new archaeological discovery. Let us suppose that some huge bones are exposed by a giant power shovel cutting a road through a hill. Archaeologists called from a nearby university carefully examine the area and find stone tools, broken bits of pottery, assorted smaller bones, and a piece of timber. They compare the tools for type with the thousands already found and carefully classified in museums. They patiently assemble the bits of pottery to determine the culture stage of the craftsman by like comparison. The bones tell them the kind, age, and size of each animal there.

Botanists, geologists, chemists, and physicists determine other facts about the findings. The annual rings of growth in the piece of timber are matched with specimens already dated for various periods. They reveal the kind of tree from which it came, its age, and much about the climatic conditions under which it grew.

Study of the layers of rock gives evidence of the geologic age involved. Microscopic examination of pollen grains in the dust yields further data on the climate and plant life of the period. Moreover, tests of the

3

The Challenge of Archaeology • *Scientists use many methods to explore the past. After careful measurement of fossil remains (left), prehistoric animals can be reconstructed with amazing accuracy. Though hidden for centuries under sand and rubble, ancient centers of culture, such as Persepolis (below), yield their historic treasures to patient excavators. A close-up of the famous Persian staircase found here is shown on page 42. The diver (right) helps to wrest the past from the depths of the sea. Here he glides over jars of grain and wine on the wreck of a Roman galley in the Mediterranean.*

Telling Time by the "Atomic Clock" · A *scientist performs one of a series of steps in the method for measuring the natural radioactivity of Carbon 14 in organic materials. Carbon 14 is manufactured from nitrogen in the atmosphere through bombardment by cosmic rays. It is assimilated as carbon dioxide by all living things and provides a known percentage of "tagged atoms" whose rate of decay can be measured with considerable accuracy up to 20,000 years.*

5

Of Ice and Men · The most recent geologic age of the earth is the Ice Age (Pleistocene). During this million-year period four frozen tides of ice (glaciers) crept at a rate of two or three inches a year from the Arctic over central Europe and North America. Each advance was followed by a warmer period of thousands of years during which the sheet of ice melted in retreat.

Proof that the climate of France and Germany was once warm and humid is given by the fossil bones of such subtropical animals as elephants, rhinoceros, and zebras found there. The fact that these were supplanted by such forest animals as bear, deer, and lynx, and these by reindeer and arctic fox, give evidence of the ice sheet creeping on. Pollen analysis of the plants on which the various animals fed shows a corresponding sequence.

The date of man's origin is estimated to be sometime in the early Pleistocene period. His place of origin is equally uncertain. Scientists question the old theories that man descended from a single "missing link," and that "the cradle of mankind" was in central Asia. Indeed man's fossilized remains have been found in such widely separated places as China, Java, South Africa, and Australia as well as Germany, England, and France. These fossils give evidence of the stages in his development. But it is from the stone tools found with the human remains that we get most of our knowledge of man's way of life. We call the earliest stone-tool-using stage of human culture the Paleolithic or Old Stone Age. It parallels the Pleistocene Ice Age in period of time.

The Long Struggle for Survival · The earliest Stone Age men of whom we have any knowledge were hairy creatures who lived pretty much like the African Bushmen

radioactivity of the pieces of bone by the Carbon-14 dating process tell with amazing accuracy the years which passed since the creatures died. In short, all the powers of modern scientific knowledge are employed to identify and describe the original people and their culture.

6

of today. They wandered through forests and across plains, seeking food where they could find it—wild fruits, roots, seeds and berries, and animals weaker than themselves. They built no homes and slept where darkness overtook them. To seize a cave required a contest with tooth and claw.

Men had four advantages over other animals which led to their control of the earth. (1) A larger brain gave them greater capacity for thought. (2) The ability to walk upright gave them a new dimension and freed their forelegs for other uses. (3) Their hands were capable of grasping and throwing objects. (4) A superior vocal mechanism enabled them to communicate more effectively.

In their long struggle for survival Stone Age men made discoveries, accidentally or otherwise, which added to their advantages. Fire caused by lightning must have been a fearful sight at first. But amazing uses for fire were soon discovered. The *borrowed* fire, when carefully fed, stayed "alive." It shed light, gave warmth, cooked food, smoked meat, hardened clay, discouraged insects, and frightened animals. Later men learned to *make* fire when they needed it by rubbing sticks or striking rocks together. Fire is only one example. Each improvement stimulated others. The effect was cumulative. New methods were spread by imitation and by word of mouth. Language thus became a means of group protection as well as progress.

Our hungry ancestors learned by bitter experience that a club was better than bare hands in getting a supply of meat and keeping it. Those who survived *taught* their young accordingly. A long, pointed stick (spear) was later found to be better. Then spears were thrown and the advantage increased. Fixing a splinter of bone or flint

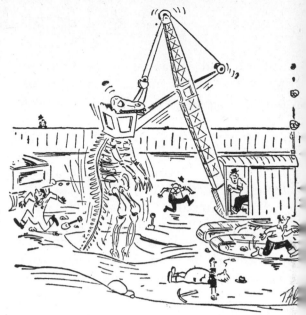

"Quick, someone call the Museum of Natural History."

at the point of the spear added to its effectiveness. Later, bows with strings could project small spears (arrows) much farther than they could be thrown. Or tiny spears (darts) could be blown through hollow tubes with deadly accuracy. The tools of the hunters plus skill in their use were measures of their culture. By studying these tools today we can determine the stage of a people's development.

CHECK ON YOUR READING
1. *Describe the work of the archaeologist, the geologist, and the anthropologist.*
2. *How do we know about climate and human culture during the Ice Age?*
3. *What four advantages helped man survive?*
4. *How did fire, language, and experience help?*

2. Life in the Stone Ages

Tools and Weapons of the Old Stone Age · The most common weapons of paleolithic hunters were called *fist hatchets*. These almond-shaped stones could be held for striking, hammering, hacking, or boring, like those in the picture on this page. Pieces could be struck from large stones to make smaller tools.

After thousands of years had passed, men learned to flake off pieces of flint by skillfully pressing with a hard bone. This discovery made possible implements with a fine cutting edge. Knives, drills, chisels, and scrapers followed. With sharper tools men could cut and fashion bone, ivory, and

Stone Age Tools (neolithic) · *From top to bottom are a flint scythe, saw, chisel, knife, dagger, and (left) a grinding stone. For what purpose might each have been used?*

horn into spoons, ladles, scrapers, spearheads, and fishhooks. With scrapers they cleaned the skins of animals, and with needles from bone splinters and thread from tendons they sewed skins or furs together for clothing.

Art and Magic of the Cave Dwellers · The earliest examples of human art are pictures of fish and animals carved by Stone Age men on their bone and ivory implements. In France and Spain lifelike pictures of animals have been discovered on the walls and ceilings of caves as well. Study the picture on the next page. Such drawings had a magical purpose. The cavemen painted the picture of the animal they intended to hunt and then performed the ritual of killing him in advance by striking the drawing with spears.

Later pictures show medicine men or witch doctors dressed as animals, dancing around their victims. Such practices are comparable to those of the Stone Age American Indians and African Bushmen with which we are more familiar. To primitive man creation of the likeness of his enemy gave power over him. The superstition persists today when disliked persons are hanged in effigy.

Climate and the Late Stone Age · In the Late or New Stone Age (Neolithic), which followed the retreat of the last great glacier 9000 years ago, men laid the foundations of civilization as we know it today. And climate played a vital role in the process. The region south of the Mediterranean, linked by narrow land bridges (via Sicily and Gibraltar) to Europe, did not suffer from extreme cold. Indeed the moisture which in Europe froze everything

Old Stone Age Cave Painting Found near Altamira, Spain · *The unknown artist (about 20,000 B.C.) used natural bulges of rock in the cave ceiling to give these buffalo lifelike roundness. How did he show action? power? wild terror? How was magic involved?*

in its icy grasp fell as rain in Africa. The Sahara plateau and Egypt were covered with meadows and forests. But with the coming of a warmer period the ice area in Europe shrank, and rains ceased to fall in north Africa. Plants withered and died. The Sahara became the desert land it is today.

As this dry period progressed, the Nile valley with its water supply became a refuge for the hunters of north Africa. Man and beast sought food and drink in its green valley. It was here, consequently, rather than in the less favorable climate of Europe, that man first advanced to the higher civilization known as the Late Stone Age.

Agriculture Revolutionizes Life · During the Old Stone Age men had chipped or flaked flint tools. In the Neolithic period they discovered how to grind or polish the edges of their stone implements much as one might grind metal tools today. Again, great advantages followed. But these were soon surpassed by a discovery which ranks with the use of fire in its importance to civilization. This was the discovery of agriculture. Men learned to sow the seeds of wild grasses—which yielded increasing crops of wheat, barley, and millet. Farming not only was less dangerous than hunting, but it resulted in a larger and more stable food supply.

Moreover, as wild cattle came in great numbers to the river's edge, men captured and tamed them. Eventually herds of cattle and flocks of sheep and goats guaranteed supplies of meat and milk, as well as material for clothing. Some animals were trained as beasts of burden.

"Here they come!" What possible danger lies below? or opportunity? What determined cave ownership? How did cave life differ from community life?

In short, agricultural discoveries revolutionized life. Men were no longer dependent upon the chance factors of *finding* berries or *stalking* game. They learned to *raise* what they needed. Some became shepherds, following their flocks from one green grassland to the next. Others tilled fields as farmers, moving only as the fertility of the soil became exhausted. But those fortunate enough to find rich river valleys established permanent homes and communities which became cradles for civilization.

Community Life · With their better sharp-edged tools men built huts, crude furniture, and household utensils. They molded clay into jars, bowls, and dishes, and hardened them in the fire. Women spun thread out of the fibers of flax and wove coarse cloth for garments. The many occupations required to supply the needs of the community resulted in a *division of labor*. While some men tended the herds, farmed, fished, hunted, or built shelters, others were busy at crafts, such as making pottery or tools. The women cared for the homes and worked in the fields.

The possession of houses and herds and farms awakened a sense of the value of property and the necessity of guarding it from outsiders. The safety of the community required observance of customs, simple laws, and forms of government.

With a more plentiful supply of food assured, the population increased and the demand for food and supplies grew. This created various forms of business and trade within a community. Then communities began to exchange their surplus goods for others which they lacked. This swapping of goods is called *barter* and is the earliest form of commerce. Since ideas were carried with the products exchanged, knowledge spread quickly and far. Indeed, we shall find throughout our study of history that cultural growth is stimulated by increased contacts between peoples. In this sense, isolation retards progress.

The Swiss Lake Dwellers · While civilization was progressing in the warm river valleys, the cave dwellers of Europe were still struggling against the cold. But gradually they began to make contact with other Stone Age peoples in Egypt and western Asia. From them they learned to grow grain, breed cattle, make ground-edged tools, and build homes.

Traces of the settlements of the Late Stone Age men in Europe have been found, together with their tools and weapons, on the lake bottoms of Switzerland. Fragments of their wooden houses have been discovered lying among the piles on which they were built along what previously had been the shores of these lakes. Pieces of chests, stools, dippers, and spoons show that these people had wooden furniture and utensils. Clay jars and kettles, and a stone spinning whorl, tell us that, like the Egyptians, they had learned the arts of pottery and weaving. Seeds of barley, other grains, vegetables, and fruits show that they too had a variety of crops. Taken together these remains give us a fair picture of life in Europe in the Late Stone Age.

Of Time, Life, and Religion · Primitive men first thought of time primarily in relation to themselves. To the American Indians, for example, night was "a sleep," and day, "an awakening." But they soon discovered that periods of day and night were related to the coming and going of the flaming sun in the sky. Sunrise dramatically opened a period of light and warmth and life. Sunset ushered in the darkness, cold, and dangers of the night. Doubts and fears haunted the shadows, and death had a way of striking while men slept. No wonder then that primitive peoples came to look upon the sun as a god, light as good, and darkness as evil. Fire became a religious symbol and remains so today.

Men noted the moon as it waxed and waned in a regular cycle. This gave them a unit of time which became the *month.* Later they came to recognize that the position of the sun was related to the four *seasons.*

The names men gave to the stars and star groupings likewise tell us much about their way of life. The hunter, longing for the season of the chase, watched the skies for signs of the Bear and for the coming of the Mighty Hunter swinging his stick which curved like a boomerang. The shepherd

Spearing Fish · *In Australia descendants of primitive aborigines still live by such skills.*

saw by the sign of the Ram that his flock would prosper. The farmer, too, looked skyward to see whether the Ploughman was visible when he began to till his soil, and the Water-pourer in sight when the crops needed rain. Men lived close to nature, and nature foresaw all and provided for everything. Their thinking, like that of the American Indian, was thus expressed in terms of the environment about them: "What is life? It is a flash of a firefly in the night. It is a breath of a buffalo in the wintertime. It is as a little shadow that runs across the grass and loses itself in the sunset."

Of Continuity, Heritage, and History · Where men were limited by their environment, they made no further advance. But in the fertile valleys of the Nile, Tigris-Euphrates, Indus, and Hwang rivers civilization went forward. Here between 4000 and

Cradles of Civilization

Cradles of Civilization · *How do river valleys "cradle" civilization? What climate characterized the areas above? Into what water bodies do the five rivers run?*

3000 B.C. men made two immense discoveries which marked the next steps in human progress—the invention of writing and the use of metals. These were turning points of great significance in our history. But they would have been impossible without the discovery of language and fire and similar gains of the prehistoric period.

We need to remind ourselves that the stream of history is an on-going process having what we call *continuity*. This makes it possible for each new generation to draw upon the vast reservoir of experience accumulated by all who have gone before. This is our *heritage* from the past. The fruits of the present are rooted in the past. Too often we take them for granted. Endless examples can be cited of modern dependence upon simple tools, language, fire, and agriculture.

As we turn to succeeding chapters in our story, therefore, we should keep in mind that history is to mankind what memory is to the individual. History gives us countless opportunities to benefit by the experiences of our past without going through the long and costly trial-and-error process by which such knowledge was acquired.

CHECK ON YOUR READING

1. *Describe the tools and weapons of the Early Stone Age. How were they improved in the Late Stone Age?*
2. *Why was the development of agriculture a step forward for man?*
3. *What discoveries made in Switzerland give a picture of life in Europe in the Late Stone Age?*

∼∼∼∼∼ *Learning Activities* ∼∼∼

Think about the chapter

1. Climate has a great influence on the development of civilization. Show how changes in climate affected the way of life of early man. How does climate affect us today?

2. It is probable that more new discoveries are being made in the time it takes you to read this statement than were made in 1000 years during the Stone Ages. Can you explain why this is so?

3. Why did barter encourage progress?

4. What characteristics of a modern community were present in a Late Stone Age community?

5. Why did government of some kind become necessary to men of the Late Stone Age?

6. *Map study*: Trace on a map of Europe, Asia, and North America the extent of the ice sheet during each of the four Ice Ages. In what parts of the world was man's development unaffected by the Ice Ages? An encyclopedia will help you.

Go beyond the text

7. Find out about the prehistoric era of your own region, the geology of it, and whether any evidence has been found of prehistoric animals or man. Most state histories have a chapter on this.

8. Horses existed during prehistoric days, but they were quite different from the animals we know today. Trace the development of the horse from prehistoric time to the present.

9. You will be interested in reading about the Piltdown Hoax. The *Readers' Guide* will give you the names of articles on this famous mistake. How did the carbon-dating process play a part in exposing the hoax?

Follow up your special interests

10. You will find that the culture of a people is reflected in their art. Why not start a class scrapbook showing the history of art? To begin it, find magazine reproductions of the primitive cave paintings.

11. Try to imagine how man discovered fire or speech. Write a short story telling of this marvelous event.

12. Those who like to draw can prepare an excellent bulletin-board exhibit by sketching Stone Age tools and weapons.

13. Many American Indian tribes had a Stone-Age-type culture. Arrange an exhibit of Indian arrowheads and tools.

READ FURTHER

Basic readings: (1) BAUER and PEYSER, *How Music Grew*, Chaps. 1–2. (2) BREASTED, *Ancient Times*, Chap. 1. (3) CHEYNEY, *World History of Art*, Chap. 1. (4) HOFFMAN, *News of the World*, No. 1. (5) VAN LOON, *Story of Mankind*, Chaps. 1–3. (6) YEAR'S *Pictorial History*, pp. 34–36.

Special accounts: (7) R. ANDREWS, *Meet Your Ancestors*. Biography of primitive man. (8) E. BAITY, *Americans Before Columbus*. Prehistoric age in the Americas. (9) M. EDEL, *The Story of People* and *The Story of Our Ancestors*. Anthropology for young people. (10) H. and I. GOLDMAN, *First Men*. Up-to-date interpretations of anthropology. (11) M. and C. H. B. QUENNELL, *The Old Stone Age*, and *The New Stone, Bronze and Early Iron Ages*. Give comparisons of life of present-day primitive groups with prehistoric times, well illustrated. (12) "How Old Is It," *National Geographic*, August, 1958. (13) Public Affairs Pamphlet, No. 85, *The Races of Mankind*.

Fiction and biography: (14) C. COBLENTZ, *Sequoya*. Story of lame Sequoya's efforts and success in developing a written language for the Cherokees in the nineteenth century. (15) T. HEYERDAHL, *Kon-Tiki*. Account of a trip across the Pacific by raft to test a theory that the pre-Inca Indians came to America from Polynesia. (16) R. KIPLING, *Puck of Pook's Hill*. Short stories that recreate scenes of prehistoric and Roman Britain. (17) J. KJELGAARD, *Fire-Hunter*. Hawk, Chief Spear-Maker, broke a tribal law and is left behind with Willow, a lame girl, to perish. They learn the secrets of fire making and are able to keep alive.

"Those who cannot remember the past are condemned to repeat it." —SANTAYANA

"The supreme purpose of history is a better world. Yesterday's records can keep us from repeating yesterday's mistakes." —HERBERT HOOVER

CHAPTER 2

What the Egyptians Accomplished

CHAPTER OUTLINE

1. *Progress in the Nile Valley*
2. *The Achievements of the Pyramid Age*
3. *Civilization of the Empire*

KEY WORDS AND DATES

delta	sculpture
irrigation	feudal
hieroglyphics	diffusion
papyrus	Hyksos
Osiris	Karnak
Re	Thutmose
mummy	Tutenkhamon
4241 B.C.	Ikhnaton
Great Pyramid	empire
Pharaoh	monotheism
craftsmen	Champollion
Sphinx	Rosetta Stone

WE HAVE FOLLOWED MAN as he struggled upward from savagery to the more comfortable life of the Late Stone Age. In this chapter we shall see how he continued to improve his lot and achieve a rich and varied civilization in Egypt. We shall find that thousands of years ago the early Egyptians discovered many things, such as picture-writing and the use of metals.

We are indebted to them for our calendar of twelve months and 365 days. Their engineers designed and built huge pyramids and magnificent temples. Their skilled craftsmen fashioned beautiful jewelry, vases, glass objects, and glazed tiles—which match the best today.

The Egyptians devised an alphabet and materials for writing. The fragments of their libraries reveal their thinking about science and mathematics. Their ships carried goods into the Mediterranean and helped to influence the civilization of other peoples.

Egypt was a power in the ancient world for 3000 years. Her Pharaohs once ruled an empire stretching from the headwaters of the Nile to the islands of the Aegean and into Palestine and Syria. During the next 3000 years (1150 B.C.–1936 A.D.), however, Egypt was largely under foreign rule. Today her influence in world affairs lies in Arab nationalism and control of the strategic Suez Canal.

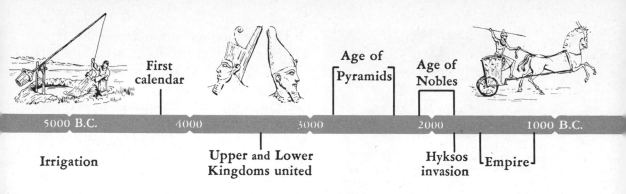

First calendar

Age of Pyramids

Age of Nobles

5000 B.C.   4000   3000   2000   1000 B.C.

Irrigation

Upper and Lower Kingdoms united

Hyksos invasion

Empire

1. Progress in the Nile Valley

Why Civilization Began in the Nile Valley · The story of Egypt is the story of the Nile. The very land itself is "the gift of the Nile," which yearly brings rich new soil in its flood waters and deposits it on the river banks. Along the narrow valley, at some places only ten miles wide, Egyptian civilization developed and its great cities grew up. The river furnishes a highway for the country and an outlet to the sea. Moreover, the Nile, in the centuries of cutting this deep gorge through the arid land of northern Africa, has given Egypt a natural shelter. The valley is protected from invasion on both side by barren cliffs and desert sands.

Before man could make any progress toward a civilized life, he had to be assured of a supply of food and water the year round. Only then could he give up the weary search for something to eat and drink and settle down, build houses, and cultivate his fields. With food and water he could turn to other occupations and improve his ways of living. He could develop new industries and arts, and seek beauty and refinement in the things about him.

When the Stone Age hunters of northern Africa moved away from the parched deserts, they discovered the Nile gorge. There they found a sheltered spot, where in time they learned to plant grain and herd cattle. The soil of the valley was very fertile. The mud carried by the Nile slowly filled up a large region at the mouth where the river divides into several slow-moving streams. In this fertile triangle, called the Delta, because its shape is that of the Greek letter Δ (delta), the earliest Egyptian civilization began.

How the Egyptians Watered Their Fields · Since it seldom rains in Egypt, the farmers had to find some way of · keeping their lands moist. Far up the Nile and its tributaries there is plenty of rain in the spring. When this rain swelled the river and raised it high above its normal level in the valley, the Egyptians stored up water to use when the river was low. They invented a simple device for lifting the water from the Nile and sending it through trenches that crossed the fields.

This artificial method of supplying water to fields we call *irrigation*. Since the days of the early Egyptians it has been used in many countries, and thousands of acres of desert land have been reclaimed for profitable farming.

15

Irrigation Then and Now · *Compare the ancient shadoof (c. 1250 B.C.) used by Apuy's servant (above) with the one used today by Egyptian fellahin for raising water.*

The Beginnings of Government · It required many men to dig trenches and lift water. Sometimes men of several settlements would have to work together to clear the canals of mud. The leader of the work became a local chieftain, whose duty it was to manage the irrigation projects of the district. In payment for his services the people of the district had to bring him every year a part of their grain or flax. These were the earliest taxes. The control of the public water system and the collection of taxes were among the earliest activities of government.

Egypt United under a King · We know that very early one of these chieftains conquered his rivals in the other districts. He united all the Delta into a Kingdom of Lower Egypt. A Kingdom of Upper Egypt also developed farther up the river. About 4300 B.C. a king of Lower Egypt brought both regions under his control. It was during this period that the most important chapter of history opens.

Introduction of Farm Machinery · So far the fields had been cultivated slowly and painfully by hand with a hoe. Now a great advance was made, for the Egyptians learned how to lengthen the handle of the hoe. They fastened it so that oxen could pull the hoe blade (plowshare) through the earth. They could now plow a much larger piece of ground in less time and greatly increase the amount of their crops. The use of animal power and plows were important steps in the long history of farm machinery.

Origin of Our Calendar · The Egyptian farmers used seasons as guides to the planting and harvesting of crops. The earliest Egyptians marked three seasons of four months each, which they called Flooding, Sowing, and Harvest. Like other early peoples, they told time by the appearance of the moon. Since the moon-month is only twenty-nine and a half days long, it does not evenly divide the year. Finally, the Egyptians made a solar calendar, dividing the year into twelve months of thirty days each. They added a holiday of five feast days at the end. This gave them a year of 365 days. Modern astronomers have been able to prove that the Egyptian calendar was introduced in 4241 B.C. This is the *earliest date* known in history. This same calendar of 365 days has come down to us after six thousand years. The length of the months has in the meantime been slightly changed. The Egyptians numbered the months, but referred to the years by important events, as one might say, "The year of the Great Fire."

The Egyptians Invent Writing · No people could progress very far without an easy way of keeping records of what was said and done and of sending messages of various kinds. The Egyptians were the first to devise a system of writing. Writing grew from pictures. These pictures, or hieroglyphics, stood for objects. Later the Egyptians began to use these pictures to represent fixed sounds. For example (supposing Egyptian words to be the same as English), the sign for "man" (𝄞) might come to be used for the *sound* "man" wherever it occurred, as in *man*tle, *man*ufacturer, or *man*ner. In the same way, the sign for "bee" (🐝) might become the sign for the sound "be," and that for "leaf" (🍃) for the sound "leaf." If used together, these signs would form a new word, *belief*. These sound-signs could be used in many combinations.

Finally it was possible to express whatever one wished with the use of a limited number of characters. So writing came to

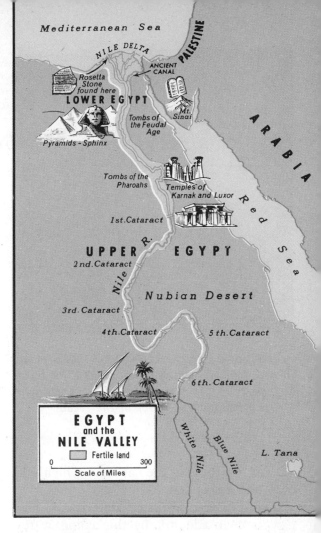

Egypt and the Nile Valley · *An excellent student can frame and answer at least ten questions about Egypt from data on this map. Can you?*

represent sounds (phonics) instead of objects. The sound-signs made it possible to write many words whose meanings could not be represented by pictures, such as *love, hate, joy*.

The Egyptians went further and devised an alphabet, or series of signs or letters representing sounds. There were twenty-four signs in this alphabet. This, the earliest alphabet known, was in use in 3500

Adoration to Osiris (c. 1000 B.C.) · *This scene shows Princess Entiu-ny offering Osiris meat and flowers. It concludes a 17-foot papyrus roll called the "Book of the Dead."*

B.C. It is probably the one from which our own has descended.

The Earliest Writing Materials · The Egyptians made ink by thickening water with a little vegetable gum and stirring in soot. They dipped a pointed reed into this mixture and found that they could write with it very well. They split and flattened out a river reed (papyrus) into thin strips and made large sheets by pasting the edges of the strips together. In this way, pen, ink, and paper came into use.

Slow Introduction of Metal · Few advances since the discovery of fire and agriculture could compare in importance with the introduction of metal. Its discovery marked a new era in the progress of man.

It was probably in the region of Sinai that the Egyptians first came upon metal (about 5000 B.C.). They may have seen pieces of copper ore lying on the ground near a fire, and were attracted by the gleaming mass that ran out of the heated ore. It was centuries, however, before men learned how to make practical use of metal. They found that copper would take a sharp edge and would make harder and better tools than they were then using.

With the copper tools they were able to cut and shape large blocks of stone. A new kind of architecture now appeared—the great stone temples and tombs of the Pyramid Age.

Egyptian Religion · The Egyptians had many gods. Each tribe had its own local divinity, whom it believed to be its special protector. Other gods, whom all the people worshiped, often represented the forces of nature. Re (pronounced "ray"), the Sun-god, who shone so gloriously every day, was one. Many temples were built in his honor. Another was Osiris, god of the mighty river which yearly brought life from the soil. The gods had human personalities, and many myths grew up as to their deeds and their relations with man.

In the temples the gods were worshiped with offerings of meat, honey, oils, fruit, and flowers. Incense was widely used. Songs were sung by the priestesses. Magic dances and religious processions were common.

CHECK ON YOUR READING

1. *What two activities of government were begun because of the need for irrigation?*
2. *Give three examples of progress made by early Egyptians.*
3. *Why was the introduction of metal important?*
4. *Name two important Egyptian gods. How were they worshiped?*

2. The Achievements of the Pyramid Age

The Pyramid Tombs · At Gizeh, not far from Cairo, stand the pyramids, tombs of Egyptian kings. This cemetery dates back to about 2800 B.C. Southward for sixty miles other groups of pyramids stand along the Nile. Each of these structures is the tomb of a king who once ruled Egypt. The whole line represents a period of five hundred years, which we call the Pyramid Age.

What the Tombs Tell Us · Much that we know about ancient Egypt we learn from its tombs. The climate of the country is so dry that after five thousand years its tombs still stand. Egyptian burial customs have made the tombs historical museums from which archaeologists have learned a great deal about Egyptian customs.

The Egyptians believed in a life after death. To obtain this life in the next world it was necessary that the body be protected from destruction and supplied with food and all the comforts to which it had been accustomed on this earth. This led to the custom of embalming and to building secure tombs in which the dead could rest undisturbed.

Bodies which were preserved by embalming are called *mummies*. They are usually the remains of kings or wealthy persons, who could afford the expense of careful embalming. The tombs of such persons were elaborately furnished and hence have given us the best examples of Egyptian workmanship.

Food, tools, furniture, jewelry, and other articles for the use of the dead were placed in the burial chambers. Sometimes the walls of a tomb were covered with scenes from the daily life of the departed one. Sometimes statuettes of his slaves and workmen were placed near him. These represented the occupations on his estate, such as counting his cattle, measuring out grain, and baking bread.

The Interior Plan of a Pyramid Tomb and a Boat Model Found Therein (c. 2000 B.C.) · *What do these tell us about the purpose of the pyramid? Egyptian life?*

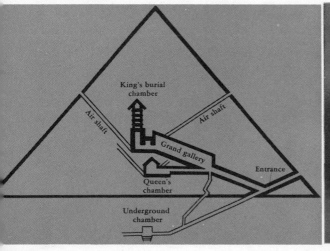

Progress in Building · Egyptian mastery in building was made possible by the use of metal tools. For centuries the tombs of kings and nobles were made of sun-dried brick. A chamber was cut in the ground and the flat roof was covered with a mound of sand and gravel. But by 2800 B.C. men had learned to cut limestone with their copper tools and to line the burial chamber with stone instead of brick. During the next hundred years tombs of stone were built *above* ground in the form of pyramids.

It was not long after that the Great Pyramid of Gizeh was built for King Khufu. This most impressive of the pyramid tombs covers thirteen acres. It consisted of 2,300,-000 limestone blocks, each weighing, on an average, two and a half tons. The Great Pyramid is proof that the Egyptians had become great engineers and organizers, as well as builders.

Power of the Pharaohs · An ancient record tells us that one hundred thousand men worked for twenty years to construct the Great Pyramid. There must have been a mighty king at the head of the government to command such a host of workers. This king was so powerful that the people believed him to be a god. His name was sacred and was never spoken by them. Instead, he was called by the name of his palace, *Pharaoh*, meaning "great house." Today we might say "The White House did this or that," meaning the President.

Life and Work in the Pyramid Age · Artists decorated these tombs for the benefit of the dead. Without realizing it, they gave to later generations a picture of the life and industries of their time. The walls were often covered from ceiling to floor with carved and painted scenes showing the daily occupations on the estate of the

Building the Pyramid of King Mycerinus at Gizeh (c. 2550 B.C.) · *Each block of limestone from a nearby quarry was levered onto a wooden sledge and pulled by slaves over greased ties up ramps of rubble. What made such vast projects possible?*

Egyptian Craftsmen Were Highly Skilled · *Metal workers polish a silver stand and shape a silver bowl on an anvil. Between them is a small furnace with blow pipe and tongs.*

buried nobleman. Scholars who can read Egyptian hieroglyphics are now able to interpret the carvings and paintings and reconstruct for us the civilization of the Pyramid Age.

The tallest or central figure of these pictures represents the dead noble, who is overseeing the work on his estate. Among the carvings we find the oldest farming scenes on record. They show sowers scattering seed and oxen drawing the plow. There are also herds of fine-looking cattle, which formed part of the wealth of the rich.

Metalworking, Pottery, and Glass · One scene shows metal craftsmen busy at their work. The coppersmith could now make many kinds of tools. He had learned how to mix tin with copper to make bronze. This is a much harder metal than copper. The goldsmith hammered and fashioned beautiful jewelry set with colored stones. Such jewelry can hardly be surpassed in craftsmanship today.

Another wall shows the potter at work. He no longer molds his jars and bowls with his fingers, as in the Stone Age, but sits before a potter's wheel. He shapes the vessel as the wheel whirls around under his fingers. When the clay vessels are finished, they are baked and hardened in furnaces. Other craftsmen are shown making glass.

This art the Egyptians had discovered centuries earlier. They spread glass on tiles, making bright-colored glazes. These adorned their house and palace walls. Later they made many-colored bottles and vases.

Skill in Weaving · The art of weaving is shown by women at work on a linen fabric. We know that the Egyptians made very beautiful fabrics. The linen wrapped around the royal mummies is so fine that a magnifying glass is required to distinguish it from silk. Modern machine-made linen is coarse in comparison with the cloth made on the ancient Egyptian hand loom.

Carpentry and Shipbuilding · In one section we find cabinetmakers at work fashioning luxurious furniture for the nobleman's house. This was often inlaid with ivory or ebony and even overlaid with silver or gold. Nearby are hulls of boats which are being made ready to carry goods to points along the river or across the sea.

In the Pyramid Age the beautiful things made by the Egyptians were sent across the Mediterranean to Europe and by land to western Asia. We have some carved and painted reliefs showing us the ships which were venturing out of the Nile into waters as far as the coast of Phoenicia. These reliefs (*c.* 2650 B.C.) are the earliest known pictures of seagoing ships.

The Great Sphinx at Gizeh (c. 2650 B.C.)

Portrait Sculpture · The portrait sculptors carved statues in wood or stone. Painted in color and with the eyes inlaid with rock crystal, they are among the most life-like portraits ever produced. The statues of the kings are often superb.

The most remarkable heroic statue of the Pyramid Age is the Great Sphinx. It stands in the cemetery at Gizeh. The head is thought to be a portrait of King Khafre; the body, that of a lion. Carved from rock, it is the largest portrait bust ever made.

Classes of Society · In the Pyramid Age we find the people divided into different classes according to their occupations and wealth. (1) There were slaves, who worked the farms and fields of the rich and performed the heavy labor. (2) There were freemen, who carried on trades and industries, and artisans, who made the many things which the people used. (3) There were also large landholders, who devoted their time to managing their estates. (4)

Above all was the Pharaoh himself, surrounded by his court officials.

End of the Pyramid Age · It was the custom of the Pharaohs to grant land from time to time to court officials in payment for their services. Finally, some of these nobles became very wealthy and powerful. They were able to make themselves independent of the king and live like princes on their own vast estates. About 2300 B.C. they overthrew the Pharaoh's government. Thus passed the period named from the great monuments which the powerful Pharaohs built as signs of their absolute power.

Feudal Age of the Nobles · There followed a long period of confusion. The nobles fought among themselves to gain greater power and more land. Sometimes one of them became stronger than the rest and united the country under his control. But such a king was not an absolute monarch, as the old Pharaohs had been. He was the head of a *feudal* state, that is, one in which there was a class of nobles who enjoyed much independence and with whom he had to deal.

Diffusion of Civilization · Some of the Pharaohs of this period sent their fleets northward to the Aegean Islands. They also conquered far up the Nile to the south. They had a channel cut eastward across the Delta, connecting the Nile with the Red Sea. The Egyptians thus came into contact with other peoples, with whom they traded goods and ideas. As knowledge and culture passed from one people to another, civilization gradually grew and spread (diffusion).

The Earliest Libraries · The tombs of the nobles of the Feudal Age lie in the cliffs near their estates, some two hundred miles south of Gizeh. In them were found fragments of the libraries of the feudal lords—

the earliest libraries in the world. These books were written on rolls of papyrus. Besides songs, poems, and stories, there are rolls dealing with science—what the Egyptians believed about the human body, about medicine and surgery. Here too are the beginnings of arithmetic and geometry.

The Hyksos Invade Egypt · Not long after 1800 B.C. foreign tribes from Asia, called Hyksos, invaded Egypt. The Hyksos kings were able to control Egypt for a century, until a native ruler appeared strong enough to drive them out. It was the Hyksos who brought horses into Egypt. With chariots to strengthen their armies, the Pharaohs established a mighty empire.

CHECK ON YOUR READING

1. *What do the pyramids tell us about Egyptian life?*
2. *Make a list of the occupations that you might have followed, had you lived in Egypt about 1800 B.C.*
3. *Give three examples of progress made during the Feudal Age.*

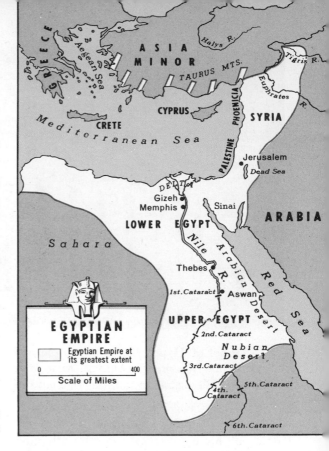

Egyptian Empire (15th Century B.C.) · *Name the geographical barriers which bound this empire. How far is Asia Minor by sea?*

3. Civilization of the Empire

The Egyptian Empire (*c.* 1580–1150 B.C.) · An empire is a group of nations which have been brought together under the control of one strong government. This is usually by conquest but sometimes with the consent of the subject peoples. The Egyptian Empire is the first empire that we meet in our story of civilization. But we shall find that an empire is a form of government that still exists.

The Egyptian Empire, made up of conquered peoples, lasted for over four hundred years. During this period the Pharaohs were generals commanding large armies. They invaded the lands of their neighbors and conquered a vast region extending from the Fourth Cataract of the Nile to the upper Euphrates (see map above).

The Temples at Thebes · The capital of the Empire was Thebes. Luxor and Karnak now occupy part of its site. Here were a large cemetery, massive temples, obelisks, and huge statues. On temple walls are sculptured reliefs showing the Egyptians in

Model of Hypostyle Hall, Temple of Karnak · *Largest building of the Egyptian Empire, the great temple of Amen covers an area 388 feet wide and 170 feet deep with 134 gigantic columns. The nave with its clerestory window stands 79 feet high.*

battle. The giant figure of the Pharaoh stands in his war chariot, scattering his enemies before him.

The greatest of the soldier-emperors was Thutmose III, who ruled for about fifty years (*c.* 1500 B.C.). He has been called the "Napoleon of Egypt." The temple walls at Karnak record the story of nearly twenty years of his campaigns. In these he subdued the kingdoms and cities of Syria and Palestine. Thutmose also built a large fleet and spread his control to the islands of the Aegean Sea.

The power and wealth of the conquering Pharaohs is shown by the size and grandeur of their statues and buildings. The great portrait statues of the Pharaohs could be seen for miles. The great temple at Karnak contains the most impressive colonnaded hall ever erected by man. The columns of its central aisle are seventy feet high. The

capital on top of each of these pillars could hold a hundred persons.

A mile and a half away is the beautiful Luxor Temple. The capitals on its columns were designed to resemble papyrus buds. The Karnak and Luxor temples were connected by a long avenue of sphinxes sculptured in stone.

Treasures of the Tombs: Tutenkhamon · Many kings and nobles were buried at Thebes. Across the Nile from Karnak, cut into the rocky cliffs which border the river valley, are hundreds of tombs. They are adorned with paintings and sculpture and were richly furnished. Because of their valuable furnishings, the tombs of the Pharaohs were early plundered by robbers.

The sole exception was the tomb of Tutenkhamon, a young king who ruled for a short while after 1360 B.C. The entrance of this burial place had been accidentally covered by stone cuttings falling from the preparation of a tomb higher up, and so its existence was forgotten. When it was discovered in 1922, it proved to be a wonderful event for archaeologists. For the first time they were able to enter an inner burial chamber that had never been seriously disturbed since the young Pharaoh was laid away over three thousand years before. They were able to view the beautiful furniture and ornaments just as they had been placed for his use in the life after death. The tomb proved to be a treasure house of Egyptian craftsmanship and art.

Religion of the Empire · The tombs of the Empire, like those of earlier periods, tell us much about the religious ideas of the time. Osiris was the chief among the Egyptian gods, and in the next world every man would have to appear before him to be judged. It was customary to place in the coffin a papyrus roll containing prayers and charms which would be useful to the departed soul. This heavenly guide we call the Book of the Dead.

Tutenkhamon's father-in-law, Amenhotep IV (c. 1375–1358 B.C.), had come to believe that there was but *one* god, who ruled the whole world. We call the belief in one god *monotheism*. Amenhotep closed the temples of the old gods and even changed his own name, in honor of the one god (Aton), to *Ikhnaton*. But the priests of the old religion made much trouble for Ikhnaton. When Tutenkhamon came to the throne, they forced him to restore the worship of the old Egyptian gods.

End of the Empire · The Empire lasted for about two hundred years after Tutenkhamon's time. It had many enemies, the most powerful of whom were at first the Hittites (p. 40). The Pharaohs of this period were unable to restore the former strength of Egypt. Finally, invaders from the northeast came in such numbers that the weakened Empire fell, about 1150 B.C. Later, Egypt came under the rule of many different conquerors. She never fully regained her independence until within our own time (in 1936). But today Egypt is once more dreaming of power.

Influence of Egypt on Civilization · Although Egypt's importance as a great power passed away, her contribution to civilization did not perish. We shall find many instances, as we go on with our story, of the influence of her art and culture on the peoples of the eastern Mediterranean world.

The rediscovery of ancient Egypt has largely taken place within the last hundred years. Archaeologists have carefully studied her tombs and monuments. In this work they have been greatly aided by the recovery of the Egyptian language. The knowledge of hieroglyphics was lost during

Aton Shines upon King Tut and His Queen · *This throne is overlaid with gold.*

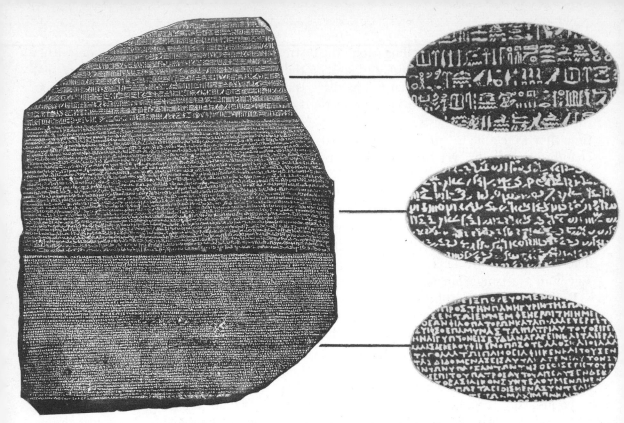

The Key to Hieroglyphics • *Napoleon's soldiers found this basalt slab near the Rosetta mouth of the Nile in 1799. It contained a public message (195 B.C.) carved in ancient hieroglyphics (top), in demotic, ordinary Egyptian handwriting (center) and in Greek. How did Champollion decipher it?*

the Middle Ages, and it was not found until 1822 when a Frenchman named Champollion deciphered the meaning of Egyptian signs from the Rosetta Stone. Since that time many others have added to his work. Now scholars are able to read the ancient inscriptions and papyri and tell us the story of this early civilization.

CHECK ON YOUR READING

1. What is an empire? How far did the Egyptian Empire extend?
2. Describe the ancient city of Thebes.
3. Why was monotheism given up? Why did the Empire fall?

". . . Sole God, to whom no other is likened
When thou wast alone thou madest the earth,
All that goes upon legs, and flieth with wings."
—from *Hymn to the Sun*
AMENHOTEP IV (Ikhnaton) 1375–1358 B.C.

Learning Activities

Think about the chapter

1. Why did the Greek historian Herodotus say, "Egypt is a gift of the Nile"?

2. Describe the different kinds of government in Egypt from the earliest days to the fall of the Empire.

3. Tell the importance of Tutenkhamon's tomb, the temple at Karnak, and the Rosetta Stone.

4. What aspects of Egyptian civilization were of permanent value to later civilizations?

5. *Map study:* On an outline map locate the Delta, Gizeh, Memphis, Thebes, and Sinai. Trace the Nile from its sources to its mouth. Compare the size of Egypt in the days of the Empire with its present size.

Go beyond the text

6. By what countries has Egypt been ruled since the fall of the Empire? The text index will help you. What form of government does Egypt have today? Compare this government with that of the Pharaohs.

7. *Fellah* (plural *fellahin*) is the Arabic word for peasant. Compare the life of a modern Egyptian *fellah* with that of a peasant in ancient Egypt.

8. Read about Howard Carter's dramatic discovery of the tomb of King Tutenkhamon.

9. Are cosmetics a modern frivolity? Investigate their use in ancient Egypt. The *Encyclopedia Britannica* has an account.

10. Animal lovers will be interested in investigating the story of the cat in Egypt.

11. Summarize the issues facing Egypt in the world today.

Follow up your special interests

12. Present a travelogue on a trip up the Nile. If possible talk to a person who has made the trip, take notes on his experiences, and borrow colored slides to show the class. Use travel folders and posters.

13. Visit the art museum nearest you to see examples of arts and crafts of the Egyptians. Add magazine pictures of Egyptian arts and crafts to your history-of-art scrapbook.

14. A science committee can keep a record of discoveries and inventions for the class in a scrapbook or by a series of posters.

READ FURTHER

Basic readings: (1) BAUER and PEYSER, *How Music Grew*, Chap. 3. (2) BREASTED, *Ancient Times*, Chaps. 2–3. (3) CERAM, *March of Archaeology.* (4) CHEYNEY, *World History of Art*, Chap. 3. (5) DAVIS, *Readings in Ancient History*, Chap. 1. (6) EVANS, *Costume Throughout the Ages*, Chap 1. (7) HOFFMAN, *News of the World*, Nos. 2–3. (8) TAYLOR. *Fifty Centuries of Art*, pp. 1–5. (9) TAYLOR, *Illustrated History of Science*, Chap. 1. (10) VAN LOON, *Story of Mankind*, Chaps. 4–6. (11) Year's *Pictorial History*, pp. 36–44.

Special accounts: (12) M. CHUBB, *Nefertiti Lived Here.* Fascinating tale of a girl who joined an expedition in Egypt. (13) E. MEADOWCROFT, *Gift of the River.* History of Egypt from 6000 B.C. to 600 B.C.; easy reading. (14) D. MILLS, *The Book of the Ancient World.* Written especially for high-school readers. (15) A. WHITE, *Lost Worlds.* Narrative of archaeological discoveries told in fast-moving style. (16) *Life*, "The Art of Writing Hieroglyphic" and "The Epic of Man: Egypt," October 1, 1956. (17) *National Geographic*, "Daily Life in Ancient Egypt," October, 1941; "Kyaks Down the Nile," May, 1955; "Fresh Treasures from Egypt's Ancient Sands," November, 1955.

Fiction and biography: (18) O. COOLIDGE, *Egyptian Adventures.* Short stories featuring the common people. (19) E. McGRAW, *Mara: Daughter of the Nile.* A slave girl is part of a royal intrigue. (20) L. MORRISON. *The Lost Queen of Egypt.*

3

Civilizations of Western Asia

KEY WORDS AND DATES

Fertile Crescent	Phoenicians
Semites	David
Tigris-Euphrates	Solomon
cuneiform	Jehovah
Sargon	Old Testament
Babylonians	Hittites
Hammurapi	Indo-European
Assyrians	612 B.C.
Nineveh	Cyrus
Chaldeans	Darius
Nebuchadnezzar	Persepolis
astrology	Crete
astronomy	Mycenaean Age

OUR STORY NOW TAKES US to western Asia, whose lands, like those of Egypt, border on the Mediterranean. Here in the valley of the Tigris and Euphrates rivers, we shall find that men early passed beyond the life of the Late Stone Age and built up a high civilization. In point of time our story begins with the rise of Sumerian civilization about 3000 B.C. Some 2500 years later the whole of western Asia was controlled by the Persians.

The account of western Asia includes the history of many Biblical peoples. Among these were the Babylonians, Assyrians, Chaldeans, Persians, Phoenicians, and Hebrews. We shall find a record of progress but also of brutal conquest. There was always the struggle among men for fertile land, for wealth, and for power over one another. But these early peoples accomplished much in spite of their many wars.

To them we are indebted for many great discoveries. Among these are methods of irrigation, coinage of money, the arch, basic codes of law, beginnings in astronomy, the first use of iron, the horse, and the chariot, the Old Testament, monotheism, and many ideas of government. It was the civilization of the Near East, together with that of Egypt, which crossed the Aegean and Cretan "bridge" to the mainland of Europe and thence came down to us.

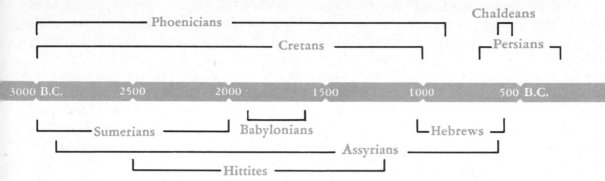

1. Early Kingdoms in Babylonia

Civilization Developed in the Fertile Crescent · In western Asia archaeologists have been pushing farther and farther back into the distant past. They have discovered the traces of a high civilization which already existed at the time when the pyramid tombs were being built on the banks of the Nile (*c.* 2800 B.C.). This was the civilization of a people whom we call the Sumerians.

These people of western Asia, like those of Egypt, were first able to make progress where the climate was warm and the soil fertile. If you will look at the map (p. 30), you will find a region between the mountains and the desert. It is shaped like a crescent, with the open side facing the Arabian Desert. Its western end lies along the Mediterranean, and its eastern part reaches the Persian Gulf. The eastern area is sometimes called Mesopotamia, which means the land between the rivers. We shall find that the history of western Asia was a constant struggle for the possession of this Fertile Crescent.

The Semites of the Arabian Desert · Arabia is a vast desert land where little vegetation can be found. It has no rivers and no rain except during a few weeks in winter. The people of this barren country come from a branch of the white race called Semites, made up of many different peoples. We are familiar with at least two of these—the Arabs and the Hebrews.

The desert peoples had no fixed homes, but were wanderers, or *nomads*. They moved up and down the arid plains, seeking food and water for themselves and their flocks. In the spring they pressed northward, where the desert, after the winter rains, was thinly covered with grass. If they found a good place in which to settle, they might give up their wandering life to plant crops and establish permanent homes.

The Early Sumerian Civilization · The earliest civilization known in western Asia developed just north of the Persian Gulf. Recent excavations at the site of the ancient city of Ur show that by 2900 B.C. a people known as the Sumerians were living there. They had come down from the north and established themselves on the Plain of Shinar near the mouths of the Tigris and Euphrates rivers. Here they reached a high state of civilization.

How the Sumerians Lived · Because there was little rainfall, the Sumerians, like the Egyptians, early learned to irrigate their fields. They raised barley and wheat. They used copper tools, and worked skillfully in silver and gold. They had wheeled carts and chariots pulled by donkeys. These are the earliest known examples of wheeled vehicles. They carried on an active business with people at Mohenjo-Daro in the Indus River valley. Archaeologists tell us that this river-valley civilization had as high a culture as that of the Sumerians.

Sumerian Writing · The Sumerians, like the Egyptians, developed a system of writing. At first they made crude pictures scratched on clay. Soon they simplified these pictures into strokes, or lines, made with the tip of a reed. When the writer pressed the end of the reed into soft clay, it left wedge-shaped marks like ▽ and ◁. These stood for sounds. We call this writing *cuneiform*, from a Latin word (*cuneus*) which means "wedge." Thousands of their clay tablets have been discovered in the ruins of ancient towns in western Asia. Modern scholars have been able to decipher these strange cuneiform signs.

The Sumerians had a system of numbers, not based on tens, as ours is today, but on sixties. A large number was given as so many sixties; that is, 120 would be two six-

The Ancient Near East · *What clues can you find on this map for the invasions which swept the Fertile Crescent? How do you account for the change in the Persian Gulf coast line? What states occupy the Near East today?*

Cuneiform Tablet from Ur (c. 1900 B.C.) · *It was not until c. (from* circa, *about) 1850 A.D., some 3750 years later, that Henry Rawlinson solved the mystery of wedge-shaped writing.*

ties, and so on. The unit of sixty led to our division of the hour into sixty minutes, the minute into sixty seconds, and the circle into three hundred and sixty degrees.

Sumerian City-States (2900–2350 b.c.) · Today nothing is left of the ancient Sumerian towns but mounds of earth and crumbled brick. Buried deep in these piles of rubbish, however, have been found hundreds of tablets of cuneiform writing. These reveal household accounts, letters, government records, notices of the building of palaces and temples, and descriptions of wars and conquests. Household utensils, tools, weapons, works of art, and many other relics tell us more about these people.

We learn that in the Sumerian cities there was a class of landholders, who had slaves to work on their estates. They traded with caravans and with small boats coming and going along the river. Over these free citizens there were government officials and priests. These formed an upper, or aristocratic, class. At the head of a community was a priest-king.

The city and the outlying fields for a few miles around formed a little city-state, or kingdom. Sumer (as the land of the Su-

merians was called) was made up of a number of these city-states. Records which have survived make it possible for us to follow their history for four hundred years.

Sargon Conquers the Sumerians · The Sumerian civilization did not continue to develop in peace. The city-kingdoms fought among themselves, and were threatened by an enemy from outside. Semitic tribesmen who had been for some time moving down the valley finally established a kingdom known as Akkad, north of Sumer. About 2350 b.c. a bold chieftain named Sargon descended the Euphrates, defeated the Sumerians, and set up the first Semitic kingdom known in history.

The more backward Akkadians gradually learned much from the Sumerians, with whom they now lived. They began to write their own Semitic language with the wedge-form signs. They also used the Sumerian calendar, numerals, weights, and measures, and imitated Sumerian art, especially sculpture. Although there was much fighting between the two peoples, they finally formed one nation, called Sumer and Akkad. The rulers of this kingdom (2350 b.c. and after) brought a large portion of western Asia under one government, and a great increase in trade resulted.

How Civilization Was Spread through the East · In the Stone Age, people bartered their products. As farming developed, barley and wheat became a useful measure of value. If a piece of land or an ox or something else could not be exchanged for something of *equal* value, it might be partly paid for by measures of grain. Then gradually the increase of precious metals made possible their use as a medium of exchange in buying and selling. Pieces of silver about the size of our dimes were used. They weighed a *shekel*, or one-sixtieth of a pound.

Hammurapi Receives Code from Sun God.

The wide trading of Sumer and Akkad resulted in an interchange not only of goods, but of ideas. Different peoples came to know of one another's customs in government, laws, religion, language, and art, as well as in business and industry.

Babylonia · About 1800 B.C. a tribe of Amorites came down the Euphrates, as the Akkadians had done earlier, and seized the little town of Babylon. One of the Amorite kings, Hammurapi, about 1700 B.C., finally succeeded in conquering the whole region of Shinar.

Hammurapi was a good fighter and an able ruler. Babylonia prospered under his leadership. The chief business of the country was trade, and Babylonian merchants traveled far and wide with their goods. These were grain, dates, leather, and wool. The weaving of woolen cloth was an important industry. Babylonian clay-tablet bills were sent out with caravans of merchandise. These had to be read by the merchants of other countries. Thus a knowledge of cuneiform writing became necessary throughout western Asia.

Hammurapi's Code of Laws · In order to establish order throughout his lands, Hammurapi made one body of laws for his people. He collected all the old statutes and customs going back to Sumerian times. He arranged and improved them, and made new laws where they were needed. This great code was engraved on a stone shaft and set up in the temple of the chief god, Marduk. There all could read it and know their rights. It is the earliest code of laws that has come down to us. To us it appears cruel to take an eye for an eye and a tooth for a tooth. But the code was a landmark of justice at that time. It limited the powerful to taking a tooth, where previously they could have taken a life.

Babylonian Art and Religion · Hammurapi's city of Babylon has disappeared, for its buildings were all of brick. Indeed, very little remains of either Babylonian art or architecture. We know, however, that by this time the arch was used over doorways. There seems to have been no painting, and the few examples of sculpture which we have cannot compare with the work of the Egyptians or that of the earlier Akkadians.

The Babylonians still worshiped the old Sumerian gods, but their own Semitic god Marduk was over all. Their religion centered in the effort to please the gods and so receive their benefits. One of the gifts of the gods was the power to foretell the future. Coming events were forecast by priests who interpreted the marks on the liver of a sheep which had been slain as a sacrifice. Sometimes the future was foretold by studying the position of the stars and planets. Both of these practices we shall find surviving among later peoples. And the reading of horoscopes (using signs of the Zodiac) is still common among the superstitious today.

Decline of Babylonian Civilization · After Hammurapi's death his successors were unable to protect the country against invaders from the northeast and northwest. By 1500 B.C. a primitive tribe called the Kassites had made themselves masters of the country. For nine hundred years progress in civilization in Babylonia ceased.

CHECK ON YOUR READING

1. Why did the desert nomads settle in the Fertile Crescent?
2. Describe the government of the Sumerians, their way of making a living, and their major contributions to civilization.
3. Why would the story of the Babylonians be important in a history of law? a history of architecture?

2. Assyrians, Chaldeans, and Phoenicians

Who the Assyrians Were · Assyria took its name from the little settlement of Assur, a fertile land to the north of Babylon. Here, about 2900 B.C., there was a small community of Sumerians and Assyrians who spoke a Semitic language. This group formed a little city-kingdom and profited by the civilization of its Sumerian neighbors. But the land was often invaded by enemy tribes, who sometimes brought Assur under their rule. Obliged to defend themselves for over a thousand years against attacking tribes, the Assyrians became hardened to war. They built up a powerful military machine.

The Assyrians Conquer the People of Western Asia · Assyria early grew rich from its trade. Its merchants eagerly sought the silver which was to be had in Asia Minor, where they had set up trading stations.

Assyrian War Chariots · *While the main attack was mounted by archers and heavy infantry, fearsome chariot forces swept around the enemy flanks to create panic and exploit any breakthrough.*

Assyria was an inland country, and its rulers were determined to reach the seacoast and control the trade routes between east and west. By 1300 B.C. her armies had marched westward across the Euphrates. But their further progress was checked by strong Semitic kingdoms that lay in their path. These were (1) the Arameans, a commercial people who had built up powerful cities in Syria; (2) the Hebrews, who occupied Palestine; and (3) the Phoenicians, who held wealthy city-kingdoms on the Mediterranean.

For centuries the Assyrian kings led their armed hosts against all who stood in their way. The Assyrians had early used horses and chariots in their armies, and until about 1100 B.C. had equipped their soldiers with weapons of bronze. After that time they had weapons, battering rams, and siege machinery made of iron. Wherever the terrible Assyrian forces swept through the land, they left a trail of death and destruction.

Empire of the Assyrians (c. 750–612 B.C.) · By 700 B.C. the Assyrian kings had gained possession of the whole Fertile Crescent and the country to the north almost to the Black and Caspian seas. Their empire was now a great military state composed of the nations they had conquered.

Sennacherib (who became emperor in 705 B.C.) established a magnificent capital at Nineveh. Here Assyrian monarchs ruled the western Asian world with an iron hand and collected tribute from their subject peoples. Moving along the roads that led to the palace might be seen herds of cattle, flocks of sheep, and long lines of camels laden with the treasure of defeated nations.

Civilization of Assyria · With these riches the Assyrian emperors lived in luxury. The entrance to the palace was made of triple arches faced with glazed brick in brilliant colors. On each side were placed colossal figures of human-headed bulls carved of alabaster. Inside the palace,

Assyrian, Chaldean, and Persian Empires · *Which was the largest? smallest? In what time order did they come? Find and name the capital city of each.*

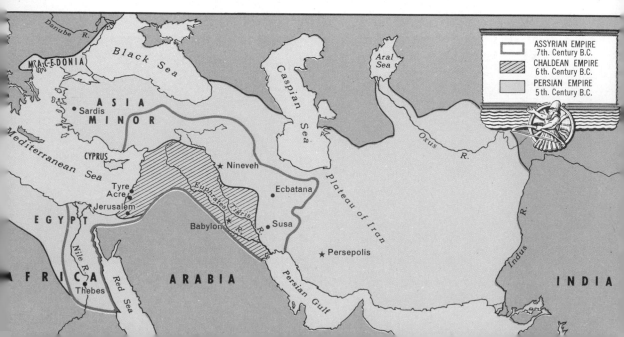

bands of sculptured reliefs pictured the mighty deeds of the ruler.

The Assyrian sculptors were most successful in their figures of wild animals. Assyrian art and industry, however, were largely borrowed from other peoples. The Assyrians were indebted to Egypt for the art of glazing brick and for many of their decorative designs. Their architects copied the arched doorways of Babylonia.

In the ruins of the palace of Assurbanipal (668–626 B.C.), grandson of Sennacherib, archaeologists found a collection of twenty-two thousand clay tablets. These were the books of Assurbanipal's library—the earliest we have from western Asia. They tell us much of what the Assyrians had learned.

Fall of Nineveh (612 B.C.) · The Assyrian kings were able to enjoy the spoils of conquest for over a century. But continual war undermined the strength of the state by cutting off the peaceful enterprises necessary to produce and maintain wealth. So the farm lands were gradually ruined or left idle. The peasants were taken from the fields to fill the ranks of the armies. Revolts within the boundaries of the empire increased, and dangers from outside began to be serious. Finally, the empire could no longer hold off invading tribes.

By 616 B.C. a Semitic people, the Chaldeans, had mastered Babylonia. A few years later they joined with the Medes, a tribe from the mountains to the northeast. Together they marched on the capital. In 612 B.C. Nineveh, the mighty city of the Assyrians, was no more.

Brief Glory of the Chaldean Empire (612–538 B.C.) · The Chaldean conquerors of Assyria were the last Semitic rulers of Babylonia in ancient times. They rebuilt Babylon into a magnificent capital for their empire, which included the entire Fertile

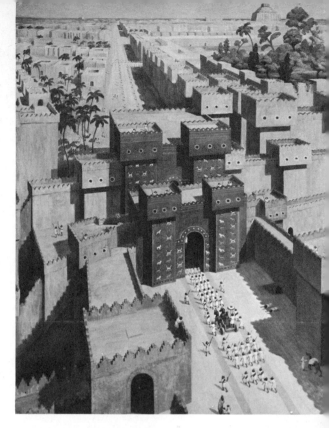

Nebuchadnezzar's Babylon · *Note the massive Ishtar Gate, the gardens on the palace roof, and the temple of Marduk in the background.*

Crescent. But the Chaldean supremacy lasted less than a century.

The greatest of the Chaldean rulers was Nebuchadnezzar (604–561 B.C.). His lavish display is vividly described in the Bible. It was Nebuchadnezzar who destroyed Jerusalem and took many Hebrews as captives to Babylon in 586 B.C.

The splendor of Nebuchadnezzar's capital surpassed even that of the Assyrian monarchs. Masses of rich foliage, rising in terraces, crowned the roof of his gorgeous palace. These roof gardens were the mysterious Hanging Gardens of Babylon, which the Greeks later counted among the Seven Wonders of the World.

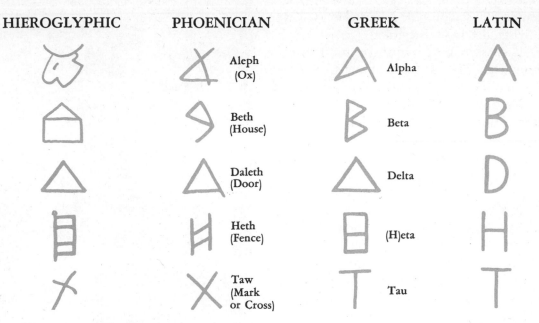

HIEROGLYPHIC	PHOENICIAN	GREEK	LATIN
	Aleph (Ox)	Alpha	
	Beth (House)	Beta	
	Daleth (Door)	Delta	
	Heth (Fence)	(H)eta	
	Taw (Mark or Cross)	Tau	

How the Alphabet Came to Us · *Why do you suppose the Phoenicians called their first letter* Aleph? *What similarities can you find? Some letters appear "backward" because the Phoenicians wrote from right to left.*

Civilization of the Chaldeans · The Chaldeans adopted the civilization they found in Babylonia. In astronomy, however, they made independent progress. This was at first only astrology, or the study of the heavenly bodies with a view to forecasting future events. The Chaldeans believed that five planets (Mercury, Venus, Mars, Jupiter, and Saturn) were divine powers which controlled the fate of men. These, with the sun and moon, made seven great divinities.

As Chaldean religious ideas spread westward, it became customary to worship each divinity on a particular day. This day finally became sacred to its god and bore its name. Three of our days—Saturday (Saturn day), Sunday, and Monday (Moon day)—still bear names of heavenly bodies. Beginning about 747 B.C., Chaldean astronomers made continuous observations of the heavens and recorded them for over three hundred and sixty years. Two Chaldean astronomers were able, with the help of these data, to determine with remarkable accuracy the time required for the revolution of the moon around the earth. They dated eclipses and computed the length of the year. The work of these astronomers was later used by Greek scientists.

End of Semitic Power in the East · After the death of Nebuchadnezzar the Chaldean Empire declined in power. Indeed, the long period of Semitic rule in western Asia was drawing to a close. Another great group of peoples—the Indo-Europeans—was advancing to conquer the Semitic kingdoms and to extend its empire over the entire Near East.

We must not neglect two other Semitic peoples, however. Though they never ruled over a great empire, they were of great importance in passing on the civilization of western Asia to Europe. These were the Phoenicians and the Hebrews.

The Phoenicians · The Phoenicians lived on the coast of what today is Syria and Lebanon. Before 3000 B.C., they were already shipping to Egypt timber from the forests near Lebanon. Their own industries were dyeing, textiles, and metalwork.

The Phoenicians were the first great sea traders in the eastern Mediterranean. They were the great "carriers of civilization." As such they played an important role in the interchange of the arts and industries of the peoples of western Asia, Egypt, and Europe. They adopted an alphabet of twenty-two letters (based on Egyptian hieroglyphics) from the Seirites of Sinai, and gave it to all the Mediterranean peoples.

They built up the great cities of Tyre, Sidon, and Acre. Many references to the cedars of Lebanon and the Phoenician cities can be found in the Bible. In fact the word *Bible* itself (meaning book) is derived from Byblos, a city which exported papyrus.

The Phoenicians fell under the control of Egypt during the period of the Empire (*c.* 1600 B.C.). But when Egypt was invaded by peoples from the northeast (*c.* 1200 B.C.), the Phoenician cities seized the opportunity to throw off the Egyptian yoke. After a period of freedom from foreign rule they were conquered by the Assyrians (*c.* 876 B.C.). Later they were part of the Chaldean and Persian empires. Phoenician ships and sailors made possible the Persian invasion of Greece. The great Phoenician colony of Carthage later was locked in mortal combat with Rome for control of the Mediterranean.

CHECK ON YOUR READING

1. *Why were the Assyrians so powerful? so feared? so wealthy? finally overthrown?*
2. *Why would the following people remember the Chaldeans: the ancient Greeks? the Hebrews? modern scientists?*
3. *What did the Phoenicians contribute to civilization?*

---

3. The Hebrews and Their Religion

Hebrews Settle in Palestine (1400–1200 B.C.) · The Hebrews, who belonged to these Semitic peoples, were also once wandering shepherds of the Arabian Desert. By 1400 B.C. they were moving into Palestine, which became their home. A southern group of their tribes had been slaves in Egypt, but under their great leader Moses had managed to escape.

When the Hebrews came into Palestine, they found another Semitic people, the Canaanites, already living there. The Canaanites, whose country was the crossroad between Egypt and Babylonia, had already learned much from these civilized nations. They lived in walled towns, had industries of their own, and used the cuneiform writing of the Babylonian traders. Gradually the two peoples mingled until they became as one. In the north the Hebrews finally adopted Canaanite ways of life. But in the south old nomad customs lingered on.

The Hebrew Kingdom (1025–930 B.C.) · Invasion of Palestine by the Philistines served to unite the Hebrews. A monarchy was established, with Saul as the first king. David, his successor, seized the Canaanite

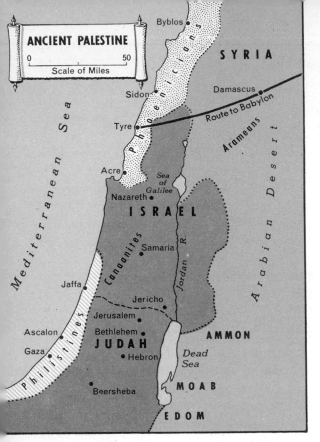

ANCIENT PALESTINE

0   50

Scale of Miles

The Kingdoms of Israel and Judah · *With which of the above locations are you familiar? What nations occupy ancient Palestine today?*

fortress of Jerusalem and made it his residence. From his new capital David was able to extend his kingdom and raise his people to a position that they had never before enjoyed.

The Hebrews never forgot the heroic deeds of King David as a warrior, nor his skill as a poet and musician. Centuries later they revered him as the author of many of their religious songs, or psalms.

Solomon's Reign and the Division of the Kingdom · David was followed by his son Solomon, who collected great riches and delighted in display. Solomon built a magnificent temple to replace the old Hebrew tabernacle, and a luxurious palace for himself. But to pay for all his projects he taxed the people heavily.

When Solomon died, the northern tribes set up a ruler of their own. The Northern Kingdom, Israel, was rich and prosperous, for its lands were fertile. The Southern Kingdom, Judah, was poorer. Aside from Jerusalem, it had no large cities, and many of its people still led the life of shepherds.

Rise of the Prophets · From time to time the Hebrew people strayed from the worship of their god, Yahveh (or Jehovah). The northern tribes, especially, had come to worship the old local *baals*, or gods, of the Canaanites.

In this religious crisis some great prophets spoke up. Elijah fearlessly denounced a king of Israel for idol worship. Amos, Hosea, and Isaiah warned the people of punishment if they offended Jehovah. This punishment would include military defeat at the hands of the foreign powers which were threatening the Hebrews at this time.

Northern Kingdom Destroyed by Assyria (722 B.C.) · The Assyrians crushed the kingdom of Israel and destroyed Samaria, its capital, in 722 B.C. The little kingdom of Judah, however, escaped the Assyrian armies. A century later Jerusalem rejoiced over the fall of Nineveh and the Assyrian power (p. 35). But she had escaped one master only to fall under another, for Chaldea followed Assyria in control of Palestine. Judah now shared the same fate as Israel. In 586 B.C. Nebuchadnezzar destroyed Jerusalem and carried away many of its people into exile.

Persian Kings Restore the Exiled Hebrews · When, forty-seven years later, a Persian king, Cyrus, conquered Babylon, the Hebrews greeted him as their deliverer. He allowed the exiles who wished to do so to return to their native land. When they returned, they rebuilt Jerusalem and attempted to restore the temple of Solomon.

How the Old Testament Came Down to Us · During the days of exile other great prophets arose among the Hebrews. They taught the people to view Jehovah as the kindly ruler of the entire universe, and emphasized the importance of a personal relationship with God. The prophets were inspired teachers of high moral conduct.

The returned exiles copied the ancient writings of their fathers. These were accounts of the patriarchs Abraham, Isaac, and Jacob, the words of the early prophets, songs, and proverbs. Now they added the teachings of later prophets. This collection has become the sacred Scripture of the Jews. It forms the first part of the Christian Bible, the Old Testament.

The first five books of the Old Testament tell the story of creation and the beginnings of the Hebrew people. They set forth early Hebrew law, including the Ten Commandments. These books are called by the Jews the *Torah*.

The scriptures were often referred to as "the law and the prophets." This literature, with its idea of one god (monotheism), is the great contribution of the Hebrews to Western religion and thought.

CHECK ON YOUR READING

1. *Trace the advances of the Hebrews through the reigns of Kings Saul, David, and Solomon.*
2. *What role did the prophets play?*
3. *What is the great contribution of the Hebrews to the world?*

---

4. The Coming of the Indo-Europeans

Who the Indo-Europeans Were · Far north of the Fertile Crescent there were peoples who pastured their flocks on the vast grasslands which reach from northeast of the Caspian Sea and the Caucasus Mountains westward all the way to the lower Danube River. We call them Indo-Europeans because when they began to migrate, they separated. One branch moved southward into India. The other moved westward across Europe to the Atlantic. These non-Semitic peoples were therefore the ancestors of the Persians and Indians, as well as of the Greeks, Romans, Slavs, Germans, English, and most Americans today.

Relation of Indo-European Languages · As the tribes wandered east, south, and west, they lost contact with one another. Although they had once spoken the same

language, the differences in the speech of the scattered peoples finally became very great. If they had happened to meet, they could no longer have understood one another. In time they lost all knowledge of their original relationship. But modern scholars have been able to show that the principal languages of Europe today have sprung from the same source.

Beginning with English and going eastward across Europe to India, we can find words which have much in common. Take, for example, the English word *mother*. In German it is *Mutter*; in Latin, *māter*; in Greek, *mētēr*; in Old Persian *mātar*; and in East Indian (Sanskrit), *mātar*.

The Hittites and Their Empire · The earliest known of these Indo-Europeans in the West had entered Asia Minor by 2500

Hittite Warrior · *Note his iron weapons, high hat, braided beard, close-fitted jerkin with broad belt, and the slippers with the turned-up toes. He could fight!*

The Hittite Civilization · It was through the Hittites that iron came into use in the Near East. Iron had long been known to man, but it was scarce and was regarded as a precious metal. By the thirteenth century B.C., however, the Hittites were working iron from the mines in Asia Minor and were trading in it. From this time on, the metal came into more general use. We speak of the Iron Age as beginning about 1000 B.C. We recall that it was the iron weapons of the Assyrian armies that made them so powerful in battle.

The Hittite Empire at its height had a good government. It also had a code of laws more humane than those of Assyria or Babylonia, with lighter penalties for minor offenses. The Hittites erected the first fine buildings of stone in western Asia. Their walled capital at Hattusas was the first large city in that area. Hittite architects introduced the portico-entrance, or porch flanked by towers. They decorated their walls with stone slabs carved in relief. These features were copied by the Assyrians and later by the Persians.

Asia Minor, lying near to the southeastern corner of Europe, was on the route over which the civilization of the East must pass on its journey westward. The Hittites handed on the civilization of the countries of Asia to their neighbors in Europe, with important contributions of their own.

B.C. They are called Hittites. They were Stone Age barbarians when they first occupied this region. But they now came into contact with merchants from Babylonia and Assyria who traded in Asia Minor. From them the Hittites learned to read cuneiform and even to write their own language in cuneiform characters. Fragments of their clay-tablet dictionaries have been found, written in three columns, Sumerian, Akkadian, and Hittite. After the Hittites had learned to write, they made great progress. By 2000 B.C. they were highly civilized.

Six hundred years later one of their kings conquered the area, and for two centuries the Hittite kings ruled over the larger part of western Asia. Then other Indo-European peoples, chief of whom were the Phrygians and the Armenians, pushed into Asia Minor. They crushed the Hittite Empire so completely that after 1200 B.C. it entirely disappeared.

CHECK ON YOUR READING

1. What languages and peoples today belong to the Indo-European group?
2. What territory did the Hittite Empire cover? What modern nation rules Asia Minor today? (See map, p. 362.)
3. What contributions did the Hittites make to civilization?

5. The Great Empire of the Persians

Separation of Aryan Tribes: the Iranians · The easternmost tribes of the Indo-European peoples, called Aryans, settled east of the Caspian Sea. About 1800 B.C. these tribes separated, and some found their way into India. Their sacred books, the Vedas, are written in Sanskrit. In them we find many references to their ancient home in the north.

Other tribes, who kept the name *Aryan* in the form *Iran*, pushed toward the Fertile Crescent. Among these were the Medes and the Persians. By 700 B.C. the Medes had established east of the Tigris a strong empire, which included the Persians. We have already noted (p. 35) how the Medes helped the Chaldeans destroy Nineveh in 612 B.C.

Rapid Rise of Persian Power · The home of the Persians was at the northeastern end of the Zagros Mountains. Sixty years after the fall of Nineveh an energetic leader, named Cyrus, united the Persian tribes into a nation. His strong army of peasants defeated the Median king and took possession of his territory. But the rapid success of Cyrus so alarmed the peoples to the west that Lydia, Chaldea, Egypt, and other countries combined against him. Without delay Cyrus marched his army all the way to Lydia. Here he captured Sardis, and took the wealthy king Croesus prisoner. Within five years the little Persian kingdom had spread to the Mediterranean Sea.

Cyrus now defeated the Chaldean army of Prince Belshazzar (*see* Daniel v). With his seizure of Babylon the control of western Asia passed from the Semites to Indo-European peoples. Five years after the death of Cyrus, his son Cambyses con-quered Egypt (525 B.C.). The empire of the Persians now included the whole civilized East, from the Nile and the Aegean coast almost to India (map, p. 34).

Government of the Persian Empire · The organization of this vast realm was a remarkable achievement. Cyrus laid the foundations of the government, but the task was completed by Darius the Great (521–485 B.C.). Darius ruled Egypt and Babylonia himself, but divided the rest of the empire into twenty provinces, or satrapies. At the head of each of these he placed a governor (satrap) responsible directly to him. This is our first example of a carefully organized provincial government.

In contrast to the cruelty of the Assyrians, the Persian kings treated conquered rulers humanely. They spared cities from destruction, and left the inhabitants in peace. Members of a subject kingdom were often made officials and generals, along with the Persians, and were rewarded for their services with grants of land. Subject nationalities were permitted to enjoy their local independence as long as they were (1) loyal to the emperor, (2) paid their regular tribute of taxes, and (3) furnished troops for the army.

In the eastern part of the realm tribute was still paid in produce, as of old. But in Lydia and the west the use of coined money was common by 600 B.C. Darius began to coin gold and allowed his satraps to coin silver.

Persia, the First Great Sea Power · Darius had the coast explored from the mouth of the Indus to the Isthmus of Suez. Moreover, he cleared out the ancient canal connecting the Nile with the Red Sea (p. 22).

Persepolis · *The splendid capital of ancient Persia was built by Darius and Xerxes and burned by Alexander. The figures to the right of the double staircase depict subject peoples bringing tribute. The eight figures to the left are the king's guards.*

Great stone tablets along the canal read: ". . . the canal was dug as I commanded and ships sailed from Egypt through the canal to Persia according to my will."

Darius was friendly with his Phoenician subjects, and with their help organized a war fleet in the Mediterranean. Thus this enlightened ruler made Persia the first great sea power of Asia. A system of roads was begun connecting the various parts of the empire. And a postal service was maintained by royal messengers.

Civilization of the Persian Empire · The Persians brought together in one empire all the civilized peoples of the Eastern world. They made use of the knowledge and art already existing instead of creating anything original of their own.

The royal palace excavated at Persepolis shows the Babylonian influence in its great terraces. The winged bulls at the palace gate were copied from Assyria, as was the use of decorative relief pictures in stone. The vast colonnade—the first in Asia—had originated two thousand years earlier in the valley of the Nile. Glazed-brick walls also had been used by the Egyptians and copied by the Assyrians, from whom they came to the Persians.

Decline of the Persian Empire · The later Persian emperors were neither as able nor as wise as Cyrus and Darius. They preferred to live in luxury and left the task of ruling to officials. The government finally became so inefficient and corrupt that the power of Persia declined. After two hundred years of prosperity this great empire lost its position of leadership in the Eastern civilized world.

CHECK ON YOUR READING

1. *How are the Indians, Medes, and Persians related?*
2. *How did Darius (a) govern his empire? (b) make Persia a sea power?*
3. *What did the Persians contribute to civilization?*

6. Civilization Reaches the Aegean World

The Aegean Bridge · We must now turn back in our story to find out what was happening in Europe. In doing so we find that civilization first developed in the region of the Aegean Sea. Egyptian ships, sailing northwest, would sight in a few days the mountains of Crete. Merchants making their way westward across the Fertile Crescent and Asia Minor would reach at length the shores of the Aegean. The Aegean Islands formed, therefore, a kind of bridge over which the civilization of Egypt and the Near East passed to the Western world.

Rise of Cretan Civilization · The most important of the Aegean Islands was Crete. As early as 3000 B.C. Egyptian ships brought copper to the little villages of the island. Later the Cretans learned to mix tin with copper and to mold bronze. This gave them stronger and more durable tools and weapons. They also devised a system of writing by means of hieroglyphics. During the Pyramid Age the Cretans learned many things from the Egyptians.

By 2000 B.C. the Cretans were a busy and prosperous people. Cnossus was the capital city of their kingdom. Here the kings built a fine palace, modeled on those of Egypt. With ships for trade and war these rulers are sometimes called "the Sea Kings of Crete." Cretan metalwork and pottery were carried to many places throughout the Mediterranean.

Grand Age of Crete (1600–1400 B.C.) · In the seventeenth century B.C. Cretan civilization reached its highest level. Excavations have revealed a magnificent palace, with colonnaded halls, open courts, and fine stairways. The walls were brilliantly painted or decorated with glazed figures. The pottery of this period was beautiful in design and decoration. The ivory carvings and exquisite work in gold and bronze rank with the finest craftsmanship of any people.

Cretan Civilization Reaches the Mainland · Although Egyptian and Cretan ships traded with the mainland of Greece, civilization in Europe was far behind that of the East. About 1500 B.C. certain chieftains, probably Aegeans, crossed over to Greece and settled in the plain of Argos. To protect themselves against the raids of wandering tribes from the north, they built great strongholds with massive stone walls. The ruins of such castles have been found in modern times at Tiryns and Mycenae.

Works of art in pottery and metal have been recovered in the remains of palaces and tombs. These are the oldest remains of a high civilization on the mainland of Europe. The period is known as the Mycenaean Age (about 1500–1200 B.C.) because the remains of this civilization were discovered at Mycenae. (See map, p. 51.)

How Civilization Spread through Europe · For many centuries this higher civilization was found only near the coast. Farther north and west the life of the European people remained that of the Late Stone Age. Traders, however, gradually pushed up the river valleys, carrying the products of the Near East into central Europe. Following the course of the Danube, they passed to the Rhine and on to the North Sea. Others, turning southward, followed the Rhone and came to the western Mediterranean and the coasts of Spain.

Most important of the wares that these wandering merchants brought to the Stone Age settlements of the north and the west

The Bull Leapers of Crete · *In this wall painting from the palace at Cnossus (c. 1500 B.C.) we see girls performing the dangerous ritual of seizing the horns of a charging sacred bull and somersaulting over his back.*

were copper tools. We have already seen how the use of metal tools promoted the progress of earlier peoples. Gradually a knowledge of metal spread through Europe, and men gave up the use of their crude stone tools. Although at first they had only copper, later they learned to make bronze by melting it with tin.

CHECK ON YOUR READING

1. *Why do we call the Aegean Islands a "bridge"? (Check with map, p. 51.)*
2. *Describe the Cretan civilization.*
3. *How did civilization spread into Europe?*
4. *Locate on a map: Cnossus, Argos, Tiryns, and Mycenae.*

~~~~~~~~ *Learning Activities* ~~~~~~

Think about the chapter

1. Why is the history of the Fertile Crescent made up of the rise and fall of many people, while in the Nile valley the Egyptians, for the most part, dominated the area?

2. How were the practices and ideas of the Near East made part of Western culture?

3. Make a chart showing the permanent contributions to world civilization made by the peoples of western Asia in the fields of religion, art and architecture, use of tools, science, government and law, literature, and commerce.

4. What do you think of the Persian plan of governing an empire? Why?

Go beyond the text

5. Find out how scholars learned to read cuneiform writing. What place did cuneiform have in the development of our alphabet?

6. Look up Hammurapi's Code, comment on its harshness or humaneness, and compare it with our laws today.

7. What is the significance of the "Dead Sea Scrolls"? To what period in history do they relate?

Follow up your special interests

8. Special reports prepared by individuals or committees will tell about other interesting developments in this long period. Reports can be in the form of essays, short talks, stories, or drawings. Here is a list of possible topics: Hanging Gardens of Babylon, Ashurbanipal's Library, Gilgamesh Epic, Hebrew Prophets, Trade Routes and Cargoes of the Phoenicians, David—Psalmist and King, Babylonian Captivity, Croesus and Lydia, Religion of Zoroaster, Trojan War, Life in Crete, and Solomon's Temple.

9. Committees working on the history-of-art scrapbook and the record of scientific discoveries will want to include the contributions made by the people of western Asia.

10. Draw the diagram of a huge tree of civilization with roots extending into the past and branches representing the present. Label each root with some contribution made by people you have studied thus far. For example: Stone Age men, *fire*; Sumerians, *unit of sixty*, etc. Then label each branch with fruits of the present which have grown out of these roots. For example: *furnace*; *minutes and hours*.

11. It is important to remember that this chapter covers a period longer than that from the time of Christ to the present day. Construct a detailed time line showing the rise and fall of the peoples of the Near East, milestones in the development of civilization, and important events in these 2500 years.

READ FURTHER

Basic readings: (1) BAUER and PEYSER, *How Music Grew*, Chap. 3. (2) BREASTED, *Ancient Times*, Chaps. 4–8. (3) CERAM, *March of Archaeology*. (4) CHEYNEY, *World History of Art*, Chaps. 2, 4. (5) DAVIS, *Readings*, Chaps. 2–3. (6) EVANS, *Costume Throughout the Ages*, Chap. 1. (7) HAGEDORN, *Book of Courage*. Moses, Saul. (8) HOFFMAN, *News of the World*, Nos. 3, 4. (9) TAYLOR, *Illustrated History of Science*, Chap. 1. (10) VAN LOON, *Story of Mankind*, Chaps. 7–12. (11) *Year's Pictorial History*, pp. 44–54.

Special accounts: (12) The *Bible*, Psalm 137, Babylonian captivity; I Chronicles, Chap. 28; II Chronicles, Chaps. 1–4; I Kings, Chap. 5. Accounts of building the Temple and dependence on Phoenician crafts and materials. (13) C. CERAM, *The Secret of the Hittites*. (14) E. CHIERA, *They Wrote on Clay*. Gives an account of the importance of the cuneiform tablets and the development of the alphabet. (15) A. POWELL DAVIES, *The Meaning of the Dead Sea Scrolls*. (16) J. GAER, *Young Heroes of the Living Religions*. Well written and beautifully illustrated. (17) W. KELLER, *The Bible as History*. (18) D. MILLS, *Book of the Ancient World*. (19) O. OGG, *Twenty-six Letters*. Covers the ideographs and writing materials of all the ancient nations. (20) *Life*, "The Epic of Man: Sumer," June 4, 1956. (21) *National Geographic*, "Mesopotamia," January, 1951.

Fiction and biography: (22) J. BAIKIE, *Sea Kings of Crete*. (23) F. GERE, *Boy of Babylon*. (24) G. MALVERN, *Behold Your Queen*. Story of Esther. Also *The Foreigner*, by same author. Story of Ruth and Naomi.

"If a man owe a debt, and through lack of water grain have not grown in the field, he shall not make any return of grain to the creditor, and he shall not pay the interest for that year." —*Hammurapi's Code*

CHAPTER 4

How the Greeks Lived
and Governed Themselves

CHAPTER OUTLINE

1. *The Story of the Greek City-States*
2. *The Greeks Drive Off the Persians*
3. *"A House Divided against Itself"*
4. *Life and Thought of the Greek People*

KEY WORDS AND DATES

city-state
Troy
tyrants
Solon
Clisthenes
Assembly
Marathon—490 B.C.
Thermopylae
Themistocles
Salamis
Delian League
democracy
Peloponnesian Wars
Pericles
460 B.C.—429 B.C.
oligarchy
Homer
kinship
oracle
Olympic games

INTO THE AEGEAN WORLD came waves of barbarians from the north whom we call the Greeks. These crude tribesmen knew nothing of the arts and industries of the people whom they conquered, and so destroyed much of what they found. Yet once again we shall watch a primitive people slowly emerge from their barbarism. By learning from their neighbors they developed a way of life that surpassed that which their forefathers had destroyed. Indeed, after a period of fifteen hundred years the Greeks built up a civilization higher than any the world had ever known.

To them we are indebted for Homer's great epic poems, the basic ideas of citizenship and democracy, and symbols of great courage such as Thermopylae, of victory such as Marathon, of sea power such as Salamis. We are privileged to share their fierce love of independence and of truth, beauty, art, philosophy, and service.

We shall find out how the Greeks governed themselves and how they united to resist Persian invasions. We shall see that their religious beliefs gave them a strong sense of kinship but that the rivalry of Sparta and Athens led finally to wars and then loss of independence.

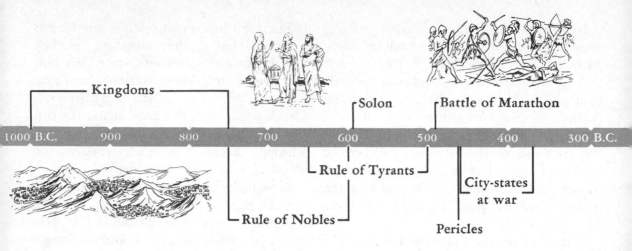

Kingdoms

Solon

Battle of Marathon

| 1000 B.C. | 900 | 800 | 700 | 600 | 500 | 400 | 300 B.C. |

Rule of Tyrants

City-states at war

Rule of Nobles

Pericles

1. The Story of the Greek City-States

Crude Greek Tribes Conquer the Aegean World · Among the Indo-European peoples of the northern grasslands, there was a large group of tribes whom we call the Greeks. They gradually moved westward along the Black Sea and into the pasture lands along the lower Danube River. By 2000 B.C. some of these crude tribesmen, with their families in rough carts, had already reached the lands of northern Greece.

We know very little about the invasions that followed, for these Greeks could not write. It seems clear, however, that their various tribes kept on pushing down the peninsula. By 1500 B.C. they were established in southern Greece. A century later one of their tribes crossed over to Crete, laid waste the city of Cnossus, and seized the whole island, as well as other islands in the south Aegean.

By 1000 B.C. the Greeks had taken possession of the entire Aegean world, including the coast of Asia Minor. Here, in the twelfth century B.C., a Greek expedition had captured and burned the great city of Troy. The story of this has become immortal in the pages of Homer's *Iliad*. The central coastal region of Asia Minor was settled by Greek tribes known as Ionians. They were to play an important role in Greek history.

The splendid civilization which the Aegeans had developed was destroyed by the crude invaders, and this region sank back into a state of barbarism. Those of the Aegeans who did not flee gradually intermarried with the conquerors. Their descendants were a highly gifted people, whose achievements we are to follow. The remnants of Aegean industries, arts, and crafts that survived provided a foundation on which the Greeks would one day build a great civilization of their own.

The Greeks Slowly Change Their Ways · For a long time, however, the barbarian Greeks remained a simple people, continuing to tend their flocks and herds. But gradually each tribe settled down, gave up its nomadic life, and began farming. The former war leaders became "shepherd kings" of their tribes. Soon little villages grew up and the people came to own their land. They needed some kind of government to settle disputes, to make laws, and to see that the laws were obeyed.

In the course of time a group of villages would merge into a city. Each of these cities became a little state in itself. Each had its own armed force, its own laws, its own gods. And each citizen had a strong patriotic feeling toward his own city and no other. The king was the chief ruler, and the guardian of the city gods. With the help of a council of important men he administered and defended his little state. There were in time hundreds of these Greek city-states.

The Phoenicians Teach the Greeks · The Greek tribesmen at first were not even able to write. And building and manufacturing were new to them too. They were glad to buy the goods that the Phoenician ships brought to their shores (p. 37). Thus they were able to get rich fabrics and clothing, gold and alabaster perfume bottles from Egypt, ivory combs beautifully carved, porcelain and silver dishes, and jewelry.

But the Phoenicians brought the Greeks a gift of even greater value: an alphabet. The Phoenician merchants wrote their bills and invoices with these characters on Egyptian papyrus. The Greeks began to write Greek words with the same signs. In this way an alphabet for the first time reached Europe. From it all others used in the Western world have been derived.

Geography Influences Government · The city-states never united in Greece to form a strong central government. The people were separated by mountain ranges and by great bays that cut the coast into different communities. Moreover, the Greeks on the mainland were at some distance from those living on the islands and in the cities of Asia Minor. These communities, separated by land and water, developed independent governments with their own laws and their own ways of living. Each was a little nation (map, p. 51).

Greek and Phoenician Colonies · *Who controlled the shores of the Aegean Sea and the Black Sea? Whose ships enabled Persia to invade Greece? Use the index to see how colonies at Syracuse and Carthage later affected history.*

The Four Chief City-States · There were, however, four distinct regions on the mainland where the geography of the country favored the union of the little communities into a larger city-state. (1) The oldest of these was Argos, where the ancient strongholds of Tiryns and Mycenae had been located. (2) Sparta dominated the two peninsulas in the south and the land to the west of them. (3) In the north Thebes headed the Boeotian League of regional city-states. (4) Athens controlled the entire Attic peninsula. These larger city-states were the only permanent unions among the Greek peoples, and of these the most prominent were Athens and Sparta.

Rise of a Noble Class · For several centuries (1000–750 B.C.) each city-state was ruled by a king, aided by a council and an assembly of all weapon-bearing men. During this period, however, a class of wealthy nobles got possession of much land. They were skilled warriors who had often defended the city-state in time of war. They finally controlled the council, and the assembly lost all importance.

By 750 B.C. they had taken away from the king almost all the powers he had formerly enjoyed. In Athens the nobles chose officials from their own number (archons) to take charge of the different departments of the government. In Sparta there were two kings, one acting as a check on the other. Elsewhere the nobles took complete control of affairs, and kingship disappeared.

Under the government of the nobles (750–600 B.C.) the rich grew richer, and the poor became poorer. Many of the farmers sank into debt and had to give up their land to the rich. They became day laborers or even sold themselves into slavery to meet their debts. As laborers and slaves, they had no vote and no rights in the courts.

Growth of Colonies and Business · These conditions led many Greek farmers to seek new homes in new lands. The vessels of Greek merchants had already ventured into the Black Sea. In that far-off region the unhappy farmers found plenty of land on which to begin life over again. By 600 B.C. Greek settlements encircled the Black Sea and reached the grainfields of the Danube and the iron mines of the old Hittite country (p. 40).

Greek seamen sailed westward to the shores of Italy fifty miles away. Here Greek colonists founded many settlements along the coast. They called the region Great Greece. Sailors also crossed to the island of Sicily, where Syracuse later became an important Greek city. (See map, p. 48.)

The founding of colonies created new business and increased wealth. A large market was opened up for Greek products. This stimulated manufacturing in the home cities. Greek merchant ships began to take metalwork, woven goods, and pottery to distant towns. They brought back raw materials, foodstuffs, and the fine bronzework of the Etruscans in northern Italy.

As a result of this business activity, a new class of persons became important in the state. This was the *middle* class. They were neither nobles nor slaves, but were businessmen, merchants, and manufacturers who were growing rich from industry and trade. These men began to oppose the autocratic methods of the nobles and to demand that they be given some share in the management of public affairs.

Solon's Reforms Help the People · In 594 B.C., a noble named Solon was elected to high office in Athens. He introduced a number of reforms to aid the poor, especially debtors. He canceled all mortgages and returned the land to its owners. He set free those who had become slaves be-cause of debt, and made it unlawful to take away a man's liberty on this account. Solon also set a limit to the amount of land which a noble might hold. And anyone who lost a lawsuit was given the right to carry the case to a jury of citizens elected by lot.

It was Solon's code of written laws which first gave to all Greek freemen equal rights in the courts. Solon made a new constitution which permitted every citizen a share in the control of the state. The citizens were graded into classes according to their income. The wealthy still held the highest offices. But even the humblest had a right to vote in the Assembly and to gain one of the lower posts in the government.

The Greek Tyrants, or Dictators · It now often happened that an ambitious noble, by championing the cause of the people, would gain enough of a following to place himself at the head of the government il-legally. These men, whom the Greeks called *tyrants*, were much like our modern bosses or dictators.

Sometimes they were good rulers who did much for the poor. Such a ruler was Pisistratus, who became tyrant in Athens about fifty years after Solon. He made many public improvements, thereby giving work to the unemployed. He invited skilled craftsmen from other cities to settle in Athens. Athenian manufacturing and commerce flourished as never before.

Tyrants were never revered as kings, be-cause they had no royal ancestry. Their position was always unconstitutional and insecure, for they were dependent entirely upon their popularity with the people. Tyrants ruled at various times in the differ-ent city-states. But the Greeks always had a prejudice against those who seized power, and the tyrants often were killed.

An Ostrakon · *This potsherd ballot was cast against Themistocles, who with Pericles proved to be one of the greatest of Greek statesmen.*

Athens Moves toward a Democracy · Some years after the rule of Pisistratus an-other Athenian noble, Clisthenes, also championed the cause of the people. He reformed the system of voting so that the right of the nobles to vote as a group and manage affairs was taken away from them (508 B.C.). In order to prevent the rise of a new tyrant in Athens, Clisthenes made a law that the people might vote once a year to banish any dangerous citizen from the state for ten years.

To cast his vote a citizen had only to write the name of the man on a piece of broken pottery (*ostrakon*), and place it in the voting vase at the market place. From this came our word *to ostracize*—that is, to banish or exclude from society or common privileges. Clisthenes thus freed Athens from dictators and by his reforms made the government more democratic than it had ever been before.

CHECK ON YOUR READING

1. *What were the results of the Greek con-quest of the Aegean world?*
2. *Why did the Greeks form city-states as their type of government?*
3. *What reforms were made by Solon and Clisthenes?*

2. The Greeks Drive Off the Persians

Persia Threatens Greece · At the opening of the fifth century B.C. the Greeks found themselves face to face with the terrible power of Persia. For while the Greeks were founding colonies and developing trade in the Mediterranean, the Persians, under Cyrus and his successors, had built up a vast empire in the East (p. 41). The Persians then conquered the highly civilized Greek cities of Asia Minor.

Although these tiny Ionian cities were no match for the Persian Empire, they nevertheless revolted. During the struggle which followed, the Athenians sent a number of ships to aid their relatives. This furnished an excuse for the Persians to attack Greece.

How the Greeks Met the Persian Invasions · The story of how the little Greek armies defended their homeland against the mighty forces of Persia is one of victory

Ancient Greece · *Locate Athens, Sparta, the Hellespont, Mt. Athos, Marathon, Thermopylae, Salamis, and Plataea in relation to the Persian invasion.*

ANCIENT GREECE

MAINLAND DIVISIONS

1. Epirus
2. Thessaly
3. Acarnania
4. Aetolia
5. Locris
6. Doris
7. Phocis
8. Boeotia
9. Attica
10. Euboea
11. Megaris
12. Argolis
13. Achaia
14. Elis
15. Arcadia
16. Messenia
17. Laconia

0   85

Scale of Miles

over tremendous odds. In the end, a free people triumphed over a despotic monarch. The names of *Marathon* and *Thermopylae* still stand for us as symbols of endurance and courage.

The Persians made three attempts by sea and land to overcome Greece. (1) The first Persian fleet was wrecked as it rounded the rocky promontory of Mt. Athos (492 B.C.). At the same time, the army lost many of its men in the long march across the Hellespont and through Thrace. (2) The second expedition (490 B.C.) brought the Persian ships into the Bay of Marathon. Here they landed twice as many men as the Greeks could put into the field. The Greeks, under Miltiades, took up their position in the hills, where they could overlook the Persians on the plain of Marathon. When the Persians attempted to march along the shore road to Athens, the Greeks charged down upon them. At close quarters the Persian bowman was no match for the Athenian with spear and sword. Fleeing to their ships, the Persians left six thousand dead upon the field. The Battle of Marathon, illustrated below, became a turning point in history. It gave the Greeks time to prepare for a third invasion, which came ten years later.

Themistocles Urges a Strong Navy · In the meantime Themistocles, the leading statesman at the time, urged the Athenians to build a strong navy. He realized that the little Greek armies would have great difficulty in defeating the massive forces which the Persians could bring against them. But he found it hard to rouse his countrymen to action. Finally the Athenians awoke to the fact that the enemy was making extensive preparations for a new attack. They then agreed to build a fleet of one hundred and eighty vessels. An effort to unite all the Greeks against the Persian invaders was unsuccessful. But the Spartans joined with the Athenians on condition that they be given command of the allied fleets.

Athens Is Destroyed · (3) In the summer of 480 B.C. the Persians advanced against Greece for the third time by sea and land. Their numbers were enormous. The only hope for the Greeks lay in stark courage and careful strategy. The decision was to delay the Persian hordes in the narrow confines of the pass at Thermopylae. Here, Leonidas, king of the Spartans, with five hundred men fought to the death against two hundred thousand Persians.

While the Persians pushed onward, Themistocles had the Athenian people removed to the islands of Salamis and Aegina for safety. As they looked northward, they could see the Persian fleet drawn up before the port of Athens, while high over the

| c. 2800 B.C. | 490 B.C. | 490 B.C. | 1944 A.D. |

The Great Pyramid is to the Battle of Marathon as the latter is to D-Day.

hills the flames and smoke from the burning city showed against the sky.

Final Defeat of the Persians · Themistocles wisely placed the Greek fleet in the narrow bay of Salamis and then tricked King Xerxes into making an attack. With its forces divided by the tiny island of Psyttalea, and cramped for lack of space to maneuver, the huge Asian fleet was soon in confusion. By nightfall it was almost completely destroyed. Xerxes thereupon withdrew into Asia. But he left some fifty thousand men to winter in Thessaly.

The following spring a united army of Greeks overwhelmingly defeated the Persian force at Plataea (479 B.C.). Greek triremes then destroyed the remnants of the Persian fleet in the waters near Asia Minor and took possession of the Hellespont. No Persian army ever again set foot in Greece.

CHECK ON YOUR READING

1. *Why did the Persian king send his army to conquer the Greeks?*
2. *What course of action did Themistocles urge? Why?*
3. *Why are Greeks so proud of the following: Marathon? Thermopylae? Salamis? Plataea? Locate these on the map.*

3. *"A House Divided against Itself"*

Growth of the Athenian Empire · In spite of these great victories, the Greeks still feared their Asian enemy. Athens therefore persuaded the Aegean Islands and the Ionian cities to join her in forming a league for self-defense. The members of this confederation were to supply ships or money toward a fleet to be commanded by the Athenians. The union was called the Delian League (477 B.C.) because the treasury was located for safety at the temple of Apollo on the island of Delos.

This fleet kept the Persians out of the Aegean Sea and cleared the pirates out of Mediterranean waters. As a result Greek trade with the East flourished as never before. Athens became the most prosperous and powerful city of Greece. It was but a step for her to transform this naval league into an empire.

But the Aegean Islands and the Greek cities of Asia Minor began to resent Athenian domination. When some of them wished to withdraw from the League, they were not permitted to do so. Athens sent out her fleet, conquered them, and forced them to pay tribute. Sometimes their people were driven from their land, and their farms were taken by Athenian settlers.

Athens also interfered in their local affairs and required them to bring certain cases to her courts for trial. Yet she did **not** grant

Athenian democracy was direct, not representative.

them Athenian citizenship. There was no longer any unity or equality in the League. Indeed, Athens now treated her allies as subjects (477–463 B.C.). The Delian League had become an Athenian Empire.

Rivalry of Sparta and Athens · Sparta jealously watched the growing prosperity and power of Athens. While Athens became a great and cultivated city, Sparta remained little more than a military camp. The wealthy citizens of Sparta lived on the income from their lands and the taxes squeezed out of subject towns. By devoting themselves to military training they became the greatest soldiers of Greece.

Instead of being a united people, the Greeks were divided into hostile factions. Sparta represented an aristocratic tradition of a privileged military class supported by the labor of an enslaved population. Athens represented democratic institutions and interest in learning and art.

The Athenian Democracy · We may well ask how Athens could be the autocratic ruler of an empire and at the same time a champion of democracy. Athens did seek, for the sake of prestige and power, to domi-

nate a union of Greek states. In the government of her own citizens, however, her progressive statesmen favored a policy of increasing the rights of the people. Under the leadership of Pericles (460–429 B.C.) Athens reached the height of her influence as the capital of an empire, and also made great progress in democratic reform.

Solon's laws had given the people the right to hold the lower offices in the state and to bring their cases before citizen juries. Pericles secured a law providing for the payment of jurors. Any citizen might now serve in these courts. These juries were so important that they became a kind of judicial body which prepared and interpreted the laws made by the popular Assembly. The citizens also succeeded in gaining the right to be chosen by lot for any office in the government except the highest—that of the generals-in-chief. Pericles was elected year after year as the leader of the ten generals who headed the Athenian state.

Duties of Athenian Citizenship · Athenian citizenship gave many privileges, but it also required certain duties. All citizens had to serve in some branch of the army or navy. The wealthy citizens had to contribute large sums for public expenses, and the less well-to-do had to pay smaller sums, somewhat like our taxes. But Athens was not a complete democracy in our sense of the term. All *citizens* could vote and be members of the Assembly, it is true. But there were thousands of slaves, freedmen, and others not admitted to citizenship.

The City-States Fight One Another · The ambition and success of Athens began to arouse the hostility of the other Greek cities. The alliances she made with Argos, Megara, and Thessaly increased suspicion against her. When the prosperous island of Aegina attached itself to Sparta for protection, Athens laid siege to the island by land and sea. There was a general fear in Greece that the Athenians wished to build up an empire on the mainland, as well as in the Aegean.

Finally, war with Sparta broke out. The civil wars which followed lasted, with intervals, for half a century. They are usually called the Peloponnesian Wars from the name of the peninsula on which Sparta was located. At the end of the first conflict (459–446 B.C.) both sides were exhausted.

A second war, even more disastrous, followed (431–421 B.C.), when the Athenian possessions in the north Aegean revolted and received support from Corinth and Sparta. The Athenian leaders were unable to match their combined enemies. They therefore gathered the neighboring people into the city and within the walls leading down to the port of Piraeus. Here a plague caused the death of perhaps a third of the population, including Pericles.

In a third hopeless conflict Athens was completely exhausted. A large fleet and army sent to capture the mighty city of Syracuse in Sicily were bottled up and forced to surrender. Athens now faced lack of leadership at home, revolts in her colonies, and even Persian aid to Sparta. A final disaster came with the capture of 180 Attic triremes as they lay drawn up on the beach in the Hellespont. Then Spartan vessels blockaded Piraeus and cut off the Athenians' food supply. Starvation forced the city to surrender. The fortifications of Athens were torn down, her foreign possessions were taken from her, and she was forced to enter the Spartan League. The Athenian Empire had come to an end (404 B.C.).

Last Years of Greek Independence · Sparta managed to maintain her leadership of the Greek states for over thirty years. But the government she established proved even more distasteful to the Greek cities than the tyranny of Athens. Small groups of nobles ruled the cities, with soldiers to assist them. (This rule by a few is called an *oligarchy*.) Opponents were murdered or banished and their fortunes seized.

Finally, the city of Thebes combined with Athens and after a long war crushed the power of Sparta (371 B.C.). But Thebes was no more successful than Athens or Sparta in uniting the Greek people. No Greek city-state was willing to submit to the rule of another. Indeed the principal city-states had taken turns in crushing one another. Divided as they were, the Hellenic people were soon to fall into the hands of a conqueror from the north—Philip of Macedon. Before we turn to his story, let us see how the Greeks lived and what they thought about.

CHECK ON YOUR READING

1. *Why was the Delian League formed? How did Athens transform it into an Athenian Empire?*
2. *How did Pericles make the government more democratic?*
3. *What were the causes and results of the Peloponnesian Wars?*

4. Life and Thought of the Greek People

Hero Songs: Homer · Long before the Greeks could write, they loved to dwell on the deeds of their national heroes. Into the songs of the distant past were woven stories and legends of great battles. Especially was this true of the war in which the Greeks had captured the splendid city of Troy in Asia Minor. As early as 1000 B.C. these songs were familiar in the Ionian cities. Here it became customary for bards to entertain the guests at the feasts of the nobles and kings. They sang poetic tales to the music of the harp. Gradually these separate songs grew into long narrative poems of heroic action, called *epics*. They were added to over the centuries, and were finally written down after 700 B.C.

The most famous of the ancient bards was one whose name was Homer. He was supposed to be the author of two great epics. The *Iliad* told the story of the Greek expedition against Troy (Ilium). The *Odyssey* was the tale of the long journey home from Troy of the hero Odysseus.

Religious Beliefs of the Early Greeks · The blind Homer became the great religious teacher of the Greeks. The Homeric songs and ancient myths told how the gods dwelt among the clouds on the top of Mt. Olympus. Zeus, the sky-god, controlled the lightning and was the ruler of them all. Apollo, the sun-god, guarded the fields and shepherds. Apollo also knew the future. When consulted at his shrine (*oracle*) at Delphi, he could reveal to inquirers what the future held for them.

Athena, the great warrior goddess, protected the Greek cities with her shining weapons. She also watched over the people as they worked in time of peace. She was the wisest of the many Greek gods, for an old tale related how she had sprung full-armed from the brain of Zeus.

The Greeks pictured the gods in heroic human form, possessing both good and bad human traits. Homer tells of the family quarrels between Zeus and his wife, Hera. Other stories showed the gods as having the same weaknesses as men.

The Greeks believed that at death all men passed into a gloomy kingdom beneath the earth, called Hades. Here the fate of the good did not differ from that of the bad. Great heroes, however, enjoyed a life of endless bliss in the beautiful Elysian Fields somewhere far to the west.

Greek Sense of Kinship · We have seen that the barriers of land and sea divided the Greek world into separate communities. In

Athena (Minerva) · *She won Athens by creating the gift most useful to mortals—the olive. Here she sadly reads the names of heroes who fell in her city's defense.*

56

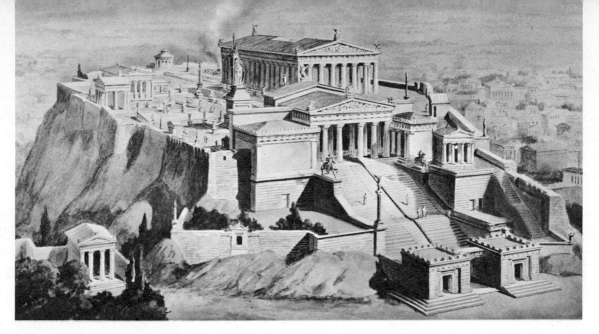

The Acropolis at Athens · *This hill was first used as a fortress and later was consecrated to Athena. This reconstruction shows the (1) marble steps, (2) entrance building, (3) Temple of Nike, (4) Erechtheum, and (5) the Parthenon.*

fact, excessive love of independence prevented the Greeks from becoming a united people. But, in spite of their rivalries, the Greeks had a sense of kinship to one another. This was strengthened by ties which set them apart from non-Greeks.

(1) One of the ties binding them together was their belief that they had all descended from the same ancestor. Since his name was Hellen, they gradually came to call themselves *Hellenes.* The rest of the world was to them composed of "barbarians." (2) To this kinship was added the use of the same language. (3) They also shared certain legends of their past history, especially the heroic stories of their great poet Homer. (4) There were also some great gods, such as Zeus and Apollo, at whose temples all Greeks worshiped. (5) As early as 776 B.C. the Greeks began to hold athletic contests at Olympia every four years in honor of Zeus. In these Olympic games all Greeks had a chance to take part. (6) Councils of representatives from the various city-states had charge of other festivals as well and took care of the temple of Apollo at Delphi.

Athens, "the School of Greece" · Until the middle of the sixth century B.C. it was in the Greek cities of Asia Minor and the Aegean Islands that literature, art, science, and industry made most progress. After the Persian Wars, Athens became the leading city not only in military affairs, but also in manufacturing, trade, literature, and art. The foremost Greek thinkers, writers, artists, and craftsmen came there to live.

Pericles made Athens the most beautiful city in Greece and the center of learning and culture in the Greek world. Thus hereafter in our story we shall be speaking chiefly of the Athenian Greeks.

Social Classes · After the Persian Wars the population of Athens was made up of

Athenian School (c. 480 B.C.) · *This red-figured cup by the painter Duris shows boys being taught to play the lyre and to read and write Greek. Why are ceramic objects like the above of so much interest to historians?*

several classes. (1) The nobles, or aristocracy, were wealthy citizens who lived on the income from their lands. (2) Rich businessmen hastened to buy land to improve their social position. (3) There were hundreds of craftsmen, who carried on the business life of the city. These artisans were beginning to organize into guilds of carpenters, masons, potters, jewelers, somewhat like our modern craft unions. (4) Below this class were the unskilled laborers, freemen but little better than slaves. (5) There were also a large number of farmers and peasants in Attica. All these classes, from rich to poor, were citizens.

(6) On the other hand, there was the colony of foreigners living in Athens, men in various arts and in business and also teachers, philosophers, artists, and poets. However celebrated they might be, these aliens could not enjoy the privileges of Athenian citizenship. (7) Nor could slaves, who were born of slave parents or who were captives of wars.

How the Greeks Lived · Although Athens was the most important Greek city, it would have seemed to us a very primitive place. The houses were of brick and had no windows. The front of even a wealthy man's house was simply a blank wall, in which there was a door leading into a court, around which the rooms were built. The court was open to the sky and was surrounded by a sort of porch with columns. As the climate of Greece was mild, the family could use this porch much of the time for their various activities. From the court a number of openings led into a living room, dining room, bedrooms, storerooms, and a kitchen.

The house had no conveniences. There was no chimney, and the smoke from the kitchen fire, though intended to go out through a hole in the roof, often filled the room instead. In winter, drafts blew into the house, for many entrances were without doors. The only stove was a pan of burning charcoal. Daylight came into the rooms through the doors to the court, for windowpanes were still unknown. At night there was only the dim light from an olive-oil lamp to help the family to see.

There was no plumbing or piping in the house, no drainage, and no sanitary arrangements. The water supply was brought in jars by slaves from the nearest well or spring. The simplicity of the house itself was in marked contrast to its rich furnishings. For the Greek craftsmen were now producing beautiful furniture, metal utensils, and lovely pottery.

The city was about a mile wide and somewhat more in length. The houses were clustered around the Acropolis, a fortified hill on which in early times had stood the residence of the kings. After the disappearance of kingship, the shrines and holy places were still preserved as religious buildings. The famous temples which now stand in ruins on the Acropolis were built by Pericles after the Persian Wars.

The streets of the city were narrow and crooked alleys, winding between the bare mud-brick houses. There was no pavement or sidewalk, and when it rained the street became a mass of mud. All the household rubbish and garbage was thrown directly into the street. Since there was no sewer system, disease spread easily and plagues were common.

How an Athenian Boy Was Educated · Athens had no public schools supported by the state. The amount of education that an Athenian youth received was largely dependent on the wealth of his parents. When a boy was old enough, he was sent, in care of a man-slave (*paidagogos*), to the home of a private teacher. These elementary teachers were generally poor and had no social standing. They taught the young boys reading, writing, counting, and a little music. During the day the children might be taken to a playground, where they had gymnastic exercises and played games. The girls did not go to school.

As the boys grew older, they might study grammar, drawing, and geometry, and memorize long passages from the poets. At the age of eighteen the sons of citizens were given two years of military training by the state. After this service those who wished to prepare themselves for public life might attend courses of lectures given by teachers called *Sophists*. These teachers were lecturers who moved from city to city. They trained their pupils in public speaking and gave them a wider knowledge of ethics, government, history, religion, and science.

Athletic Training · The Athenians admired a sound and beautiful body, as well as a well-trained mind. Hence gymnastics and athletics formed a part of all education. Athletic contests were an important feature at all entertainments and religious festivals. But perfection and grace in performance were valued more highly than the setting of a new record.

The Discus Thrower · *The great Greek sculptor Myron portrays the beauty, perfection, and grace of the human body in action. What is the latest Olympic record for the discus?*

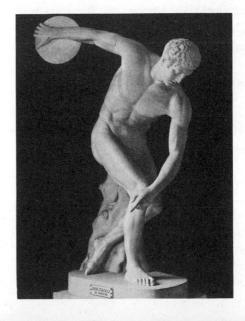

Wealthy young Athenians spent much of their time on the new athletic fields. On the north of Athens was the field known as the Academy, and on the east was the Lyceum. Later, courses of lectures were given in these places, and this custom gave to the words *lyceum* and *academy* the associations which they have for us today.

The chief events in the athletic contests were boxing, wrestling, running, jumping, casting the javelin, and throwing the discus. To these contests were afterward added chariot and horseback races.

How a Spartan Boy Was Educated · The schooling of a Spartan boy was quite different from that of an Athenian. When he was seven years old, he was taken from home to live in a camp with other boys of his own age. Here he was given a strict military training by officers whom he had to obey without questioning. If he disobeyed orders, he was brutally punished.

In the camp the boys slept on the ground, wore no shoes, and had to bathe in the river, even in winter. This severe routine was intended to harden them to the conditions of war. They were sometimes even obliged to steal their food in order to learn how to forage for food in wartime.

Contrast between Athenian and Spartan Ideals · The education of the Spartan boy was a preparation to serve the state. The Spartans believed that the individual was important only as he was of service to his country. Moreover, it was the idea of a state-at-war that molded his education.

The Athenian youth, on the other hand, was educated to serve the state at peace. He was expected to speak publicly on questions of general policy and to influence the government. The Athenians believed that the state existed to serve the individual. The Spartans, on the other hand, believed that the individual existed to serve the state.

These conflicting theories as to the relative importance of the individual and the state have survived to our own time. Many countries which constitute the "free world" today hold to the Athenian view. But behind the Iron and Bamboo curtains men are mere puppets in the hands of the all-powerful state.

CHECK ON YOUR READING

1. *Identify Homer's great epic poems. How did they come to be written?*
2. *Briefly summarize the religious beliefs of the early Greeks.*
3. *Cite six factors which strengthened the Greek sense of kinship.*
4. *Describe life in Athens under these topics: social classes, homes, furnishings, conveniences, temples, streets.*
5. *Contrast the education and the ideals of the Athenians and the Spartans. Which do you favor? Why?*

"Nothing in excess."
"Know thyself."
  —*Sayings from the temple at Delphi*

"Athens is the school of Greece."
  —PERICLES as quoted by THUCYDIDES

Think about the chapter

1. Trace the steps in government from the rise of the kings to the democracy of Athens.

2. If you had lived in the fifth century B.C., would you have preferred to be a citizen of Sparta or a citizen of Athens? Why?

3. Some tyrants—for example, Pisistratus—were wise rulers. Why, then, did the Athenians hate tyrants? How did a tyrant then, differ from a tyrant today?

4. How could Athens be the autocratic ruler of an empire and at the same time a champion of democracy?

5. *Map study:* Draw a large-scale map of Greece and locate on it the Peloponnesus, Isthmus of Corinth, the four chief city-states, Piraeus, Hellespont, Mt. Olympus, Delphi, Marathon, Thermopylae, Salamis, and Delos.

Go beyond the text

6. You will find that the Greek myths make interesting reading and that it is helpful to understand the many references to Greek mythological characters in literature. You will often find phrases such as "Pandora's box" or "Herculean labor." Read one of the myths and tell the story to the class.

7. Many words in common use today have a connection with Greek history. Among these are *oracle, ostracism, Olympian, solons, laconic, Spartan, marathon, lyceum, academy, sophist, odyssey.* Consult a dictionary and write sentences using these words in their present meaning. In parentheses explain the source of the word from Greek history.

Follow up your special interests

8. Many cities in the United States have Greek names, many ending in *polis.* What does this mean? On a large map of your state or of the United States, mark with red ink any cities with Greek names.

9. How have the athletic contests of the Greeks influenced modern athletics? Read some accounts of the Greek Olympic games and then look up an account of the latest Olympics and write a comparison of the two.

10. Make a relief map of Greece and show the class why the Greeks did not unite.

11. Prepare a bulletin-board display of drawings that give the highlights of the *Iliad* and the *Odyssey.*

READ FURTHER

Basic readings: (1) Botsford, *Source Book,* Chaps. 6–27. (2) Breasted, *Ancient Times,* Chaps. 9–17. (3) Davis, *Readings,* Chaps. 4–10. (4) Hagedorn, *Book of Courage.* Socrates. (5) Hoffman, *News of the World,* Nos. 4–7. (6) Van Loon, *Story of Mankind,* Chaps. 13–20. (7) Year's *Pictorial History,* pp. 66–82.

Special accounts: (8) T. Bulfinch, *Mythology.* Comprehensive and easily read. (9) W. Davis, *A Day in Old Athens.* Activities of the Greeks. (10) T. Giankoulis, *The Land and the People of Greece.* (11) R. Halliburton, *The Glorious Adventure.* You follow the route of Odysseus. (12) D. Mills, *The Book of the Ancient Greeks.* (13) *Life,* "How a Democracy Died," January 1, 1951. Deals with the Peloponnesian Wars. (14) *National Geographic,* "Fish Men Discover a 2,200 Year-old Greek Ship," January, 1954.

Fiction and biography: (15) G. Atherton, *The Immortal Marriage.* The love story of Pericles and Aspasia—for good readers. (16) W. Davis, *The Victor of Salamis.* The story of Glaucon, a Greek athlete, in the days of Leonidas and Xerxes. (17) C. Snedeker, *The Perilous Seat.* Adventures in Delphi, home of the famous oracle. (18) C. Snedeker, *The Spartan.* Was Aristodemus a coward because he was the sole survivor of Thermopylae? (19) G. Trease, *The Web of Traitors.*

5

What the Greeks Gave to Civilization

KEY WORDS AND DATES

fables	Plato
lyric	Aristotle
tragedy	Parthenon
Sophocles	Alexander
Aristophanes	Hellenistic Age
Herodotus	Stoic
Thales	Epicurean
Pythagoras	Euclid
Democritus	Eratosthenes
Hippocrates	Archimedes
Socrates	323 B.C.—31 B.C.

THE ACHIEVEMENTS OF THE GREEKS are part of the civilization we call our own. In all fields of intellectual and artistic endeavor the Greeks set standards which are difficult to surpass today. Their greatest poetry and prose are still masterpieces (classics). To the Greeks we owe the beginnings of drama, both tragedy and comedy. The principles of art which they developed are still sound. The finest examples of their architecture and sculpture have never been excelled.

They made a notable start in natural science by turning away from familiar superstitions to the study of nature and its laws. Their scholars laid the foundations of mathematics and physics. They began to write about invisible atoms, evolutionary processes, planetary motion, and many other problems which have been worked out in the laboratories of modern times. Their philosophy still inspires our present-day thinkers. In politics the Greeks began to work toward those ideals of human equality which are the basis of our democratic way of life.

Greek culture owes much of its widespread influence to Alexander the Great. This young Macedonian king carried forward his father's ambition to unite the Greeks under one rule. He then proceeded to bring the entire Near East under his control. For three centuries Greek civilization flourished in the ancient world.

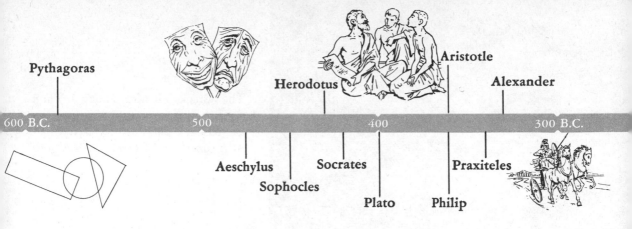

1. The Marvelous Achievements of the Greeks

Early Greek Poetry and Fables · The earliest Greek literature was poetry. Most of it has disappeared. The epics of Homer stressed the brave deeds of ancient heroes and the life of the gods. The first poet to describe the everyday life about him was Hesiod (750–700 B.C.). In his *Works and Days* this poor farmer-poet tells of the daily toil of the peasant and the reward that comes from hard work.

Besides these early poems, there were little stories called *fables*, which mothers told to their children. In these tales animals talked and acted like human beings. There was always a moral lesson in the story which made it plain how one ought to act. Many of these animal stories have come down to us in a collection called *Aesop's Fables*. Everyone knows the ancient tales of the fox and the grapes, the lion and the mouse, and the tortoise and the hare.

Lyric Poetry · Following the Epic Age of gods and heroes there developed a form of poetry called *lyric*. It was sung to the accompaniment of the lyre, a kind of harp. Lyric poems are shorter than epics. The lyric does not tell a story but reflects a passing mood. It is a personal expression of the poet's own experience. The greatest of Greek lyricists was Pindar. Another famous lyric singer was the poetess Sappho.

The Beginnings of Drama · The drama of the Greeks began with religious festivals in honor of the gods. At rural feasts the country people loved to hear a chorus sing of the life of the gods. The singers, who marched in a procession, wore goatskins and had their faces hidden behind masks. The leader of the chorus might sing a part or with gestures depict the story told in the song. He was a kind of actor. Later, when a second actor was added, the two might have a dialogue, but the chorus still told most of the story.

This kind of musical play the Greeks called a tragedy (meaning "goat-song"), probably because the chorus wore goatskins. A tragedy usually depicted a series of unhappy events ending in disaster. Later, as the Greek drama developed, the chorus became less important. Sometimes it interpreted to the audience the action of the play. Again it told of the feelings of the audience as it watched the story unfold.

The Greek Theater · Plays were always given out of doors. The Greek theater

63

The Greek Theatre Today · *Thousands witness performances of ancient Greek plays at the festival held each summer at Epidaurus in Argolis.*

would seem strange to us today. Although there was a place for the stage, there was little or no scenery, and no curtain. The theaters were usually located on the sloping side of a hill, so that the people could look down on the stage below.

Writers of Tragedy · The first important Greek playwright, Aeschylus (525–456 B.C.), was a great moral teacher and poet. His plays dealt with gods and heroes and important events. They were written in a dignified style and in majestic language.

The realistic characters of Sophocles (496?–405 B.C.) awakened great sympathy in the audience. In moderation, refinement, and beauty his plays were the perfection of dramatic art.

Euripides (480–406 B.C.) was a skeptic—a person who questions what he is told rather than accepts information on faith. He was also a realist; that is, he described things about him just as he saw them. His plays, therefore, are full of human conflict and emotion. He shocked old-fashioned people by doubting the existence of the gods and questioning many things which people took for granted.

Comedies of Aristophanes · The great tragedies were given in the morning, and in the afternoon the people were ready for less serious plays (comedies). These plays made fun of the leading politicians, writers, and philosophers, and the Athenian multitudes roared with laughter.

The best-known writer of comedies was Aristophanes (446?–385 B.C.). In *The Frogs* he ridiculed his fellow townsman Euripides. In *The Clouds* he represented the great philosopher Socrates, who was very progressive for his time, as an old fake. Aristophanes pretended to have no sympathy for the new ideas which were abroad in his day.

The First Historians · In contrast to the legends of former times, which were revived in the theater, the Greeks now began to have accounts of actual events in their own recent past. Herodotus, the first great historian (c. 484–424 B.C.), had traveled widely through Egypt, Asia, and the Mediterranean world. In his history he told about what he had learned in his journeys and closed with an account of the great war between Greece and Persia. He described

Athens as playing the leading part in the struggle. Herodotus is often called "the father of history." But he represented the fortunes of nations as due to the will of the gods.

Thucydides (*c.* 460–*c.* 399) came a generation later. His point of view was more like that of modern historians. He traced historical events to their earthly causes in the world of men. His impartial account of the Peloponnesian Wars is still one of the world's great classics.

Greek Science and Medicine · The inquiring genius of the Greeks early turned to the study of man himself and the world in which he lives. In the sixth century B.C. there arose in the Ionian cities a group of men interested in what we call natural science. They wished to know more about the origin of the universe, the laws that control it, and the things they saw about them.

Prominent among these early philosophers was Thales of Miletus (*c.* 640–546 B.C.). Thales had traveled in Babylonia and become interested in the astronomical observations taken there (p. 36). He is said to have predicted that an eclipse of the sun would take place in the year 585. When it occurred his fame spread far and wide. Thales and his fellow philosophers taught that the movements of the heavenly bodies followed natural laws.

Another Ionian thinker held that the higher animal forms developed from lower ones. This idea resembles somewhat the later theory of evolution. He also studied the land and sea formations and made the earliest known world map.

Pythagoras (born *c.* 582 B.C.) was interested in numbers and believed that mathematical principles underlay all things. He made important discoveries in geometry and raised mathematics to the level of a science. He also made a great contribution to astronomy, which, unfortunately, was disregarded for a long time. He saw the earth as a globe revolving in space around a luminous body. When Copernicus (p. 202) later made his great discovery that the earth revolves around the sun, he declared that Pythagoras's doctrine of planetary movement had given him the first hint.

Democritus (*c.* 470 B.C.), the greatest of the physical philosophers, explained the universe on the basis of motion. He asserted (1) that all things are composed of innumerable invisible atoms, or particles, and (2) that the behavior of all phenomena can be attributed to the changes and rearrangement of these atoms. This has been called the mechanical theory of the universe.

Greek physicians gave up the older belief that disease was caused by evil demons. Hippocrates (born *c.* 460 B.C.) was the greatest Greek physician. He ruled out priestcraft, horoscopes, and charms, and based the practice of medicine on careful observation. He believed in "the healing power of nature." He was the founder of scientific medicine.

Greek Physician · *"Whatsoever things I see or hear in my attendance on the sick I will keep as sacred secrets."—Hippocratic Oath.*

The Death of Socrates · *The great thinker, who applied philosophy to human affairs, poses one more question before accepting his cup of hemlock. The question* Why *has been called "the most explosive question in history."* Why?

The Greek students opened up a new world of philosophy and science. Their method lay in seeking the explanation of natural phenomena in law and fact rather than in mythical stories of the gods. This was one of the greatest intellectual revolutions ever made by man.

Greek Philosophy: Socrates · To question the power of the gods and their importance in human affairs was disturbing to the old-fashioned Greeks. They were shocked by the teachings of some of the Sophists (p. 59) and by the plays of Euripides. The raising of doubts about accepted ideas confused and angered those who did not want to change their ideas. It still does.

The one who did most to encourage the discussion of important matters was a homely and hen-pecked philosopher named Socrates. He was accustomed to stand about in the market place all day long, entering into conversation with anyone he met. What is more, he had the embarrassing habit of asking people questions which were very hard to answer. For instance, he asked what was meant by *justice, virtue, duty, love,* and *reason.* He urged his listeners to think about things which they had previously taken for granted. And this was dangerous, for once started, it set off a sort of mental chain-reaction. His method of teaching was by question and answer. It is known today as the Socratic method.

But the aims and noble efforts of Socrates were misunderstood. His keen observations seemed to undermine all the old beliefs. The Athenians finally summoned this human gadfly to trial for corrupting the minds of the young. Then the court voted the death penalty. His life might have been spared had he agreed to stop asking questions. But he said, "The unexamined life is not worth living." He chose to spend his last days in peaceful conversation with his friends, and in their presence quietly drank the fatal hemlock poison (399 B.C.).

Plato (427–347 B.C.) · Plato was the most gifted student of Socrates. He wrote out much of his master's teachings in the form of imaginary conversations between Socrates and those who flocked around him to discuss the problems of man's nature and duty. In Plato's writings Greek philosophy and prose reached their height.

The *Dialogues* give us a lively idea of the informal way in which the intellectual Athenians met in the market place or in one another's houses and discussed the good, the true, and the beautiful. Among the most famous of the *Dialogues* are those describing Socrates' defense of his teaching against his accusers. They reveal the calm manner in which he cheerfully discussed the immortality of the soul with his companions while he sat in prison. It is through the writings of Plato that we learn most of what we know of Socrates, who wrote nothing.

Aristotle and His Influence · Aristotle (384–322 B.C.) was Plato's best student. He was destined to gain a reputation through the ages even greater than that of his master. With the help of his own advanced students Aristotle wrote on many subjects. Among these were treatises on politics, ethics, economics, psychology, zoology, astronomy, poetry, and the drama. Indeed, it seems to have been his ambition to summarize and present all that had ever been discovered.

His skill and knowledge were so great that in the Middle Ages he was regarded as the "master of those who know." His books were almost the only ones studied in the medieval universities, and his theories were strongly endorsed by the Church. He is still revered as one of the greatest scholars of all time. Certainly the writings of no other man have ever enjoyed such long and widespread and unquestioned authority.

The Great Buildings of Greece · The greatness of Greek genius also found full expression in architecture, sculpture, and painting, and in the many beautiful things which the Greeks created for everyday use. In their simplicity, composition, balance, symmetry, and proportion, and in their careful use of decoration, the Greek artists have been our teachers.

Because Greek patriotism was closely related to religion, their great public buildings were temples. And since the Greeks believed that the gods protected their city-states, they constructed magnificent buildings in their honor. The Greek temple was the residence of a god and contained an image of the deity. It was there that offerings to the god were placed.

Styles of Greek Architecture · An important feature of the Greek temple is the series of columns surrounding it (the colonnade). The Greeks developed three styles of columns—the Doric, Ionic, and Corinthian. The *Doric* pillar is sturdy and rests directly on the foundation, without a base. It has a simple capital. The Lincoln Memorial in Washington, D.C., is of Doric design.

DORIC   IONIC   CORINTHIAN

The *Ionic* style has a more slender and graceful column, which rests on a base. Its capital has a roll, or volute, on each side. Between these volutes is an ornamental design. The *Corinthian* pillar also rests on a base, but has an elaborate capital, decorated with acanthus leaves.

Athens in the Age of Pericles · Greek architecture reached its height in the latter part of the fifth century B.C. This period is called the Golden Age, or Age of Pericles, in honor of the great Athenian leader. Pericles dreamed of creating a new and splendid capital which should control all Greece. When the Athenians came to share his vision, they voted to spend a vast sum to beautify the city and to restore the temples destroyed by the Persians.

The most important temples of the city were on the Acropolis (p. 57). The chief of these was the Parthenon, the temple of the patron-goddess Athena. This was rebuilt on a scale of magnificence never before known in Greece. It is one of the most celebrated buildings in the world. Made of gleaming Pentelic marble, it is a perfect example of the Doric style of architecture. It has seventeen columns on each side and eight across each end.

Parthenon and Frieze · *This temple later served as a Christian church (6th century), a mosque with minaret (1456), and a Turkish powder magazine (1697), which exploded and caused great damage.*

Greek Sculpture · Phidias, the greatest of the Athenian sculptors, designed the famous frieze of the Parthenon. This band of carved marble reliefs extending completely around the building portrayed the people of Athens moving in a stately religious procession. The figures of the men and horses are of unrivaled beauty and grace. Inside the temple stood the ivory and gold statue of Athena, also by Phidias.

On the athletic fields the Greek sculptors had an excellent opportunity to study the human form in various poses. They caught the beauty of line, balance, and rhythm which have given their art its perfection. (See the statue of the discus thrower on page 59.)

As time went on, sculpture changed. The statues of men and women were no longer modeled in the severe and heroic form which had prevailed earlier. Praxiteles, the greatest sculptor of the fourth century (364–330 B.C.), carved his marble gods and goddesses so that they appear as very lovely human beings.

Painting; Arts and Crafts · Although the Greeks made important progress in the technique of painting, almost all examples of this art have perished. We know about Greek painting principally from descriptions of ancient writers. Students have, however, been able to follow the development of pictorial art from paintings on vases which archaeologists have found.

The Greek potters made the most beautiful earthenware that had so far been known. Besides dishes, bowls, and jars they made handsome vases of lovely design and decoration. The earliest vases had black-glazed figures on a red clay background. Later, in the more perfected art the figures are red on a black-glazed ground. Examples of these vases can be seen in our museums today.

Ajax versus Achilles at Checkers.

The Greek love of beauty was shown not only in great works of art but also in the objects which were made for everyday use. Later craftsmen excelled in metalwork, fine woodwork, and in the use of inlays as well.

CHECK ON YOUR READING

1. *Explain and give examples of Greek epics, lyrics, and fables.*
2. *Why are the writings of Thucydides more "modern" than those of Herodotus?*
3. *Describe Athens in the Golden Age.*
4. *Identify the Doric, Ionic, and Corinthian styles of architecture.*
5. *Who were the important men in the following fields: drama, science, philosophy, and sculpture? What was the major accomplishment of each?*

2. How Greek Civilization Spread to Other Lands

Greek States Conquered by Macedonia · While the Greeks were wasting their resources in civil wars, Macedonia, a new power to the north, was slowly gaining in strength. Its first king of importance was Philip, a great admirer of Greek culture. When he came to the throne in 360 B.C., he realized the weakness of the rival Greek states and determined to make himself their master. With the aid of his new and powerful army he extended his kingdom northward to the Danube and eastward to the Hellespont. Here he soon came into conflict with the Greek states which controlled cities in this region. Of these states Athens was the most important.

After a long series of hostilities Philip finally defeated the Greeks at the battle of Chaeronea (338 B.C.). He then established himself as the head of a league of all the Greek states except Sparta, which still held out against him. Two years later Philip was murdered, and the kingship passed to his twenty-year-old son, Alexander.

Alexander Becomes Ruler of Greece · Alexander had been tutored by the great Greek philosopher Aristotle. And he had learned to know and love the masterpieces of Greek literature, especially the heroic songs of Homer.

The Greek leaders fancied that they could easily overthrow the young Alexander. But when Thebes revolted against him, Alexander captured and completely destroyed the city, thus teaching all Greece to fear and respect his power. Thereupon the Greek states, with the exception of Sparta, formed a league and elected Alexander as their leader and general. All sent troops to strengthen his army.

King Darius Flees from the Charge of Alexander's Cavalry at Issus · *Where is Alexander? Darius III? This mosaic panel is from Pompeii, 3rd century B.C.*

Alexander Strikes at Persia · Alexander now became the champion of Hellas against Asia and its Persian rulers. Leading his army into Asia Minor he met the enemy at the river Granicus (334 B.C.), where he scattered the forces of the Persian king. Marching southward he retook the Greek cities long subject to the Persians and freed all western Asia Minor forever from the Persian yoke. (See map on next page.)

Alexander then pushed boldly eastward. At Issus he met the Persian army, swept the troops from the field, and forced them to retreat until they had crossed the Euphrates. Darius III, the Persian king, offered Alexander all Asia west of the Euphrates. Alexander's friends advised him to accept the terms, but he waved aside his counselors and determined to conquer the whole Persian Empire.

Alexander Conquers the Ancient East · Alexander first captured the Persian sea-

ports and cut off the fleet. He then quickly subdued Egypt and returned to Asia. Marching eastward along the Fertile Crescent he crossed the Tigris and met Darius near Arbela, where he had gathered his forces for a last stand. Although their numbers were smaller, the Macedonians crushed the Persian army. In a few days Alexander was living in the winter palace of the Persian king in Babylon.

Less than five years had passed since the young Macedonian had entered Asia, and for the first time the valley of the Nile and the Fertile Crescent were in the hands of a European power.

Last Campaigns of Alexander the Great (330–323 B.C.) · In the course of the next few years Alexander pushed his conquests to the north, and then marched southeast. He crossed the frontiers of India, where at last the complaints of his weary troops forced him to turn back. At points all

460 B. C.

323 B. C.

1797 A.D.

1933 A.D.

From Pericles to Alexander is as from Washington to Franklin D. Roosevelt.

along his line of march Alexander had founded cities, which he often named after himself. He likewise had set up kingdoms which were to be centers of Greek culture as far as the frontiers of India. His dreams of conquest were still unsatisfied.

But in the midst of preparations for further campaigns in the west the great conqueror fell sick and after a few days died.

Division of Alexander's Empire · After a generation of wars among Alexander's commanders, his empire fell into three main parts. (1) In Europe, Macedonia was in the hands of Antigonus (grandson of Alexander's ablest general of that name), who also tried to control Greece.

(2) In Asia most of the former Persian Empire was under the rule of Alexander's commander Seleucus. He founded the important city of Antioch.

(3) In Africa, Egypt was held by Ptolemy, one of the ablest of Alexander's leaders. He was the first of a dynasty (family) of kings whom we call the Ptolemies. These rulers lived at Alexandria.

CHECK ON YOUR READING

1. *Trace Alexander's marches on the map. What peoples did he conquer?*
2. *How did he spread Greek culture?*
3. *How was Alexander's empire divided?*

Alexander's Empire · *Trace Alexander's march from Pella to the scene of his death in Babylon. What historic cities did he enter? What great rivers did he cross?*

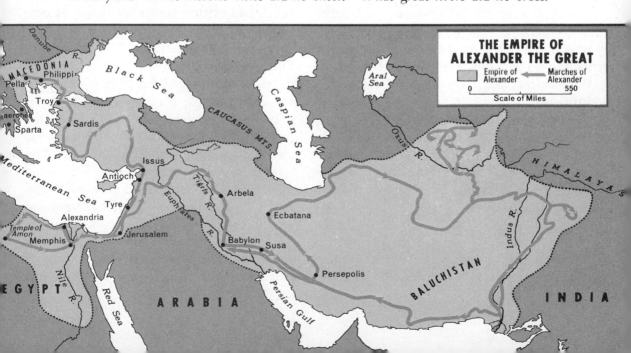

THE EMPIRE OF
ALEXANDER THE GREAT

Empire of Alexander — Marches of Alexander

0   550
Scale of Miles

3. The Hellenistic Age

Civilization of the Hellenistic Age · The three centuries following the death of Alexander are called the Hellenistic Age because during that period Greek civilization spread throughout the ancient world. The people of Egypt and western Asia now had Macedonian rulers, who spoke Greek and who carried on the affairs of government in that language. The people had constant dealings with Greek merchants, read Greek books, and attended Greek plays. Greek thus became the prevailing language of the eastern Mediterranean world. Yet Greek civilization was itself profoundly modified by the cultures of the Near East.

The new cities of the Hellenistic Age were laid out on a systematic plan. In Pericles' time the great buildings had been temples, but now fine buildings were erected for government offices. These occupied the center of a city, where the palace of the king had once stood. Near by was an open market place, surrounded by colonnades, where the people transacted their business.

There were also gymnasiums and baths, a race track, and a theater. The streets now had a drainage system. The houses of well-to-do citizens were more comfortable than before, and they were now elaborately furnished.

Alexandria, the Leading City · In population, commerce, and wealth and in all the arts of civilization Alexandria was the greatest city of the Hellenistic world. As the traveler sailed by the great lighthouse and into the spacious harbor, he might see ships laden with merchandise from all parts of the ancient world. Alexandria, with its marble buildings set in masses of tropical foliage, presented a magnificent spectacle.

Here, under the rule of the Ptolemies, science and learning were encouraged and supported. At the *Museum*, a kind of university maintained by the Ptolemies, scholars were able to devote themselves to study and research. Equipped with its library and laboratories, this was one of the first scientific institutions to be founded and supported by a government. The scientists of the Hellenistic Age, especially the group at Alexandria, were pioneers in systematic research. Their books were regarded as authorities for nearly two thousand years.

Science and Invention in the Hellenistic Age · The most famous mathematician at the Museum was Euclid. His work on geometry was used as a textbook in England down to our own day. At the astronomical laboratory built by the Ptolemies important observations and discoveries were made.

Eratosthenes, an astronomer, computed the size of the earth to within fifty miles of its true diameter. He also wrote a geography which was more accurate than any which had existed before his time. It contained the first map having a cross-net of lines indicating latitude and longitude. This enabled him to show the location of any place on the earth far more exactly than had been possible before.

Most gifted of all was Archimedes, the greatest of ancient mathematicians. He was also a physicist and an inventor. By his experiments in physics he discovered what we today call specific gravity. Archimedes lived in Syracuse, but corresponded with his friends at the Museum. One of the feats which made his name famous was based upon his arrangement of a series of levers and pulleys. These so multiplied power that the king was able, by turning a light crank, to launch a large ship which stood fully loaded at the dock.

The Hellenistic Age was one of mechanical inventions. The scientific principles discovered were used to make devices which would assist men in their everyday life. We read of such things as an automatic door-opener, a washing machine, a water-sprinkler operated by water pressure, and an olive press which was managed by screw pressure. By the use of screws, cogwheels, levers, and derricks, machines were made which would raise heavy weights.

The Library at Alexandria · In addition to the advancement made in science, great progress was made in the study of literature. The great library of the Ptolemies at Alexandria far surpassed all other libraries of the time. It contained over half a million books. An immense amount of editing and copying by hand was required to make the accurate editions needed for this collection.

In order to correct older texts a critical knowledge of language was necessary. Hence Alexandrian scholars began to compile dictionaries and to write the first grammars. The copies of texts made by these scholars became the standard editions, on which other libraries and copyists depended. It is from these Alexandrian editions that most of the manuscripts preserved in the libraries of Europe are descended. Our printed editions of Homer and other Greek authors have come from these.

Schools of Philosophy · Athens was still the chief center of philosophy. The successors of Plato still continued his teachings in the Academy where he had once taught. Plato's pupil Aristotle, after having been the teacher of the young Alexander, had returned to Athens. There he had established a school of his own at the Lyceum.

The First Jet Engine (*above*) *was invented by Hero of Alexandria about 100 B.C. How did it work? Below, we find* **Hipparchus in his observatory at Alexandria.** *He used trigonometry to calculate star positions and to predict eclipses of sun and moon.*

Two other schools of philosophy which became famous also were founded at Athens. (1) The first was that of the Stoics (founded by Zeno). It derived its name from the *stoa*, or porch, where it met. The Stoics believed in one god who had arranged all natural things for man's benefit. They taught the fatherhood of God and the brotherhood of man. They held that the life of happiness could be achieved by rising above all temporary discomforts and misfortunes and placing one's faith in God. We use the word *stoic* for one who shows great courage even in the face of misfortune.

(2) The second school was founded by Epicurus. He taught that man should seek happiness by not worrying about the gods and death. The Epicureans did not believe that the gods had made man or took any interest in him, either to help or to punish him. They further denied that there was any life after death.

Epicurus and his early followers believed in leading a simple life, since that caused less worry. But their denial that the gods were concerned with man's conduct and their denial of the immortality of the soul gave them a bad name. They were accused of making pleasure the only goal in human existence. Our word *epicure* has come to mean one who pays much attention to good eating and drinking.

The school of Epicurus, like that of the Stoics, attracted many disciples. Many men among the educated class had given up the older ideas about the gods. The new philosophies served as their religion and guide in life.

Greek Civilization Carried to the West · The older Greek states had become part of a larger world which had grown up as the result of Alexander's conquest of Greece and Asia. And this Hellenistic world was destined (about 200 B.C.) to fall under the control of a new military state in the West. For three centuries the city of Rome had been developing in power. It was now to unite the East and West into one great empire which would embrace the whole region of the Mediterranean. But just as Greek culture had dominated the Hellenistic world, it continued to live and to influence the civilization of the larger world of the new Roman Empire.

CHECK ON YOUR READING

1. *What, when, and where was the Hellenistic Age?*
2. *Describe the buildings, schools, and famous library at Alexandria.*
3. *What scientific discoveries were made during the Hellenistic Age?*
4. *How did the Stoics and the Epicureans differ?*

"It is easy to be brave from a safe distance." —AESOP

"The things which we are to do . . . we learn by doing."
—ARISTOTLE, *Nicomachean Ethics* II:1.

"I am a citizen of the world."—DIOGENES

"Give me but one firm spot on which to stand, and I will move the earth." —ARCHIMEDES

Think about the chapter

1. Many groups in the modern world owe much to the Greeks. Name five professions whose members are indebted to the Greeks. What contributions did the Greeks make to their fields?

2. Characterize the type of play written by each of the four great Greek dramatists to show how each differed from the other.

3. What scientific ideas were investigated by the Greeks? Which ideas contain the roots of present-day advances?

4. What is meant by philosopher or "philosophical turn of mind"? How did Socrates try to learn the truth?

5. *Map study:* Show on a map of the Near East the extent of Alexander's empire. Indicate the important places in his campaigns.

Go beyond the text

6. Read from a collection of *Aesop's Fables* and report on several of them.

7. Why is Greek pottery important as a source of information?

8. What basic ideas are contained in the oath of Hippocrates? What insignia of the medical profession came from ancient Greece?

9. Prepare a biographical sketch of Alexander the Great. Include the following incidents: the taming of Bucephalus; cutting the Gordian knot; death of Clitus; visit to the oracle of Zeus Amon in Egypt.

10. What were the Seven Wonders of the Ancient World?

Follow up your special interests

11. For a bulletin-board display make drawings of the three types of Greek columns and find pictures of modern buildings that use them.

12. Try to write a modern fable. Read James Thurber's *Fables for Our Time* to see how interesting modern fables can be.

13. Add to your record of discoveries and inventions. Demonstrate some scientific principle discovered during the Hellenistic period.

READ FURTHER

Basic readings: (1) BAUER and PEYSER, *How Music Grew*, Chap. 4. (2) BOTSFORD, *Source Book*, Chaps. 6–27. (3) BREASTED, *Ancient Times*, Chaps. 18–21. (4) CHEYNEY, *World History of Art*, Chaps. 5–6. (5) DAVIS, *Readings*, Chaps. 4–10. (6) EVANS, *Costume Throughout the Ages*, Chap. 2. (7) HAGEDORN, *Book of Courage*. Socrates. (8) MACY, *Story of World Literature*, Chaps. 5–9. (9) TAYLOR, *Fifty Centuries of Art*, pp. 6–12. (10) TAYLOR, *Illustrated History of Science*, Chap. 1.

Special accounts: (11) W. S. DAVIS, *A Day in Old Athens*. (12) D. MILLS, *Book of the Ancient Greeks*. (13) M. and C. H. B. QUENNELL, *Everyday Things in Ancient Greece*. (14) A. TOYNBEE, (ed.), *Greek Civilization and Character*. (15) A. WHITE, *Lost Worlds*. The accounts of archaeological expeditions read like detective stories. (16) National Geographic Society, *Everyday Life in Ancient Times*. Selected articles on Egypt, Mesopotamia, Greece, and Rome.

Fiction and biography: (17) *Aesop's Fables*. (18) *The Iliad* and *The Odyssey*. (19) H. LAMB, *Alexander of Macedon*. The author traveled over the routes of Alexander's conquests to write this vigorous story. (20) C. MASON, *Socrates: The Man Who Dared to Ask*. (21) PLUTARCH, *Parallel Lives*. Vivid biographies, much used by later fiction writers. Read about Pericles, Demosthenes, and Alexander the Great.

How Rome Became the First Great Capital in the West

KEY WORDS AND DATES

Tiber	146 B.C.
Etruscans	The Gracchi
republic	Marius and Sulla
patricians	Julius Caesar
plebs	44 B.C.
tribune	Augustus Caesar
Punic Wars	Mark Antony
Hannibal	Cleopatra
Carthage	Hadrian
Scipio	Marcus Aurelius

ROME BEGAN as a tiny trading station on the river Tiber in Italy. The people who lived there were called Latins. They were surrounded by unfriendly tribes, who were always threatening to seize the settlement for themselves. But the Latins were sturdy farmers and courageous fighters. Somehow they managed to overcome one enemy after another until they established a small city-state.

From these simple beginnings Rome gradually grew in power. She triumphed over her neighbors and extended her control over all Italy. Then she sent her legions to conquer rivals to the east and west until she had subdued the whole Mediterranean world. These conquered lands were then brought together into one vast empire. Rome became the first great power in the West.

In this chapter we shall meet such history makers as Hannibal, Caesar, Mark Antony, Cleopatra, Augustus, Nero, and the philosopher-emperor Marcus Aurelius.

But before studying Rome at the height of her glory, let us find out who these Latins were and how they laid the foundations of her greatness in the little market place on the Tiber.

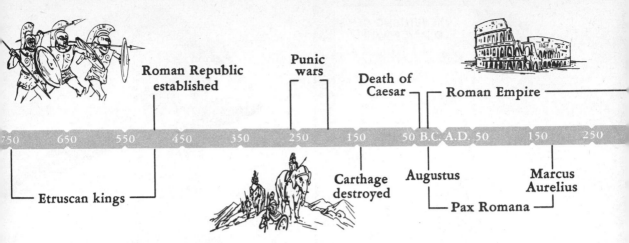

Roman Republic established

Punic wars

Death of Caesar

Roman Empire

| 750 | 650 | 550 | 450 | 350 | 250 | 150 | 50 B.C. | A.D. 50 | 150 | 250 |

Etruscan kings

Carthage destroyed

Augustus

Pax Romana

Marcus Aurelius

1. The Building of Roman Power

The Indo-Europeans Reach Italy · About the same time that the Greeks were entering the lands of the Aegean, another branch of the Indo-European peoples moved into the western Mediterranean world. Those settling in the central and southern parts of the Italian peninsula were the Italic tribes, which gave the land its name.

They were not so fortunate as the Greeks. The land had no fine cities and flourishing industries and arts, such as those of the Aegean world. They found a warm and sunny climate, rich valleys, and fertile plains suitable for farming, it is true. But the people whom they discovered in northern Italy were still in the Early Bronze Age of civilization.

It took the descendants of the Italic invaders a long time to reach the highest level of their achievement. This was because they had no earlier high civilization from which to learn. And Italy was not in close contact, as was Greece, with the progress of the eastern Mediterranean world. Hence, while Athens was the leader of the civilized world, Rome was fighting for her existence against her warlike neighbors.

Dangerous Neighbors of the Italic Tribes · The Italic tribes were for a long time a simple farming folk who tilled their fields and tended their flocks. They were ignorant, but brave and hardy. Two powerful peoples from the eastern Mediterranean barred them from controlling the entire peninsula.

The first of these were the Etruscans, a bold, sea-roving people who migrated from Asia Minor. Before 1000 B.C. they invaded the west coast of Italy. In time they gained control of the north-central part from the Tiber to the river Arnus. They were far more advanced than the Italic tribesmen, for they brought with them the knowledge, skill, and business experience of the East. They were prosperous merchants and traders. Their ships sailed from the Tyrrhenian (or Estrucan) Sea into the Mediterranean and carried on trade throughout the area. (See map, p. 78.)

The second rival of the Italic tribes were the Greeks. Their colonies had spread along the entire southern shore of Italy and in Sicily (p. 48). From both of these rivals the Romans learned much.

77

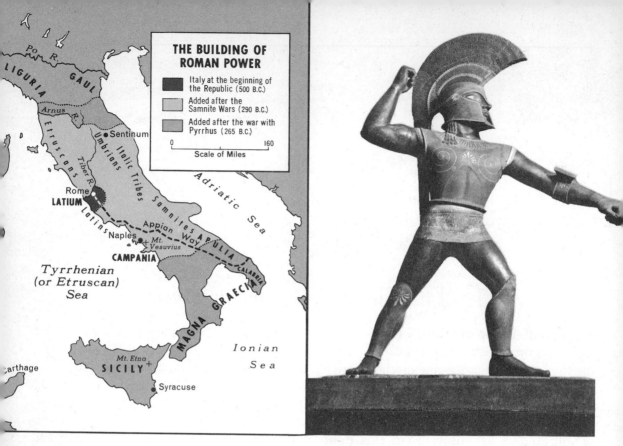

Rome Conquers Italy · *Name the peoples absorbed in Rome's conquest of the peninsula.*

Etruscan Warrior or God of War (c. 500 B.C.) · *What weapon do you think he bore?*

The Beginnings of Rome · Little is known about the early history of Rome because the Italian peoples did not learn how to write until long after they founded their city. The most trustworthy information available comes from archaeologists, whose discoveries are used to trace the gradual development of the early dwellers in Italy.

It seems that by 1000 B.C. one of the Italic tribes—the Latins—had established themselves south of the Tiber on a small plain which they called Latium. When they wished to exchange their grain and oxen for the tools and weapons of the neighboring Etruscans, they went to a little trading post at a narrow point of the river. Around this market place were a few scattered villages, and on one of the near-by hills (the Palatine) a stronghold. These little communities developed into the city of Rome.

Rome under the Etruscan Kings (750–500 B.C.) · The Latin tribes to which the Romans belonged were in constant terror of the powerful Etruscans across the river. Their fears were well founded, for about 750 B.C. one of the Etruscan princes crossed the Tiber and took possession of Rome and its stronghold on the Palatine. From this little fortress the Etruscans extended their rule over the surrounding plain of Latium.

For two centuries Etruscan kings ruled in Rome, but the Latins managed to keep their own language. The Etruscans greatly improved the city. They erected better buildings and made a great stone drainage system. They brought to the simple Romans a much more civilized way of life than they had known before.

The Romans became familiar with their manufactures, pottery, and metalwork. They also saw the Greek wares which Etruscan ships brought into the harbor. Thus the early Roman peasants learned something of the arts and crafts of the eastern Mediterranean world. The Etruscan princes were so cruel, however, that about 500 B.C. the Latins overthrew them.

The Roman Republic · When the Etruscan princes had been expelled, the government fell into the hands of nobles, called *patricians*. They arranged that two of their number should be elected each year as heads of the state. These two magistrates, called *consuls*, were to have equal power and serve for one year. They were chosen by an *Assembly* composed of all the fighting men in the state, but dominated by the patricians. Rome thus became a *republic* in form, since the common people had a voice in electing their consuls, or presidents. But there was also a *Senate*, or advisory body of nobles, which really possessed the chief power in the government, so that the people soon became dissatisfied with their share.

When the rule of the patricians became too oppressive, the common people, called *plebs*, left Rome and threatened to form a city of their own. The nobles knew that they needed the help of the plebs as soldiers. They therefore agreed to give them a larger part in the management of public affairs. They allowed them to elect each year two officials called *tribunes*. These officials had the power to veto any measure passed by the Senate and in this and other ways to protect the interests of the common people against certain kinds of injustice. But they were not powerful enough to secure for them such privileges as the right to become a consul, to marry into a patrician family, or to become a senator.

The Plebs Struggle for Power · For a hundred and fifty years after the founding of the Republic, the plebs struggled to win equal rights with the patricians. Their first important gain was a *written* code of laws (450 B.C.). These laws were engraved on twelve tablets of bronze and set up in the *Forum*, or market place, for all to see.

The old Assemblies gradually freed themselves from control by the Senate and gained the right to make laws. The plebs were given equal voting rights with patricians. By 367 B.C. they were permitted to hold any public office, including that of consul or senator. The office of tribune was made more important. Its right to veto any measure passed by the Senate was recognized as part of the constitution.

As the plebs came to have more to do with the making of the laws, they were able to get a greater share of the lands that Rome conquered. There thus grew up in time a new nobility of plebeians who owned land and who held public office.

Latin terms in use today · What do they mean? Can you add others?

1. *Anno Domini*
2. *post mortem*
3. *bona fide*
4. *habeas corpus*
5. *e pluribus unum*
6. *pro tempore*
7. *status quo*
8. *vox populi*
9. *per se*
10. MCMLX
11. *pax vobiscum*
12. *et cetera*

The Roman Senate · The Senate was, at first, a council made up of patricians only. It advised the consuls and carried on the business of the state. But the plebs steadily gained power until they too were able to become members of this high body. It had long enjoyed respect as the greatest power in the Republic. Its members were largely ex-consuls and skilled statesmen.

As Rome extended her boundaries, many of her allies were too far away to come to the city to vote and willingly left public questions to the care of this group of men. The Roman Senate became the most famous council of statesmen that developed in the ancient world.

Rome Begins to Grow · When the Etruscan princes were overthrown, the territory of the tiny Republic was only the city and a few miles around. Rome did not even control all of Latium. The Latin tribes soon found, however, that they needed the aid of Rome in time of war and made a defensive alliance with her against all outsiders.

The Roman Senate · *This wise and patriotic group of men guided the Republic safely through its darkest hours and was responsible for many of its greatest achievements.*

Fortunately for the Romans, their most dangerous enemies, the Etruscans, were conquered by others. The Greeks destroyed the Etruscan fleet (474 B.C.), and the barbarian Gauls laid waste the Etruscan cities in northern Italy. Relieved of pressure from this powerful enemy, Rome was able to beat off the Italic tribes which had been threatening the city. By 400 B.C. she had conquered her neighbors and won a strip of territory which protected her on all sides.

Rome Gains Control of All Italy · Rome administered these annexed districts very wisely. She founded colonies of citizens or granted the conquered peoples business privileges and even citizenship. Such treatment made them her faithful allies. She was thus able to draw from her friendly territory a growing army of loyal citizen-soldiers. With their help she now proceeded to subdue all Italy.

Although severely defeated by the Gauls, who sacked the city of Rome (about 390 B.C.), she was able to save herself from disaster by the payment of a ransom to the invaders. The Gauls then returned to their home in the Po Valley. The Romans now built strong walls around their city and fortified it against future attack.

In 338 B.C. (the year that the Greek cities fell to Philip of Macedon, p. 69), Rome conquered certain Latin tribes which had revolted against her. Later she decisively defeated a combination of her enemies, Gauls, Etruscans, and Italic tribes called Samnites, at the battle of Sentinum (295 B.C.). After this she was able to seize the cities of her rivals and to beat back the Gauls until she finally controlled Italy to the river Arnus. (See map, p. 78.)

The Greek cities of the south, alarmed at the growth of Roman power, appealed for outside aid, but later deserted the Greek general who had come to help them and surrendered to the Roman army. By 270 B.C. all Italy was under the control of Rome.

As Rome extended her power she also developed her commerce and trade. But whenever Roman merchants sailed forth, they found the western Mediterranean already ruled by a powerful rival. This was the ancient city of Carthage.

Carthage and Her Empire · In the ninth century B.C., the Phoenicians had founded a colony at Carthage on the African coast opposite Sicily. This colony, in time, became the leading business center in the western Mediterranean. It built up an empire which extended along the African shore from the city of Cyrene to the Atlantic. In addition, Carthage had colonies in Sardinia and Corsica, held a large part of Sicily, and seized southern Spain. (See map, p. 48.)

She prevented her weaker neighbors from trading freely with one another, and closed the ports under her control to all foreign ships. Vessels venturing into these waters were promptly sunk. The Romans bitterly resented all these restrictions, which interfered with the growth of their own business. They especially rcscntcd not being able to trade with the thriving towns of Sicily. It was finally clear that war between Rome and Carthage could not be avoided. The Punic Wars (from Latin *Punicus*, meaning "Carthaginian") lasted over a century.

How the Rivals Compared · At the opening of the struggle Carthage was a splendid city, far larger and more impressive than Rome. Her navy controlled the western seas. But her land forces were composed of hired soldiers, for she had no large peasant class from which she could recruit an army.

The Romans could put a force of six hundred thousand citizens and allies in the field. But the Romans had no sea power.

Rome vs. Carthage: the First Punic War · *How did geography influence this struggle? Why was the Strait of Messina so important? What territory did Rome gain?*

Rome Defeats Carthage: the First Punic War (264–241 B.C.) · War broke out when a Carthaginian force seized Messina on the strait between Sicily and the mainland. The Romans now crossed this narrow strait, defeated the Carthaginians, and soon gained possession of the eastern part of Sicily. But the war dragged on, year after year, because the Romans could never muster enough ships to beat a great sea power like Carthage.

Finally a great fleet was built by the subscriptions of patriotic Romans and sent against the enemy. This time the enemy's

81

navy was overcome, and the Carthaginians were forced to make peace on Rome's terms. They were required to give up Sicily and pay a large money indemnity. Later Rome seized Sardinia and Corsica.

The Second Punic War (218–201 B.C.) · When the war began again, Hannibal was a brilliant young Carthaginian general in Spain. He conceived the daring plan of leading an army through Gaul and across the Alps to surprise the Romans from the north. After a terrible climb over the snow-covered mountains the little Carthaginian force reached the valley of the Po. It had lost many men on the way. But even under these circumstances Hannibal was able to defeat the Romans in two engagements. This so impressed the Gauls that they aided the Carthaginian leader with troops.

Hannibal now pushed on and won a brilliant victory at Lake Trasimene. He was unable, however, to capture Rome for lack of siege machinery. At Cannae he anni-

hilated the Roman army sent against him. Later southern Italy deserted Rome and joined Hannibal. But the Roman Senate, with fine leadership and dogged resolution, raised new forces, which recaptured one by one the allied cities that had deserted to the enemy. Hannibal struggled on in southern Italy but without reinforcements.

Meanwhile the Romans had placed their army in Spain under the command of an able young general named Scipio. Scipio drove the Carthaginians out of Spain and then went to Africa, where he twice defeated the enemy. Carthage now called Hannibal home. But at Zama, Scipio met Hannibal and overwhelmed his army.

In the treaty of peace the Carthaginians were forced (1) to pay a large sum to the victor, (2) to give up all but ten of their warships, and (3) to promise to ask Rome's permission before making war against any other power. Hannibal escaped and later went into exile in the East. Here he tried to stir the leaders to combine against Rome.

Hannibal's Army Crossing the Rhone · *Note the crude rafts supported by pig-skin floats. How were the elephants used? What topography lay ahead?*

Rome Destroys Carthage: the Third Punic War (149–146 B.C.) · For fifty years the Carthaginians continued to carry on their trade. But some of the Roman leaders (especially Senator Cato) never forgot about Hannibal's invasion. Cato insisted that Rome would never be safe until Carthage was destroyed. On a slight excuse Rome attacked her old enemy again. In the three years' war that followed, the ancient city of Carthage was utterly destroyed. Her land was taken from her to form the Roman Province of Africa. Rome had now conquered her only rival in the West. Let us see how she had already disposed of her rivals in the East.

How Rome Conquered the East · While Rome was making her conquests in the West, the successors of Alexander the Great were fighting among themselves for the possession of the various parts of his empire. Hannibal, during his war in Italy, had made an alliance with the Macedonian king. The Romans therefore sent an expedition to Macedonia, defeated its army at Cynoscephalae, and made the country a dependency (197 B.C.). The Greek cities that had been taken by Philip and Alexander were now given their freedom, but Rome kept a strict eye on them.

The war with Macedonia brought Rome into conflict with Antiochus the Great, who ruled the Asian part of Alexander's empire (p. 71). Antiochus began to seize portions of the Macedonian realms which the Romans had declared independent. Moreover, Hannibal, who was now with Antiochus, was urging an invasion of Italy. The Romans therefore moved against the Asian forces and defeated them at Magnesia (190 B.C.). The lands of western Asia Minor were thus brought under Roman control.

Two of the great divisions of Alexander's empire were conquered. Before long Egypt too became a dependency of Rome (168 B.C.). Soon the Greek cities also became Roman vassals. With the destruction of both Corinth in the East and Carthage in the West (146 B.C.), Rome was supreme in the entire Mediterranean.

CHECK ON YOUR READING

1. *Why did civilization come later to the West than the East?*
2. *What did the Romans learn from each of their powerful neighbors?*
3. *What part did each of the following play in the Roman Republic: patricians, plebs, tribunes, code, Forum, consul, Senate, Assembly?*
4. *Use the map to explain how Rome gained control of (a) Italy, (b) Carthage, (c) the East.*

---

2. *From Republic to Empire*

How Conquests Affected Rome · At the end of the Carthaginian wars, Rome was the greatest power in the world. She had acquired new lands, many people, and much wealth. But she had also taken on great responsibility. She had to govern these foreign realms and, at the same time, meet entirely new conditions at home.

Rome now had the huge task of governing her many different peoples, each with its own laws and customs. The new state was very complex. (1) There were first the citizens of Rome, (2) then those of the Latin cities and colonies. (3) Next there were the allies, both in Italy and beyond the sea. They were bound to the capital by treaties of friendship and mutual advantage. (4) Finally, there were the provinces, whose conquered peoples were subjects of Rome.

Misrule in the Provinces · Most of the provinces were ruled by Roman governors with unlimited powers. The people of a province were not permitted to have an army of their own. They were obliged to pay whatever taxes the governor demanded. The laws for the provinces were made by the Senate and were usually reasonable. But there was no means of compelling the governors to follow them.

The governors lived in luxury and were eager to make a fortune during their term of office. They plundered the provinces to fill their pockets and returned to Italy rich men. Sometimes "contractors" were allowed to collect the taxes for the state. They usually took enough to be able to keep out plenty for themselves.

Roman businessmen of all sorts came to the provinces to make fortunes. Later all these men, as well as the generals, returned to the city with their loot. There thus grew up in Rome a wealthy class that had become rich through the profits of war.

Effects of Wealth on Rome · The wealthy class at Rome now included not only the old aristocratic families, but these war profiteers. Their demand for luxuries of all sorts greatly increased foreign trade and created a group of prosperous businessmen and merchants. One new group made fortunes from contracts to build ships and roads, another from the profits of working mines, quarries, and forests. Some men grew rich merely by lending money at high rates of interest.

The growth of this *capitalist* class at Rome had a serious effect on the land situation. Formerly the large landholder had lived on his estate. But there now grew up a system of what is called *absentee ownership*. The rich owners moved to the city, but nevertheless continued to buy up and hold land. On these large tracts, armies of slaves produced oil and wine, which their masters sold at high prices.

Ruin of the Farming Class · The small farmers, who had once been the mainstay of the country, were being brought to ruin. The campaigns of Hannibal had laid waste much of their land, and they were never able to cultivate it again. As the wealthy added farm after farm to their estates, few small homesteads remained.

Fathers and sons who had been serving in the Roman legions returned to find their families scattered and their farms in many cases sold for debt. Those who still had small holdings found that the owners of great plantations, whose slaves received practically nothing, could sell grain cheaper than they. So they often abandoned their farms and became hired workers or else drifted to the city to increase the miserable group of unemployed already there.

Position of Slaves · The hundreds of slaves who toiled on these great estates had been brought to Rome as captives of war and sold to the landholders. The life of these unhappy prisoners was little better than that of beasts of burden. When the supply of war captives failed, slave pirates carried on wholesale kidnaping.

Italy and Sicily were flooded with slaves. The brutal treatment they received was so unbearable that at various places they revolted. In Sicily sixty thousand gathered and slew their masters. It took an army several years to subdue them.

The Gladiators · *Why is the victor looking at the crowd? What is its answer? Do we have any comparable contests today?*

Politicians Become Corrupt · The evil effects of the wars were also to be seen in the government at Rome. Politicians now sought office with the hope of making themselves rich for life. Office-seekers tried to win favor by bribery or by providing bread and entertainment for the voters.

They arranged chariot races at the great circular tracks (called *circuses*), and contests between gladiators (*gladius*, "sword"). These swordsmen, who were captive slaves or criminals, were compelled to fight to the death for the amusement of the crowds. Later, contests were held between men and wild beasts. These barbarous entertainments took place in a great stone *amphitheater*. (See illus. above.)

The Senate was no longer the wise and efficient body it had formerly been. It was now composed of selfish aristocrats, eager to increase their fortunes at the expense of the Republic.

Civil War in Rome · The situation finally became so desperate that the people's cause found sympathizers even among the nobles. Two of these, Tiberius Gracchus and later his brother Gaius, were elected tribunes. They proposed to save Italy by limiting the amount of land a rich man might own and restoring a fair living to the farming class

(133–121 B.C.). Both met violent death for these proposals.

During the next hundred years the history of Rome is one of civil wars between rival generals for control of the state. Some military commanders were supported by the Assembly, others by the Senate.

A change in the method of recruiting armies aided ambitious military leaders. Instead of drafting property-holding citizens, the generals now recruited volunteers. These were poor men who hoped to be granted a bonus in land when their term of service was over. These soldiers developed great loyalty to their commanders.

One of these generals, Sulla, was the first to use a Roman army *against* the citizens of Rome. A bloody struggle followed as first the followers of Sulla and then of his rival Marius gained control.

Finally, Sulla, as dictator, put to death his enemies and reorganized the government. He deprived the Assembly and the tribunes of their power. By a series of laws he restored control to the Senate. To his credit he then retired to private life.

Rise of Julius Caesar · After Sulla's death the people selected Pompey to be their leader. He repealed the hated laws of Sulla, cleared the Mediterranean of pirates, and gained important victories in the East. He added Syria to the Roman realms and brought Jerusalem under Roman control.

In the meantime, Julius Caesar, a new champion of the people's cause, had arisen at Rome. Pompey, Caesar, and Crassus, a wealthy aristocrat, now formed a combination (sometimes called a *triumvirate*) which gave them control of affairs.

Caesar was elected consul for the year 59 B.C. He at once made himself popular by proposing new land laws for the benefit of the people. Realizing that the way to power lay through the command of a strong army, he had himself appointed governor of Gaul. This great territory lay on both sides of the Alps. In eight years Caesar subdued the Transalpine Gauls and added their lands to the empire. This vast dominion corresponds roughly to modern

At the Base of Pompey's Statue Great Caesar Fell · *"Yesterday his word might have stood against the world. Now lies he there, and none so poor to do him reverence."*

France and Belgium. Caesar also invaded Britain as far as the Thames River.

Caesar now wished to become permanent head of the state. He used every available opportunity to bring himself to the attention of the people. One of his cleverest ideas was to publish a history of his campaigns in Gaul. Thus its readers might know of his vast conquests and what they owed to the governor in that province. Strangely enough, this account, which was intended for the Romans, has become the most widely known Latin book among foreigners. Every Latin student reads Caesar's *Gallic Wars*.

Caesar Supreme in Rome · The senators, who were afraid of having a new dictator, dreaded the return of Caesar. They persuaded Pompey to oppose him and support their party. But Caesar disregarded the command of the Senate to disband his army.

In 49 B.C. he crossed the Rubicon, which marked the boundary of his province and beyond which he had no legal right to move his forces. He then marched on Rome, taking the city by surprise. Pompey fled to Greece. After having been elected consul, Caesar pursued Pompey and inflicted a crushing defeat on his army at Pharsalus.

Caesar soon became head of the whole Roman world. This was the first time that the Republic had ever been under the command of one man. He made his position legal by having himself made dictator for life.

Death of Caesar (44 B.C.) · Caesar intended to reform thoroughly the corrupt government of Rome. He also planned to rebuild the city and laid out new roads to make travel easier throughout the realm. He introduced the Egyptian calendar (later called Julian) to replace the older one used by the Romans. Our month of *July* is named for him. It was Caesar who really established the Roman Empire and became its first emperor in fact, if not in name.

But there were still those who opposed the rule of one man. They thought that the Republic could still be saved. On March 15 (the Ides of March), just before he was to leave for a campaign in the East, Caesar was murdered.

Octavian Becomes Head of the Government · Caesar had legally adopted his grandnephew Octavian and made him his sole heir. At the time of Caesar's assassination Octavian was only eighteen years old. In spite of his youth and inexperience, he immediately started for Rome to find supporters and secure a military command.

Two years later he was able to defeat all who opposed him, including Caesar's assassins (Brutus and Cassius), in the battle of Philippi (42 B.C.). During the following eight years he made his position so strong that at twenty-eight he almost completely controlled the eastern and western portions of the Roman realms.

Octavian Defeats Mark Antony · Octavian's last struggle was with his former friend and supporter Mark Antony, who had become infatuated with the charming Egyptian queen Cleopatra. It was reported to Octavian that Antony and Cleopatra were planning to become rulers of Rome. With Senate approval Octavian advanced against Antony and defeated him in a naval battle at Actium (31 B.C.), off the west coast of Greece.

The next year Octavian landed in Egypt, which had long been under Roman influence (p. 83). Antony, probably forsaken by Cleopatra, took his own life. The proud queen, unwilling to be displayed at Octavian's triumph at Rome, died at her own hand. She was the last of the Ptolemies, the ruling family of Egypt established by Alexander's general nearly three hundred years before. Octavian now made Egypt a Roman territory, and the entire Mediterranean world was under a single ruler.

CHECK ON YOUR READING

1. *How was Rome changed by her conquests?*
2. *How did Julius Caesar make himself the ruler of Rome?*
3. *How did Octavian bring the Mediterranean world under his control?*

---

3. *The Roman Empire at Its Height*

Augustus, the First Roman Emperor (30 B.C.–14 A.D.) · When Octavian returned in triumph from his wars, he was hailed as the savior of the commonwealth. The Senate now appointed Octavian to a series of offices which placed him in complete control of the state. He was given command of the greater provinces. He was made head of the army and was given great authority over the laws. It was he who made war and peace.

The Senate also conferred upon him various titles of honor. He was called *Augustus* ("the Revered"), and *Imperator* to signify his power over the army. It is from this title that our word *emperor* is derived.

Octavian, whom we will now call Augustus, was one of the ablest rulers that the

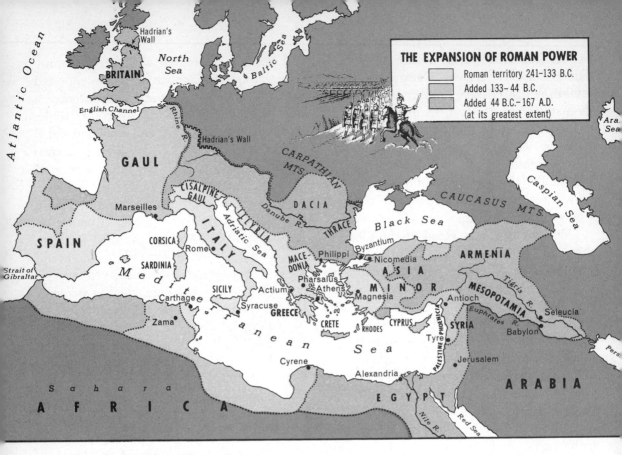

THE EXPANSION OF ROMAN POWER

- Roman territory 241-133 B.C.
- Added 133-44 B.C.
- Added 44 B.C.-167 A.D. (at its greatest extent)

The Roman Empire (241 B.C.–167 A.D.) · *Name the rivers, mountains, deserts, and seas which marked the boundaries of Roman power at its greatest extent. What conclusion can you draw as to the influence of geography here?*

state ever had. He devoted his life to giving the people the good government that they had so long lacked.

The task of administering the vast Roman Empire was huge. Its boundaries now extended from the Rhine and Danube to the Sahara Desert and Red Sea, and from the Atlantic Ocean to the Euphrates River. (See map above.) To guard these long frontiers a standing army of about 200,000 men was necessary. These troops were recruited chiefly from the provinces. Foreigners who entered the ranks were given citizenship so that the tradition of a loyal citizen army might be maintained.

Government Reform in the Provinces · For many years the provinces had been mismanaged and plundered by dishonest men. Augustus now proposed to change all this by making the provinces departments of the state. He himself appointed the governors of the important provinces and held them personally responsible for performing their duties. Only those whose work he approved could retain their posts. He abolished the old system of extortion and had the taxes collected by imperial officers. The most effective check on the abuse of power by the governors was the right of every citizen to appeal to the emperor.

Augustus turned back to the provinces part of the revenue collected from them. These funds were then used for internal improvements, such as new roads, harbors, aqueducts, bridges, and public buildings. In many other ways, he tried to unite the scattered Roman possessions into one great state. And his success was shown by the fact that the Empire enjoyed a long period of prosperity and peace.

The Successors of Augustus · After the death of Augustus four members of his family, related either by blood or adoption, succeeded him. This line of emperors ruled for fifty years, completing a century of peace which began with the rule of Augustus.

As Augustus had no male heir, his stepson Tiberius now became head of the state (14 A.D.). Tiberius had a strong sense of duty and was an able ruler. But he was stern and unadaptable and often disagreed with the Senate. In his last years he became more and more tyrannical.

Claudius (41–54 A.D.) tried to follow the policy of Augustus and Tiberius, but he lacked the same resolute purpose and energy. During his rule the southern part of Britain was conquered and became a Roman province. It was this conquest that probably first introduced Latin elements into the English language.

We can mention only a few of the emperors who followed. Some were good and efficient rulers. But others, such as Nero (54–68 A.D.), were extravagant, moody, and wicked.

How the Emperors Strengthened the Frontiers · An able general named Vespasian became emperor in 69 A.D. With him began a second century of general peace. Honest and efficient rulers brought the Empire to the height of its prosperity. Vespasian reorganized the various branches

Augustus: First of the Roman Emperors · *His statesmanship brought domestic peace, secured the frontiers, and helped preserve civilization.*

of the government and gave special attention to strengthening the frontiers.

The northern and eastern boundaries were constantly in danger of attack from the German barbarians. Vespasian and his successors built walls and forts along these boundaries to protect them. By cutting down expenditures and levying new taxes, Vespasian restored prosperity. He was even able to erect many public buildings. One of these is the famous Colosseum at Rome.

On the lower Danube the emperor Trajan (98–117 A.D.) captured the stronghold of the Dacians. He built a massive bridge across the Danube, and made Dacia a Roman province. The descendants of these

Triumph of Marcus Aurelius · *Surrounded by his victorious legions, whose banners wave on high, the emperor accepts the surrender of defeated German chieftains.*

colonists still call their land *Rumania* or *Romania* (Latin, *Romanus*).

Hadrian (117–138 A.D.) was equally energetic. The whole northern boundary was strengthened with walls. Remains of these may still be seen in the long stretch between the Danube and the Rhine, and on the northern boundary of Britain. (See map, p. 88.)

Roman Law Becomes the Law of the Empire · Hadrian formed a permanent council of jurists to aid him in the administration of justice. Italy was divided into four judicial districts, with officials in charge of each. And the narrow *city*-law of Rome was now extended so that it might meet the needs of the whole Empire.

In spirit Roman law was fair, just, and humane. It did much to unify the peoples of the Mediterranean world into a single nation. The various peoples were no longer regarded as members of different nations, but as subjects of the same great state. To all was extended the same protection of justice, law, and order.

Marcus Aurelius, Emperor and Stoic Philosopher (161–180 A.D.) · When Marcus Aurelius became emperor, he had to face a very serious situation. The barbarian hordes from the north broke through the frontier defences and poured into the Empire. Unable to expel them, the emperor finally permitted some of them to settle within the frontiers on condition that they would help defend the Empire against their fellow Germans. This policy had very unhappy results, as we shall later see.

Marcus Aurelius was a student and philosopher whose fate it was to spend most of his years in a long military campaign against invaders. In the midst of his battles, however, he found time to write a little book in Greek called *Meditations*. This gives a very good picture of the Stoic philosophy, which comforted and strengthened the emperor in the midst of his trying duties. But no ruler, however high-minded and courageous, could stop the forces which were now undermining the Roman world.

CHECK ON YOUR READING

1. *What facts prove that Augustus was one of the most able Roman rulers?*
2. *What defense measures did the emperors take?*
3. *How did Roman law help to unify the Empire?*

Think about the chapter

1. Which gains made by the plebs do you consider most important? Why?
2. Contrast the government of the Roman Republic with that of our own.
3. What did Caesar mean by saying, as he crossed the Rubicon, "The die is cast"?
4. Why was Caesar assassinated?
5. *Map study:* On an outline map draw in the boundaries of the Empire at its greatest extent. Label the main provinces. (Map, p. 88.)

Go beyond the text

6. Report on the career of Hannibal.
7. What effects did the Roman conquest of Britain have on that country?
8. How did Julius Caesar change the calendar? How similar is ours today?

Follow up your special interests

9. Those interested in drama will want to read Shakespeare's *Julius Caesar*. Act III, Scene II, is excellent for dramatization.
10. Read a translation of Caesar's *Gallic Wars*. Report to the class on its highlights.
11. Write a biographical sketch of the beautiful Cleopatra. You may want to read Shakespeare's play *Antony and Cleopatra*, or G. B. Shaw's *Caesar and Cleopatra*.
12. The Romans were great builders. Collect pictures for a bulletin-board display to show some examples.

READ FURTHER

Basic readings: (1) BOTSFORD, *Source Book*, Chaps. 28–47. (2) BREASTED, *Ancient Times*, Chaps. 22–26. (3) DAVIS, *Readings*, Vol. 2, Chaps. 1–6. (4) HAGEDORN, *Book of Courage*. Hannibal. (5) HOFFMAN, *News of the World*, Nos. 8, 9, 11. (6) VAN LOON, *Story of Mankind*, Chaps. 22–27. (7) Year's *Pictorial History*, pp. 84–108.

Special accounts: (8) W. DAVIS, *A Day in Old Rome*. (9) G. FOSTER, *Augustus Caesar's World*. (10) E. HAMILTON, *The Roman Way*. Excerpts from Caesar, Cicero, Horace, and Virgil. (11) D. MILLS, *Book of the Ancient Romans*. (12) National Geographic Society, *Everyday Life in Ancient Times*.

Fiction and biography: (13) P. ANDERSON, *Swords in the North* and *With the Eagles*. Caesar's famous Tenth Legion in action in Britain. (14) M. COLES, *Great Caesar's Ghost*. A mystery story. (15) M. DOLAN, *Hannibal of Carthage*. The story is told by the Greek who was Hannibal's tutor. (16) W. DAVIS, *A Friend of Caesar*. Story about Cleopatra. (17) S. and E. GODWIN, *The Roman Eagle*. The scenes are laid in Rome, Galilee, and Gaul. (18) I. LAWRENCE, *The Gift of the Cup* and *Theft of the Golden Ring*. Stories of Julius Caesar, revolts of Greek colonies, and tales of pirates. (19) C. SNEDEKER, *The Forgotten Daughter* and *The White Isle*. The first story is of the time of the Gracchi and the second is about a Roman girl who traveled to Britain.

"Iacta alea est." (The die is cast.)
"Veni, Vidi, Vici." (I came, I saw, I conquered.)
—JULIUS CAESAR

7

Roman Civilization
and Its Influence on the West

KEY WORDS AND DATES

Pax Romana	Colosseum
Diocletian	Pompeii
Constantine	Justinian Code
Cicero	aqueducts
Virgil	Christianity
Tacitus	311 A.D.
Plutarch	Paul of Tarsus
Pliny	Romance languages
Ptolemy	fifth century A.D.

FOR TWO CENTURIES the Roman world was at peace. During this so-called *pax Romana* the Empire reached the height of its achievement, prosperity, and power. Then, under incompetent and wicked rulers, the great state gradually weakened from within. At the same time it was invaded by enemies from without. Finally, at the end of the fifth century A.D., it disappeared altogether in the West. If we are to benefit most from the lessons of history we should be alert to discover the causes of each great civilization's decline.

But the tradition of a universal empire, embracing many peoples united by the bonds of government, law, and trade, lived on in Europe as an ideal long after the Western Empire itself had ceased to exist. Now that we have followed the history of the Roman state, we can better understand the widening interests of its people. We shall see what the Romans learned from other civilizations and what contributions they themselves made to the later progress of mankind. They were especially successful in borrowing from the cultures of others, but they also made notable strides of their own in law and government.

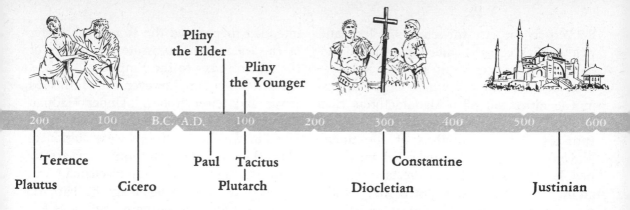

Pliny
the Elder

Pliny
the Younger

200   100   B.C. A.D.   100   200   300   400   500   600

Terence   Paul   Tacitus   Constantine

Plautus   Cicero   Plutarch   Diocletian   Justinian

1. Decline of the Empire in the West

Difficulty of Uniting the Empire · A number of conditions weakened the Empire until it was unable to withstand the invasion of the barbarous tribes from the north. In the first place, the Empire included a hundred million people of widely different cultures. Italians, Greeks, Gauls, Iberians (Spaniards), Britons, Germans, North Africans, Egyptians, Arabs, Jews, Phoenicians, Syrians, and Armenians were among the more important.

The Empire at its height was able to hold these peoples together. But the emperor was a long way from most of them, and when his government was not efficient there was little to bind these nations into a unified state. Moreover, they had no voice in the choice of the emperor.

No Legal Method for Choosing the Emperor · Lack of a legal method for choosing a new emperor was a serious defect. The various divisions of the army discovered finally that *they* had the power to set up an emperor and also to depose him. Thus, crude and barbarous soldiers, few of whom were citizens, became the chief controlling power in the state. There were often several of these "barrack" candidates for the throne fighting among themselves.

In 212 A.D., citizenship was granted to all freemen within the Empire. The various provinces then felt that they had as much right as Italy to select a new ruler. Here was a cause for great confusion and disorder.

Decline in Farming · In spite of its seeming prosperity, the Empire had for a long time been suffering from a steady decline of farming. The small farmers gradually disappeared as the land continued to fall into the hands of the rich, whose vast estates were called *villas*. These villas covered not only Italy, but Gaul, Britain, Spain, and other provinces as well.

The discouraged farmer, unable to bear the burden of heavy taxes, would often become the *colonus*, or laborer, of some rich landlord. By this arrangement he and his descendants were assured the right to work the land. But they were bound to it by law and passed with it from owner to owner when it changed hands. Though not actually slaves, the *coloni* were not free to leave their farms. They were the forerunners of medieval serfs.

Growth of the Unemployed · The disappearance of the small farms was one of the chief causes of the weakening of the Empire. Many of the country people

93

flocked to the city for relief. As less land was cultivated, the amount of food decreased and prices went up.

Since there were fewer to buy, business in the cities fell off. Manufacturers then had to discharge more workmen, who in turn swelled the numbers of the unemployed. The cities became filled with poor people standing in lines to receive the free grain, wine, and meat distributed by the government. A vast "depression" paralyzed the economy.

Heavy Taxation · A constant increase in taxes was needed to keep up the luxurious court of the emperor, to pay the armies, and to supply food and amusement for the idle in the cities. It became customary to require a group of wealthy men to become responsible for collecting the taxes of their district. The state enacted laws forbidding men to give up their business. Sons were required to follow the trades and professions of their fathers. Wages and the prices of goods were fixed by law. Thus the once free Roman citizen, whether rich or poor, in country or city, had almost no independent life of his own.

Changed Character of the Army · Under Augustus the army had been made up of Roman citizens or of freemen from the provinces. They were granted citizenship on entering the service. This policy was intended to preserve the Roman character of the legions and so assure the loyalty of the armed forces to the Empire.

As time went on, however, Italy furnished fewer and fewer troops. Under Hadrian the legions were recruited from the provinces in which the troops were stationed. Thus the character of the armies was greatly changed. The more cultured element was replaced by a growing body of barbaric soldiers. Italy and southern Gaul were left without defense, while the large professional army was protecting the far-flung frontier. It became out of touch with the more civilized parts of the Empire and had no interest in orderly government or respect for civil authority.

The permanent fortifications along the boundaries also had an important effect. The legions were scattered thinly along the stretches of the frontier. They were unable to mobilize quickly in time of emergency. Moreover, when the soldiers stationed at the garrisons were given land, they cultivated their farms and reared their families. This domestic life reduced their military vigor. And the fortifications were not equal to withstanding the assault of large numbers of invading barbarians. When the Germans finally pushed across the borders, there were no forces able to drive them back.

Retail Pork-Butcher at Work · *Behind the butcher is a spare chopper, and his steelyard with weight and scale pan. His wife keeps the accounts. Note the familiar chopping block.*

The Roman Empire Becomes an Oriental Monarchy · Under Diocletian (284–305 A.D.) the Empire became an absolute monarchy. The emperor, now supported by the army, exercised complete authority over the state. Diocletian deprived the Senate of all power except that of governing Rome. It finally lost all importance.

The emperor now assumed the outward symbols of an Oriental monarch. Among these were the diadem (ornamental headband or crown), the gorgeous robes, and the throne and footstool. All who entered his presence had to kneel. He was regarded as an Oriental sun-god, and his birthday was publicly celebrated on the twenty-fifth of December. Sacrifices in Oriental fashion were to be offered by all to the emperor as a divine ruler.

As Diocletian was kept busy in the East by his wars with the New Persians, he lived most of the time at Nicomedia in Asia Minor. He therefore appointed another emperor to rule jointly with him and watch over the western part of his realms. He had no intention of dividing the Empire, but this sharing of authority finally led to the separation of the East and the West.

Diocletian and his successors reorganized the government into new districts. Great numbers of officials were appointed to run them. The expense of this vast organization, together with the luxury of the imperial court, was tremendous. And it all had to be met by increased taxation.

Constantine and His New Capital (324–337 A.D.) · When Constantine became emperor, he determined to establish a new capital on the eastern borders of the Balkan region. He selected the ancient Greek town of Byzantium on the Bosporus. Named Constantinople, it stood just between Europe and Asia, well situated to

Diocletian's Palace at Split on the Adriatic.

be a center of power in both continents. The emperor stripped many an old town of its works of art to adorn his new city. And before the emperor's death Constantinople had become a magnificent capital.

The Empire Is Divided · The transfer of the capital of the Empire to the East tended to bring about a real separation of the East and the West. After Constantine's time there often were two emperors. One was likely to live in Italy, the other at Constantinople. As we shall see, the West was taken over by Germanic peoples in the fifth century A.D. But the Roman Empire in the East stood the test until overcome by the Turks almost a thousand years later.

CHECK ON YOUR READING

1. List the causes of the decline of the Roman Empire from the time of Marcus Aurelius to Constantine.
2. What actions of Diocletian and Constantine helped divide the Empire?

2. Everyday Life of the Romans

How the Roman People Lived · The story of the Roman state, which we have been following, covers over one thousand years. During these many centuries the Romans were busy with many other things besides fighting and governing their territory. Most people were far removed from both these occupations. They were pursuing the routine of their daily lives as farmers, laborers, businessmen, traders, or craftsmen. They were building houses, laying roads, or making the things they needed for everyday use. Some of them were writing books or plays or planning great public works or monuments. In short, during these years the Romans were slowly building up a civilization.

Comparison of the Greeks and Romans · The Greeks, as we have seen, were a creative

My Lady's Hairdo · *Four maids help this noble woman arrange her coiffure. What do you suppose is the responsibility of each? Does the wicker chair look familiar?*

people. They learned much from the Orient and the Aegean world. But after many years they finally surpassed their teachers in many ways. They added greatly to what had been known before. They set new standards of perfection in literature, art, and science.

The Romans seem to have had less originality than the Greeks. They were practical rather than imaginative, but they too appreciated the achievements of others and were deeply influenced by them. They adopted what suited their tastes and made it their own. It was in this way that much of the civilization of the Hellenistic world lived on.

The Romans Learn First from the Etruscans · The Etruscans were the first to bring civilization to the simple farmers of Italy. It was before 1000 B.C., we may recall, that these seafarers from Asia Minor had brought the traditions of the eastern Mediterranean world to the west coast of Italy. The excavations of Etruscan tombs in their early cities have brought to light a rich store of objects and wall paintings. From these we learn of this first civilization in the Italian peninsula.

Bowls, dishes, jars, and vases in bronze and silver, and the carvings on ivory show that their art was Oriental in character. Indeed the scenes and designs were taken from Assyrian and Egyptian models. There is also a large collection of beautiful jewelry in gold. The tomb furnishings include even a bronze bed and chariots in which Etruscan nobles rode. Frescoes on tomb walls show scenes from daily life and the games and amusements that these early people enjoyed.

Etruscan Mourning Dancers (c. 5th Century B.C.) · *One dancer plays a double flute, the other a lyre. What evidence can you find of Greek influence?*

The Etruscans were good craftsmen and carried on a thriving industry in pottery and metalwork. After the seventh century B.C. Etruscan art shows the growing influence of the Greeks, with whom they traded. It was this Greco-Etruscan civilization which affected the Romans when the Etruscan princes took possession of their city.

How the Romans Learned from the Greeks · It was from the Greek merchants that the Romans received their alphabet. They gradually learned to read the Greek letters on their bills and began to use these letters themselves, changing them somewhat to suit their own language. Thus the Phoenician alphabet was brought one step nearer to us.

The Romans also gave up barter, their primitive way of paying for goods with grain and cattle. They began to use money, as the Greek traders did. For a long time they used lumps of bronze of different weights and sizes. Later they made bronze coins. But when they conquered the Greek cities of the south, they copied the use of silver coins, and finally (268 B.C.) minted silver themselves. They also adopted Eastern weights and measures.

But the Romans learned more than business methods from the Greeks. They saw the beautiful temples of the Greek cities. They attended Greek plays and watched their races and athletic contests. The Greeks became their teachers.

Greek Culture Spreads to Rome · We recall how greatly the wealth which came from the Roman conquests affected the political and social life of the people. More important than this was the change that took place in the culture of the Roman world. A great enthusiasm for all Greek things grew up. For the Romans appreciated the high character of Greek culture and wished to become part of the Greek civilized world.

They brought home to Italy all the art treasures they could find and imitated the luxuries that were known in the East. They tried to copy Greek literature, drama, and art, and even identified the Greek gods with their own. Educated Romans learned Greek, read Greek books, and sought Greek tutors for their children. Greek civilization thus found a new home in Italy.

Some of the old-fashioned Romans were heartily against this craze for adopting foreign customs and ideas. They declared that the people were losing the simplicity and the rugged virtue of the days of the early Republic. But the people recognized that Greek culture was far superior to their own, and they had the good sense to borrow freely from it.

Roman Houses · The early Roman houses were of sun-dried brick and had but one room. In this the family slept and ate and received their friends. After the conquests the wealthy Romans began to build beautiful new homes like those in the Hellenistic cities.

In the finer houses the original room, or *atrium*, was converted into a reception hall. There statues and paintings from Eastern cities were displayed. Suites of rooms or alcoves which opened off the atrium could be used as living rooms or dining halls. Behind the atrium was a colonnaded court, around which more rooms were grouped. The court was decorated with fountains, plants, and flowers. This court led into the garden, at the back of the house.

The floors were of tile, marble, or mosaic, of various colors. Often the mosaic was in beautiful patterns and took the place of carpets. The walls were sometimes painted. Curtains of tapestry or colored wool might hang at the doorways. In the wealthiest homes the tables, chairs, couches, lamps, and pedestals for statues were rich in material and design. The kitchens had pots and pans of bronze and a great variety of pottery, glass, and silver tableware.

The fine homes also had pipes for running water and a sewer system. In later days they were warmed with hot air carried through pipes from a central heating system. This was a great improvement over the open hearth or the pan of glowing charcoal which was all the earlier Romans had had to make them comfortable.

The wealthy Roman usually had two houses. One was in town, and the other was a villa, or country estate, where he spent the summer.

In sharp contrast to the luxurious homes of the rich were the tenements of the poor. These were built in blocks like modern flats, several stories high. They were crowded, dirty, and unsanitary. Rich men often owned these tenements as investments and charged high rents for them.

Roman Villa at Pompeii · *Note the tile roof and the garden court with statues, flower beds and fountain pool. What ideas shown here are still used in your own community?*

Roman Schoolmaster and Schoolboys · *The textbooks consist of papyrus scrolls. Is the boy at the right tardy? volunteering? or trying to say "It's time for lunch"?*

Greek Influence on the Theater: Plautus and Terence · Educated Romans appreciated the beautiful Greek works of art, which their sculptors and painters were now trying to copy. They also enjoyed Greek plays. The plays of Plautus (c. 254–184 B.C.) and Terence (c. 190–c. 159 B.C.) were modeled on the new Greek comedy of the day. Although they were supposed to deal with Greek characters, the Romans recognized much that was part of their everyday life. They laughed heartily at the jokes on themselves.

Plautus and Terence were the founders of comedy as we know it today, for European comedy followed the rules that they established. The Romans soon built a theater. But they protected it with an awning and placed seats in the orchestra, which in the Greek theater was the place for the chorus.

Roman Education · The Greeks also influenced Roman education. In the old days, when there was any training at all, it was given in the home. But in the late Republic and Empire, Roman parents began to send their boys to schools kept by Greek freedmen. The young children took up simple subjects and memorized short verses. Later they learned either Greek or Latin poetry. They were taught to read well and know something about grammar.

Higher studies included oratory and philosophy. Very little science was taught, as it was among the Greeks. Sometimes a youth of high family would be sent to Athens to complete his education.

Growth of Latin Literature · During the conquest of Macedonia a thousand educated Achaeans had been brought as hostages to Rome. Among these was a Greek statesman of great ability, named Polybius. He was taken into the family of the Scipios (p. 82) and saw the destruction of both Carthage and Corinth. He later wrote a history in Greek of the Roman wars.

The presence of educated Greeks in such numbers at Rome had a great influence on the development of literature. Poets and writers now arose among the Romans. And educated Romans began to collect libraries of Greek and Latin works.

CHECK ON YOUR READING

1. *How did the Etruscans and the Greeks contribute to the growth of Roman civilization in use of metal? conduct of business? art? religion?*
2. *Describe (a) the home of a wealthy Roman, (b) a Roman tenement.*
3. *How did the Greeks influence Roman theaters? education? literature?*

3. Civilization of the Roman World

Latin Literature · In the age before Augustus, a lawyer, statesman, and remarkable orator named Cicero had done much to perfect the Latin tongue in his speeches before the Senate. Late in life he wrote treatises in Latin on various subjects, such as friendship, duty, old age, and the gods. They are so beautifully expressed that they have come to be regarded as models of Latin prose. They are still read in the schools and colleges where Latin is studied.

From Livy's great history of Rome we get a large part of our information about the development of the Roman state.

During the life of Augustus the writing of Latin reached its Golden Age. Horace wrote gay, and sometimes sad, little poems about joys, loves, and ambitions, which are still quoted. Virgil was the most beloved of Latin writers through the ages. He described country life in his earlier poems and then wrote his famous *Aeneid*. In this epic he described the fall of Troy and the coming to Italy of Aeneas, whom he represented as the ancestor of the Caesars.

Later Latin Writers · After the Age of Augustus literature tended to decline. Writers were too content to imitate the great works of the past. However, there were a few prose writers of ability. Seneca wrote essays and letters in an admirable style. Plutarch wrote in Greek his remarkable *Lives of Famous Men*, which has charmed and inspired readers ever since. Tacitus prepared histories of current events. These are celebrated for their compact style and keen estimates of the leading men of this time.

Science: Pliny and Ptolemy · The Romans showed little curiosity about the natural causes of things and made no advance in science. Pliny the Elder, however, devoted himself to scientific studies. He collected all sorts of information from Greek writers, which he presented in an encyclopedia called *Natural History*. He mixed with his facts many stories of imaginary animals and men and of magical properties of germs and plants. Yet people were so ignorant of science that Pliny's book was later regarded during the Middle Ages as a great authority.

Ptolemy, who lived in Alexandria about the time of Hadrian, wrote on geography and astronomy. He summed up the previous discoveries of the Greeks so well that in the Middle Ages his books too were widely accepted. He mistakenly held that the sun revolved around the earth, and his explanation of the movements of the planets is known as the *Ptolemaic system*. It was not until the time of Copernicus (1543 A.D.) that men discovered Ptolemy's great error.

Buildings of the Empire · Augustus had undertaken to rebuild Rome and make it the leading art center of the world. He boasted that he had found Rome a city of brick and left it a city of marble. In the new architecture the Roman builders used Greek and Oriental features, especially the arch and colonnade.

By the time of Trajan and Hadrian, Rome had become the most magnificent city in the world. Palaces, temples, and theaters had been added by emperor after emperor. Vespasian had erected the Colosseum, a vast amphitheater seating forty-five thousand spectators.

The most important architecture reflects to some degree the character of the Roman

Ancient Roman Bridge and Aqueduct (upper level) near Nîmes, France · *It stands 155 feet high and 880 feet across the river Gard. Note the massive stone columns and arches which support the bridge and the covered waterway above it.*

state. Its buildings were solid and durable and very impressive. The public halls, theaters, and amphitheaters were built to accommodate vast crowds. The practical genius of the Romans is illustrated in magnificent bridges and aqueducts. And the arches or gateways to celebrate victories are symbols of Roman military might.

Provincial Cities: Pompeii · Remains of Roman buildings may still be seen throughout the Mediterranean world. The best-preserved of these Roman cities is Pompeii. In the year 79 A.D. an eruption of Mt. Vesuvius smothered it with volcanic ashes. Modern excavations show its streets, public buildings, and ways of life preserved just as they were in the hour when death enveloped it like a cloud.

"All Roads Lead to Rome" · The magnificent system of roads remains as evidence of the ability of Roman engineers. Miles of highways were smoothly paved with blocks of stone. Crossing rivers by great stone bridges, all roads led to Rome. Some of the Roman bridges are still in use today. The speed of travel was fully as high as that in the days before the steam railway. A Roman merchant could send a letter by sea to his agent in Alexandria in ten days.

The Roman Law · One of the most important contributions of the Romans to later civilization was their system of law. It grew and developed as the city-state expanded into a republic and later an empire. Roman *private*, or civil, law dealt with such matters as property, inheritance, marriage, and divorce. *Public* law had to do with such matters as voting, taxation, citizenship, and the right of securing justice in the courts.

Mars, the Roman God of War · *His four sons were aptly named Terror, Trembling, Panic, and Fear. Why?*

Able Roman judges in Hadrian's time, we recall, began to organize the existing laws so that there might be a uniform system of justice for the whole Empire. Under the emperor Justinian (527–565 A.D.) the Roman law was re-examined and brought together into what became known as the Justinian Code. This collection later became the basis of law in a large part of Europe and Latin America.

The Religion of the Romans · The early Latin farmer believed in a great number of spirits or powers which affected him for good or ill. Because he was in fear of these unseen powers, religion consisted chiefly in ceremonies to win their favor. There were spirits that presided over every important event in life and all parts of the household. *Vesta* was the goddess of the hearth and cooking. *Janus*, the two-faced god, stood at the front door to keep out evil. Other gods guarded the storerooms and watched over the fields. The farmers joined together in festivals to celebrate the seasons. They appealed to *Jupiter*, the god of the sky, and to *Ceres*, who governed the fruitfulness of the grain fields (cf. "cereal"), to grant them plentiful harvest.

As the community grew into a state, the informal worship of the household developed into a state religion. Special places of worship were built and a regular calendar of celebrations was planned in honor of the gods. Priests appointed by the state took the place of the father of the family in performing the ceremonies. Jupiter became the supreme god and Janus, the god of the city gate.

The Romans Accept the Gods of Other Peoples · As Rome extended its boundaries, the people were attracted by foreign gods, especially those of the Greeks. They adopted the Greek gods and identified them

---

Our Debt to Roman Law

The law codes of Italy, France, Spain, Japan, Scotland, Latin America, and Louisiana are based on Roman law.

It strongly influenced Moslem law and the canon law of the medieval church.

English common law borrowed such terms as *posse*, *habeas corpus*, and *juror*. International law contains many Roman legal principles.

Roman maxims form the basis of our law of equity. To the Romans we owe the idea that a person must be held innocent until proved guilty.

Christian Martyrs · *There was standing room only in the Circus Maximus while Christians were burned at the stake or devoured by wild beasts. Why? Yet their membership multiplied with every martyr's death. Why?*

with their own deities, so that Zeus became Jupiter, Dionysus became Bacchus, Aphrodite became Venus, and Ares became Mars.

In the latter days of the Republic many educated Romans questioned the old religions. They turned to the teachings of Greek philosophy, especially the philosophy of the Stoics. On the other hand, many Romans were fascinated by the mysterious religions coming in from the East. Shrines and even temples to the Egyptian Isis were to be found in the larger cities. Today tiny statuettes and other symbols of the Egyptian goddess are found even along the Seine, the Rhine, and the Danube.

Rise of Christianity · Among all the faiths of the East the common people were more and more following that of the Christian missionaries. These men told how their Master, Jesus, a Jew born in Bethlehem in the days of Augustus, had preached for a few years his faith of human brotherhood and of divine fatherhood, until he was put to death in the reign of Tiberius.

A Jewish tentmaker, Paul of Tarsus, became the leading Christian missionary. He preached the new gospel in Asia Minor, in Athens, and finally in Rome itself. Christian churches began to grow up. Some of Paul's letters to the churches which he founded were widely circulated.

There were also four accounts in Greek of the life and teachings of Jesus that came to be regarded as authoritative. These are the Four Gospels. With Paul's letters and some early Christian writings they were brought together to form the New Testament. As time passed, increasing numbers learned of Jesus and joined the Christians.

Persecution of Early Christians · The early Christians, like the Jews, refused to offer sacrifices to the emperor as a god, as all good Roman citizens were supposed to do. They even predicted the downfall of the Roman state. Their religious beliefs brought them under suspicion, for they prevented Christians from paying the usual respect to the emperor and the government. Though the Roman government was usually very tolerant in matters of religion, it could not overlook what it believed to be disloyalty. Hence the Christians came to be regarded as political enemies and were frequently persecuted.

The Early Christian Churches · But in spite of persecution, Christian churches steadily increased in number. The officers of the churches came to be called the *clergy*. Ordinary members were called the *laity*. Those in charge of the smaller country congregations were called *presbyters*, meaning "elders." From *presbyter* our word *priest* is derived. Over the group of churches in each city was a *bishop*. And in communities where there were several bishops an *archbishop* had general authority.

Thus the despised sect of Christians gradually grew into a strong organization. In 311 A.D. the emperor Galerius issued an edict granting the Christians the same rights under the law as followers of other religions in his territories. This decree was broadened by Constantine to include the whole Empire. Constantine himself was converted to Christianity, and later emperors finally abolished other sects. Christianity was made the official religion of the realm under Theodosius I (379–395 A.D.).

Contribution of the Romans to Civilization · Before leaving the ancient world we may mention briefly some of the elements of Roman civilization which were handed down to later times. (1) Latin was the universal language of the medieval universities and of the learned class in Europe for over a thousand years. As late as the seventeenth century, English scholars wrote their important works in Latin so that the scholars of other countries might be able to read them. Latin has always been the official language of the Roman Catholic Church everywhere. Latin terms are still retained in various branches of science, such as zoology, botany, and medicine. The modern Romance languages—for example, Italian, French, and Spanish—are derived from Latin. English is enriched by many words of Latin origin.

(2) Roman architecture continues to furnish models for public buildings in our own time. Some of our libraries, courthouses, capitols, banks, and stadiums, have been copied from the Romans, who modified the Greek style and introduced the Oriental arch. (3) The Roman system of numerals is still often used in the engraving of dates on public buildings, to number the chapters in books, and on clock-faces.

(4) Many have regarded as the greatest achievement of the Romans their contribution to the development of law. (5) Their ability to organize and rule a great empire was likewise significant. (6) Very important for Western progress too was the fact that the Romans admired and conserved much of the Greek culture and that through them Greek books survived, though often only in translation.

(7) Finally, in the later Empire, Christianity was protected by the state and became the official religion of the realm. Rome remained the capital of the Christian world, though her political importance had long since passed away.

CHECK ON YOUR READING

1. *Identify five of the great writers of Latin literature.*
2. *Why were the Romans weak in science? What mistake was made by Pliny? Ptolemy?*
3. *Why is Roman law so important?*
4. *Why were the early Christians persecuted?*

"The good of the people is the chief law." —CICERO, *De Legibus*

"Greece, taken captive, took captive her rough conqueror and brought the arts to rustic Latium."—HORACE

Think about the chapter

1. Our immigrant ancestors came from different backgrounds with different languages, customs, and habits. But they were quickly "Americanized." How successful was Rome in "Romanizing" the 100 million people of the Empire? Explain the difference in success.

2. Horace, a Latin poet, said, "*Victi victores vicerunt*" ("The conquered have conquered the conquerors"). He was speaking of the Greeks and Romans. What did he mean?

3. In what way is the importance of Tutenkhamon's tomb similar to the importance of Pompeii?

4. What relation to Christianity did the following people have: Jesus, Augustus, Tiberius, Paul, Galerius, Constantine, Theodosius I?

5. Summarize the great contributions of the Romans to later civilizations.

6. *Map study:* Locate on a map: Constantinople, Pompeii, Alexandria, Bethlehem. Write an explanation of the importance of each.

For further inquiry

7. Choose an aspect of Roman life (sports and amusements, dress, or food) and find out all you can about it.

8. What adventures did Aeneas have in the *Aeneid?*

9. Read about the life of one of the early martyrs.

Something to do

10. Make a "Who's Who" of the famous Roman writers and scientists. Include the important facts on the life and work of each one.

11. Prepare an illustrated talk on "Roman architecture in the U.S.A." Find pictures of buildings in the Roman style. (The Capitol Building in Washington, D.C., is one.) Be sure to look in your community for examples. Your pictures may be posted, or projected by an opaque projector.

12. What buildings of ancient Rome are still standing today?

READ FURTHER

Basic readings: (1) BAUER and PEYSER, *How Music Grew*, pp. 43–45. (2) BOTSFORD, *Source Book*, Chaps. 28–47. (3) BREASTED, *Ancient Times*, Chaps. 27–29. (4) CHEYNEY, *World History of Art*, Chap. 7. (5) EVANS, *Costume Throughout the Ages*, Chap. 3. (6) HOFFMAN, *News of the World*, Nos. 12–14. (7) MACY, *Story of World Literature*, Chaps. 10–13. (8) TAYLOR, *Fifty Centuries of Art*, pp. 12–13. (9) TAYLOR, *Illustrated History of Science*, Chap. 1. (10) Year's *Pictorial History*, pp. 84–108.

Special accounts: (11) W. DAVIS, *A Day in Old Rome*. (12) G. FOSTER, *Augustus Caesar's World*. (13) J. HALL, *Buried Cities*. This tells you what you can see today in Pompeii. (14) D. MILLS, *Book of the Ancient Romans*. (15) *National Geographic*, "The Grandeur That Was Rome," November, 1946.

Fiction and biography: (16) E. BULWER-LYTTON, *The Last Days of Pompeii*. (17) L. DOUGLAS, *The Robe*. Story of the effect on Marcellus, the Roman soldier who won the robe of Christ in a dice game. (18) J. GAER, *Young Heroes of the Living Religions*. (19) H. SIENKIEWICZ, *Quo Vadis*. Lives of the Christians in Rome at the time of Nero—for good readers. (20) L. WALLACE, *Ben-Hur*. A chariot race is the climax of this exciting story. (21) J. WILLIAMS, *The Roman Moon Mystery*. The scene is laid in the slums of Rome.

The Middle Ages

600 B.C.   1500 A.D.

B.C. A.D.

4000   2000

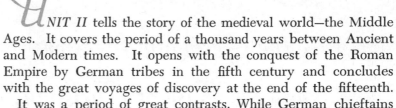

UNIT II tells the story of the medieval world—the Middle Ages. It covers the period of a thousand years between Ancient and Modern times. It opens with the conquest of the Roman Empire by German tribes in the fifth century and concludes with the great voyages of discovery at the end of the fifteenth.

It was a period of great contrasts. While German chieftains fought for control over portions of a once proud empire, priests and monks of the Christian church patiently worked to preserve what remained of classical culture. For a time Charles the Great (Charlemagne) established a great Christian Empire in the West, but upon his death confusion again prevailed. To establish order and give protection to the people a system known as feudalism developed. Peasants worked as serfs on manors of the feudal lords in return for their protection. Feudal Europe witnessed soaring cathedrals and quiet monasteries, privileged nobles and lowly serfs, great walled castles and peasant huts, mounted knights and footmen dependent on the bow. It was an age of great romance, grinding poverty, and mass illiteracy.

But at Constantinople (Byzantium) in the eastern part of the old Roman Empire classical civilization continued to thrive. And in the Arab world a brilliant culture flourished. The prophet Mohammed started a new religion which swept the Near East and northern Africa and Spain.

In the Far East, civilizations which had developed in ancient times continued to flourish. The teachings of great philosopher-leaders, such as Gautama (the Buddha), Confucius, and Lao-tse, continued to influence civilization in Asia. China under the T'ang emperors was highly civilized, and her influence spread to neighboring Japan.

Turning again to Europe we trace the rise of national states. In France and England the kings eventually overcame the feudal lords and built strong central governments. The English nobles were able to win a charter and parliament from their king, but in France autocracy reigned. Germany remained divided.

The leaders of Christian Europe launched great Crusades for recovery of the Holy Land from the Turks. These great military expeditions re-established contacts between East and West. As a result business and trade boomed, towns grew, and thriving business enterprises led to voyages of discovery and exploration. Thus the medieval period which opened with a note of gloom and doom in the destruction of the Western Roman Empire closed with a Renaissance (New Birth) of ideas and activities which greatly affected modern times.

CHAPTER

The Germanic Invasions
and the Rise of Christianity

KEY WORDS AND DATES

500–1500 A.D.	Byzantine
Goths	Papacy
Odoacer	Gregory the Great
Theodoric	Saint Benedict
476 A.D.	monks
Justinian	monasteries
Lombards	Augustine
Franks	Canterbury
Clovis	Gothic

THE MIDDLE AGES (500–1500 A.D.) once were thought of as a dark period of warfare and confusion during which little happened that was important to the later progress of man. They were commonly referred to as the "Dark Ages." We now know that, in spite of the ignorance and disorder that overtook Europe for several centuries, the foundations of many of our institutions were then being laid: (1) During the Middle Ages, Christianity became the religion of the Western world. (2) Modern national states had their beginnings. (3) Universities were founded. (4) The languages of present-day Europe developed. (5) Through the Middle Ages some part of what man had previously achieved was handed on to later generations. (6) Civilization spread into northern Europe.

We shall see how and with what effects the German barbarians overran the Roman Empire. Meanwhile, in the East the great Byzantine city of Constantinople preserved our classical traditions. And in the West the Christian Church provided a refuge from disorder and chaos, founded monasteries and missions, and built the great cathedrals which symbolize the religious spirit of the age.

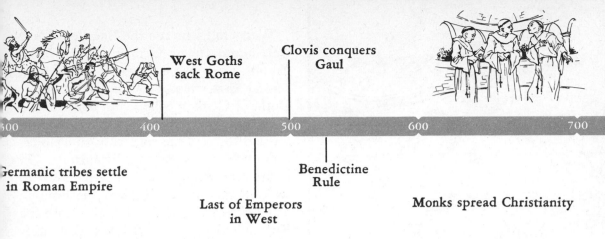

West Goths
sack Rome

Clovis conquers
Gaul

300   400   500   600   700

Germanic tribes settle
in Roman Empire

Benedictine
Rule

Last of Emperors
in West

Monks spread Christianity

1. German Chieftains Set Up Governments in the Empire

Invasions Common in History · The barbarian invasions of the Middle Ages were not a new thing in man's history. Our study of the Ancient World has shown us how common it was for primitive peoples to attack their richer and more civilized neighbors. We have seen how the Sumerians were overcome by the Akkadians, and how the prosperous Akkadian kingdom was later seized by the Babylonians. We have seen how Babylonia fell victim to the Assyrians, who in turn were conquered by the Chaldeans and they by the Persians. The world saw one civilization after another fall before the forces of an invading enemy.

Who the German Barbarians Were · The German tribes that pushed their way into the Roman Empire belonged to the same great group of Indo-European peoples as did the Persians, the Greeks, and the Romans themselves. Like their earlier kinsmen, they too were given to wandering about and seizing the lands and possessions of others. Just as Greek tribes had overwhelmed the Aegean world, so now German peoples from central and eastern Europe overran the Empire and established themselves within its borders.

How the Germans Lived · The Germans must have looked like giants to the Romans, for they were tall and very strong. They had fierce blue eyes and fair hair, which they sometimes dyed red. This fashion, it is said, was adopted by Roman ladies.

In the forests of their native lands the German peoples had not advanced much beyond the Late Stone Age in their civilization. They settled in villages of about a hundred families, with a head man over each village. Their houses were huts of rough timber plastered with mud. They got their food by hunting and shifted their homes often. Sometimes they kept cattle or raised a few crops. They did not know how to write or to make many things. They spent most of their time in fighting and plundering.

How the Germans Fought · Their love of pillaging led them to wander about, followed by their wives and families in heavy wagons. An entire people might include some fifty villages. But each village group remained together, protected by its body of about a hundred warriors, the heads of the village families. In battle each hundred held together as a fighting unit of a larger

109

GERMANIC MIGRATIONS

Germanic Migrations (Fifth Century) · *Trace the movements of these peoples fleeing before the Huns. Which tribes finally took over Italy? France? Britain? Spain? North Africa?*

army. Hardened by their rough outdoor life, these bands of kinsmen with their fierce eagerness for battle were hard to defeat.

How the Germans Got a Foothold in the Empire · Different groups of German barbarians had long been a serious threat to the peace of the Empire. We have already seen how the Roman armies and fortifications had held them off. But they kept on coming in an irresistible tide pouring through the crumbling Roman line.

Some were hired to fill the ranks of the Roman legions. Others fought as Roman allies. Finally, *entire* German peoples were allowed to settle permanently within the Empire. Their leaders were given offices in the government or rose to high places in the army. Some even married Roman women of high rank.

Over an extended period these Germans were becoming partially Romanized, and the Romans partially Germanized. This gradual process might have continued had not the Huns suddenly caused an upheaval.

West Goths Invade the Empire · There were already many Germans living in the Empire when the Mongolian Huns from central Asia swept down upon the West Goths, a German tribe living north of the Danube. The terrified Goths begged permission to cross the river and gain protection within the Roman boundaries. In return for food and land, they promised to serve in the army and guard the frontier. The Goths soon fell out, however, with the Roman officials, who did not deal fairly with them. In the battle of Adrianople in 378 A.D., they defeated the Romans and killed the emperor Valens. (Locate Adrianople on map at left.)

As a result of their victory, the Goths established themselves permanently within the Empire. Thus the battle of Adrianople may be said to mark the beginning of the conquest of the Western Roman Empire by the barbarian tribes. For some years the West Goths (*Visigoths*) kept the terms of peace made with the emperor, and some of them served as soldiers in the imperial armies.

The Sack of Rome (410 A.D.) · Among the Germans who gained important positions in the Roman army was Alaric, the leader of the West Goths. After a while he became dissatisfied with the treatment he received from the emperor. He set out for Italy and decided to march on Rome. In 410 the great capital fell into Alaric's hands, and for three days his followers plundered the city. They then moved on to southern Italy.

West Goths and Vandals · Alaric died in 410, and his followers soon wandered into Gaul and later into Spain. Here they came upon another German tribe, the Vandals. The Vandals had earlier crossed the Rhine and devastated Gaul, and were now settled in Spain. The Goths finally got the better of their rivals and took possession of a large part of the Spanish peninsula. The Vandals pushed on across the Strait of Gibraltar and established their kingdom in North Africa (map, p. 113). In 455 they attacked Rome, where their destruction of beautiful works of art has given us the term "vandalism."

Huns Defeated at Châlons (451 A.D.) · It is unnecessary to follow the confused history of the many bands of restless barbarians who wandered at will over Europe in the fifth century. Scarcely any part of the continent was left untroubled by them. Even Britain was conquered by German tribes, the Angles and the Saxons.

To add to the universal disorder, the Huns, who had been devastating the Eastern Empire, now turned to the West. Under their leader, Attila, these savage Asian people invaded Gaul. But the Romans and Goths united against this dreaded foe and defeated them at Châlons. Attila died soon afterward, and the Huns never troubled Europe seriously again.

Last of the Roman Emperors in the West · Most of the Roman rulers in the West had for some time been weak and incompetent. The barbarians had moved about as they pleased, and their armies in the Roman service had been able to set up and depose emperors to suit themselves.

Finally, in 476, Odoacer, the most powerful of the German generals, overthrew the feeble emperor. He then assumed the title of "Patrician," and made Italy a practically independent kingdom. Though the Eastern emperor still ruled at Constantinople, he had no control over the West.

Theodoric and the East Goths Control Italy · Odoacer did not maintain his kingdom long. In 493 he was conquered by Theodoric, the king of the East Goths (*Ostrogoths*), who for some time had wished to establish a kingdom within the Empire. The East Goths had at first threatened Constantinople, but they later came to friendly terms with the emperor there. He encouraged them to move on to Italy and seize Odoacer's kingdom.

Theodoric established his capital at Ravenna. Beautiful buildings which were erected there in his time may still be seen. Theodoric adopted Roman customs, kept the old offices and titles of the Empire, and encouraged learning. Goth and Roman lived peaceably together under the same Roman law.

Justinian Recovers Part of the Empire · The year after Theodoric's death one of the greatest emperors of the East, Justinian, came to the throne (527–565). Justinian's ambition was to regain for the Empire the provinces in Africa and Italy which had been seized by the Vandals and East Goths. One of his generals overthrew the Vandal kingdom in North Africa in 534. After a long struggle, the East Goths were so completely defeated that they left Italy. What became of the remnants of this people is unknown.

The Justinian Code · Justinian's name has come down to us in connection with the vast body of Roman laws which his experts revised and put into permanent form (p. 102). The Justinian Code contains (1) the *edicts* of the emperors; (2) a *digest* of the decisions of celebrated Roman judges; (3) a textbook, called the *Institutes*, for law students; and (4) *new statutes* made to supplement the older laws. This great collection—*corpus juris*—became the foundation of the civil law in medieval Europe and continued to be studied until our time.

The Lombards Settle in Italy · Soon after Justinian's death the Lombards pushed into Italy. The last of the German peoples to establish themselves within the former Empire, these newcomers occupied the region north of the Po River, an area which has ever since kept the name Lombardy. They then extended their conquests southward, pillaging the country as they went. As time passed, they became more civilized and adopted the customs and religion of the people among whom they lived. Their kingdom lasted for two hundred years.

CHECK ON YOUR READING

1. *How did the Germans step by step gain a foothold in the Empire? Show where the various tribes settled.*
2. *Explain the importance of (a) Adrianople, (b) Châlons, (c) Odoacer, (d) Theodoric.*
3. *What did the Justinian Code contain?*

---

2. Effects of the Germanic Migrations

The Frankish Kingdom in Gaul · In Justinian's time Gaul, the area which we now call France, was coming under the control of the most powerful of all the German peoples—the Franks. The Franks succeeded in founding an important and a lasting kingdom. In the early part of the fifth century the Franks had occupied the region which is Belgium today, as well as lands to the east of it. In 486 their king, Clovis (the name later became *Louis*), began a series of conquests. These continued until he controlled all Gaul except the Rhone valley and the Mediterranean coast.

In the midst of one of his battles Clovis pledged himself to be baptized in Jesus' name if Jesus would help the Franks to victory over their enemies. When Clovis won the battle, he kept his word and was baptized, together with three thousand of his warriors. Clovis died in 511 at his capital, Paris, but his successors continued to enlarge the Frankish kingdom until it included what today are France, Belgium, Holland, and western Germany.

Most of the other kingdoms of the barbarians disappeared. But the Angles and Saxons, who conquered the Roman island of Britain, laid the foundation for modern England.

The Eastern, or Byzantine, Empire · Although the political unity of the Roman Empire in the West was shattered by the Germanic kingdoms, the flame of civilization still burned brightly in the East. The Byzantine Empire managed to survive for another thousand years. Throughout this time it was often attacked by invaders, who occupied portions of its lands. The emperors were constantly at war, and sometimes there was no government at all within the realm.

Many different peoples settled within its borders, but the tradition of the old Roman glory united them under one rule. Greek instead of Latin became the official language of the government and the Church. But the Justinian Code of Roman law remained in force.

While the West was in a state of constant turmoil, Constantinople was the chief center of art and literature in Europe. Examples of gold, silver, bronze, and enamel work of this period are chiefly

Byzantine. The influence of Byzantine architecture can still be found in Italy and southern France. Constantinople was also the center of trade between the East and the West, and here were manufactured fine fabrics of silk and metal thread.

It was at Constantinople that something of the ancient Greek and Roman culture was preserved. And while our story now turns to the West, we must not forget that this vast reservoir of civilization lay to the East. When tapped by the Crusaders a thousand years later, it pours forth again in what we call the Renaissance. It was not until the capture of Constantinople by the Turks in 1453 that the Eastern Empire came to an end.

Civilization Still Persists · The Germanic migrations set Western civilization back. The crude German tribes of forest and plain knew little of the learning, art, and mode of life which had prevailed in lands they overran. Great centers of culture such as Milan, Rome, and Alexandria were partially destroyed. Libraries and works of art were ruined, and learning was neglected.

The Germans infused fresh vigor into the stale Roman system. During the period of intermingling between the Germans and the Romanized peoples whom they conquered, the basis was laid for a new flowering of civilization.

Despite much destruction, therefore, what mankind had achieved was too widespread

Germanic Kingdoms and the Byzantine Empire · *The Eastern Empire lasted 1000 years. Which Germanic tribes laid the basis for England and France?*

to be wiped out. Islands of culture existed in scattered places throughout the Empire. The Eastern (Byzantine) Roman Empire still prospered, and contacts with it and the Orient were never completely lost.

Moreover, there was one great social institution which continued to grow and spread until its influence reached all the peoples of western Europe—the Church.

CHECK ON YOUR READING

1. *Why are the Franks, Angles, and Saxons considered especially important in the period of the early Middle Ages?*
2. *Why is the Byzantine Empire important in the history of Europe?*
3. *Explain why the civilization of Rome was not entirely destroyed by the German migrations.*

3. Growth of the Christian Church

The Influence of Christianity in the Empire · We have seen how, from simple beginnings, Christianity grew in influence until it was placed by imperial edict (311 A.D.) on an equal footing with other religions in the Empire. In the fifth century the Theodosian Code—a collection of laws made under the emperor Theodosius II— affirmed Christianity as the sole religion of the realm (438 A.D.). Its doctrines were to be accepted, and unbelievers were judged guilty of heresy and were threatened with punishment by the government. The Code set the clergy apart as a separate class. Because of their sacred duties, the clergy were freed from taxation and all public burdens. Subjects of the Empire were invited to bequeath a part of their wealth "to the holy and Catholic church."

The Teachings of the Church · But Christianity had more than a legal hold on the minds and lives of the people. In a time of hardship and warfare the gospel of Jesus offered to poor and rich alike a message of comfort and hope. It preached righteousness and peace in a world of cruelty and bloodshed. It promised to the faithful a life of happiness in a world to come. Some of its teachings, such as the fatherhood of God and the brotherhood of man, were already familiar to many as part of the philosophies existing in the Empire (see the Stoics on page 74).

The Church Takes on the Duties of the State · Besides spiritual comfort, the Church gave practical aid to a sorely distressed people. As the Empire fell apart, the Church began to perform some of the duties that had formerly belonged to the state. The barbarian chiefs were seldom able to maintain peace in their kingdoms. There was much fighting as wealthy landholders settled their grudges against one another in local or neighborhood wars.

In the midst of this lawlessness it was the Church that tried, by threats or by persuasion, to restore order. It endeavored to see that contracts were honored, that the wills of the dead were carried out, and that marriage obligations were observed. The Church also protected defenseless widows and orphans and gave aid to the poor.

Since very few besides the clergy could read, the Church provided such education as there was. As time went on, the kings became more and more dependent on the clergy because of their learning. Members of the clergy were appointed by the kings to be secretaries and ministers of state. As Christian rulers and their people gave lands and money to the Church, it became a great landholder. It built up, in addition to its spiritual authority, a great earthly (*temporal*) power.

Rise of the Papacy · The title "Pope," meaning "father," was originally given to all bishops and priests. But by the sixth century it began to be especially applied to the bishop of Rome. Pope Gregory VII (d. 1085) was the first to declare plainly that the title should be used only by the bishop of Rome. By the eleventh century the Church had become the most powerful institution in Europe, and Rome, though no longer of political importance, was now the seat of the Holy Roman Apostolic Church.

Gregory the Great and His Missions · One of the most distinguished of the early Popes was Gregory the Great (590–604). During his reign ancient Rome, the former capital of a *political* empire, was already changing into medieval Rome, the seat of a *religious* empire. Gregory had great power and grave responsibilities. He was not only the spiritual leader of his people, but a skillful statesman as well. He had to defend central Italy against the Lombards, who were pushing down from the north (p. 112). He had also to govern Rome, for the authority of the Eastern emperor now no longer existed in the West save in name.

His most important work, however, was to Christianize the countries which are today called England, France, and Germany. Gregory, before he became Pope, had been a devoted monk. He now turned to the monks as his missionaries to convert the people of these heathen lands and bring them within the fold of the Church.

CHECK ON YOUR READING

1. *What duties of the state were taken over by the Church?*
2. *How did the Church build up temporal power as well as spiritual authority?*
3. *Why is Gregory the Great considered to be one of the most able of the Popes?*

---

4. Life and Work of the Monks

Who the Monks Were · An important part of the early Christian faith was the belief that man's stay on this earth was but a preparation for a better life to come. To atone for his daily sins he must fast and pray, do good works, and set his mind on things heavenly. It was praiseworthy to scorn the comforts of the body, because the body is mortal, whereas the soul is immortal, or eternal.

Some Christian enthusiasts longed to withdraw themselves entirely from the world and devote their whole time to repentance, prayer, and praise. Others preferred to form small communities, or orders. Women who joined such orders came to be called *nuns* and lived in nunneries, or convents. Men belonging to religious orders were called *monks* and lived in monasteries.

In following the monastic life these people gave up everything they had formerly possessed, even their own wills. They vowed absolute obedience to the rules of their order. Religious orders founded in the Middle Ages still exist today.

What Monastic Life Offered · There were other reasons besides piety which made the monastic life seem attractive.

A Medieval Scribe at Work · *Books were handwritten (L. manuscript) in Gothic letters on vellum (calf skin) or parchment (sheepskin). Initial letters of pages were often ornamented with gold and the margins with pictures.*

The monastery offered a secure and peaceful life to thoughtful persons who wished to escape the dangers of a disordered world. For even pagan warriors hesitated to attack these communities, where holy men were believed to be devoting themselves entirely to the service of God.

The monasteries provided a refuge for the homeless, the friendless, the unfortunate, and the disgraced. They offered food and shelter even to the lazy, who otherwise would have had to earn their living. Kings and wealthy persons, for the good of their souls, often gave lands on which to found these retreats. In time there were many such communities, which provided an escape from the world, its temptations, its dangers, and its responsibilities.

The Benedictine Rule · About 526 Saint Benedict wrote out a set of regulations for the monastery of Monte Cassino, of which he was the head (*abbot*). Through the influence of Pope Gregory the Great this gradually became the rule by which most of the Western monks lived.

The Benedictine Rule provided that everyone wishing to enter a monastery should first go through a period of testing (the *novitiate*) before he was fully accepted. Every monk was required to take the solemn vows of obedience, poverty, and purity. He was to obey the head of the monastery in all matters without question. He was to keep nothing for himself, not even a book or pen. He must promise never to marry.

Besides prayer, meditation, and reading, the monks were required to do their own work. This included cooking, laundering, and farming their land. Those unable to work outdoors were given lighter tasks, such as the copying of books.

What the Monks Did for Civilization · In the work done on their fields the monks set an example of careful cultivation, and they improved farming methods in the regions where they were settled. They lodged pilgrims and wayfarers at a time when there were few inns to provide shelter.

One of the most important services of the monks to civilization was the copying of books. Because of the destruction of libraries and the general neglect of learning, it was necessary to make new copies of manuscripts. Poor and incorrect as these copies sometimes were, they were better than nothing. Almost all the Roman books disappeared during the Middle Ages, but from time to time a monk would copy the poems of Virgil, Ovid, or Horace, or the speeches of Cicero. In this way, many of the works of the chief Latin writers were preserved.

The Missionary Work of the Monks · The monks rendered great service to the cause of Christianity by carrying the gospel to heathen lands, converting the people, and bringing them into the Church. In the middle of the fifth century Ireland was converted to Christianity by Saint Patrick whose feast day (March 17) is still celebrated. The Irish monasteries were centers of culture, and even Greek was studied there. From these communities Irish missionaries went forth to spread the gospel in Scotland, England, and Gaul.

Pope Gregory the Great sent a company of monks to England, under the leadership of Augustine (597). They were given an ancient church at Canterbury which dated from the Roman occupation. Here they established a monastery and from this center gradually converted the whole island. Canterbury has always retained its pre-eminence among the churches of England. The Archbishop of Canterbury today occupies the highest office in the English Church and is called "the Primate of all England."

In 718 Boniface, an English monk, was sent to convert the Germans. He won to Christianity some of the more remote German tribes east of the Rhine.

CHECK ON YOUR READING

1. Why did the life of the monasteries and convents attract so many people?
2. What were the rules of monastic life laid down by Saint Benedict?
3. How did the work of the monks benefit the world?

---

5. The Great Cathedrals

The Church Dominated Each Town · The most important and imposing building in every medieval town was its church. Here the life and interests of the people were centered. No modern churches equal in beauty and grandeur the finest of the great cathedrals of the Middle Ages. They stand as memorials to the power of the medieval Church and as a symbol of the religious spirit of the Middle Ages.

In those days everybody belonged to the one great Catholic Church. Therefore everyone, however humble, contributed to the building of the church. The cathedrals represent the devotion of many hearts and the labor of many hands, the riches of the wealthy and the savings of the poor. Humble workers and skilled craftsmen labored together to make these great buildings a worthy expression of their faith and art. The building of a cathedral, or bishop's church, sometimes took centuries.

Gothic Style of Architecture · In the twelfth century, French architects developed a new method of constructing buildings which came to be known as the *Gothic* style. This was a great change from the Romanesque architecture, hitherto the

The Cathedral at Chartres, France (c. 1194–1260) · *Note the flying buttresses (right), the stained-glass windows, the "cross" plan of the roof. The left spire was built in the 12th century, the other in the 16th.*

prevailing style. Romanesque churches, patterned after the old Roman public halls (*basilicas*), had thick walls to support the thrust of a heavy stone roof. The French architects filled most of the wall space with high, graceful windows. They could do this by bracing the walls with buttresses at special places (see illustration above).

Since the walls were no longer needed as the chief support for the vaulted stone ceiling, the facade and sides of the building could be opened up with windows as high and wide as the architect wished. Instead of the round arches and horizontal lines of Romanesque, the Gothic style used the pointed arch in window and ceiling, carrying the eye upward to a great height. The pointed arch permitted great variety in design and structure.

Stained-Glass Windows · The cathedrals were now adorned with exquisite stone trac-ery in which were set great stained-glass windows. Through them the light shone as through jewels. Sometimes the windows portrayed sacred characters or scenes from the Bible. Instead of the gloomy interior of the Romanesque church, the interior of such a Gothic building is suffused with a glorious mellow light. By far the greater part of this magnificent glass has been destroyed. The examples that do remain are highly prized and carefully preserved, for the work of this period has never since been equaled.

CHECK ON YOUR READING

1. *In what respects are the cathedrals the most important symbol of the Middle Ages?*
2. *What are the characteristics of a Gothic cathedral?*

Think about the chapter

1. What events in Ancient Times can be compared to the Germanic invasions of Rome?

2. Where does the word *vandalism* come from? What does it mean?

3. How was the Christian Church able to become so powerful in western Europe?

4. *Map study:* Locate the boundaries of the German kingdoms and the Byzantine Empire.

For further inquiry

5. What are the characteristics of Byzantine architecture? Saint Sophia in Constantinople (Istanbul) and Saint Mark's in Venice are good examples. Try to find pictures of them.

6. Why was the location of Constantinople strategic in the Middle Ages? Why today?

7. What were the *chronicles* kept by the monks? How do they help historians?

8. How were the interiors of the great cathedrals decorated? Show pictures of some.

Something to do

9. Read some of the myths of the Germanic peoples. What characters appear in some well-known operas by Wagner?

10. Try to find a recording of Gregorian chant for the class to hear. Explain it.

11. Write a biography of one of the great missionaries: Augustine, Patrick, or Boniface.

12. Draw a floor plan of a medieval monastery. Explain each of its sections.

13. In the center of a bulletin board mount a small map of Europe. Around it arrange pictures of some famous cathedrals. Connect the pictures to their location with colored strings.

READ FURTHER

Basic readings: (1) BOTSFORD, *Source Book,* Chaps. 44–45. (2) BREASTED, *Ancient Times,* Chap. 30. (3) CHEYNEY, *Short History of England,* Chaps. 4–5. (4) CHEYNEY, *World History of Art,* Chaps. 11, 15. (5) DAVIS, *Readings,* Vol. 2, Chap. 10. (6) HOFFMAN, *News of the World,* No. 15. (7) Life's *History of Western Man,* Introduction. (8) ROBINSON, *Readings in European History,* Chaps. 2–4. (9) SCOTT, HYMA, and NOYES, *Readings in Medieval History,* Chaps. 5–7; 16–17. (10) Year's *Pictorial History,* pp. 102–111.

Special accounts: (11) *Anthology of Great Operas.* For reference on Wagnerian opera using Norse mythology. (12) BULFINCH, *Mythology.* Germanic legends. (13) B. FLETCHER, *History of Architecture on the Comparative Method.* (14) L. LAMPREY, *All the Ways of Building.* From lake dwellings to skyscrapers. (15) D. MILLS, *The Middle Ages.* Excellent chapters on Germanic invasions and Byzantine Empire. (16) H. VAN LOON, *The Arts.* Chap. 13 on Byzantine art.

Fiction and biography: (17) J. BALDWIN, *The Story of Siegfried.* (18) H. GUERBER, *Myths and Legends of the Middle Ages.* (19) V. HUGO, *The Hunchback of Notre Dame.* (20) E. JEWETT, *Hidden Treasure of Glaston.* The search for the Holy Grail. (21) H. PYLE, *The Story of the Grail and the Passing of Arthur.* (22) K. SEREDY, *The White Stag.* A hero tale of the founding of Hungary.

"This is now to be said, that whilst I live I wish to live nobly, and after life to leave to the men who come after me a memory of good works."
—ALFRED (848–901) *Boethius*

How Feudalism Developed in Medieval Europe

KEY WORDS AND DATES

feudal system
Mayor of the Palace
Papal States
temporal power
Charlemagne
800 A.D.
Northmen
Magyars
vassal
fief
homage and fealty
Truce of God
knight
donjon
manor
serf

THIS CHAPTER tells about European society, with its division into an upper class (the nobles and higher clergy) and a lower class (the common people). In the period of confusion that followed the barbarian invasions, the kings had little money. They had to give away much of their land to pay the leaders who fought for them. These men finally grew so powerful that they ruled as independent princes on their vast estates, and paid little attention to their kings. This group of landholders became the *nobility*. The rest of the folk (other than the clergy), who farmed for them and supplied their needs, were the *common people*.

The nobles, in order to increase their armed forces, often granted the use of part of their land to lesser nobles, who promised to fight for them. This relation of lord and followers, based on land, is called the *feudal system*. The nobles were free to spend their time in fighting or hunting, while the peasants had to do all the work for a mere living. This division of Europe into privileged and unprivileged classes lasted long after the kings had put down the nobles and regained control of the government. It was the source of much trouble in later times.

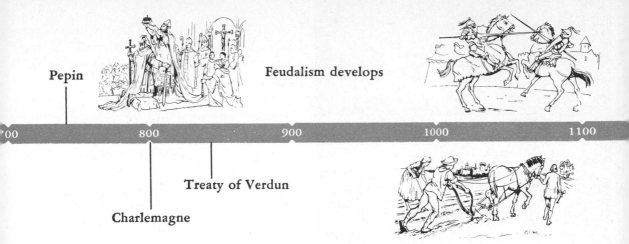

Pepin

Feudalism develops

'00   800   900   1000   1100

Treaty of Verdun

Charlemagne

1. How the Empire Was Revived in the West

Kings and Popes Aided Each Other · We have seen that most of the governments set up by Germanic chiefs within the Roman Empire soon disappeared. However, the Franks under Clovis and his successors conquered a large territory covering what today is western Germany and France.

As time went on, the Frankish kings became so lazy and incompetent that they left to others most of the task of governing. Chief among the king's officials was the Mayor of the Palace. He managed the royal household and estates, received the taxes, and led the army in war. Those who fought under him looked up to him as the real leader of the state. Charles Martel, an able Mayor of the Palace who had defeated the Moslems (p. 136), died in 741. His son Pepin, who succeeded him, determined to get rid of the "do-nothing" ruler and make himself king in his place.

But Pepin decided to make sure of the support of the Church before taking so dangerous a step. He therefore appealed to the Pope, Boniface, who replied that the one who had the power should also have the title. The council of Frankish nobles also

rallied to Pepin's cause. The feeble ruler was removed, and Pepin was crowned. He was also anointed by Saint Boniface. This religious ceremony, which declared the ruler to be "God's anointed," was very important. It gave to kingship a sacred character, which later monarchs made much of.

Pepin was soon able to repay the Pope for his assistance. The Lombards, who had been overrunning Italy for some years (p. 112), were threatening Rome. Pepin finally overcame the Lombards and presented their conquered cities to the Pope. Over this territory, which became the foundation of the so-called Papal States, the Pope reigned as sovereign. The papacy thenceforth could claim a *temporal* (worldly), as well as a *spiritual*, power.

How Charlemagne Built an Empire · Pepin and his successors are called the *Carolingian* kings because of the name of Pepin's famous son *Charlemagne*. (Charlemagne is the French form of *Carolus Magnus*, Charles the Great.)

Charlemagne, who became king in 771, was the greatest of medieval rulers. His ambition was to bring all the German

121

Charlemagne (by Albrecht Dürer) · *How does Dürer (who came 700 years later) emphasize the emperor's power? religion? wealth? Why the German eagle and lily of France?*

peoples together into one Christian empire. For over forty years he was busy subduing the peoples within his own boundaries and conquering his hostile neighbors. (1) To aid the Pope, who was again threatened by the Lombards, Charlemagne crossed the Alps into Italy. He shut up the Lombard king in a monastery and then renewed his father's donation of the Lombard lands to the Pope.

(2) Later he marched into Spain, where he conquered a wide strip north of the Ebro River which became known as the *Spanish March*.

(3) To the east, Charlemagne added the territory of the Duke of Bavaria to his realms.

(4) But Charlemagne's most difficult task was subduing the heathen Saxons, who occupied the region east of the Rhine. It took him thirty-three years of almost constant warfare before he was able to conquer them. He then forced them to accept Christianity and become part of the Frankish state, whose. border was thus extended to the river Elbe.

The Pope Crowns Charlemagne Emperor (800) · Charlemagne finally brought most of western Europe under his control. His realms included much of the former Roman Empire in the West as well as non-Roman territory east of the Rhine.

In the meantime Leo III had become Pope (795) and was heartily disliked by the Romans. Charlemagne had to go to Rome to settle the quarrels between Leo and his enemies. On Christmas Day, as Charlemagne knelt at prayer in St. Peter's, the Pope placed a crown upon his head while the crowds hailed him as "Emperor of the Romans."

This extraordinary act had some important consequences. It seemed to revive the Empire in the West. Moreover, it formed the basis of the later claim of the Popes that they could make and unmake emperors. Charlemagne is said to have been much displeased by the Pope's action. This may have been because he feared that it would cause trouble with Constantinople, or because he did not wish to wear the crown *as the gift of the Pope*. We do not know the real reason. At any rate, he later

(810–812) made a treaty by which Constantinople recognized him as emperor in the West. In return Charlemagne ceded Venice and the Dalmatian coast to the Eastern Empire. Before his death he saw to it that his son placed the imperial crown upon his own head.

CHECK ON YOUR READING

1. *How did Pepin I become king?*
2. *How was the temporal power of the papacy increased?*
3. *How did Charlemagne revive the Empire in the West?*

2. Breakup of Charlemagne's Empire in an Age of Disorder

Charlemagne's Empire Soon Divided · The Empire in the West was short-lived. The task of governing this vast domain was difficult, even for the able and energetic Charlemagne. It was quite beyond the power of any of his successors.

By the Treaty of Verdun (843) the grandsons of Charlemagne divided the empire into three kingdoms. (1) The West Frankish kingdom, corresponding roughly to modern France, went to Charles. The language of its people was derived from the *spoken* Latin and later developed into French. (2) The East Frankish kingdom, now Germany, was given to Louis. Here the German language was spoken. (3) Lothair's kingdom included Italy and a wedge of territory between the other two. By the Treaty of Mersen (870) this wedge was split between the two large kingdoms. In Italy the spoken Latin of the people finally became Italian.

Reasons for General Disorder · There were several reasons for the general disorder which prevailed after the Treaty of Mersen. (1) The medieval king had little power to govern his realm properly. It was very difficult for him to get an army quickly from one part of the kingdom to another in case of rebellion. The old Roman roads had fallen into ruin and no new ones had been built. Many Roman bridges had been washed away by floods. Progress was slow and laborious, by foot or on horseback.

(2) The king was poor. There were but few gold or silver mines in western Europe, and no supply of metal was coming in from outside, since business had largely died out after the breakup of the Roman Empire. The king had no money to keep up an army or to pay his officials. All he had to give the dukes and counts who supplied him

Division of Charlemagne's Empire, 843 · *Charles and Louis and Lothair received areas now France, Germany, and Italy respectively.*

with soldiers was land. But in giving away his lands he was handing over his kingdom, piece by piece, to the nobles. They soon became richer and more powerful than their ruler.

(3) When these independent lords had any grievance, they readily resorted to fighting. Thus constant local warfare added to the general confusion of the time. (4) Besides, there was constant danger from invaders who terrorized all parts of Charlemagne's empire and England as well.

Invaders from Every Side · The Moslems had begun to get possession of Sicily (in 827) shortly after Charlemagne's death. They finally conquered the whole island and harassed the people of Italy and southern France.

On the east the Slavs, whom Charlemagne had defeated, still made occasional trouble for the German rulers.

The Magyars, a savage people from Asia, entered Hungary in the ninth century. They swept over Germany, plundered Lombardy, and even devastated Gaul. Finally, they were driven back eastward and settled in Hungary, where they later became the ruling class.

Most fearful and destructive of all the invaders of the ninth and tenth centuries were the Northmen. These fierce and cruel pirates came from the Scandinavian countries in their small open boats. They burned and pillaged the towns along the coasts and then found their way up the rivers to the interior of Germany and France. Here they plundered and destroyed cities as far south as Bordeaux, massacring or enslaving the people and carrying off large stores of booty.

Europe was now in such a state of disorder that danger threatened from every side.

CHECK ON YOUR READING

1. How was Charlemagne's empire divided after his death? What modern nations developed from these divisions?
2. Why were the medieval kings unable to keep order in their kingdoms?
3. What different peoples threatened western Europe with invasion?

---

3. Feudalism and What It Offered

How Feudalism Developed · When governments could no longer protect their subjects, people had to find some other means of defense. Men, therefore, attached themselves to some stronger man in the community by promising to fight for him in return for his support. If a noble had but a few followers, he would put himself and his men at the service of a more powerful lord. In this way he gained greater security by strengthening the forces of his master.

The relationship which developed between *lord* and *vassal* was a contract for their mutual security. Each promised to perform a needed service for the other. This political relationship, defining the obligations between nobles, is called *feudalism*.

Feudalism Based on Land · The feudal system did not come into existence by any royal decree or through any series of statutes. It developed gradually, at different times in different places. Its agreements rested on solemn promises and the principle of honor. Its forms and usages varied with the time, the place, and the preferences of the nobles involved.

There were, however, certain characteristics which generally prevailed. In the first place, the feudal system was based on land. Owners of large estates were glad to turn over part of their domain to persons who would bind themselves to render certain services in return. One who received such a grant promised to fight for his lord, lend him other aid when he needed it, and above all be faithful to him and guard his interest. In return, the lord promised to protect his man, or vassal. Land granted on these terms to a vassal was called a *fief*.

Ceremony of Homage and Fealty · One desiring to become a vassal had first to go through a solemn ceremony. *Homage* bound him as a vassal to his lord and declared the lord's right over him. He must kneel, place his hands in those of his lord, and declare himself his "man" for such and such a fief. Thereupon the lord gave the kiss of peace and raised him to his feet.

The vassal then took an oath of *fealty* (loyalty), swearing on the Bible to be faithful in everything to his lord. The ceremony of homage and fealty was the first duty of a vassal. The lord then *invested* his man with a fief by giving him some object as a symbol that he had handed over the land to him.

Duties of a Vassal · The vassal pledged himself to perform a number of services for his lord. He must help to guard the lord's castle and follow him to war when necessary. He must be present at important celebrations, such as a marriage in the lord's family. He must attend the lord's court to hear cases and adjust differences among the vassals, and aid his master in administering justice.

The vassal was often required to make money payments when the lord was at heavy expense. Such occasions were when

A Squire Becomes a Knight · *The king confers the* accolade *of knighthood upon a vassal's son. Why were ceremonies of homage, fealty, and knighthood impressive? expensive?*

he knighted his son, or when his daughter was married, or when he set out on a crusade. The vassal was also expected to entertain the lord and his escort when they passed his castle. This finally became such a burden that agreements had to be made as to how many followers the lord might bring and what he and his followers were to have to eat during their stay.

The Confusing Character of Feudalism · There were fiefs of all grades of importance. They ranged from the great provinces of the dukes and counts, who held their land directly from the king, to the small portion of the knight, whose bit of land barely supported the horse on which he rode to

Jousting in a Medieval Tournament · *Describe what has happened. Why the trumpets and banners? Why do certain ladies look concerned? Is the combat mock, or mortal?*

war. One who had a large fief might grant portions of his land to vassals on the same terms as those by which he held his own estate. The vassal of a vassal was a *subvassal*—but *all vassals were nobles.*

A man might hold fiefs from several lords and in turn grant parts of these to vassals of his own. Thus he might be both lord and vassal at the same time, and also owe allegiance to more than one overlord. The subdivisions of fiefs became very confusing when, in case of war, one might owe aid to conflicting sides. It finally became necessary, on accepting a fief, to require that the lord who granted it state just what services were due.

How Feudalism Weakened the Power of the Kings · Originally the feudal agreement was good only for the life of those making

it. The lord could reclaim the fief at the vassal's death. But in time the fief (or its use) became hereditary in the vassal's family, passing down to the eldest son from generation to generation. So long as the vassal remained faithful to his obligations, neither the lord nor his heirs could regain possession of the land.

The great vassals, who held their domains directly from the king, became practically independent of royal control. As time went on, their many vassals, who owed allegiance directly to them and not to the king, paid little attention to royal commands. Thus from about the tenth to the thirteenth century, in the feudal states of Germany and France, the king did not rule *directly* over his subjects. They did not owe him first obedience and were not bound by oath to fight for him. As a feudal lord, he had the right to demand assistance from his great vassals. But the mass of the people, over whom he was nominally king, lived on the lands of other feudal lords and so were more or less independent of him.

Constant Warfare of the Feudal World · Every noble was a warrior by training and profession and made war on his enemies at will. Indeed, war was the common law of the feudal world. Rival nobles found many excuses for waging war on each other, for in the noble class fighting was not only a business but a pleasure. *Jousts* and *tourneys* were arranged to fill in the time between real wars. These were mock combats in which single knights or opposing bands would meet in contest on the open field. The idea was to unsaddle one's opponent. Sometimes these combats were as serious as real wars.

The Truce of God · The constant disorder of the period was so terrifying to the common people and so destructive of life and property that the Church tried to check it. The Church forbade attacks on churches and monasteries, and on pilgrims, merchants, and other defenseless people. Later, church councils in France decreed what is known as "the Truce of God." This prohibited fighting during Lent, on certain holy days, and at the end of each week. During these periods all people must be allowed to go about without fear of being molested by soldiers.

┌─ **CHECK ON YOUR READING**

1. *Define feudalism. Why did it develop?*
2. *What were the duties of the vassals? of the lords?*
3. *How was the king's power weakened?*

4. How People Lived in Feudal Times

Privileged and Unprivileged Classes · In feudal times society was divided into rigid classes—the privileged and unprivileged. Almost everyone accepted this as the natural and unchangeable order of things. To belong to the privileged (upper) class, one must possess wealth, which was usually in the form of land. Nearly everyone, therefore, who owned much land was a noble. To this class also belonged the higher clergy. Owing to the vast gifts of land to churches and monasteries, the bishops and abbots were often great feudal lords.

The rest of the people constituted the lower class. A bishop once described the population as consisting of the nobles, who did the fighting; the clergy, who did the praying; and the others (peasants), who did the work.

The Education of the Young Noble for Knighthood · Every young noble was educated to become a *knight*, or warrior. He was often sent at an early age to the estate of some important lord. Here he served as a *page*, assisted the lord in dressing, waited at table, and learned the manners of courtly life. Later he was taught to mount a horse, to handle arms, to scale a ladder, to hunt, to ride, and to hawk. Then, as a *squire*, he attended a knight on the field. After he had finished his training and reached the proper age of young manhood, he was ready, if wealthy enough, to become a knight.

In order to be admitted to knighthood, he had to go through a ceremony of initiation. He was required to perform some feat of arms. Then he had to be dubbed a knight by one already of that rank, and receive the *accolade*. This was a blow on the shoulder or neck with the fist or the flat of a sword.

Estates of the Nobles · By the tenth century there were few small landholders in Europe. Almost all land formed part of large estates held by nobles. Most small landowners found it easier to turn over their land to the great landholders in return for safety and support. The lord then allowed them to use the land on certain terms.

The houses, or castles, of the nobles varied in accordance with the rank and fortune of their owners. The Roman landholders during the days of the declining Empire had fortified their houses or villas against the raids of the barbarians. These forts were wooden buildings situated on a mound of earth and surrounded by a deep ditch and a palisade of wooden posts.

The methods of warfare changed in the Middle Ages. The wooden castles were

battered by heavy missiles hurled by stone-throwing machines. Great square towers of stone began to be built. Later, round towers were used, since these were even stronger.

The Medieval Castle · The castle of the wealthy noble was a mighty fortress. It was usually built on a rocky hill or other elevation. Thus it had a commanding view of the countryside all round and was hard to approach. If it was on the edge of a rocky slope, it could not easily be attacked by movable towers and siege machinery. If it was on lower ground, it was encircled by a deep moat, filled with water. This prevented the enemy from scaling the walls on ladders. The moat was crossed by a bridge which could be drawn up if the castle were attacked.

The doorway was protected by a heavy iron grating which could be dropped like a curtain to shut out the enemy. The walls and towers were of massive stone, with narrow slits here and there from which arrows could be shot at the foe. From the top of the wall stones could be hurled, or boiling oil or pitch could be poured on the heads of the besiegers. Inside the walls the chief tower, or *donjon*, was the residence of the lord of the castle and his family. Other buildings housed the guard and stored supplies and arms, and there was also usually a chapel. The donjon often had a great hall, where the lord could hold court or entertain his followers. Our word "dungeon" gets its meaning from the prison-like underground rooms of the donjon.

The Medieval Manor · Around the castle or great house lay the estate of the lord, where his dependents and tenants lived. The estates were called *vills* or *manors* (English) and some resembled the Roman villas of earlier days. In a society where

*The Mighty Alcazar of Segovia, Spain, was built in the 14th century. What made it mighty? Around it stretched the domains of the lords and the strip fields of the peasants as shown in the **simplified manor plan below.***

Waste

Woodland

Lord's Domain

Fallow Land

Spring Planting

Fall Planting

Pond

Church

Village

Stream

Common Pasture

Mill

Fields of the Parish Church
Fields of the Lord's Domain
Fields of the Peasants
Strips farmed by one peasant

part of the people were free to spend their time in fighting or amusing themselves, the rest of the population had to do all the work. The common people kept everyone fed, clothed, and supplied with other things that were needed.

A portion of the estate was reserved by the lord for his own use. The rest was divided among the peasants and tenants for their own farming. The medieval manor was a self-sufficient, but narrow, little world in itself. Here a community of peasants and artisans raised food and made clothes, tools, furniture, and all the other necessities of life. The manor had its guard of armed followers, its court of justice, and its parish church. With few exceptions most of its inhabitants lived and died within a few miles of its boundaries.

How the Serfs Lived · The peasants, who were generally *serfs* (from the Latin *servus*, meaning "slave") were not free. They were bound to the land that they farmed. They were sold or transferred with the land from owner to owner. But the serf could not be deprived of the land's use if he performed the services and paid the dues demanded by its owner.

There was no one to restrain the lord, however, and he often squeezed as much as he could out of his peasants. The serf was not free to go where he pleased. He might not even marry without his lord's consent. His wife and daughters performed the indoor tasks at the manor house, such as spinning, weaving, and candle-making, in addition to doing their own work.

The peasants lived in little wooden huts with thatched roofs. There was often but one room, in which the family ate and slept. If there was a window, it had no glass to keep out the cold. In the center of the room was the fire, but there was no chimney

Scenes from Duc de Berry's Book of Hours · *In February (above) at Poitiers, there were trees to cut, stock to feed, and chilled fingers to blow. In July (below) there were wheat fields to reap, and sheep to shear—near King Charles's chateau.*

to carry off the smoke. Often there was no bed, and the family slept on pallets of straw on the earthen floor.

The peasant's land usually consisted of a few strips scattered over the lord's estate. In return for the right to farm his portion, the peasant worked a part of his time for his master and paid him numerous dues. These might vary according to the disposition of the lord. But they were always heavy enough to make the peasant's life one of monotony and toil.

Duties of the Serfs · The serfs had to do all the heavy work on the estate. They plowed the fields, reaped and carried in the crops, dressed the vines and made the wine. They chopped and fetched firewood, mended the roads and bridges, and cleaned the moats and fish-pond. They repaired buildings and fortifications.

In addition, the lord found a way of collecting various fees in money, labor, or produce. The lord required his peasants to grind their flour at his mill, use his wine press, bake their bread at his ovens, and use his weights and measures. For all these and other services they had to pay something. Moreover, the peasant, from his own farm land, had to give his lord yearly a portion of whatever he produced. The collection of these taxes was in the hands of a superintendent, who made his living by keeping a share of everything collected.

Not all the peasants who lived on the estate were serfs. Some freemen simply paid the lord a yearly rent for their land. They were free to go as they pleased.

The Gradual Decline of Serfdom · Towns began to grow up in the twelfth and thirteenth centuries and business revived (p. 176). Then serfs could sell some of their produce at neighboring markets. This gave them money to pay their dues to their lord, instead of working out what they owed. The lords were often glad to get the money because with it they could hire laborers. They could also buy with it some of the luxuries which began to appear in the shops or fairs.

Lords sometimes freed their serfs for a fixed sum of money. The peasant might then work for his former master as a paid laborer. This new relation between landholder and worker tended to break up the medieval manor. In France at the end of the thirteenth century serfdom was beginning to disappear. It disappeared somewhat later in England. In Prussia and Russia the serfs were not freed until the nineteenth century. In parts of the world today where there are semi-feudal landlords, conditions approaching serfdom still exist.

Notes on Medieval Peasant Life

Clothes—Coarse—linen, wool, leather.
Diet—Limited, monotonous, unhealthful.
Formal education—None.
Attitudes—Extremely superstitious.
Amusements — Crude — wrestling, cockfighting, bull-baiting. (Example: Two blindfolded men, swinging clubs, attempt to find and kill a pig let loose in an enclosure.)
Sanitation—The devil was said to have refused to accept more peasants because they smelled so bad.
Famine—A constant and terrible threat.
Life span—Short. **Death rate**—High.

CHECK ON YOUR READING

1. *Contrast the lives of nobles and serfs.*
2. *Explain how the feudal way of life made a manor self-sufficient.*
3. *What caused serfdom to decline?*

Learning Activities

Think about the chapter

1. Why did Charlemagne object to being crowned by the Pope?

2. Why might medieval castles be described more as fortresses than homes?

3. Why was it difficult for serfs to rise in the social scale?

4. Why do conditions resembling serfdom still persist in parts of the world today?

For further inquiry

5. What place did women have in feudal society? Compare the status of women then to the status of women today.

6. What sort of person was Charlemagne? Find out about his appearance, his early life, his family, his ambitions, his reputation.

7. How were tournaments of the Middle Ages conducted?

8. How was justice meted out in feudal courts?

9. Describe the clothes and food of serfs and nobles.

10. Find out about the semi-feudal Dutch patroon system that once existed along the Hudson River in New York.

Something to do

11. Draw a diagram to illustrate the distribution of land under the feudal system.

12. Make a collection of pictures of medieval castles still standing today.

13. Many common family names describe the occupation of the head of the family in medieval days. Miller, Carpenter, Smith are examples. List as many others as you can.

14. Write sentences that might appear in a news story today using these words: accolade, chivalrous, homage, privileged classes, serfdom, tournament.

READ FURTHER

Basic readings: (1) BOTSFORD, *Source Book*, Chap. 46. (2) DAVIS, *Readings*, Vol. 2, pp. 370–79. (3) HOFFMAN, *News of the World*, Nos. 18–19. (4) Life's *Picture History of Western Man*. Secs. I–II (5) ROBINSON, *Readings in European History*, Chaps. 7–9. (6) SCOTT, HYMA, NOYES, *Readings in Medieval History*, Secs. 6–8. (7) VAN LOON, *Story of Mankind*, pp. 144, 155–161. (8) Year's *Pictorial History*, pp. 139–45.

Special accounts: (9) T. BULFINCH, *Mythology*. Includes legends of Charlemagne's time. (10) G. HARTMAN, *Medieval Days and Ways*. Brings to life the people and their customs. (11) D. MILLS, *The Middle Ages*.

Fiction and biography: (12) F. ANDREWS, *For Charlemagne*. Sigmund of Fulda comes to court to study under Alcuin and becomes involved in stirring adventures. (13) I. M. BOLTON, *Son of the Land*. England in the 14th century; the Peasant's Revolt; the hero is a 16-year-old boy who tries to escape serfdom. (14) M. CHUTE, *The Innocent Wayfaring*. A gay story of an English girl who ran away from home. (15) W. DAVIS, *Life on a Medieval Barony*. A picture of a typical feudal community in the 13th century in northern France. (16) E. GRAY, *Adam of the Road*. Story of a minstrel boy in England. (17) M. TWAIN, *A Connecticut Yankee in King Arthur's Court*. Good-humored satire on knighthood.

"Let every monastery and every abbey have its school, where boys may be taught the psalms . . . singing, arithmetic, and grammar. . . . *Decree of Charlemagne*, 789

The Near East and the Far East

KEY WORDS AND DATES

Mohammed	Gautama
Mecca	Buddhism
622 A.D.	Asoka
Islam	Guptas
Koran	Taj Mahal
mosques	Lao-tse
Tours—732 A.D.	Great Wall
caliphs	Confucius
Baghdad	Kublai Khan
Mohenjo-Daro	Shinto
caste system	samurai
Hinduism	Shogun

EUROPEAN CIVILIZATION during the Middle Ages was temporarily declining. But in the Near East and the Far East culture and learning were flourishing. Wealth and luxury were enjoyed, though only by the privileged few. Great Asian rulers supported the arts and the study of science and medicine, mathematics and philosophy. Religious fervor inspired magnificent architecture and decoration of temples.

From Arabia, Moslems spread the new religion of Islam. Baghdad rivaled Constantinople in trade and splendor. And Moorish Spain attained a high degree of culture.

In India the great religions of Hinduism and Buddhism developed. Literature and art reached a peak during the Golden Age of the Guptas—only to fall before barbarian invasions as in Europe.

The Han, T'ang, Sung, and Ming dynasties made China supreme in the East. Great was the respect for education and for the philosophy of Confucius. Many discoveries such as silk, paper, porcelain, gunpowder, and printing later spread to Europe.

Japan was protected from invasion, and yet she was near enough to benefit from the advanced civilization of China. The emperor, though worshiped as a god, found his power weakened by wealthy nobles and military dictators.

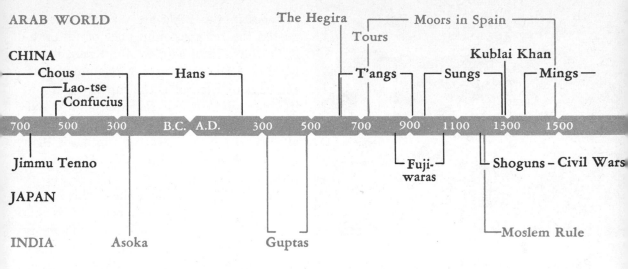

ARAB WORLD

CHINA

— Chous —   — Hans —   The Hegira   — Moors in Spain —

Tours

      Lao-tse   Kublai Khan

      Confucius   — T'angs —   — Sungs —   — Mings —

700   500   300   B.C. A.D.   300   500   700   900   1100   1300   1500

Jimmu Tenno   Fuji-   Shoguns – Civil Wars
                                waras

JAPAN

INDIA   Asoka   Guptas   — Moslem Rule

1. The Moslem World

Mohammed Founds a New Religion · At the same time that the Christian faith was being preached to the pagan tribes of Europe by missionaries of the Pope, a new religion was growing up in a distant city of Arabia. Like Christianity, this new religion spread widely until it too became one of the great religions of the world. The new faith was built on the teachings of a young Arab dreamer of Mecca named Mohammed. Today Moslems number at least three hundred and twenty millions.

The Arabs are a branch of the Semitic peoples. Before Mohammed's time they had neither a central government nor a national religion. The scattered tribes in town and desert had their own tribal deities and religious practices. Mecca, however, was regarded by *all* Arabs as a holy spot. In Mecca there was a cube-shaped temple, the Kaaba, containing many idols. Chief among these was a black stone (probably a meteorite), which was held to be especially sacred. Each year the warlike tribes ceased fighting for a period so that the people might journey to Mecca in peace and pay their reverence at the Kaaba.

Mohammed Preaches Islam · Mohammed, though of a prominent family, had been left an orphan as a child and had become a camel-driver. From his early years he had always been of a religious nature. When he became a man, he would retire from time to time to a cave alone, for fasting and prayer. When he was about forty years old, he became convinced that in these retreats God was sending him messages commanding him to preach a new religion to the world.

For some years Mohammed made only a few converts, although he felt a divine call to preach the religion of one God. But when he began finally to attack the worship of false idols at the Kaaba, his enemies threatened to kill him. Mohammed fled with his followers to the town of Medina, where he had friends. This flight, which took place in 622, the Arabs call the Hegira. To the faithful it marks the beginning of a new era—the Year One for Moslems.

Pilgrims Circle the Kaaba in Mecca · *They kiss the sacred black stone imbedded in the wall of the black-draped, cube-shaped* (Ka'bah) *shrine.*

After the Hegira, Mohammed gained many disciples, who frequently fought against the people at Mecca. By 630 he had a force strong enough to capture the city. He then destroyed the idols of the Kaaba, sparing only the sacred black stone. By the time of his death (632) Mohammed's new religion was widely spread throughout the Arabian peninsula.

The Arabic name of Mohammed's religion is *Islam,* meaning "surrender" or "submission" to the will of Allah, the sole God. Its members are called Moslems (Muslims). They do not worship Mohammed, and prefer not to be called Mohammedans.

The Koran and Its Teachings · From time to time as Mohammed received revelations, he would relate them to his followers. His sayings were committed to memory or written down on anything that lay at hand. After the prophet's death the fragments of the sayings were collected into a volume called the *Koran.* Similarities with

passages in the Bible are many, for it reflected the religious influences of its time.

To the faithful Moslem the Koran is the word of Allah dictated to Mohammed. As the basis of Islam it is the supreme authority and guide in all religious and moral matters. Like the Bible, its teachings have affected the lives of so many millions that it must be considered one of the most important books in history.

The Koran contains the beliefs and duties required of the followers of Islam. The chief articles are these: (1) There is one supreme God, Allah, and Mohammed is his prophet. (2) There is a resurrection of the body and a final day of judgment, when each man shall receive the reward for his deeds on this earth. Those who have refused Islam shall be banished to hell, there to be burned and tormented forever. The believers who have obeyed the Koran, especially those who have died fighting for Islam, shall enter a garden of delight to enjoy constant pleasures.

The good Moslem has certain religious duties. He must pray five times a day. He must fast during the month of *Ramadan* every day, though he may eat at night. He must deny himself what he loves in order to give alms to the poor. And he must make at least one pilgrimage to Mecca. Other precepts forbid gambling, the drinking of wine, and the eating of certain articles of food.

The Moslem Churches, or Mosques · Islamic mosques are temples for worship, prayer, and reading the Koran. They have no altars. Representations of human beings in pictures or images are forbidden.

Some of many beautiful mosques are those in Jerusalem, Constantinople, and Cairo. They have inner courts with covered colonnades and are adorned with

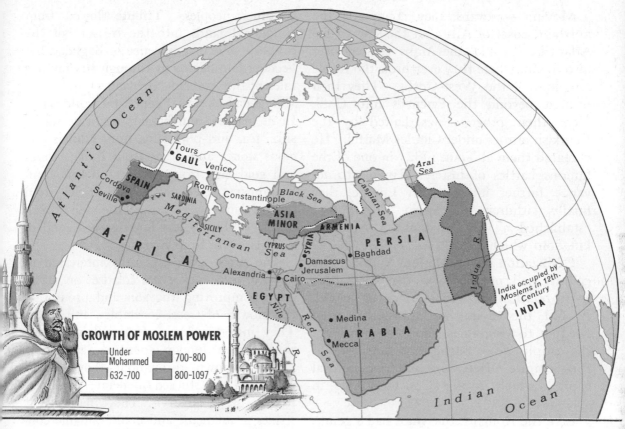

Growth of Moslem Power · *Note the sweep of Moslem faith through North Africa and the Middle East. Later it was carried into the Balkans, India, and Indonesia. See map of* Major Religions of the World, *page 647.*

mosaics and marbles. Their windows are of lovely stained glass, and the walls bear inscriptions from the Koran. The floors are covered with rich rugs, and the worshiper must remove his shoes before he enters so as not to defile the temple. From the tower, or minaret, the faithful are called to prayer five times each day.

Moslems Build an Empire by Conquest · Islam soon became a religion of war and conquest. Mohammed had attacked his enemies on the ground that they were unbelievers and idolators. His successors, called *caliphs,* organized the untamed des-

ert tribes into powerful armies. United for the first time by religious zeal, the Arabs went forth to a series of bold conquests.

Within a few years after the prophet's death they had taken all Syria, including the Holy Land, Armenia, and Egypt, from the Eastern Empire. Its territory was thus reduced to Asia Minor and a portion of southeastern Europe. At the same time, they crushed the empire of New Persia and brought the Sassanian line of kings to an end in 640. The Moslems were now able to extend their power to the frontiers of India.

Moving westward, they conquered the northern coast of Africa all the way to the Atlantic. In 711 the Arabs crossed over into Spain, where they overthrew the feeble kingdom of the West Goths. They then pushed beyond the Pyrenees into Gaul. Here their progress was halted by the Frankish armies under Charles Martel. He defeated them at Tours (732) in one of the famous battles of history. Unable to advance farther into western Europe, they finally withdrew into Spain. There they established a west Moslem, or Moorish, kingdom which lasted until 1492.

Civilization of the Moslem World · The caliphs had now become the rulers of a great *political,* as well as *religious,* world. In 661 the capital was transferred from Medina to Damascus, and a century later the caliphs chose Baghdad as the center of their empire. Here they built a new royal capital which rivaled Constantinople in splendor.

Like the Romans, the Arabs had a genius for adopting and spreading the civilization of other peoples. Tribute flowed from conquered lands into the treasury of the caliphs. The magnificence of Baghdad has become familiar to us through the famous tales of the Arabian Nights.

Baghdad became a center for world trade. In its markets and bazaars could be found silks, tea, and porcelains from China; precious stones and drugs from India; ivories and gold dust from Africa; and furs from Scandinavia. To the many articles from foreign lands were added the rich woven fabrics, perfumes, and fine rugs of Baghdad, and glassware from Syria.

The Arabs were especially interested in agriculture. They wrote treatises on methods of improving the soil and promoting the growth of trees, vegetables, and fruits. They introduced rare fruits, flowers, and shrubs from foreign countries, and these became known throughout the Moslem world. They studied alchemy, the forerunner of chemistry. They made great strides in medicine and made valuable contributions to mathematics. Our figures (1, 2, 3, 4, etc.) were borrowed by the Arabs from India. They replaced the awkward Roman numerals and made calculations much easier. The Arabs also developed algebra and trigonometry.

The caliphs were often patrons of learning and art and founded schools and universities. Arab scholars translated and wrote commentaries on the works of Greek philosophers and scientists, and also wrote treatises and poems of their own. Many large libraries were collected in various parts of the Moslem empire. The Arabic language spread widely throughout the Mediterranean world. Such familiar words as *alcohol, almanac, coffee, cotton, muslin, sherbet, sirup,* and *sofa* show how Arabic civilization affected western Europe.

Avicenna (980–1037 A.D.) · *The medical textbook of this famous Persian pharmacist, physician, and philosopher was used in the West as late as the 17th century.*

Above: *Egyptian students at work in the mosque of Al Azhar at the University of Cairo. Note the intricate geometric designs in the beautiful rugs, windows, and wall mosaics which characterize Moslem art.* **Right:** *Each Moslem mosque has one or more towers* (minarets) *from which a crier, or* muezzin, *calls the faithful to prayer.*

Moorish Civilization in Spain · Spain had broken away from the East and was ruled by an Emir of Cordova. Yet Spain shared the culture of the Oriental Moslem world. While most of Europe was living in the ignorance of the Middle Ages, the Moors were enjoying a high degree of civilization and were eager students of literature and science. Some beautiful buildings, such as the great mosque (now cathedral) at Cordova and the Alhambra of Granada, still bear witness to the culture of Moorish Spain.

CHECK ON YOUR READING

1. *What are the main beliefs and rules of Islam? How were they spread?*
2. *Describe the highly developed Moslem civilization.*

2. Civilization in India

The Land of India · The map on page 363 shows that India (today India and Pakistan) is a large triangular area lying between what we call the Middle East and the Far East. Half the size of the United States, it is a great peninsula jutting into the Indian Ocean. On the north it is bordered by mountains. The Himalayas contain the highest peaks in the world, but they also have mountain passes through which traders and invaders have entered and left India over the centuries.

Early Indian Civilizations · The very earliest civilization that we know about in India existed in the Indus Valley. It flourished at Mohenjo-Daro and Harappa at about the same time that ancient Egypt and Babylonia were flourishing. The people lived in large cities where there were brick houses and plumbing systems. They made beautiful bronze, copper, and silver implements as well as glazed pottery. They even grew and wove cotton thousands of years before it was known in the West.

In some way unknown to us this civilization was destroyed before 2000 B.C. The next important era of Indian history was marked by a series of invasions by an Indo-European people called the Indo-Aryans (p. 41). These invaders came into northern India during the thousand years from 2000 to 1000 B.C., driving south and conquering the native Dravidians who inhabited a large part of India.

The Caste System Develops · During the years from 1000 B.C. to 500 B.C. the Aryans moved south and eastward in India. There was a good deal of fighting during this period. Stories of it have been preserved in the great Indian epic poems, one of which has over 100,000 stanzas! Despite the fighting, cities were established and trade developed.

During this time the caste system took on the form which it kept up to modern times. A caste is a division of society which has its own standards of conduct, privileges, and duties. No person born into one caste could change to another. Four castes developed: (1) the priests, (Brahmans), (2) the soldiers, (3) the farmers and merchants, and (4) the serfs. Below these was a group of people, often made up of those captured in war, who belonged to no caste. These Untouchables, or Outcastes, had to do the lowest and dirtiest work. Each of the castes

The Six-Armed Goddess Kali · *Hindus revere the goddess of death and destruction as defender of the faith.*

in India was divided into many sub-castes, according to various occupations. In 1947 untouchability was outlawed, but many problems arising from caste divisions remain.

Hinduism and Buddhism · Hinduism, the religion of most people in India today, developed gradually over about a thousand years. It is a very complex religion with many gods and a profound philosophy. Basically, Hindus believe that life is evil and the aim of all existence is for the soul to be merged in the world soul or spirit, *Atma*. This goal can be attained only very gradually. Each person must go through a series of reincarnations, or separate lives, before it is possible. The caste system here becomes part of Hinduism, for a person progresses from the lowest caste up to the Brahman in his successive rebirths. As a Brahman he is close to deliverance.

Buddhism arose in the sixth century B.C. It was started by Gautama Sakyamuni, later called the Buddha, as a reform movement. Buddhism kept a number of Hindu beliefs but gave up many of its gods, priests, and rituals as well as the caste system.

Buddhist teaching is based on the *Four Noble Truths:* (1) Suffering is universal. (2) The cause of suffering is craving or selfish desire. (3) The cure for suffering is to give up craving. (4) The way to give up craving is to follow the Noble Eightfold Path, or the Middle Way. *The Noble Eightfold Path* consists of (1) right knowledge, (2) right intention, (3) right speech, (4) right conduct, (5) right means of livelihood, (6) right effort, (7) right mindfulness, (8) right concentration.

There is more to Buddhism than this. But from this it is clear that it preached a way of life based on self-discipline, inner peace of mind, and good works. It spread out of India, as we shall see later, to em-

Gilt-Bronze Chinese Buddha · *The "Enlightened One" sits in meditation. His expressive hands denote teaching.*

brace most of Asia. In India itself Buddhism disappeared, merging back into Hinduism after about a thousand years.

Emperor Asoka (273–232 B.C.) · We have seen how Alexander the Great conquered the northern border of India (p. 70) but that he died before he could carry out his plans for further conquests. Just at this time a new dynasty of emperors arose in northern India. One of them was Asoka.

Asoka became a Buddhist early in his reign and gave up all war and bloodshed. He even gave up hunting and refused to have animals killed for meat. He beautified the country, building roads, a magnificent palace, and many Buddhist shrines. Asoka played an important part in the spread of Buddhism by sending missionaries to Ceylon, southern India, Burma, and Egypt.

The Taj Mahal at Agra, India, is of white marble inlaid with precious stones.

At Asoka's death his empire began to decline. Northern India was again overrun by bands of nomads. Various kingdoms rose and fell in north and south India.

Golden Age of the Guptas (320–480 A.D.) · All of north India was united again under the dynasty known as the Guptas. Great sculptors decorated Hindu temples and created magnificent images of Buddha. Buddhist paintings have survived on the walls of the Ajanta caves. Indian literature, in the language known as Sanskrit, included poetry, plays, fables, and fairy stories.

Colleges and universities flourished. Mathematicians developed our "Arabic" numerals, the zero, and the decimal system. Cloth making, the making of dyes, and metallurgy reached a high level.

Indian culture and the Buddhist religion were spread widely through Asia at this period. There were many contacts with the Arabs, who thus could pass on to us important Indian achievements.

This golden age was brought to an end by a series of invasions carried out by groups of Huns beginning in 455 A.D. The resulting decline in civilization continued for 500 years until the Moslem conquest of India began.

The Moslem Conquest of India · By 1000 A.D. Islam had become the religion of Central Asia (Afghanistan, Turkestan), and it was from this region that the Moslem Turks attacked India.

The Hindus resisted desperately the fierce attacks. But the Moslems felt they were waging a holy war against infidels. They gradually occupied the country. From 1206 to 1526 there was a Moslem Sultanate in India with its capital in Delhi. In 1526 it was replaced by the Mogul Empire, also Moslem, which lasted up to 1707.

India now had a new religion, and a new art and architecture developed. Great mosques were built, and many Indians became Moslems, though more of them remained Hindu. After 1526 there was religious toleration, and a new golden age seemed to be coming to India. The most famous structure built during the Mogul Empire in India is the magnificent Taj Mahal. It was completed in 1648 as the tomb of the Mogul Emperor Shah Jahan and his wife. It is a masterpiece of Persian-Indian design and architecture.

CHECK ON YOUR READING

1. *Explain the caste system.*
2. *What are the basic beliefs of Hinduism and Buddhism?*
3. *Summarize the achievements (a) of Asoka, (b) of the Golden Age of the Guptas.*

The Ancient Far East · *Which Indian empire was larger? which Chinese? How do modern India and China compare in size with these empires? Find Agra.*

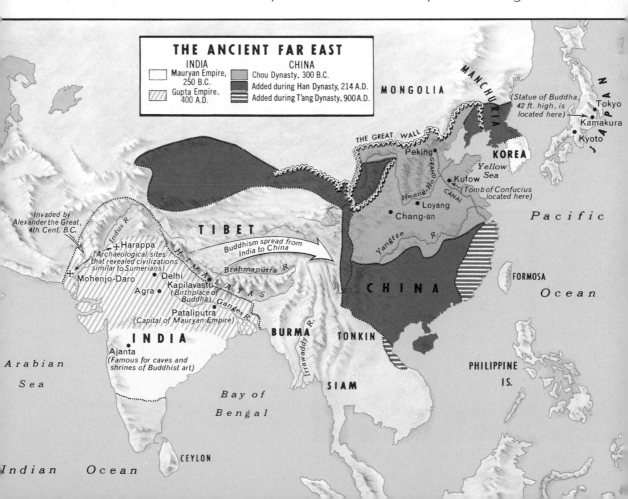

THE ANCIENT FAR EAST

INDIA
☐ Mauryan Empire, 250 B.C.
▨ Gupta Empire, 400 A.D.

CHINA
▨ Chou Dynasty, 300 B.C.
▨ Added during Han Dynasty, 214 A.D.
▨ Added during T'ang Dynasty, 900 A.D.

3. China Develops an Advanced Civilization

The Greatness of China · While Europe was still in the early Middle Ages, China was the most cultured nation on earth. Its civilization furnished the model for the less progressive countries of the Far East, including Korea, Burma, Thailand, Annam, Tibet, and Japan. China maintained close contacts with India, from which the Buddhist religion had spread over all China by 800 A.D.

China in the Chou Dynasty (*c.* 1122–256 B.C.) · Events in Chinese history are usually associated with the name of a dynasty, or line of rulers. The Chou dynasty controlled China for a period of nearly nine hundred years. In this early period the ruler of China was also the high priest. He was regarded as holding his power directly from heaven and ruling by "divine right." He was the highest authority of the country as a whole. But there were also, as we have found in many other nations, certain heredi-

Confucius Teaches Moderation · *Vessels reasonably full remain balanced. Too much, causes loss of all. Moral: nothing to excess.*

tary princes governing more or less independent provinces. They were nominally vassals of the monarch, but from time to time they disputed the imperial power.

The population was divided into two distinct classes. The nobles were members of clans tracing their descent from some great ancestor. They owned the land and held the high offices in the government. The larger part of the population, however, was composed of the common people. They were artisans or peasants and did all the work. Religion was partly the worship of a higher power and partly reverence for one's ancestors. In China the family has always been the most important unit in society. The wishes of the individual are second to the will and honor of the family.

Confucius and Lao-tse · The Chinese look back to the Chou dynasty as their classic age. It was the era of China's great thinkers and philosophers. Confucius (b. 551 B.C.) and Lao-tse (b. *c.* 609 B.C.) are the best known in the West. To this age belong the Classics—the great literature of China. This consists of the Four Books (the sayings of Confucius and his disciples) and the Five Canons (on Changes, History, Poetry, and Rites, and the Spring and Autumn Annals). For twenty centuries these works exercised an enormous influence on Chinese civilization.

The proverbs of Confucius and his insistence on the faithful observance of ancient rites and ceremonies fostered a great respect for the past. They furnished a pattern of daily life to the people. Confucius believed that the most intelligent class should aid the prince, and that statesmen should be scholars. This gave rise to the custom of holding competitive examinations for those who wished to become government officials.

Lao-tse saw less virtue in rites and ceremonies. He believed that right living consisted in putting oneself in harmony with the order of nature and seeking peace through curbing one's worldly desires. His philosophy was mystical rather than practical, and later many superstitions became mixed with it. Centuries after his death Lao-tse was regarded as a god, and a temple was built in his honor. Taoism (*tao*, "path" or "way"), as the beliefs of his followers were called, became one of the great religions of China.

The Great Chinese Wall · In the later centuries of the Chou dynasty weaker rulers succeeded to the throne. The power of the central government was greatly reduced, and China fell apart into a group of independent states, whose princes made constant war on one another. Out of this confusion there arose a military leader who was able to conquer the other feudal nobles and to unite China once more. Calling himself the "First Emperor," he was an able administrator and a great warrior.

In order to protect the northern boundaries against invasions of the nomadic tribes of the desert, he completed the Great Wall. This wall extends for hundreds of miles along the frontiers of the Eighteen Provinces. Following the "First Emperor" there was a period of civil strife before another powerful general emerged to found the great Han dynasty.

Contact with the West in the Han Dynasty (206 B.C.–214 A.D.) · The four centuries of the Han dynasty correspond to the last two centuries of the Roman Republic and the first two centuries of the

The Great Wall · *It was 25 feet high, 12 feet wide at the top, and ran for 1500 miles. Why didn't it stop the invaders?*

Roman Empire. In China it was a period of military conquest. The interest of these victories for us is not so much in the extension of the Chinese empire as in the subduing of the tribes of central Asia, which opened up an overland caravan route to the Near East.

It is from the days of the Han monarchs that the earliest evidence of contact with the West has come down to us. Modern archaeologists have discovered along this ancient route arrowheads, bits of leather armor, utensils, and pottery. There are also the remnants of fortifications that show that the Han emperors had outposts to guard the way that travelers took between China and the Mediterranean world.

Some of the Roman emperors, including Marcus Aurelius, sent embassies to the Chinese monarchs. Chinese silks were worn by Roman ladies. Certain products from the West, such as glass and grapevines, were introduced into China, as well as some

143

Chinese Ladies Preparing Newly Woven Silk · *This scene is part of a painted silk scroll showing the beating, winding, and (left) ironing of silk. Note the flowing gowns and upswept hairdos, which were later adopted by the Japanese.*

knowledge of Western civilization. But the interchange with the West was not very great, for the journey was long and perilous.

Civilization under the Han Dynasty · During the Han period the power of the emperor was supreme, but he was aided by a large body of able officials. Realizing the value of having scholars as statesmen, the emperor in 124 B.C. established a college to provide a body of scholars with thorough training in the philosophy of Confucius. Candidates who passed the severe system of examinations were eligible for appointment to office on the basis of merit.

Scholarship was aided by the important discovery of the art of making paper and ink. This invention, as we shall see, found its way to Europe in the Middle Ages. Confucius was revered by the intellectual classes, while the superstitions of Taoism had a strong hold on the common people. Literature reached a high level of excellence, and progress was made in sculpture and in pottery.

Buddhism Influences China · After four centuries of rule, the Han emperors no longer were able to maintain their authority, and the dynasty disappeared. There were numerous invasions from the north and

west. Although the outsiders were gradually absorbed by the Chinese nation, they introduced new elements of race and language. Even today there is a difference in physical characteristics and dialect between the northern Chinese and the people of the south.

It was during this period that Buddhism gained a wide hold on the people. Buddhist priests came into the country, and Chinese converts and priests made pilgrimages to India—the holy land of their new faith. The spread of Buddhism influenced not only the religion and philosophy of China, but its art. Buddhism especially affected the character of Chinese temples, pagodas, and religious sculpture. In the sixth century, Buddhism spread to Korea and thence to Japan, where it was warmly accepted.

The T'angs and Their Conquests (618–907 A.D.) · Four centuries of confusion passed after the fall of the Hans before an able general arose to found the great T'ang dynasty. It was destined to endure for three hundred years. The rule of the T'ang emperors is one of the most brilliant in Chinese history. Under their guidance China was united and reached a position of great military power and high culture. The T'ang generals subdued the restless tribes of Mongolia and central Asia and greatly enlarged the boundaries of the empire. They brought Tibet and Korea into tributary alliance, and extended Chinese rule over southern Manchuria and most of Tonkin and Annam.

Chinese Civilization Spreads through Asia · Freed from civil war and the threat of invasion, China enjoyed a period of peace and prosperity. Again there was contact with the West, over the old caravan route. Traders, chief among whom were the Arabs, also came from India by sea to Chinese ports. (This explains why the ink invented by the Chinese came to be called "India ink" in the West.) Many other foreigners found their way into China, and Chinese civilization was spread through the less advanced countries of Asia.

The T'angs encouraged education by founding schools and academies. They developed further the civil-service examinations as an essential feature of their political system. Poetry and prose reached new heights, and the painting of the period often showed great delicacy and beauty.

Printing was developed long before it was known in the West. The first printed book in China appeared in 868 A.D., five hundred years before books were printed in Europe. The T'ang dynasty corresponds in time to the misnamed "Dark Ages" of early medieval Europe. China at this period was probably the most highly civilized country in the world.

Chinese Culture under the Sungs (960–1280 A.D.) · The rulers who followed the T'angs were much occupied by struggles with the Tatar tribes of Mongolia. One of these tribes established control over northern China.

In 960, however, a new ruling house—the Sung dynasty—was established. This dynasty held its power for over three hundred years. Though the territory of the Sungs was not so large as the T'ang empire, their reign was noted for its high culture. The literature of the period showed great refinement of feeling, and painting reached its highest development.

The greatest scholar of his day was Chu Hsi (1130–1200), whose commentaries on the Classics have remained the standard authority on these ancient writings. It was through Chu Hsi's works that the philosophy of Confucius began to enjoy the great favor and popularity which it has had in China until modern times.

The Mongol Empire of Genghis and Kublai Khan · The Sung rulers were not great military leaders, and they were overwhelmed by the Mongol invasions of the thirteenth century. Genghis Khan (1206–1227) and his successors overran northern China, central Asia, northern India, and eastern Europe. By 1280 they had completed the conquest of China and disposed of the last of the Sungs.

The Mongols wrought great destruction. But the establishment of their great empire, extending from the Yellow Sea to the Black Sea, removed all barriers throughout the continent of Asia and brought Europe into contact with the Far East.

Kublai Khan (1260–1294) now made his capital at Peking and became the emperor of China (Yüan dynasty). Under his leadership China was once again united, as it had been under the T'angs. This was the China known to medieval Europe as *Cathay.*

Kublai Khan built an astronomical observatory on the city wall at Peking. He restored the Grand Canal (map, p. 141).

Kublai Khan (1260–1294) · *He favored Europeans, literature, astronomy, paper money, a pony express, and lavish entertainment.*

The Ming Rule in China (1368–1644) · After the Mongols had ruled less than a century, they were driven out by a Chinese general. He united the country and founded a new ruling house—the Mings.

The Mings ruled over a territory much smaller than that of the Mongol emperors, though they still continued to collect tribute from Burma, Annam, and Ceylon. On the whole, the time was one of peace and prosperity. Population increased, and Chinese emigrated to the Philippine Islands and to the Malay States. The period was famous for its porcelain and for its lacquer and bronze work.

China's Supremacy in the Far East · Strife among the tribes of central Asia after the death of Kublai Khan made travel too dangerous along the overland route. As a result the lively interchange which had been carried on with the West was interrupted. But the Ming emperors greatly raised the prestige of China in the Far East. Some of the Burmese states, Korea, and the Ryukyu Islands soon acknowledged themselves vassals of the Chinese monarchs.

The Ming rulers sent out embassies to Japan, the Philippine Islands, and the East Indies. A flourishing trade was carried on with the Malay world during the fifteenth century. Many of the rulers of the islands sent tribute to the Ming emperors.

Postal relays of some 200,000 horses were established on great imperial roads. Hospitals and charitable relief were provided for aged scholars, orphans, and the sick. Surplus food was purchased and stored against the time of famine. Paper money was used, and gunpowder and the compass needle were known.

Envoys and missionaries who visited the camps of the Great Khan brought back to the West stories of the skilled craftsmanship of the people and told of the richness of the country. It was the brilliant court of Kublai Khan which Marco Polo described in his *Travels*. From his account of China the Europeans got their notions of the fabulous wealth of Cathay. But Marco Polo was only one of many merchants and missionaries who visited Cathay and were made welcome by the great Eastern ruler.

CHECK ON YOUR READING

1. *What were the beliefs and teachings of Confucius and Lao-tse?*
2. *Why is the period of the Han dynasty of especial significance to the West?*
3. *What were the contributions of the T'ang, Sung, and Ming dynasties?*
4. *Summarize the work of Genghis and Kublai Khan.*

4. Ancient and Medieval Japan

Japan's Island Kingdom · Japan's separation from the mainland of Asia has had an important effect on her history. It has protected her from foreign invasions. Even the great Kublai Khan twice failed to get possession of her islands. Yet at the same time Japan is near enough to Asia to have benefited from the advanced civilization which early developed in China.

The Japanese are a mixed race. Various peoples from the Asian continent through the ages made their way to the islands and settled there. The latest comers, who became dominant, were a group of independent tribes, or clans. Each was under a hereditary leader, who was both chieftain and high priest. The most powerful of the clans occupied the district called Yamato. In time, the Yamato chief was recognized as holding a position superior to those of the other leaders, and finally he became emperor of the entire nation.

Early Religion and Government · The early religion of Japan was a combination of ancestor and nature worship. This is clearly seen in the belief that the Yamato chief was directly descended from the sun-goddess, who had ruled the islands for untold ages. This myth gradually grew into a state religion, known as *Shinto*. It centered in reverence for the emperor, who held his throne by "divine right." Shintoists were expected to honor the gods and faithfully serve their descendants, who were the emperor and those close to him.

Official Japanese history begins with the emperor Jimmu Tenno, in 660 B.C., and claims an unbroken line of hereditary monarchs down to the present time. But as writing was not introduced into Japan until the fifth century A.D., the early records of the country are largely based on tradition and myth.

The Japanese Imitate the Chinese · In the fifth century A.D., Chinese refugees fleeing before invading Tatar tribes sought safety in Korea and later in Japan. From these newcomers the Japanese learned many things. Among them was the cultivation of the silkworm (sericulture) and silk-weaving, which became one of Japan's most important industries.

The Chinese character writing was introduced in the early part of the fifth century. This was the only system that the Japanese had until the ninth century, when they developed a script based on syllables. Buddhism reached Japan from the continent in

Shinto Temple at Kyoto · *Militarists used Shintoism, "the way of the Gods," to glorify aggression. But in 1946 Emperor Hirohito destroyed its basis by denying his divinity.*

the sixth century, and soon found favor in court circles.

During the brilliant period of the T'ang rulers (p. 144) the influence of Chinese culture in Japan was at its height. Embassies were sent to the Chinese imperial court, and scholars went to China to study. These travelers brought back Chinese institutions and customs, which the Japanese eagerly adopted. They imitated their continental neighbor in much the same way that they later imitated the Westerners in the nineteenth century (page 461).

Educated Japanese mastered the Chinese language, and poets made their verses on Chinese models. Architecture, painting, and sculpture all drew their inspiration from Chinese art. Standard weights and measures were introduced and also the use of gold, silver, and copper coins. The Japanese also adopted certain features of the Chinese government and revised their laws according to the legal code of the T'angs.

The Aristocratic Tradition of Japan · The Japanese were not mere imitators. They altered what they took from others to suit their own ideas. For example, the Japanese had a strong belief in the inherited superiority of the noble class. Therefore, though they agreed with the Confucian teaching that government officials should be men of sound scholarship, only nobles were allowed to take the training for the examinations required of candidates for public office. Thus in Japan the high posts in the government were reserved for the aristocracy. In China youths of all classes might rise to important positions if they had the ability.

In 794 Kyoto was chosen as the imperial capital. A beautiful city was built on the model of the capital of the T'angs at Chang-an. Kyoto remained the capital for over a thousand years. (See map, p. 141.)

Feudalism: the Daimio and Samurai · The power of the Japanese aristocracy was based on land ownership as well as on holding high public office. Sometimes land was granted as payment for services to the ruler. Sometimes it came through marriage to members of the imperial family. Some of the nobles grew very rich by amassing vast estates.

The most powerful of these feudal lords were called *daimio* ("great names"). As their land was exempt from taxes, the emperor lost a large part of his income and his power. There was much rivalry and fighting. Each daimio had his band of military retainers, called *samurai*. Like the medieval knights, the samurai were pledged to assist the lord in battle. A feudal society thus existed in Japan very much like that of Europe, in which the ruler was little more than a figurehead.

Power of the Fujiwara Family (842–1042) · Actual control of the central government finally fell into the hands of the most powerful family in the imperial court—the Fujiwara. The head of the Fujiwara controlled the appointments to political offices and advised the emperor. If the monarch was a child, the head of the Fujiwara acted as regent. The emperors were obliged to marry Fujiwara ladies. Thus successive emperors were Fujiwara themselves on their mothers' side.

For two centuries the head of this great family was the real "power behind the throne." At first the Fujiwara were able statesmen. But their successors paid less attention to the details of government and allowed the court to become extravagant and wasteful. Heavy taxes were imposed on the lower classes to pay for the luxuries of the court. The provinces were neglected, and there was much fighting and disorder.

The Emperor Flees from His Burning Palace · *The emperor* (right) *is protected by faithful samurai archers, who proceed gingerly in fear of ambush. This is the last detail from a 13th-century scroll painting, 23 feet wide.*

Origin of the Shogunate · A new military aristocracy now grew up throughout the country. It was composed of the provincial daimio and the descendants of the younger branches of the royal family, for whom there were no high offices in the government.

By 1192 a warrior noble named Yoritomo, who had overthrown all his rivals and set up his military headquarters at Kamakura, was appointed by the emperor to be *Shogun,* or generalissimo. This office was one of great importance because it gave the holder supreme authority over the armed forces of the empire. In former days the emperor had appointed a Shogun only in times of national danger. When the crisis was past, the Shogun would give up his command. But Yoritomo was now appointed Shogun for life, with the power to name his successor.

Military Dictatorship of the Shoguns · There was thus established, side by side with the imperial court, a hereditary military dictatorship. Though the emperor still reigned at Kyoto, the real ruler was at Kamakura. From his "camp court" the Shogun directed the civil as well as the military affairs of the government.

The early Shoguns maintained a high order of military discipline and of simplicity in their administration. During this period the Shoguns prevented the invasion of the islands by the Mongol forces of Kublai Khan. The Kamakura Shogunate lasted 141 years.

The Ashikaga Shoguns (1338–1583) · The Ashikaga Shoguns established their headquarters at Tokyo. The third ruler of this family (1367–1395) re-established friendly relations with China and Korea

Mt. Fuji · *Fujiyama, a dormant volcano rising 12,389 feet southwest of Tokyo, is held in reverence by all Japanese. To ascend its snowy peak, which Buddhists compare to the white bud of the lotus, is considered a sacred duty.*

after the Mongols were driven beyond the Chinese Wall. He was eager to develop trade with the continent and to enrich his treasury. He and his advisers also wished to keep in contact with the Chinese Buddhists, whose scholarship they greatly admired. The Shogun even acknowledged the overlordship of the Ming emperor.

As a result of the close relationship with China, Kyoto again became a center of culture and of luxury, as it was in the days of the Fujiwara. Chinese architecture and painting were copied, and Chinese and Buddhist philosophy were earnestly studied. Flower arrangement and landscape gardening were taken up.

It was at this time that the tea ceremonial, a distinctive feature of Japanese life, was developed. This was a social function in which strict rules of etiquette were carefully followed. It was regarded by the Buddhists as cultivating courtesy and dignity and an attitude of repose, which were favorable for the acceptance of Buddhism.

Decline of Ashikaga Power · The Shoguns allowed themselves to become involved in court intrigues. Military discipline relaxed, and the efficiency of the administration declined. Though life at Kyoto was prosperous, the rest of the country suffered. The peasants remained poor and ignorant and weighed down by heavy taxes. The Shoguns neglected the outlying provinces, so that the daimio once more asserted their independence. For a century (after about 1462) the country was without any effective central government, and was torn by feuds and civil wars.

CHECK ON YOUR READING

1. *How did Japan benefit from its nearness to China?*
2. *How did the Japanese modify what they learned from China?*
3. *Explain how the feudal system and the Shogunate developed. What was accomplished by the Shoguns up to about 1400?*

Think about the chapter

1. Why was the battle of Tours significant?

2. Compare the "golden age" of India with that of Greece and Rome.

3. How did the Moslem conquest affect the culture of India? In what parts of Europe and Africa were the Moslems in control during the corresponding period of time?

4. Why was the Great Wall of China built?

5. Compare the characteristics of the period from 907 A.D. to 1230 A.D. in China with the characteristics of western Europe during this same period (the early Middle Ages).

6. *Map study:* Show on a map of Asia the outline of modern China. Draw in the Great Wall and mark Peking. Shade and label all the areas that came under Chinese influence in the period covered by this chapter.

7. *Map study:* On a map similar to the one on page 135, mark the extent of the Moslem conquests in the Middle East, North Africa, and Europe. Locate Tours.

Go beyond the text

8. Which ideas in the Koran are similar to those in the Bible?

9. What countries of the world are today predominantly Moslem?

10. What is the sacred Rama epic of Hinduism?

11. Why does much California architecture show Moslem influence?

Follow up your special interests

12. Read some of the *Arabian Nights* stories and report to the class.

13. Make a collection of pictures of the art of India and southeast Asia.

14. Prepare a bulletin-board display of Chinese landscape painting and other art.

15. Investigate the traditions of Kabuki dancing and the Nō dramas of Japan.

READ FURTHER

Basic readings: (1) BAUER and PEYSER, *How Music Grew*, Chap. 5. (2) CHEYNEY, *World History of Art*, Chaps. 8–10, 12, 27. (3) EVANS, *Costume Throughout the Ages*, Chap. 19. (4) DAVIS, *Readings*, Vol. 2, Chap. 11. (5) HOFFMAN, *News of the World*, Nos. 16, 17, 32, 35, 36. (6) MACY, *Story of World Literature*, Chap. 3. (7) SCOTT, HYMA, NOYES, *Readings*, Chaps. 18–22. (8) TAYLOR, *Fifty Centuries of Art*, pp. 15–27. (9) VAN LOON, *Story of Mankind*, pp. 138–143, 241–251. (10) Year's *Pictorial History*, pp. 56–61, 122–137, 178–188.

Special accounts: (11) M. DILTS, *Pageant of Japanese History*. A beautifully illustrated brief history of Japan. (12) F. FITCH, *Allah: the God of Islam*. Useful for an understanding of the culture of the Moslems as well as their ways of worship. (13) J. GAER, *How the Great Religions Began*. Easy reading; stories of the leaders of eleven religions. (14) E. SEEGER, *The Pageant of Chinese History*. Written especially for young people, it makes far-off places and people easier to understand. (15) C. SPENCER, *The Land of the Chinese People*. Portraits of Nations series. (16) C. SPENCER, *Made in India*. All the arts of India, ancient and modern. (17) *Life*, "The World of Islam," May 9, 1955. (18) *National Geographic*, "India's Sculptured Temple Caves," May, 1953.

Fiction and biography: (19) R. ANDREWS, *The Quest of the Snow Leopard*. Fictional account of a young man's experience on a scientific expedition to southwestern China. (20) J. GAER, *Young Heroes of the Living Religions*. Mohammed, and the great figures of the religions of India and the Far East. (21) J. GAER, *The Adventures of Rama*. A beautifully written account of the ancient epic of India. (22) M. KOMROFF, *The Travels of Marco Polo*. One of the best books about Kublai Khan's "publicity agent."

CHAPTER 11

Germany, France, and England in the Middle Ages

CHAPTER OUTLINE

1. *The Holy Roman Empire*
2. *French Kings versus Feudal Lords*
3. *England Builds a National State*
4. *The English People Get a Charter and a Parliament*
5. *The Hundred Years' War and the Wars of the Roses*

KEY WORDS AND DATES

Holy Roman Empire
investiture
Gregory VII
Canossa
Concordat of Worms
Philip Augustus
Alfred the Great
William the Conqueror (1066)
Domesday Book
Henry II
trial by jury
common law
Thomas Becket
Magna Carta (1215)
Model Parliament
Robert Bruce
1337–1453
Agincourt
Joan of Arc
Wars of the Roses
Henry Tudor

NOW WE TURN again to the West. In the midst of the disorder that followed the breakup of the Roman Empire, the ideal of restoring world unity haunted the minds of medieval rulers. Charlemagne had revived the Empire in the West, but it had fallen apart after his death.

This chapter tells how a German king temporarily revived the Empire for a second time. But the would-be emperors soon found themselves in conflict with the mighty princes of the Church. Their Holy Roman Empire, as it was later called, was to prove to be neither "Holy," nor "Roman," nor an "Empire."

In the meantime feudalism had reduced the power of the kings of France and brought that country into a long conflict with England. But the English kings had begun to unify their realm. They laid the foundations of an orderly national government.

So strong was England that the war with France became the Hundred Years' War. At its end England had lost its territory on the continent. The French monarchs had overcome the nobles and were on the way to building up a strong national government. Germany, on the other hand, remained divided for centuries.

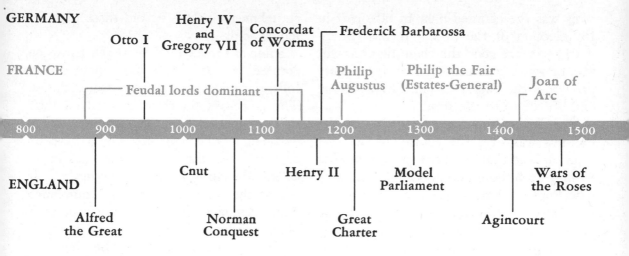

GERMANY

Henry IV
and
Gregory VII — Concordat — Frederick Barbarossa
Otto I of Worms

FRANCE
Philip | Philip the Fair
Augustus | (Estates-General) | Joan of
Arc

Feudal lords dominant

| 800 | 900 | 1000 | 1100 | 1200 | 1300 | 1400 | 1500 |

Cnut Henry II Model Wars of
Parliament the Roses

ENGLAND

Alfred Norman Great Agincourt
the Great Conquest Charter

1. The Holy Roman Empire

Otto I (936–973) Revives the Empire in the West · The East Frankish kingdom (Germany) had fallen apart like the western part of Charlemagne's empire. Its feeble rulers could not keep the powerful nobles from making war on one another and on the kings themselves.

When Otto I came to the throne in 936, he determined to put an end to this feudal anarchy. He succeeded in overcoming a number of his more troublesome vassals and handed their lands over to his own relatives. He also granted large fiefs to churchmen to gain their support.

Then in 951 he crossed the Alps to aid one of the warring factions in Italy. There he defeated his opponents and was recognized as king of Italy. Some ten years later the Pope appealed to Otto for assistance against his enemies. Again the German king restored order, and the grateful Pope crowned him emperor as Charlemagne's successor (962).

Thus the Empire in the West was restored a second time. But the Holy Roman Empire (as it was later called) was even less like the empire of the Romans than the empire of Charlemagne had been.

The Holy Roman Empire and Germany · Otto's coronation as emperor in Italy had an important effect on the future of Germany. Instead of devoting their energies to unifying their own realms, the German kings thereafter were constantly distracted by conditions in Italy. They had to make costly journeys across the Alps to restore order and keep their power there. During their absence their German vassals had an excellent opportunity to revolt against them.

Thus Germany remained divided, while France and England became strong national states. Study the map on page 154. You will see that the Holy Roman Empire was a sprawling group of duchies, bishoprics, principalities, and even separate cities. Each had its own ruling prince or duke, or other official, and had only a loose connection with the Holy Roman Empire.

However proud the German monarchs might be of their title of Emperor, it did not give them any more power than they had as German kings, except for one thing.

This was the claimed right to take part in the election of the Pope. It was the attempt to make good this claim that brought the emperors into conflict with the mighty princes of the Church. The Church in the end proved to be the stronger.

The Investiture Struggle · One of the quarrels was over the control of the vast tracts of land that had been given from time to time to bishops and abbots in Germany. The Pope, as head of the Church, claimed the right to influence the selection of the German bishops and abbots and to enjoy part of the income from the church lands which they held. The emperor, on the other hand, regarded the lands held by churchmen much as he did those of other feudal lords.

Some of these churchmen even had been granted the right to coin money, collect tolls, and perform other government duties. The emperors, therefore, insisted on their right to appoint them and require homage of them. Otherwise they would have no authority over them. This long conflict is called the struggle over *investiture*. It meant the right to *invest* the churchmen with their lands and the symbols of their office (bishop's ring and pastoral staff).

Gregory VII's Views of the Papacy · The Popes determined to reform the Church and take it out of the hands of kings and

Europe about 1000 A.D. · *Five competitors in Europe during this period were the Holy Roman emperor, the Byzantine emperor, the Moslems, and the English and French kings. What areas were held by each?*

princes. A decree issued in 1059 deprived the emperor and other rulers of all part in the election of the Popes. Henceforth the Popes were to be chosen by the leading Roman prelates (later called *cardinals*).

In 1073 Gregory VII, the most celebrated of the medieval Popes, ascended the papal throne. Gregory believed that the Pope was supreme, not only over the Church, but over temporal rulers as well. Gregory claimed that the Pope could even depose emperors and "free subjects from allegiance to an unjust ruler."

Long Conflict between Popes and Emperors · One of Gregory's first acts was to forbid the German bishops to receive investiture from the emperor. This so angered the young ruler, Henry IV, that he ordered the Pope deposed as a wicked man. The Pope in turn deposed Henry, whereupon Henry's vassals deserted him. Henry then hastened to Italy to plead for the Pope's forgiveness. Before the castle at Canossa, where the Pope was staying, Henry stood barefoot awaiting pardon (1077). The spectacle of a German prince in tears before the Pope has always been regarded as a striking illustration of the power of the medieval Church.

But the famous scene at Canossa settled nothing. The struggle was carried on for many years by the Popes and emperors who followed Gregory and Henry. A settlement of the question of investiture was finally reached in 1122 in the Concordat (agreement) of Worms. The emperor agreed that the Church should elect the bishops and abbots and invest them with the symbols of their spiritual authority. But the elections were to take place in the presence of the emperor, who must invest the bishop or abbott with his lands before he could be consecrated.

Germany and Italy Remain Divided States · The quarrel between the emperors and the Popes now turned on the question of Italy. Here the emperors had great difficulty in maintaining their authority. The northern Italian towns had grown rich from their trade and resented the interference of a foreign power. Finally, they joined together and in 1176 defeated the emperor Frederick Barbarossa. The emperor was forced to let them go their own way.

Frederick II (grandson of Frederick Barbarossa) continued to hold on to the kingdom of Naples and Sicily. But with his death (1250) the Empire's power in Italy may be said to have come to an end. Few of the German kings took the trouble to go to Italy to be crowned or made any serious effort to recover Italian territory.

Germany and Italy remained hopelessly divided, not to be unified until 1870. The flourishing Italian towns established independent governments, while the Pope retained a troubled hold on the States of the Church. In the south the kingdom of Naples fell into the hands of the French. The Popes had called them in, hoping to get rid of the German rulers. Sicily drifted under Spanish control. Germany was in the hands of many dukes, counts, bishops, and abbots, all independent of the weak ruler of the "Holy Roman Empire."

CHECK ON YOUR READING

1. *How did the establishment of the Holy Roman Empire affect Germany's future?*
2. *Explain the investiture struggle. How was it finally settled?*
3. *How and why was Italy divided?*
4. *Identify (a) Otto I, (b) Gregory VII, (c) Henry IV, (d) Canossa, (e) Concordat of Worms.*

2. French Kings versus Feudal Lords

The Great Fiefs Become Independent States · After the Treaty of Mersen (870) the West Frankish kingdom, or France, fell into the hands of nobles (p. 123). They built castles, had their armies of fighting men, and acted as independent rulers on their own estates. The king had little left but his title and his crown. If ever the kings were to regain their position and unite France into a strong state, they must recover their lands and subdue the ambitious nobles who defied them.

These great nobles included the dukes of Normandy, Brittany, and Burgundy, and the counts of Flanders, Champagne, Anjou, and Aquitaine. Of all these great fiefs none was more important than Normandy. Its people were descendants of the fierce Northmen.

A Norman Duke Becomes an English King · Normandy became a source of much trouble for the French kings in 1066. In that year Duke William laid claim to the throne of England, invaded that country, and made himself its king. We shall speak first of the results which the Norman Conquest had on the history of France. In the next section we shall tell of its effects on the English people. We shall see that the affairs of the two countries were entangled for centuries because of the successful expedition of the Norman duke.

How England Controlled Much of France · By the time of Henry II (1154–1189), the great-grandson of William the Conqueror, the English king controlled vastly more of France than the French king himself. Henry held Normandy and Brittany as a descendant of William. From his father he inherited Anjou and Maine.

And when he married Eleanor of Aquitaine, he doubled the size of his French possessions. (See map, p. 154.) Thus the French kings, already deserted by their vassals, saw more than half the territory within their borders in the hands of a foreign power, the Plantagenet kings of England.

How Philip Augustus Strengthened the Monarchy (1180–1223) · A strong king came to the throne of France in the person of Philip Augustus. Philip was an able ruler and was determined to get the better of his rebellious vassals, whether French or English.

An excuse soon arose for seizing the greater part of the French fiefs of the English kings. King John, Henry's youngest son, was guilty of having deserted his wife and marrying a lady betrothed to one of his own vassals. As John's overlord, Philip summoned him to appear at the French court to answer the charges against him. When John refused, Philip stirred up John's vassals to revolt against him. Philip finally succeeded in taking over almost all John's French lands, leaving the English king only the southwest corner of France.

Philip also got back the lands of some of his French vassals. By the end of his reign he had brought a large part of his realms once more under royal control.

He further strengthened the monarchy by appointing officials who were directly responsible to himself. He encouraged trade and increased the importance of the towns by including their representatives in his assemblies, along with the nobles and clergy. He protected the interests of all classes, but saw to it that they made substantial contributions to his treasury.

Parlements and Estates-General Established · Saint Louis (1226–1270) and Philip the Fair (1285–1314) continued these policies. (1) They established the supremacy of the royal courts, or *parlements,* by receiving appeals from the feudal courts of the nobles. This brought in fees and fines to their government.

(2) Philip the Fair strengthened the royal treasury by securing loans or gifts from the nobles and levying taxes on property, income, and trade. (3) He established a French national assembly, called the *Estates-General* (1302). This was composed of members of the three estates, or classes of people, in the nation: the clergy, the nobility, and the town merchants.

Philip called the assembly occasionally when he wished new taxes. But he did so only in order to collect funds more easily, for he claimed the sole right to levy taxes.

CHECK ON YOUR READING

1. *Which great French fiefs became practically independent?*
2. *How did an English king come to control much of France?*
3. *How did Philip Augustus and his successors strengthen the French monarchy?*

---

3. *England Builds a National State*

Britain under the Angles and Saxons · When the barbarians began seriously to invade the Empire at the opening of the fifth century, Rome was forced to withdraw her legions from Britain in order to protect her frontiers on the Continent. The island was thus left to be conquered by Germanic peoples—chiefly Angles and Saxons—who came across the sea from the region south of Denmark. The Celtic inhabitants either were killed or fled to the mountainous districts of Wales or merged with the invaders into one people.

Many small kingdoms were established by the Saxons and Angles, and the island finally came to be called *England* (Angleland). About 830 these various kingdoms were brought together under the overlordship of Egbert, chief of Wessex (land of the West Saxons).

Alfred the Great and the Danes · Not long after this a group of Northmen, the Danes, invaded England. Alfred the Great (871–901) was able to defeat them, and in 876 forced them to accept Christianity. A few years later he made a treaty with them, restricting them to the eastern part of England.

But after Alfred's death the Danes continued their invasions. Sometimes they were bought off for a time by money payments (a tribute called the *Danegeld*). Finally a Danish chief, Cnut, made himself king of England (1017). Cnut and his sons ruled for twenty-five years.

In 1042 another Saxon king, Edward the Confessor, came to the throne. He had been brought up in Normandy. His mother was the daughter of the Norman duke, and his father had fled to Normandy when he was driven from his throne by Cnut. Edward, called back to England as king, brought with him many of his Norman relatives and retainers.

For some years the country had been divided into five or six provinces. These

Ninth-Century England · *Which areas were controlled by the Norsemen? the Anglo-Saxons? With what can you associate Hastings? Canterbury? Runnymede? Bannockburn?*

earldoms were ruled by almost independent nobles. During most of Edward's reign the government was largely in the hands of Godwin, Earl of Wessex, and later of his son Harold.

William of Normandy Conquers England (1066) · At Edward's death in 1066, Harold was chosen to succeed him. Thereupon one of the most important events in the history of England took place. The powerful William, Duke of Normandy, immediately claimed the throne.

William was a cousin of Edward the Confessor. He based his claim to the English throne on this relationship and on a promise which he declared Edward had made to him. Since Harold refused to acknowledge this claim, William prepared to invade England.

Unfavorable winds delayed the invasion. Harold, in the meantime, faced an invasion from the Norwegian king, a descendant of Cnut. Just when Harold was drawn north to fight the Norwegians, the winds changed, and William landed in England.

After decisively defeating the Norwegians, Harold and his men hastened south, marching two hundred miles in five days. They met the Norman invaders at Hastings. Though they fought valiantly they were defeated, and Harold was killed. William was now known as "the Conqueror."

William was subsequently chosen king by an assembly in Westminster Abbey. He was crowned on Christmas Day, 1066.

William Creates a Strong Monarchy · William built a strong and efficient monarchy. He retained the familiar council of nobles and bishops (the Saxon *Witenagemot*) and consulted it on important matters. He issued a code of laws based on those of earlier times, but made a few changes and additions.

William placed Normans who were faithful to him in the important positions in each locality. He gave them the estates of Saxon nobles who had resisted him. But he made sure that no lord was strong enough to muster a great force against him. Moreover, he compelled all landholders to take an oath of allegiance to him *directly*. Thus subvassals would owe fidelity to him first, and to their immediate overlord second.

William had his officials make a survey, or census, of the country. This showed the exact number of tenants, the size and value of their estates, and the payments they owed the crown. The information was written down in two volumes called the

The Death of Harold · *This scene concludes the pictorial story of the Norman Conquest of England. It was embroidered in colored wool on a 231-foot strip of linen for display as a tapestry in the Cathedral of Bayeux, Normandy.*

Domesday Book. William's ability to collect this information from his people and have it presented in such a clear report is evidence both of his authority and the efficient methods of government that he had established.

Henry I Strengthens the National Government (1100–1135) · William's fourth son, Henry I, still further increased the royal authority. He kept his powerful nobles well in hand. (1) He required them to pay taxes and to submit to the decisions of his courts. (2) Lawsuits between nobles or cases involving land and taxes which were of concern to the crown were tried before the *curia regis*, or king's council. (3) Justices representing the *curia regis* were sent to the different parts of the country to settle difficulties, thus making the king's authority respected throughout the land.

(4) Still another means of centralizing power was the annual meeting of the *Exchequer*. On these occasions the king's ministers sat around a table marked with squares like a checkerboard. On these squares the officials could easily calculate accounts by means of counters or coins. The sheriffs of the counties and the representatives of the nobles had to appear before the group to give a report of the taxes, dues, and other payments owed to the crown. All difficulties were settled on the spot by the ministers, and the decisions and payments recorded.

The Exchequer thus became a tax court and an accounting office. The British still call their national treasury the Exchequer. Its head, the Chancellor of the Exchequer, is a member of the cabinet, corresponding to our Secretary of the Treasury.

Importance of the Norman Conquest · The conquest of England by a Norman-French duke was much more than a change of kings. (1) It brought to the country a vigorous new people, whose influence upon the national development was of highest importance. (2) The Norman kings laid the foundations of a strong national state. England became unified and strengthened under a well-organized central government.

and nobility, while Anglo-Saxon remained the speech of the mass of the people. Latin continued to be used in the Church and in the law. This combination greatly enriched the national language as it developed into the English that we speak today.

Henry II (1154–1189); Trial by Jury · Henry II, with the aid of his ministers, built up his kingdom by the enforcement of the law, by the introduction of better methods of trial in the courts, and by a fairer treatment of all classes of English subjects.

Henry's justices developed a more efficient type of procedure in the courts, which grew into what we call *trial by jury*. A number of men—usually twelve—were ordered to investigate the facts of a case. Then they were to attend court and to make a sworn statement, or *verdict*, as to which party had the better claim. These men were called jurors (from Latin *jurare*, "to swear") because they had to swear to tell the truth.

Henry II also introduced the *grand jury*, which we still use. This was a group of men, selected in each neighborhood, whose duty it was to bring anyone suspected of wrongdoing before them. If there was sufficient evidence against him, they would accuse, or *indict* him. He must then stand trial before the law.

The Common Law · The king's council had kept a record of the opinions handed down by the justices in earlier times. These judges decided legal cases according to what they believed most people would consider was right. They relied on the customs and beliefs of the people.

Henry's officials, when traveling through the country, made their decisions on the same principles. Let us suppose that one person charged his neighbor with failure to honor an agreement. The king's official

Early English Law Court · *An usher swears in the jury (right). Find the king's justices, clerks, attorneys, and the prisoner.*

(3) Merchants, weavers, and many other skilled tradesmen, brought into the country new occupations, new methods of manufacture, new arts and crafts, and new interests and ideas. (4) The Normans also brought another language to the island. French became the language of the court

would try to find if a similar case had been decided earlier. His own decision would then be based on the judgment of the earlier case. This body of opinion and custom which grew up through practical experience was called the *common law*, for it was common to the whole kingdom. Lawyers and judges learned common law by reading reports in which judges gave reasons for their decisions. The common law, together with the written statutes of the realm, governs the English people. The common law was brought by the colonists to America. It is still used in many court cases in our country.

The power to enforce the law, together with the fairer methods of trial, tended to bring more and more cases before the king's courts. As the king's officials held sessions in small districts, even the local courts came under the king's control, and the courts of the feudal lords became less important.

Henry II Creates a National Army · Henry greatly strengthened the monarchy by creating a national militia. Every freeman was required by law to be armed and ready to fight when called to the king's service. Those of the rank of knight had to provide themselves with full armor and a horse. Those of lower station must be equipped, each according to his means.

Henry's Relations with the Church · William the Conqueror had received the Pope's approval of his invasion of England. Nevertheless he refused to take an oath of submission when it was demanded by Gregory VII. William went even farther. He forbade his subjects to recognize any Pope, attend any church council, or receive any papal demands without his consent. His successors also were careful to safeguard the crown against any serious interference from Rome.

By Henry II's time the Church owned a large amount of property in England. It had its own laws and courts. Church courts settled cases affecting the clergy, as well as many matters having to do with property, wills, inheritance, and marriage. The question naturally arose as to how far the Church and its officers should be under the control of the king. Henry was determined to keep his authority over the Church in England. He intended to punish churchmen like other offenders for their crimes, to force bishops and abbots to fulfill their feudal promises, and to abolish appeals from his authority to the Pope.

Henry was constantly opposed in his efforts by the equally determined Archbishop of Canterbury, Thomas Becket. The conflict grew so serious that Henry, in an angry moment, is reported to have said, "Is there no one to rid me of this miserable churchman?" Unfortunately, some of the king's followers took his remark seriously, and Becket was found murdered in his cathedral at Canterbury.

The power of the medieval Popes is clearly shown in the crisis which followed. For when the Pope threatened to excommunicate the king, Henry promised to return to Canterbury all the property he had taken. He promised also to send money and even to lead a crusade to recapture Jerusalem, which had fallen into the hands of the Moslems.

CHECK ON YOUR READING

1. *What different groups of people lived in Britain during this period?*
2. *How did William the Conqueror and Henry I centralize the government?*
3. *What changes were made by Henry II?*

4. The English People Get a Charter and a Parliament

John Grants the Great Charter (1215) ·
We have already seen (p. 156) how King
John (1199–1216), Henry's son, lost most
of the possessions of the English kings in
France. This event was important in the
unification of France. It was also important for the future of England. For when
the king proposed to take a new army to
France to retake these lands, his vassals
refused to go. They insisted that they
were not pledged to fight for him abroad.

King John replied by levying huge taxes
on the barons who objected. And they
responded by marching against him. The
barons met the king at Runnymede, not
far from London. Here, on June 15, 1215,
they compelled him to grant a list of demands which they and the townsmen of
London had drawn up. A portion of this
great document is shown at the right.

The Great Charter (*Magna Carta*)
forced the king to acknowledge for the first
time that the government was not for his
benefit alone, but also for that of the people. The Charter revived an old feudal idea
which was being forgotten. This was that
government is a *contract* between the lord
and his subjects in which good government
is to be given in return for loyal service. If
the king fails in his obligation to his people,
they have the right to hold him to account.
The Charter admitted that the nobles have
certain *rights* which the king could not
remove. These basic principles were later
repeated in the English Bill of Rights and
our Declaration of Independence.

What the Great Charter Proclaimed ·
(1) It was clearly stated in the Charter
that the king was to impose no tax, besides
the feudal dues, without the consent of the
Great Council. (2) The Charter promised
that "to no one will we . . . deny or delay
right or justice." (3) No freeman may be
arrested, imprisoned, or deprived of his
property unless he is immediately sent before a court of his equals for trial. (4) The
Charter further provided that merchants
should be safe to come and go without being subject to "evil tolls." (5) No official
may take away a person's goods or chattels
without immediately paying for them in
money. (6) Fines must be just.

Limits of the Charter · It should be
noted that the nobles, churchmen, and
townsmen who drew up this document represented only about one-sixth of the population. Nothing was said of the serfs or
lowly freemen, who formed the mass of the
people at the time.

Yet the Charter was a notable achievement. Later the common people did appeal
to the Charter when attempts were made to
oppress them. The right to a fair trial by
a jury of one's equals was later claimed by
all freemen. And English kings were reminded from time to time that they could
not levy taxes without consent.

The Model Parliament (1295) · During
the thirteenth and fourteenth centuries an
important political institution slowly developed. It gave to the English people an
increasing part in the government of their
country.

The Great Council was composed of
nobles, bishops, and abbots who met with
the king to discuss important matters.
The name *Parliament* (from French *parler*,
"to speak" or "discuss") was gradually
adopted for it when representatives of a
new group began to be regularly included.

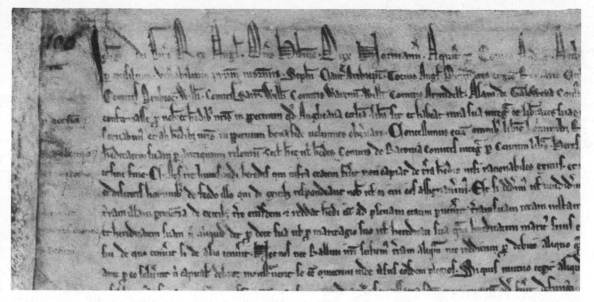

Magna Carta, 1215 A.D. · *Latin originals of the charter still exist in the cathedrals of Lincoln and Salisbury and in the British Museum, from which the above is taken.*

This new group was the middle class, or the *commons.* The increase of business and trade in the country had by this time produced a large group of landholders and merchants. Although they were below the rank of the nobility, they were rich and energetic. Since the king could no longer tax the people without their consent, one of his main reasons for summoning Parliament was to obtain grants of money. He soon saw that the wealthy middle class was an important source of income.

In 1295 Edward I summoned a Parliament which set certain precedents. Some historians have called it the Model Parliament. To this gathering the king invited not only the nobles and higher clergy, but also two knights representing each county and two townsmen representing each city or borough in the county.

The Model Parliament established a principle which is the very foundation of representative government. No Parliament since then has met without representatives of the commons. Gradually the lords and the commons began to meet separately as an upper House of Lords and a lower House of Commons.

The Growing Power of Parliament · Parliament soon found that it was able to place a check on the king and his officials. It began to demand a "redress of grievances" before it consented to a grant of money. This meant that the king must promise to remedy any act of which Parliament complained before Parliament would levy new taxes. Moreover, instead of meeting wherever the king happened to be, Parliament began to hold its sessions in the city of Westminster, now part of London.

In 1327 Parliament further showed its power by deposing an incompetent king (Edward II) and declaring his son the rightful ruler. Edward III's wars with France (p. 165) kept him in constant need of money. Nearly every year he had to ask

Meeting of Parliament · *Below King Edward I are seated Alexander III, king of Scotland; Llewelyn, prince of Wales; and the Archbishops of Canterbury and York.*

Parliament for additional funds. On each occasion Parliament gained some reform or new law before it granted the king's request. It thus was able to improve the government of the country and to establish itself as a lawmaking body. No new law was passed without the consent of Parliament.

Edward I Conquers Wales · In the days of Edward I (1272–1307) the English kings did not yet rule over all Britain. To the west of their kingdom lay the mountainous district of Wales, which had never been conquered by the Angles and Saxons. The people still spoke the Celtic tongue of their forefathers and kept their independence under their native chieftains.

Shortly after he became king, Edward marched into Wales with a large army and defeated the Welsh. Llewellyn, their

prince, was killed, and all resistance to the English was finally put down. Edward divided the country into shires, or counties, and introduced English laws and customs. Later, at a public ceremony, he presented his son to the Welsh as their prince. Since that time the eldest son of the English king has borne the title "Prince of Wales."

Edward I Fails to Subdue Scotland · It was a far more difficult task to conquer Scotland. Scotland was the home of two different peoples. Those of the north, called Highlanders, were mainly descended from the Celts and spoke Gaelic. Those of the south, Lowlanders, were descended from the Anglo-Saxon invaders and spoke English. There was much conflict between the two sections, but finally they united under Scottish kings, who established Edinburgh as their capital.

When the old line of Scottish rulers died out, Edward I was asked which claimant should become king. Before making his choice, Edward demanded that the one selected should hold Scotland as a fief from the English ruler. John Baliol was chosen king, but he soon renounced his homage to the king of England. Moreover, he made an alliance with Edward's enemy Philip the Fair of France (p. 157). Edward thereupon marched into Scotland (1296) and put down the rebellion.

He now declared that Baliol had forfeited his fief and that he himself was king of Scotland. The crown and the famous Stone of Scone, upon which the Scottish kings had always sat to be crowned, were carried to London.

But the Scots continued to resist under a heroic leader, Robert Bruce, whom they acknowledged as their king. In 1314 Bruce defeated Edward II in the famous battle of Bannockburn. The English ruler still refused to acknowledge the independence of Scotland, and the two countries carried on a border warfare for centuries. Not until a Scottish king, James VI, succeeded to the English throne as James I (1603) were the warring neighbors permanently united into one kingdom. Then the Scots joined the English on a basis of equality rather than as a conquered people.

CHECK ON YOUR READING

1. *What basic ideas did the Magna Carta revive? What rights did it secure? For whom?*
2. *Describe Parliament: its origin, membership, and powers.*
3. *How did Edward I try to unite Britain? With what success?*

5. The Hundred Years' War and the Wars of the Roses

An English King Claims the French Crown · The English rulers had continued to pay homage to the French monarchs for their possessions in France for many years. But in the time of Edward III of England (1327–1377) the old line of French kings came to an end when none of Philip the Fair's sons had a male heir. Thereupon Edward III declared that he was the rightful ruler of France because his mother was a daughter of Philip and sister of the last French king.

This claim led to a series of conflicts between France and England, known as the Hundred Years' War (1337–1453). It was, of course, only part of the long struggle which had been going on between the two countries ever since the Norman Conquest. Actual fighting did not take place during the whole of the hundred-year period. There were long stretches of time when there was a truce between the enemies. Indeed, two treaties were made in this century in the hope of ending the conflict. But both treaties were disregarded, and each time the war was renewed.

Progress of the War · Edward III landed in France in 1346. Although the English bowmen won several important victories over the French knights, the English could not occupy all of France. Nor would the French give in and accept a foreign ruler. By the end of Edward's reign the English had lost almost all their French possessions. Then the war ceased for forty years.

When fighting began again, the Burgundians allied themselves with the English against their own monarch. Again the English were victorious, winning a great battle at Agincourt (1415). Fifteen years later the English, with the aid of the Burgundians, had succeeded·in occupying a great part of French north of the river Loire.

Joan of Arc · In the south the feeble heir to the French throne (Charles VII) was doing nothing to check the English. While the English were besieging the great town of Orléans, help came to the hard-pressed French from an unexpected quarter. A peasant girl, Joan of Arc, was inspired by visions which bade her go forth to the help of her poor king. She begged Charles to give her a few troops that she might try to save Orléans. She met with many objections, but finally her belief in her divine mission persuaded her hearers that she was sent by God. Joan put on a soldier's uniform and rode at the head of her troops.

Impressed and inspired by her faith, the fainthearted French took courage. Orléans was relieved, and the French made a victorious attack on their enemies.

Under Joan's direction the French continued to be successful. But the king was too weak to be guided by Joan's councils. Finally, the Maid of Orléans, as she was called, was allowed to fall into the hands of the English. They surrendered her to a French ecclesiastical court to be tried as a witch who had been aided by the devil. She was condemned as a heretic and burned at the stake (1431). The example of Joan, however, had given hope to the French.

The Relief of Orléans · *Joan of Arc led the French in storming the bastille, and later the bridgehead, which broke the English siege of the city.*

After her death the English won no more victories. By 1453 all their possessions except Calais were in French hands.

How France Developed a National Government · France had suffered greatly in the long conflict with England, for all the fighting had been done on French soil. Yet at the same time a number of changes had taken place which had made the king stronger than ever before. (1) The nobility had suffered great losses in men on the battlefield and had lost much of their land. A middle class of small tenant farmers was growing up. (2) The tradespeople in the towns were becoming more prosperous and influential. These wealthy men were of great service to the king in supplying him with loans.

(3) The king now had a permanent standing army, supported by state funds. The Estates-General agreed to an annual tax, called the *taille*, to pay the cost of a regular army. The king need no longer sacrifice his land and his authority to his nobles for their aid.

(4) But there were still powerful vassals in France who were very jealous of the king's authority. They did not hesitate to plot against him. The task of subduing these subjects and regaining their lands fell to the able and cunning Louis XI (1461–1483). We cannot recount the various schemes by which Louis outwitted his enemies. But at his death, except for Artois, Burgundy, and Brittany, he had recovered nearly all the territory included in modern France. Louis's son, Charles VIII, added Brittany to the crown lands by marrying the heiress to that province.

(5) The nobles were now forbidden to coin money, maintain armies, or tax their subjects. (6) The king's judges were given authority throughout the land. Business

and industry had increased the wealth of the middle class. This group was loyal to the king because only under a unified and peaceful government could trade flourish. France was on the way to becoming a strong modern state.

Wars of the Roses (1455–1485) · At the close of the Hundred Years' War, England was divided by civil wars as members of rival branches of the royal family struggled over the succession to the throne. The two main branches were the house of York, whose emblem was a white rose, and the house of Lancaster, symbolized by a red rose. These conflicts have therefore come to be called the Wars of the Roses. They were marked by treachery and cruelty. Richard III (a Yorkist who, legend says, had his two little nephews murdered in the Tower of London) was killed at the battle of Bosworth Field. The victor was Henry Tudor, a kinsman of the Lancastrians. He came to the throne as Henry VII (1485). This first Tudor king put an end to the feud by marrying Elizabeth of York.

Absolute Rule of the Tudors · Henry VII restored the absolute power of the monarchy. (1) Most of the nobles had perished in the civil war. Those who remained and made trouble for the king were put to death. (2) The many great estates seized by Henry gave him new wealth, power, and independence. (3) He saw to it that all the old dues, duties, and grants payable to the crown were collected and increased wherever possible.

(4) He avoided costly wars and so did not need to ask Parliament for money. Parliament was therefore summoned less often, but when it did meet it seemed willing to carry out the king's wishes. The Tudors, although despotic rulers, knew how to get along with Parliament.

Choosing Sides in the Temple Gardens · *Richard Plantagenet (left) chooses the white rose of York. The Earl of Somerset (right) prefers the red rose of Lancaster. Which won?*

(5) Business and trade had increased by Henry VII's time, and the laws which were made were usually favorable to the middle class, or commons. Since order was essential to prosperity, this class, like its counterpart in France, was very loyal to a king who could maintain peace.

CHECK ON YOUR READING

1. *What part did the following play in the Hundred Years' War: Edward III, Agincourt, Burgundians, Joan?*
2. *How did France develop a national government?*
3. *How did the Tudors gain the throne of England?*
4. *How did Henry VII strengthen the monarchy?*

Learning Activities

Think about the chapter

1. How do you account for the strengthening of the monarchy in France and England, but not in Germany?

2. Compare the struggle between monarch and Pope in Germany and England.

3. Explain the contributions of Henry II to the English constitution.

4. Why were *parlements* and *Estates-General* significant steps in the development of France as a nation?

5. Why is the Norman conquest one of the most important events in English history?

6. *Map study:* On a map of Europe outline the Holy Roman Empire about the year 1000. Then locate the following places which are significant in the period 1100 to 1400: Kingdom of Naples, Sicily, Normandy, Agincourt, Orléans, Calais, Westminster, Canterbury, Edinburgh.

Go beyond the text

7. Compare the Great Charter and the Bill of Rights in our Constitution. What rights are similar? What ones are missing from the Great Charter?

8. Compare the work of the grand jury and petit or trial jury of Henry II's time with the same juries today. A civics book will tell you how a trial is conducted today.

9. Why was Joan of Arc found guilty of heresy? Was her punishment the usual one for heresy? Read one of the several plays written about her.

10. Investigate further the story of Scotland's fight to remain free. Who was Wallace? What is the history of the Stone of Scone? How was a spider supposedly involved in one of Bruce's battles?

Follow up your special interests

11. Look up a picture of Canterbury Cathedral and read about its history. When was it founded? What events are connected with it? Why did pilgrims go to Canterbury?

12. To illustrate how developments discussed in this chapter have directly affected American history and institutions, draw a tree, showing the roots as the English beginnings and the branches as the American institutions that have grown from them. What will you label the trunk?

13. Very good readers who are interested in drama and literature might enjoy reading Shakespeare's historical plays dealing with this era. Many of you have probably seen the film adaptations of *Richard III* and *Henry V*. Choose a dramatic scene to read to the class. Be sure you can explain the historical background.

READ FURTHER

Basic readings: (1) CHEYNEY, *Readings in English History*, Chaps. 4–12. (2) CHEYNEY, *Short History of England*, Chaps. 6–10. (3) EVANS, *Costume Throughout the Ages*, Chaps. 4, 10, 11. (4) HAGEDORN, *Book of Courage*. Joan of Arc. (5) HOFFMAN, *News of the World*, Nos. 19–20, 22, 26–28. (6) ROBINSON, *Readings*, Chaps. 11–14. (7) SCOTT, HYMA, NOYES, *Readings in Medieval History*, Secs. 10, 19. (8) Year's *Pictorial History*, pp. 148–152.

Special accounts: (10) D. MILLS, *The Middle Ages*. (11) M. and C. H. B. QUENNELL, *Everyday Things in England*, Vols. I-II. Simply written; good drawings.

Fiction and biography: (13) N. BAKER, *Robert Bruce: King of Scots*. See also *William the Silent* by the same author. (14) M. BARNES, *Tudor Rose*. Unusually fascinating story of Elizabeth of York. (15) T. COSTAIN, *The Moneyman*. Jacques Coeur, the financier of Charles VII, becomes involved in intrigues for the royal succession in France. (16) A. CONAN DOYLE, *The White Company*.

Exploits of English bowmen in the early part of the Hundred Years' War. (17) A. KELLY, *Eleanor of Aquitaine and the Four Kings.* As Queen of France, she went with Louis VII on the Second Crusade, later married Henry II of England, and was the mother of Richard the Lion-Hearted and King John. (18) M. LEIGHTON, *Judith of France.* The story is based on the life of Judith, the granddaughter of Charlemagne. (19) H. MUNTZ, *The Golden Warrior.* King Harold of England and the Norman Conquest. (20) A. PAINE, *The Girl in White Armor.* Joan of Arc. (21) W. SCOTT, *Ivanhoe.* A classic dealing with the rivalry between the Anglo-Saxons and Normans. (22) G. B. SHAW, *St. Joan.* A celebrated playwright's interpretation of Joan of Arc. (23) R. STEVENSON, *The Black Arrow.* A tale of the days of the Wars of the Roses.

The English Kings from William the Conqueror to Edward III

The table shows the basis of the claims of English kings to French lands.

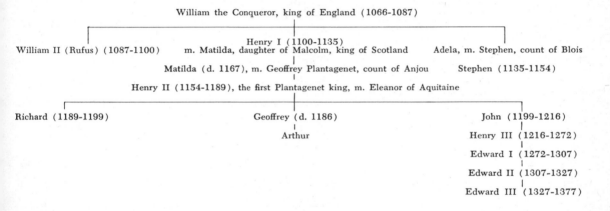

William the Conqueror, king of England (1066-1087)

William II (Rufus) (1087-1100)　　Henry I (1100-1135) m. Matilda, daughter of Malcolm, king of Scotland　　Adela, m. Stephen, count of Blois

Matilda (d. 1167), m. Geoffrey Plantagenet, count of Anjou　　Stephen (1135-1154)

Henry II (1154-1189), the first Plantagenet king, m. Eleanor of Aquitaine

Richard (1189-1199)　　Geoffrey (d. 1186)　　John (1199-1216)

Arthur　　Henry III (1216-1272)

Edward I (1272-1307)

Edward II (1307-1327)

Edward III (1327-1377)

The Rival Houses of Lancaster and York and the First of the Tudor Line in England

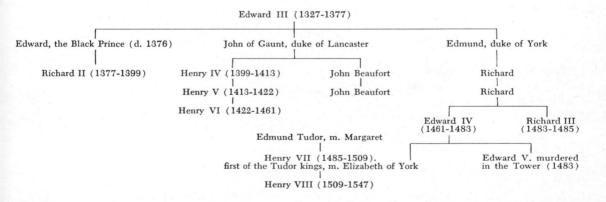

Edward III (1327-1377)

Edward, the Black Prince (d. 1376)　　John of Gaunt, duke of Lancaster　　Edmund, duke of York

Richard II (1377-1399)　　Henry IV (1399-1413)　　John Beaufort　　Richard

Henry V (1413-1422)　　John Beaufort　　Richard

Henry VI (1422-1461)

Edward IV (1461-1483)　　Richard III (1483-1485)

Edmund Tudor, m. Margaret

Henry VII (1485-1509). first of the Tudor kings, m. Elizabeth of York　　Edward V. murdered in the Tower (1483)

Henry VIII (1509-1547)

12

The Crusades and the Towns
Promote Trade and Progress

KEY WORDS AND DATES

Byzantine Empire	guilds
Seljuk Turks	Hanseatic League
Greek Orthodox	fairs
Urban II	bourgeoisie
1096	Renaissance
Crusades	Venice
Holy Sepulcher	Florence
Saladin	Medici
Richard	Marco Polo
charters	1492

ALTHOUGH THE EMPIRE in the West disappeared in the fifth century, the Byzantine Empire in the East held out against invaders for a thousand years. At the end of the eleventh century Emperor Alexius appealed to the Pope for aid against a new and powerful invader. The Seljuk Turks had overrun the Holy Land and were seriously threatening Constantinople itself.

When the Pope called on Western Christians to join in rescuing the Holy Land from the "infidels," thousands of persons were fired with enthusiasm to make the long journey to Jerusalem. These *Crusades*, or Wars of the Cross (Latin, *crux*), continued during 150 years.

The Crusades began as a religious undertaking, but they had also an important effect on progress. They brought the West into contact with the more highly civilized Byzantine East. Europeans saw new things, learned new ways, and received many new ideas. This hastened the change which was already beginning in western Europe. Towns were developing and business was reviving, especially in Italy. A new and prosperous *middle class* arose. The Middle Ages were coming to an end, and Europe was entering a new era.

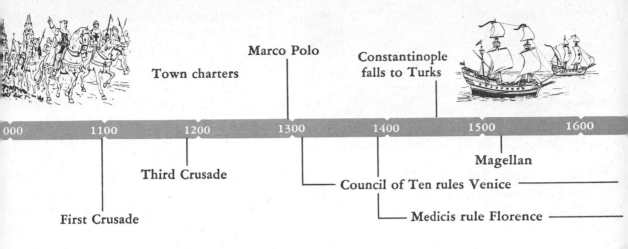

Town charters

Marco Polo

Constantinople
falls to Turks

000   1100   1200   1300   1400   1500   1600

Third Crusade

Magellan

Council of Ten rules Venice

First Crusade

Medicis rule Florence

1. The Byzantine Empire

Why the Byzantine Empire Was Envied · While the Empire in the West had fallen into the hands of barbarian chieftains, the Eastern Empire managed to maintain itself until Constantinople (Byzantium) was captured in 1453. But outsiders often invaded and took over parts of its territory. Constantinople itself was besieged from time to time. But because of its location on a peninsula, its strong natural defenses held off all foes.

Constantinople's fine landlocked harbor made it a great and active trading center in the Middle Ages. Furs, amber, honey, and wax were brought from the north by Scandinavian and Russian merchants. Spices, drugs, ivory, and precious stones from the Orient came overland by caravan or by Byzantine ships from Alexandria. This trade brought great prosperity and a high level of culture, which was reflected in its brilliant art, but it also aroused the envy of other nations.

Enemies of the Empire · The Byzantine Empire was directly exposed to the wandering tribes from Asia. The Avars, a tribe from southern Russia, invaded its boundaries from time to time but sometimes were bought off. Then the Slavs, driven by the Avars, established themselves permanently in the Balkan Peninsula. Other troublesome tribes included the Bulgars, the Russians, and the Magyars, or Hungarians. They plundered the provinces of the Empire and settled where they wished.

The Empire was still suffering from long wars with the Persians when its eastern portions fell victim to the Moslems (map, p. 135). Their attempt to take Constantinople was a failure. The struggle between Christians and Moslems continued for two hundred years. However, by the year 1000 the emperors had freed Asia Minor.

Seljuk Turks Threaten the Empire · In the eleventh century a new and powerful enemy appeared. This was a nomad people from Turkestan called the Seljuks, from the name of their leader. After overwhelming the Persian kingdoms, these Turks adopted the religion of Islam. Then, fired with religious zeal, they set forth on new conquests.

Greek Flame Throwers · *"Greek Fire" was made of highly inflammable naphtha. The Byzantines used it against their enemies with deadly effect.*

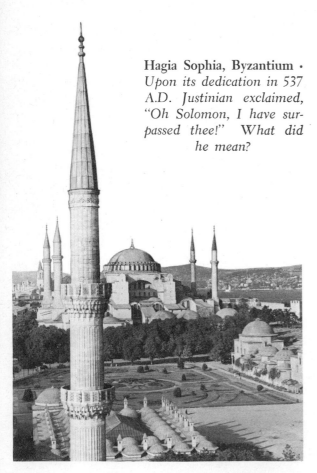

Hagia Sophia, Byzantium · *Upon its dedication in 537 A.D. Justinian exclaimed, "Oh Solomon, I have surpassed thee!" What did he mean?*

When Jerusalem fell into the hands of the Arab Moslems (p. 135), Christian pilgrims were permitted to visit there. But the Seljuk Turks treated the Christians with great cruelty. In 1071 they defeated the emperor and took possession of Asia Minor. They then occupied the fortress of Nicaea, across from Constantinople. There they were a serious danger to the capital. It was in this crisis that Emperor Alexius called on Pope Urban II for aid.

The Western Roman and Eastern Greek Churches · The emperor appealed to the Pope as the leader of the Roman Catholic Church. He did not acknowledge him as head of the Eastern or Greek Orthodox Church. The Eastern Church was under the direct control of the emperor, and its spiritual leader, the "patriarch," was but a representative of the crown. The churches of East and West had split in 1054 after repeated disputes over doctrine.

When the emperor appealed for the help of Western Christendom against the Moslems, the Pope responded to the call. Three practical considerations may have influenced his decision: (1) He could head a movement which would unite all Christians against a common foe. (2) The Greek Church might once more be joined with the Western Church under the headship of Rome. (3) There was a real danger that the Turks might overcome the emperor and then invade Europe.

CHECK ON YOUR READING

1. Why was the Byzantine Empire envied?
2. Use the map to show which enemies threatened the Empire.
3. Why did the Pope agree to help the emperor?

172

2. The Crusades and Their Effects

Motives of the Crusaders · Pope Urban II answered the emperor's plea at a great church council at Clermont in France (1095). He asked knights and soldiers of all ranks to give up warfare against one another and go to the aid of fellow Christians in the East. He warned that the Turks, if unchecked, would extend their sway more widely over the Christian world.

Thousands eagerly responded to the Pope's appeal. Their motives were many. Earnest Christians started on the long pilgrimage in the simple faith that they were doing God's work. Realists saw the practical need for unity in the face of a common enemy. The romantic and adventurous were caught up in the excitement of the undertaking. Discontented nobles hoped to gain a bit of territory for themselves in the East. Merchants saw an opportunity for new business. The bored and restless simply wished to escape from home and its responsibilities. Even criminals grasped at a chance to escape the results of their misdeeds, for the Pope promised to the loyal Crusader freedom from punishment for past sins.

Behavior of the Crusaders · The behavior of the Crusaders when they reached foreign lands reflected their motives. Some sacrificed their lives and fortunes for the greater good. Others seized every opportunity for selfish gain. Many of the people through whose lands they marched had reason to regret their coming.

Among those who preached the Crusade was a poor monk named Peter the Hermit. Throngs followed him around, determined to join the expedition. By the spring of 1096 a great crowd of simple folk, including women and children, started off blindly to reach the Holy Sepulcher. They were led by Peter the Hermit, Walter the Penniless, and simple knights utterly unfitted to manage unruly crowds.

Many of these "Crusaders" were killed by the Hungarians, who rose to protect themselves against the plunderings of this motley horde. Others died by the way. Some of them reached Nicaea, only to be massacred by the Turks.

The First Crusade (1096) · It was nearly a year after the Council of Clermont before the first organized armies of fighting men were ready to start. Groups under noble lords from France and southern Italy took different routes, but agreed to meet at Constantinople. Upon their arrival the Crusaders found that they had little more in common with the Greeks than with the Turks. Bitter conflicts soon arose. The emperor wished to use the Western allies to force back the Turks from his territory. But much time was spent while the various princes set up kingdoms and interested themselves in worldly gains.

In the spring of 1099 twenty thousand warriors were at last able to move on Jerusalem. After two months of hard fighting the city fell into their hands. The Crusaders showed no mercy to the people, but murdered the inhabitants with shocking barbarity. Godfrey of Bouillon was chosen ruler and took the title of Defender of the Holy Sepulcher.

Crusaders' States in Syria · The Crusaders founded four small kingdoms (map, p. 175). In addition they took possession of some important coastal towns, but they were never able to subdue the country.

Knights Departing on a Crusade ·
What kinds of armor did they wear?
What weapons did they bear?
How did the Crusade affect them?

Friendly relations were gradually established, and the Crusaders began to adopt native customs. They soon learned to respect the superior knowledge and achievements of the Moslems in certain fields, especially in medicine.

Later Crusades · The Second Crusade (1147–1149) was a terrible failure. Then, in the year 1187, Jerusalem was recaptured by Saladin, the most distinguished of all the Moslem rulers of the period. The loss of the Holy City led to the famous Third Crusade. The kings of Germany (Frederick Barbarossa), England (Richard the Lion-Hearted), and France (Philip Augustus) took part. These rulers quarreled among themselves, but they and the Moslems were beginning to win each other's respect. This was due in part to the character of Saladin. In 1192 Richard concluded a truce with Saladin by which the Christian pilgrims were allowed to visit the holy places in comfort and safety.

Further Crusades were undertaken. In one of them the leaders were persuaded by the Venetians, who were furnishing ships and supplies, to attack Constantinople. The city was captured, and its treasure divided among the invaders. A Latin empire was set up, which lasted for nearly sixty years (till 1261). This disgraceful enterprise against a Christian city hurt the whole crusading movement. By 1291 the Westerners had lost all their possessions in the Holy Land.

Results of the Crusades · From a military point of view the Crusades were unsuccessful. But much good came of them nonetheless. (1) There was a revival of religious faith. (2) During the 150 years of the Crusades thousands of Europeans went to the East. They broke free from the narrow, local environments which bound them in. (3) The long journey taught them many things. They saw new lands, enjoyed Eastern luxuries, mingled with strange peoples and found customs and ideas different from their own. The tales they told of the life and customs of the Orient found their way into songs, stories, and histories which became familiar to Europeans.

(4) The Crusades affected business and trade. Italian merchants furnished ships and supplies for the Crusaders and were well paid for their services. When they aided in a successful siege of a town, they

arranged that a definite quarter should be assigned to them where they could have markets and carry on a permanent business.

(5) This new trade with the Orient brought the West into permanent relations with the East. Products from India and the Far East—silks, spices, camphor, ivory, and pearls—were carried by Moslems from the East to the commercial towns of Palestine and Syria. Then through Italian traders these products found their way into France and Germany.

(6) The transportation of pilgrims and their equipment necessitated the building of larger vessels. On their return voyages these ships could bring merchandise into Europe. (7) Manufacturing also was stim-

ulated. Europeans in some places began to imitate the East in the making of rugs, cloth, and silk.

(8) The Crusades influenced European methods of warfare. The Western soldiers learned from the Greeks the use of machinery for attacking castles and walled towns. Heraldry, or the use of "coats of arms," also developed during the Crusades.

CHECK ON YOUR READING

1. *What motives led people to join the Crusades?*
2. *How do you account for the successes? failures?*
3. *What were the results of the Crusades?*

The Crusades · *Who led them? Which Crusade stressed the land route? the sea route? both? Which European ports benefited? What places were taken?*

THE CRUSADES

First Crusade 1096
Second Crusade 1147
Third Crusade 1189

Scale of Miles
0 — 320

3. The Towns Revive Business and Trade

Country Life in the Middle Ages · Up to the twelfth century most of the people of western Europe lived on great estates, or manors. Each manor was a world unto itself and had little contact with life outside its borders. Sometimes a peddler would come along, bringing various novelties in his pack. Sometimes wandering minstrels or players would stop at the manor house to entertain the lord and his guests. But the life of the peasants in the little huts of the village was bounded by their own community.

Moslem conquests from the seventh to the ninth centuries had interfered with normal trade between East and West. The Mediterranean had become in reality a "Moslem lake." Such few products of the East as still made their way into Europe were brought by occasional wandering merchants, usually Syrians or Jews.

Without foreign trade there was no flow of money into the country from outside. Business declined, and the towns lost their importance and disappeared. The estates, which had formerly sold their extra produce to the townspeople, now raised only what they needed for themselves.

Reappearance of Towns · Towns are the chief centers of progress and enlightenment. When people live near one another they exchange ideas and plan improvements that carry civilization forward. We recall that the Greek and Roman cities were the leaders in the civilization of their day. Later the city of Byzantium was a great center of culture.

In the eleventh century the population of western Europe began to increase. Industry and trade revived, and towns gradually developed. Many of the towns occupied the sites of former Roman settlements favorably located for trade. Some were communities which had survived the numerous invasions. Other towns grew up around a castle or monastery. The French name for town, *ville*, comes from the Latin *villa*, meaning "estate." The term still survives in the names of modern cities, such as Jacksonville, Louisville, or Nashville.

As the need for defense was still very great, the towns were surrounded by walls to protect them from attack. Crowded within these walls, the medieval cities were closely built up. The streets were narrow, crooked alleys above which the overhanging upper stories of the houses nearly met. Aside from the market square near the church, there were few open spaces. Sanitary conditions were appalling.

Trade, Taxes, and Charters · European towns, except those of Italy, were small in the eleventh and twelfth centuries. As the new goods from the East began to come into Europe, however, the townsmen were eager to make and sell more things in order to obtain the novelties from distant countries. Towns grew with the growing trade. Artisans learned to make things for a wider market.

Increased trade required greater freedom for townsmen to manage their own affairs. But feudal laws and taxes were oppressive. As long as a town remained under the control of the lord or abbot on whose land it was situated it had little chance for growth. The merchants found that when they were successful in business the landlords taxed them more heavily in order to share the profits.

As a consequence the townsmen frequently rose in revolt. The lords were then forced to give the towns *charters*, or written agreements. In these charters the rights of the townsmen, as well as of the lords, were clearly stated. They also listed the rules by which the communities were to be governed. The old feudal obligations of the townsmen to the lords were usually abolished or changed into money payments.

Business, Interest, and Profit · In the Middle Ages businessmen were looked down upon by the nobles and clergy as men of a lower order. Business was regarded as a strictly private affair without legal protection. Those who engaged in it had to look after their interests as best they could.

We all know that for business to grow, money or some system of credit is necessary. But in the Middle Ages money was scarce throughout western Europe, and there was no system of credit and banking such as we have today. Further, there was a prejudice against the taking of interest for a loan of money. Accepting interest was considered wicked because it appeared to be taking advantage of the embarrassment and need of others. The Church forbade "usury," as the taking of even a moderate interest was then called. So moneylending was left to the Jews, who did not have to obey the rules of the Church.

As Jews were kept out of the guilds (p. 178), they turned to moneylending as a business. Undoubtedly this had much to do with their unpopularity in the Middle Ages and caused them to be ill-treated by the Christians. The kings allowed them to make loans, but reserved the right to extort their profits from them when the royal treasuries were empty.

The whole question of profits was viewed differently from what it is today. It was

A Medieval Market (c. 1460) · *Find the druggist, seamstress, moneylender, and liveryman. Note the men's jackets, tights (leotards), swords, and pointed shoes.*

believed that everything had what was called a "just price." It was considered outrageous to charge more than this for any article. This price was merely enough to cover the cost of materials and repay the worker for the labor involved. Modern businessmen maintain that they are justified in seeking *profits* in addition to the cost of making the article. This repays them for the risks they take and covers the interest on the capital which they have invested in their enterprises.

Restrictions on Trade · The medieval businessman faced other restrictions. Tolls and payments were demanded by the lords across whose property his goods might pass.

Exam Time for Journeymen · *To become a master craftsman each mason and carpenter had to complete a* masterpiece *acceptable to the judge of the guild.*

Charges were levied for crossing bridges and fords and for using highroads. Streams were sometimes blocked so that a boat could not pass without paying for the privilege. In some cases parcels of merchandise were opened, and a small portion was taken by a lord or abbot as his payment for letting the goods cross his domain. At the markets fees were charged for the use of the lord's scale and measures. Moreover, the many local coinages caused much confusion.

On land the merchant and his wares were in constant danger from robbers. On the sea, pirates might seize a vessel and its cargo and sell the crew into slavery.

Coasts were dangerous and lighthouses were few. False signals were often used to lure vessels to shore, where robbers were lying in wait to plunder them.

Craft Guilds · As business grew, medieval artisans and merchants began to discover that the members of a class must organize to promote their interests and to make their power felt. They began to form associations to control the manufacture and sale of merchandise.

The tradesmen in the medieval towns were both manufacturers and merchants. They made, as well as sold, articles in their own shops. Those engaged in the same line of trade formed themselves into groups called *guilds*. There were, for example, guilds of bakers, tanners, weavers, hatters, armor-makers, candlemakers, and goldsmiths. These groups were organized to protect the industry. No one was allowed to carry on a craft unless he was a member of the proper guild.

The guilds fixed the hours and conditions of labor, the quality of the material to be used, the kind of workmanship required, and the price to be charged for finished articles. Since the work was done by hand and sold directly to a purchaser in the maker's house, the craftsmen usually took pride in their work. The guilds also helped to keep up a high standard of workmanship and to prevent any craftsman from taking advantage of another in the quality of his materials or the price that he charged.

There were *apprentices, journeymen,* and *master workmen* in a guild. In order to become a member, a young man had to spend several years in learning a trade. During this time he lived in the house of a master and worked as his apprentice, but received no wages. An easy trade might require three years' apprenticeship, but it took as many as ten years to learn a difficult one, such as that of goldsmith. When the apprentice had finished his training, he became a journeyman, or one who works by the day (French, *jour*) for wages. Finally, a journeyman might become a master by passing an examination or producing a "masterpiece," proving his skill. Usually he must also have enough money to start in business for himself.

The number of apprentices in any one trade was strictly limited so that there might not be too many journeymen to make a living in that trade. The members of a guild elected officials and had a treasury, to which all contributed. From this fund aid was given to the members and their families in time of sickness or other trouble.

Merchant Guilds · There had been a few traveling merchants even before the reappearance of the towns. But with the revival of trade with distant countries and the increase of business there gradually developed a large merchant class. This group devoted all its time to buying and selling. The merchants too formed guilds to protect their special interests. Competition was strictly regulated. The merchant guilds prohibited any member from buying up goods before they reached the market. They also forbade selling short weight, or asking more than the established price.

The merchants bought goods in large quantities to sell in the various towns, and they supplied raw materials to the craft guilds. The merchant guilds built and maintained offices and warehouses, improved harbors, built ships and docks, and insured their members against loss. They had their own meeting places, or guild halls. As the merchants were the richest class in the communities, they soon were able to obtain special privileges from those who governed the towns.

The Hanseatic League · Some of the towns formed unions for mutual defense. The most famous of these united the cities along the northern coasts of Europe. It was called the Hanseatic League (German, *Hanse*, "merchant guild"). Lübeck was the leader, and at one time or another seventy towns were members of the League. The union controlled settlements in Bergen, London, Venice, and Novgorod in Russia. It controlled nearly all the trade in the Baltic and the North Sea.

The League made war on pirates, and it also did much to reduce the perils of sea traffic. Its ships sailed in fleets under the protection of a man-of-war. For two hundred years before the discovery of America the League played an important role in European trade.

Leading Commercial Cities · The leaders in foreign commerce with the East were the Italian and Flemish (Belgian) cities. While the rest of Europe was cut off from the East, Venice had been able to remain in contact with Constantinople. She had greatly profited from her trade with this great commercial city. To it she exported wheat and wine from Italy, wood from Dalmatia, and salt from her neighboring lagoons.

The prosperity of Venice led other Italian towns to follow her example. It was not long before the Italian cities, especially Genoa and Pisa, succeeded in recapturing Sicily, Sardinia, and Corsica from the Moslems. Trade in the Mediterranean was reopened.

We recall that the Italian towns did a flourishing business during the Crusades, transporting pilgrims to the Holy Land and carrying all sorts of provisions and supplies for the Crusaders. On their return journeys

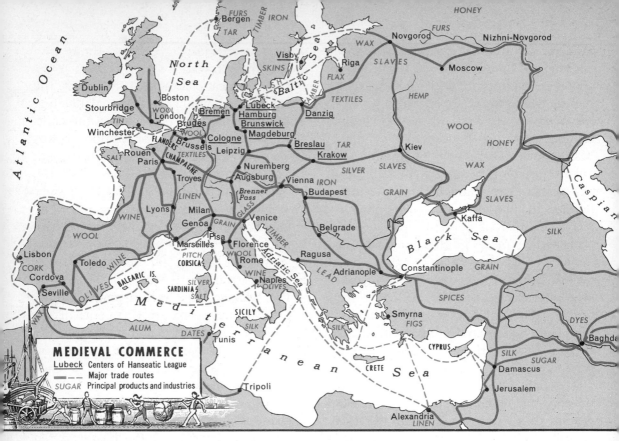

Medieval Commerce · *Locate the sources of such products as dyes, silk, spices, sugar, honey, cork, salt, tin, linen, textiles, furs, fish, grain, and glass. What cities prospered because of the water routes? the land routes? the fairs?*

the ships brought into Europe the luxuries of the East. These towns set up business quarters in various cities in the Levant (eastern Mediterranean). There they traded directly with the merchants who brought, by sea or by caravan, the products of India, the Spice Islands, Persia, and Arabia to the coast towns of the Near East.

Eastern goods reached northern Europe by way of the Brenner Pass and the Rhine. Some were sent by ship to the coastal towns of France and Spain and the Flemish cities. Flanders was fortunately situated to be the center of trade between England, the Scandinavian countries, and the Baltic ports. At the same time it was on the main overland route to the north. In exchange for foreign goods Flanders sent her fine woolen cloth to all parts of Europe and the East.

By the thirteenth century, business centers had developed in the German cities of Bremen, Lübeck, and Hamburg. Augsburg and Nuremberg, in southern Germany, also attained importance on account of their location on the line of trade between Italy and northern Europe. (The map above will help you to locate these important cities and trade routes.)

Trade Stimulates Manufacturing · By the twelfth century there was an eager demand in Europe for the luxuries from far-away lands. Some of these articles so delighted the Europeans that they began to try to make them themselves. Venice manufactured silk and made glass, an industry in which her craftsmen achieved great success. The people of the West learned to weave silk and velvet fabrics, as well as linen and cotton. Manufacturers used the eastern dyes, and Paris soon imitated the tapestries of the Orient.

Medieval Fairs · One of the chief centers of wholesale trade was the great medieval fair. Fairs had usually been local markets, where the products of the country and neighboring towns were sold. They were numerous and popular in the Middle Ages.

The fairs not only offered a chance to obtain a greater variety of goods than usual but were a welcome break in the dreary monotony of country life. Here people could meet one another, hear the news, and be entertained by the amusements that the fairs always provided. From the twelfth century on, some of the fairs in the larger cities came to be great exchanges for foreign goods and were an element of tremendous importance in medieval economic life.

At a time when transportation was difficult and dangerous, the annual fair provided a definite time and place where merchants who dealt in valuable merchandise on a large scale could meet other merchants and be sure of a crowd of eager buyers. They were the centers for wholesale trade.

Most famous of the great medieval fairs were those of Champagne in France. Here one could find the finest fabrics, jewels, and furs as well as foodstuffs, wine, cattle, horses, and articles of everyday household use. Whole streets were set apart for the dealers in special lines of goods, such as woolens or leathers.

Other important fairs were those of the Flemish towns; of Stourbridge and Winchester in England; and later of Leipzig in Saxony and Nizhni Novgorod in Russia.

Rise of the Middle Class, or Bourgeoisie · One of the most important results of the growth of business and towns was a change in the class structure of society. (1) At the bottom of the scale was a poor working class made up of former serfs who had left the manors. (2) Just above them were the growing number of skilled artisans and tradesmen. (3) But a middle class of businessmen and merchants now appeared. They clamored for privileges previously held by (4) the upper class of landed, wealthy nobles.

These wealthy townsmen began to put up fine houses and buy the luxuries that were now available. Their representatives were called to attend parliaments. The kings were eager to favor a wealthy group that could give them substantial aid in times of need.

The rise of the business class, or bourgeoisie (*bourg* means "town") was one of the most far-reaching changes in the Middle Ages. And the role of the middle class was destined to become even more important as time went on.

CHECK ON YOUR READING

1. Describe early medieval towns.
2. Why were trade, taxes, and charters important?
3. What restrictions were placed on business? interest? profits? trade?
4. What were the purposes of the craft guilds? merchant guilds? the Hanseatic League? medieval fairs?
5. Summarize the class structure of the medieval town.

4. The Italian Cities and the Beginning of the Renaissance

Importance of the Italian Towns · We have already seen that the Italian towns were the first to become important. During the disorder of the early Middle Ages some of these towns set up governments under their local dukes. Then during the long struggle between the emperors and the Popes (p. 155) many towns were able to achieve complete independence. In the fourteenth and fifteenth centuries it was these Italian cities which led in the revival of learning and art which we call the *Renaissance*.

Italy at the beginning of the fourteenth century was still divided into three zones. In the extreme south was the kingdom of the Two Sicilies (Naples). In the central portion were the States of the Church,

The Doge's Palace · *This elegant pink marble palace reflects the wealth of Venice. Note the domes of St. Mark's Cathedral.*

stretching diagonally across the peninsula. To the north and west lay a group of city-states, chief among which were Venice, Florence, Milan, and Genoa.

The Government of Venice · Venice was called a republic, but it was really an *oligarchy* (p. 55). Its constitution changed from time to time, but after 1310 the chief governing body was a Council of Ten, elected annually by the Great Council (resembling a senate). The *Doge*, or duke, of Venice was the nominal head of the state. Government affairs were conducted with no public discussion of political questions. But the Council of Ten ruled efficiently. Since the state and the people were prosperous, the citizens were satisfied.

Venice and Its Rivals · The Venetians manufactured glass, cloth, silk, and leather products. But the greatness of the city was built on its commerce. It became the chief exchange center in the Mediterranean. In order to keep this supremacy, the city made many laws favorable to its own shipping. Venice also forced as much of the trade of other cities as possible to flow through its port. Heavy duties were imposed on incoming and outgoing goods. Sometimes Venice itself bought the goods in order to sell them again at higher prices. The city fought successfully with its chief commercial rival, Genoa, as well as with other towns, including Florence and Milan.

The Italian cities were very jealous of one another. They were constantly at war over boundaries, rights, tolls, and trade. Moreover, there was frequent strife within the towns themselves because of feuds be-

Lorenzo the Magnificent, a Portrait by Vasari · *Lorenzo de' Medici was a great patron of arts and letters. He made Florence a city of great beauty and culture.*

to govern well and even to patronize artists and literary men who brought honor to the state.

The Republic of Florence · The history of Florence differs from that of Venice and the northern despotisms like Milan. Florence was a republic, under the control of the representatives of the guilds. All classes claimed a right to share in the government. This led to many changes in the constitution and to a constant scramble for office by inexperienced men. The result was much confusion and frequent revolution. When one party got the upper hand, it drove the defeated faction out of the city. Exile was a terrible punishment to those who loved their native city.

Florence Ruled by the Medici · In 1434 Cosimo de' Medici, a wealthy banker, got control of the government. Though he retained the republican forms, he took the real power of the state into his own hands. By secretly controlling the selection of city officials he governed without letting it seem that the people had lost their privileges. Cosimo taxed the wealthy, but was lenient toward the lower classes and the peasants of the neighboring countryside.

The most distinguished member of the house of Medici was Lorenzo the Magnificent (d. 1492). Under his rule Florence not only prospered in industry and commerce, but also reached the height of its glory in art and literature. Lorenzo was a sincere admirer of men of genius and generously supported them. As a result Florence abounds with beautiful churches, monasteries, and public buildings. Marvelous works of art fill the Florentine museums today. They show that the Italian genius never reached a higher expression than it did in Florence under the rule of the despots.

tween lordly families or opposing political factions. These sometimes led to revolution and the exile of the defeated group.

The Italian Despots · The towns frequently fell into the hands of strong rulers, or despots, much like the old Greek tyrants. If a usurper could establish himself firmly in power, his rule sometimes passed to his descendants. Thus arose such famous family despotisms as those of the Visconti in Milan or the Medici in Florence.

The position of the despot was apt to be insecure because of other ambitious leaders who might wish to overthrow him. There are many tales of the unbelievable cruelty of the Italian despots. But some of these rulers saw that it was to their own advantage

The Restoration of Rome · During this time Rome was likewise being transformed. For over seventy years (1305–1377) the Popes had been Frenchmen, and the papal palace had been at Avignon in France. When the Pontiffs once more took up their residence in the ancient capital, they found Rome in a neglected and dilapidated condition. For years they were able to do nothing to restore it, since the Church was weakened by the existence of a rival line of Popes, who continued to live in their palace at Avignon.

After forty years this quarrel (the Great Schism, p. 215) came to an end, and the European nations once more acknowledged the Pope at Rome as the true head of the Church. There was great enthusiasm for restoring the glory of the ancient mother city. Architects and painters were handsomely paid by the Popes to erect and adorn magnificent buildings, and learned men were commissioned to collect a great library for the papal residence.

St. Peter's and the Vatican · The old basilica of St. Peter's was gradually torn down, and the present cathedral, with its vast dome and great wings, took its place. The Lateran Palace, where the government of the Church had been located for a thousand years, was deserted. A new palace, the Vatican, was built to the right of St. Peter's and was added to by successive Popes. This massive building, with its innumerable rooms, was adorned by the most gifted of the Italian artists. Its museum contains the choicest collection of Greek and Greco-Roman sculpture in existence. The great Vatican library possesses many priceless and rare manuscripts.

CHECK ON YOUR READING

1. *Describe the governments of Venice and Florence.*
2. *Why was Rome neglected and dilapidated in 1377?*
3. *What was done to restore Rome?*

5. How Commerce Led to Exploration

Commerce Leads to Exploration · By the fifteenth century there was a far greater demand in Europe for foreign goods than its merchants could supply. The gradual growth of *world* commerce began when enterprising western Europeans determined that they would no longer be dependent upon Moslem traders and Italian merchants. They broke free from the Mediterranean and decided to seek for themselves new routes to the riches of the East. This resolve eventually led to the exploration by Europeans of the whole globe, most of which was unknown at that time.

The Greeks and Romans had learned much through trade with countries bordering upon the Mediterranean. But the size of their ships and the instruments for navigation restricted their area of exploration. They therefore knew little about the world beyond southern Europe, northern Africa, and western Asia. And even the little they knew had since been forgotten. But the Crusades brought many Europeans for the first time as far east as Egypt and Syria. The luxuries they found there made them think about the lands much farther off, from which these products came.

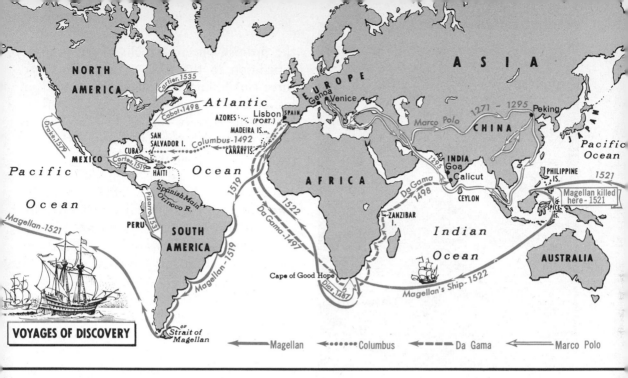

 VOYAGES OF DISCOVERY

Magellan · · · · · · · Columbus · - - - - Da Gama ← — — Marco Polo

Voyages of Discovery · Who journeyed to China?   the Cape of Good Hope?
Calicut?   San Salvador?   New England?   Mexico?   Peru?   the St. Lawrence?
the Philippines?   How did each of these affect history?

The Travels of Marco Polo · By the thirteenth century we begin to have stories of travelers who made their way into Asia and visited the court of the Great Khan, the ruler of the Mongolian Empire (p. 145). About 1260 two Venetian merchants, the Polo brothers, visited China and were kindly received by the emperor at Peking. On a second journey Marco Polo, the son of one of them, went along. Marco lived for twenty years in China and other parts of Asia. When he returned to Venice in 1295, he wrote an account of his experiences. His description of the gold of Japan and the spice markets of the Moluccas and Ceylon greatly excited his readers.

Explorations of the Portuguese · By the middle of the fourteenth century mariners from Portugal had discovered the

Canary Islands, and Madeira and the Azores were also known. During the fifteenth century Portuguese expeditions ventured farther and farther down the west coast of Africa.

At last, in 1487, Bartholomeu Dias reached the southern tip of the continent and rounded the Cape of Good Hope. Eleven years later (1498) Vasco da Gama sailed around the cape and up the east coast of Zanzibar. Then, aided by an Arab pilot, he crossed the Indian Ocean and reached Calicut, in Hindustan (India).

Portugal's Direct Route to the East · The desire to obtain spices was at this time the main reason for the exploration of the globe. Spices were essential to flavor and preserve food.

Up to this time the Moslem merchants had enjoyed a monopoly of the spice trade.

185

Aztec Goldwork · *This superbly wrought breastplate and mask of the god of Death was found by a Mexican archaeologist in 1931.*

They were not powerful enough, however, to prevent the Portuguese from making treaties with the native princes of India and establishing trading stations at Goa and elsewhere. In 1512 the Portuguese reached Java and the Moluccas. Portugal now had become the greatest sea power in Europe and had secured a direct route by which spices reached Lisbon.

The Discovery of America (1492) · A number of informed people in the Middle Ages knew that the earth is a globe. Indeed, the chief authority on the form and size of the earth was the ancient astronomer Ptolemy, who lived about 150 A.D. But no one suspected that western continents lay between Europe and Asia.

In 1492 an experienced Genoese navigator, Christopher Columbus, persuaded the Spanish queen, Isabella, to sponsor an expedition to the East. He got together three small ships and started westward on his journey. Thirty-two days from the time he left the Canary Islands, he came to the island of San Salvador. Going on farther he discovered the islands of Cuba and Haiti.

Then he returned to Spain with tales of his marvelous discoveries. Later he made three more expeditions and sailed down the coast of South America as far as the Orinoco. He died believing that he had explored the Indies and the coast of Asia.

Further Spanish Expeditions · In 1519–1522 an expedition headed by Magellan succeeded in sailing around the globe. Magellan himself was killed in the Philippines.

In 1519 Cortés began the Spanish conquests in the western world by subduing the Aztec empire in Mexico. A few years later Pizarro established the Spanish power in Peru by conquering the Incas. The great wealth from her western lands now gave Spain the lead over Portugal as the greatest European sea power.

By 1600 the Spanish Main (the northern coast of South America) was frequently visited by mariners who were merchants, slavers, and pirates. Many of these adventurers came from England, and it is to them that England owed the beginning of her commercial success. We shall see later how the exploration of the globe led to world commerce and vast empires.

CHECK ON YOUR READING

1. *How did commerce lead to exploration?*
2. *How did Portugal come to dominate the Eastern trade?*
3. *What was the significance of Columbus? Magellan? Cortés? Pizarro?*

Learning Activities

Think about the chapter

1. What was going on in England and France at the time of the Third Crusade? (See Chapter 11.)

2. Why are towns important for the advancement of civilization? Why did the Italian towns have a head start on towns in other parts of Europe?

3. How did the Atlantic come to replace the Mediterranean as the center of trade?

4. In your opinion which of the voyages of exploration was most significant? Why?

5. *Map study:* Locate on a map the routes by which the Crusaders traveled to the Holy Land. From what places on their routes would they be likely to learn the most?

6. *Map study:* On a map of Europe and the Near East locate (1) the chief Italian cities, (2) the important Hanseatic League towns, (3) the overland trading routes within Europe, and (4) the sea routes between Europe and the Near East.

Go beyond the text

7. What similarities and differences between medieval craft guilds and modern trade unions can you point out?

8. What was the Children's Crusade?

9. Who was Machiavelli? What does the word "Machiavellian" mean today?

10. Describe the ships and navigating equipment used by the early explorers.

11. Describe a medieval fair. What goods were sold? What entertainment was given?

Follow up your special interests

12. Choose one of the events of the Crusades and write it up as a news article.

13. Prepare a poster showing the results of the Crusades.

14. Make a collection of pictures to show what some of the medieval towns mentioned in this chapter look like today.

READ FURTHER

Basic readings: (1) BAUER and PEYSER, *How Music Grew*, Chaps. 8–9. (2) CHEYNEY, *Readings in English History*, Chap. 9. (3) CHEYNEY, *World History of Art*, Chap. 14. (4) HOFFMAN, *News of the World*, Nos. 21, 23–25. (5) Life's *Picture History of Western Man*, Part IV, "The Glory of Venice"; Part V, "Age of Exploration." (6) ROBINSON, *Readings in European History*, Chaps. 15, 18. (7) SCOTT, HYMA, NOYES, *Readings in Medieval History*, Secs. 11–12, 14, 21. (8) VAN LOON, *Story of Mankind*, pp. 174–205. (9) Year's *Pictorial History*, pp. 158–162.

Special accounts: (10) K. GIBSON, *The Goldsmith of Florence*. A book of great craftsmen and their work. (11) G. HARTMAN, *Medieval Days and Ways*. (12) H. LAMB, *The Crusades*. (13) D. MILLS, *The Middle Ages*. (14) *National Geographic*, "Crusader Lands Revisited," December, 1954.

Fiction and biography: (15) T. COSTAIN, *The Black Rose*. Two English boys, inspired by lectures by Roger Bacon, travel to China. (16) W. DAVIS, *The Beauty of the Purple*. How imperial Constantinople repulsed the Saracens. (17) W. DAVIS, *God Wills It*. The Crusades. (18) F. DONAUER, *The Long Defense*. Rivalry of Genoa and Venice and the final downfall of Constantinople. (19) A. HEWES, *A Boy of the Lost Crusade*. Roland Arnot comes to Syria with a monk to find his Crusader father. (20) A. HEWES, *Spice and the Devil's Cave*. An Arabian girl plays a part in Vasco da Gama's voyage around the Cape of Good Hope, "the devil's cave." (21) L. LAMPREY, *In the Days of the Guild*. Fictionalized account of the various activities in the medieval towns. (22) W. SCOTT, *The Talisman*. Saladin and Richard the Lion-Hearted are the main characters. (23) S. SHELLABARGER, *The Prince of Foxes*. The intrigues of the Italian princes under the Borgias—for good readers.

Beginnings of the Modern World

1200 1800

B.C. A.D.

4000   2000

*T*HE RISE OF CITIES, the development of trade, and contacts with Oriental civilizations stirred Europe. By 1500 the older ways and ideas of the Middle Ages were being challenged by the new. Scholars turned again to study the civilizations of the Greeks and Romans in a revival of learning. There were new inventions and startling scientific discoveries. Art flourished. Historians call this surging period the "Renaissance" or "Rebirth" of civilization.

At the same time the ferment of change was at work within the most powerful institution in medieval Europe, the Christian Church. Reformers criticized its theories and practices. Some protesting groups actually broke away. In Germany Martin Luther, supported by the Princes, led the revolt. It spread to Switzerland under Zwingli and Calvin. In England the Tudor rulers established a separate national church. But as the Protestant Reformation spread through northern and western Europe the Catholic Church launched a great Counter-Reformation under the leadership of the Jesuits and the Council of Trent.

For over a hundred years terrible wars raged. Philip of Spain fought against England and the Netherlands. French Protestants struggled against French Catholics. Many nations engaged in a fierce and bloody religious war on German soil. Finally the wars became cruel struggles for worldly power.

By 1500 national states such as we know them today were firmly established in Europe. And they fought for power and land. King Louis XIV of France was the supreme "divine right" ruler in the seventeenth century. In an age of absolutism he was considered the model for other autocrats to follow. However, when the English kings tried to rule without considering the wishes of their people, there was revolution. At first the English established a Commonwealth under Oliver Cromwell. Later they restored the monarchy but made it subject to the will of the people. Meanwhile, the rulers of Russia, Prussia and Austria fought for position and power.

As the European nations struggled on the Continent, they also sought land and wealth in India and America. Spain and Portugal led the way in exploration and trade. They were soon rivaled by the Dutch, and then by the English and the French. By 1763, however, the English had defeated the French for the struggle for control of India and North America.

But England was not able to keep all her colonies. Restrictive trade policies led to revolt of the English colonists in America. Aided by the French they won their war for independence.

13

How Europe Regained the Past and Made New Progress

KEY WORDS AND DATES

Chaucer	Leonardo da Vinci
Dante	Copernicus
scientific method	Galileo
Peter Abelard	Newton
Thomas Aquinas	1492
scholasticism	Ferdinand
Roger Bacon	Isabella
Petrarch	1453
humanism	Hapsburgs
Renaissance	Charles V
Florence	Francis I

WE HAVE SEEN HOW, after centuries of ignorance and disorder, the growth of towns stimulated the people of Europe to many new kinds of activity. In this chapter we shall see how some of the features of our modern civilization emerged in the medieval world: (1) Modern languages developed. (2) An interest in learning revived. (3) Universities had their beginnings among the groups of professors and students who gathered to discuss law, philosophy, and theology.

(4) Some bold thinkers proclaimed new and startling truths, which they had discovered as the result of experiment. (5) New and useful inventions were made, among them the art of printing. (6) Scholars recovered some of the literature of the Greeks and Romans. Having caught up with the past, people pressed forward in their thinking to the fuller and richer life of modern times.

(7) One of the most important features of the change from medieval to modern life was the growth of closely knit nations out of the confused feudal territories of western Europe. We have seen the beginnings of France and England. Here we shall trace the development of other new national states.

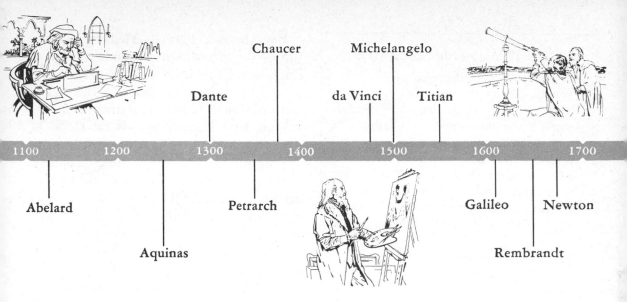

Abelard | Aquinas | Dante | Petrarch | Chaucer | da Vinci | Michelangelo | Titian | Galileo | Rembrandt | Newton

1100   1200   1300   1400   1500   1600   1700

1. Beginnings of Modern Languages

Contrast between Written and Spoken Language · Today we use one language for speaking or writing. But this has not always been the case. In some countries there has been a *spoken* tongue for ordinary conversation, and an older and more elegant language for writing books and other formal works. This is still true in China.

One major difference between *written* and *spoken* speech is that a spoken language changes more. New words are added and meanings are altered. Abbreviations and slang sometimes gradually become a part of the language. The written language, changes more slowly because those who use it take pride in holding to the fixed rules and standards of the past.

Importance of Latin in Western Civilization · Latin was the language used throughout the Roman Empire. It continued to be used in the Church both in its services and in its administration. The standard version of the European Bible was in Latin. Latin was also the language of the civil law.

Many terms which we use today show how it has persisted in law, in medicine, and in natural science.

All scholarly books were written in Latin for centuries. It was not until 1700 in Germany that more books were published in German than in Latin. In England such famous men as Francis Bacon, John Milton, and Sir Isaac Newton wrote some of their important works in Latin.

A universal language like Latin was of great service. It enabled the Pope to keep in touch with the clergy throughout Western Christendom. It made it possible for monks and students to be understood when they went from one country to another. Learned men in all parts of Europe could read one another's books and exchange letters. The Roman law could be understood throughout Europe because every educated person began his training with the study of Latin. Latin, together with Greek, became the basis of a liberal education in the Western world.

How Modern Languages Developed · Though Latin was understood by the educated, most people knew nothing about the ancient tongue. The northern people who overran Europe kept the languages that they were accustomed to. Gradually the vernacular (Latin, *verna,* "household slave") tongues, or the speech of the common people, began to be written down. A literature of the people then developed in the various countries.

The German peoples kept their own particular dialects. From these have come modern German, English, Dutch, Swedish, Norwegian, Danish, and Icelandic. The *Romance* languages (Italian, Spanish, Portuguese, Rumanian, and French) grew from the *spoken* Latin of the soldiers, merchants, and common people.

English and French Medieval Literature · Anglo-Saxon is the oldest form of English. The earliest Anglo-Saxon epic poem, *Beowulf,* dates back to the eighth century. In this long narrative poem the warrior hero Beowulf stands for Good in the great struggle against the dragon Evil.

King Alfred (871–901) translated various Latin works into Anglo-Saxon and encouraged the writing of the *Anglo-Saxon Chronicle.* This was a history of England which was continued down to 1154. It is not until the fourteenth century that we come to the first great English poet, Chaucer (*c.* 1340–1400). His *Canterbury Tales* are still read with pleasure.

The French took the lead in prose and poetry from the eleventh to the thirteenth century. Their first great works were also epics, dealing with the heroes of the Frankish people. The most famous was the *Song of Roland,* which related the marvelous exploits of one of Charlemagne's generals. The chief interest of these romances for the modern reader is the picture they give of life in the Feudal Age.

Knighthood and Chivalry · The heroes of medieval poetry were the knights, with their daring adventures and their romances. In an earlier chapter we learned how a man became a knight (p. 127). The knights formed a special class, with a code of conduct supposed to be fitting to their high order. It was an ideal society, to which even a king was proud to belong.

The knight was a brave Christian soldier, and must defend the Church on all occasions. He must fight the infidel Moslems with all his power. He must be the champion of right against injustice. He must aid the weak and helpless and give generously to the poor. He must never break his word and must be faithful to his lord. He must defend his lady and her honor always. These standards of conduct, according to which a Christian soldier and gentleman must live, are called *chivalry*.

King Arthur and His Knights · In the latter part of the twelfth century a famous cycle of romances developed. These celebrated the deeds of King Arthur and his Knights of the Round Table. They were very popular in western Europe, and some of the characters are still familiar to us today. Arthur was supposed to have been an early king or general of Britain who fought the invading Saxons.

Sir Thomas Malory, an Englishman, wrote the stories of the hero and his knights —Tristan, Lancelot, Percival, and others— in a book called *Morte d'Arthur* ("Death of Arthur"). In the nineteenth century Tennyson, in his *Idylls of the King*, wrote a poetic version of the legends of Arthur.

The Troubadours · It was in the songs of the *troubadours* of southern France that the ideals of chivalry found their fullest expression. These songs give a picture of a gay and polished society at the courts of the feudal princes. The rulers encouraged the poets, and many of them became troubadours themselves.

The troubadours sang their verses to the accompaniment of the lute. They traveled about from one court to another in France, Germany, and Italy and thus greatly influenced the poetry of those countries. In Germany the chivalric poets were called *Minnesingers* (from the German *Minne*, the poetic word for "love").

Dante and Italian Poetry · The first great name in Italian literature is that of Dante (1265–1321). Dante was a scholar familiar with the philosophy of Aristotle and with theology and science. He was also a dreamer, a mystic, and a loyal Catholic.

Dante Alighieri · *This portrait of Italy's national poet was painted by his friend Giotto. Research: In the* Divine Comedy *who guided Dante through hell? paradise?*

Dante admired the language of the people. He wrote his immortal *Divine Comedy* in his native Italian so that all might be able to read it. In this poem Dante is led through hell and purgatory up to heaven, and on the way sees and converses with the great men of the past.

CHECK ON YOUR READING

1. *Contrast written and spoken language.*
2. *Why was Latin so important?*
3. *How did Romance and Germanic languages develop?*
4. *Give examples of the early literature of England, France, and Italy.*

2. Medieval Science and Education

What We Mean by Modern Science · You sometimes hear it said that we live in a Scientific Age. *Science* is a general term which really means "knowledge" (Latin, *scientia*). The word with us has come to refer especially to those branches of study whose data can be observed and measured and about which certain facts can be proved. Among these are the study of the stars (astronomy), of the earth (geology), of animals (zoology), and of plants (botany). We also study the elements of which matter is composed (chemistry) and the properties and behavior of matter (physics).

The method of studying these subjects includes examining data with an unbiased mind, testing hypotheses, weighing, measuring, experimenting, and basing conclusions only on precise knowledge. This is called the *scientific method* of study. It dares to ask *Why?* It challenges superstition in all its forms.

Medieval Science and Superstition · What medieval men considered science was not based on the scientific method. Rather there were fantastic notions about the world, based on authority, fear, old wives' tales, and folklore. People accepted all kinds of stories of magic, and did not consider challenging them. They believed in strange and imaginary animals, such as the unicorn, the phoenix, and dragons. Such superstition was born out of fear and ignorance of the world about them.

Before people could make much progress in learning, they would have to have a new and critical attitude toward what they heard. They would have to observe for themselves the things about them instead of accepting, without question, everything that they were told.

Astrology and Alchemy · Two medieval "sciences" illustrate the differences between that time and ours. The study of the stars was called *astrology*. Its purpose was not to gather exact information, as in *astronomy* today. Rather, the stars were believed to influence a person's character and his fate. The position of the stars and planets at a person's birth supposedly determined the kind of temperament he would have and the kind of trade he would follow. Astrology was taught in the universities because it was believed that physicians should choose times when the stars were favorable for particular kinds of treatment.

The Alchemist · *Which objects can you identify? What gives this scene an air of mystery or magic? What did the alchemist seek?*

Medieval *alchemy* was as different from modern *chemistry* as astrology from our astronomy. The chief aim of alchemy was to turn less valuable metals into gold. Though they never succeeded in this aim, the alchemists performed many experiments and learned a good deal about metals.

Renewed Interest in Learning · The early Middle Ages are sometimes miscalled the Dark Ages because people seemed not to be interested in learning and progress. Ignorance was widespread, even in the Church. Most people could neither read nor write. But by the eleventh century there were a few scholars and historical writers. A number of schools developed, connected with cathedrals and monasteries.

With the growth of towns and commercial contacts with the more cultured East opportunities for learning increased. There were many more teachers who attracted students to hear them. The chief subjects were "grammar" (or the study of Latin writings in order to acquire a good Latin style in speaking and writing), philosophy, astronomy, and theology.

One of the most famous of medieval teachers was Peter Abelard (1079–1142), who lectured at the cathedral school at Paris. Abelard was a master of logic (dialectic), or the art of reasoning and debate. The main subjects of discussion were problems of philosophy and theology. Instead of copying out and accepting the statements of the authors of the past, Abelard taught that the way to arrive at truth was to examine, question, and discuss subjects with an open mind—in short, to use one's reason. But Abelard was ahead of his time. This attitude later got him into trouble with the Church, which held that some matters were not to be settled by human reason but were to be accepted by faith.

The First Universities · By the end of the twelfth century the teachers in Paris had become so numerous that they organized themselves into a guild to protect their interests. This union of professors was called by the Latin word for corporation in the Middle Ages, *universitas*. From this term our word *university* is derived. Kings and Popes both favored the universities. They granted teachers and students many legal privileges, such as freedom from arrest except for a serious offense.

About the same time that a university was developing in Paris, other institutions of learning were growing up at Bologna in Italy and at Oxford in England. At Paris the chief attention was given to theology, while Bologna became a famous center for the study of law, both civil and canon (church) law. Cambridge University, as well as numerous institutions in France, Italy, and Spain, developed in the thirteenth century. The German universities were established in the fourteenth and fifteenth centuries.

What a Medieval University Was Like · The students of a medieval university were of all ages from thirteen to forty. There were at first no university buildings. When the professors and students did not like the treatment they received in one town, they could easily move to another. The lectures were held in hired halls. Often the students had to sit on the floor. There were few textbooks. The lecturer read from his book, line by line, commenting as he read. The language used was Latin. The students could, if they wished, take down his words and make a textbook of their own.

Influence of Aristotle's Works · Gradually separate faculties, or departments, were organized. These included the liberal arts, law, medicine, and theology. Most of the

At the University of Paris · *The teacher leads his scholars in discussion. Scepters held by three students contain holy relics. Note the caps and gowns.*

courses of study were devoted to the explanation of some one of the numerous works of Aristotle. So confident were medieval thinkers that the Greek philosopher had discovered the truth in every branch of knowledge that his conclusions were accepted without question.

It was curious that the ideas of a pagan philosopher were so completely accepted by Christian authorities. But the medieval teachers were impressed so by his learning and logic that two of the great religious masters of the time, Albertus Magnus (d. 1280) and Thomas Aquinas (d. 1274), prepared elaborate commentaries on his works. In these they reconciled his ideas with the doctrines of Christianity. Thus Aristotle was accepted by the Church as an authority not only in philosophy, but in all branches of science.

Scholasticism is the name given to the beliefs and method of reasoning of the medieval religious teachers and writers. They discussed and wrote about God's nature, man's soul, the essence of things, and many other deep matters.

University Degrees · When the student had completed his studies at the university, he was examined by the professors. If successful he was admitted to the guild of teachers and became a "master." A university degree in the Middle Ages was, therefore, really a license to teach. Many students who did not desire to become professors, nevertheless liked the honorary title and so were called masters of arts. The titles of *master*, *doctor*, and *professor* all had about the same meaning in the thirteenth century.

The degree of bachelor of arts, which comes at the completion of our four-year college course today, also originated in the Middle Ages. A bachelor was one who had passed part of his examinations and was permitted to teach certain elementary subjects before he finished the work for the master's degree. Thus in the medieval universities, as with us, the bachelor's degree (B.A.) was lower in rank than the master's degree (M.A.). It was necessary to study for at least six years before becoming a master.

CHECK ON YOUR READING

1. *Contrast medieval and modern science.*
2. *Describe medieval universities: origin, locations, methods, degrees.*
3. *What did these men contribute to learning: Abelard, Aristotle, Aquinas?*

3. Progress in Inventions

Roger Bacon Urges Experimentation · As early as the thirteenth century some scholars were condemning the practice of relying entirely on Aristotle. One of these was an English monk, Roger Bacon (d. 1294). To Bacon there appeared to be various stumbling blocks in the way of reaching the truth. Among these were three arguments often used by those who wished to hold on to old ways: (1) "This is the way of our ancestors. The old ways are best. Beware of the new." (2) "This is the custom. We've always done it this way." (3) "This is the common view. Why be different?" These arguments still persist.

Bacon declared that men should study the everyday things around them. They should rely less on what they are told and more on what they can find out for themselves. "Experiment starts us on the way to marvelous inventions which will change the face of the world," said Bacon. He predicted that the time would come when men would be able to fly, and would have carriages which needed no horses to draw them. He also foretold the development of suspension bridges and of ships that would move swiftly without oars.

Progress in Mathematics · Inspired by those who dared to think for themselves, men began to make great advances in knowledge and invention. They owed much to the Moslems, who handed on to Europe what they had learned from the East and much that they had added to it. Algebra was introduced. Arabic numerals replaced the awkward Roman letters which had stood for numbers. The Arabic numerals greatly simplified all arithmetic because they were easier both to write and to read (for example 88 instead of lxxxviii, or 49 instead of xlix). Thus mathematics increasingly became the basis for the scientific thinking which was to follow.

An Age of Inventions · Progress was made along many other lines. (1) Mirrors and lenses began to come into use. We hear for the first time of spectacles to assist failing eyesight. Later, lenses were used to make microscopes and telescopes, which greatly aided progress in science.

(2) The compass helped men to find their way at sea and encouraged geographical exploration. While the Chinese seem to have known about the compass, the fact that a magnetized needle, when free, will turn to the north was probably discovered by Europeans. Sailors could now tell in what direction they were going, even on the darkest night when there were no stars to guide them. (3) The invention of the astrolabe (the ancestor of the modern sextant) was also significant. With it mariners in clear weather could find the positions of their ships by observing the sun and stars.

(4) Quite a different type of discovery was that of gunpowder. This was an explosive composed of sulphur, saltpeter, and charcoal. Its discovery revolutionized methods of warfare. Bows, arrows, and lances were given up, and firearms took their place. Metal armor was discarded since it was found to be of no protection against bullets. Stone castles could not withstand the blasts of cannon, and the old town walls offered but a feeble means of defense. Kings began to live in unprotected palaces, and towns turned to other means than their medieval walls to secure safety.

Gutenberg's Printing Press · *Johann Gutenberg made brass moulds and matrices by which type could be cast. His press at Mainz, Germany, produced the first Bible ever printed.*

Printing Is Invented · (5) The invention which proved to be of widest benefit in improving the life of mankind was that of printing with movable type on paper. In the Middle Ages the only copies of books available had been slowly written out by hand on parchment (sheepskin). This parchment was so expensive that the invention of printing would not have greatly increased the number of books had not a cheaper substitute been found. Paper fitted this need. The art of making paper had been learned from the Chinese by the Arabs as early as the eighth century. Paper had become so common in Europe by the thirteenth and fourteenth centuries that it was already replacing parchment before the invention of printing.

With printing by movable type on paper, copies of the ancient books now increased in number and new books were written. The first book of any considerable size to be printed was the Bible, which appears to have been completed at Mainz in the year 1456. A year later the Mainz Psalter was finished.

By the year 1500 there appear to have been at least forty printing presses in the various towns in Germany, France, Italy, the Netherlands, and England. It is estimated that these presses had already turned out eight million volumes. Greek and Latin manuscripts were printed, and there was now no danger that the works of the ancient authors would be lost again.

Great libraries were formed containing thousands of volumes. More people began to read the same things, so that there grew up a common body of knowledge on many subjects.

This accumulated knowledge was the very basis of civilization, for it was the written record of what men had thought and accomplished from earliest times. Men no longer had to depend on what they were told. They could read for themselves. They could follow new discoveries and learn about the ideas of educated men.

> **CHECK ON YOUR READING**
>
> 1. *What "stumbling blocks" did Bacon encounter? How would he overcome them?*
> 2. *What progress was made in mathematics?*
> 3. *Cite five great inventions. How did each affect civilization?*
> 4. *Why was the invention of printing especially important to a revival of learning?*

4. The Revival of Learning: Renaissance

Petrarch, Founder of Humanism (1304–1374) · Dante wrote his great work, the *Divine Comedy*, in his native tongue. But another Italian, Petrarch, fell so in love with the books of the ancient Romans that he preferred to use Latin for his prose works. He composed imaginary letters to Cicero and other classic authors whom he greatly admired, and even letters to his own friends, in elegant Latin. He eagerly sought for the works of his favorite authors and copied them for his own library. Petrarch's enthusiasm was largely responsible for the development of a new movement for the study of classic literature. It was called *Humanism*, that is, the study of writings (the humanities) which deal with man's nature and interests rather than with religious subjects.

The Humanists Revive Greek · At the end of the fourteenth century Greek professors began to come to Italy to lecture. A great interest in the study of Greek now developed. Scholars often went to Constantinople and brought back copies of all the ancient writers they could find. By 1430, after a thousand years of neglect, Greek books were once more known and prized in the West.

The Humanists valued the ancient literature for its content, as well as for the beauty of its language and literary form. To some it gave a new idea of the value of the present world. This contrasted sharply with the medieval emphasis on the vanity of earthly things and the importance of the life to come.

The Renaissance · The name *Renaissance*, meaning "rebirth," has been given to this period by some historians. This is because the interest in arts and letters indicates that Europe had at last awakened from a long "winter sleep" of ignorance. The term also includes earlier signs of enterprise and renewed mental vigor. We have already discussed many—the development of towns, the study of Roman law, the founding of universities, and progress in science and invention.

The interest in the Greek and Roman writers is also called the Revival of Learning. Not only was part of the ancient literature recovered, but it was carefully studied. Copies which had been ignorantly made were corrected. Improved texts of ancient writings were prepared for printing. New grammars and dictionaries were compiled, and literary form was given great attention. This study laid the foundations of literary criticism and *philology* (study of language).

Greek and Latin versions of the Bible and the writings of the early Christian Fathers also were reread, and better texts and commentaries were prepared. After the discovery and re-editing of classic literature came the formation of famous libraries by Popes, princes, and scholars. As time went on, the universities gave up the exclusive study of Aristotle and included other Greek and Latin works in their lectures.

The Revival of Learning was more than the recovery of ancient manuscripts. It was the discovery of the ancient world. A genuine enthusiasm for classic literature spread throughout Europe. It gave men a knowledge of the great achievements of the past and bridged the gap between their own time and that of classic civilization. Having caught up with the past, they were now ready to progress more rapidly in scholarship, in literature, philosophy, and history.

Italian Art of the Renaissance · Italy took the lead in art as well as literature in the Renaissance period. In the fifteenth and sixteenth centuries Italian art reached such a high degree of perfection that it set the standards for all western Europe. Florence was the great center of artistic activity in the fifteenth century. The foremost sculptors and painters either were natives of Florence or did their best work there.

During the first half of the century there were a number of outstanding sculptors, among whom were Donatello and Ghiberti. When Michelangelo first saw Donatello's lifelike statue of "St. George," he exclaimed, "March!" And Ghiberti's bronze doors of the baptistery at Florence were called by Leonardo da Vinci worthy of being the gates to Paradise.

Florence reached the height of her glory as an art center during the reign of Lorenzo the Magnificent (p. 183). With his death (1492), Rome took the leadership in art.

Renaissance Art at Its Height · During the sixteenth century the art of the Renaissance reached its highest development. Among the names of this period three stand out above all others. (1) Leonardo da Vinci (1452–1519) was a master in the three arts of architecture, painting, and sculpture. He was a musician, poet, engineer, and inventor as well. His great paintings include "The Last Supper" and the "Mona Lisa." But his great influence on the art of his time came from his many-sidedness, his originality, and his unflagging interest in the discovery and application of new methods.

(2) Michelangelo (1475–1564) was appointed architect for the rebuilding of St. Peter's cathedral in Rome. His frescoes and his ceiling paintings of the Sistine Chapel in the Vatican are famous. And his statue of "David," rising eighteen feet high in the Florentine square, is a masterpiece of sculpture.

(3) Raphael (1483–1520) likewise left behind him magnificent frescoes. But his Madonna paintings, among which is the beautiful "Sistine Madonna," caused him to be called the "Prince of Italian painters."

Another important center of artistic activity in the sixteenth century was Venice. Here the "material splendor and freedom" of the Renaissance were pictured by the great painters Titian, Tintoretto, and Veronese. They achieved for color what the Florentines had done for form.

Titian became so famous for his portraits that the Emperor Charles V made him court painter and named him Knight of the Golden Spur. His name has come down to us in the word "titian," a warm red-yellow hue of which he was master.

Tintoretto's painting of "Paradise," measuring 30 x 74 feet with over 500 figures, is the largest oil canvas in the world. Veronese was known for his "cool, clear color harmonies." The "Triumph of Venice" is one of his best.

Painting in the Northern Countries · It was natural that artists living in the northern countries of Europe should be attracted to Italy by the fame of its great masters. After studying there they returned home to follow their art in their own fashion. Two Flemish brothers, the Van Eycks, who lived at the beginning of the fifteenth century, improved oil painting by a superior way of mixing their colors.

Later, when painting had reached its height in Italy, the Germans Albrecht Dürer and Hans Holbein the Younger vied

The Sistine Madonna (right) by **Raphael** · *It is now in Dresden. Below is the* Prophet Jeremiah, *by* **Michelangelo,** *a detail from the ceiling of the Sistine Chapel in the Vatican.*

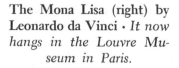

HIEREMIAS

The Mona Lisa (right) by **Leonardo da Vinci** · *It now hangs in the Louvre Museum in Paris.*

with the Italians in the mastery of their art. Dürer is celebrated also for his wonderful woodcuts and exquisite copperplate engravings, a field in which he has never been excelled. Holbein, like Dürer, made many drawings, but is chiefly known for his portrait-painting.

In the seventeenth century Dutch and Flemish masters—especially Rubens and Rembrandt—developed a new and famous school of painting. Van Dyck, another Flemish master, made many notable portraits of historically important persons. In the seventeenth century Spain gave to the world a painter who ranks with the greatest artists of Italy, Velásquez (1599–1660). His genius, like that of Van Dyck, is especially clear in his portraits.

The Beginnings of Modern Science · Modern science may be said to have begun in the sixteenth century. The discovery of the classic literature helped stimulate it, because some of the Greek thinkers had made shrewd and correct guesses as to the workings of nature. But the distinguishing characteristic of the new science was that it based its conclusions not on tradition, but on experiment.

Scientists began to observe, experiment, test, and measure for themselves, with the help of such apparatus as they had, and based their opinions on proved facts. As a result, they sometimes reached conclusions which were in opposition to accepted theories and so found themselves in trouble with the Church. The Church in those days determined what was to be believed not only in religious matters but also in many other fields as well.

The Startling Discovery of Copernicus · Of great assistance to the scientists in their investigations was the progress which was being made in mathematics, physics, and mechanics. In 1543 a Polish astronomer, Copernicus, published a work entitled *Concerning the Revolutions of the Celestial Bodies.* This book announced a startling discovery. Copernicus rejected the Ptolemaic theory of the universe, taught in the universities and upheld by the Church. This theory held that the earth was a fixed body around which the sun and stars revolved. Copernicus said that the *sun* is the center around which the planets, including the earth, revolve. The reason why the heavenly bodies seem to go around the earth each day is that our globe rotates on its axis.

Copernicus had been encouraged to write this book by a cardinal and had dedicated it to the Pope. Nevertheless, Catholic as well as Protestant theologians declared that the new theory contradicted the teachings of the Bible. They therefore condemned the book, and its author was forced to denounce his findings (recant). But we now know that Copernicus was right and that the theologians and universities were wrong.

Galileo and Newton · Two of the great geniuses among the modern scientists were an Italian named Galileo and an Englishman named Newton. Galileo was a mathematician who understood mechanics and optics as well as astronomy. He was also a brilliant lecturer and writer and an inventor who made an air thermometer and an astronomical clock. By the use of a telescope which he had perfected, Galileo could see many heavenly bodies never visible before. He was able also to find the mountains and valleys on the moon, and to watch Jupiter's moons revolving around the planet.

In 1611 Galileo discovered the spots on the sun. As he followed these spots on the moving sphere, he knew that the sun was

Newton Experimenting with Light · *"White" light passing through a prism becomes a rainbow of seven colors. Newton invented the reflecting telescope and developed the calculus.*

Progress in Medical Science · There was much progress in medical knowledge. A way was found to use a thermometer for measuring the temperature of the body. An Italian physician advanced the theory that disease is caused by the presence of living organisms. Another physician pointed out the fact that the operations in the body are chemical, and showed the important relation of medicine to chemistry.

In 1628 an English court physician, William Harvey, published a book in which he announced the discovery of the circulation of the blood. Harvey began his work with an apology for contradicting the older theories on the subject, but described his own experiments and offered many proofs of his daring theories.

The microscope made it possible for the human eye to see the great world of minute things never before beheld by man. Rude and simple microscopes were used as early as the seventeenth century. Leeuwenhoek, a Dutch merchant, improved his lenses so that he discovered (1665) the corpuscles in the blood and the tiny organisms of various kinds found in pond water and elsewhere. This was but the beginning of the marvelous story of what the microscope has revealed to man.

Societies to promote scientific research were founded. Their object was to learn more about the universe by carrying on new investigations and experiments.

not a perfect, unchanging body, as Aristotle had declared. It was a body that rotated on its axis, as Copernicus had said. His desire to have the theory of Copernicus accepted brought him under suspicion. His theories were condemned and he was imprisoned by the church authorities.

The year that Galileo died, a great English mathematician, Isaac Newton (1642–1727), was born. Newton carried forward the work of the earlier astronomers, using his great knowledge of mathematics to aid him. His name became famous through his description of the universal law of *gravitation* (the force, or attraction, that causes bodies to fall and holds the planets in their orbits).

CHECK ON YOUR READING

1. *What is Humanism?*
2. *What developments ought to be included when one uses the term Renaissance?*
3. *What were the great contributions of Copernicus, Galileo, and Newton to scientific knowledge?*

5. The Rise of National States

Appearance of National States · By the sixteenth century *national* states began to appear. The map of Europe about 1500 shows distinct areas with familiar names, such as England, France, Spain, and Portugal. In these countries the feudal lands had been united in the hands of ruling monarchs. In these states the people had a common language, a common literature, and traditions which set them off from their neighbors. They were loyal to the reigning sovereign, who became a symbol of the bonds uniting his subjects. They were no longer mere states; they were *nations*.

We have already seen how England and France developed strong central governments. As the monarchs in these countries became powerful enough to maintain order, business and trade flourished and wealth increased. The kings now had sufficient income to support a standing army and were no longer dependent on the loyalty of feudal vassals.

The Unification of Spain · *What five kingdoms finally merged? Locate the Pyrenees, Madrid, Granada, Palos, and Cadiz.*

Moors Driven out of Spain · Spain, we recall, had been conquered in the eighth century by the Moslem Arabs (p. 136). During the following two hundred years the Arabs had developed there a great civilization. Gradually, however, a number of small Christian kingdoms—Castile, Aragon, Navarre, and Portugal—appeared in northern and western Spain.

A long fight to drive out the "infidel" invaders began. Castile pushed the Moslems back until its kingdom extended to the southern coast and included the great Moorish cities of Cordova and Seville. For two centuries longer the Moors were able to hold the mountainous kingdom of Granada. But in 1492, after a long siege, the Christians captured the city of Granada and destroyed the last remnant of Moslem power in the peninsula.

Spain Becomes a Great European Power · In 1469 the two leading kingdoms in Spain had been united by the marriage of Queen Isabella of Castile to Ferdinand, heir to the crown of Aragon. With the union of Aragon and Castile the importance of Spain as a European power begins.

The year 1492 was a momentous one in Spanish history. It saw not only the final conquest of the Moors, but also the first of the Spanish discoveries in the New World. This opened up prospects of untold wealth beyond the seas. Through the diplomacy of Ferdinand, Spain was also gaining an important position among her European neighbors. The greatness of Spain in the sixteenth century, however, was chiefly due to the riches from her American possessions (p. 186). The looting of Mexican and Peruvian cities' by Cortés and Pizarro and the discovery of silver mines brought fabulous wealth to Spain for a while.

Spain's glory was brief, however, because of her unwise policies. (1) Her income from the New World was wasted in wars. (2) Her economy was completely dominated by the government. Private enterprises were not encouraged. (3) Religious persecution drove the Jews and Moors out of the kingdom. These people were among the most skillful and industrious of the Spanish population.

Portugal as a Sea Power · On the western coast of the Spanish peninsula was Portugal, which established itself as an independent Christian kingdom as early as 1263. Although small in size, Portugal became an important state because of its business enterprise and its explorations and discoveries. In the sixteenth century Portugal, as we have seen, controlled a direct overseas trade between Lisbon and the Far East. For a time it was the leading sea power in Europe.

The Netherlands · The Netherlands, or Low Countries, included seventeen provinces stretching for a hundred miles or more along the coast of the North Sea. These provinces later became the kingdoms of Holland and Belgium. By the fourteenth century there had grown up in this region important manufacturing and trading towns. They included Haarlem, Leiden, Amsterdam, and Rotterdam, in the north, and Ghent, Bruges, and Antwerp, in the south. The immense business carried on by the merchants of these cities brought great wealth to the Low Countries.

In 1384 the county of Flanders had come into the hands of the Duke of Burgundy through marriage, and one by one the provinces were added to his possessions. At the death of Charles the Bold (1477) this region was inherited by his daughter Mary. The marriage of Mary of Burgundy to the emperor Maximilian added these lands to the possessions of the Austrian rulers, whom we shall discuss in a moment.

The Eastern Empire Falls to the Turks (1453) · The Crusades ended in failure, as we have seen, and the last of the Christians were driven out of Syria by 1291. Some years later the Ottoman Turks invaded Asia Minor. They subdued the other Turkish peoples in the eastern-Mediterranean region and built up a strong military state. Gradually they took possession of the provinces of the Eastern Empire until they had all Asia Minor under their control. By 1350 the Empire had been reduced to Constantinople, a part of Thrace, and a narrow strip along the Aegean Sea.

The leaders of the Ottoman Turks, who were called Sultans, were not only great fighters, but able rulers as well. Having secured Asia Minor they crossed the Dardanelles and conquered the Slavic peoples in southeastern Europe. Soon they dominated the Balkan Peninsula. Constantinople, now hemmed in on all sides by the enemy, was helpless. After a long siege the Eastern capital finally surrendered to the Turks in 1453. Constantine's city, after more than a thousand years, fell into the hands of Moslem invaders. The last piece of the ancient Roman Empire disappeared.

After the capture of Constantinople, the Ottoman Turks continued to add to their realms. They took Baghdad and the valleys of the Tigris and Euphrates from the Persian rulers. By 1520 one of their Sultans had conquered Syria and Egypt. He then took the ancient Arab title of Caliph, which signified that he was the head of all orthodox Moslems. The Ottoman Empire lasted until the twentieth century.

EUROPE ABOUT 1560
Boundary of the
Holy Roman Empire
▢ Austrian
Hapsburgs
▨ Spanish
Hapsburgs

Europe about 1560 ·
*Name five of the many
states within the Holy
Roman Empire. What
areas were held by the
Austrian Hapsburgs?
the Spanish?*

The Holy Roman Empire · The Holy Roman Empire in the sixteenth century was still composed of many independent principalities. These two or three hundred states, which the French called the "Germanies," were of every size and character. There were important principalities, ruled by dukes, counts, or margraves. There were ecclesiastical states, in the hands of archbishops, bishops, or abbots. There were *free* cities, such as Nuremberg and Frankfurt, which were as independent as the great duchies of Saxony, Bavaria, and Württemberg. Besides these there were the tiny possessions of the knights, which might be little more than a castle with a wretched village lying at its foot.

The rulers of all these territories jealously guarded their independence, and the emperor had little means of controlling his vassals. The real power was in the hands of the more important lords, seven of whom

had the right to choose the emperor. The seven electors, as they were called, were the Count Palatine of the Rhine, the Duke of Saxony, the Margrave of Brandenburg, the king of Bohemia and the archbishops of Cologne, Mainz, and Trier.

Although the emperors were often succeeded by their sons, the office was not inherited. Each new ruler had to be elected before he could take office. The great nobles who controlled the choice of emperor were thus in a position to bind the candidate by solemn promises not to interfere with their privileges.

The Holy Roman Empire had a national assembly, called the *diet*, composed of the princes and more important nobles. But the rivalries existing among the various states prevented the formation of any policy advantageous to the empire as a whole. The diet met irregularly, first in one town and then another, wherever the emperor happened to be. The Holy Roman Empire had no capital city. The towns were not permitted to send representatives to the diet until 1487. The knights and lesser nobles, who were not members, often refused to be bound by the diet's decisions.

The Title of Emperor Passes to the House of Austria · Rudolf of Hapsburg was chosen emperor in 1273. His family was to play a leading role in European affairs for many centuries. Rudolph established his position by gaining the duchies of Austria and Styria, which later were to become the center of the great Hapsburg possessions. After 1438 the German electors began regularly to choose as emperor the ruler of the Austrian realms. Thus the imperial title

Emperor Charles V, by Titian (1548) · *Though ruler of a vast empire (see map), the tired face and sad eyes reflect the weariness which finally led Charles to abdicate the throne.*

became, to all intents and purposes, hereditary in the Hapsburg line.

But the Hapsburgs were far more interested in increasing their family holdings than in advancing the interests of the empire. It is important to bear in mind that they owed their continued power not to the shadowy title of Emperor, but to the vast territories which the family directly controlled.

Maximilian Lays the Foundation of the Hapsburg Power · There is an old saying that some families fight their way, others intrigue their way, to power. The Hapsburgs married their way. It was Maximilian I (1493–1519) who laid the foundation of the family fortunes by arranging an unusual number of profitable marriages. As a young man, he had married Mary, daughter of Charles the Bold. He thus gained the Burgundian inheritance, especially the Netherlands. His son Philip wed Joanna, the daughter of Ferdinand and Isabella of Spain, adding the prospect of still greater territory for the Hapsburg heirs.

Vast Possessions of Charles V · Philip succeeded his mother as nominal sovereign of the Netherlands at an early age. Here in 1500 a son, Charles, was born to Philip and Joanna. Charles was to rule over a wider empire than had ever fallen to any Christian prince. All through his youth, lands and titles showered upon the young Charles. At six he inherited from his father the crowns of the Netherlands and Castile. At sixteen, on the death of his grandfather Ferdinand, there came to him the far-flung Spanish possessions in Europe and America. When he was nineteen, Maximilian died, leaving the great Hapsburg realms in his hands. In 1519 he was elected Holy Roman Emperor, and he ruled as Charles V for thirty-seven years.

By this election a king of Spain who had been brought up in the Netherlands became the ruler of the confused territories of the Germanies. It was a bewildering task for the young prince to govern such widely scattered dominions, with their different peoples. Although they now had the same ruler, they had no love for one another and no natural ties. The problems which confronted Charles greatly taxed his energy, and his relations with other European powers kept him almost constantly at war.

How Francis I and Charles V Fought over Italy · Italy in the sixteenth century, like Germany, was still hopelessly divided. The Italians would never lay aside their quarrels and combine, even against an invader. Knowing this, the various European monarchs made continual attempts to add portions of the peninsula to their domains. So it was that Italy became a battleground of European powers and remained disunited until 1870.

In 1515, Francis I came to the French throne. Francis was a man of gracious manner and chivalrous conduct, and his proudest title was "the Gentleman King." Like his contemporaries Pope Leo X, son of Lorenzo de' Medici, and Henry VIII of England, he was a generous patron of artists and writers. Francis, who was eager to win military glory, opened his reign with a brilliant victory. He led his troops into Italy over a mountain pass which had hitherto been believed too steep for cavalry and defeated the Swiss—who were hired by the Pope—at Marignano. He then occupied Milan and made terms with Leo X.

The Pope agreed that Francis should retain Milan, and Francis agreed to support the rule of the Medici family in Florence. Some years later the republic of Florence became the grand duchy of Tuscany. It was governed by a line of petty princes, and never regained its former glories.

Francis I and Emperor Charles V engaged in almost constant warfare over their claims to Italian territory and other matters. These wars were but the beginning of a conflict lasting over two centuries between France and the Hapsburgs.

The wars with France were by no means all the troubles that wearied the hardworking Charles. V. At the very outset he was confronted by the problem of a young university professor, Martin Luther, who was accused of writing heretical books and attacking doctrines of the Church.

CHECK ON YOUR READING

1. *Why was Spain a great nation? What policies weakened her?*
2. *How do you account for the rise of Portugal? the Netherlands?*
3. *Show the extent of the Ottoman Empire.*
4. *Describe the Holy Roman Empire.*
5. *How did Charles V grow so powerful?*

"Anyone who conducts an argument by appealing to authority is not using his intelligence; he is just using his memory."
—LEONARDO DA VINCI

"By doubting we are led to questioning, and by questioning we arrive at truth." —PETER ABELARD

Learning Activities

Think about the chapter

1. In what ways was the world of 1460 different from the world of 1160? Consider political organization, business and trade, education, science, art, and philosophy.

2. How do Roger Bacon's words show the spirit of the Renaissance?

3. Show how the scientific method is used today.

4. What is nationalism? How did the growth of nations aid the progress of civilization? Where is nationalism strong today?

5. *Map study:* On a map of Europe and the Near East show the limits of the Holy Roman Empire, the Ottoman Empire, and the Hapsburg possessions. Locate Paris, Oxford, Bologna, Florence, Rome, Venice, Castile, Aragon, Granada, Constantinople.

For further inquiry

6. The "complete man" was the Renaissance ideal. Look up the story of Leonardo da Vinci's life. How did he fit the ideal?

7. Investigate the everyday life of the Renaissance. Find out about the styles of clothing, the architecture of homes and public buildings, amusements, and education.

8. How did the printing press help bring about the end of the Middle Ages? Prepare a report on book production through the ages.

Follow up your special interests

9. Galileo's telescope magnified objects thirty-three times. Compare this telescope with the powerful telescopes used today.

10. Prepare reports on the lives of the following Renaissance writers: Dante, Boccaccio, Petrarch, Rabelais, Cervantes, Chaucer, Sir Thomas More, Edmund Spenser, Francis Bacon, Christopher Marlowe, Ben Jonson, and William Shakespeare. Tell the class the story of the *Canterbury Tales* and *Don Quixote.*

11. Add to your history-of-art scrapbook reproductions of Renaissance paintings.

12. Guide the class on a picture tour through Renaissance Europe.

READ FURTHER

Basic readings: (1) BAUER and PEYSER, *How Music Grew,* Chaps. 7, 11. (2) CHEYNEY, *World History of Art.* Chaps. 16–18, 20–23. (3) COTTLER and JAFFE, *Heroes of Civilization.* Copernicus, Galileo, Newton. (4) EVANS, *Costume Throughout the Ages,* Chap. 5. (5) HOFFMAN, *News of the World,* Nos. 29–31. (6) MACY, *Story of World Literature,* Chaps. 14–18. (7) Life's *History of Western Man,* Parts III, V, VI. (8) ROBINSON, *Readings in European History,* Chaps. 12–14, 19, 24. (9) SCOTT, HYMA, and NOYES, *Readings in Medieval History,* Secs. 13, 15, 21. (10) TAYLOR, *Fifty Centuries of Art,* pp. 29–115. (11) TAYLOR, *Illustrated History of Science,* Chap. 2. (12) Year's *Pictorial History,* pp. 167–172, 188–190, 198–224.

Special accounts: (13) D. MILLS, *Renaissance and Reformation Times.*

Fiction and biography: (14) A. ARMITAGE, *The World of Copernicus.* (15) C. CHAUCER, *Canterbury Tales.* (16) M. CHUTE, *Geoffrey Chaucer of England.* (17) F. GOUDGE, *Towers in the Mist.* Life at medieval Oxford. (18) H. GUERBER, *The Book of the Epic.* (19) W. IRVING, *The Alhambra.* Life around this monument of the Moorish occupation of Spain. (20) E. KELLY, *From Star to Star.* Story of the medieval university in Cracow, Poland. (21) E. KYLE, *Apprentice of Florence.* (22) L. LERMAN, *Michelangelo.* (23) E. LEVINGER, *Galileo: First Observer of Modern Things.* (24) D. McMURTIE and D. FARRAN, *Wings for Words.* The story of printing. (25) E. RIPLEY, *Leonardo da Vinci.* (26) K. SINCLAIR, *Valiant Lady.* About the Dutch revolt. (27) H. SOOTIN, *Isaac Newton.*

14

The Breakup of the Medieval Church

KEY WORDS AND DATES

catholic	Henry VIII
heresy	Anglican
Inquisition	Dissenters
Saint Francis	Armada
schism	1588
Wycliffe	Council of Trent
Luther	Jesuits
Protestants	*Vulgate*
indulgences	*Index*
Zwingli	Loyola
Calvin	dispensation

FOR CENTURIES the Roman Catholic Church was the most powerful institution in Europe. It brought to trial all those who questioned its doctrines, and it turned over obstinate offenders to the state, which put them to death. Aided by the civil government, the Church was safe against any serious rebellion.

In the early sixteenth century, a young German professor, Martin Luther, openly attacked some of the chief doctrines of the Church. But instead of arresting him, as the Pope and emperor commanded, the Elector of Saxony protected the heretic. In this way the first successful revolt from the Church began. Certain German princes, following Luther's teachings, now set up their own churches.

Other reformers arose in Switzerland and France. In England the king threw off the authority of the Pope and established a national church under his own leadership. Those who left the Roman Catholic Church came to be known as *Protestants*.

A Catholic or Counter-Reformation strengthened the Church in southern Europe and extended its influence overseas. A long church council restated the Catholic beliefs to counter the Protestant arguments. And a strong new religious order, the Jesuits, spread Catholic teachings to many parts of the world.

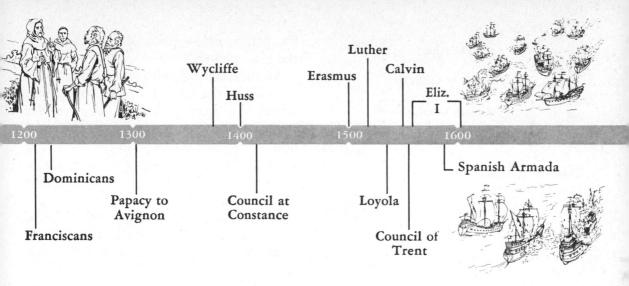

Franciscans
Dominicans
Papacy to Avignon
Wycliffe
Huss
Council at Constance
Erasmus
Luther
Calvin
Eliz. I
Loyola
Council of Trent
Spanish Armada

1. The Church Universal

Power of the Church · The Catholic Church was the most powerful institution in the Middle Ages. It claimed spiritual authority over all men as their sole means of salvation. Because of its religious authority, the Church was *universal,* or *catholic.* Every child of Christian parents was born into the Church, as one is born into the state today. And the Church was *permanent.* Kingdoms might come and go, and empires rise and fall, but the Church stood firm through the years. The Church alone kept alive man's ideal of a unified empire. It served as almost the *only common bond among the peoples of Europe.*

The medieval Church was very wealthy. It had a vast revenue from its lands, its offices, and its fees. Every person had to pay one-tenth (a *tithe*) of his income to the Church. In return the Church met his spiritual needs, looked after the sick and the helpless, and provided education.

Finally, the Church was a great *temporal* power. It ruled the Papal States and it held vast lands throughout Europe. It con-trolled the appointment of all important Church officials. The Christian rulers of Europe owed it their allegiance. The Church also had its own system of law— canon law—and its own courts.

How the Church was Organized and Governed · As the head of the Church the Pope was the supreme lawgiver. His decisions were binding on all members. The Pope could set aside any church law, however ancient, so long as it did not seem to be commanded by the Scriptures or Nature. He could, according to his judgment, make exceptions to purely human laws. For example, he could annul marriages or free a monk from his vows. Such an exception was called a *dispensation.*

The Pope was also the supreme judge. And he was able to exercise control over the Church in distant countries by means of *Papal legates,* or messengers, who were his special representatives.

Next in rank to the Pope were the *cardinals.* They were eminent churchmen appointed by the Pope to serve as a sort of

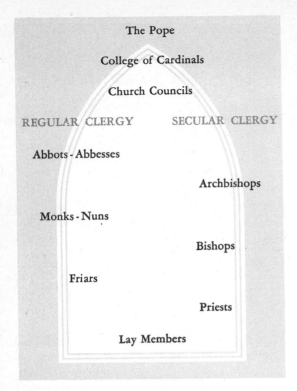

The Pope

College of Cardinals

Church Councils

REGULAR CLERGY   SECULAR CLERGY

Abbots - Abbesses

Archbishops

Monks - Nuns

Bishops

Friars

Priests

Lay Members

Organization of the Church

council to aid him in the supervision of the Church. The College of Cardinals, after 1059, had the duty of electing the Popes.

The Church was divided into various administrative districts. An *archbishop* was a bishop whose power extended over a large province and who had a certain control over all the bishops in his territory. A *bishop* was in charge of a *diocese*, or subdivision of a province. Each bishop had his special church, called the *cathedral*, which was usually the most important church in the diocese in size and beauty. The bishops supervised not only the clergy, but the lands and other possessions belonging to their diocese. The bishop was therefore usually a feudal lord and was often himself a vassal of the king or of some neighboring lord. The smallest division of the Church was

the parish, whose priest was in charge of the local church.

All these officials, who were charged with the care of the Church in the world, were called the *secular* clergy. The *regular* clergy were the members of monastic orders. They had retired from the world and lived according to a *regula*, or rule, under the supervision of the heads of their orders and the Pope.

Importance of the Clergy · In the Middle Ages the clergy was a distinct class. Its members could act as mediators between God and man. They officiated at Masses, heard confessions, absolved the guilty from their sins, and administered the sacraments.

They owed their first allegiance not to their earthly ruler, but to the Pope. They were excused from paying taxes and had the privilege, if accused of wrongdoing, of being tried in church courts. This right was called the "benefit of clergy."

The clergy was the only educated class. In the early Middle Ages very few outside the clergy could read or write. Even Charlemagne could hardly sign his own name. All teachers came from the ranks of the clergy, and from this group the civil rulers often chose their ministers and secretaries.

How the Church Punished Heretics · Those who dared to defy the authority of the Church or question its teaching were guilty of the supreme crime of *heresy*. To the faithful believer nothing could exceed the guilt of one who rejected the religion handed down in the Church from the immediate followers of Jesus. Besides, heresy was revolt against the most powerful institution in Europe.

A special system of courts was established by the Pope to search out cases of unbelief and bring the guilty to judgment. These courts were called the *Holy Inquisition*.

Those suspected of heresy were encouraged, often by torture, to confess. The statement of the victim that he was not an unbeliever carried no weight, because it was assumed that he would naturally deny his own guilt.

If the suspected person renounced his heresy, he was forgiven and received back into the Church. But he had still to suffer imprisonment for life as a means of cleansing himself from sin. If he persisted in his heresy, he was turned over to the civil power, which burned him alive. The suffering imposed on the victims has made the name of the Inquisition infamous. Yet the inquisitors were often earnest and upright men, acting according to their conscience, and the methods of the Inquisition were not more cruel than those used in other courts of the period.

Founding of Mendicant Orders · The wealth and power of the Church and the privileges enjoyed by the clergy led to individual excesses. Worldly persons sought rich appointments for themselves or their relatives and friends. Weak members of the clergy were tempted to use church resources for their own personal benefit.

There were some within the Church who saw that it was sadly in need of reform. They believed that the failure of some of the clergy to lead simple lives and perform their religious duties was responsible for the evils of the time. It was this conviction that led to the founding of two great orders—the Franciscans and the Dominicans. The members of these associations were called *mendicant friars*, or begging brothers, because they depended entirely on charity for their support. They gave up their possessions, led a life of sacrifice, and tried to awaken in the people a love of spiritual things.

Saint Francis of Assisi (1182–1226) · Born in Assisi, in central Italy, Saint Francis was the son of a well-to-do merchant. In his youth he lived a gay life and had everything that money could buy. But he was of a sensitive and chivalrous nature. The contrast between the luxury of his surroundings and the poverty of others began to trouble him. After a serious illness when he was about twenty, he began to visit the poor and forsaken, especially the lepers. Finally, he decided to give up his inheritance.

He cast aside his riches, put on the worn-out garments of a gardener, and became a

St. Francis Preaching to the Birds · *This beautiful legend is preserved in a fresco painting in the Church at Montefalco, Italy.*

Basilica of St. Peter's in Rome · *An obelisk in the piazza is flanked by two fountains and semicircular colonnades. The basilica was started in 1506 and completed in 1626. R and M are the initials of two of its famous architects.*

homeless wanderer. He soon began to preach in a simple fashion. Others joined him, and the little band, barefoot and penniless, went about Italy, preaching the gospel of Christ.

The Franciscans and Their Work · Some years later, the group received the approval of the Pope (1210). The organization, which had greatly grown in size, then started missionary work on a large scale. Soon the Franciscans, in their patched gowns, with ropes around their waists, were to be seen in many countries of Europe. Filled with Christian faith the Franciscans went from place to place to convert men to a deeper religious life.

Saint Francis did not wish his group to become rich and powerful lest they cease to follow in the footsteps of Christ. But after his death much wealth was given to the Franciscan order. A stately church was built at Assisi to receive his remains. Later many other beautiful churches and monasteries were built by the Franciscans.

The Dominican Order · Saint Dominic, the Spanish founder of another great order, was a learned churchman. Shocked by the amount of unbelief that he met in France, he decided to spend his life trying to win men to Christ. As soon as Dominic had received the permission of the Pope, he sent forth his followers to preach just as the Franciscans were beginning their first missionary journeys. By 1224 the Dominican order was thoroughly organized and it had sixty monasteries throughout western Europe.

The Dominicans were called "the Preaching Friars." They were carefully trained in debate in order that they might be able to refute the arguments of the heretics. The Pope entrusted to them especially the task of conducting the Inquisition. Two of their most distinguished teachers of the thirteenth century were Albertus Magnus and Thomas Aquinas (p. 196).

CHECK ON YOUR READING

1. *Why was the Church so powerful? How was it organized and governed?*
2. *How did the Church punish heresy?*
3. *Describe the founding and work of the Franciscan and Dominican orders.*

2. Conflict between Church and State

Church and State Become Rivals · The activities and the wealth of the Church were bound to bring it into conflict with the new national states. (1) As the kings began to get the better of the feudal lords, the Church seemed to some of them a great obstacle to the building of a unified government. Within their realms were many churchmen who owed their first allegiance to a foreign sovereign, the Pope. (2) The kings could collect no taxes from the vast Church lands or from the clergy.

(3) There was still the old difficulty about whether the king or the Pope had the sole right to select the bishops and abbots. Both were eager to place their friends in these high positions and enjoy the large gifts which were made on the granting of a benefice.

(4) The kings were also irritated by the large number of cases which could be tried in church courts, whose fees thus went to the Church instead of to the royal treasury. (5) Finally, there was the question of how far the Pope, as head of the Church, had a right to interfere in the affairs of a state when he did not approve of the actions of the ruler.

"The Babylonian Captivity" · When Philip the Fair of France decided to impose a tax on both clergy and laity alike, he came into bitter conflict with Pope Boniface VIII. After the death of Boniface (1303), Philip determined to put an end to all such difficulties. He had a French archbishop chosen as head of the Church, with the understanding that he would move the papacy from Rome to France.

The new Pope, Clement V, remained in France during his entire reign. His suc-cessors built a great palace at Avignon, where they lived in luxury for sixty years. This long exile of the Popes from Rome is called "the Babylonian Captivity." It was suspected that these Popes (all French) were controlled by the French kings. This tended to weaken the influence of the holy office in other countries.

The Great Schism (1378–1415) · A further misfortune befell the Church after the Popes had returned to Rome. When a new Pope was to be chosen, the Roman people demanded an Italian, and one was elected. But when the new Pontiff attempted to introduce some much-needed reforms, the cardinals asserted that they had been forced to choose Urban VI against their will. They met and elected a second Pope, Clement VII. Clement re-estab-lished the papacy at Avignon.

Thus for forty years there were *two* popes, each claiming to be the true head of the Church. Likewise there were *two* colleges of cardinals. All Europe was divided in its loyalty. Peace and unity were finally re-stored at the Council of Constance (1415). A new Pope, Martin V, was elected and the schism in the Church officially came to an end. But the questions raised by the Great Schism were to have serious conse-quences.

Reformers in the Church: Wycliffe · There were many faithful Catholics who be-lieved that the evils that had grown up in the Church should be corrected. Among these early reformers was a former professor at Oxford, John Wycliffe (*c*. 1320–1384). Wycliffe criticized the enormous political power of the Pope. He thought that many of the clergy were more interested in wealth

215

and property than in religion. He would have preferred to see the Church poor, as in the time of the apostles. Wycliffe boldly attacked many of the familiar practices of the Church, which he considered superstitions. So eager was he to have the people learn the nature of true religion from the Bible that he translated it from the Latin into English. He also prepared a great number of sermons for people to read.

Wycliffe's Influence on Huss · Soon Wycliffe's ideas reached Bohemia, where they had a great influence on John Huss, rector of the University of Prague. Huss asserted that because many of the clergy were sinful, men should not be forced to obey them. This highly dangerous teaching roused the Church to action. Huss was tried as a heretic at the Council of Constance in 1415 and condemned. He was turned over to the government and burned at the stake.

Erasmus of Rotterdam (*c.* 1466–1536) · One of the most famous of the early reformers was Erasmus, a Dutchman by birth. He was a serious student of theology, which is the study of religion and religious beliefs. Erasmus wrote hundreds of letters, pamphlets, and books urging people to use plain common sense in determining their religion. His writings influenced the educated class all over Europe.

In one of his famous books, the *Praise of Folly*, Erasmus criticized some of the beliefs and customs that had grown up in the Church. He held that only through education and enlightenment would men give up their superstitions. Men should read the Bible, he urged, if they wanted to know the truth about religion.

Church Councils and Reform · The Church councils, which were assemblies of churchmen from all Christendom, tried to

Desiderius Erasmus, by Hans Holbein the Younger · "*No man of the Renaissance did more to realize the ideal of intellectual liberty*" than Holland's great humanist.

cure some of the outstanding evils. Although they accomplished little, it was arranged that a council should be held every ten years. Thus it was hoped that the absolute power of the Pope would be controlled in some measure and that the councils would share in making Church laws.

CHECK ON YOUR READING

1. Name five causes for conflict between kings and the Church.
2. Why were the "Captivity" and Schism so unfortunate?
3. What reforms were urged by Wycliffe, Huss, and Erasmus?
4. What was the purpose of the Church councils?

3. The Protestant Revolt in Germany

The Church Divided · As the result of a number of successful revolts against the authority of the Pope, the unity of the Christian Church in western Europe was shattered. We have already seen how at an earlier time the Church in the Eastern Empire broke away (p. 172). Now the rulers of portions of western Europe withdrew from the Mother Church and established independent religions. Western Christendom was henceforth divided into *Catholics* and *Protestants*. The Protestant organizations not only declared themselves separate from Rome, but also rejected certain teachings and practices of the ancient Church.

Germany Dissatisfied with the Papacy · The trouble began in the German part of the Holy Roman Empire. The German people were good Catholics. But they had become suspicious of the Popes, whom they regarded as foreigners receiving large revenues from the German lands. The great German churchmen were expected to contribute no less than ten thousand gold guldens to the papal treasury on having their elections approved by Rome. The Pope had the right to fill many important offices in Germany. To many of these he appointed Italians. They collected the income, often without troubling to go to Germany to perform their duties. Sometimes one clergyman held several such posts.

Luther and His Teachings · Martin Luther was the son of a poor miner, but his father wished him to be a lawyer and sent him to college. As a young man, Luther was very religious and decided to become a monk. Later he was chosen as professor of theology in the new University of Wittenberg. Luther believed in a simpler form of Christianity and began to criticize freely the older system. When he was about thirty years old, he suddenly found himself in the midst of a controversy with the leaders of the Church.

Indulgences Issued by the Pope · In Luther's younger days the Popes had begun the rebuilding of St. Peter's at Rome. To raise the necessary money Pope Leo X had arranged that those who made contributions should receive special *indulgences*, or pardons as the people called them.

One of the doctrines of the Church was that when men died, they did not immediately enter heaven. They must first pass a long period in *purgatory* (a place between earth and heaven). Here they were purified of sin by some form of punishment. An *indulgence* was a pardon (usually issued by the Pope) which freed the person to whom it was granted from some of his suffering in purgatory. It did not forgive his sins or take the place of penance. It only reduced the punishment which the repentant sinner would otherwise have to endure before he could enter heaven.

Eager to collect as much money as possible, the fund-raisers did their best to induce everyone to secure an indulgence for himself or one of his friends in purgatory. They succeeded in raising a great deal of money, and criticism too, as we shall see.

The Ninety-five Theses · In October, 1517, a Dominican monk named Tetzel began preaching indulgences in the neighborhood of Wittenberg. He made claims about them which Luther believed had no foundation in Christianity. Luther thereupon wrote out a series of statements about

Luther Preaching at Wartburg Castle (painting by Hugo Vogel) · *As a result of his influence, most of the people of North Germany, Denmark, Norway, and Sweden are Lutherans today.*

indulgences. According to the custom of the time, he posted these *theses* on the church door, inviting anyone interested in the matter to debate the subject with him.

The ninety-five theses, written in Latin, were expected to attract only learned men. But Luther soon found that everyone, high and low, was eager to talk about indulgences. The theses were translated into German and scattered throughout the land. One of Luther's chief contentions was that neither pardons nor "good works" brought forgiveness, but only faith in God and true repentance.

Luther Widens His Attack · There were many in Germany who sympathized with Luther's views. A widespread discussion now developed, which soon included many topics besides indulgences. Luther became more and more outspoken in his writings. He not only attacked the papacy, but called on the German rulers themselves to reform the Church. He denied that there was anything sacred about a clergyman except the duties he performed. He recommended reducing the number of monasteries and declared that pilgrimages and church holidays interfered with daily work.

The Pope Excommunicates Luther · The Pope now *excommunicated* Luther. This meant that he was outside the Church and was denied its sacraments. A papal *bull* or edict warned that any place sheltering the heretic was to be placed under an *interdict*. This was an order to the clergy to close all the churches and stop holding public services.

But an unexpected thing happened. Some of the German princes, instead of obeying the Pope, refused to arrest the young professor. Far from taking back his statements, Luther summoned his students to witness a "pious religious spectacle." He publicly burned the papal bull, together with a copy of the laws of the Church and a textbook on theology which he specially disliked.

The Edict of Worms (1521) · The following year Emperor Charles V summoned Luther to appear before the diet (parliament) held at Worms to answer the serious charges against him. In the presence of the emperor, the nobility, and the clergy, Luther acknowledged his writings against the Church and maintained that he believed them to be true.

The emperor thereupon issued an edict. It named Luther an outlaw, since he had defamed the Pope, denied the authority of the Church, stirred up the people against the clergy, and made himself a danger to Church and State alike. Everyone was forbidden to give him food, drink, or shelter. Anyone who could was required to seize and deliver him to the emperor. No one was to print, buy, sell, or read the writings of the "notorious and stiff-necked heretic." But few were willing to pay any attention to the edict. Charles V left Germany for Spain and for the next ten years was occupied with his many wars.

Luther Translates the Bible · As Luther was on his way home from Worms, he was kidnaped by his friends and taken to the Wartburg, a castle belonging to his local ruler, the Elector of Saxony. Here he was to remain until the danger from the edict of the emperor should pass. During his months of hiding he occupied himself with a new translation of the Bible from Greek into German. Before he left the Wartburg, he had finished the New Testament. The completed work was of such force and beauty that Luther's Bible became a classic.

Spread of Luther's Teachings · Luther's teachings soon spread throughout Germany, for they appealed to many classes of people: (1) the rulers, who coveted the church lands; (2) the pious, who were shocked by the evils in the Church; and (3) the peasants, who hoped to escape from the heavy taxes of the nobles and higher clergy. These simple folk thought that the seizure of the church property by the rulers would in some way right the wrongs from which they suffered. Some of those who took Luther's teaching seriously now began to put them into practice.

The Peasant Revolt · Luther warned the people against taking matters into their own hands, but they did not heed his advice. In 1525 the peasants rose, in the name of "God's justice," against their masters. There were some fanatics among them who proposed to kill the "godless" priests and nobles. Violence soon broke out and hundreds of castles and monasteries were destroyed. Some of the nobility were brutally murdered. Luther tried to control the people. When they ignored his warnings, he bade the government put down the uprising without pity.

Scene from the Peasant Revolt · *The peasants were called Buntschuh (colored shoe), hence the emblem on their banner. In this woodcut they use their pitchforks to overcome a knight.*

The nobles followed Luther's advice and took fearful revenge. Some ten thousand peasants were put to death. Few of the landlords made any reforms, and the condition of the serfs following the revolt was worse than before.

Origin of the Term *Protestants* · After the Peasants' War it became clear that some of the German rulers were going to adopt Luther's ideas and take over the church property in their domains, and that other princes would remain loyal to the Pope. In the absence of the emperor there was no one to act for the whole of Germany.

The diet which met at Speyer in 1526, therefore, decided that for the present each ruler in the Holy Roman Empire should live and reign according to the dictates of his own conscience. This meant that each ruler might determine the religion of his subjects. In general, southern Germany remained Catholic, but many of the northern princes decided to break away from the Church.

The Catholic emperor, however, commanded the next diet, which met at Speyer in 1529, to enforce the Edict of Worms against the heretics. Thereupon the Lutheran princes drew up a *protest*, declaring that the majority had no right to set aside the unanimous decision of the diet of 1526. Those who signed this appeal came to be called *Protestants*. Thus originated the name which came to be applied to Christians who did not accept the rule of the Roman Catholic Church.

Religious Peace of Augsburg · At the Diet of Augsburg (1530) a statement of the Lutheran beliefs was presented to the emperor. It became the recognized creed of the Lutheran churches and remains so today. But the religious question was not settled in Germany. A temporary solution was provided by the Peace of Augsburg (1555). This stated that each prince and knight was free to choose for himself and his subjects between the Catholic Church and the Lutheran.

Everyone was supposed to be Catholic or Lutheran, and no provision was made for any other form of belief. The settlement did not establish religious liberty as we know it, except for the rulers. Every German had to conform to the official religion of his state or leave it. No one suggested that each individual should be permitted to worship God according to his own beliefs.

CHECK ON YOUR READING

1. *How was the Church divided?*
2. *Why did the revolt occur in Germany?*
3. *Explain: indulgences, theses, excommunicate, interdict, Protestant.*
4. *Why did Luther's teachings spread?*
5. *What did the Peace of Augsburg provide?*

---

4. *Protestant Reformers in Switzerland*

How Switzerland Was Formed · One of the earliest centers of Protestantism was Switzerland. During the Middle Ages this region was part of the Holy Roman Empire. In the thirteenth century the three Swiss *cantons* (states) on the shores of the Lake of Lucerne formed a union to protect themselves against their neighbors, the Hapsburgs.

By brave fighting, the Swiss were able to keep the Hapsburgs from conquering them. Several districts, including the region lying on the Italian side of the Alps, joined the Swiss union. Later, a number of areas were annexed in which French was spoken. Since most of the Swiss were German-speaking people, the result was that three languages—German, French, and Italian—came to be spoken in Switzerland. Gradually the union freed itself from the empire and in 1499 became practically an independent country.

Zwingli, Revolt, and Civil War · The first leader of the revolt in Switzerland was a young priest named Ulrich Zwingli. As he says, he "began to preach the Gospel of Christ in the year 1516, before anyone in my locality had so much as heard the name of Luther."

Zwingli began to denounce the evils in the Church, as well as the shameless hiring out of Swiss soldiers to foreign governments. In 1518 he was appointed preacher in the cathedral at Zurich and in this prominent position continued to attack the Church. He denied the authority of the Pope and proclaimed the Bible to be the only guide of man in faith and morals.

Zwingli's teaching soon led to uprisings against the Church. Some of his enthusiastic listeners began to demolish the churches and destroy their ornaments. When, in 1523, the Pope intervened, the canton of Zurich declared its independence of the Catholic Church. The revolt spread throughout Switzerland, except in the original cantons on the Lake of Lucerne, which still held to the old faith.

In 1531 civil war broke out between Catholics and Protestants, and Zwingli fell in battle at Kappel. A truce was then arranged, under which each canton was left free to choose its own religion. Switzerland has remained to this day part Catholic and part Protestant.

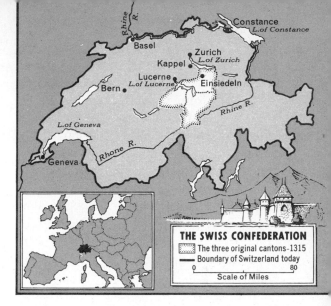

THE SWISS CONFEDERATION
☐ The three original cantons-1315
— Boundary of Switzerland today
0   80
Scale of Miles

The Swiss Confederation · *Between what nations is Switzerland a buffer? What river headwaters does she control?*

John Calvin · *He ruled Geneva with a very strict hand. What countries were most affected by his ideas?*

John Calvin (1509–1564) · A reformer who had an even greater influence in the spread of Protestantism than Luther or Zwingli was John Calvin. Born in northern France, Calvin was early influenced by Luther's teachings. A persecution of the Protestants under Francis I drove Calvin from France, and he lived for a time at Basel, Switzerland. Here he published his great work, *The Institutes of the Christian Religion.* This was the first complete statement of the principles of Christianity from a Protestant standpoint and became the most widely used book on Protestant theology.

Calvin later went to Geneva where he became the chief reform preacher and had an important part in directing the affairs of the town. Calvin had very strict ideas about what a Christian should be and frowned upon gaiety and frivolity.

Noted for his ideas of church government, he believed that the New Testament taught that the Church should be under the care of ministers and elders (*presbyters*) rather than bishops. He is regarded as the founder of the Presbyterian Church. His teachings spread into France, England, Scotland, and later to America. The early Protestantism in these countries was that of Calvin rather than Luther.

CHECK ON YOUR READING

1. *How was Switzerland formed?*
2. *How does it happen that three languages are spoken in Switzerland today?*
3. *What were the short-term and long-term results of Zwingli's preaching?*
4. *Why is Calvin an important figure in the history of Protestantism?*

RELIGIOUS SITUATION 1560

- ▦ Anglicans
- ▨ Lutherans
- ▢ Roman Catholics
- ◈ Calvinists and Zwinglians

Religious Groupings in 1560 · *In which countries were the Christians largely Catholic? Protestant? Although ruled by the Ottomans, most Balkan peoples retained their Greek Orthodox faith.*

5. England Establishes a National Church

England Revolts from the Papacy · For some time England had been dissatisfied with the interference of the Popes in national affairs and over the wealth that was sent to Rome. In 1351 the government had put an end to papal control over appointments to church positions in England. Wycliffe and Erasmus had called attention to the abuses existing in the Church. The writings of Luther had been read and studied at Oxford and Cambridge.

A few years after the protest at Speyer (p. 220) England rejected the authority of the Pope and established an independent Church.

Henry VIII's Quarrel with the Pope · The final break with Rome was connected with a personal struggle between the Pope and King Henry VIII. The famous quarrel resulted from the question of the king's divorce. Henry had come to the throne when he was only eighteen years old. His first wife was Catherine of Aragon, the widow of his older brother, and the aunt of Charles V. Only one of their children, Mary, lived to grow up. The king was very eager to have a son to succeed him on the throne and besides had grown tired of his queen, who was older than he.

In marrying Catherine, Henry had been granted a papal *dispensation* from the Church law which forbade a man to marry his brother's widow. He now pretended to fear that he was committing a sin by living with Catherine. He urged the new Pope, Clement VII, to annul his marriage on the ground that it was unlawful. Henry's real reason, however, was that he had fallen in love with a sixteen-year-old young lady at the court, Anne Boleyn.

The Pope was in a difficult position. To grant Henry's request, Clement would have to nullify the dispensation of one of his predecessors. Moreover, he would anger the queen's nephew, the powerful Charles V. When Henry found that he was not able to influence the Pope, he lost patience and secretly married Anne Boleyn. The Pope then excommunicated him.

England Breaks with the Papacy · By a series of laws (1530–1535) Parliament, which was completely under the king's control, made a complete separation of England from Rome. It established an independent (Anglican) national Church and declared in the Act of Supremacy that the king was its supreme head.

The clergy was required to submit to the sovereign instead of to the Pope. The king was given the right to appoint all the prelates and to receive the income which formerly went to the papal treasury. Parliament forbade appeals to Rome. Every officer was required to take an oath acknowledging the king's supremacy or suffer the penalty of treason.

Henry VIII Dissolves the Monasteries · Henry VIII continued to believe most of the doctrines of the Catholic faith and never accepted the teachings of Luther, Zwingli, or Calvin. However, on the excuse that the monasteries were centers of superstition and scandals, the king ordered these communities dissolved.

But Henry's real reason for breaking up the monasteries was that he needed money, and some of the English abbeys were very rich. The royal commissioners took possession of the buildings and disposed of every article of value, even the bells and

Henry VIII · *This robust Tudor king established the Church of England, was "Father of the Navy," and built a national state. How does Holbein portray Henry's vanity?*

the lead on the roofs. The lands were handed over to the king, who sold them or gave them to nobles whose favor he wished to secure.

Six Wives and Three Children · The fickle king soon tired of Anne Boleyn, and three years after their marriage she was beheaded. Henry's third wife, Jane Seymour, became the mother of his son and successor, Edward VI. Jane died a few days after her son's birth, and later Henry married three other women, who left no children as claimants to the crown. By an act of Parliament Henry arranged that his three children — Mary, Edward, and Elizabeth (daughter of Anne Boleyn), all of whom were one day to reign — should be given their place in the line of succession.

England Becomes Protestant under Edward VI · At Henry's death (1547) Edward, a boy of ten, came to the throne. During the six years of his reign those in charge of his government favored the Protestant party. Protestants were placed in high church positions and reformers were brought over from the Continent to be teachers in the universities.

Parliament further declared that the clergy should be free to marry. Masses for the dead were abolished, and sums of money that had been left for that purpose were handed over by Parliament to the king. So intolerant did the feeling against the Catholic faith become that a general destruction of shrines, sacred images, and stained-glass windows in the churches took place.

Mary Restores Catholicism (1553–1558). Edward was succeeded by his Catholic half-sister Mary, the daughter of Catherine of Aragon. The new queen at once undertook to return England to the Church of Rome. Her Parliament repealed all the acts of her father and brother that had separated England from the papacy. The Catholic cause seemed still further strengthened when the queen married the Spanish prince Philip, son of Charles V. But although Philip persecuted Protestants in his own realms, he never gained any control over England.

Mary's determination to root out heresy, however, resulted in the most serious religious persecution in English history. Nearly three hundred persons were put to death and hundreds more left to suffer in the miserable prisons of the time.

But Mary's dream came to nothing. As she had no children, she was succeeded by her sister Elizabeth, the daughter of Anne Boleyn. Since the Church had never sanctioned the marriage of Anne to Henry VIII, it was natural that Anne's daughter should feel no allegiance to Rome.

Anglican Church Permanently Established under Elizabeth I (1558–1603) · When Elizabeth came to the throne, the Church of England once more became Protestant. The laws of Henry VIII and Edward VI establishing independence from Rome were revived, and the statutes of Mary were repealed. Parliament gave the queen the powers of the head of the Church.

The Anglican Church, as it was finally established, followed a middle course between the older Church and that of the Protestant reformers. Its outward form remained much like that of the Catholic organization, with its archbishops and bishops. But in doctrine it was Protestant, following the ideas of Calvin and the Swiss reformers rather than those of Luther.

In Scotland, John Knox, a second Calvin, secured the introduction of the Presbyterian faith, which still prevails in that country.

The Dissenters · Unfortunately, the religious settlement did not bring peace and harmony. Loyal Catholics, of course, wished to have the Church under the headship of Rome. But some Protestants believed that the reformation had not gone far enough. They wanted to "purify" the Anglican Church of any traces of the Roman Catholic religion which remained.

The *Puritans* objected to the vestments of the clergy and certain of the ceremonies. Later they bitterly opposed the rule of the bishops. They demanded that the Church should be placed under the management of ministers and elders.

Various sects developed, each with its own ideas of what a "true Church" should be. Those Protestants who refused to conform to the national Church were classed as *Dissenters*. Their complaints were troublesome enough, but Elizabeth considered the hostility of the Catholics most dangerous. For the Catholics secretly hoped to remove her and place a Catholic, Mary Stuart, on the throne.

Queen Elizabeth I Loved Pageantry · *The ornate sedan chair of the dazzling queen is borne by six knights. She is going to the marriage of Anne Russell, her maid of honor, who follows on foot.*

Mary Stuart, Hope of the Catholics · Mary, Queen of Scots, was only nineteen when she landed in Scotland after the death of her French husband, Francis II. She was descended from the Stuart kings of Scotland. But she had been brought up at the French court and was almost a stranger to her subjects. Her grandmother was a sister of Henry VIII, so that Mary claimed to be the rightful heir to the English as well as the Scottish throne. Mary soon became the hope of all who wished to bring England and Scotland back to the Catholic Church. Chief among these was Philip II of Spain.

The hapless young queen soon lost favor with her subjects. Mary's second husband was mysteriously murdered. Both Mary and a nobleman named Bothwell came under suspicion. How far the queen was responsible for her husband's death was never known, but later, when she married Bothwell, her Protestant subjects deposed her as a murderess. After vain attempts to regain her power, Mary abdicated in favor of her infant son, James VI, and fled to England for protection. But Elizabeth took good care to keep the young Catholic queen a prisoner (1568–1587).

Catholic Plans to Depose Elizabeth · In 1569, soon after Mary's arrival in England, some of the nobles led a rebellion in her favor. The revolt was put down, but the next year the Pope excommunicated Elizabeth and released her subjects from allegiance to their heretical queen. Parliament now passed severe laws against the Catholics, with heavy penalties for those who stirred up sedition. Several priests were hanged.

Nevertheless plots to depose or assassinate Elizabeth continued, and some of these plans were discovered. They usually included asking help from abroad, so that an invasion by France or Spain was known to be a danger. In 1587 Mary Stuart became involved in a plot to kill the queen. Parliament now realized that so long as Mary lived, the queen was not safe. As a result Mary was beheaded (1587).

The Spanish Armada · Philip II was now more resolved than ever to establish the authority of the Pope in England. In 1588 he collected a great fleet of warships, proudly called by the Spaniards "the Invincible Armada." This was to sail to the Netherlands to bring over the Spanish commander there and his soldiers. They expected soon to make an end of Elizabeth's troops.

When the Armada approached, it was allowed to pass up the English Channel in a strong wind, which later became a gale. The English ships gave battle under Admiral Howard and such famous sea captains as Drake, Hawkins, and Frobisher. Both fleets were driven past the coast of Flanders. Of the hundred and thirty Spanish vessels only about fifty returned home. The rest were destroyed by the English or by successive storms, to which Elizabeth ascribed the victory. The defeat put an end to the danger from Spain, and England remained a Protestant country. Furthermore, for over 350 years thereafter (with rare exceptions) "Britannia ruled the waves."

CHECK ON YOUR READING

1. What events led to the English revolt from the papacy?
2. How were Protestants and Catholics treated under Edward VI? Mary? Elizabeth?
3. Describe the Anglican Church, the Dissenters, Mary Stuart.
4. Why was the defeat of the Spanish Armada important?

6. The Catholic Reformation

The Catholic Program of Reform · While England, northern Germany, Scandinavia, and other portions of the Continent withdrew from the Roman Catholic Church, Italy, Spain, France, and other areas remained loyal. Many critics wished only to see the Church purified from within so that it would continue to hold the faith and affection of the people.

The Catholic Church, therefore, set itself the task of a thoroughgoing reform. (1) A line of able Popes saw the importance of filling high offices only with men of piety and learning. (2) A great council was summoned to restate the principles of the Church and enforce its discipline. (3) A new religious order taught the Catholic faith to the young and carried on missionary work in foreign fields. As a result the Church retained the loyalty of the people of southern Europe and extended its influence overseas.

The Council of Trent (1545–1563) · The church council, which met at Trent, had a twofold task: (1) It restated clearly and positively the dogmas of the Catholic faith in order to refute the arguments of the Protestants. (2) It provided for a number of important reforms in the Church and for a new edition of the Bible in Latin, the *Vulgate*.

Strict measures were taken to check the spread of heretical and immoral ideas among Catholics. A list of books which the people were forbidden to read was to be drawn up. After the council closed, the Pope issued the first *Index* [or list] *of Prohibited Books*.

Founding of the Jesuit Order (1540) · The Church was greatly strengthened at this time by the work of a new monastic order. Its founder was Ignatius Loyola, a Spaniard. Loyola had been a soldier in his younger days. Then during a long illness he read the lives of the saints and became filled with a desire to equal their deeds. He dedicated his life to the work of the Church, put on a beggar's gown, and started

Ignatius de Loyola · *He was founder and first General of the* Company of Jesus *for "soldiers of God under the banner of the Cross." Can you translate his motto?*

on a pilgrimage to Jerusalem. Later he went to Paris to study.

In 1534, with a few followers, Loyola went to Rome to place himself at the service of the Pope. The little group called itself the Society of Jesus. At Rome the Jesuits worked out the rules of a new order and received papal sanction in 1540.

As a soldier, Loyola believed in absolute and unquestioning obedience. To the monastic vows of poverty, purity, and obedience, the members of the new order added a further pledge of special allegiance to the Pope. They were to undertake any journey that he might command and to obey their superiors in all things. The long and strict training of the Jesuits was the secret of their success.

Work of the Jesuits · Many members of the order were priests who went about preaching and hearing confessions. But the Jesuits were also famous teachers. They opened schools and seminaries and served as the schoolmasters of Europe.

Their great missionaries went throughout the world. We owe to the Jesuits' reports much of our knowledge of the condition of America when white men first began to explore Canada and the Mississippi Valley. They also furnished reports about China, where they went as early as the sixteenth and seventeenth centuries.

CHECK ON YOUR READING

1. *Summarize the threefold Catholic program of reform.*
2. *Identify these terms: Council of Trent, Vulgate, Index.*
3. *Describe the work of the Jesuits.*

"A mighty fortress is our God
A trusty shield and weapon."
—LUTHER, *Ein Festeburge*

Learning Activities

Think about the chapter

1. List the strengths and weaknesses of the Church before the time of Luther.

2. How did both nationalism and economic factors affect the Reformation in England?

3. How did people of the sixteenth century define freedom of religious worship?

4. Why is the Catholic Reformation sometimes called the Counter-Reformation?

5. *Map study:* Draw a map of Switzerland. Locate the famous lakes on the borders and Lake Lucerne; the cities of Zurich, Kappel, Basel, and Geneva.

Go beyond the text

6. What countries today still have a tax-supported church? Does this violate the principle of freedom of religion?

7. Make a "Who's Who" of religious reformers *not* mentioned in the text, giving concise and pertinent information about each.

8. Who were the English "Sea Dogs"? What part did they play in the defeat of Spain?

9. Check newspapers and news magazines for current information on today's religious leaders, such as the Pope, the Archbishop of Canterbury, Patriarchs of the Orthodox Churches, great rabbis, and outstanding Protestant churchmen. What part do they play in world affairs?

10. Name some Jesuit missionaries connected with the exploration and settlement of the New World. Give the major accomplishments of each.

11. Report on the Church Council proposed by Pope John XXIII in 1959.

Follow up your special interests

12. Read more about the story of St. Francis. If there is a Franciscan monastery in your vicinity, you may be able to report on it.

13. Show on a world map the principal religions of the world today. In which countries are the majority of the people Roman Catholic? Protestant? Eastern Orthodox? Moslem? Buddhist? Shintoist? Jewish? Animist?

14. William Tell is the legendary national hero of Switzerland, and Rossini wrote an opera about him. Relate the story and play the *William Tell Overture.*

READ FURTHER

Basic readings: (1) BAUER and PEYSER, *How Music Grew,* Chaps. 7, 11. (2) CHEYNEY, *Readings in English History,* Chaps. 13–14. (3) CHEYNEY, *Short History of England,* Chaps. 12–13. (4) HAGEDORN, *Book of Courage.* St. Francis, Savonarola, Luther, Elizabeth, Drake. (5) HOFFMAN, *News of the World,* Nos. 31–34. (6) Life's *History of Western Man,* Sec. VI. (7) MACY, *Story of World Literature,* Chap. 21. (8) ROBINSON, *Readings in European History,* Chaps. 24–27. (9) VAN LOON, *Story of Mankind,* pp. 251–261. (10) Year's *Pictorial History,* pp. 232–235, 250–254.

Special accounts: (11) W. DAVIS, *Life in Elizabethan Days.* (12) D. MILLS, *Renaissance and Reformation Times.*

Fiction and biography: (13) M. ANDERSON, *Elizabeth the Queen* and *Mary of Scotland.* Plays by an excellent dramatist. (14) N. BAKER, *Sir Walter Raleigh.* (15) W. DAVIS, *Friar of Wittenberg.* There is much detail of Luther's life before and after the break with the Church. (16) M. IRWIN, *Elizabeth and the Prince of Spain.* A fascinating story of the sojourn of Philip in England as the husband of Mary and his partiality to the young Elizabeth. (17) S. JEWETT, *God's Troubadour.* Tells the story of St. Francis of Assisi. (18) C. KINGSLEY, *Westward Ho.* A long, detailed account involving Raleigh, Drake, and the Spanish Armada, worth making the effort to read.

CHAPTER 15

Wars of Religion and Political Ambition Change the Map of Europe

CHAPTER OUTLINE

1. *Philip II and the Revolt of the Netherlands*
2. *How Protestants Fared in France*
3. *The Thirty Years' War in Germany*
4. *The Age of Louis XIV in France*
5. *Louis Makes War and Loses an Empire*

KEY WORDS AND DATES

Philip II
Duke of Alva
William the Silent
Huguenots
St. Bartholomew's Day
Henry IV
Bourbons
Edict of Nantes (1598, 1685)
Richelieu
Thirty Years' War (1618–1648)
Gustavus Adolphus
Treaties of Westphalia
Louis XIV
Mazarin
intendants
divine right
Colbert
Versailles
Molière
Spanish succession
Treaty of Utrecht (1713)

SOME OF THE DARKEST PAGES in history tell of wars that have been waged in the name of religion. We have seen that the Romans persecuted the Christians, that the Moslems spread their religion by the sword, and that Christians fought the Moslems.

But now in the sixteenth and seventeenth centuries Christians began fighting *one another* because of differences over doctrine and worship. These so-called "religious wars" slowly taught men the need for tolerance.

It must be pointed out, however, that wars fought in the name of religion often were motivated by political and territorial ambitions. French cardinals allied with Protestant princes in their war against Catholics in Austria and Spain. And Protestant mercenaries, hired by Catholic princes, attacked Protestant towns in Germany.

French wars against the Hapsburgs were continued by Louis XIV. But the attempts of the "Sun King" to extend his power resulted only in great losses of empire and near bankruptcy.

The power of Louis XIV and the lavishness of his court at Versailles have led historians to call his long reign "The Age of Louis XIV." French culture dominated western Europe.

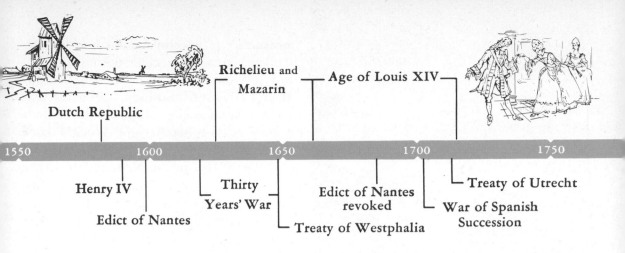

Richelieu and Mazarin

Age of Louis XIV

Dutch Republic

1550   1600   1650   1700   1750

Henry IV

Edict of Nantes

Thirty Years' War

Edict of Nantes revoked

Treaty of Westphalia

Treaty of Utrecht

War of Spanish Succession

1. Philip II and the Revolt of the Netherlands

The Spanish and Austrian Hapsburgs · Emperor Charles V, crippled with gout and old before his time, decided at the age of fifty-six to give up the task of governing and retire to a monastery. From this time on, we find two lines of Hapsburg rulers, the Austrian and the Spanish. To his brother, Ferdinand, who had acquired the kingdoms of Bohemia and Hungary, he transferred all his German possessions. Ferdinand was also chosen to succeed him as emperor. To his son, Philip, he gave Spain with its great American colonies, the kingdom of Naples and Sicily, and the Burgundian realms of the Netherlands.

Philip II of Spain (1556–1598) was one of the chief champions of the Catholic cause against Protestantism. Already we have seen how he plotted to regain England for the papacy by overthrowing Elizabeth and placing a Catholic on the throne (p. 226). Let us now see how he tried to crush heresy within his own realms.

Philip's Unwise Government in Spain · Philip II was upright and sincere, but utterly ruthless. He believed that a monarch had absolute power to rule as he thought best. He had two great ambitions. One was to unify the Spanish peninsula and make it the greatest country in the world. The other was to restore the former power of the Church by crushing its Protestant enemies. In both these goals he failed. When he died, he had also lost one of his fairest provinces, the Netherlands.

Philip abolished local government in Spain and required that every detail of administration pass through his hands. He disregarded the *Cortes* (parliament) and ignored the advice of the nobility. He imposed unwise taxes and ruined the industries of the country. In 1580 he annexed Portugal to Spain. He revived the Inquisition and terrified his subjects by his actions.

Philip's Treatment of the Netherlands · Philip's greatest failure, however, was in the Netherlands. This region had become rich and prosperous through the industry and thrift of its people. Large tracts of lowlands, formerly under the sea, had been reclaimed for farm land by the building of dikes. The towns were famous centers of manufacturing. Their linen and woolen cloth was sent to all parts of Europe.

231

GRONINGEN

FRIESLAND

DRENTHE

HOLLAND

Zuider
Zee

Zaandam
Haarlem
Edam

OVERYSSEL

Amsterdam

Leiden

Utrecht GELDERLAND

The Hague
Delft
Rotterdam

UTRECHT

North
Sea

Rhine R.

ZEELAND

BRABANT

Meuse R.

R.

Bruges

Antwerp

Dunkirk

FLANDERS

Ghent

Scheldt R.

Brussels

Liége

LIMBURG

ARTOIS

HAINAUT

NAMUR

LUXEMBURG

FRANCE

Meuse R.

measures. It is estimated that fifty thousand persons were executed during his reign. But this terrible persecution had not put down Protestantism. Philip, in the first year after he became king, revived all his father's decrees against heretics and brought back the Inquisition.

Duke of Alva in the Netherlands · After suffering this despotic cruelty for ten years, some five hundred nobles protested against Philip's rule. Instead of listening to their grievances, the Spanish king now took a step which finally led to the revolt of the provinces. He sent to the Low Countries the heartless Duke of Alva, whose inhuman conduct made his name notorious. The news that Alva was coming caused many to flee from the country. Alva brought with him an army of well-equipped Spanish soldiers. His method of dealing with the situation was to kill all who opposed "the best of kings." As long as Alva remained in the Netherlands (1567–1573), there was bloodshed and terror.

William the Silent (1533–1584) · At last the Netherlands found a leader in William, Prince of Orange and Count of Nassau. William now undertook the almost hopeless task of freeing his people from the tyranny of a distant king. His main support came from the northern provinces, of which Holland was the chief.

The Spanish had little trouble defeating the Dutch troops, but the Dutch had some success on the sea. They hired privateers to prey on the enemy ships. These "sea beggars," as they were called, captured many Spanish vessels and sold them in England. Holland and Zeeland now chose William for their governor, though they did not yet dare to throw off their allegiance to Philip. These two provinces became the center of the United Netherlands.

The people of the northern provinces (now Holland) were related to the Germans. The people of the southern provinces (now Belgium) were mainly related to the French. But the Flemish, in Flanders, spoke a Dutch dialect.

Instead of trying to win the affection and loyalty of his subjects in the Netherlands, Philip did everything to antagonize them. (1) He increased their taxes and interfered with their commerce to favor Spanish interests. (2) He sent Spaniards to occupy high government offices, depriving prominent Dutchmen of their positions. (3) The people were forced to house the insolent Spanish soldiers. (4) To these acts of tyranny Philip added the terrors of the Inquisition. Charles V had attempted to curb heresy in the Netherlands by severe

William the Silent, Father of the Dutch Republic · *Under his leadership, the Calvinists of Holland won their independence from Spain.*

Independence of the United Provinces (1581) · Alva recaptured some of the towns which revolted. But his merciless slaughter of the inhabitants aroused the southern provinces to join in the rebellion. Alva was recalled to Spain, and a more moderate general was sent in his place. But the new leader soon died. The army, left without a general, followed Alva's example and engaged in an orgy of robbery and murder. The "Spanish Fury," as it was called, led to a union of all the Burgundian provinces against the Spanish tyrant (1576).

The more reasonable governors whom Philip now sent won back the Catholic southern provinces (later Belgium) for the king. They remained in Hapsburg hands for two centuries longer. They were called the Spanish, and later the Austrian, Netherlands.

The northern provinces went their own way. In 1581 they declared their independence as the United Provinces, or the Dutch Republic. William of Orange was made hereditary governor of the new republic. Philip realized that William was the soul of the revolt and offered a title of nobility and a large reward to anyone who would make away with the Dutch patriot. He was assassinated in 1584.

The construction of the great Armada to invade England interfered with further attempts to recover the United Provinces. But Spain refused to acknowledge their independence until 1648.

CHECK ON YOUR READING

1. *Locate the territories of the Hapsburgs.*
2. *What were Philip's two ambitions?*
3. *How did he treat the Spanish? the Dutch? Why?*
4. *What were the results of his policies in these two countries?*

---

2. How Protestants Fared in France

France Remains a Catholic Country · In France the majority of the people clung to the old faith. The French kings knew how to retain their independence and yet remain on friendly terms with the papacy. During the years that the Popes lived at Avignon, they were in no position to defy the French kings. Later it was definitely agreed that the Pontiff was not to interfere in church elections or levy taxes on the French people. Francis I virtually controlled the appointments and wealth of the

233

Church and therefore had no quarrel with the papacy.

When Lutheran ideas began to make progress in France, Francis I took severe measures to suppress the reformers. The Inquisition was set in action, and many heretics were burned or driven into exile. It was during these persecutions that Calvin fled to Switzerland, where he became the leader of the Protestant movement at Geneva.

Henry II (1547–1559) swore to wipe out the Protestants, and hundreds were burned. His three weak sons, the last heirs of the House of Valois, succeeded in turn to the throne. During their reigns France was distracted by civil wars. Catholics and Protestants fought each other not only because of religious differences, but because each sought to control the government.

The Huguenots · In spite of persecution, however, the Protestants in France became a strong minority. They were called *Huguenots* and followed the religious teachings of their fellow countryman Calvin.

The Huguenots formed a prosperous and intelligent class, and many of them belonged to the nobility. They demanded not only religious toleration, but a more responsible government, with meetings of the Estates-General (Parliament) as a check on the royal power. They found great support in Henry of Navarre, who belonged to the younger branch of the royal family, the *Bourbons.*

Both Catholics and Huguenots tried to dominate the government. Catherine de' Medici, regent for her young son Charles IX, favored first one side and then the other. A limited amount of toleration was granted to the Huguenots, permitting them freedom of worship in certain places. But any concessions to the Huguenots angered the Guises, a powerful noble family which headed the Catholic party.

Massacre of Saint Bartholomew's Day (1572) · In 1570 a brief peace was made. The Huguenots were to be tolerated. Certain towns were given to them where they might defend themselves in case of attack. For a time Charles and his mother were under the influence of the Huguenot leader, Admiral Coligny, who acted as a sort of prime minister. But the Duke of Guise soon persuaded Catherine that she was being deceived by Coligny, and an unsuccessful attempt was made to murder him.

Catherine was now afraid that her son would discover her part in the plot, so she invented a story of a great Huguenot conspiracy. The innocent king was deceived. The Catholic leaders arranged to put to death Coligny and all the Huguenots who were to gather in Paris for the marriage of the king's sister to the Protestant Henry of Navarre.

On the morning of Saint Bartholomew's Day (August 24, 1572) the Huguenots were set upon suddenly. Before the next day was over, no fewer than two thousand of them had been murdered in the city. The news of the attack spread, and at least ten thousand more Protestants were put to death throughout the country.

Henry IV (1589–1610) and the Edict of Nantes · When the third son of Henry II died, the man with the best claim to the throne was the Protestant Henry of Navarre. He became the first of the Bourbon line of French kings. Henry had many enemies among the Catholics. In order to restore peace he decided to accept the religion of the majority of his people and was readmitted to the Catholic Church (1593).

But Henry also tried to aid the Huguenots. In 1598 he issued the *Edict of*

Nantes. (1) This order granted them the right of private worship throughout France and of public worship in certain specified towns and castles. (2) It promised government support to Protestant schools and allowed the publication of Protestant books. (3) Political and civil rights were now granted to Protestants, and they were henceforth to be permitted to hold government offices. (4) A most important provision was the right to hold for a period of years some two hundred fortified towns.

Henry Tries to Restore France · Henry IV found the kingdom in a wretched state after long years of civil war. With the aid of his minister Sully, an able Huguenot, Henry set about the task of restoring order and prosperity. Sully cut down grants to palace favorites and reduced the size of the army. He encouraged farming and stock-raising, and interested the king in promoting manufacture and trade. A merchant marine was built up by government aid, and a navy was started.

In the midst of this great work for France, Henry IV was assassinated (1610). His widow ruled as regent for their young son, Louis XIII. Sully was dismissed, and the queen surrounded herself with courtiers who wasted the resources of the country. They soon undid all that Sully had accomplished. The kingdom was again torn by warring factions.

Richelieu Governs France (1624–1642) · Finally, the young king Louis forced his mother to retire and placed in control Cardinal Richelieu. Richelieu was perhaps the greatest minister France has ever had. His ambition was to build up the absolute power of the monarchy. He therefore determined to suppress the Huguenots.

Ever since the Edict of Nantes the Protestants had constituted a real danger to the

Cardinal Richelieu · *To strengthen the French monarchy, he did not hesitate to crush the nobles, suppress the Protestant Huguenots, or oppose the Holy Roman Emperor.*

monarchy, for they had their own officers and judges, as well as their fortified towns. Richelieu deprived them of these strongholds by force of arms and forbade them to hold political meetings. Although he still allowed them freedom of worship, he removed all threat of armed opposition from the Protestant party in France.

CHECK ON YOUR READING

1. *Why did France remain Catholic?*
2. *Identify: Huguenots, Bourbons, Guises, St. Bartholomew's Day.*
3. *Summarize the Edict of Nantes.*
4. *How did Sully prove "able," and Richelieu "great"?*

3. The Thirty Years' War

Character of the Thirty Years' War · The last great conflict between Catholics and Protestants was the Thirty Years' War (1618–1648). It was really a series of wars on German soil, but with Denmark, Sweden, Spain, and France playing prominent parts in the struggle.

It is important to note that though the Thirty Years' War began as a quarrel between Catholics and Protestants, it was soon concerned with other matters than religion. In the end, Catholic and Protestant rulers were aiding each other against members of their own faith in their eagerness to gain land and power.

Why War Came · The Peace of Augsburg failed to settle the religious question in Germany (p. 220) for a number of reasons. (1) The treaty provided that only Protestants of the Lutheran faith were to be tolerated. Now the Calvinists, who had increased in numbers, were demanding equal rights with their fellow Protestants. (2) The seizure of church property by the Protestant princes had continued, in spite of the terms of the settlement.

(3) The reform movement had grown and spread into the Austrian possessions of the Hapsburgs, especially Bohemia. (4) With the hope of gaining further concessions from the Hapsburg emperor, Ferdinand, a Protestant union of princes was formed in 1608 under the leadership of Frederick, Elector of the Palatinate, on the Rhine. (5) The next year a Catholic League was organized under the Duke of Bavaria, with the object of revising the treaty and recovering church property.

The War Begins in Bohemia · Here, in 1618, the Protestant nobles revolted against the Hapsburg emperor and declared their independence. They chose Frederick, Elector of the Palatinate, as their king. The Bohemians looked to England for help since Frederick was the son-in-law of James I. But James failed to act, and the emperor, aided by Spain and the Catholic League, soon put down the rebellion.

The "Winter King" (as Frederick was called because he reigned for only one season) was driven into exile. Protestantism was forbidden in Bohemia, and the Palatinate was handed over to the Duke of Bavaria. The first stage of the war ended with a victory for the Catholics and an increase in the territory that they controlled.

The Danish King Joins the War (1625) · In 1625 the Protestant king of Denmark, Christian IV, entered the war to aid his fellow princes. But Ferdinand now had a vast army. It was led by Wallenstein, a brilliant soldier who had offered his services in return for the spoils of war. The Danes were severely defeated and after four years of fighting retired from the struggle. The second stage of the war ended with another success for the Hapsburgs.

Edict of Restitution (1629) · The emperor now issued an edict ordering the Protestants to give back any church property seized since the Peace of Augsburg. All Protestant sects except the Lutherans were to be suppressed. As a result, the Catholics recovered a number of bishoprics and monasteries and some thirty towns.

Wallenstein was going to carry out this order with his army of mercenaries in his usual manner. But the Catholic League was shocked at the barbarity of Wallenstein's troops and jealous of this ambitious

Gustavus Adolphus's Triumphal Entry into Munich, May 18, 1632 · *Behind him rode the King of Bohemia and the Elector of Saxony. The Swedish king's military genius won him the title "Lion of the North" and saved German Protestantism.*

and powerful general. The League, therefore, persuaded the emperor to dismiss Wallenstein.

Sweden Enters the War · Just at this time a new enemy to the Catholics arrived on the scene. Gustavus Adolphus, king of Sweden, sincerely wanted to aid the Protestants and also wanted to gain territory for his growing kingdom.

Sweden was at this time a strong national state, and Gustavus Adolphus was a very talented general. In 1631 he defeated the Catholic forces at Leipzig and the next year he was again victorious at Munich. The emperor, in alarm, now recalled Wallenstein to command his forces.

In November, 1632, Gustavus met Wallenstein on the field of Lützen. After a fierce struggle, the Swedes won the victory. But their king was killed. The Swedes continued, however, to take part in the war.

The struggle now became a series of raids, in which the soldiers of both sides slaughtered the people and devastated the land.

Wallenstein was deserted by his soldiers and finally murdered in 1634. That same year the emperor's forces won an important battle.

France Enters the War against the Hapsburgs · The German princes were now quite ready to end the war. If it had ended at this point, the Hapsburgs would have fared quite well. But just at this critical moment the French decided to prolong the struggle. Richelieu believed that it was to the interest of Louis XIII to enlarge his country at the expense of the Hapsburgs. He therefore had no hesitation in joining Catholic France with the Protestant princes.

France was surrounded by Hapsburg lands, with no natural boundaries (rivers or mountains) to protect her against her powerful neighbors. Richelieu determined therefore to make the Pyrenees Mountains the border line between France and Spain. He planned also to extend France toward the Rhine River, and to add a number of

Europe after the Peace of Westphalia · *Trace the boundary of the Holy Roman Empire. What Austrian Hapsburg territory lies outside? What power almost surrounded France? How were Holland and Switzerland affected by the treaties?*

fortified towns in the north as a protection against the Spanish Netherlands.

The cardinal had already formed an alliance with the chief enemies of the House of Austria and had furnished money to the Protestant leaders. He now openly declared war on Spain (1635). For a decade longer the armies of the allies continued to despoil the German states. Richelieu died in 1642, but his foreign policy was carried farther by his successor, Cardinal Mazarin. The war went on under the leadership of brilliant French generals.

The Treaties of Westphalia (1648) · By 1644 it was agreed that the nations involved should confer on the terms of peace. After four years of negotiation in Westphalia, a series of treaties were signed. The chief provisions were six: (1) Religious toleration in Germany was extended to include the Calvinists, as well as the Lutherans. (2) The Protestant princes were to keep the lands which they possessed in the year 1624. Each ruler was to determine the religion of his own realm. (3) The breakup of the Holy Roman Empire was practically acknowledged by permitting the individual states to make treaties among themselves and with foreign countries.

(4) Though portions of Germany were given to Sweden, this territory was to remain part of the Empire. Sweden was allowed three votes in the German diet. (5) To France, the emperor gave the fortified towns of Metz, Toul, and Verdun and all his rights in Alsace except the city of Strasbourg. (6) The independence of the United Netherlands and Switzerland was acknowledged.

How Germany Came out of the War · The devastation caused by the Thirty Years' War in Germany was almost unbelievable. A large proportion of the towns were destroyed. In some regions the population was reduced one half. The misery and poverty of those who remained were pitiful. Large sections of the country were now mere wasteland. As the German princes secured their independence, even the shadow of unity which the Hapsburgs had maintained in the Empire faded away.

CHECK ON YOUR READING

1. *What were the causes of the war? What nations were involved?*
2. *Why did Wallenstein, Adolphus, and Richelieu enter the war?*
3. *Summarize the treaties of Westphalia. What happened to Germany?*

---

4. The Age of Louis XIV in France

France Defeats the Spanish Hapsburgs · By the Peace of Westphalia France had added to her territory in the northeast and defeated the Austrian Hapsburgs. Cardinal Mazarin, who managed the government for the young Louis XIV, now sent the French armies against the Spanish Hapsburgs. Eleven more years of war ended with the Peace of the Pyrenees (1659). By its terms (1) Spain ceded to France the province of Roussillon, thus making the Pyrenees the natural frontier. (2) France received, in addition, a strip of the Spanish Netherlands. (3) Moreover, the Spanish king gave his daughter in marriage to the young French ruler, Louis XIV.

This treaty marked the end of Spain's supremacy. Her strength and resources were nearly exhausted by her long wars. France, on the other hand, had risen to be the chief power in Europe.

Louis XIV (1643–1715) the "Grand Monarch" · Louis XIV was only five years old when he came to the throne. For eighteen years Cardinal Mazarin ran the government for him, just as Richelieu had done for Louis XIII. These two great cardinal-ministers had made the monarchy supreme in France. Richelieu had transferred most of the powers of the nobles to royal officers (called *intendants*) directly responsible to the king. Many castles had been destroyed. Conspiracies among the courtiers were rooted out. Mazarin had put down a last uprising of the rebellious nobility. Thus when Mazarin died in 1661 and Louis XIV took up his duties as king, he found the stage set for him to play the role of "grand monarch."

Under Louis XIV absolute monarchy reached its height in France. The king was the sole authority, and the welfare of the people rested entirely in his hands. Louis could even dispose of the lives of his subjects without interference. There was no parliament to check his actions, or to which he must apply for funds. More important, he controlled a superb army. His power and the influence of the French court on Europe was so great that this period is sometimes called the Age of Louis XIV.

What is more, Louis XIV looked "every inch a king." He was handsome, of a commanding appearance, with courtly and elegant manners. While not brilliant, he had a quick understanding. He spent much time attending personally to the details of government. Louis regarded his ministers merely as his assistants to carry out his ideas. He believed that no one approached him in military talents, in plans and enterprises, or in governing ability. Louis chose the sun as his emblem, to show that the nation depended on him as the earth depends on the sun.

"Divine Right" of Kings · The "Sun King" not only played the role of grand monarch with perfect mastery, but believed that he was divinely chosen to do so. The idea that a king was given to his people by God was an old one, going back to the Bible (1 Samuel ix). When the Pope anointed Pepin as ruler of the Franks, he acknowledged anew the sacred character of kingship. Early in Louis's reign the ancient theory was clearly explained by a learned French bishop for the benefit of the people. God had given kings to men, he wrote, to rule over them as his representatives. Therefore it was sacrilege to disobey them.

The Estates-General of France had not met for nearly half a century when Louis began his reign, nor was it summoned again until 1789. The French people had no Magna Carta like England's. Moreover, the French depended far more on their king than did the English. France was surrounded by neighbors ready to invade the country at any sign of weakness in the government. Therefore the French felt that it was better to leave matters in the king's hands, even if they sometimes suffered from his tyranny.

How Colbert Strengthened France · Although Louis's pride prevented him from realizing what he owed to his ministers, much of the glory of his reign was due to the experts who surrounded him. Among these was the great economist and finance minister, Colbert.

(1) Colbert reformed the business methods of the government and put an end to the wasting and stealing of large sums of money by officials. He could not change the system of taxation, which freed the nobility and clergy from payment and robbed the defenseless peasants. (2) But he imposed new customs duties, which fell alike on all classes.

(3) Colbert encouraged farming and cattle-breeding, (4) improved roads and canals, (5) favored new industries and (6) protected the rights of inventors. (7) He set up high tariffs to keep out foreign goods that would compete with home products. (8) He established government control over the quantity and the quality of manufactured goods. (9) With the aid of government subsidies he built up merchant shipping and constructed docks and shipyards. (10) He enlarged the French navy and (11) began to secure colonies overseas as markets for French goods.

Unfortunately the increased wealth was squandered by the king on expensive palaces, on lavish gifts to his palace favorites, and in maintaining a costly army to fight a series of useless wars.

King Louis XIV and His Heirs ·
*From left to right: Louis's second
wife, his eldest son, the Sun King,
and his grandson. The little child,
his great-grandson, was crowned
Louis XV in 1715.*

The Glory of Versailles · The reign of the "Sun King" was one of splendor and display. At Versailles, near Paris, Louis had constructed an enormous palace. It had innumerable rooms, apartments, and mirrored salons, all furnished in the most costly and lavish style. The palace was set in a vast park beautified by groves, gardens, terraces, and marvelous fountains.

The luxuries of life at court and the magnificent entertainments were calculated to entice the nobles to leave their estates and flock to Versailles. Here they might share in the gay life at the palace and compete for the royal favor.

The ceremony at Versailles was as elaborate as a great pageant. Nobles who in their own castles lived like princes now eagerly sought the privilege of waiting upon the king. They saw him to bed at night and in stately procession greeted him in the morning. It was a high honor to assist him in dressing or to hand him a table napkin.

Louis as a Patron of Arts and Letters ·
Louis surrounded himself with artists, writers, and men of learning. Their genius reflected glory upon their patron king.

Molière, the foremost of French dramatists, delighted the court with his comedies. Racine was the great tragic playwright of the time. Madame de Sévigné wrote charming letters describing the brilliant life at Versailles. Many artists and scientists added luster to the reign of Louis XIV.

Colbert encouraged the growth of the French Academy, which had been created by Richelieu. This body gave special attention to perfecting the French language. French became the language of polite society and diplomacy in Europe. Colbert had an astronomical laboratory built in Paris. There too the Royal Library was beginning to grow into the great collection which in recent times has attracted scholars from all parts of the world.

CHECK ON YOUR READING

1. *What did the Peace of the Pyrenees mean to Spain? to France?*
2. *Explain Louis's idea of the "grand monarch" and "divine right."*
3. *How did Colbert strengthen France?*
4. *Describe the "glory of Versailles."*

5. Louis Makes War and Loses an Empire

Louis Seeks Glory in War · Louis was ambitious. Not satisfied with the realms he inherited, he dreamed of winning for France the natural boundaries of the Rhine and the Alps.

Much of the land that Louis coveted belonged to his rivals the Hapsburgs. He began to invent various claims to pieces of adjoining territory. He turned first to the north, claiming that the Spanish Netherlands rightfully belonged to his wife, the elder sister of the Spanish king. His armies in 1667 easily captured a number of border towns and then, moving south, completely conquered Franche-Comté (map, p. 238). But Holland persuaded England and Sweden to join her in a Triple Alliance to stop the French king's advance. Louis was forced to make peace. Though he retained some of the towns, he was obliged to return Franche-Comté to Spain.

Louis Turns against Holland (1672) · Louis was greatly angered that a little country like Holland should dare to oppose him. Besides, he was envious of Dutch trade and colonial successes overseas. He broke up the Triple Alliance by secretly bribing Charles II of England to help France in a new war against Holland. Louis's army then crossed the Rhine and conquered the southern part of that country.

For the moment the Dutch were in grave danger. But William of Orange showed the courage of his great ancestor William the Silent. The dikes were opened. This let in the sea and flooded the land, so that the French advance was checked.

The emperor also sent an army against Louis. The English Parliament, discovering Charles's secret treaty with the French king, compelled him to renounce it and make peace with the Dutch. The result of Louis's second war was that Holland was left intact, but France this time was given Franche-Comté.

Persecution of the Protestants · Louis adopted a very shortsighted policy in dealing with his Protestant subjects. Chiefly engaged in manufacture, trade, and banking, the Huguenots formed a thrifty and prosperous class in the nation. But Louis had very little sympathy with them and found excuses to persecute them. Finally in 1685 he revoked the Edict of Nantes. The Protestants in France were now outlaws, and their ministers were liable to the death penalty. Thousands of them fled to Germany, England, and America. The loss of their skills and industry was a serious drain on the French economy.

Louis Attacks the Palatinate (1689–1697) · Louis now decided to take possession of the rich country of the Palatinate. But this time the alliance that was formed against him included England. Louis's enemy William of Orange had just become its king (p. 255). After eight years of indecisive war Louis agreed to make peace.

Louis Covets the Spanish Crown for His Grandson · Louis's fourth and last war was the most important for its effects on the future of France. Louis was eager to gain a crown for his grandson and to widen the power of the Bourbons in Europe. He therefore risked a war which put an end to all prospects of a great French empire overseas. It was England that emerged victorious from the conflict and began to build up a great colonial empire in America and India.

The king of Spain, Charles II, had no children. All Europe was interested in what would become of his vast realms when his sickly life should end. Louis XIV and Emperor Leopold of the Holy Roman Empire had married sisters of Charles. The two rulers had often discussed how the Spanish possessions should be divided. If Louis's descendants should inherit the Spanish crown, a great Bourbon monarchy might be established, reaching from Holland to Sicily. If Leopold's family, the Austrian Hapsburgs, inherited the domains of the Spanish Hapsburgs, he would control a realm as vast as that of Charles V.

When Charles II died, it was found that he had made Philip, grandson of Louis, his heir on condition that the Spanish realms should never be divided. Louis now had a momentous decision to make. If he accepted the will, the Bourbons would have vast possessions in Europe and overseas as well. He knew that neither the English king nor the emperor would tolerate this increase of French power without a struggle. But the temptation was too great. He accepted the will and permitted his grandson to become Philip V of Spain.

War of the Spanish Succession (1702–1713) · King William of England now headed a new alliance of all Louis's old enemies. England, Holland, and Austria were the most important members. William died soon after the fighting began, but Queen Anne (1702–1714) carried on vigorously the War of the Spanish Succession.

The great English general, the Duke of Marlborough, and the Austrian commander, Prince Eugene of Savoy, drove the French out of the Netherlands, the Holy Roman Empire, and Italy. Even in America there was fighting between French and English colonists. Here it was known as Queen Anne's War. All the more important battles on land and sea went against the French. After ten years of misfortune, Louis was finally ready for a settlement.

The Great Treaty of Utrecht (1713) · The Treaty of Utrecht made many changes in the map of Europe. (1) Philip V was allowed to retain Spain and her colonies, but only on condition that the Bourbon Spanish and French crowns should never be united. (2) Austria was given the Spanish Netherlands (afterward called Austrian Netherlands). She also received the Spanish possessions Naples, Milan, and Sardinia. In this way she got a firm hold on Italy which she retained until 1866. (3) Savoy received Sicily and was recognized as a kingdom. (4) Holland won back certain border fortresses and was now protected from France by the Austrian Netherlands.

(5) England profited most from the war. From Spain she received the island of Minorca and the great fortress of Gibraltar. This put her in command of the narrow

Treaties of 1713–1718 · What territorial gains were made by England? Austria? Savoy? What important exchange was made in 1720? How did the treaty affect the New World?

entrance to the Mediterranean Sea. Her principal gains, however, were not in Europe but in the New World. Here she obtained Nova Scotia, Newfoundland, and the Hudson Bay region, and so began to push the French out of North America.

End of Louis's Reign · Although France lost none of her home territory in Europe, the nation had had to pay a terrible price for its king's ambition. The war had emptied the treasury and brought the people to the depths of misery. Taxes were increased and the currency was debased, for the country was now bankrupt. After a reign of seventy-two years the once magnificent Louis handed down to his great-grandson (Louis XV) an impoverished kingdom and a shrunken empire. Such was the record of the most glorious of kings, who had made a mockery of "monarchy by the grace of God."

CHECK ON YOUR READING

1. Why did Louis fight the Hapsburgs? Holland?
2. How did the persecution of the Huguenots affect France?
3. What were the causes and results of the War of the Spanish Succession?
4. How did the Treaty of Utrecht remake the map of Europe? of North America?

~~~~~~ *Learning Activities* ~~~~~~

Think about the chapter

1. What lessons can we learn from Philip II's treatment of Holland?

2. How did each of the following affect the history of France: Catherine de' Medici, Sully, Richelieu, Mazarin, Colbert, Louis XIV?

3. Why were both the issuing and the revocation of the Edict of Nantes significant?

4. In which wars in this period was religion an important factor? In which wars was the struggle for power and territory important? Explain.

5. Explain how the "Age of Louis XIV" was both glorious and inglorious.

6. *Map study:* On a map of Europe locate the Dutch Republic, Nantes, Bohemia, Denmark, Sweden, Leipzig, Lützen, Pyrenees Mountains, the Rhine, Westphalia, Versailles, Franche-Comté, Palatinate, Naples, Milan, Sardinia, Sicily, Austrian Netherlands.

Go beyond the text

7. The Duke of Marlborough was an ancestor of Winston Churchill. Read about Marlborough's life. How did court politics influence his career?

8. A French bishop made a statement of principles on which the theory of the "divine right of kings" is justified. You may be interested in looking it up and comparing present ideas as to the principles on which governments are based. (See HAYES, *Political and Cultural History*, Vol. 1, p. 291.)

9. Read further and report on one of the following: William the Silent (or his successors), Catherine de' Medici, Coligny, Wallenstein, Gustavus Adolphus.

10. Read about the construction of the Palace of Versailles. Try to find pictures of it as it is today. Why is the Hall of Mirrors so famous?

11. Find out how Spain controlled her New World colonies in the time of Philip II. Why were they easier to control than the Netherlands?

12. Read about the rise of Sweden as a national state. What was the Union of Calmar? Who was Gustavus Vasa?

Follow up your special interests

13. Try to find a reproduction of Pieter Brueghel's painting, *The Massacre of the Holy Innocents*. You will notice that Brueghel, by setting a biblical subject in a Flemish village of his own time, is comparing the cruelties of Herod with those of the Spanish rulers.

14. All Europe copied the styles in dress and the manners of the French court. Drawings of some costumes would make a good bulletin-board display. Be sure to include both men's and women's dress.

15. Louis XIV was called the "Sun King." Can you draw a cartoon that expresses this idea?

16. Many Huguenots emigrated to America. Try writing an original story about a family who settled in one of the colonies.

READ FURTHER

Basic readings: (1) BECKER, *Modern History*, Chap. 4. (2) CARR, *Men of Power*. Richelieu. (3) EVANS, *Costume Throughout the Ages*, Chap. 6. (4) HOFFMAN, *News of the World*, Nos. 34, 35, 37, 39. (5) MACY, *Story of the World's Literature*, pp. 236–241, 249–252. (6) ROBINSON, *Readings in European History*, Chaps. 28, 29, 31. (7) TAYLOR, *Fifty Centuries of Art*, pp. 116–145. (8) Year's *Pictorial History*, pp. 238–245, 260–264, 270–277, 308–313.

Special accounts: (9) A. BARNOUW, *The Land of William of Orange*. (10) L. BRAGDON, *The Land of Joan of Arc*. (11) T. COSTAIN, *The White and the Gold*. Events and personalities of the age of Louis XIV. (12) D. MILLS, *Renaissance and Reformation Times*. Chaps. 17–18. (13) D. OGRIZEK, *France: Paris and the Provinces*. Good for descriptions of Versailles and outstanding features of France. (14) F. SCHEVILL, A *History of Europe*. Chapter 15 is excellent on Louis XIV.

Fiction and biography: (15) M. CERVANTES, *Don Quixote*. A famous satire on Spanish chivalry. (16) T. COSTAIN, *High Towers*. The struggle for the rich furs of New France and the founding of New Orleans. (17) A. DARK, *Twelve Royal Ladies*. Catherine de' Medici and Queen Christina of Sweden are included. (18) A. DUMAS, *The Black Tulip*. Events in Holland at the time of William of Orange. Others by the same author are *The Man in the Iron Mask* and *The Three Musketeers*. (19) R. KNIGHT, *It Might Be You*. Short stories including one of a Huguenot boy in Paris on the eve of the massacre of St. Bartholomew's Day. (20) E. RIPLEY, *Rembrandt*. Life of the greatest of the Dutch painters, illustrated with many reproductions of his work. (21) C. SUBLETTE, *The Scarlet Cockerel*. An account of the attempt of the Huguenots to make a settlement in Florida.

"I want there to be no peasant in my kingdom so poor that he is unable to have a chicken in his pot every Sunday." —HENRY IV of France

The Making of Modern England

KEY WORDS AND DATES

Stuart kings
King James Bible
Shakespeare
Francis Bacon
William Harvey
Petition of Right (1628)
Puritans
Separatists
Presbyterians
Long Parliament
Archbishop of Canterbury
Cavaliers and Roundheads
"Rump Parliament"
Cromwell
Lord Protector
Commonwealth
Dissenters
Glorious Revolution
constitutional monarchy
Bill of Rights (1689)
Hanoverian kings
Whigs and Tories
cabinet system
prime minister
Robert Walpole
George III

AT THE VERY MOMENT when Louis XIV was ruling as absolute master of France, an English king was beheaded for attempting to override an unwilling Parliament. Monarchy by "divine right" flourished successfully in France. In England it met a strong challenge.

In the seventeenth century in England a long struggle took place to decide whether the supreme power should belong to the king or to the representatives of the people. As a result of this conflict, England adopted many of those forms and principles of government which have ever since been followed in Great Britain. England emerged from her "Glorious Revolution" a *constitutional monarchy*. The king was subject to the will of Parliament, and soon a *cabinet* of ministers began to exercise authority for the king. Political parties began to play an important role in government.

During this century England also settled her religious problem and firmly established the Anglican Church. The Revolution of 1688 not only reaffirmed the civil rights of the people, but granted them some measure of religious liberty. Protestants who "dissented" from the national Church were in general given the legal right to believe and worship according to their conscience. Out of the struggle for religious liberty, political liberty was born.

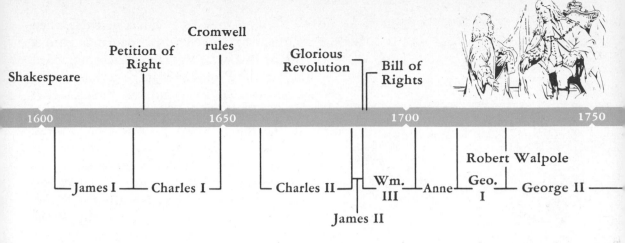

Shakespeare

Petition of
Right

Cromwell
rules

Glorious
Revolution

Bill of
Rights

1600   1650   1700   1750

James I —— Charles I   Charles II   Wm. III   Anne   Geo. I   Robert Walpole   George II ——

James II

1. The Struggle between King and Parliament

Character of the Stuart Kings · At the opening of the seventeenth century a new royal family came to the throne of England. In 1603 Queen Elizabeth died. James VI of Scotland, son of Mary Stuart (p. 226), became King of England as James I. The Stuart family ruled England, with two short interruptions, for over a century. The first four Stuarts were highly autocratic. During most of their reigns they were engaged in a losing battle with Parliament for control of the government.

The Stuart kings favored policies that were highly unpopular, and persisted in them in the face of open opposition. Yet it has been said that the very faults of the Stuarts proved a blessing to the English people. Had these rulers been wise and brilliant leaders, they might have fastened on England the chains of a strong monarchy. Parliament might have been reduced to a mere name. But their blind insistence on royal authority roused the people to assert their ancient rights. Parliament emerged as the supreme power in the British nation.

James I Antagonizes Parliament (1603–1625) · The English people, unlike the French under Louis XIV, were not impressed by Stuart claims to "divine right" rule. For one thing, James failed to command respect. He was awkward in appearance, and he spoke in an unpleasant voice with a Scottish accent. Moreover, he was peevish and had a quick temper. He scolded the members of Parliament as if they were children, telling them that they had no business to meddle in "deep matters of state."

From the very start, James met opposition. All his domestic and foreign policies seemed to be contrary to the wishes of Parliament. Unsympathetic and even hostile to the Puritans, he treated their representatives with great rudeness. Yet the Puritans were growing in numbers, gaining seats in Parliament, and exercising great influence among the people.

The Puritans, you will recall, favored a national church but wished to remove from it Catholic influences (p. 225). Because James had not interfered with the estab-

247

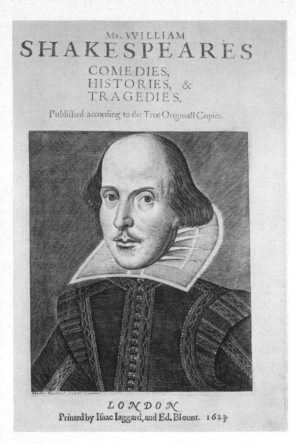

Mr. WILLIAM
SHAKESPEARES
COMEDIES,
HISTORIES, &
TRAGEDIES.

Published according to the True Originall Copies.

LONDON
Printed by Isaac Iaggard, and Ed. Blount. 1623.

Title Page of the First Shakespeare Folio ·
"He was not of an age, but for all times."
What does this mean?

lished Presbyterianism of Scotland, the Puritans had high hopes that he would favor their cause. Presbyterians and Puritans held many ideas in common. But James promised to "make them conform . . . or harry them out of the land." Thousands emigrated to Massachusetts.

James was eager for a union between Scotland and England, which neither nation then desired. He favored friendly relations with England's old enemy Spain, and even conspired to have his son wed a Spanish princess. He had great difficulty with Parliament over his extravagant spending.

Matters came to a climax in 1621, when Parliament replied to his demands with a list of its own. Parliament recommended aiding the Protestants in their war on the Continent (p. 236) and enforcing the laws against Catholics. It urged that the heir to the throne marry a Protestant princess, and not, as James wished, a Catholic. It asked for the reduction of expenses.

Angered at these suggestions, James forbade the mention of such matters in Parliament. This led to the drawing up of the *Great Protestation*. In this Parliament entered on the record a statement of its rights, privileges, and jurisdictions. James, however, sent for the journal, tore out the page, and dismissed Parliament. He had prepared the way for a very serious conflict, which was to end disastrously for his son.

Literature and Science under James I ·
It was during the reign of James I that some of the most gifted of all English writers flourished. Shakespeare is generally admitted to be the greatest dramatist that the world has ever produced. He wrote many of his plays before the death of Elizabeth. But some of his finest works—for example, *Othello*, *King Lear*, and *The Tempest*—belong to the time of James.

It was in James's reign that a new translation of the Scriptures was undertaken by a group of scholars. The *King James Bible*, or *Authorized Version*, is still highly esteemed because of the beauty and eloquence of its language.

Francis Bacon, a master of English prose, was writing his *Advancement of Learning*. In it he urged the careful study of animals, plants, and chemicals, instead of the works of Aristotle.

Among those who were making direct observations instead of relying on ancient authorities was William Harvey, a physician. He made the great discovery (1608) that the blood circulates from the heart through the arteries, capillaries, and veins back to the heart.

Charles I (1625–1649) Has Trouble with Parliament · Charles I succeeded James. He was a handsome man and more kingly in appearance than his father. But he was just as stubborn. Moreover, he made promises only to break them when he saw fit.

He began immediately to quarrel with Parliament. With his favorite, the Duke of Buckingham, he soon had the country at war with Spain, the Netherlands, and France. The wars proved miserable failures, and Charles was in need of funds. When Parliament refused to grant his demands unless he dismissed Buckingham, he sent the members home.

Since he could not obtain money from the government, Charles now resorted to questionable ways of getting it. His officials extorted loans from the people. When several prominent persons refused to make such forced loans, they were arrested and thrown into prison. Another thing that angered the people was the quartering of soldiers with private families. This meant supporting them in their homes, however distasteful this might be.

The Petition of Right (1628) · Such interferences with the liberties of the people led Parliament to draw up the *Petition of Right* in 1628. This was one of the most important documents in English history.

The petition reminded the king of the unlawful acts of his agents. It "humbly prayed" (1) that hereafter no free man should be imprisoned except according to the laws of the realm, (2) that the people need pay no tax or loan without the consent of Parliament, and (3) that soldiers be no longer lodged in private houses. Very unwillingly Charles signed this document, setting a limit to the kingly powers. But it was not long before he disregarded it.

Charles Defies Parliament and Rules Alone · In spite of his pledges, Charles continued to raise money by illegal means. He had his officials collect duties on the import and export of certain goods, such as wine and wool, without the permission of Parliament. When that body protested, he declared that this was not a tax but a customs duty. Parliament now summoned to trial customs officers who had seized the goods of those refusing to pay the tax. But Charles forbade his officers to appear. After several stormy sessions, he dissolved Parliament again.

For eleven years (from 1629 to 1640) the king ruled England without calling

Charles I, Cavalier · *While "principalle paynter" at the Stuart court, Anton Van Dyck did many such portraits.* Describe a Cavalier.

England in the 17th Century · *Why are pictures placed near Plymouth? Canterbury? Stratford? Research: Which two victories decided the Civil War?*

Parliament. New funds were raised in all sorts of illegal ways, and this made Charles and his advisers very unpopular. Old feudal dues were revived and special taxes were levied on property. Fines were collected for the breaking of ancient and forgotten laws. An old tax, called "ship money," formerly levied on seaport towns only, was extended to all towns. This was done on the pretext that the revenue was needed for the defense of the country.

How Charles Dealt with the Religious Situation · The ill feeling between king and Parliament was increased by religious differences. The king had married a French Catholic princess and was known to be sympathetic to the Catholic cause. There had been a tendency to restore some of the older ceremonies in the Anglican Church. Parliament, on the other hand, was growing strongly Puritan in membership.

William Laud, Archbishop of Canterbury, was the king's adviser in religious affairs. He made every effort to enforce obedience to the Anglican Church. Clergymen who refused to use the Anglican Book of Common Prayer or objected to any of the Anglican services were brought to trial and might lose their parish. Many outspoken Puritans were tried for their speeches and writings.

Some cases were tried by the Court of High Commission, consisting of Anglican church officials. Others went before the Court of Star Chamber, made up of the king's advisers and two judges. The accused were practically condemned before their cases were tried. The Puritans came to think of their cause as the cause of liberty and the rights of Parliament. Their sufferings seemed to increase rather than diminish their number.

The Protestants outside the Anglican Church at this time were divided into a number of sects. The largest was the Presbyterian, but there were also Quakers, Baptists, and other less well-known groups. There were an ever-increasing number of Independents, or Separatists. Their earliest leaders had been extreme Puritans who had come to believe that reform within the established church was impossible. They believed that every religious congregation should be free to govern itself. The Church and the state, they declared, should be entirely separate. Under the persecution of James and Charles many Puritans were driven into this movement. Among them were the Pilgrims of Plymouth colony.

The Scots Rebel · Charles's personal government was brought to an end by events in Scotland. There the Presbyterian form of religion had been established (p. 225). Charles wished to have the Scottish Church similar to the Anglican. When an attempt was made to compel the Scots to use a prayer book much like that of the Church of England, a riot broke out. In 1638 many of the Scots signed a National Covenant, pledging themselves to restore the "purity and liberty" of the Gospel. A Scottish assembly defied the commissioners sent by the king and re-established their own form of worship.

Charles now determined to punish this act of rebellion by going to Scotland with an army. But he found that he could not carry on a war without funds. He was therefore forced to summon Parliament once more.

The Long Parliament (1640–1653) · The so-called Long Parliament lasted thirteen years. It was in no mood for compromise. (1) It began by arresting those who had oppressed the people and accusing them of high treason. Some of Charles's ministers escaped. But his chief adviser and the Archbishop of Canterbury, William Laud, were tried and executed.

Parliament next provided (2) that it could not be dissolved without its own consent and (3) that it should meet every three years even if the king failed to summon it. (4) It abolished the hated special courts and (5) prohibited the collection of the illegal taxes which the people had been forced to pay. (6) The Anglican Church was temporarily overthrown, and the management of the Church was placed in the hands of a General Assembly. (7) It drew up a *Grand Remonstrance*, boldly stating the king's offenses and proposing a number of reforms. Parliament thus put an end to the despotic government of Charles I.

Civil War · England was soon plunged into civil war. Those who supported Charles were largely of the landed nobility

Oliver Cromwell · *Man of action though he was, Cromwell loved art and enjoyed music. John Milton was his Latin secretary.*

and were called *Cavaliers*. The king was strongest in northern England and part of Ireland, where the royal and Catholic causes were popular.

Members of the Parliamentary party were nicknamed *Roundheads* because some of them cropped their hair to show their dislike of the long locks of their aristocratic enemies. Most of them were middle-class people engaged in trade and business.

The Roundheads soon found a stalwart leader in Oliver Cromwell. He was a country gentleman who was a member of Parliament and an Independent. Cromwell organized an army of God-fearing men, who marched on their enemies singing Psalms.

The war continued for several years. After the first year it went, in general, against the Cavaliers. The king, defeated on every side, finally put himself into the hands of the Scottish army. It soon turned him over to Parliament. For two years Charles was kept a prisoner.

Execution of Charles I (1649) · There were many in the House of Commons who were still loyal to the king. They carried on negotiations in the hope of restoring him to the throne. But while these discussions were in progress, Charles was secretly seeking help from the Scots, Irish, and French.

In December, 1648, Parliament attempted to make peace with the king. The next day, however, all who were known to be friendly to Charles were prevented from entering the House by a body of soldiers stationed at the door. Thus the House of Commons was reduced to a small number of men who were enemies of the king. This remnant of the House, known as the "Rump Parliament" by its critics, declared themselves to be the supreme power in England as representatives of the people.

They chose a High Court of Justice, made up of Charles's sternest enemies, to pass judgment upon him. The king was declared guilty of being a tyrant, traitor, and murderer. On January 30, 1649, he was beheaded in front of his palace of Whitehall in London. It was not the nation at large that demanded Charles's death, but a small group of extremists who claimed the powers of the people.

CHECK ON YOUR READING

1. *How did James I antagonize Parliament?*
2. *What did Shakespeare, Bacon, Harvey, and the translators contribute?*
3. *Summarize the Petition of Right.*
4. *How did Charles I manage to rule alone?*
5. *Why were the Puritans and sects alarmed?*
6. *What did the Long Parliament do?*
7. *Describe the causes, participants, and results of the Civil War.*

---

2. The Commonwealth and the Restoration

England Becomes a Commonwealth · On May 19, 1649, the "Rump Parliament" proclaimed England to be a "Commonwealth." That meant a republic without a king or House of Lords. The government was in the hands of Parliament, but Cromwell was the real ruler.

Cromwell was supported by the Independents, but his main strength was his well-organized army of fifty thousand men and his own skill and energy as a leader. Otherwise the republic would not have lasted more than a few months. There were many who opposed it and were shocked at the "murder" of the king. Even the Presbyterians regarded Charles's son as the rightful heir to the throne.

Cromwell Subdues Ireland and Scotland · Cromwell found himself faced with revolt in Ireland. The nobles and the Catholics there proclaimed Charles II king and raised an army to overthrow the Commonwealth. Cromwell, therefore, set out for Ireland, and by 1652 the island was conquered for the Commonwealth. A large part of the land was taken over by the English, and the Catholic landowners were driven into the hills.

In the meantime Charles II, who had taken refuge in France, landed in Scot-

Cromwell Dismisses the Long Parliament, 1653 · *"Be gone, you rogues, you have sate long enough." This Dutch print uses a poodle, a nearsighted owl, and a peacock to satirize the British lion, and the blindness and vanity of the Lords.*

land (1650). When he promised that he would be a Presbyterian king, the whole Scottish nation was ready to support him. But Cromwell subdued Scotland even more speedily than he had Ireland and completely destroyed its army.

Brief War with the Dutch · Cromwell found time, in the midst of all his other activities, for a brief war against the Dutch. Both England and Holland had been increasing their trade overseas. But the skill and enterprise of the Dutch sailors and merchants had made them the most successful traders in Europe. This rivalry between the English and the Dutch led to many disputes.

Finally, in 1651, Parliament passed a Navigation Act. By its provisions Dutch ships could bring to England only goods produced in Holland. After a series of battles between the English and Dutch fleets, the Dutch were forced to recognize the Navigation Act (1654).

Cromwell as the Lord Protector (1653) · In April, 1653, Cromwell put an end to the unpopular "Rump Parliament" and summoned one made up of men chosen by himself and his army officers. Then in December a group of the more practical members got up early one morning. Before the others had a chance to protest, they declared Parliament dissolved and placed supreme authority in the hands of Cromwell.

Cromwell, as "Lord Protector," was practically king, though he refused to take the title. He was, in reality, a dictator with a strong army behind him. His greatest success was in his relations with foreign states.

Coronation of Charles II in Westminster Abbey · *All English rulers since William I have been crowned here. The church is a gothic monument as well as a famous national shrine.*

At home he was opposed by two groups: those who wished to restore a king and the Anglican Church, and those who favored a more democratic form of government. In 1658 Cromwell died. A great storm passed over England at the time, and the Cavaliers asserted that the devil had come to fetch home his soul.

Restoration of Charles II (1660–1685) · In the confusion that followed the death of Cromwell, it was soon clear that the people were weary of a military government and of the drabness of life under the Puritans. Under Cromwell theaters had been closed, many amusements forbidden, and strict observance of the Sabbath enforced.

The new Parliament that assembled in 1660 received a message from the exiled prince in France. He offered to pardon all those who had taken part in the rebellion, to permit confiscated royalist property to remain in the hands of its present owners, and to grant religious toleration.

On reading this declaration, Parliament resolved that "according to the ancient and fundamental laws of this kingdom, the government is, and ought to be, by king, lords, and commons." A few weeks later Charles was welcomed with joy by the people of England. The Puritan revolution was over. Life became gay again as people indulged in pleasures forbidden by the Puritans.

Charles II swore to uphold the Great Charter, the Petition of Right, and other statutes safeguarding the liberties of the people. The full powers of Parliament, if not its supremacy, were recognized.

Charles was quite as fond of having his own way as his father. But he had sad reminders to warn him how far he could go. Although he was lazy and pleasure-loving, and might try to outwit Parliament, he never stubbornly defied it. He did not intend, he said, to let anything send him on his travels again.

Parliament Re-establishes the Anglican Church · The Parliament which met in 1661 was made up almost entirely of Cavaliers. Charles got along with it so well that he did not dissolve it for eighteen years.

A number of laws were now passed to establish the Anglican Church in its former position of power. An attempt was made to keep Presbyterians and Independents out of town offices. An Act of Uniformity required every clergyman and schoolteacher to accept fully the teachings of the Anglican Prayer Book or lose his position. About two thousand ministers resigned rather than act against their conscience.

All Protestants who differed in belief from the Anglican Church were thrown into one legal class, the Dissenters. They included Presbyterians, Baptists, Quakers, Independents, and minor sects. Since some had taken part in the rebellion, they were regarded as dangerous unless strictly regulated by law.

The King Favors Toleration · It was Parliament rather than the king that wanted the Anglican Church to be supreme. Louis XIV had secretly bribed Charles to support France against Holland (p. 242) *and to extend Catholicism in England.* In 1672 Charles issued a Declaration of Indulgence. It suspended the enforcement of the laws punishing Roman Catholics and Dissenters for their failure to conform to the Established Church. But when Parliament protested, Charles withdrew the declaration.

Fearing the return of the Catholics to power, Parliament now passed the Test Act. This kept everyone from public office who did not accept the views of the Anglican Church and take the Communion according to its usage. This intolerant law remained in force in England until the nineteenth century.

War with Holland Again · The old war with the Dutch broke out again over the rivalry in trade and colonies in the East and West Indies and in North America. Neither side could gain a decisive victory. However, the English were able to seize some of the West Indian islands from the Dutch. In 1664 they captured the settlement of New Amsterdam, which they renamed New York in honor of the king's brother, the Duke of York. Peace was made in 1667. The English retained their conquests and ceded the Spice Islands to Holland.

· **CHECK ON YOUR READING**

1. *Summarize Cromwell's rule and his military successes.*
2. *Why did Parliament restore the monarchy?*
3. *How were Anglicans, Dissenters, and Catholics treated under Charles II?*
4. *What were the causes and results of the two wars with Holland?*

---

3. *England Establishes a Constitutional Monarchy*

How James II Antagonized His People (1685–1688) · Charles was succeeded by his brother James II. James was a tactless and stubborn man who was soon thoroughly disliked by the people. He had all the Stuart ideas of kingly privilege but none of the quick wit and adaptability which helped Charles out of difficult situations.

James was an ardent Catholic. Most of his troubles came from his determination to favor the Catholic cause. He appointed Catholics to government and university offices and dissolved Parliament when it opposed his actions. He finally suspended all laws against Catholics and Dissenters.

The English people tolerated James as long as they believed that his Protestant daughter Mary, who had married William of Orange, would succeed him. But then a son was born to James and his Catholic second wife. At this event representatives of Parliament were sent to Holland to invite William and Mary to come to England as king and queen.

The "Glorious Revolution" (1688) · William landed in November, 1688. As he marched with his Dutch troops toward London, most of the nobility announced their intention of supporting him. James, finding himself deserted, fled to France.

Parliament now declared the throne vacant. James, they said, had broken the original contract between the king and the people, had violated the fundamental laws, and had withdrawn from the kingdom. They listed James's illegal acts, restated the rights of the people, and offered the throne to William and Mary. In accepting the crown for himself and his wife, William promised to observe the laws and govern with the advice of Parliament.

Thus, in the so-called "Glorious Revolution," Parliament, without bloodshed, deposed a hereditary king and elected one of its own choosing. England rid herself forever of monarchy by "divine right," and the supremacy of Parliament was established.

The Bill of Rights (1689) · On the accession of William and Mary, Parliament passed the Bill of Rights. Like the Great Charter and the Petition of Right (1628), this is one of the great documents of the British constitution. Unlike the United States Constitution, the British constitution does not consist of a particular group of articles and amendments. It is rather made up of all fundamental acts of Parliament plus many usages never put down in writing.

The Bill of Rights once more defines the rights of the people and sets a limit to the powers of the king. Among other things it (1) declares that the king may not suspend the laws or free subjects from obedience to the law. (2) He may not levy taxes or maintain an army without the consent of Parliament. (3) He may not interfere with the free election of members to Parliament or with the freedom of speech and proceedings of the governing body.

A Toleration Act was also passed (1689). It freed Dissenters from penalties for failing to attend the Anglican services and permitted them to have their own churches. Catholics were not included in the Toleration Act, but they were allowed to hold their meetings undisturbed.

Protestantism Assured · The Bill of Rights decided, once and for all, that England was to remain a Protestant country. It stated that no Catholic, or one who should "marry a papist," should ever inherit the crown.

The Act of Settlement (1701) provided for the Protestant succession to the throne. As there was no Protestant heir in the Stuart family, Parliament arranged that after the death of Queen Anne (p. 257), the crown should go to her nearest Protestant relative.

Religious toleration, though extended, was not fully achieved. The Dissenters were recognized by law but were not allowed to hold public offices. These were reserved for Church of England men. The Catholics and Unitarians were not granted toleration, but they worshiped privately and were no longer persecuted. Although many of the old harsh laws remained, they were generally neglected.

England Becomes a Constitutional or Limited Monarchy · The most important result of the Glorious Revolution was the settlement of the permanent form of the English government. The struggle between king and Parliament was now at an end. Henceforth the king would owe his crown to the will of Parliament.

Two measures increased still further Parliament's control over the government. (1) A large part of the taxes formerly granted to the king for life were now awarded for a year at a time. (2) The funds

An English Coffee House · *In such centers of wit and learning, gentlemen might trade stories, argue politics, engage in spritely conversation, read the magazines, or otherwise pass the time while sipping the popular new drink from Arabia.*

for the upkeep of the army were to be voted annually. These acts prevented the king from gaining personal control of the armed forces or accumulating large amounts of money. The powers of the sovereign were now strictly limited by law.

Scotland and England Unite (1707) · William III outlived Mary by some eight years and during that time ruled alone. At his death, Mary's younger sister came to the throne. It was during Anne's reign (1702–1714) that the final union of Scotland and England took place.

The two countries had been under the same ruler since the days of James I, but each had its own parliament and system of government. Finally they agreed to unite. Forty-five members of the British House of Commons were thereafter to be chosen in Scotland. Sixteen peers took their seats in the British House of Lords. The whole island was joined under one government, and the Union Jack became the national flag of the United Kingdom of Great Britain.

The House of Hanover (1714) · Since none of Anne's fourteen children survived her, the Act of Settlement gave the crown to her nearest Protestant relative. This was the son of James I's granddaughter Sophia, who had married the Elector of Hanover. George I came to England, but continued to rule Hanover and to serve as an elector of the Holy Roman Empire. Members of this family still reign in England today, but during World War I they changed their name to Windsor.

Political Parties in England · There were no political parties in England before the seventeenth century, although the members of Parliament took sides on questions that came up before them. But during the time

Sir Robert Walpole · *Hogarth shows England's first Prime Minister (left) conversing with the Speaker and the Clerk of the House.*

of Charles I two distinct groups arose in Parliament. One, the Cavaliers, supported the king. The other, the Roundheads, upheld the rights of Parliament (p. 251).

During the reign of Charles II the power of Parliament so increased that permanent political parties developed. In time, the successors of the Cavaliers came to be called *Tories*, and the successors of the Roundheads became known as *Whigs*.

In general, the Tories were the party of the landholding gentry and the supporters of the Anglican Church. The Whigs represented the business class, the Dissenters, and a small portion of the nobility. Later the Tories became the Conservatives and the Whigs the Liberals.

How the Cabinet System Developed · William III had at first chosen his ministers from *both* political parties. But as there were frequent disputes that delayed action, he finally decided to select advisers only

from the party that had the majority in the House of Commons. The custom gradually developed that a small group of the king's most important advisers met frequently to discuss the affairs of the country. This group came to be called the *cabinet* because it held its sessions in a cabinet, or private room.

Today the English cabinet is responsible for the direction of the government. Headed by its spokesman, the first, or *prime*, minister, it proposes the policies to be followed. These are submitted to Parliament to be debated and voted upon. If they are approved, they are carried out as the will of the people.

If, however, Parliament rejects the policies of the cabinet, the ministers may resign as a body. The king will then ask the leader of the Opposition (the strongest party opposed to the one in power) to form a cabinet.

A cabinet whose measures are rejected may prefer not to resign, but ask for a general election to determine the wish of the country. In this case the leader of the party which wins the largest number of seats in Parliament is asked to select a new cabinet and formulate new governmental policies.

When a law has been passed by both houses of Parliament, it is presented to the king for his signature. Today this is a matter of courtesy only, for the king no longer has the power to veto an act of Parliament and prevent it from becoming law. Also today the House of Commons is really supreme. The House of Lords has no power over money bills and can only delay other measures.

Origin of Office of Prime Minister · The important office of *prime minister*, as we know it today, did not develop until the time of George I. Because he could speak no English, he soon ceased to attend the meetings of his ministers and left affairs in their hands.

Robert Walpole, a man of great financial ability, was called into the government at a time of crisis. He became First Lord of the Treasury and Chancellor of the Exchequer. He showed such general wisdom that he soon rose to prominence and was recognized by both the king and Parliament as leader of the cabinet.

Walpole continued his service under George II (1727–1760). For twenty-one years, as spokesman for the cabinet, Walpole was really prime minister. He was friendly and judicious. By maintaining peace at home and abroad he enabled the country to build up its business and trade and to enjoy prosperity.

George III (1760–1820) attempted to recover some of the power formerly held by the English kings. He created a party known as the "King's Friends," which helped him to run the country as he wished. In spite of the restrictions of Parliament, he managed to rule in a highhanded and head-strong way. George III was practically his own prime minister. It was during his reign that the American colonies won their independence from the mother country.

Parliament Represented a Minority · England had made great progress in establishing parliamentary control over the government. But Parliament was not yet truly representative of the entire people. Some towns had declined over the years or disappeared altogether, yet still had members to represent them in Parliament. On the other hand, new manufacturing cities might have no members in Parliament at all.

The House of Commons in the eighteenth century represented only a small minority of landowners and businessmen. Only those who had a certain amount of property had the privilege of voting. The English system, in spite of parliamentary rule, was still aristocratic. The rich enjoyed privileges that were denied to the poor.

Yet England had laid the foundations of a system of government which could be greatly improved as one class after another gained the vote. In the nineteenth century there was a thoroughgoing reform of Parliament. No such revolution as the French suffered was necessary to create a modern democracy in England.

CHECK ON YOUR READING

1. *What were the causes of the "Glorious Revolution"? What problems did it settle?*
2. *Summarize the Bill of Rights.*
3. *What other parliamentary measures helped to prevent absolutism?*
4. *How did the union of England and Scotland affect Parliament?*
5. *How did political parties, the cabinet system, and office of Prime Minister each develop? How does the cabinet system operate today?*

"Give me the liberty to know, to utter, and to argue freely according to conscience, above all liberties."
—JOHN MILTON, *Areopagitica*

Learning Activities

Think about the chapter

1. Compare the ways used by Charles I to raise money with those used by Colbert and Louis XIV (see Chapter 15).

2. Explain: "The faults of the Stuarts proved a blessing to the English people."

3. Do you think Charles I had a fair trial? Why did some refer to his execution as murder?

4. Explain why Parliament in the eighteenth century was not really representative.

5. *Map study:* Draw a map of the British Isles and northwestern Europe showing northern France and the Low Countries. Label England, Scotland, Ireland, Wales, London, Dublin, Edinburgh, and the bodies of water surrounding the British Isles.

Go beyond the text

6. Make a report on one of the following topics: Cromwell and the Civil War; Richard Cromwell; Guy Fawkes and the Gunpowder Plot; John Hampden and the Ship Money; Samuel Pepys and His Diary.

7. Contrast life under the rule of Cromwell and under Charles II. Why did the English welcome the Restoration?

8. The Pilgrims, Puritans, and Catholics settled three colonies while James I and Charles I were ruling. Why?

9. John Milton lived in this period (1608–1674). Report on his political activities and his writings.

Follow up your special interests

10. Read the amusing poetry about Pilgrims and Puritans in *The Book of the Americas* by Stephen and Rosemary Benét.

11. You are familiar with the stories of the Dutch settlements in New Amsterdam. Try writing a dramatization of Peter Stuyvesant's surrender to the English in 1664.

12. Make a chart or poster showing steps taken in England toward political democracy from 1215 to 1760.

13. See if you can find the words and music to "The Skye Boat Song." It is in many collections of folk songs. How are the words connected with this chapter?

14. Read and report on one of the many fine selections listed below.

READ FURTHER

Basic readings: (1) BECKER, *Modern History*, Chap. 3. (2) CARR, *Men of Power*, Cromwell. (3) CHEYNEY, *Readings in English History*, Chaps. 14–17. (4) CHEYNEY, *Short History of England*, Chaps. 14–17. (5) EVANS, *Costume Throughout the Ages*, Chap. 12. (6) HOFFMAN, *News of the World*, Nos. 36–38. (7) Life's *History of Western Man*, Sec. VIII. (8) MACY, *Story of World's Literature*, Chaps. 24, 26, 29. (9) ROBINSON, *Readings in European History*, Chap. 30. (10) VAN LOON, *Story of Mankind*, pp. 279–295. (11) Year's *Pictorial History*, pp. 264–269, 314–317.

Special accounts: (12) M. and C. H. B. QUENNELL, *Everyday Things in England from 1500–1799*. (13) A. STREET, *The Land of the English People*. (14) *Life*, "High Venture and Civil War," November 12, 1956. From Churchill's *History of the English-Speaking Peoples*.

Fiction and biography: (15) M. BARNES, *With All My Heart*. A story of Charles II and England under the Restoration. (16) C. HAWES, *Dark Frigate*. An English lad runs away to sea and is captured by pirates. (17) H. MORROW, *Yonder Sails the Mayflower*. A story of the Pilgrims during their last weeks in England. (18) H. READ, *Fighters for Freedom*, Chaps. 32–33. (19) G. TREASE, *Cue for Treason*. Tells the adventures of a boy who joins a company of actors and becomes a friend of Shakespeare.

Tudor, Stuart, and Hanoverian Kings in Britain

Tudors

Stuarts

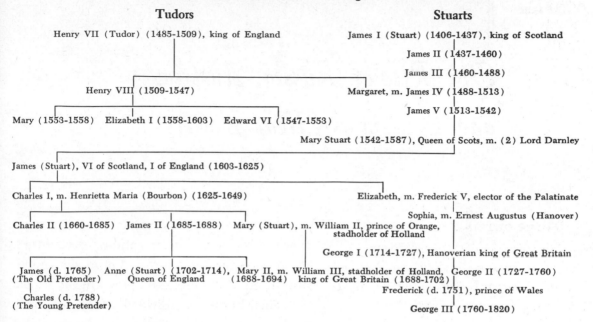

Later British Hanoverians and Related Ruling Houses

This table is incomplete, but gives sufficient detail to show how, in the twentieth century, some of the reigning families of Europe are related.

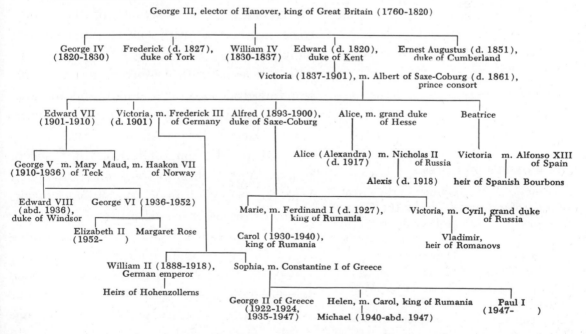

CHAPTER 17

The Rise of Russia, Austria, and Prussia as Great Powers

CHAPTER OUTLINE

1. *The Rivalries of National States*
2. *Russia Becomes a European Nation*
3. *The Austrian Empire of the Hapsburgs*
4. *Prussia Becomes a Great Power*

KEY WORDS AND DATES

autocracy	Catherine the Great
balance of power	Frederick the Great
dynasties	Hohenzollerns
Slavs	Maria Theresa
Scandinavian	Hapsburgs
Genghis Khan	Silesia
tsars	Seven Years' War
Romanovs	1756–1763
Peter the Great	benevolent despots
Duma	Partitions of Poland

WE OFTEN SPEAK TODAY of great or small "powers" when we mean nations or countries. The term *power* came into use in modern times with the growth of national states. In the Feudal Age, when Europe was divided into many principalities, there was no such thing as a power. But with the triumph of monarchy came central governments, standing armies, national policies, and the development of clearly defined powers. These modern states, because of their unity, could act or treat with one another much as individuals do.

In the seventeenth century France and England forged ahead as the leading European states. The eighteenth century saw the rise of Russia, Austria, and Prussia. All these nations were destined to play important roles in modern times. With their ambitions and rivalries they kept the map of Europe constantly changing, as one or the other gained or lost a bit of territory. International relations are much influenced by long-standing traditions of friendship or enmity. We may be better able to understand the Europe of today if we see how the powers developed and how they dealt with one another from the first.

262

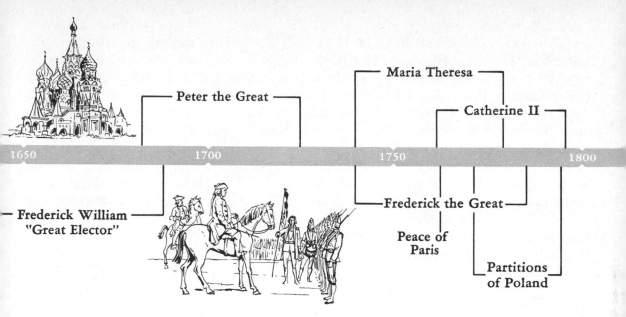

Peter the Great

Maria Theresa

Catherine II

1650 1700 1750 1800

Frederick William
"Great Elector"

Frederick the Great

Peace of
Paris

Partitions
of Poland

1. The Rivalries of National States

Keeping a "Balance of Power" · Europe has been fought over for centuries and its lands have passed back and forth through countless hands. The development of highly nationalistic states intensified the struggle for land and power. For protection various nations would often make agreements with one another to prevent an ambitious monarch from becoming *too* strong and thus threatening the fortunes of the rest. This was called maintaining the "balance of power."

Different nations threatened the balance of power at different times. We have already seen that a Triple Alliance was formed against France when Louis XIV tried to seize the Netherlands (p. 242). At an earlier time Spain had threatened the balance of power in Europe.

In the eighteenth century three new powerful states emerged. The ruling dynasty in each sought to extend its territory and match the power of the Bourbons of France. (1)

The kingdom of Prussia and house of Hohenzollern dominated Germany. (2) The Austro-Hungarian Empire of the Hapsburgs controlled much of southeastern Europe. (3) Russia under the Romanovs was transformed from an Asian to a European country.

Autocracy and Dynasty · Two ideas of government were held by most eighteenth-century monarchs. (1) They believed in *autocracy* and the divine right of kings. This is best summed up in the famous remark of Louis XIV: *"L'état, c'est moi!"* ("I am the state!"). James I of England said, "Kings . . . have power . . . of life and death over their subjects, . . . accountable to none but God only."

(2) They believed in *dynasty*—the continued rule of the same family. They regarded their realms as personal possessions to be handed down from generation to generation to the nearest heir. In this way European states were hereditary in a

263

few dynasties. The initials **B. H. H. H. R.** (Bourbon, Hanover, Hapsburg, Hohenzollern, Romanov) may help you keep these ruling families in mind. These dynasties dominated the major countries of Europe until the end of World War I.

Methods Used to Increase Power · Most of the eighteenth-century autocrats were ambitious. They were eager to enlarge their realms and gain more glory for themselves. There were several ways in which they could achieve these ends. (1) Through the marriage of a member of one royal family with a member of another their lands might be consolidated. Younger sons and princesses in one country became kings or queens of another by such marital arrangements. The relationship between the various royal houses thus became bewilderingly complicated.

(2) Treaties and military alliances were made in which each ruler tried to outwit the others and gain some advantage. Friends one day might be enemies tomorrow. Principalities and populations were shifted about like pawns in a clever game.

(3) The monarchs readily resorted to war in the hope of gaining what they desired. They believed that might made right, the end justified the means, and that to the victor belonged the spoils.

CHECK ON YOUR READING

1. *Explain the ideas of "balance of power," autocracy, and dynasty.*
2. *What great powers and ruling families dominated Europe?*
3. *By what three methods did autocratic monarchs seek power and prestige?*

---

2. Russia Becomes a European Nation

Who the Slavs Were · We must now turn our attention to the Slavic peoples, to whom the Russians, Poles, Serbs, and other groups of eastern Europe belong. The Slavs outnumber the other peoples on the European continent. They were settled along the Don, Dnieper and Vistula rivers as early as the beginning of the Christian Era. After the East Goths pushed into the Roman Empire, the Slavs followed their path and conquered a great part of southeastern Europe.

The three chief branches of the Slavic peoples are (1) the Russians; (2) the group living in what is now Poland and Czechoslovakia, which includes the Poles, Bohemians, Moravians, and Slovaks; (3) the southern Slavs (Yugoslavs) of the Balkan region, including the Serbs, Croats, and Bulgarians.

Earliest Russia · Russia began with the gradual expansion of the Slavic tribes living on the eastern slopes of the Carpathian Mountains. Pushing their way through the forests of what is now central Russia, these tribes made clearings and founded villages.

In the ninth century bands of Northmen invaded the districts east of the Baltic Sea. These adventurous Northmen—known as the Varangians—moved down the riverways of western Russia until they came to the Black Sea. They established communities and trading stations. In the later tenth century, they hired themselves to the emperor at Constantinople as soldiers of his bodyguard.

The Scandinavian invaders had a great influence on the development of Russia. Indeed, the early rulers mentioned in the chronicles of the time have Scandinavian, rather than Slavic, names. It is from *Rus*, the Slavic word for the Northmen, that Russia derives its name.

The Mongols Overrun Russia · Russia is geographically an extension of the vast plain of northern Asia and so was exposed to invasion from the east. In the thirteenth century the Mongols, a powerful tribe originally from the region north of China, swept into the country. Their great leader, Genghis Khan (1206–1227), conquered northern China, central Asia, northern India, Turkestan, and Persia and reached the shores of the Black Sea.

The bands of fierce horsemen sent by Genghis Khan's successors overran Russia, which had fallen apart into numerous principalities. The Russian princes became dependents of the Great Khan. They were required frequently to visit his far-distant court at Peking. There the Khan might, as he chose, give them crowns or cut off their heads.

Among the Russian princes who went to prostrate themselves at the foot of the Great Khan's throne was the prince of Muscovy, or Moscow. But in due time the power of the Mongols began to decline. Then the prince of Moscow refused to pay tribute any longer and threw off the Mongol yoke.

The Mongol occupation, however, had greatly affected Russia. The princes of Moscow imitated the oriental despotism of the khans and the emperors at Constantinople, rather than the rulers of western Europe. As a matter of fact, they knew nothing of western Europe. The Mongol invasions, which reached as far west as Poland and Hungary, must have been one

The Duel, by Mikhail Avilov · *The Russian champion meets and defeats the Mongol champion at the battle of Kolikovo.*

means of bringing oriental ideas and products into Europe.

Russia Becomes a Monarchy · The princes of Moscow now began to extend their own power and dominion. Ivan the Great (1462–1505) and his son subdued the other independent Russian principalities. They created a vast monarchy under the autocratic rule of Moscow.

Christianity had been brought into Russia from Constantinople, and the Russians had acknowledged the patriarch of the Greek Orthodox Church as the head of their church. After the Turks captured Constantinople (1453), however, the Russian emperors (*tsars* or *czars*, from *Caesars*) liked to think of themselves as the successors of the Eastern Christian emperors and as protectors of the Orthodox Church.

In 1547 Ivan the Terrible (Grandson of Ivan the Great) had himself crowned "Tsar

Peter I, the Great · *Peter created the Russian navy and placed Vitus Bering, a Danish sea captain, in command. He later financed Bering's first exploration west of Alaska.*

and Autocrat of all the Russias." He deprived the nobles, or *boyars*, of their hereditary estates and made his power absolute. But he enforced his authority with such cruelty and bloodshed that his reign was a nightmare of terror.

After Ivan's death there followed a period of civil war and anarchy. It came to an end with the election of a new tsar, Michael. The choice of Michael (1613) brought to the throne of Russia the Romanov family, which ruled for three hundred years, down to the revolution of 1917.

Peter the Great · The most noted of the Romanovs was Peter I, the grandson of Michael. It was he who brought Russia into the family of European nations. Peter the Great was a giant of a man, seven feet tall and of enormous strength and energy. He was shrewd and practical and combined some idealism with a good deal of coarse brutality. He ruled from 1689 to 1725.

When Peter came to the throne, Russia was still a semibarbarous state. Its customs and manners were oriental, and the country was almost entirely unaffected by the progress in government and learning which had been made in Europe. Russia was far behind the countries of western Europe.

Peter knew that his crudely equipped soldiers could not cope with the well-disciplined armies of the West. He realized that without a warm-water port and ships Russia could not trade or take part in world affairs. He therefore determined to Westernize his realms and make a "window" through which Russia could look abroad.

Peter Learns Many Things in Europe · In 1697–1698 Peter, in disguise, visited Europe. His purpose was to investigate for himself the improvements that had been made in science and art and in manufacturing methods. Nothing escaped the keen eyes of this half-savage giant. He put on the wide breeches of a Dutch laborer and for a week worked in the shipyards at Zaandam. In England, Holland, and Germany he engaged architects, scientists, workmen, ship captains, and military experts to help him modernize his country.

Peter was called home by a revolt of the Russian nobles of the royal bodyguard. He took a terrible revenge on the rebels and is said to have cut off many heads himself. He left the bodies lying about all winter unburied so that all might see the fearful results of revolt against his power.

Peter Establishes the Absolute Power of the Tsar · Peter now determined to make his authority absolute throughout his realms. (1) He recruited a large standing army, directly under his control. He had his troops trained by foreign officers, who were responsible to him. (2) He reorganized the country into provinces. At the head of each he placed a military officer, who was to collect sufficient taxes from his district to support a certain number of regiments. (3) Peter abolished local self-government and brought the country under the management of his own officials. (4) He replaced the old assembly of nobles, the *Duma*, by an advisory council of nobles, whom he himself selected.

(5) Peter prevented any possible trouble with the Church by making it virtually a department of the government. He replaced the patriarch of Moscow by a religious council. But he himself appointed the members of this body, so that the religious activities of the Church were completely under his control.

Serfdom in Russia · The peasants in Russia had formerly been free to move from place to place, so long as their debts had been paid to their landlords. As time went on, however, many of them were unable to keep up their dues and so fell under the power of their masters. When they could not meet their taxes, they sometimes handed over their bit of property to the Church or to a noble and became tenants.

In the early seventeenth century a number of decrees were passed which took away the former freedom of the serfs and set a strict watch over the payment of their debts. In this way, the serfs became merely a part of the lord's estate and were sold or exchanged along with the land itself. The laws passed by Peter tightened this slavery and created an ever-widening gap between the privileged upper classes and the miserable peasants. The latter had no means of protecting themselves and were completely at the mercy of their masters. Sometimes they had to suffer flogging and torture.

Peter Westernizes Russia · Along with organizing the government and army on Western models, Peter determined to give his kingdom a European appearance. He invited foreigners to settle in Russia and sent young Russians abroad to study. He made the people give up their beards and flowing garments. They were to dress like Europeans. He forced the women of the upper classes, who had been kept in seclusion, to appear at social gatherings as did women in the West. But these were superficial changes only.

More important for the economic future of Russia was Peter's success in gaining territory which gave the country access to the sea. Peter had longed to extend his power

Growth of Russia, 1689–1796 · *What territory did Peter add? at whose expense? What did Catherine add? at whose expense? Which new ports were won?*

THE GROWTH OF RUSSIA

Russia before 1689
Added by Peter the Great, to 1725
Added by Anne and Elizabeth, to 1762
Added by Catherine II to 1796

0   550
Scale of Miles

Catherine II, the Great · *She read the liberal French philosophers, encouraged Russian literature, colonized Alaska, and expanded Russian frontiers. But the peasants suffered.*

Catherine the Great Makes Russia a Great Power · The most important ruler of Russia after Peter the Great was a German princess of remarkable ability, Catherine II (1762–1796). Catherine had come to Russia to be the wife of the heir to the throne. Her husband, who ruled for six months, proved to be a worthless fellow. Catherine won over the imperial guard and had herself proclaimed empress. Her husband was forced to abdicate and was carried off and put to death, probably with Catherine's consent.

It has been said that Peter made Russia a *European* power but that Catherine II made it a *great* power. Catherine was ambitious and unscrupulous, but shrewd in the choice of her ministers. All her measures were directed toward increasing the royal authority, for she was a thorough despot.

As the result of a successful war against the Ottoman Turks, Catherine gained Azov and territory north of the Black Sea. Russian ships were now granted the right to pass through the Bosporus, the Sea of Marmora, and the Dardanelles and thus to reach the Mediterranean Sea. Catherine also pushed her boundary westward by taking a part of Poland. A glance at the map (p. 267) will show how much territory was added by Peter and by Catherine.

to the shores of the Black Sea, but here he was confronted by the Ottoman Turks. He therefore turned to seek a boundary on the Baltic Sea.

In 1718, after much fighting, Peter forced the Swedes to cede to him Livonia (later Latvia), Estonia, and other territory. This gave him the outlet he needed. He built a fine new capital, St. Petersburg (now Leningrad), on part of the land which he had won from Sweden. He drained the marshes along the Neva and created Russia's first seaport. Handsome buildings were built in European styles. Then he moved the seat of the government from Moscow to the new capital, his "window" to the West. It became one of Europe's brilliant capitals.

CHECK ON YOUR READING

1. Show the importance to Russia of the Slavs, Northmen, and Mongols.
2. What did the Ivans do to lay the foundations for centralized government?
3. How did Peter the Great establish absolute power? modernize Russia?
4. How did Catherine make Russia a great power?

3. The Austrian Empire of the Hapsburgs

The Scattered Hapsburg Territories · The Hapsburgs had little control over the Holy Roman Empire. They kept the title of Emperor only for the glory that it lent their name. But the emperor was actual ruler of a large territory of his own. It included Austria, Bohemia, Hungary, Transylvania (central Rumania), and other family possessions (see map below).

The Treaty of Utrecht (p. 243) awarded the Hapsburgs a part of the Netherlands, the duchy of Milan, Naples, and Sardinia. Austria thus gained a hold on Italy, and also a valuable region on the North Sea. But the scattered territories of the emperor caused many problems.

Trouble with the Turks · The possession of Hungary brought the Hapsburgs into a long conflict with the Turks. After the Ottoman Turks conquered Constantinople in 1453, they began to press into southeastern Europe and push northward. The republic of Venice and the Hapsburgs tried to hold them in check, but they continued to advance and occupied part of Hungary. Then they invaded Austria with a large force and besieged Vienna (1683). Fortunately, the king of Poland came to the assistance of the Hapsburgs, defeated the Turks, and freed the city.

The success of the Moslem invasion so alarmed the Christian powers of Europe that from this time they furnished money and troops to aid the emperor. After a long struggle the Hapsburgs regained all of Hungary and Transylvania. In 1699 the Sultan acknowledged the right of the Hapsburgs to these lands.

Trouble with Nationalities · In Austria the people were mainly Germans. In Bohemia there were Germans and a Slavic people called Czechs. There were Hungarians (or Magyars), Rumanians, and other smaller groups in Hungary and Transylvania. To the south were Serbs, Croats, and Slovenes (all Slavs). There were Italians in Milan and southern Italy, and Flemish and Walloons in the Netherlands.

The task of governing such a miscellaneous group of peoples, each with its own language and customs, was a stupendous one. There was no bond between them save that of a common ruler. And they were likely at any time to rise up in revolt.

In spite of their difficulties with peoples of many nationalities and religions, the Catholic Hapsburgs retained their scattered empire more or less intact. They remained one of the chief reigning families until the end of World War I. They were related

Austrian Possessions, 1730 · *What did the Hapsburgs possess in Italy? in the Balkans? Why were minority peoples a "problem"?*

Maria Theresa's Family · *The Hapsburg Empress (right) is shown with H.R.E. Francis I, and 13 of their 16 children. She made Vienna a center for the arts and music.*

Trouble with Prussia · At the death of the last male heir of the Spanish Hapsburgs a European war had broken out to determine who should inherit the kingdom. A similar fate overtook the Austrian Hapsburgs a generation later.

In 1740 Emperor Charles VI died, leaving his daughter, Maria Theresa, to rule over his various realms. Charles had taken great care to secure from the other European rulers a promise that they would respect his will, leaving his possessions to his daughter. But no sooner had Maria Theresa come to the throne than her greedy neighbors disregarded the "Pragmatic Sanction," as their agreement was called. They ruthlessly prepared to seize her lands. Her chief enemy was the newly crowned king of Prussia, Frederick II. We must now see how it was that a German prince had become strong enough to be a danger to the ancient Hapsburg power.

CHECK ON YOUR READING

1. Locate the Hapsburg territories. How were they secured?
2. Explain the trouble with the Turks.
3. Which peoples governed by the Hapsburgs are now nations?

---

by marriage with other ruling families and they shared with their fellow sovereigns the belief in the powers and privileges of absolute monarchy.

4. Prussia Becomes a Great Power

The Hohenzollerns Build Prussia · The beginnings of modern Germany may be traced back to 1415. In that year the Electorate of Brandenburg was given by the emperor to a family of landowners named Hohenzollern. Beginning with this strip of territory extending about a hundred miles to the east and west of a town called Berlin,

the Hohenzollerns built up the kingdom of Prussia. By 1870 Prussia occupied nearly two-thirds of Germany.

It was the pride of the Hohenzollern family that almost every one of its rulers added something to what he inherited. Their first annexations are unimportant. But about the time of the Thirty Years'

War the electors of Brandenburg inherited Mark and Cleves and thus got their first hold on the Rhine. A few years later they inherited the duchy of East Prussia on the Baltic. When Frederick William came to the throne in 1640, his territories ranged from the Rhine to the Vistula and beyond.

The Great Elector Unifies His Realms (1640–1688) · The Great Elector, as Frederick William was called, was well fitted for the task of welding these various domains into a unified state. He was hard-working and conscientious, but heartless with opponents and treacherous in dealing with other rulers. He set himself, with great determination, to enlarge his territories and build up his personal power.

By shrewd tactics during the closing days of the Thirty Years' War the Great Elector secured the bishoprics of Minden and Halberstadt and the duchy of Pomerania. This increased his shore line on the Baltic.

To unify his government, he abolished all local self-government. He brought the administration, finances, and army all under his own control. He built up farming and industry. He organized a strong army and joined in the wars of his neighbors, helping first one and then the other. Gradually his military power began to be respected and feared. He welcomed the persecuted Huguenots of France, offering them special inducements to settle in his domains.

Frederick William was succeeded by his son Frederick, who was permitted by the emperor to change his title from "Elector of Brandenburg" to "King in Prussia" (1701). Thus the ruler of Prussia was recognized as an independent sovereign.

King Frederick William I and His Army (1713–1740) · Very early the Prussian rulers showed an interest in military affairs. Frederick William I was a rough and boor-

ish king. As soon as he came to power, he discharged a large number of servants. He sold the family jewels, had the silver coined into money, and reduced the extravagance of his court to Spartan simplicity. His chief pride was in collecting stalwart, tall soldiers.

Frederick William I built up the Prussian army until it was almost equal in size to that of France or Austria. Because he was constantly drilling his men, Thomas Carlyle called him the great "Drill Sergeant" of the Prussian nation. The drilling and regimenting affected not only the army but every aspect of Prussian life.

As he was strongly opposed to all forms of luxury, Frederick William was able to leave to his son not only a fine army, but a large amount of gold. These helped to make possible the remarkable achievements of Frederick II.

Frederick II, Called "the Great" (1740–1786) · In his youth Frederick II disgusted and angered his stern father by his love of books, music, and finery. The crown prince appeared to lack entirely those soldierly qualities necessary for a Prussian monarch and a Hohenzollern. When Frederick became king, however, he proved to have such energy, ability, and skill in warlike undertakings that he gained the title of "the Great."

Frederick Seizes Silesia · In the same year that Frederick II ascended the throne, Maria Theresa became ruler of the Hapsburg realms. Frederick decided to use this opportunity to seize the province of Silesia. This was a strip of Hapsburg territory southeast of Brandenburg, populated by Germans. Brandenburg had an ancient claim to it. The province was rich and fertile. Besides, Frederick was eager to possess it so that he might add this large number of Germans to his population.

Frederick II, the Great · *Whether playing the flute at Sans-Souci, or reviewing his troops at Potsdam, this enlightened despot insisted upon excellence. He was a great administrator, military strategist, and patron of the arts.*

Frederick knew that Maria Theresa's ill-equipped forces were no match for his large and well-disciplined armies. He therefore marched into Silesia and easily took possession of the capital city of Breslau. He did not even stop to declare war or give a good reason for his invasion.

War of the Austrian Succession · France and Bavaria joined the attack on Maria Theresa. It seemed for a time as if the struggle to keep her realms would be in vain. But her people, stirred by her courage, came to her aid. The French and Bavarians were thrown back, but Frederick held Silesia. In 1745 Frederick was formally granted the province and retired from the war.

England and Holland had entered the war to support Austria, for they were determined to prevent France from seizing the Austrian Netherlands. In 1748, however, all the countries decided to stop fighting. They agreed to leave things as they were before the fighting began. Francis of Lor-

raine, Maria Theresa's husband, became emperor of the Holy Roman Empire as Francis I.

The Powers Combine against Frederick · Maria Theresa did not give up her determination to drive out Frederick and regain her lost province. First, she undertook to improve conditions in her own country and increase her army. Then she looked about for friends to aid her. She easily gained the consent of Russia, Sweden, and Saxony to join in an attack on Prussia, whose growing power they feared. Her ambassador at Paris achieved a brilliant success in inducing the French, after two hundred years of hostility to the Hapsburgs, to join in an alliance with Austria (1756).

The war that followed—the Seven Years' War—was one of the most important in modern history in its effects. Not only did almost every European power become involved, but there was fighting all over the world, from India to the American continent (pp. 283, 286). In this chapter we shall mention only that part of the war in which the king of Prussia played such a remarkable part.

Frederick's Success in the Seven Years' War · As the forces of his many enemies came from all directions, it seemed as if the Prussian king and his armies might be destroyed. But it was in this war that Frederick earned his title of "the Great." He dealt with his enemies with amazing courage and ability. He defeated the French and his German foes at Rossbach. This was, perhaps, the most famous of his battles (1757). A month later he put the Austrians to flight at Leuthen, not far from Breslau. Thereupon the Swedes and Russians retired from the war.

The English soon occupied the attention of the French, and money paid to Frederick by the English government helped to keep his army going. Fortunately for Frederick, a new tsar, who was an ardent admirer of the Prussian king, came to the throne. This caused Russia to make peace. Maria Theresa thereupon agreed to give up the struggle. Shortly afterward England and France came to terms, and a general settlement was made at Paris in 1763.

The So-Called Benevolent Despots · Frederick the Great, Maria Theresa, her son Joseph II, and Catherine the Great are sometimes called "enlightened despots" or "benevolent despots." This is because they were better educated and more willing to making certain reforms than some of their predecessors. They read books and interested themselves in the newer ideas in science, philosophy, and religion which were spreading through Europe. They sometimes corresponded with and supported

Brandenburg-Prussia Expands · *What region was the core of the Hohenzollern possessions? Tell the importance of East Prussia, Pomerania, West Prussia.*

The Partitions of Poland · *A contemporary cartoon shows Catherine II, Joseph II, and Frederick II, making the first partition while King Stanislaus II clings to his crown in great despair. When the three partitions were finished what areas had been taken by Russia? Austria? Prussia? When did Poland rise again?*

famous writers, such as Voltaire (p. 298). This enlightenment, however, did not prevent them from being despots. They made sure that none of their reforms would lessen their absolute authority.

Weakness of Poland Tempts Her Neighbors · Frederick, Catherine, and Maria Theresa, while "enlightened," did not hesitate to lay hands on any territory within their reach. And a most tempting and unprotected region was the huge kingdom of Poland. Its population was thinly scattered and consisted of Poles, Germans, and Russians. Invasion presented no difficulty, since the country was a vast plain with no natural protective boundaries. Moreover, the government was weak and helpless.

Poland was in a condition of feudal anarchy. A large class of nobles lived on their estates, while the peasants had sunk to a miserable condition of servitude. Each new ruler was elected by a diet of nobles. And the European powers regularly interfered to secure a candidate who might favor their interests.

The king had no real power. He could not make war or peace, levy taxes, or make a new law without the consent of the diet. Yet the diet amounted to very little, for no measure could be passed if any *one* of the many nobles vetoed it! Since the members rarely agreed, the meetings usually broke up without accomplishing anything. Poland had no national armies that could compete with those of her neighbors.

Prussia, Russia, and Austria Partition Poland (1772, 1793, 1795) · Each of these neighbors desired a piece of Polish territory. Frederick's kingdom was cut off from East Prussia by a large Polish province known as West Prussia, which extended up to the Baltic Sea. Frederick decided to add West

Prussia to his kingdom. He well knew that Poland was in no condition to defend her territory.

Catherine the Great had established Russian influence in Poland by having one of her favorites made king in 1764. She was as eager as Frederick to prevent any improvement in Poland's internal affairs. Thus Russia might be able to profit from the disorder and move her frontiers considerably westward. Marie Theresa was particularly interested in the Polish areas around Krakow and Lemberg.

Using convenient pretexts which arose in 1772, 1793, and 1795 the greedy despots thrice partitioned this unfortunate kingdom. The map on page 274 shows what each obtained. As a result the Polish king was compelled to abdicate. Poland disappeared from the map of Europe for more than a century. She was not to rise again as a nation until after World War I.

CHECK ON YOUR READING

1. Show on the map the piece by piece growth of the Hohenzollern state.
2. What methods were used to unify and strengthen Hohenzollern territories?
3. How do the wars of this period illustrate the "balance of power" principle?
4. Who and what were the "benevolent despots"?
5. Why and how was Poland partitioned?

Learning Activities

Think about the chapter

1. What are some causes for the rivalries of national states?

2. How is a "balance of power" maintained?

3. How is the geography of Russia an important factor in its history?

4. What special problems confronted the Austrian Hapsburgs?

5. How has "militarism" come to be associated with Germany?

6. What lessons may be drawn from the partition of Poland?

7. Map study: Comparing a map of modern Europe and one of the eighteenth century, note what states (whether independent or satellite) now occupy the area of the three great powers studied in this chapter.

Go beyond the text

8. What seemed to be the criteria for giving rulers the title of "Great" in the eighteenth century? If we used the same criteria now who would be some of the persons who might be called "great"? What standards do you think should be applied? By your standards whom would you place on the list of "great" rulers today?

9. Who built the Kremlin? What has it been used for through the centuries? What do we mean today when we say "the men in the Kremlin"?

10. Why may the Seven Years' War be truly considered a world war? Give the provisions of the Treaty of Paris and evaluate its effects on England and France.

11. Read further on the benevolent despots of the eighteenth century. Is the term a contradiction of words?

12. George Washington lived from 1732 to 1799. He was a contemporary of Louis XV and Louis XVI, Frederick the Great, Catherine of Russia, and Maria Theresa. In Genevieve Foster's George Washington's World, read and report on: (a) the "Petticoat Plot" against Frederick; (b) the relations between

Frederick and Bach, and Frederick's friendship with Voltaire; (c) how a fourteen-year-old German princess journeyed to Russia and became Catherine the Great; (d) the great German poet Goethe, who was not sure that Frederick was "the Great."

Follow up your special interests

13. Who were some of the great German and Austrian musicians who lived in the eighteenth century? For example, Mozart played at the court of Maria Theresa when he was eight years old.

14. Make a collection of pictures relating to Russia. You might include icons, the interior of a Greek Orthodox Church, St. Basil's Church, the Kremlin, and Red Square.

15. *Stormy Victory*, the story of Tchaikovsky, by Purdy, has descriptions of the life of the serfs, miners, boatmen, and the poor of the cities, and excerpts of some of their songs. Could you write a story based on this material?

READ FURTHER

Basic readings: (1) BAUER and PEYSER, *How Music Grew*, Chaps. 17–18. (2) BECKER, *Modern History*, Chap. 5. (3) CARR, *Men of Power*. Frederick the Great. (4) HOFFMAN, *News of the World*, Nos. 33–40. (5) ROBINSON, *Readings in European History*, Chap. 32. (6) VAN LOON, *Story of Mankind*, pp. 296–316. (7) Year's *Pictorial History*, pp. 278–280, 318–323, 332–337.

Special accounts: (8) G. FOSTER, *George Washington's World*. Important events of the eighteenth century told in story form with dramatic emphasis on personalities. (9) H. LAMB, *Genghis Khan and the Mongol Horde*. (10) J. MARTIN, ed, *A Picture History of Russia*. An invaluable source of material on all periods of Russian history. (11) A. NAZAROFF, *The Land of the Russian People*. Excellent treatment of early history and good descriptions of the different regions of Russia. (12) E. SEEGER, *The Pageant of Russian History*.

Fiction and biography: (13) N. BAKER, *Peter the Great*. A vivid account of the man and the changes he brought to Russia. (14) S. DARK, *Twelve Royal Ladies*. Tells about Maria Theresa and Catherine the Great. (15) D. EWEN, *Haydn: A Good Life*. This biography of an important composer gives you a good insight into eighteenth-century Austria, then the center of cultural achievement. (16) M. Goss, *Deep-flowing Brook: The Story of Johann Sebastian Bach*. This is a colorful story of the composer of great religious music, of his large family, and of the royal personages who were his patrons.

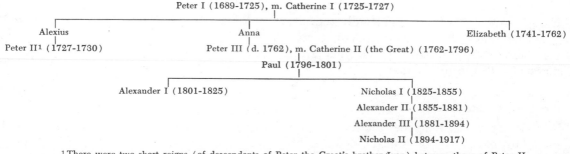

The Romanov Rulers of Russia

Peter I (1689-1725), m. Catherine I (1725-1727)

Alexius — Anna — Elizabeth (1741-1762)

Peter II[1] (1727-1730) — Peter III (d. 1762), m. Catherine II (the Great) (1762-1796)

Paul (1796-1801)

Alexander I (1801-1825) — Nicholas I (1825-1855)

Alexander II (1855-1881)

Alexander III (1881-1894)

Nicholas II (1894-1917)

[1] There were two short reigns (of descendants of Peter the Great's brother Ivan) between those of Peter II (1727-1730) and Elizabeth (1741-1762).

The Austrian Hapsburgs and the Italian House of Savoy

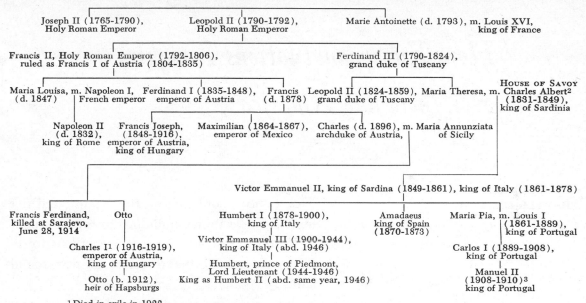

Maria Theresa of Austria, queen of Bohemia and Hungary, m. Francis I, duke of Lorraine, Holy Roman Emperor (1745-1765)

Joseph II (1765-1790), Holy Roman Emperor

Leopold II (1790-1792), Holy Roman Emperor

Marie Antoinette (d. 1793), m. Louis XVI, king of France

Francis II, Holy Roman Emperor (1792-1806), ruled as Francis I of Austria (1804-1835)

Ferdinand III (1790-1824), grand duke of Tuscany

HOUSE OF SAVOY

Maria Louisa, m. Napoleon I, French emperor (d. 1847)

Ferdinand I (1835-1848), emperor of Austria

Francis (d. 1878)

Leopold II (1824-1859), grand duke of Tuscany

Maria Theresa, m. Charles Albert[2] (1831-1849), king of Sardinia

Napoleon II (d. 1832), king of Rome

Francis Joseph, (1848-1916), emperor of Austria, king of Hungary

Maximilian (1864-1867), emperor of Mexico

Charles (d. 1896), m. Maria Annunziata archduke of Austria, of Sicily

Victor Emmanuel II, king of Sardina (1849-1861), king of Italy (1861-1878)

Francis Ferdinand, killed at Sarajevo, June 28, 1914

Otto

Humbert I (1878-1900), king of Italy

Amadaeus king of Spain (1870-1873)

Maria Pia, m. Louis I (1861-1889), king of Portugal

Charles I[1] (1916-1919), emperor of Austria, king of Hungary

Victor Emmanuel III (1900-1944), king of Italy (abd. 1946)

Carlos I (1889-1908), king of Portugal

Otto (b. 1912), heir of Hapsburgs

Humbert, prince of Piedmont, Lord Lieutenant (1944-1946) King as Humbert II (abd. same year, 1946)

Manuel II (1908-1910)[3] king of Portugal

[1] Died in exile in 1922.
[2] Charles Albert was a member of the House of Savoy, which, since the eleventh century, had ruled over the territories of Savoy and Piedmont. In 1720 Sardinia was added, and henceforth the rulers were styled "King of Sardinia" until they became Kings of Italy in 1861.
[3] After a revolution in 1910 Portugal was declared a republic.

The Hohenzollerns in Prussia and Germany

Frederick William (the Great Elector) (1640-1688)

Frederick III of Brandenburg, Frederick I of Prussia (1688-1713), m. Sophia Charlotte (Hanover)

Frederick William I (1713-1740), m. Sophia, daughter of George I of England

Frederick II (the Great) (1740-1786)   Augustus William

Frederick William II (1786-1797)

Frederick William III (1797-1840)

Frederick William IV (1840-1861)   William I, king of Prussia (1861-1888), German emperor (1871-1888)

Frederick III (1888), m. Victoria, daughter of Queen Victoria of England

William II (1888-1918) (d. 1941)   Sophia, m. King Constantine of Greece

Hohenzollern heirs

How European Nations Fought over India and America

KEY WORDS AND DATES

seafaring powers	Wolfe
trading companies	Peace of Paris, 1763
Mogul	Navigation Acts
sepoys	Stamp Act
Dupleix	Burke
Clive	1776
Cartier	Saratoga
Champlain	Franklin
seaboard colonies	Lafayette
Pitt	Yorktown

THE NATIONS bordering on the Atlantic did not limit their territorial ambitions to the continent of Europe. Instead they sent expeditions to explore and exploit the resources of new found lands in Asia and the Americas.

For a time Spain and Portugal were powerful enough to split the wealth of the East and West Indies between them. But then the Dutch took over the East Indies. And English privateers reaped fabulous rewards on the Spanish Main.

English and French trading companies established posts in India and played off native princes against each other. Under Clive the British won the contest. The French were left with a few small trading posts along the coast.

In the great struggle for the control of North America the advantages of leadership and Indian allies at first favored the French. But the long-term advantages were heavily on the side of the English. By 1763 England reigned supreme in North America.

Unwise restrictions on their trade and threats to their rights as Englishmen led the American colonists to revolt. Against great odds, General Washington kept an army in the field. With French aid, independence was finally won.

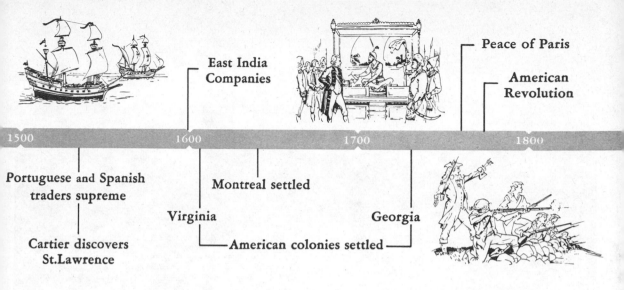

East India
Companies

Peace of Paris

American
Revolution

1500   1600   1700   1800

Portuguese and Spanish
traders supreme

Montreal settled

Virginia

Georgia

Cartier discovers
St. Lawrence

American colonies settled

1. European Rivalry over World Trade

Review of Overseas Ventures · We have had occasion from time to time to notice the activities of various seafaring powers. These were the seaboard countries of Portugal, Spain, Holland, France, and England. They soon became bitter rivals in their attempts to establish colonies and develop trade. This rivalry was another cause for the wars of the sixteenth to eighteenth centuries.

Spain and Portugal led the race for overseas possessions (p. 185). They even agreed for a time to divide all newly discovered lands between them. The Pope drew a line in the Atlantic, assigning to Spain the territory to the west of it and to Portugal the lands to the east. Under this arrangement Spain claimed the Americas except for the eastern part of Brazil.

Portugal soon established trading stations at Ormuz in Persia, at Diu and Goa in India, on the islands of Ceylon, Java, and Sumatra, and in the Spice Islands. Lisbon grew in wealth and importance, while the prosperity of the Italian cities declined (p. 179).

While Portugal was busy in the East Indies, Spain was profiting from her vast empire in America. The wealth of the gold and silver mines in Mexico and Peru (p. 186) had raised her to a leading position in Europe. Moreover, in 1580 Philip II annexed Portugal. He thus gained control for a time of the Portuguese trade and possessions in the East.

Decline of Spain and Portugal. · The unwise policies of Philip II, however, hurt both Portugal and Spain. He closed the port of Lisbon to France, England, and Holland. The Dutch, with whom he was at war, took this opportunity to seize the trade of Portugal and establish themselves in many of the Portuguese settlements.

Philip's meddling in English affairs (p. 226) led to the destruction of his magnificent armada. After this time (1588) Spanish naval patrols for her American colonies were too small to offer any real protection.

First Dutch Fleet from the Indies, 1597 · *The Dutch East India Company owned 150 East Indiamen,* designed *"to outrun the Spanish and outcarry the English."*

The seventeenth century was the golden age of piracy. English, French, and Dutch freebooters roamed the Atlantic and Caribbean at the expense of Spain.

In Spain itself agriculture and industry were neglected. High taxes ruined the trade with the colonies. And the Spanish nobles wasted the treasure that came to them from the New World.

The Dutch Take Over in Asia · After the Dutch gained their freedom from Spain (p. 233), they turned their attention to the sea. They built up a strong fleet of ships to increase the already flourishing trade of their rich cities. In 1595 they sent out their first expedition to India by way of the Cape of Good Hope.

The success of this expedition aroused great enthusiasm among the Dutch. By 1602 between sixty and seventy vessels had sailed to India and the Malay Archipelago. In the same year the Dutch East India Company was formed to regulate and protect the growing trade. This company rapidly established trading houses. One by one it seized the most favorable Portuguese trading stations, until by 1700 only Goa and a few minor posts remained of Portugal's commercial empire.

The Dutch continued to enjoy a profitable foreign trade during the eighteenth century. They controlled some very important possessions. The Cape of Good Hope served as a halfway post to India. They held Ceylon and several important settlements in India. In addition, they were the chief European power in the Moluccas, or Spice Islands, Java, Sumatra, Borneo, Celebes, the Malaccan (Malay) peninsula, and Siam (Thailand). They controlled the trade with Japan.

The English Check the Dutch · For a while the Dutch had made enormous profits from the goods that they brought to England to sell. But in 1600 London merchants organized the East India Company.

The government granted them a charter which gave them the entire control of the English trade with India. They were further granted the power to govern themselves and to defend themselves against their Dutch and French rivals.

A few years later the English East India Company was permitted to coin money, administer justice, punish independent English merchants who sailed ships into Eastern waters, and even to make war and peace with non-Christian states. The English succeeded in establishing a number of trading agencies in India, including one near Calcutta. In 1640 they built a fort at Madras on the southeast coast of India.

At this time the Netherlands owned half the merchant ships of Europe and controlled a large part of the carrying trade between Europe and the East. Hoping to increase English shipping at the expense of the Dutch, Parliament in 1651 passed a Navigation Act. It provided that only English vessels should be permitted to bring to Britain goods from Asia, Africa, and America. This led, as we know, to a short war on the sea between the Dutch and the English (p. 253).

Stricter provisions were added to the Navigation Act under Charles II. As these were aimed at the Dutch, war again broke out between the rivals (p. 255). In 1664 the English got possession of some of the Dutch West Indies, as well as the island of Manhattan. On the other hand, the Dutch drove the English out of the Spice Islands.

When William of Orange became king of England in 1689, the Dutch no longer opposed the English in India. Thus it was not the Dutch, but the French who were to fight it out with the English for the control of India and North America.

CHECK ON YOUR READING

1. Point out the Portuguese and Spanish overseas possessions in 1600.
2. Why did Portugal and Spain decline?
3. What did the Dutch take over in Asia?
4. How did the English check the Dutch?

---

2. The Contest of France and England over India

India in the Eighteenth Century · When we last discussed India (p. 141) it had been invaded by the Moslems. A line of emperors called the "Moguls" established a magnificent court at Delhi. But they were never able to gain complete control over all India. Many of the native princes continued to rule their own provinces.

When the great Mogul Emperor Aurangzeb died in 1707, the empire began to fall apart. The emperor's officials, the subahdars and nawabs (nabobs), as well as the Hindu princes, got control of various districts. Though an emperor still held court at Delhi, he had little power. Thus the foreigners who began in the eighteenth century to get a foothold in India dealt with the local rulers whose lands they desired. They were able to play one off against the other and thus "divide and conquer."

English and French Rivalry in India · In the time of Charles I (1639) the English East India Company purchased a village which grew into the important trading station of Madras. About the same time trading posts were established in the district

Robert Clive, Baron of Plassey · *He destroyed French power in India, and governed Madras and Bengal with great efficiency.*

India about 1775 · *What areas were held by the British? French? Dutch? Portuguese?*

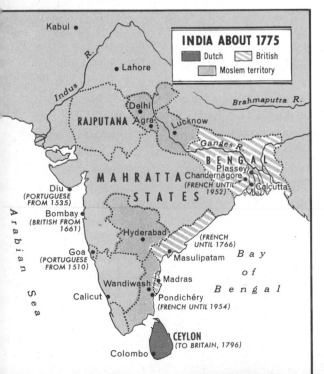

INDIA ABOUT 1775

Dutch British

Moslem territory

Kabul

Lahore

Indus R.

Delhi

RAJPUTANA Agra

Lucknow

Brahmaputra R.

Ganges R.

B E N G A L

Plassey

Chandernagore
(FRENCH UNTIL 1952)

Calcutta

M A H R A T T A

Diu
(PORTUGUESE
FROM 1535)

S T A T E S

Bombay
(BRITISH FROM
1661)

Hyderabad

(FRENCH
UNTIL 1766)

Goa
(PORTUGUESE
FROM 1510)

Masulipatam

Bay

of

Bengal

Wandiwash

Madras

Calicut

Pondichéry
(FRENCH UNTIL 1954)

A r a b i a n   S e a

CEYLON
(TO BRITAIN, 1796)

Colombo

of Bengal, and later Calcutta was fortified. Bombay was already an English station.

The Mogul emperor at first scarcely noticed the presence of a few foreigners on the shores of his extensive realms. But before the end of the seventeenth century there were clashes between the East India Company and the native rulers.

In 1664 Louis XIV granted a charter to the French East India Company. The charter gave it a monopoly of trade for fifty years and permitted it to raise troops, to garrison posts, and to make war and peace in the name of the sovereign. The king also assisted the company with grants from the royal treasury. In 1669 the company's first expedition established an agency near those of the English and Portuguese.

Three years later the French became the rivals of the English in Bengal by fortifying themselves at Chandernagore, just north of Calcutta. They also purchased a plot of ground on the southeastern shores of India. Here Pondichéry, the center of the French dominion in India, was built. Pondichéry had a population of sixty thousand, of which only two hundred were Europeans.

Dupleix, the French governor, had great ambition and energy. He was determined to use the quarrels between native princes to make himself leader in India and drive out the English. He formed alliances with natives of importance and fortified Pondichéry. He began to enlist natives. This practice was quickly adopted by the English. These Indian soldiers, whom the English called *sepoys*, were trained to fight in the European manner.

Clive Defeats the French in India · The English discovered among the clerks in Madras a leader equal in skill and energy to Dupleix himself. This was Robert Clive, a young man only twenty-five years old.

Englishmen in India · *The new rulers of India brought with them British customs and traditions. In this painting by John Zoffany they take time out for a "spot of tea." Note the Indian servants and the costumes of the period.*

Clive organized a large force of sepoys and gained a remarkable influence over them by his astonishing bravery.

Just as the Seven Years' War (p. 272) was beginning in Europe (1756), word reached Clive that the nawab of Bengal had imprisoned 146 Englishmen in a little cell (the "Black Hole" of Calcutta) where most of them died of suffocation before morning. Clive hastened to Bengal and forced the nawab to hand over Calcutta to the English. Later, he won a brilliant victory over the nawab at Plassey (1757).

As France and England were at war, Clive took possession of the French settlement at Chandernagore. Before the Seven Years' War was over, the English had won Masulipatam and Wandiwash, and captured Pondichéry. They had thus deprived the French of their former power in the region of Madras.

Although the French received back the towns which the English had taken from them, they had lost their influence over the native rulers because of their defeat. Clive, on the other hand, had made Britain's name feared among the rulers. The forces of the English East India Company not only had put an end to French control in India, but had begun the conquest of Bengal. It became the center from which British power spread throughout India.

CHECK ON YOUR READING

1. *Locate the French and British strongholds in India. How were they obtained?*
2. *What part did trading companies play in English-French rivalry?*
3. *Identify: Dupleix, Clive, the "Black Hole," Plassey.*
4. *What did Robert Clive accomplish?*

3. The Rivalry of England and France in North America

French Possessions in America · The great struggle between France and England for supremacy in commerce and colonies was also fought in North America. French explorers had early established claims in the New World. Jacques Cartier, seeking the East Indies, had discovered instead the St. Lawrence River (1534–1535). Making his way up the St. Lawrence he took possession of the land in the name of his sovereign. In 1604 a French company succeeded in establishing a permanent settlement at Port Royal in Acadia (now Nova Scotia).

Four years later Champlain founded a colony at Quebec. From this base French explorers and missionaries worked their way westward and southward. In 1642 Montreal was permanently established. French explorers and missionaries, pressing westward to find the Pacific, discovered the Great Lakes and laid claim to all the surrounding lands.

The French companies offered many inducements to their countrymen who would agree to settle in Canada. But the severe climate and hard life in the New World kept back all but the most adventurous.

Exploration of the Mississippi · In 1673 Father Marquette, a Jesuit missionary, and Joliet, an explorer and trader, undertook to follow the course of the Mississippi. Untroubled by the warnings of the Indians that the river was full of monsters, the brave adventurers found their way southward almost to the Gulf of Mexico.

La Salle, a French nobleman, completed their work. In January, 1682, he set out from Lake Michigan and in April reached the mouth of the Mississippi. La Salle then claimed all the region watered by the great river for France. He named it Louisiana after his king, Louis XIV.

England's Seaboard Colonies · While the French were roaming about the Great Lakes and the Mississippi Valley, the English were occupying the Atlantic coast from New England to Florida. In 1607, a year before Champlain founded Quebec, Englishmen had established their first successful colony. They named it Jamestown after their king, James I.

In 1620 a little band of separatists— the Pilgrims—landed at Plymouth. They had come to seek a land where they could worship God according to their own conscience. The richest and most important colony in the north was that of the Massachusetts Bay Company, founded in 1628 by a group of prosperous Puritans. One group from Massachusetts established themselves as a colony in Connecticut, another in Rhode Island.

Maryland, granted to Lord Baltimore in 1632, became a refuge for Roman Catholics, who were persecuted in England. The Carolinas were settled by English courtiers to whom Charles II had granted a large tract south of Virginia. Pennsylvania, founded by William Penn (1681), became a thriving colony of Quakers. New Hampshire became a separate colony in 1679 and Georgia was founded in 1733. Delaware remained under the management of Pennsylvania until the Revolution.

Henry Hudson, an English mariner sailing under the Dutch flag, in 1609 discovered the river which bears his name and the island of Manhattan at its mouth. On this island the Dutch established the colony of New Amsterdam. They occupied the valley of the Hudson and what is now New Jersey. But the short history of the Dutch in America came to an end in 1664, when their possessions were taken by the English.

England Gains Nova Scotia and Other French Territory (1713) · The wars in Europe were usually accompanied by little wars among the colonists of the various nations involved. The War of the Spanish Succession was called Queen Anne's War by the colonists. During it New England settlers captured the French stronghold of Port Royal in Nova Scotia (then Acadia). By the Treaty of Utrecht France gave Nova Scotia to England and acknowledged England's right to Newfoundland and the Hudson Bay region.

Advantages and Disadvantages of the French and English in America · By trading and intermarrying with the Indians the French won their valuable support. But they had several important disadvantages. (1) The territory they claimed in America was too large to protect with a scattered population. (2) The French who came to America were mainly explorers, traders, and missionaries. They were not interested in forming permanent settlements. (3) The exhausting wars of Louis XIV had checked emigration and prevented the sending of sufficient financial support to the colonies. (4) The French king kept strict control over his overseas possessions. He permitted practically no self-government.

The situation in the English settlements was quite different. (1) A large proportion of the population lived within a short distance of the seacoast. The people could get together more easily than the French to protect themselves. (2) They were also in closer communication with the home country than the French, who had pushed far into the interior of the American continent.

A Comparison of North America before 1754 and after 1763 · *What two nations made great territorial gains during this period? at whose expense? With what historic events can you associate St. Augustine? Jamestown? Plymouth? Quebec? Louisburg? Ft. Duquesne? Boston? Yorktown?*

The Taking of Quebec, September 13, 1759 · *This photo of an old contemporary engraving shows the British advancing up the St. Lawrence, scaling the heights, and winning on the Plains of Abraham. Why was the victory vital?*

Although the English colonies differed in size, population, and religion, they had a common bond of loyalty to the mother country. (3) England left her colonies comparatively free in the conduct of their local affairs. Each colony had its own government and laws, subject to the approval of the king. (4) Moreover, the English had come to the New World to establish permanent homes. Their industry and trade were growing. By 1750 the English colonists numbered nearly a million and a half. This was fifteen times the French colonial population.

The Seven Years' War in America · The French and English began their contest for the New World in 1754. For several years this "French and Indian War" went badly for the British. Their officers knew nothing about Indian-type fighting in the forests, and they scorned the advice of the frontiersmen.

In 1756, however, the struggle became part of the Seven Years' War, which was now raging in Europe. The situation changed as William Pitt, a great British statesman, became head of the government. He immediately sent re-enforcements to the hard-pressed colonists and permitted colonial officers to command their own forces. The colonists raised new troops and money. They now took Louisburg, on Cape Breton Island, and Fort Duquesne, which they renamed Pittsburgh. They also drove the French from western New York.

In the following year the English began the conquest of Canada. They took Fort Ticonderoga and Crown Point on Lake Champlain and Fort Niagara. Under General Wolfe, English forces made their way up the St. Lawrence and finally captured Quebec, the key to French power in Canada. Both Wolfe and the French general Montcalm were killed in this battle. From this time on, the conquest of Canada proceeded rapidly. When Montreal was captured in 1760, the French gave up the struggle and withdrew their troops.

The Peace of Paris (1763) · By the Peace of Paris at the end of the Seven Years' War, France surrendered her territory in North America. (1) To England she ceded Canada and all the region east of the Mississippi, as well as several islands of the West Indies. (2) To Spain she gave the territory west of the Mississippi, together with New Orleans. (3) Spain, on her part, ceded Florida to England in return for Havana and Manila, which the English had captured. Thus England got possession of practically all that part of North America which had been developed, with the exception of Mexico.

CHECK ON YOUR READING

1. *Locate the French and English settlements in the New World. Identify the key leaders thereof.*
2. *Contrast the French and English colonies.*
3. *Summarize the highlights of the French and Indian War.*
4. *Why was the Peace of Paris (1763) so important?*

---

4. England Loses Her American Colonies

Trade Restrictions Arouse the Colonists · England granted greater freedom to her colonial settlements than did France or Spain. But like other European nations, England regarded her overseas possessions chiefly as a source of profit. She therefore enacted a number of navigation and trade laws to control the commerce of the colonies in the interest of the mother country. These regulations were not intended to injure the colonies, but to protect British trade against its French, Dutch, and Spanish rivals. To the colonists, however, these measures seemed an attempt to deprive them of their rights and to interfere with their prosperity.

The Navigation Acts, or trade laws, required (1) that goods produced in Asia, Africa, and America should be imported into England or her colonies only in English ships. (2) Goods from Europe could not be imported into the colonies unless they were shipped by way of England and carried in English ships or those of her colonies. (3) If an American merchant wished to sell his products to a foreigner, he had to send them in English ships and by way of England.

(4) Certain articles, including sugar, tobacco, cotton, and indigo, could be sold only to England or her colonies. (5) Other articles the Americans were forbidden to

export at all or even produce. Although they had plenty of furs, they were forbidden to ship them to any foreign country, or even to England.

The Colonists Break the Trade Laws · In spite of these restrictions, the colonists built up their home industries and carried on a flourishing trade with other countries. The laws at first were not strictly enforced. As a result businessmen were able to engage for a long time in a good deal of smuggling of foreign products into the country. England was occupied with European wars. And for twenty years after the Treaty of Utrecht the prime minister, Robert Walpole, was unwilling to interfere with the colonies.

The English Enforce the Laws after 1763 · After the close of the Seven Years' War, however, and the addition of Canada and the Ohio valley, the attitude of the English government changed. It held that the colonists should pay part of the cost of the war, which had benefited them. The colonists should also help to meet the expense of keeping an army to protect the new territory against the Indians.

England now undertook to enforce the trade laws and to collect the duties levied on silk, wine, coffee, and other articles imported by the colonies. Finally, Parliament decided to raise a fixed revenue by means of direct taxation.

The Stamp Act Angers the Colonists · In 1765 Parliament passed an act requiring stamps costing from a few pence to several shillings to be affixed to all legal and business papers. Such papers included wills, leases, mortgages, and bills of sale, as well as newspapers and pamphlets. This act angered the colonists as no previous measure had done. Everywhere protests arose against the new bill. It was asserted that it

introduced "taxation without representation," since the colonists were not *directly* represented in Parliament, which had levied the tax.

Colonial assemblies denounced the measure, and a petition was sent to the king. The excitement became so great that the Stamp Act was repealed. Parliament now tried to secure revenue by placing duties on glass, paper, and tea. But again the protests of the colonists were so violent that all duties were removed except that on tea. This was retained because of the influence of the East India Company.

The "Boston Tea Party" (1773) · The colonists, however, objected to paying even a small duty on tea. The effort to force on the Boston market the East India Company's tea at a very low price produced trouble. Those who had supplies of smuggled tea on hand and were likely to be undersold even after the low duty was paid began to raise again the cry of unjust taxation. A band of young men boarded a tea ship in Boston harbor and threw the cargo into the water. This so-called "Boston Tea Party" served to increase the hard feeling that existed between the colonies and the mother country.

There was a division of opinion in Parliament as to how the colonists should be treated. Edmund Burke, perhaps the most able member of the House of Commons, urged that the Americans be left free to tax themselves. But the king and the Tory party insisted on taking measures to put down the opposition. Believing that the trouble was confined to New England, Parliament closed Boston harbor, so that goods could neither enter nor leave the port. The holding of town meetings in the Massachusetts colony was forbidden without the permission of the governor. Also its high

Signing the Treaties of Commerce and Alliance between France and the United States, 1778 · *From left to right, William Temple Franklin (Franklin's grandson), Monsieur Gerard de Reyneval, Benjamin Franklin, Arthur Lee, and Silas Deane.*

officials were henceforth to be chosen by the king.

The Continental Congresses · Instead of bringing Massachusetts to terms, these measures caused general alarm. A congress of representatives from all the colonics was called at Philadelphia to see what could be done. This was the first united action of the colonies in defense of their liberties.

The First Continental Congress (1774) declared that trade with Britain should cease until the grievances of the colonies were remedied. In the following year the Americans met the British troops at Lexington and Concord, and made a brave stand against them in the battle of Bunker Hill.

The Second Continental Congress (1775) raised an army and placed it under the command of George Washington. On July 6 it finally declared war on England.

Declaration of Independence (1776) · Up to this time few of the colonists had openly urged the separation of the colonies from the mother country. The war was begun merely to recover the rights which the Americans believed had been taken from them. But the king charged the colonists with being rebels and increased the number of British troops in America. Finally, on July 4, 1776, Congress declared that "these united colonies are, and of right ought to be, free and independent states."

The party that favored separation was at first a minority of the population. The so-called Loyalists, or Tories, who opposed a break with England, were perhaps as numerous as the "patriots," who believed in the war for freedom. At least one-third of the colonists seemingly were indifferent.

France Aids the Colonists · The Revolution aroused great enthusiasm in France, where the people were glad of any setback for their old enemy England. The colonies sent Benjamin Franklin to Versailles to ask aid from the French king. The French hesitated as they were at first uncertain whether the colonies could carry on a struggle against the powerful mother country.

After the Americans defeated Burgoyne at Saratoga (1777), France made a treaty with the colonies, recognizing the independence of the new republic. This was equivalent to declaring war on England. The French aided the colonies with supplies and loans. A number of the younger nobles, notably the Marquis de Lafayette, crossed the Atlantic to fight as volunteers in the American army. So likewise did other liberty-loving Europeans, such as Kosciusko, Pulaski, Baron de Kalb, and Baron von Steuben.

The American Revolution Succeeds · There was much difference of opinion in England as to the advisability of the war. Influential members of Parliament openly sympathized with the colonists and urged reconciliation. George III found it necessary to hire Hessian troops as mercenaries. And British generals did not press their military operations with vigor.

Nevertheless the Americans found it no easy task to win the war. In spite of the heroic self-sacrifice of Washington and the bravery of his troops, the Americans lost more battles than they won. The French fleet was of great aid in bringing the conflict to a successful close by helping force General Cornwallis to surrender at Yorktown (1781).

The chief result of the American Revolution was the recognition by England of the independence of the United States, whose territory was to extend to the Mississippi River. West of the Mississippi the vast region of Louisiana still remained in the hands of Spain. Florida, which England had held since 1763, was returned to Spain. Spain and Portugal were able to keep their American possessions a generation longer than England kept her colonies. In the end, however, practically the whole Western Hemisphere freed itself from European rule.

CHECK ON YOUR READING

1. *What were the purposes of the trade laws? Why did they arouse such resistance?*
2. *What part did each of the following play in the American Revolution: Stamp Act, tea tax, Boston, Burke, Continental Congress, Washington, Franklin, Saratoga, Yorktown?*
3. *Why and how did France aid the colonies?*
4. *What was the result of the American Revolution?*

"We hold these truths to be self-evident: That all men are created equal; that they are endowed by their Creator with certain unalienable rights; that among these are life, liberty, and the pursuit of happiness."—JEFFERSON

Learning Activities

Think about the chapter

1. Why were the European nations such rivals over world trade?

2. What is a trading company? What powers were given to them by England and France?

3. Why were the wars in the eighteenth century essentially world wars?

4. What advantages did the Dutch have in the competition for overseas trade?

5. How do you account for the British victories in India? in North America?

6. Why did the British lose their Thirteen Colonies?

7. *Map study:* Draw a map of India showing important geographical features and locate the most important places involved in the colonial empires of England and France.

8. *Map study:* On a map of North America show (a) the changes made by the Treaty of 1763, and (b) the changes after Yorktown.

Go beyond the text

9. Choose one of the men of this period for further study. Find out about his life, his personality, and his influence on his times. The following are particularly interesting: Clive, Pitt, Burke, Wolfe, Montcalm, Lafayette, Franklin.

10. What territory in India does Portugal still hold? Why has it been in the news in recent years?

11. What possessions in the Western Hemisphere are still held by the Dutch? the French? the English?

12. Read about the Englishman John Locke, whose ideas are reflected in the Declaration of Independence.

Follow up your special interests

13. You are living in a part of the United States that was once English, Swedish, Spanish, French, Dutch, or Russian territory. Make a collection of pictures and objects for a display showing the influence of these cultures.

14. Prepare an oral or written report on one of the excellent books listed below.

READ FURTHER

Basic readings: (1) BECKER, *Modern History*, Chap. 5. (2) CHEYNEY, *Readings in English History*, Chaps. 17–18. (3) CHEYNEY, *Short History of England*, Chaps. 17–18. (4) HOFFMAN, *News of the World*, Nos. 39–42. (5) ROBINSON, *Readings in European History*, Chap. 33. (6) Year's *Pictorial History*, pp. 280–85.

Special accounts: (7) T. COSTAIN, *The White and the Gold*. (8) G. FOSTER, *George Washington's World*. (9) M. LUCAS, *Vast Horizons*. Development of trade routes to the Indies is recorded in dramatic fashion. (10) H. PRIESTLEY, *The Coming of the White Man, 1492–1848*. Good detail on the French in Canada and the Spanish settlements. (11) *American Heritage*, "LaSalle and the Discovery of the Mississippi," April, 1957. (12) G. SCHEER and H. RANKIN, *Rebels and Redcoats*. Eye-witness accounts of the American Revolution.

Fiction and biography: (13) W. CATHER, *Death Comes for the Archbishop*. Tells of the Spanish in New Mexico. *Shadows on the Rock*, by Miss Cather, tells of early days in French Canada. (14) J. EATON, *That Lively Man, Ben Franklin*. Franklin at the court of Louis XVI and how he obtained aid for the colonists. (15) A. NEVINS, *St. Francis of the Seven Seas*. The adventures of St. Francis Xavier as a missionary in India, Malabar, and the Spice Islands. (16) C. NORDHOFF and J. HALL, *The Bounty Trilogy*. Exciting tales of the British navy in eighteenth-century sailing days. (17) E. SWENSON, *South Sea Shilling*. The toss of a shilling started Cook on the voyages that added important lands to the British Empire.

The Struggle for Democracy

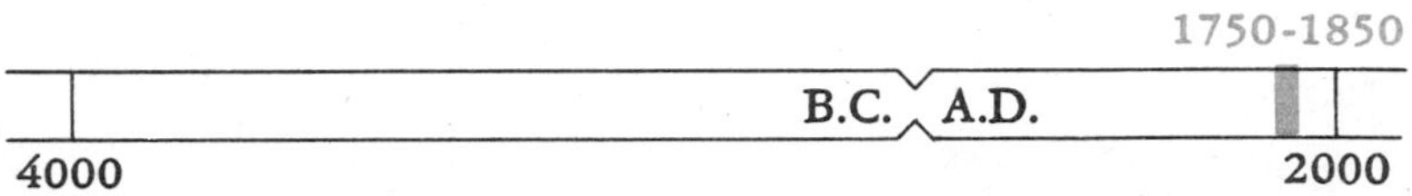

1750-1850

B.C. A.D.

4000

2000

*W*HEN Cornwallis surrendered at Yorktown at the end of the American Revolution, the band played "The World Turned Upside Down." And the world *was* turned upside down. For the next sixty or seventy years the Western world was torn by revolutions, some peaceful, most violent. The new struggled against the old. As Charles Dickens said, "It was the best of times, it was the worst of times."

Perhaps the greatest changes began in the minds of men. Scientists turned away from the accepted authorities and experimented for themselves. Philosophers challenged the *Ancient Regime*. Men rose up against their oppressors and demanded liberty. The cry was for freedom.

The result was the French Revolution. The old order was swept away. Tumbrels rattled through the streets of Paris carrying to the guillotine the aristocracy of France. The common people demanded the right to liberty, equality, and fraternity. A republic was established, then a reign of terror.

Into the confusion and disorder which followed came a man determined to make himself not only a ruler of France but also ruler of all Europe. The fiery and ambitious Napoleon swept along on a wave of successes. He became Emperor of France. His armies conquered most of Europe. But the Russian winter, the British fleet, and the allied armies finally brought about his defeat and exile to St. Helena.

His great empire was broken up. The men of the Congress of Vienna sought to suppress freedom and set the clock of history back. But they did not reckon with the revolutionary temper of the times. Men insisted upon governing themselves. As a result, new revolts broke out in Greece, Belgium, France, Poland, Germany, Hungary, and Italy. Some failed, others succeeded. Independence was won by Greece and Belgium. France again became a republic. In Latin America the Spanish and Portuguese colonists gained their independence and came under the protection of the British fleet and the Monroe Doctrine.

Meanwhile another kind of revolution was quietly taking place. New inventions were changing the way men lived. Manufacturing turned from homes to factories. Men flocked to cities to work for wages, form unions, and struggle for a higher standard of living. The Machine Age began, and with it great changes in our political, social, and economic institutions.

293

The French Revolution: Its Causes and Its Course

KEY WORDS AND DATES

Voltaire
Diderot (*Encyclopedia*)
Rousseau
parlements
Third Estate
Marie Antoinette
cahiers
Bastille
departments
Declaration of the Rights of Man
emigrant nobles
Committee of Public Safety
Jacobins and Girondists
Reign of Terror
Commune
Robespierre
Directory
1789

POLITICAL EVENTS are only part of the story of the eighteenth century. How were the masses of the people living? Wars of conquest, far from benefiting the common people, sacrificed the lives of many and weighed down the poor with crushing taxes. Any gains from added territory or overseas adventures seemed to find their way into the pockets of the nobles or merchant class.

A growing number of reformers were pointing out the unfairness of the old order and demanding a greater share of liberty, justice, and opportunity for all. In the year 1789 a momentous event took place in France. In the country where absolute monarchy had achieved its most spectacular triumph, the old order of things suddenly came to an end. The throne, the aristocracy, and all special privileges were swept away by a wave of revolt. France became a republic in which all Frenchmen alike were "citizens."

The overthrow of ancient institutions was followed by a period of bloodshed and terror. This led to a reaction and later to an empire and the return of monarchy. But many reforms lived on and spread through Europe. They ushered in a new era of hope for the common man. The struggle for liberty and the rights of man continued.

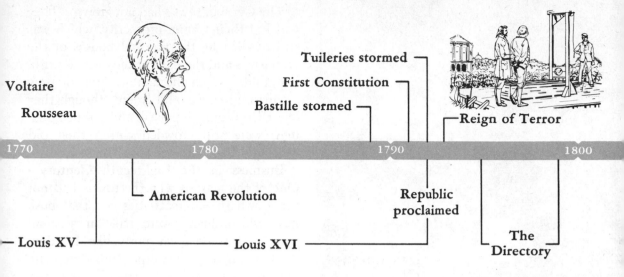

Voltaire
Rousseau

Bastille stormed

First Constitution

Tuileries stormed

Reign of Terror

1770   1780   1790   1800

American Revolution

Republic
proclaimed

The
Directory

Louis XV   Louis XVI

1. Life and Thought in the Eighteenth Century

Serfdom Lingers in Europe · In medieval times the serf was considered as part of the land. If he ran away and was caught, he could be punished. In the eighteenth century such conditions persisted in Prussia, Russia, Austria, Hungary, Italy, and Spain.

In parts of western Europe serfdom had begun gradually to disappear as early as the twelfth century. In England and France by the eighteenth century the peasant was no longer bound to the land, but was free to move about as he wished. He could marry without the lord's consent and could now rent the land or work for wages.

We shall see, however, that in France the nobles retained many privileges (p. 300). But they no longer provided essential services. Their irresponsibility finally led to a revolution.

Condition of the Peasants · The peasant worked in the same way and with the same crude tools that his ancestors had used. He still had a wooden plow to break the earth. He cut the wheat with a sickle and the grass with an unwieldy scythe. The farm carts still had only wooden rims on their wheels.

Nor had the conditions of living grown better with the lapse of centuries. The houses were often mere hovels with dirt floors and thatched roofs. There was little light or ventilation. The pigs and cows were often as well off as the peasants, for the barn and the house were parts of the same building. The drinking water was bad and the drainage poor.

There were no amusements to relieve the dreariness of country life, not even a newspaper to tell of something going on in the outside world. But then even in England it is said that not one peasant in five thousand could read.

Medieval Character of the Towns · The appearance of the towns was much as it had been in the Middle Ages, though some were larger. The streets were still narrow and crooked and were darkened by the overhanging upper stories of the buildings. They were often unpaved.

Dancing the Minuet · *Eighteenth-century society was very elegant. For it, Mozart composed many charming and graceful minuets.*

In London, with its half-million inhabitants, a person without a private carriage had to walk or take one of the few public coaches or be carried in a sedan chair. The poorly lighted streets were supposed to be guarded at night by watchmen, who went about with lanterns. But they were so few as to be of no real protection. Gentlemen who went forth after dark had to carry arms to defend themselves against attack.

Paris was somewhat larger than London and had spread beyond its medieval walls. The great park, the "Elysian Fields," and many of the boulevards which now beautify Paris were already laid out. But the streets were still narrow and winding. There were few sewers to carry off the water. The people had to rely for their water supply on easily polluted wells or the river Seine.

The German towns had not grown. They had lost their former prosperity, which was still recalled by the fine old houses of the merchants and the halls of the once flourishing guilds. Even the famous cities of Italy —Milan, Florence, and Rome—though they had their beautiful palaces and public buildings, were still crowded within their old walls and had dark, crooked streets.

Business in the Eighteenth Century · One of the reasons why the towns had not yet grown to be great cities was that business and industry were still on a small scale. At some great ports like London, Amsterdam, and Antwerp, goods were coming from and going to colonies overseas, and there were some warehouses and business buildings. But there were only a few cities. There were no railroads, steamships, and factories, such as we have today. The medieval guilds (p. 178) still controlled the making and selling of goods.

Social Classes · The old medieval division of society into privileged and unprivileged classes lasted into the eighteenth century. There was a rigid social scale according to wealth, rank, and occupation. It extended from the king, nobility, and clergy down to businessmen, artisans, and peasants. The nobles still formed a wealthy and powerful class. The unwillingness of the French nobles to give up their privileges finally led to their downfall.

The clergy, especially in Catholic countries, enjoyed many rights and exemptions that set them off from the people at large. The higher clergy were members of the nobility, and many lived at the court. They took a prominent part in affairs of state, even acting as ministers to the king. They controlled the vast wealth of the Church, which had accumulated through the years from gifts of money and lands.

Censorship of the Press · Both the Catholic and the Protestant Church were still intolerant. In this they were usually supported by the government, which was ready to punish any who refused to conform to the religion of the realm. Books and pamphlets were carefully examined by a censor in order to see whether they contained anything intended to undermine the authority of the Church or of the king. As late as 1757 the king of France issued a decree prescribing the death penalty for those who wrote, printed, or distributed any work which appeared to be an attack on religion.

Nevertheless books calling for reform in both Church and state constantly appeared and were freely circulated. The writers took care not to place their names or those of the publishers on the title pages. Many such books were printed in England, Switzerland, or Holland, where greater freedom prevailed. The books of the English reformers especially had great influence on the French.

Men of Science Challenge the Old Ways · In the eighteenth century, more and more people began to recognize that what had often passed for wisdom and fact in the old days was sheer ignorance and superstition. They set themselves to discover the truth about many kinds of things.

It was above all the men of science who broke the hold of the past on men's minds. They rejected authority and tradition as a basis for knowledge, and substituted the evidence of man's eyes and the use of his reason. We have already seen how the discoveries of Copernicus, Galileo, and Newton revolutionized the idea of the physical universe and revealed many of its important laws.

Many other patient workers were observing nature's processes. Scientists in their

Antoine Lavoisier and Wife, 1743–1794 · *Lavoisier was a founder of modern chemistry. He developed the theory of combustion and explained the role of oxygen in respiration.*

laboratories were laying the foundations of our modern sciences of chemistry, physics, botany, geology, zoology, biology, and medicine. These scholars cast aside the old authorities and made observations and experiments for themselves. Microscopes, telescopes, barometers, thermometers, clocks, and balances assisted them to make more accurate measurements than had been possible in the days of the Greeks and Romans, who had none of these instruments.

Others saw that many of the old laws and institutions stood in the way of progress, and should be changed or given up. Accordingly, with an increase in knowledge came a growing demand for reform. This included a struggle for religious toleration and for political liberty.

Bronze Bust of Voltaire, by J. A. Houdon ·
*The artist admirably expresses the sardonic
humor of the versatile penman whose genius
enlivened French literature for fifty years.*

John Locke's Revolutionary Theory ·
A number of thinkers and writers were impressed with the importance of the new discoveries. They used them to criticize the practices of the Church and the government. They asserted that man's *reason* was sufficient to guide him to live according to the laws of God and nature. They said that man was entitled to believe what he discovered, even if it was in opposition to the opinions of kings and theologians. This doctrine was very shocking to political and clerical leaders everywhere.

Among the revolutionary thinkers and writers was the English political philosopher John Locke. In *Two Treatises of Government*, published in 1690, he justified the right of Englishmen to dethrone their "divine-right" king. Locke made three points. (1) All men are born with certain *natural rights,* such as life and liberty. (2) Men set up governments by consent to protect these rights. (3) Whenever government ceases to protect these rights, the people who made it may overthrow it. This doctrine of government of, by, and for free men made the autocratic James II the villain, and the liberty-loving people not rebels but heroes.

American colonial leaders read Locke with enthusiasm. And Thomas Jefferson echoed Locke's arguments in justifying the revolt against King George III. We shall see how Frenchmen seized upon these revolutionary ideas to attack the autocracy of the Bourbons.

The Influence of Voltaire (1694–1778) ·
Voltaire was a young and gifted Frenchman whose critical writing caused his exile to England. There he was deeply impressed by Parliament, the free press, freedom from arrest, and the rights enjoyed by Englishmen. On his return he wrote his *Letters on the English*. It was promptly burned by the hangman, and Voltaire narrowly escaped imprisonment.

During the rest of his long life Voltaire advocated reliance on reason and confidence in the progress of mankind. He hated tyranny and bigotry in all its forms. He believed that liberty for one was impossible without free speech for all—especially for minority opinion. Said he, "I wholly disapprove of what you say [but] will defend to the death your right to say it."

The *Encyclopedia* · Voltaire had many admirers and allies in his work of reform. Among these were Denis Diderot and a group of scholars who prepared articles for a new French encyclopedia. This work was intended to give the public a summary of the new scientific knowledge and awaken interest in progress and reform.

The *Encyclopedia* was an important influence in bringing about the French Revolution. Its articles attacked the slave trade, religious intolerance, unfair taxation, the brutality of the criminal law, and other evils of the time. Although the editors tried to avoid stirring up ill feeling, they were bound to contradict old theories and expose bad institutions.

The clergy believed (with considerable truth) that the work was dangerous to the authority of the Church and the king. The first two volumes (which appeared in 1752) were banned. This added immensely to their popularity and increased the circulation of the volumes which followed.

Rousseau's Plea for Democracy · The most famous French writer devoted to reform in government was Jean Jacques Rousseau (1712–1778). He believed that all human beings are equal and that every man has a natural right to share in the government. "Men are born free," he said, "[yet] are everywhere in chains."

In a famous little book, *The Social Contract*, which was to become the "Bible of the French Revolution," he declared that the only lawful government is that which rests on the will of the people. The *people* may appoint a king to manage the state for them. But *they* should make the laws *themselves*, since it is *they* who must obey the laws once they are made. To Locke and Voltaire these italicized words meant the middle class. To Rousseau they meant *everybody*.

Rousseau's ideas of liberty, equality, and fraternity became very popular with the people. His influence is shown in the first French constitution (p. 310). It defines law not as the decrees of a monarch, but as "the expression of the general will."

CHECK ON YOUR READING

1. Describe eighteenth-century life under these topics: (a) peasants, (b) towns, (c) business, (d) social classes, (e) the press.
2. How did men of science challenge authority?
3. Explain Locke's revolutionary theory.
4. What did (a) Voltaire, (b) the Encyclopedia, and (c) Rousseau contribute to the revolution in men's minds?

---

2. How the French Revolution Came About

Why There Was Discontent · The revolutionary ideas we have discussed do not bring revolutions unless they have discontent to feed on. When Louis XVI came to the throne of France in 1774, there was discontent everywhere. Part of the trouble was that the state was a patchwork of provinces, each retaining its own ancient laws and privileges. As a result, tolls and customs duties varied throughout the country and caused great confusion.

Moreover, the different districts did not all pay the same amount of taxes to the central government. Some even kept the right of deciding for themselves what they would give. Thus there was much bickering and bargaining between the royal intendants and the local officials as to the amount that would be levied.

All this was bad enough in times of prosperity. But now the country was on the brink of bankruptcy. The state was reaping

Crushing Burdens on the Peasants · *Identify the specific estates and taxes shown in this satirical engraving of 1789. Was the cartoon for, or against, the Revolution?*

the harvest of costly wars and extravagant court life.

Heavy Taxes of the Peasants · People as well as provinces were taxed unequally. The taxes imposed on peasants sometimes amounted to 80 per cent of their whole income. These included the land tax (*taille*) and the poll tax (*capitation*, or tax per head). Another burden on the peasants was the *corvée*, which was the duty to do unpaid labor on the public roads.

Also there were *tithes* to be paid to the Church and the old feudal dues still demanded by the lords of the manors on which the peasants lived. The government, moreover, obtained a large revenue from various taxes on food, wine, and tobacco. These the peasants paid *indirectly* in the increased prices that they were charged for these articles.

Sometimes the taxes were "farmed" out to collectors, who arranged to get for the government a certain amount from each district. These farmers-general, as they were called, then got all they could out of the people. After paying the agreed sum to the government, they pocketed the rest.

Privileges of the Clergy and Nobility · The clergy and nobility formed what were called the *First* and *Second Estates*. They did not have to pay the heavy land tax and escaped other burdens which the common people (the *Third Estate*) had to bear.

Much of the revenue of the Church went to the higher clergy—the archbishops, bishops, and abbots. These churchmen lived like lords and often left the work to be done by the lower clergy, who received but little for their labors. Thus it was that when the Revolution came, the parish priests in general sided with the people rather than with their bishops.

Originally the nobles had been excused from paying taxes because they had defended the country. By the eighteenth century, however, the nobles had laid aside their swords and in their velvet coats were gathered around the king at Versailles. Though they no longer performed their former *services*, the old custom still prevailed which freed them from the *taille* and other taxes.

The stewards who managed the estates of their absentee lords squeezed all they could out of the farmers to pay the expenses of their idle masters at the court. The nobles also had the exclusive privilege of hunting, which was their favorite pastime. The game which they preserved for their amusement often did great damage to the crops. Yet the peasants were forbidden to kill the deer and hares and thus spoil the sport of their lords. Many of the estates had large pigeon-towers with a thousand or more nests. These were especially detested by the farmers because the flocks of pigeons often devoured newly planted seeds.

Other Grievances of the Third Estate · Although the peasants were the largest group within the Third Estate, leadership in the coming struggle was assumed by a much smaller one. In this group were the lawyers, merchants, bankers, doctors, teachers, and other professional people from the rising middle classes of the cities.

Although better off than the peasants or the unskilled laborers in the cities, the middle classes had real grievances of their own. The higher offices in the army and in the Church, and the most desirable appointments at the king's court, were reserved for the nobles. Talented and ambitious middle-class people bitterly resented their exclusion from all participation in the government and saw no hope for improvement.

Despotic Powers of the Crown · The king had unlimited power. He levied the hated *taille* and could spend what he pleased without being questioned.

The king also had the power to issue orders for the arrest and imprisonment of any person. These notorious orders of arrest were called "sealed letters" (*lettres de cachet*). Anyone who had influence with the king or his favorites could easily obtain one to use against an enemy. The victim, without being told of what he was accused or having any trial, could be cast into a dungeon, such as the *Bastille*. He might lie there until the king happened to remember him or was reminded of him by the poor man's friends. *A Tale of Two Cities* by Charles Dickens gives an excellent account of such an experience.

The *Parlements* Could Protest · There remained certain ways in which the protests

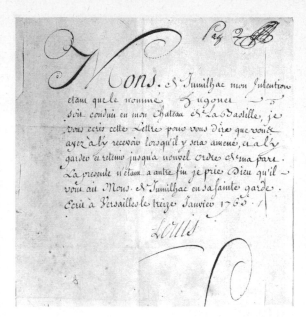

Lettre de Cachet · *This letter, written at Versailles, January 13, 1765, tells Monsieur Jumillac that Louis wishes one named Lugones to be taken to the Bastille and held until . . . .*

of the French people could find voice. The high courts of justice, called *parlements*, did not confine themselves to trying lawsuits. They maintained that when the king made a new law, it must be sent to them to register. Otherwise they would not be able to make their decisions in reference to it.

Sometimes, instead of registering an edict which they disliked, they would send a protest (*remonstrance*) to the king, urging that his ministers had misled him. They would have their protest printed and sold on the streets for a penny so that the people might know that the *parlements* were defending them against the tyranny of the royal officials.

How Public Opinion Was Aroused · We have seen how philosophers and reformers like Voltaire and Rousseau had openly attacked the evils around them and helped

Queen Marie Antoinette · *Despite many extravagances, her life was not a happy one. Her son died in prison, and she on the guillotine (childhood picture, p. 270).*

to spread serious discontent in France. Poems, stories, and plays had laid bare the existing abuses and demanded reform. The *Encyclopedia* had promoted the idea that it was the common people in a nation whose lot ought to be the main concern of the nation's government.

Above all, the French were impressed by two successful revolutions. They had seen the English in the "Glorious Revolution" of 1688 limit the powers of their king. And their leaders had read the powerful arguments of John Locke. Their own Lafayette had fought in the American Revolution, and the republic established in the New World had broken completely with the old regime and proclaimed all men to be "free and equal."

The French people were nearly ready to follow America's example by the time the American Revolution had been successfully brought to an end. All kinds of political activities were going on. Political clubs were formed, where people could discuss questions of government and religion.

There were few newspapers, but great numbers of pamphlets were written and circulated. Everyone who had a grievance or who thought strongly about some idea of reform rushed to print it (though without signing his name). Thousands of pamphlets were eagerly read and discussed. All this ferment of ideas helped to arouse public opinion and inspire rebellion.

Louis XV Prepares the Way for Revolution (1715–1774) · During the reign of Louis XV the evils of the old regime grew steadily worse. The monarchy became more overbearing and oppressive without having any constructive policy for running the country. The king himself was bored with government matters. His personal life was scandalous and given over entirely to pleasure. He lavished money and estates on his favorites and allowed them to meddle in matters of state.

The gulf between rich and poor grew ever wider, and the oppressed peasants became more bitter over the unfair treatment that they received. Finally, the disastrous war in which France lost her hold in India and all her American possessions (1763) brought the country to the verge of bankruptcy and convinced the middle classes that the country was being misgoverned. In the early years of his reign Louis XV had been nicknamed the "well-beloved," but as time went on he lost all claim to that title. When at last he was carried off by smallpox, everyone hailed with hopes of better times the accession of his grandson, Louis XVI.

Louis XVI (1774–1793) and Marie Antoinette · The new king was twenty, heavy-looking, poorly educated, kind in heart, and lazy. He was fond of hunting and puttering about in a workshop, where he spent his happiest hours. Now and then he tried to attend to the tiresome business of government. He had good intentions but was indecisive. He continually relied on the advice of others, lacking the will power to take responsibility himself.

The new queen was Marie Antoinette, the beautiful daughter of Maria Theresa of Austria. The marriage had been arranged in 1770 to maintain the alliance between France and Austria that had been so skill-fully concluded during the Seven Years' War.

The Austrian princess was nineteen, light-hearted, and eager for pleasure. But she soon wearied of the formal etiquette of the court at Versailles and often shocked people by her thoughtless pranks. She learned how to manage her easygoing husband and did not hesitate to interfere in the government when she wished to help a favorite or harm an enemy.

Turgot Recommends Economy · As the finances of the country were in a desperate condition, Louis XVI appointed a brilliant economist, Turgot, as controller-general. Turgot immediately recommended cutting down expenses. The vast amount spent on the luxurious court at Versailles, he urged, must be reduced. The various royal estab-lishments cost the nation annually about twelve million dollars.

Besides, the French kings had long been accustomed to grant "pensions" in a reck-less manner to their favorites. These cost nearly twelve million dollars more. But attempts to reduce this amount aroused the opposition of the courtiers, and it was the

Louis XVI · *Dull, shy, and indecisive, Louis ruled reluctantly in a court teeming with jeal-ousy and intrigue. What circumstances led to his death? How would you have voted?*

courtiers who really controlled the king. They soon persuaded Louis to dismiss Turgot (May, 1776), and most of his reforms were undone.

Necker Presents a Financial Report · Necker, who shortly succeeded Turgot, was a banker. It was hoped that with more businesslike management he could remedy matters without touching the privileges of the rich. But Necker had to borrow vast sums to aid the American colonists in their war against England, and this further drained the treasury. When he planned economies, he too created enemies, chief of whom was Marie Antoinette. The indul-gent king could not bear to deprive the queen and her friends of their accustomed pleasures, and so he sent Necker off.

Convocation of the Estates–General at Versailles, May 5, 1789 · *Can you identify the king? each of the three estates? When had they last met? Why was this body called? How was history affected thereby?*

In one way Necker helped bring on the French Revolution. In 1781 he presented a report to the king on the financial condition of the country. This was published, and for the first time the people could see how much the *taille* took from them and how much the king spent on himself and his favorites. Necker's suggestion to levy the *taille* more equally was scorned by the nobles.

Bankrupt Condition of France · The new minister, Calonne, was at first popular with the king and courtiers. He succeeded in getting new loans and spent money recklessly. But the time soon came when he was forced to inform the astonished king that the country was nearly bankrupt. The treasury was running behind every year by some 25 million dollars. This was a huge sum for those days.

In 1787 Calonne persuaded the king to call an assembly of *Notables* (nobles, bishops, and government officials). He hoped that they would agree to a new system of taxation by which the upper and lower classes would pay alike and much more money could be raised. But the Notables were unwilling to give up their exemptions. So the king sent them home and dismissed Calonne.

The Estates-General Summoned · Louis then tried to get the *parlements* to approve new taxes, but they refused. The *parlement* of Paris declared that "only the nation assembled in the Estates-General can give the consent necessary to establish a permanent tax." Only the nation, they asserted, could destroy the existing evils and injustices.

The king replied by abolishing the *parlements*. But this action aroused a wide protest and a general demand for the calling of the representatives of the nation. Finally, the king yielded and summoned the Estates-General, which had not met since 1614.

┌─ CHECK ON YOUR READING

1. *Why were the French people discontented with (a) government organization? (b) the tax system? (c) privileges of clergy and nobles? (d) lettres de cachet?*
2. *How was public opinion aroused?*
3. *How did Louis XV, Louis XVI, and Marie Antoinette influence matters?*

3. *The National Assembly Brings Reforms* (1789-1791)

The Estates-General and Its Method of Voting · The Estates-General, which met in May, 1789, was made up of representatives elected by the (1) clergy, (2) nobility, and (3) Third Estate. Each estate ordinarily sent an equal number of delegates, even though there were far more members of the Third Estate in France than of the other two estates combined. Each group met as a house by itself and cast one vote. Thus the First and Second Estates could outvote the Third Estate two to one. They were likely to do so whenever a question of their privileges was involved.

To offset this advantage the Third Estate insisted that it have twice as many deputies (about six hundred) as either of the other orders. And the king's ministers finally agreed. But this did not affect the outcome so long as the voting was done by estates. Yet the king refused to allow the assembly to sit as one body.

The People Voice Their Grievances in the *Cahiers* · According to an ancient custom, every town and village was invited to prepare a list of its complaints and the reforms it desired. These grievances really took the form of petitions, which the delegates could use as a basis for their discussion. They were officially known as *cahiers* ("kà yā'")—literally, "notebooks."

The *cahiers* prepared in the local groups give an excellent idea of the widespread discontent in France. Though all showed great loyalty to the king, they revealed a general distrust of the court. The lower classes complained of the heavy taxes, which they were unable to bear, while the rich were allowed to escape this burden. They asked for the abolition of the old feudal dues and privileges, which made their lives so hard.

The *cahiers* pointed out the confusion existing in the country and prayed for a uniform system of laws for the realm. They asked that "sealed letters" be abolished and that the prisons be improved. They urged greater economy and a balanced budget.

The National Assembly (June, 1789) · With these ideas in mind, the deputies assembled at Versailles and held their first session on May 5, 1789. In spite of the king's commands, the representatives of the Third Estate refused to organize themselves

FRANCE IN 1789

0   225
Scale of Miles

Dunkirk
Brussels
ARTOIS
Meuse R.
Rhine R.
Neerwinden
Amiens
Rouen
Verdun
Varennes
Seine R.
Metz
Versailles
Paris
Valmy
Lunéville
Chartres
Toul
Orleans
BRITTANY
Nantes
Tours
Loire R.
Chambord
VENDÉE
F R A N C E
Saône R.
Bay of
Biscay
Clermont
Lyons
Rhône R.
Bordeaux
Dordogne R.
GIRONDE
Garonne R.
Avignon
Toulouse
PROVENCE
Nice
PYRENEES MTS.
Marseilles
S P A I N
Toulon

France in 1789 · *How were these places head-lined: Paris? Versailles? Varennes? Ven-dée? Gironde? Lyon? Toulon? Valmy?*

as a separate class. They invited the deputies of the clergy and nobility to join them to discuss the great problems of the nation. Some liberal nobles—Lafayette, for example —and a large minority of the clergy wished to accept the suggestion. But they were outvoted.

The representatives of the Third Estate finally lost patience. Asserting that they represented 96 per cent of the nation, they declared themselves a National Assembly (June 17). This transformed the old feudal Estates-General, voting by class, into the first national representative assembly on the continent of Europe.

The Tennis-Court Oath · Three days later, when the members of the Third Estate came to their regular place of meeting, they were not permitted to enter. The excuse given was that the building was under repair. They thereupon betook themselves to a neighboring building, some-

times used as a tennis court. Here, on June 20, amidst great excitement, the members took the famous Tennis-Court Oath. They pledged *"to come together wherever circumstance may dictate, until the constitution of the kingdom shall be established."*

The king now tried to restore the old system by holding a royal session of the three estates at which he presided in person. He presented a long program of reforms and then ordered the estates to meet separately as formerly. When he had finished, most of the bishops, some of the parish priests, and a great part of the nobility obeyed. The rest sat still, uncertain what they should do. The master of ceremonies ordered them to obey the king's commands.

Then Mirabeau, the most distinguished statesman among the deputies, told him bluntly that they would not leave their places except at the point of the bayonet. The king immediately gave in. A few days later he directed all the deputies of the two privileged orders who had not already done so to join the Third Estate in the National Assembly.

Bastille Day, July 14, 1789 · The National Assembly now began in earnest its great task of reform. It was soon interrupted, however, by events at Paris. On July 14 a mob stormed the ancient Paris fortress of the Bastille. This castle had long been used as a prison for offenders against the state and for those arrested under "sealed letters."

When the crowd demanded admission, it was fired on, and nearly a hunded were killed. The mob now forced its way into the building, but found only seven prisoners. One poor fellow had lost his wits, and another had no idea why he had been kept there for years. The captives were freed amidst great rejoicing, and the people soon

Paris Mob Storming the Bastille, July 14, 1789 · *This massive prison-fortress was a symbol of autocracy. The frenzied mob tore it to pieces. Its fall was prelude to the overthrow of the hated* ancient regime.

set to work to demolish the walls. This was the first act of violence in the Revolution. Bastille Day is still celebrated as the national holiday of France each July 14.

The Assembly Abolishes Feudalism, Reforms Taxation, and Creates Departments · About the first of August news began to reach the Assembly in Versailles of serious riots in the provinces. In some cases the peasants burned the country houses of the nobles so as to destroy the records of the feudal dues which they owed.

On the night of August 4, 1789, the Assembly passed a momentous resolution. (1) It did away with all the survivals of feudalism in France. The exclusive right of the nobility to hunt and maintain pigeon-houses was abolished. The peasants were now permitted to kill game which they found on their land. (2) Exemptions from the payment of taxes were done away with, and equal taxation for all classes was proclaimed. The tithes of the Church were abolished. (3) All citizens, without distinction of birth, were thereafter to have the right to hold office. (4) Moreover, all

the special privileges in the various provinces were revoked. All France was to have the same laws. Its citizens everywhere were henceforth to be treated in the same way by the state. The Assembly soon went a step farther in unifying France. (5) It wiped out the old provinces altogether and redivided the country into districts of convenient size, called *departments*.

Declaration of Rights, August 26, 1789 · The Declaration of the Rights of Man is one of the most notable documents in the history of Europe. It not only aroused general enthusiasm when it was first published, but appeared over and over again, in various forms, in later French constitutions. It has been the model for similar declarations in many other European countries. Each article represented the correction of some long-standing evil.

The Declaration proclaimed that "men are born and remain equal in rights." It provided that no one should be accused, arrested, or imprisoned except according to the law. Every citizen was guaranteed freedom of speech, of the press, and of religion. Read some statements from the Declaration on page 317.

Rumors Make the People Suspicious · The king hesitated to ratify the Declaration of the Rights of Man. In October rumors spread that under the influence of the courtiers he was calling troops together to put an end to the Revolution. It was also reported that the new national colors— red, white, and blue—had been trampled underfoot at a banquet at Versailles in the presence of the queen. All these rumors, together with the fact that food was scarce, aroused the excitable Paris populace.

The King Is Forced to Return to Paris (October, 1789) · On October 5 several thousand poor women, together with a number of armed men, marched out to Versailles to demand bread of the king. Rumor had it that there were plenty of provisions at the court, and the people still believed in the king, however suspicious they might be of his friends.

The mob declared that the king must accompany them to Paris, and he was obliged to consent. So they gayly escorted the "baker, the baker's wife, and the baker's boy," as they jocularly termed the king and queen and the little crown prince, to the Palace of the Tuileries. There the king took up his residence, practically a prisoner. The National Assembly soon followed him and held its sittings in a riding school near the Tuileries. (See map below.)

This transfer of the king and the Assembly to the capital was the first great misfortune of the Revolution. It placed the National Assembly at the mercy of the leaders of the disorderly elements of Paris.

The Assembly Takes Over Church Property (November, 1789) · In the meantime the financial condition of the country was growing ever worse. Business was suffering, food was scarce, and many were living on charity. The treasury could not arrange new loans, nor collect new taxes. Under these circumstances the wealth of the Church offered a great temptation.

The Church owned one-fifth of the land of France. This land brought in a vast revenue, yet the Church was free from taxation. As this was part of the old order, the Assembly finally decided to seize the lands of the Church and sell them to raise money.

The tithes had been abolished in August, along with feudal dues. On November 2 a decree was passed taking Church possessions. It provided that the nation must provide "for the expenses of maintaining religious services, for the support of those who conduct them, and for the help of the poor." In February, 1790, the monasteries and convents also lost their property.

Control of the Clergy (July, 1790) · The Assembly now passed measures which completely reorganized the Church and made it a part of the state. The 134 bishoprics, some of which dated back to the

Paris · Which of these famous places can you identify? Why is Paris considered the "heart" of France?

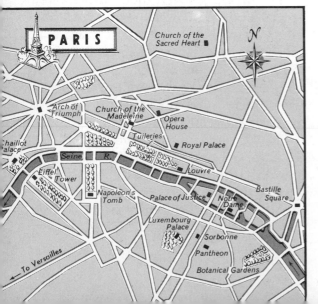

Roman Empire, were replaced by eighty-three. These corresponded to the *departments* into which France had been divided. Each of the new districts became the diocese of a bishop. Bishops and priests were regarded as officers of the state. They were to be elected by all citizens, including non-Catholics, who had the right to vote for other state officials.

The Civil Constitution of the Clergy, as the new regulation was called, was a serious mistake on the part of the Assembly. It was true the Church in France sadly needed reform. But the introduction of state control and the proposal to have the people elect the bishops and priests shocked thousands who hitherto had enthusiastically welcomed the reforms of the Assembly.

The resistance of the clergy led the Assembly to commit another grievous error. It required the clergy to take an oath to be faithful to the new constitution. The Pope forbade the French clergy to take the oath, threatening to excommunicate those who did so. On the other hand those who refused were to be deprived of their salaries by the Assembly and might be imprisoned. Nevertheless, forty-six thousand parish priests refused to take the oath. Later, the punishment for such refusal became worse.

The Jacobins · Enthusiasm for the Revolution was greatly increased by the newspapers, pamphlets, and political clubs. The most famous club was that of the Jacobins. It was founded by representatives of the Third Estate when the Assembly moved to Paris. The members of the society met in a room in the monastery of the Jacobin monks. Here they discussed questions which were to come up before the Assembly and decided how they should vote.

Though few in number, the Jacobins soon had branches in many French towns

Sans–Culotte · *Too poor for knee breeches (culottes) and silk stockings, the common man wore pantaloons, sabots, and liberty cap.*

and exercised a considerable influence on public opinion throughout France. The secret of their strength was in careful organization. Among their leaders were Mirabeau, Marat, and Robespierre.

The Emigrés Conspire to Help the King · Some of the nobility, under the leadership of the king's youngest brother, the Count of Artois, had left the country. They were called *émigrés*. Joined later by other nobles, they collected a little army on the frontier. With it they hoped to invade France.

By means of newspapers, pamphlets, and plots the *émigrés* kept up a continual conspiracy against the government. They were in touch with the king. On the night of June 21, 1791, Louis XVI and Marie Antoinette fled secretly from the palace, hoping to join them. But the royal party was stopped at Varennes and brought back to Paris. The National Assembly pretended that the king had not really fled, but had been kidnaped by his bad advisers.

The queen's brother, Emperor Leopold II of Austria, to whom Marie Antoinette had been appealing secretly for help, was greatly disturbed by the arrest of the royal family. Together with the Prussian king, he issued an appeal to the European powers to unite in forcing the French people to give back to Louis XVI his former rights. But this call on foreign monarchs to help the *émigré* nobles re-establish the old regime only angered the people and created bad feeling against the king.

The First French Constitution Establishes a Limited Monarchy (1791) · At last the National Assembly, after two years of work, put the finishing touches on the new constitution for France. The king had no choice but to sign it. This was the first important *written* constitution in any European country.

Like the American Constitution, it provided for the "separation of powers." The law-making powers were placed in the Legislative Assembly. It was to be indirectly elected by the people. The executive authority was centered in the king, but the king no longer had power over local governments or the army and navy. Thus France was changed from a despotism to a constitutional monarchy in which the **powers** of the king were limited.

CHECK ON YOUR READING

1. *How did each of the following influence reform: (a) the three estates? (b) the cahiers? (c) the Tennis-Court Oath? (d) Bastille Day?*
2. *Summarize the chief reforms of the Assembly regarding (a) feudalism, (b) taxes, (c) departments, (d) Rights of Man, (e) Church property, (f) the clergy.*
3. *How did the following influence the Revolution: (a) rumors? (b) the king's flight? (c) the loyalty oath? (d) the émigrés? (e) the Jacobins?*

---

4. The Legislative Assembly and Its Problems (1791–1792)

Difficulties Facing the New Government · The new Legislative Assembly met for its first session on October 1, 1791. It faced many difficulties.

Some people thought the National Assembly had gone too far and others felt that it had not gone far enough. There was general distrust of the king and hatred of the foreign queen. The emigrant nobles were known to be conspiring on the borders. Foreign kings had threatened to invade France to restore the old regime. In France many were opposed to the laws concerning the Church.

The Legislative Assembly now added to the discord by issuing severe orders against

Seizure of Louis XVI and His Family in the Courtyard of the Tuileries · *This print shows Louis being made a sans-culotte. The Republic soon followed.*

the emigrant nobles and the non-cooperating clergy. All Frenchmen assembled on the frontier were ordered to return to France by January 1, 1792 under penalty of death. Clergymen who refused to accept the Civil Constitution of the Clergy and the new constitution of France were looked upon as suspects and were finally ordered to leave the country. In this way, the Assembly aroused the active hostility of a great part of the priests, who had formerly favored the Revolution. Moreover, it antagonized the great mass of Catholics, who would not desert their spiritual leaders.

France at War with Austria and Prussia · The Assembly suspected that Louis was negotiating with foreign powers to secure their interference in French affairs. It believed that a war against Austria would unite the people and force the king to show his true character. In April, 1792, the Assembly declared war on Austria and forced Louis to sign the declaration.

Prussia immediately joined Austria, and the allies raised a large army to invade France. When the French armies met with a series of defeats, the unpopularity of the king increased because it was believed that the royal family was betraying military secrets to the enemy. In June a Paris mob invaded the Palace of the Tuileries and forced the king to appear before the people, wearing the "cap of liberty," the badge of "citizen patriots."

As the Prussian and Austrian armies approached the French boundaries, it became clear that the king was utterly incapable of defending France. The Assembly seriously considered deposing him. To complicate matters, the Duke of Brunswick, who was at the head of the Prussian forces, took the very worst means of helping Louis. He issued a manifesto in which he threatened to destroy Paris should the king suffer any harm.

The Commune Revolts · Angered by this declaration, the populace of Paris again invaded the Tuileries, on August 10, 1792. The king was now obliged to take refuge in the building in which the Assembly was in session.

Radicals were determined to get rid of the monarchy altogether and to establish a republic. They had already entered the city hall and taken the government of Paris into their own hands. In this way, the members of the Paris city government, or the *Commune,* became the leaders of the new revolution, which established the First French Republic.

On August 10 the Assembly, which agreed with the Commune in desiring a republic, voted to suspend the king. They also arranged that the people should elect delegates to a National Convention. It would draw up a new constitution for France to replace the existing constitution of the limited monarchy.

Until the meeting of the Convention on September 20 France was practically in a state of anarchy. The functions of all the offices of the government were at a stand-still. The royal family was sent to the prison called the Temple.

September Massacres (1792) · Late in August the Prussians crossed the boundary of France, and on September 2 took the fortress of Verdun. Fear grew that the invading armies would march on Paris. The Commune, by arresting and imprisoning more than three thousand citizens as "traitors," brought discredit on the cause of liberty. From September 2 to 6 it executed hundreds of royalists by means of the guillotine, with scarcely a pretense of a trial. Similar massacres occurred in the provinces.

At the same time, the leaders of the Commune were rallying the French armies. General Dumouriez replaced Lafayette as head of the nation's forces. On September 20 the armies of the invading allies were stopped at Valmy and forced to retreat.

CHECK ON YOUR READING

1. *How did the Legislative Assembly meet its difficulties?*
2. *Why did France declare war?*
3. *Explain: Brunswick Manifesto, Commune, September Massacres, Valmy.*
4. *How did the Paris Commune change the course of the Revolution?*

---

5. Republic, Reign of Terror, and Reaction

The Convention Proclaims a Republic and Executes a King · The newly elected National Convention immediately abolished the monarchy and proclaimed France a republic (September 22, 1792). This date was reckoned as the first day of the Year One of French liberty, since it seemed to the enthusiasts of the time that a new era had dawned.

But the new Convention still had to decide the serious question of what to do about the king. A sizable group felt that he was guilty of treason in secretly encouraging foreign powers to come to his aid. The discovery of certain compromising papers in his possession sealed his fate. He was brought to trial. When it came to the final vote, he was condemned to death by a small majority. On January 21, 1793, Louis XVI went to the guillotine with the dignity and courage of a martyr.

War with England (February, 1793) · Meanwhile after General Dumouriez had stopped the allies, he had pursued their armies across the Rhine and taken several towns. He had also invaded the Austrian Netherlands, where part of the people hailed the French as deliverers.

The success of its armies led the Convention to think of itself as the deliverer of Europe from the old regime. It now proposed to assist any country that wished to throw off the yoke of monarchy. It even suggested a republic to the English people. But England, irritated by its loss of trade and horrified by the execution of Louis XVI, refused to recognize the French Republic. France then declared war. Great Britain proved to be her most persistent enemy from this time forward.

Alliance against France · Up to now the rulers of Prussia and Austria had been suspicious of each other. They were afraid too that Russia would seize more than her share in the second partition of Poland (p. 275) while they fought France. All differences were now forgotten in the horror at the execution of Louis XVI. The allies joined in a plan to invade France from every side. In March, 1793, Spain and the Holy Roman Empire joined the alliance. Now France was at war with all her neighbors.

The Austrians defeated Dumouriez and drove the French out of the Netherlands. Dumouriez, disgusted by the failure of the Convention to support him and shocked by the beheading of the king, deserted to the Austrians with a few hundred soldiers who consented to follow him.

The Committee of Public Safety · The loss of the Netherlands and the treason of

The Execution of Louis XVI by Guillotine · *This instrument of vengeance was named after the French physician who proposed its use. How do you explain its popularity?*

the best French general made a deep impression on the Convention. If the Republic was to defend itself against its enemies both at home and abroad, it could not wait until a permanent constitution was drawn up. It must have an efficient government immediately to keep the people loyal to the Republic and to raise and equip armies. Accordingly, the Convention put the government into the hands of a Committee of Public Safety, which was given practically unlimited powers.

The Jacobins Expel the Girondists and Bring Civil War · Within the Convention there were two parties, which came into bitter conflict over the methods to be pursued. One was the *Girondists*, whose leaders came from the department of Gironde in southwest France. Though they earnestly desired a republic, the Girondists had no liking for the Paris mob and the extreme actions of the Paris Commune. They sat on the right and were now looked upon as conservatives. This was because some had voted against the execution of the king.

Opposed to them were the extreme radicals, the active *Jacobins*, led by Robespierre, Marat, and Danton. They were called the *Mountain* because they occupied a high bank of seats on the left in the Convention. The Jacobins believed that everything that recalled the tyranny of despots should be wiped out.

All who were suspected of having the least sympathy with the nobles or the persecuted priests were branded as counter-revolutionary. The Jacobins were willing to resort to any methods whatsoever to rid the nation of these traitors. The Girondists proposed that the Paris Commune be dissolved and that the Convention be removed to another town where it would not be at the mercy of the mob. The Jacobins then accused them of "royalism." With the aid of the mob, they now expelled the Girondists from the Convention.

This act of violence aroused great resentment in the provinces. The first serious trouble came in Brittany, especially in La Vendée. There the peasants rose against the government which had killed their king and persecuted their priests. The cities of Bordeaux, Marseilles, and Lyon, which hated the Jacobins and the Paris mob, joined the counter-revolutionists. But the Committee of Public Safety quickly sent troops to put down these uprisings and to wreak a terrible vengeance on those who dared revolt against its authority.

The Republic Repels Foreign Armies · The Committee of Public Safety at the same time took measures to meet its foreign enemies. A general draft of troops was

Robespierre, 1758–1794 · *Called both "the incorruptible" and "a demagogue," he sacrificed much (and many) for the Republic.*

called for. Carnot, a distinguished military strategist, became a member of the Committee. He soon had an army of over 750,-000 men. The English and Hanoverians, who were besieging Dunkirk, were defeated. The Austrians were driven back across the Rhine.

At Toulon the royalists had admitted the English and Spanish, and their ships lay in the harbor. The situation was saved, however, by a young artillery officer named Napoleon Bonaparte. In December, he shelled the fortress of Toulon from a high promontory. The enemy fleet sailed away, leaving the unhappy royalists to the mercy of the republican army. By the close of 1793 all danger from invasion was past, at least for the moment.

The Reign of Terror · A special court, called the Revolutionary Tribunal, was established to try all those suspected of being enemies of the Republic. The wives, fathers, mothers, and even children of the emigrant nobles were imprisoned. Those convicted of being "counter-revolutionists" suffered death by the guillotine. In October the queen was executed in Paris after a trial in which many false charges were brought against her.

But the most horrible acts of the Reign of Terror, as it is called, took place in the provinces. Deputies were sent out from Paris to these areas with orders to crush rebellion. A representative of the Convention had thousands of the people of Nantes shot or drowned. The Convention did not carry out its proposal to destroy the great city of Lyon, but thousands of its citizens were executed.

Death of Robespierre Ends the Terror · Soon the members of the Jacobin party, which was in control of the government, began to disagree among themselves. Some believed that the Terror was no longer necessary. Others felt that the Revolution was not yet complete.

The most powerful member of the Committee of Public Safety was Robespierre, who enjoyed a great reputation for loyalty to the Republic. He disapproved of the leaders of both the moderate and the extreme factions, and they were executed.

But Robespierre's companions in the Convention soon began to fear that he would demand their heads next. A conspiracy was formed against him, and the Convention ordered his arrest. With his supporters he was sent to the guillotine (July, 1794).

Now that he was gone, the country was filled with relief. Public opinion forced the government to adopt a more lenient policy. Hundreds of suspects were released. The Revolutionary Tribunal was reorganized.

It turned against those responsible for the worst atrocities and condemned them to death. In a few months the Jacobin Club was closed, the Paris Commune was abolished, and greater freedom in political opinion was tolerated. Thus the Reign of Terror came to an end.

The Constitution of 1795 · Freed from the danger of being overthrown by the extremists, the Convention at last turned its attention to the important task for which it had been summoned. It drew up a constitution for the Republic. This is known as the Constitution of the Year Three.

The lawmaking power was to be vested in a legislature of two houses. The lower house was called the Council of Five Hundred and the upper chamber the Council of Elders. The executive powers were to be in the hands of a Directory of five persons, to be chosen by the two chambers.

Bonaparte's "Whiff of Grapeshot" Saves the Convention · In order to protect the Republic against the plots of the royalists, the Convention decreed that two-thirds of the new legislature should be chosen from its own membership. It also provided that a body of troops should be assembled near Paris to assure order. These measures so aroused the royalist groups in Paris that they began to gather armed forces to oppose the Convention. That body, however, put its defense in the hands of Napoleon Bonaparte, who had distinguished himself at Toulon.

On October 5 the royalists assembled to march on the Convention, but found themselves facing an array of cannon. When the attack began, Bonaparte's guns fired a "whiff of grapeshot," which soon dispersed the rebels and cleared the streets near the Convention. The army had saved the government. Shortly afterward Bonaparte was

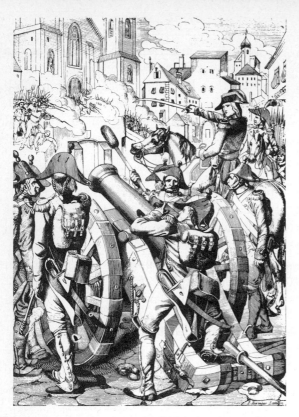

The Whiff of Grapeshot · *Napoleon suppressed the royalist uprising by bombarding their forces on the steps of the Church of Saint-Roch.*

rewarded by being appointed commander in chief of the Army of the Interior.

Accomplishments of the Convention · In October, 1795, the Convention finally dissolved itself after having governed the country during three years of excitement, danger, and disorder. Though it was responsible for the Reign of Terror, it had carried France through the terrible crisis of 1793.

Among its accomplishments were these: (1) The civil war had been brought to an end. (2) The foreign enemies of the Republic had been defeated. (3) Committees of the Convention had been working on the problem of bettering the system of education, which the state had taken out of the hands of the clergy. (4) Progress had also been made toward establishing a single system of law for the whole country. (5) The metric system adopted by the Convention is used throughout the world.

The Directory (1795–1799) · The members of the new legislature who took over on October 26, 1795, were moderates but stanch friends of the Revolution. To avoid trouble they selected as the five directors men who had voted for the execution of Louis XVI. There was now little danger from enemies at home or abroad, but France was not to have peace for many years.

The country was in a wretched condition. (1) There was poverty and hunger among the people. (2) The national debt was enormous and the currency was hopelessly depreciated. (3) Commerce was all but destroyed. (4) The majority of the directors were ignorant, selfish, and corrupt. (5) They determined that war was the best means of maintaining their power. So they staked their fortunes on the French armies, thus providing a golden opportunity for the ambitious Napoleon Bonaparte.

CHECK ON YOUR READING

1. Why did the National Convention (a) execute the king? (b) declare war on England? (c) set up a Committee of Public Safety?
2. Contrast the Girondists and Jacobins.
3. Describe the Reign of Terror: (a) causes, (b) methods, (c) consequences.
4. What part did these men play during the Revolution: (a) Dumouriez, (b) Carnot, (c) Bonaparte, (d) Robespierre?
5. What did the Convention accomplish?
6. Cite evidences of the wretched condition of France under the Directory.

Excerpts from **The Declaration of the Rights of Man and Citizen, August 26, 1789.**

1. Men are born and remain free and equal in rights. . . .

2. The aim of every political association is the preservation of the natural and imprescriptible rights of man. . . liberty, property, security, and resistance to oppression.

4. Liberty consists in the power to do anything that does not injure others. . . .

5. The law has the right to forbid only such actions as are injurious to society. . . .

6. Law is the expression of the general will. All citizens have the right to take part personally or by their representatives in its formation. It must be the same for all, whether it protects or punishes. . . .

9. Every man [is] presumed innocent until he has been pronounced guilty. . . .

11. The free communication of ideas and opinions is one of the most precious of the rights of man. . . .

13. . . . A general tax is indispensable . . . to be equally apportioned among all citizens according to their means.

15. Society has the right to call for an account from every public agent of its administration.

Learning Activities

Think about the chapter

1. Why do we call the eighteenth century the *threshold* of modern times?

2. In what respects did the French Revolution differ from the Glorious Revolution of 1688 in England and the American Revolution of 1776?

3. The French Revolution may be divided into three periods in each of which there was a different governing body. These were the National Assembly, the Legislative Assembly, and the National Convention. What was the effect of each of these bodies on the course of the Revolution?

4. Why is July 14 in France equivalent to our July 4? Does the difference in the specific event each celebrates indicate any difference in the two revolutions?

5. Compare the French Declaration of Rights (see above) with our Bill of Rights.

6. *Map study:* Draw a map of western Europe and show by different markings the countries (a) that were at war with France in 1792 and (b) that joined in the alliance against France in 1793.

Go beyond the text

7. Many parallels have been drawn between the French Revolution and other great revolutions which have occurred before and since. Choose one such revolution to compare with the French Revolution.

8. Read from several sources on the results of the Revolution and make a list of its permanent accomplishments.

9. The following people played important parts in the Revolution: Lafayette, Mirabeau, Danton, Marat, Charlotte Corday, Madame Roland, Robespierre. Read further about them and note which stage of the Revolution they were connected with. In reading about Lafayette, you may find out what happened to the key to the Bastille.

10. What were some of Rousseau's views on education? Do you agree with him?

Follow up your special interests

11. Look up the "Marseillaise," composed during the Revolution, and read its verses. How does it express the spirit of the Revolution? Play a recording of it to the class.

12. Write a letter such as an émigré noble might have written, describing the events of the Revolution as they appeared to him.

13. Add some of the important discoveries and inventions of the eighteenth century to your chart of scientific discoveries and inventions.

14. Make a poster or chart of the three great documents of liberty, the English Bill of Rights, the American Bill of Rights, and the French Declaration of the Rights of Man. Underline the main statements of each that are almost identical.

15. Read and report on one of the excellent sources listed below.

READ FURTHER

Basic readings: (1) BAUER and PEYSER, *How Music Grew,* Chaps. 20–21. (2) BECKER, *Modern History,* Chaps. 6–8. (3) CHEYNEY, *Readings in English History,* Chap. 18, Sec. 6. (4) COTTLER and JAFFE, *Heroes of Civilization.* Scientists of the century. (5) HOFFMAN, *News of the World,* No. 43. (6) Life's *History of Western Man,* Secs. VII, IX. (7) ROBINSON, *Readings in European History,* Chaps. 34–36. (8) VAN LOON, *Story of Mankind,* pp. 334–348. (9) Year's *Pictorial History,* pp. 286–295, 324–327, 344–351, 360–368, 374–377.

Special accounts: (10) H. BELLOC, *The French Revolution.* Dramatic events of the period told in simplified form for the average reader. (11) G. FOSTER, *George Washington's World.* (12) G. LEFEBVRE, *The Coming of the French Revolution.* Excellent analysis of conditions leading to the outbreak—for better readers. (13) S. MATTHEWS, *The French Revolution.* Interesting details make this valuable for anyone to use. (14) *American Heritage,* "Lafayette's Two Revolutions," December, 1956.

Fiction and biography: (15) A. BILL, *The Red Prior's Legacy.* Two young Americans see the attack on the King's palace. (16) W. DAVIS, *The Whirlwind.* Exciting fictional account of the Revolution. (17) M. DAVENPORT, *Mozart.* Good for social history of eighteenth-century Austria. (18) C. DICKENS, *A Tale of Two Cities.* Unforgettable scenes of the Terror and the escape of a French girl and her father from France. (19) J. EATON, *A Daughter of the Seine.* An accurate account of the part played by Madame Roland and other main characters of the Revolution. (20) M. GOSS, *Beethoven: Master Musician.* Not only the man as a musician but also a story of events of the time. (21) B. KIELTY, *Marie Antoinette.* A sympathetic biography. (22) D. LOTH, *The People's General.* Lafayette's part in both the French and American Revolutions. (23) M. VANCE, *Marie Antoinette, Daughter of an Empress.* Brings in background of French court life. (24) J. WILLIAMSON, *Jacobin's Daughter.* The young heroine meets all the important Jacobins, but Robespierre is the central character.

"Man is born free, and everywhere he is in chains."
—JEAN-JACQUES ROUSSEAU

"O liberty! O liberty! What crimes are committed in thy name!"—MADAME ROLAND

"History is only the pattern of silken slippers descending the stairs to the thunder of hobnailed boots climbing upward from below." —VOLTAIRE

The French Kings from Saint Louis to Henry IV

The table of early French kings shows a straight line of descent from Hugh Capet (987-996) through Philip Augustus (1180-1223) and Louis VIII (1223-1226) to Louis IX, called Saint Louis. The table below indicates the origin of the Valois and Bourbon lines.

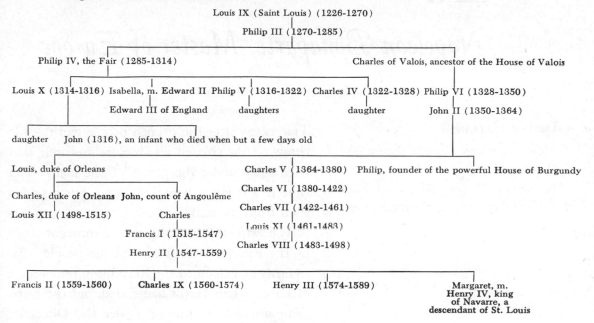

Louis IX (Saint Louis) (1226-1270)

Philip III (1270-1285)

Philip IV, the Fair (1285-1314)   Charles of Valois, ancestor of the House of Valois

Louis X (1314-1316)   Isabella, m. Edward II   Philip V (1316-1322)   Charles IV (1322-1328)   Philip VI (1328-1350)

Edward III of England   daughters   daughter   John II (1350-1364)

daughter   John (1316), an infant who died when but a few days old

Louis, duke of Orleans   Charles V (1364-1380)   Philip, founder of the powerful House of Burgundy

Charles, duke of Orleans   John, count of Angoulême   Charles VI (1380-1422)

Louis XII (1498-1515)   Charles   Charles VII (1422-1461)

Francis I (1515-1547)   Louis XI (1461-1483)

Henry II (1547-1559)   Charles VIII (1483-1498)

Francis II (1559-1560)   **Charles IX (1560-1574)**   Henry III (1574-1589)   Margaret, m. Henry IV, king of Navarre, a descendant of St. Louis

Bourbon Kings of France and Younger Line of Orleans

Bourbon   Orleans

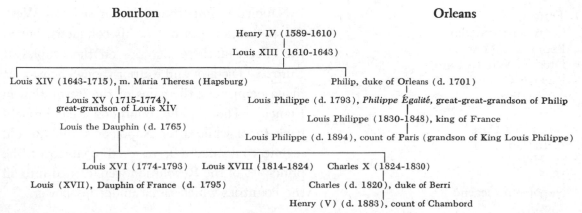

Henry IV (1589-1610)

Louis XIII (1610-1643)

Louis XIV (1643-1715), m. Maria Theresa (Hapsburg)   Philip, duke of Orleans (d. 1701)

Louis XV (1715-1774), great-grandson of Louis XIV   Louis Philippe (d. 1793), *Philippe Égalité*, great-great-grandson of Philip

Louis the Dauphin (d. 1765)   Louis Philippe (1830-1848), king of France

Louis Philippe (d. 1894), count of Paris (grandson of King Louis Philippe)

Louis XVI (1774-1793)   Louis XVIII (1814-1824)   Charles X (1824-1830)

Louis (XVII), Dauphin of France (d. 1795)   Charles (d. 1820), duke of Berri

Henry (V) (d. 1883), count of Chambord

CHAPTER **20**

Napoleon Bonaparte, Master of Europe

CHAPTER OUTLINE

1. *How Napoleon Rose to Fame*
2. *Bonaparte as Ruler of France*
3. *Napoleon Becomes Master of Europe*
4. *Collapse of the Napoleonic Empire*

KEY WORDS AND DATES

Directory
First Consul
Code Napoléon
Concordat of 1801
the allies
Tilsit
Tsar Alexander I
Nelson
Trafalgar
Continental System
Peninsular War
Duke of Wellington
Russian Campaign, 1812
nationalism
Elba
"Hundred Days"
Waterloo
St. Helena
1815
Napoleonic legend

TEN YEARS after the French people had risen to throw off the yoke of an absolute monarch, they were again under the power of one man. This time it was not a hereditary king, but a soldier risen from the ranks.

The swift and sweeping changes brought about by the Revolution had divided the people. Extremists had changed the Revolution into a reign of terror. The Terror had ended, but the European war had continued under the Directory. Because of the incompetence and corruption of this government, people began to look towards a strong leader—Napoleon Bonaparte.

How this young Corsican made himself ruler of France and master of Europe is one of the most amazing stories in history. He flashed across the horizon like a meteor and was gone. Yet for a decade he kept all Europe in a turmoil and reshaped it to his will.

Napoleon's importance in our story of Western civilization lies not in his conquests, but in the effects of these victories on the peoples of Europe. Dictator and warrior though he was, he made permanent the gains of the Revolution in France. Though the Bourbons were brought back for a while after Napoleon's fall, the old regime could never be restored. Moreover, the principles of the Revolution were carried into all the countries which came under his power.

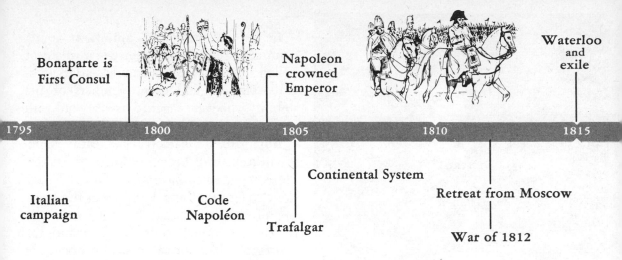

Bonaparte is
First Consul

Napoleon
crowned
Emperor

Waterloo
and
exile

| 1795 | 1800 | 1805 | 1810 | 1815 |

Italian
campaign

Code
Napoléon

Trafalgar

Continental System

Retreat from Moscow

War of 1812

1. How Napoleon Rose to Fame

Bonaparte's Early Life · Napoleon Bonaparte was born in Corsica in 1769, the year after the island came under the rule of the French. The Bonaparte family was of Italian origin and spoke Italian at home. Napoleon was the second of eight surviving children. Most of them were one day to become kings, queens, or princes as the result of their brother's exploits.

When he was ten years old, Napoleon was taken to France, where he was given a military education. At the age of sixteen he received his commission as second lieutenant and joined an artillery regiment.

This poor but proud young man had little hope of advance in the French army. The high posts always went to the members of the nobility. He therefore spent as much time as possible in Corsica, where he mixed in a number of intrigues, hoping to get control of the forces on the island. Because of this he and his family were banished and fled to France (1793).

Bonaparte was lucky in the time of his arrival, for he was soon able to be of service to the Republic, as we have seen (p. 315). The Directory was now to provide him with his great opportunity.

How France Had Dealt with the Allies · It will be recalled that after the execution of Louis XVI (1793) most of the powers of Europe had joined in an alliance against France. Despite the overwhelming forces of the allies, the French armies had managed not only to beat off their enemies successfully, but also to conquer additional territory.

By 1795 France had taken possession of the Austrian Netherlands and had established in Holland a republic under French control (Batavian Republic). She had occupied western Germany as far as the Rhine. She had concluded peace with some of her enemies. Yet Austria, Sardinia, and England were still at war with France when the Directory took office. Early in 1796 the Directory decided to send two armies against Austria—one through southern Germany and the other through Italy. Bonaparte was made commander of the latter.

Napoleon at the Battle of Arcole, 1796 · *The "Little Corporal" was only twenty-seven when he scored this brilliant victory over the Austrians in Italy.*

Bonaparte's Victorious Italian Campaign (1796–1797) · Bonaparte skillfully separated the armies of Austria and Sardinia. He defeated the Sardinians and forced their king to cede Savoy and Nice to France (April 28). In December the king abdicated and the French occupied Piedmont. The young general now carried out a brilliant campaign in which he defeated the Austrian armies and marched his victorious troops almost to Vienna.

In the Treaty of Campo Formio (1797) the emperor yielded the Austrian Netherlands and the Ionian Islands to France. Bonaparte divided the ancient Venetian republic. He gave part to Austria and made the western part into the Cisalpine Republic, subject to France. (See map, p. 323.)

In the meantime the ambitious young commander lived like a prince in a villa near Milan. Here he received ambassadors, generals, officials, and even members of the nobility who were eager to have a word with him.

Bonaparte's Character · Already Napoleon dreamed of becoming ruler of France. He is reported to have said: "What I have done so far is nothing. I am but at the opening of the career that I am to run. . . . What the French want is glory and the satisfaction of their vanity; as for liberty, of that they have no conception. . . . The nation must have a head . . . who is rendered illustrious by glory and not by theories of government, fine phrases, or the talk of idealists, of which the French understand not a whit."

This cynical young general, who already saw himself as master of his country, was a short man, hardly more than five feet two inches in height. He was thin, with a sallow complexion and dark, searching eyes. He spoke rapidly but with an imperfect French accent.

Napoleon was a dreamer, and yet was extremely practical. He was a good organizer. He was daring and utterly selfish and unscrupulous. He worked with a tireless energy. He had extraordinary military ability and knew how to inspire his soldiers and win their support. His success was due partly to his own personal qualities and partly to conditions in France.

The Expedition to Egypt (1798–1799) · The Directory received the war hero on his return to Paris with an outward show of gratitude and held fetes in his honor. Bonaparte realized, however, that he was not yet in a position to get control of the government. Until that day should come he must keep his fame alive by constant victory.

Treaties, 1795–1812 · *What areas were annexed by France? under French influence? What two great nations remained outside Napoleon's reach? Why?*

He persuaded the Directory to allow him to undertake an expedition to Egypt. The object was to cut off England's trade with the East and perhaps to seize her possessions in India. The Republic was on the eve of a new European war, and Napoleon shrewdly foresaw that the government might need to recall him to save France.

In April, 1798, Bonaparte set sail with a large expedition for Egypt. He took possession of Malta on the way and landed his army safely at Alexandria. But the English fleet under Nelson destroyed the French ships as they lay in the harbor and cut off Bonaparte from Europe.

Bonaparte easily defeated the Egyptian troops in the battle of the Pyramids (July 21, 1798). Then he undertook to penetrate into Syria, hoping to gain a victory which would make up for the loss of his fleet.

This undertaking proved disastrous. But while he was in Syria, Bonaparte received news from Europe which led him to desert his army in Egypt and hasten back to France with a few of his officers.

CHECK ON YOUR READING

1. *Describe Napoleon's early life. What part did ambition and opportunity play in his rise?*
2. *Use the maps to point out the Batavian Republic, Sardinia, Scandinavia, Savoy, Nice, Vienna, Campo Formio, Venetia, Cisalpine Republic, Milan, Malta, Alexandria, Syria.*
3. *What were the strong and the weak points in Napoleon's character?*
4. *How were these revealed in Italy? in Egypt?*

2. Bonaparte as Ruler of France

Bonaparte Becomes First Consul (November, 1799) · During Bonaparte's absence the corrupt Directory had disgraced itself at home and suffered reverses in war. After the Treaty of Campo Formio the Directory, on one pretext or another, had continued its policy of conquest. It had created a number of republics dependent on France. This widening of influence once again roused the European powers against France. England, Russia, Austria, Turkey, and some lesser states formed an alliance (December, 1798) and drove the French armies out of Germany and Italy.

The stage was now set for a dictatorship. Within a month of his return Bonaparte was able to overthrow the Directory. A constitution was shortly afterward drawn up by which the general became First Consul. Although it provided for a Council of State, a Senate, and other assemblies, the real power was in Napoleon's hands. Even local officials were appointed by him or by his chosen representatives.

It now fell to Napoleon as First Consul to rebuild the reputation of France abroad, as well as to restore order at home.

French Influence Increases in Europe · Bonaparte decided that he would first defeat Austria. In June, 1800, he led his troops over the dangerous Alpine passes into the Po valley and decisively defeated the Austrians at Marengo. A second defeat, at Hohenlinden in Germany, brought the Austrians to terms. They agreed to make a separate peace with France. This Treaty of Lunéville was the first of a series of treaties (1801–1802) signed by all the powers with which France had been at war. Even England, which had not laid down her arms since 1793, made peace with France in the Treaty of Amiens, 1802.

The Treaty of Lunéville gave France those territories lying on the west bank of the Rhine which had belonged to the Holy Roman Empire. It made the Rhine the boundary of France from the point where it left Switzerland to where it flowed into Dutch territory. In addition, France received back the Austrian Netherlands and later Piedmont. The Batavian and Cisalpine republics were under French control and contributed money and troops to promote French interests. (See map, p. 323.)

Bonaparte Reorganizes France · For the first time in ten years France was at peace. But the finances of the nation were in a terrible condition. Bonaparte restored order by introducing a revised system of taxation, which brought in an increased revenue. Rigid economy was enforced, and corrupt officials were severely punished. The worthless paper money that flooded the country was replaced. Provision was made to pay the national debt. Finally, Bonaparte established the Bank of France, which proved to be one of the soundest financial institutions in Europe.

The *Code Napoléon* · One of the grievances against the old regime had been the various confusing laws that existed in different parts of the country (p. 299). The legislative bodies during the Revolution had attempted to reduce this mass of decrees and laws to one uniform system. But it was not until Bonaparte took control that the work was carried to completion.

In 1802 the *Code Napoléon* was issued. This codification of the civil law became the permanent body of law for France.

With some modifications, it was adopted throughout a large part of continental Europe. It retained many of the gains of the Revolution, including the equality of citizens before the law, religious toleration, the abolition of feudalism, and the emancipation of the serfs.

Catholic Church Re-established (1801) · Bonaparte determined to win the support of the Catholics by adjusting the differences between the government and the Church (p. 308). In 1801 a formal treaty, called the *Concordat* (1) recognized the Pope as the head of the Church. (2) The Pope accepted the taking over of the church property by the government and the suppression of the monasteries. (3) The government for its part agreed to pay the salaries of the clergy. (4) The First Consul was to nominate the bishops, but the Pope was to invest them with their office. The priests were to be chosen by the bishops.

This agreement re-established the Catholic Church in France, but tied it closely to the government. The Concordat remained in force until 1905.

System of Public Education · The principle of equality of opportunity was carried out in education. Building on the foundations laid during the Revolution, the new state provided for a system of public instruction. Primary, grammar, and high schools were established, all under the supervision of government inspectors. Private schools and schools conducted by the clergy were permitted, but were subject to government approval.

Restoration of the Nobility · Bonaparte now made peace with the old nobility. He ordered that no more names of emigrant nobles should be added to the lists of those under suspicion. He even removed some of the names and in some cases returned

Napoleon, by J. Louis David · *He wore the uniform of a general of the Grenadiers and the medal of the Legion of Honor.*

confiscated property not already sold. Parents and relatives of emigrants were no longer barred from holding office. In April, 1802, a general amnesty (pardon) was issued, and no fewer than forty thousand families returned to France.

Gradually other signs of the Revolution disappeared. Streets which had been given republican names received their old names again. The republican calendar was finally given up. The old titles of address, *Monsieur* and *Madame*, were again used instead of the revolutionary "Citizen." Old titles of nobility were revived, and something very like a royal court began to appear in the Palace of the Tuileries. Except in name, Bonaparte was actually king of France.

Bonaparte Becomes Emperor (1804) · In 1802 Bonaparte was made Consul for life by a vote of the people. But even this did not satisfy his boundless ambition. He longed to be a monarch in name, as well as in fact, and to enjoy all the outward signs and honors of royal power. A plot to restore the Bourbons gave him an excuse for secretly urging that he be made emperor to avoid civil war.

In May, 1804, the French Senate asked him to accept the title of "Emperor of the French," which he was to hand down to his children or adopted heirs, and the Senate's action was approved by an overwhelming vote of the people.

On December 2, 1804, at an impressive ceremony in the Cathedral of Notre Dame, Napoleon Bonaparte became Emperor Napoleon I. The Pope was present on the great occasion, but the new monarch seized the golden crown before the Pope could take it, and placed it upon his own head. This was to show the world that he owed the crown not to the head of the Church, but to his own power and genius.

A royal court was established in Paris. Former aristocrats showed the new officials how to deport themselves before the emperor according to the old forms of etiquette. New state offices were created and given impressive titles, and fourteen generals became Marshals of France.

Five Successful Years · In five action-packed years Napoleon had scored many

The Crowning of Napoleon I, Notre Dame, 1804 · *Note Queen Josephine kneeling at the Emperor's feet. His mother, "Madame Mere," is smiling her approval from her seat of honor behind Pope Pius VII. Why did Bonaparte crown himself?*

successes. (1) He had defeated his foreign enemies and extended the boundaries and influence of France. (2) The government was completely reorganized with a new constitution and with himself as emperor. (3) The state finances, taxation system, and Bank were on a firm footing. (4) The Code Napoléon gave France a permanent body of civil law. (5) The re-establishment of the Catholic Church had won the support of the clergy. (6) The new system of education was popular with the people. (7) The restored nobility looked upon him with favor. (8) His armies and his marshals worshiped him.

In an amazing fashion the dreams of the young Corsican had come true. He had risen from poverty and obscurity to be the ruler of France.

CHECK ON YOUR READING

1. *How did Napoleon become First Consul? Consul for life? Emperor?*
2. *What were France's boundaries after the treaties of 1801–1802?*
3. *Describe measures taken with regard to (a) government centralization, (b) financial reform, (c) the law, (d) the Church, (e) education, (f) the nobility.*

---

3. *Napoleon Becomes Master of Europe*

Napoleon's Ambition Fed by Success · Napoleon's ambition knew no bounds. No sooner had he become ruler of France than he aspired to be master of Europe. "There will be no rest in Europe," he said, "until it is under a single chief—an emperor who shall have kings for officers, who shall distribute kingdoms to his lieutenants." This was the vision which now filled the young emperor's mind.

"I shall put up with peace," Napoleon said, "as long as our neighbors can maintain it, but I shall regard it as an advantage if they force me to take up my arms again before they rust."

England and France Again at War (1803) · Napoleon's interference in the affairs of Holland, Switzerland, and Italy, and the high import duties he imposed on English goods in these territories, greatly alarmed the British. They believed, moreover, that he was preparing for an expedition to overthrow British power in India.

In 1803, therefore, England renewed her war with France.

Napoleon declared the whole coast of western Europe, from Holland to southern Italy, blockaded against English ships. At the same time, he made preparations for an invasion of the British Isles. He collected a large army at Boulogne and made ready a great fleet of warships and transports to carry men and supplies across the Channel. He knew that he must conquer this rival which controlled the seas before he could hope to build up a colonial empire.

Napoleon Defeats the Third Coalition (1805) · In the meantime, the English formed the Third Coalition of European states to put an end to Napoleon's power. Included this time were Austria, Russia, Sweden, and England. The Continental states were to furnish troops while England provided money and sea power.

In the summer of 1805 the coalition advanced westward through southern

Germany toward the Rhine. Napoleon now abandoned his plans for an invasion of England. Before the allies could reach the French border, he had rushed his well-trained army eastward to meet the Austrians in battle at Ulm, in Württemberg. The Austrian commander was forced to surrender with all his troops. Napoleon then marched down the Danube and took the city of Vienna.

Napoleon now led his forces northward to meet the combined armies of Austria and Russia. He defeated them on December 2 in the terrible winter battle of Austerlitz. Austria was forced to withdraw from the alliance and signed the humiliating Treaty of Pressburg. By this agreement she gave up Venetia (map, p. 323) and other Italian territories, and recognized Napoleon as king of Italy. She awarded other provinces to Bavaria and Württemberg. Napoleon now made these two German states into kingdoms in return for their support against his enemies.

How Napoleon's Victories Refashioned Europe · When Napoleon's career began, Germany consisted of over three hundred kingdoms, principalities, city-states, and other tiny governments. After his victories in 1800, he took over the German territories on the west bank of the Rhine (p. 324). The diet of the Holy Roman Empire then transferred most of the German ecclesiastical states (lands held by bishops and abbots) and the free cities to the kings and princes who had lost land to France. Also many German knights were deprived of their tiny states.

The states which gained the most from the distribution were Baden, Bavaria, and Württemberg. All three had been friendly to Napoleon. In July, 1806, Napoleon organized a union of the south German states into a Confederation of the Rhine. He became its Protector in return for military support, and these states were excused from further allegiance to Emperor Francis II. Thus the Holy Roman Empire came to an end. Francis, therefore, switched his title to Francis I, Emperor of Austria.

The consolidation of small territories was the beginning of German unification. We shall see that this was finally achieved in 1870.

Napoleon now began to place his relatives on thrones all over Europe. His brother Joseph became king of Naples and Sicily. He made his brother Louis king of Holland. A brother-in-law, Murat, became duke of Cleves and Berg in Germany. Brother Lucien, with whom Napoleon quarreled, went without a kingdom. But brother Jerome was soon rewarded at the expense of Russia, as we shall see.

The Disastrous Defeat of Prussia (1806) · Napoleon was a master in the technique of "divide and rule." And treachery was a convenient tool. The timid King Frederick William III of Prussia had refused to join the European coalition against France. As a reward Napoleon had offered him the Electorate of Hanover. This act drove a wedge between the English (Hanoverians) and Frederick. Now Napoleon secretly offered to restore Hanover to the English king. He thus made certain the English would not come to Frederick's aid.

He also persuaded Prussia to disarm and then refused to remove the French troops from her territory. Such insulting treatment aroused a national protest among the people of Prussia. The reluctant king was forced to break with Napoleon and declare war on France.

The Prussian army under the aged Duke of Brunswick now advanced to meet the

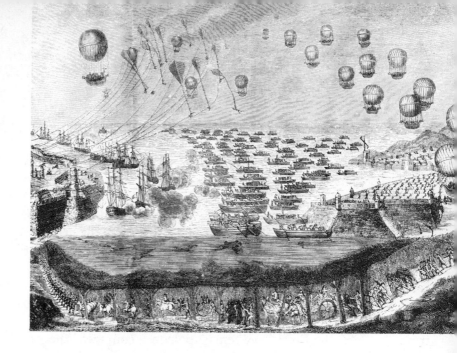

Imaginary Invasion of Britain · *This engraving made in 1801 depicts Napoleon's forces crossing the Channel by balloon, boat, and underwater tunnel. Compare this with Hitler's "Operation Sea-Lion," page 579.*

highly trained French forces without waiting for the Russians, who had agreed to help. The result was a complete rout of the Prussian armies in the battles of Jena and Auerstedt. Discouragement spread rapidly throughout the country, and fortresses surrendered without resistance. Napoleon entered Berlin in triumph, and Frederick William fled to the Russian border.

Treaties of Tilsit (1807) · Napoleon now led his army into Poland. Here he spent the winter in operations against the Russians. In June he won a brilliant victory over them at Friedland. Tsar Alexander I immediately sought peace.

In the Treaties of Tilsit, Russia came off easily, whereas Prussia was made to pay. Prussia lost all her gains in the partitions of Poland. Out of a portion of this land Napoleon created the Grand Duchy of Warsaw, to be ruled by his friend the Elector of Saxony. Out of the Prussian provinces west of the Elbe River plus Hanover, Napoleon carved the kingdom of West-

phalia for his brother Jerome (see map, p. 323). Russia escaped lightly by promising to aid Napoleon in excluding British trade from the Continent.

English Sea Power Frustrates Napoleon · England, France's most persistent enemy, was still beyond Napoleon's reach. His victories had made him master of the Continent, but England ruled the seas.

In 1798 Admiral Nelson had sunk the French squadron at Alexandria and made escape impossible for Napoleon's army in Egypt (p. 323). In October, 1805, just as Napoleon was undertaking his brilliant campaign against the Austrians, Nelson destroyed a second French fleet off the coast of Spain. Word of the disaster at Trafalgar was not allowed to reach the French people at the time.

Napoleon realized that invasion of the island was now impossible. He must find another way to crush this powerful rival. He therefore decided to strike at England's most vital point. He would ruin the industry and trade by which she existed.

The Continental System and How It Worked · Napoleon aimed (1) to prevent European countries from *importing* British goods and (2) to keep European countries from *exporting* goods to England. Thus England would be denied both the markets and the resources of the Continent.

In this plan of economic warfare Napoleon attempted to line up all Europe against England in an endurance test. It was called the Continental System. Time would tell whether the island or the Continent could last longer without the aid of the other.

Early in 1806 Napoleon closed Prussian ports to British trade, and England replied by declaring the coast of Europe closed from the Elbe to Brest. When Napoleon entered the Prussian capital, he issued the Berlin Decree. This declared a state of blockade against the British Isles, and closed all French and allied ports to ships of Britain and her colonies.

Later decrees provided that neutral vessels sailing from England or from countries occupied by British troops might be seized and even that British goods found in countries under Napoleon's control should be destroyed.

The English retaliated by declaring all vessels trading with France and her allies liable to capture. In certain instances they permitted neutral ships to proceed if they touched at a British port first and paid a heavy duty. The charges on a ship during a single voyage would sometimes amount to many thousands of dollars.

Freedom of the Seas Disregarded · These blockades and counterblockades made much trouble for neutral countries. Among these was the United States, whose trade prospered during the early Napoleonic wars. Hundreds of British sailors became naturalized Americans to enjoy the better pay, food, and treatment on American ships. England replied by impressing "American" seamen.

The enforcement of the various British regulations was so harmful to American business that the United States finally went to war with Great Britain in 1812. The serious question of the freedom of the seas has never been settled. In the life-and-death struggle between great powers, the rights of neutrals are generally disregarded.

Hardships of the Continental System · In enforcing the Continental System, Napoleon undertook to make Europe independent of British goods and of goods formerly brought in British ships. He encouraged the substitution of chicory for coffee, the cultivation of sugar beets, and the production of new dyes to replace those coming from the tropics. But the Continental System caused great hardship in Europe, as well as in England. Napoleon's attempts to enforce it finally led to his downfall.

Napoleon Seizes Portugal and Spain (1808) · Napoleon now insisted that Portugal join the Continental System and break off relations with England. The Portuguese refused. Thereupon a French army marched into the country, and the royal family fled to Brazil.

Napoleon's forces did not stop with occupying Lisbon, but continued to pour across the Pyrenees into Spain. Taking advantage of serious disagreements at the Spanish court, Napoleon was able to force both the king and the prince to give up their rights to the Spanish throne. On June 6 he promoted his brother Joseph, who had been king of Naples, to be king of Spain. The Spanish people rose in revolt.

In November the French emperor himself led a magnificent army into Spain and

The Third of May, 1808, by Francisco Goya · *This painting of the execution of citizens of Madrid who defied Napoleon's army of occupation is a memorial to the resistance heroes of all time. What resulted from such defiance?*

soon overwhelmed the ill-equipped Spanish forces. Madrid surrendered on December 4. Napoleon immediately abolished the Inquisition, the feudal dues, and internal customs lines. The next month Napoleon was back in Paris, for a new war with Austria was about to begin. He left Joseph in Spain on his insecure throne.

France Loses the Peninsular War · But the Spanish carried on a guerrilla warfare against which Napoleon's best troops were powerless. His soldiers suffered from scarcity of food and from the extreme changes in temperature. Moreover, the patriotic spirit of the Spanish was now aroused. They were determined to drive the invaders from their soil.

An English army under the command of Sir Arthur Wellesley (later the Duke of Wellington) arrived to aid the Spanish and Portuguese. The Peninsular War was a hard one and lasted for several years. Wellington, with his English and Spanish troops, slowly drove the French back across the Pyrenees.

Napoleon Once More Defeats Austria (1809) · Meanwhile the spirit of nationalism was also rising in Austria. Angered by numerous disasters that they had suffered at the hands of the French, the people began to prepare for a war of liberation from the "enemy of Europe."

Taking advantage of Napoleon's preoccupation with Spain, Austria declared war on France. But this time she found no one to aid her. The great battle of Wagram, near Vienna (July 5–6), was another victory for Napoleon. It forced Austria to accept just as harsh terms as those of Pressburg a few years earlier (p. 328).

Napoleon Marries a Hapsburg Princess (1809) · Napoleon was eager to have an heir. His first wife, Josephine, bore him no children. He therefore divorced her and married the Archduchess Marie Louise, the daughter of the Austrian emperor.

To crown all his successes the Corsican adventurer had now married into one of the oldest and proudest reigning families of Europe—the Hapsburgs. The next year a son was born, whom Napoleon proudly called the King of Rome.

CHECK ON YOUR READING

1. *What was Napoleon's great ambition?*
2. *Why was England especially frustrating?*
3. *Show on the map how Napoleon's victories refashioned Europe.*
4. *What methods did Napoleon use against the allies? With what success?*
5. *Why was each of the following important: (a) Boulogne, (b) Trafalgar, (c) Pressburg, (d) Napoleon's brothers, (e) Tilsit, (f) sea power, (g) Continental System, (h) guerrilla war, (i) nationalism.*

Napoleon Dominates Europe · *How did Napoleon control areas outside of French borders? Were his allies dependable? Locate important battle sites.*

EUROPE ABOUT 1810
- French Empire
- Controlled by Napoleon
- Allied with Napoleon

4. Collapse of the Napoleonic Empire

Some Reasons Why Napoleon Failed · Napoleon's star of destiny, which had shone so brilliantly, was fated to fade and disappear even more rapidly than it had risen. After 1808 the great adventurer's power declined. Though he still won victories, his hold on his vast empire was weakening.

What were some reasons for this? (1) To manage that great empire was beyond the ability of any one man, and Napoleon was so egotistic that he would not tolerate advice from others. (2) The new Europe was held together only by force of arms. It was ready to break apart at the first military failures of its conqueror. (3) Napoleon's despotism had created a deep hatred for him. This hatred was to flame forth later in nationalist revolts. (4) It proved impossible to shut British trade completely out of the Continent and make the Continental System an effective weapon against England.

We have seen how Napoleon's attempts to enforce the Continental System in Portugal and Spain led to the disastrous Peninsular War. Now the tsar's refusal to follow the Continental System led Napoleon, against the advice of his wisest counselors, to reopen the war with Russia.

Difficulties between Alexander I and Napoleon · There were a number of reasons for enmity between the young Tsar Alexander I and Napoleon, in spite of the peace made at Tilsit. (1) The tsar was not pleased by the closer relations between France and Austria as a result of Napoleon's marriage. (2) When the Grand Duchy of Warsaw was enlarged after the war of 1809, the tsar feared that Napoleon planned to create a new kingdom of Poland.

(3) The Continental System was hurting Russia, a farming country. The attempt to stop her from shipping grain to England caused great hardship and discontent. Alexander therefore opened up trade relations with Britain. At this Napoleon prepared for war.

Napoleon's Russian Campaign (1812) · The French emperor collected a great army of 600,000 men. It was composed of his own veteran troops and a large number of young recruits furnished by his allies. In April, 1812, Napoleon's forces began to push into Russia. Napoleon had planned to take three years to conquer the country, but he was led on by the desire to announce one great victory before the close of the season. The Russians retreated, however, and drew him farther and farther into a hostile and barren land before they would meet him in battle. At Borodino (September 7) the Russians made a stand. Though Napoleon won, his losses were terrible.

A week later he took possession of Moscow. But the city was deserted. The people and the government, as well as the Russian army, had left the city. Moreover, the town was on fire, so that it was impossible for Napoleon to quarter his troops in the devastated city for the winter. He decided to withdraw.

On October 22 began the retreat from Moscow, one of the most tragic episodes in history. As the army retraced its steps across the land which it had ravaged in its forward march, it found nothing on which to live. It was followed by the Russians, who attacked its rear all along the route. Lack of food, terrific cold, and the forced march through mud, sleet, and snow, caused

Napoleon's Retreat from Moscow, by Meissonier · *How was this military disaster influenced by* (a) *Napoleon's ego?* (b) *his lack of supplies?* (c) *"General Winter"?* (d) *the Fabian tactics of the Russians?* *See Tolstoy's* War and Peace.

thousands to fall from exhaustion. When Napoleon reached Poland in December, less than a sixth of his once magnificent army remained.

How Defeat Led to Reforms in Prussia · In the meantime a conquered Prussia had been slowly preparing for the day when she would revenge herself on the French adventurer. Her people blamed her defeat on the old-fashioned institutions. Chief among the Prussian reformers were the great minister Baron vom Stein and the chancellor, Prince Hardenberg.

The first step in the modernization of Prussia was taken in October, 1807, when the government abolished serfdom. The old system of class privileges was done away with. Henceforth anyone, regardless of social rank, peasant as well as noble, could purchase and own land. Professions and occupations that had been closed to the lower classes were now opened to them. Improvements were also made in government administration.

The old military system of Frederick the Great, which had failed so completely against Napoleon, was entirely reorganized. A new law made every able-bodied young man henceforth liable for duty in the armed forces. By instructing recruits in special shifts Prussia soon had a force of 150,000 trained soldiers at her disposal.

Growth of National Spirit in Prussia · Along with these reforms went the rise of a new national spirit in Prussia. The people were growing ever more resentful of the wrongs that they had suffered at the hands of the French invader. Napoleon had robbed them of their territory, ruined their trade, and continued to quarter his soldiers on their land. They longed to overthrow this proud tyrant.

National enthusiasm was aroused by patriotic societies, by speeches, and by writings. The philosopher Fichte even went so far as to assert that the Germans were the one really superior people in the world. He declared that the gifted Germans would one day be recognized as the leaders of the world.

"Battle of the Nations" (October, 1813) · After the retreat from Moscow, Napoleon hastened back to Paris ahead of his army. Here he entirely misrepresented the true state of affairs. As speedily as possible, he got together a new army of 150,000 raw recruits.

But he was no longer looked upon as invincible. The Prussians now decided to join forces with the Russians and Swedes to complete his overthrow.

The campaign which followed is known in Germany as the War of Liberation. For a time the French were still triumphant. Napoleon gained his last great victory at Dresden on August 26–27. Finding that the allied Russians, Prussians, and Austrians were preparing to cut him off from France, he retreated early in October. He was totally defeated in the tremendous "Battle of the Nations," as it is now called, in the vicinity of Leipzig (October 16–19).

Breakup of Napoleon's Empire · As the defeated emperor crossed the Rhine with the remnants of his army, the whole structure of his power in Germany and Holland collapsed. The members of the Confederation of the Rhine deserted Napoleon and joined the allies. Jerome Bonaparte fled from his kingdom of Westphalia, and the Dutch drove the French officials from Holland. During 1813 the Spanish, helped by the English under Wellington, had practically cleared their country of the French intruders.

Napoleon Abdicates (April, 1814) · In spite of these disasters, Napoleon refused the proposals of peace made on condition that he would be contented to rule within the "natural boundaries" of France. He still clung to the hope of victory and em-

pire. The allies consequently marched into France. Even the almost superhuman activity of the hard-pressed emperor could not prevent them from occupying Paris.

At Fontainebleau, Napoleon was forced to abdicate and renounce all rights to the throne for himself and his family. He was permitted to retain the title of "Emperor," with full sovereignty over the tiny island of Elba, in the Mediterranean, where he became practically a prisoner of the allies.

The victorious powers immediately reinstated the Bourbon dynasty on the throne of France. The Count of Provence, Louis XVI's brother, was recalled from England, where he had been living, and given the title of Louis XVIII. The boundaries of France were fixed as they had been at the beginning of 1792.

A great congress of the allies was summoned to meet at Vienna to settle the many problems of readjustment which now arose. Accordingly, there gathered in September a notable assembly of rulers and statesmen. This Congress of Vienna was faced with the task of remaking the map of Europe. Although the allies were at one in their hostility to Napoleon, they immediately began to disagree on how Europe was to be reconstructed.

Waterloo and Exile · While the Congress was in session, Napoleon managed to escape from Elba. With twelve hundred men he landed in southern France. An army of enthusiastic followers joined him on his way, and he reached the city of Paris on March 1, 1815.

Napoleon counted on the loyalty of the French people to support him. He believed that the division among the allies would prevent their making a combined attack on him. But he was mistaken. The allies quickly forgot their differences in the face of the common danger and joined to overthrow once more "the destroyer of the world's peace." It took a "hundred days."

The Duke of Wellington assembled an army of 100,000 British, Germans, and Dutch in the Netherlands. General Blücher had an equally large number of Prussians under his command. The Austrians also had a considerable force near the Rhine.

In June, Napoleon collected an army. With his old daring he marched to the Belgian frontier, hoping to divide his enemies and defeat them separately. He managed at first to drive back the Prussians. But he was overcome by Wellington's forces at Waterloo and then completely routed by Blücher's troops.

There was now no hope for Napoleon, for the allies were sending an increasing number of soldiers into the field against him. Hopelessly defeated at last, the mighty conqueror had come to the end of his career.

On July 15 Napoleon finally gave himself up to the British. This time he was sent to St. Helena, a remote island in the South Atlantic. Here the great emperor spent the remaining five years of his life, walking about his lonely island, talking to his few companions, and dictating his *Memoirs*.

The Napoleonic Legend · In his account of his life Napoleon explained away all his blunders and left to posterity the picture he wished it to have of the great Napoleon.

He posed as a true son of the Revolution, raised by the will of the people to power. He declared that he had fought always for liberty and peace. The Terror and the failure of the Directory, he asserted, proved that only a monarchy could preserve the rights of the people.

If he ruled as a dictator, it was because the state was threatened with anarchy. But he restored order, purified the Revolution, and extended the glory of France. Napoleon claimed that he was never an aggressor, but was *forced* into war by his enemies.

As the years passed, Frenchmen tended to forget the thousands of their fellow countrymen who died needlessly on the battlefields. They began to see Napoleon *as he had pictured himself.* He was remembered as the great conquering general who brought glory to France. He was "the Emperor" (*l' Empereur*). We shall see later how his influence extended beyond his death.

CHECK ON YOUR READING

1. *What caused Napoleon's downfall?*
2. *Why did he invade Russia? Account for his failure.*
3. *Describe the reforms and new spirit in Prussia.*
4. *Why did Napoleon's Europe break up?*
5. *How do these terms summarize his downfall: (a) abdication, (b) Elba, (c) "Hundred Days," (d) Waterloo, (e) St. Helena?*
6. *How did Napoleon picture himself? With what effect?*

"England expects every man will do his duty."
—NELSON at Trafalgar

"The more I study the world, the more I am convinced of the inability of brute force to create anything durable."
—NAPOLEON I

Learning Activities

Think about the chapter

1. Why did England think it necessary to conquer Napoleon?

2. What do you regard as Napoleon's greatest achievement? mistake? Why?

3. How did the Napoleonic wars affect trade? nationalism? reform? the U.S.?

4. Write a page summary of this chapter using as many of the key words and dates on page 320 as you can.

5. *Map study:* On a map of Europe locate the places where the most famous of Napoleon's battles occurred: Marengo, Ulm, Austerlitz, Jena, Borodino, Leipzig, Waterloo.

Go beyond the text

6. Russian tactics against Napoleon in 1812 were used again by Russia in 1941–1942. Report briefly on the comparison.

7. Comparisons have been made between Alexander the Great's, Napoleon's, Mussolini's, and Hitler's dreams of empire. What similarities and contrasts can you find between any two of these lives?

8. Napoleonic France set the styles for the rest of the world. Describe the dress worn by the Parisian ladies of the period.

9. Read a good biography of Napoleon. Why is there a Napoleonic legend still? Was he truly a "son of the Revolution"? Do you think he was a great man?

Follow up your special interests

10. Robert Livingston and James Monroe bought Louisiana from Napoleon in 1803. Impersonate Napoleon telling a close advisor frankly why he was selling this vast territory. How did he get it in the first place?

11. Nelson and Wellington are famous figures of this period. Prepare a debate on the topic, *Resolved,* That Napoleon was a greater military genius than Wellington.

12. If you are interested in ships, make or draw a model of the type used in the English navy at the time of the Napoleonic wars.

13. Two famous musical compositions have a connection with Napoleon. Report on the *"Eroica Symphony"* by Beethoven and the *"1812 Overture"* by Tchaikovsky. Listen for the strains of the *"Marseillaise"* and the bells of Moscow in the latter.

READ FURTHER

Basic readings: (1) BECKER, *Modern History,* Chap. 9. (2) CARR, *Men of Power.* Napoleon. (3) HOFFMAN, *News of the World,* No. 44. (4) ROBINSON, *Readings,* Chaps. 37–38. (5) VAN LOON, *Story of Mankind,* pp. 349–60. (6) Year's *Pictorial History,* pp. 352–359.

Special accounts: (7) E. C. CORTI, *The Rise of the House of Rothschild.* Interesting material on the Napoleonic period. (8) P. GUEDALLA, *The Hundred Days.* The escape from Elba to the battle of Waterloo.

Fiction and biography: (9) A. BILL, *The Clutch of the Corsican.* Easy reading about Napoleon. (10) C. S. FORESTER, The Hornblower series: *Lieutenant Hornblower; Hornblower and the Atropos; Commodore Hornblower.* (11) M. KOMROFF, *Napoleon.* An absorbing tale of his rise from obscurity to absolute monarch. (12) E. LUDWIG, *Napoleon.* By an author who admires Napoleon—for good readers. (13) A. SELINKO, *Désirée.* A woman whose life was closely linked with Napoleon's is the heroine. She married Bernadotte, one of Napoleon's generals, and became the queen of Sweden. (14) W. THACKERAY, *Vanity Fair.* This story about life in England around 1815 contains a famous description of the battle of Waterloo. (15) L. TOLSTOY, *War and Peace.* This great drama of Napoleon's invasion and retreat from Russia is also available in a condensed version.

337

21

The Age of Metternich: Restoration, Repression, and Revolt (1815-1848)

KEY WORDS AND DATES

Congress of Vienna	Bolívar
1815	San Martín
restoration	Monroe Doctrine
compensation	Iturbide
Metternich	Charter of 1814
guarantees	royalists
German Confeder-	bourgeoisie
ation	July Ordinances
Holy Alliance	1830
Quadruple Alliance	Louis Philippe
Concert of Europe	socialists
reactionary	"bloody June days"
conservative	1848
moderate	Louis Napoleon
liberal	*coup d'etat*
radical	plebiscite
Carlsbad Decrees	Leopold
Carbonari	neutrality
Miranda	Kossuth

IN THE YEAR 1815 the victorious powers held a great peace conference at Vienna. The old-fashioned kings and diplomats met to undo the work of Napoleon and of the French Revolution as well. They hated new and dangerous doctrines and loved the old ways and old ideas.

They tried to set the clock of history back. (1) First they redrew the map of Europe. They distributed the lands Napoleon had seized, with the strongest powers receiving the largest shares. (2) Then the Congress, fearing republics and republicans, largely restored "legitimate rulers" (former rulers or their heirs) to their thrones. (3) To make sure that their settlement would last, they formed a repressive alliance.

Their policy led to revolts, which were put down with great brutality. But the forces of freedom would not be denied. In Greece, Belgium, and Latin America independence was won. By 1848 the revolutionary spirit had spread to many parts of Europe. For a brief time liberal reforms were successful. Then the reactionary governments again took over. But the revolutions of 1848 served as the "handwriting on the wall." They warned that one day the old order of Europe would be cast aside forever.

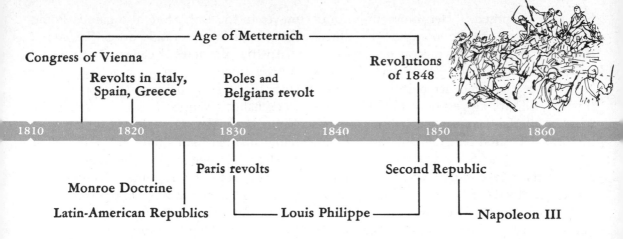

Age of Metternich

Congress of Vienna

Revolts in Italy,
Spain, Greece

Poles and
Belgians revolt

Revolutions
of 1848

| 1810 | 1820 | 1830 | 1840 | 1850 | 1860 |

Paris revolts

Second Republic

Monroe Doctrine

Latin-American Republics

Louis Philippe

Napoleon III

1. The Congress of Vienna Redraws the Map of Europe

Leaders and Work of the Congress · A brilliant array of European aristocracy assembled at Vienna in September, 1814. Tsar Alexander of Russia, Emperor Francis of Austria, King Frederick William of Prussia, and the kings of Bavaria, Württemberg, and Denmark were present, as well as a host of lesser princes. There were also numerous statesmen and diplomats. Among them were Castlereagh and Wellington of England, Nesselrode of Russia, Hardenberg of Prussia, Talleyrand of France, and Prince Metternich of Austria. The mass of people were not represented. It was the conservative Metternich who presided over and dominated the conference.

A succession of banquets, concerts, and balls was arranged by the Austrian court for the entertainment of its distinguished guests. There was no sign that in the midst of all these festivities the future of Europe was being determined.

The work of this extraordinary congress was done mostly in small committees and conferences. The main decisions at first were made by Austria, Russia, Prussia, and England. But through the skillful diplomacy of Talleyrand, France soon won an equal voice. The decisions were more or less forced on the smaller states. All the treaties and conclusions of the Congress as to the peace settlement were brought together in a "Final Act" on June 9, 1815.

There was a general agreement that the settlement should (1) restore Europe as it had been before the French Revolution. This included putting the old ruling houses back on their thrones. (2) The great powers must be compensated for their losses. (3) Measures should be taken to guarantee the peace and prevent the repetition of such disasters as had recently upset Europe.

Restorations and Guarantees · The former, or "legitimate," rulers who had been deprived of their thrones were restored. Thus the Bourbons returned to France, Spain, and the Two Sicilies. The king of Sardinia recovered his former territories.

In France Louis XVIII became king (p. 335). But France lost nearly all the territory she had taken since 1789. A heavy

339

fine was imposed. Her most important fortresses were to be occupied by allied troops for a period of years, at her expense.

Around France a "Rhine barrier" was created to guarantee her neighbors against further military aggression. (1) The Austrian Netherlands were annexed to Holland to form a United Kingdom of the Netherlands. (2) The Swiss Confederation was granted its independence, and its neutrality was guaranteed. (3) Prussia was strengthened by receiving Westphalia. This gave her territory on both banks of the Rhine and insured her support against French moves to the east. She also gained Pomerania from Sweden, and part of Saxony.

Austria Becomes Leader of Europe · Austria emerged from the peace conference with the largest share of the spoils. (1) In exchange (compensation) for the distant Netherlands she received territories which built up her kingdom in central and southern Europe. (2) She renewed her hold on Italy by regaining Venetia and acquiring the provinces on the eastern shore of the Adriatic, as well as the Duchy of Milan. (3) Hapsburg princes again ruled in the north Italian states of Modena,

Europe after the Congress of Vienna · Compare with the maps on pages 243 and 332. What states regained independence? Locate the "Rhine barrier."

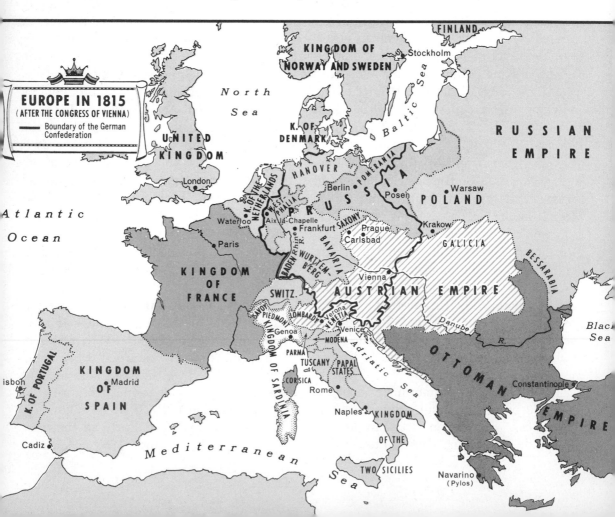

Diplomats at the Congress of Vienna · *Here in Schönbrunn palace, diplomats worked and socialized. Metternich stands prominently at left. Castlereagh sits with legs crossed. What role did Talleyrand, seated at right, play?*

Parma, and Tuscany. (4) Austria was also able to establish her authority in Germany. The former members of the Confederation of the Rhine were united into a loose union over which Austria was to preside. Thus Austria succeeded France as the dominant power in Europe.

The German Confederation (1815–1866) · Germany became a loose confederation of thirty-eight independent states. It was really an alliance of rulers dominated by Austria. It still had no king, no capital, no common government, and no federal policy.

The German people thought of themselves as citizens of Bavaria or Prussia, for example, rather than of Germany. There was a central diet (or congress) for the union, which met at Frankfurt. But this was composed of representatives not of the people, but of the rulers.

The member states retained the right to make alliances with other countries, though they pledged themselves not to enter into any agreement endangering the Confederation. They also agreed not to make war on one another. In spite of its many weaknesses, the German Confederation continued for fifty years.

Other Congress Decisions · Tsar Alexander wanted all of Poland but had to be content with the greater part of it. Prussia kept Posen and Austria retained Galicia. Russia also obtained Finland from Sweden.

In compensation for her losses Sweden received Norway from Denmark. Thus Denmark was made to pay for having allied herself with Napoleon.

A Bourbon ruler, Ferdinand I, was restored as king of the Two Sicilies. The king of Sardinia (Victor Emmanuel I, 1802–1821) recovered the former territories of the House of Savoy and to them was added the republic of Genoa. Austria, however, dominated these two Italian rulers completely (see map, p. 340).

The Holy Alliance · Having settled the affairs of Europe to their own satisfaction, the diplomats of Vienna now had to make their work permanent. Tsar Alexander proposed the formation of a kind of religious brotherhood of monarchs. They would regard themselves as "delegates of Providence," ruling over various branches of the same human family.

He got the emperor of Austria and the king of Prussia to join with him in a "Holy Alliance," as it was called. In a solemn treaty the three sovereigns declared that they would be guided in the administration of their respective states and in their relations with other governments solely by "the precepts of justice, Christian charity, and peace." Other monarchs who were willing to accept these sacred principles were invited to join the alliance.

Most of the European rulers signed the treaty to please the tsar. They did not take it seriously. To have practiced the Christianity they preached would have meant giving up the spoils of victory. Metternich pronounced it mere "verbiage" and a "sonorous nothing." The English minister, who refused to join the group, called it a "piece of sublime mysticism and nonsense."

The Quadruple Alliance and Concert of Europe · A quite different kind of alliance was presided over by Metternich. He believed that a united force would be needed to suppress any future outbreaks against the old order. This was a formal agreement, entered into by the four powers which had combined to overthrow Napoleon (Austria, Russia, Prussia, and Great Britain). It was known as the Quadruple Alliance.

In 1818 France was admitted to the alliance for certain purposes. This alliance of the great powers is known as the Concert of Europe. The members pledged themselves (1) to use every measure necessary to maintain the peace of Europe as now established and (2) to prevent the reappearance of those revolutionary principles that had destroyed France.

CHECK ON YOUR READING

1. *Describe the Congress of Vienna: (a) great powers, (b) leaders, (c) festivities, (d) three agreements.*
2. *Explain and give examples of (a) restorations, (b) guarantees, (c) Rhine barrier, (d) compensations.*
3. *Show on a map the gains made by (a) Austria, (b) Russia, (c) Prussia, (d) Sweden, (e) Sardinia, (f) the German Confederation.*
4. *Compare and contrast the Holy Alliance with the Quadruple Alliance (Concert of Europe) as to (a) membership and (b) purposes.*

---

2. Repression and Revolt

Metternich Dominates the Age · For thirty years Metternich was the leader in this *unholy* alliance. So powerful was his influence that the period between 1815–1848 has been called the "Age of Metternich." At Vienna he had restored the Hapsburg monarchy to its former position after its years of humiliation. Now, by reason of Austria's control over Italy, Germany, and her own vast dominions, her clever minister could speak with great authority.

RADICAL	LIBERAL	MODERATE	CONSERVATIVE	REACTIONARY
LEFT WING	PROGRESSIVE	MIDDLE OF THE ROAD	STATUS QUO	RIGHT WING

Political Opinions · *Why are most people moderates? What would happen if this chart were a circle? In the French parliament conservatives sat on right.*

Prince Metternich was admirably fitted for this commanding role. He was handsome and aristocratic. He combined charming manners with great cleverness and the ability to handle the most delicate situations. He was a true master of the art of diplomacy.

After the Congress of Vienna, Metternich used all his energies to guarantee the settlement that the *reactionary* statesmen had fastened on Europe. Through the Concert of Europe he claimed the right to intervene in any country to suppress *liberal* ideas and *revolutionary* outbreaks.

Common Political Labels · Before we examine Metternich's program, however, let us clarify some terms commonly used to describe political opinions. Among these we find *reactionary, conservative, moderate, liberal,* and *radical* (see chart).

The *reactionary* is one who wishes to turn the clock back to the past. He swings to the extreme right in reaction against the excesses of the radical. He is a counter-revolutionist. He believes that "old ways are best." Metternich and his colleagues were extreme reactionaries. The *radical* is an extremist too. Like a pendulum he swings to the far left, away from the old regime. He favors drastic (often revolutionary) changes with an idealist's eye to the future. His weapon is revolt. The "Jacobins" and "republicans" were radicals.

A *conservative* is cautious about change and has a skeptical attitude toward new experiments. He is inclined to believe that things are pretty good as they are. He favors a policy of "slow but sure" but he can be persuaded. His counterpart is the *liberal,* who sees errors in the past and present and believes in reforms. He welcomes change and is inclined to say, "Let's try it and see." His favorite weapons are free speech, free press, education, and the ballot. The *moderate* is the man in the middle. He prefers to avoid extremes. He tends to see some merit on both sides and is inclined to compromise.

All these labels are carelessly used. It frequently happens that persons are *called* reactionary or conservative who believe in progress. And those who have no idea of approving violence are branded as radicals by those who do not like their ideas. In this way a great deal of unfairness and ill-feeling may arise because people do not take the trouble to discover and respect what others really believe.

During the nineteenth century the contest in most countries was chiefly between reactionaries and liberals. The reactionaries supported the old monarchical style of

Metternich · *In his youth Metternich witnessed revolutionary mob violence, and this, he claimed, affected his policies. He seriously underestimated the force of nationalism.*

vised. The Church aided the state by requiring students to attend its services. Moreover, Metternich's spies were busy all over Europe to see that no dangerous ideas spread into the Hapsburg realms.

Trouble in Germany · Metternich had reason to be concerned. The demands for constitutional government and greater personal liberty were difficult to suppress.

In Prussia Frederick William III, under the influence of Metternich, refused to grant a constitution after promising one. In other German states absolutism was restored. But the spirit of liberalism did not die. Its chief center was the universities, where student societies held patriotic meetings and kept alive the enthusiasm for national unity.

Metternich in 1819 had the diet of the German Confederation issue the so-called Carlsbad Decrees. Constitutions of a "foreign pattern" were forbidden. Strict censorship was established. Spies were placed in universities to inform on professors, and secret societies were forbidden.

Uprisings in Italy and Greece · Repression breeds revolt. Secret societies kept alive the agitation for individual freedom, national independence, and constitutional government in Italy. The best known of these associations took the name *Carbonari* (charcoal-burners). It advocated revolution to achieve its aims.

In 1820 the liberals in Naples forced Ferdinand I to accept a constitution. The alert Metternich now called together the Concert of Europe to assist him in putting down the outbreak. He soon obtained the consent of Russia and Prussia to send Austrian troops into Italy. With this help Ferdinand was able to discard the constitution and revenge himself on the revolutionaries (1821).

government, while the liberals wished constitutional checks placed on the powers of the rulers. They usually believed in increasing the number of voters so that reforms would be brought about by the will of the people.

Reaction and Repression in Austria · To prevent any outcroppings of liberal ideas at home, Metternich maintained a strict censorship over books, newspapers, and plays. No foreign works containing liberal ideas were permitted to enter the country. An efficient police and spy system was organized to watch government offices and educational institutions.

Professors and students were subject to strict regulations, and textbooks were super-

In Piedmont too the people demanded a constitution. King Victor Emmanuel I abdicated, and the regent granted the constitution. But the Austrians drove out the liberals and soon gained control of the situation. In spite of these failures, the desire for a free and united Italy continued secretly to grow and await a more favorable day of triumph.

What gave them heart was the success of the revolution in Greece. Here Turkish rule was overthrown, and after eight years of bitter struggle independence was secured (p. 439). Failure of the European powers to help Turkey suppress the revolt was due to policy differences among themselves.

Restoration Leads to Despotism and Revolution in Spain · The Italian uprisings had been set off by a revolution in Spain. In 1815 the Congress of Vienna had restored Ferdinand VII as the "legitimate" ruler in Spain. Immediately this reactionary Bourbon swept away all the reforms that Napoleon had introduced into the country. The liberal constitution that had been adopted in 1812 was annulled and the Cortes (assembly) was abolished.

The king now established a thoroughly despotic monarchy. Class distinctions and privileges were revived. Monastic orders were brought back and the Inquisition was set up. Books and newspapers were censored, free speech was prohibited, and great numbers of liberals were imprisoned or executed. These measures divided the country between reactionaries and liberals. They also kept the people poor and ignorant, interfered with business and trade, and inspired secret rebellion. In the meantime the king and his favorites plundered the treasury.

For years Ferdinand VII had sent thousands of men to die of fever and wounds in the vain attempt to subdue rebellious colonists in South America. But in 1820, soldiers who were waiting in Cadiz to embark for service overseas revolted. The revolution spread to the larger cities. In Madrid a mob surrounded the palace and forced the king to take an oath to restore the constitution of 1812. This alarmed the ruling houses of Europe.

The Concert of Europe Puts Down the Spanish Revolt · The representatives of the great powers—Russia, Austria, Prussia, Britain, and France—met at Verona in 1822 to determine what should be done about the Spanish crisis.

Great Britain refused to interfere in any way. Her people sympathized with the efforts of the Spanish colonies to win their independence. Moreover, it was not to Britain's advantage to see Ferdinand regain his power and the South American trade.

The Concert of Europe, nevertheless, decided that Louis XVIII should send an army across the Pyrenees. The spirit of liberty might otherwise spread to all Europe. The French commander easily defeated the revolutionists and placed Ferdinand in a position to crush his enemies. This he did in such a bloodthirsty manner that his French allies were heartily ashamed of him. Thousands were exiled, jailed, or executed as Ferdinand stamped out liberty in Spain.

CHECK ON YOUR READING

1. *How did Metternich dominate this period?*
2. *Define reactionary, radical, conservative, liberal, moderate.*
3. *What weapons are used by each?*
4. *Which of these revolts (Italy, Greece, Spain) were (a) suppressed? (b) successful? (c) Why?*

3. Latin-American Independence

Why the Spanish Colonists Revolted · Even more serious than the unrest at home was the growing discontent in the Spanish empire across the Atlantic. Her colonies in the New World included Mexico (and the region north of it, later acquired by the United States), Central America, and most of South America.

Let us look more closely at Spain's colonies now and see why they revolted. (1) Spain had long treated her colonies merely as a source of wealth to be exploited for her own benefit. This attitude was greatly resented by the colonists. (2) Over the years the ties with the mother country had become steadily weaker. The inhabitants of the Spanish colonies began to think and speak of themselves as *americanos*, just as in North America the English colonists were gradually transformed into *Americans*. (3) The Spanish colonists were stirred by the revolutionary ideas of Locke, Voltaire, and Rousseau. (4) They were especially impressed by the successful American Revolution. Indeed in this their mother country had played a part. (5) The French Revolution likewise had a tremendous impact on their thinking. (6) Napoleon's invasion of Spain and Portugal gave them the opportunity they sought.

Miranda Leads Revolt in Venezuela · When Napoleon placed his brother Joseph on the throne of Spain (p. 330), the Spanish colonies refused to recognize him. Some hailed the worthless Ferdinand as sovereign. But many colonists doubted whether he would ever be restored to the throne. Having little respect for his character or abilities, they launched movements for independence. Revolutionary publica-

tions came from the presses of Argentina and Chile.

The first public move for independence came in Venezuela under the lead of Francisco Miranda. On April 19, 1810, a *junta* (local council) expelled all the royal officials from the province.

A year later the Congress of the "American Confederation of Venezuela" adopted a Declaration of Independence. In it they characterized Charles IV and Ferdinand as "unfit to rule over a free people." In words borrowed from the American Declaration of Independence they declared that "these united provinces are, and ought to be, from this day forth, in fact and of right, free, sovereign, and independent states. . . ." A constitution based largely on that of the United States was adopted.

But Miranda's revolutionary army was no match for the Spanish troops. He was compelled to surrender in the summer of 1812. Violating their pledge for his safety, the royalists seized him and sent him to Spain, where he died in prison four years later.

Simón Bolívar, the "Liberator" · Miranda's mantle fell on the shoulders of Simón Bolívar, a young Venezuelan of high birth and great wealth. He had been an efficient field officer under Miranda. For ten years he fought valiantly and spent his private fortune freely in the struggle against superior Spanish forces. He performed daring feats of generalship to break the Spanish resistence in New Granada (Colombia) and Quito (Ecuador).

In May, 1822, Bolívar drove the royalist commander from the last stronghold, and proclaimed the freedom of the northern provinces of the continent: Venezuela,

Colombia, and Ecuador. Two years later he won a great victory at Ayacucho in Peru. He then liberated the province of Charcas, which received the name Bolivia in his honor. The title of "Liberator" was bestowed on him, and he is often spoken of as "the Washington of South America."

San Martín Liberates Argentina, Chile, and Peru · The hero of the wars in the southern part of South America was José de San Martín. He commanded the revolutionary army in Argentina and greatly influenced that province's decision to declare its independence.

San Martín now planned to liberate Chile and Peru. Crossing the snow-covered Andes with the Chilean revolutionist O'Higgins, he defeated the royalist troops at Chacabuco in 1817. He thus cleared the road to Santiago, where Chilean independence was proclaimed the next year.

The next move was northward to Peru. San Martín's forces were now reinforced by numerous deserters from the royalist side and were aided by a fleet under the command of an English officer. They entered Lima on July 12, 1821, and the municipal council immediately voted for independence. Soon afterward San Martín, in poor health, retired to private life.

Iturbide Frees Mexico and Guatemala · In 1820 the Spanish gave Augustín de Iturbide an army to put down the persistent guerrilla warfare in Mexico. Iturbide joined the rebels instead and declared the independence of New Spain (1821). He compelled the viceroy to sign a treaty providing that some member of a royal European family be invited to take the throne of Mexico. Otherwise the Cortes was to choose a ruler.

Iturbide entered Mexico City in triumph and was hailed as the "father and liberator

San Martín and Bolívar Meet at Guayaquil · *What took place at this dramatic meeting (July, 1822) was never revealed.*

of his country." When the Spanish Cortes repudiated the treaty, Iturbide seized the crown for himself. On July 25, 1822, he was crowned Emperor Augustín I.

The new emperor now called upon Guatemala (including Central America) to recognize his rule. But before it could be incorporated into Mexico, Iturbide was overthrown. A constituent assembly thereupon met and on July 1, 1823, proclaimed Guatemala's independence as the "United Provinces of Central America."

Haiti and Santo Domingo · Only one of the Spanish island colonies in the Caribbean threw off the yoke of Spain in the revolutionary era. This was little Santo

Dom Pedro (center) Proclaims Brazilian Independence · *Near São Paulo on September 7, 1822, the regent tore from his uniform the Portuguese colors and proclaimed, "Independence or death! We are separated from Portugal!"*

Domingo, which occupied the eastern half of the island of Hispaniola discovered by Columbus.

But Santo Domingo won its independence from Spain only to fall under the rule of its far stronger neighbor, the French-speaking republic of Haiti (1822). The Haitian domination lasted for twenty-two years.

Santo Domingo finally achieved independence in 1844. But it was cursed with misrule, staggering debts, and repeated revolutions for nearly a century.

Brazil Wins Independence · When Napoleon Bonaparte invaded Portugal in 1808 (p. 330), the prince regent, Joao, left Lis-

bon with the whole royal family and court. On the advice of their British ally, they set sail for Brazil with some 15,000 troops. Arriving at Rio de Janeiro, the prince was joyously acclaimed by the populace as Emperor of Brazil.

Joao's popularity, however, rapidly declined in the following years. Revolutionary uprisings resulted from the insolence of the Portuguese courtiers, the heavy taxes laid on the people, and the revolts in the Spanish Indies. After the overthrow of Napoleon, Portugal called the regent to return home to rule as King Joao VI. He left his young son Dom Pedro as regent, but took with him most of the money in the Brazilian treasury.

The Portuguese Cortes ordered Dom Pedro to follow his father home, but he defied them and joined the party of Brazilian independence. On December 1, 1822, he was crowned Emperor Pedro I. Thus the Portuguese colony in America began its independent existence as an empire, not a republic.

The empire lasted until 1899, when Pedro II was deposed and the republic of the United States of Brazil was established.

The United States Recognizes the New Republics · The government and people of the United States strongly sympathized with the struggle of the Spanish and Portuguese colonists for independence. Henry Clay urged the recognition of "eighteen millions of people struggling to burst their chains."

But the more cautious Secretary of State, John Quincy Adams, was in the midst of negotiations with Madrid for the acquisition of the Spanish province of Florida. He preferred not to risk offending the ministers of Ferdinand VII. When the treaty ceding Florida to the United States was finally ratified by the Spanish Cortes in 1821, however, the administration was free to extend a friendly hand to the "sister republics" of the south.

Diplomatic relations with several of the Latin-American states were established beginning in 1822. Recognition by England and the other European nations followed soon afterward.

The Monroe Doctrine Guarantees the Independence of the New Republics · But recognition of the new republics was not automatic. Indeed the reactionary rulers at the Congress of Verona in 1822 (p. 345) proposed that Ferdinand send an army across the Atlantic to reconquer his rebellious Spanish provinces. This proposal roused Great Britain and the United States to protest. (1) Public opinion in Great Britain and the United States favored colonial independence. (2) Restoration of Spanish authority would close the ports which the new republics had opened to trade.

The British foreign minister Canning proposed that the two nations make a joint declaration guaranteeing the independence of the new republics. But Secretary of State John Quincy Adams persuaded President Monroe to act alone. The President's statement in his annual message to Congress of December 2, 1823, has since been known as the *Monroe Doctrine.*

President Monroe declared (1) that the American continents were closed to any further colonization by European powers. (2) Any interference with the governments which had declared their independence would be "regarded as the manifestation of an unfriendly disposition towards the United States." (3) In return, the United States pledged not to interfere in the political affairs of Europe.

President Monroe Discusses His Message · *The Monroe Doctrine might justly be called the Adams Doctrine. Adams had stated earlier the noncolonization principle to prevent Russian colonization in Oregon.*

This firm declaration became a basic principle of American foreign policy. Backed by the British fleet it proved more than sufficient to guarantee the independence of the Latin-American republics.

CHECK ON YOUR READING

1. *Why did the Spanish colonists revolt?*
2. *Use the map to show where and how each of the following served the cause of independence: (a) Miranda, (b) Bolívar, (c) San Martín, (d) Iturbide, (e) Dom Pedro.*
3. *What special problems faced Santo Domingo?*
4. *How were recognition and independence influenced by (a) Clay? (b) Florida? (c) Canning? (d) J. Q. Adams?*
5. *Explain the purpose, provisions, and result of the Monroe Doctrine?*

349

4. From Monarchy to Republic in France (1814–1848)

What the Liberals Wanted · In spite of the watchfulness of Metternich and his friends, the great reforms of the French Revolution were not forgotten. Everywhere the middle classes, the workers, and the intellectuals (professors, students, writers, and reformers) were enemies of the peace settlements of Vienna. All these liberals still cherished the principles of the Declaration of the Rights of Man (p. 317). They were eager to overthrow the reactionaries and see a new order in Europe.

The program of the liberals included the following points. (1) They wanted written constitutions in which the rights of the people and responsibilities of their leaders were clearly stated. (2) They wanted to establish parliaments which would reflect the will of the people. (3) They held that the burden of taxation should be more equally distributed. (4) They sought freedom of speech, press, religion, and assembly. (5) They demanded safeguards against arbitrary arrest, imprisonment, and loss of property. (6) Groups of people who had been forcibly brought under the domination of stronger powers should have the right of national independence.

We shall find that France became the leader in the long struggle of the liberals to reach these goals during the nineteenth century. Let us see how she fared after the downfall of Napoleon.

Louis XVIII Grants a Charter (1814) · When the allies brought stout old Louis Bourbon to Paris, they realized full well that the people would never again tolerate the abuses of the old regime. And Louis was careful to "grant" at once a constitution guaranteeing the rights of the people.

The provisions of the Charter, as it was called, clearly show the gains which the French people had made as a result of the Revolution. (1) Most of the great reforms proclaimed in the Declaration of the Rights of Man were maintained. (2) The laws were to be made by the king in co-operation with parliament. (3) No tax could be levied without the consent of parliament. (4) Every citizen was to have equal rights before the law and to be eligible to hold government office. (5) No one could be arrested without the protection of the law. (6) Religious freedom was guaranteed.

Not all the provisions of the Charter were democratic, however. (7) The nobility created by Napoleon was recognized alongside that of the old regime. But titles now had only a social value and carried no political privileges or exemptions. (8) Only those citizens who paid a certain amount of taxes could vote for deputies. This, of course, restricted the vote to those who had property and were well-to-do.

Moderate Policy of Louis XVIII · The new king regarded the throne as the "softest of chairs" and preferred to rule within constitutional limits rather than not to rule at all. Although a staunch believer in the "divine right" of monarchs, he understood the change that had taken place in France. He was faithful, therefore, to the Charter and made no effort to destroy the great achievements of the Revolution.

The French people, however, were far from united when Louis XVIII ascended the throne. There were reactionary supporters of the old regime on the one side and radical defenders of the Revolution on the other. There were moderates, as well as sympathizers with Napoleon.

The reactionary group was led by the king's brother, the Count of Artois. It tried to persuade Louis to abolish the Charter and to rule as an absolute monarch. The reactionaries became so troublesome in the parliament that the king finally dissolved it.

New elections brought moderates into control of the government, and for four years parliament worked in harmony with the king. France paid off her war debts, and foreign troops were withdrawn from her soil.

Charles X Tries to Restore the Old Order (1824–1830) · When Louis died, in 1824, his reactionary brother came to the throne as Charles X. As leader of the emigrant nobles, he had plotted with Austria and Prussia to invade France and crush the Revolution (p. 309).

Now he tried to restore the ancient Bourbon power. He re-established the influence of the Catholic Church by placing education in the hands of the priests and permitting the clergy to interfere with teaching in the universities.

The royalists (emigrant nobles) were given one billion francs to repay them for their losses in the Revolution. As the government did not have sufficient funds to meet this sum, it decided to cut the interest on its bonds. The amount thus saved would go to the nobles. This antagonized the bankers, merchants, and businessmen, who owned many of these government bonds. They objected to payments made to the nobility at their expense. From this time on, the middle classes, or *bourgeoisie*, were the bitterest enemies of the king.

Charles X Reviews the National Guard · *This Guard was the people's militia. Charles disbanded it when its members demanded reform.*

The royalists now began to lose their influence in the Chamber of Deputies, and republicans were elected to fill their places. A struggle between the king and parliament followed. Charles finally took matters into his own hands and in July, 1830, issued a set of decrees designed to put down all opposition to his policy.

These "July Ordinances" (1) curbed the liberty of the press, (2) restricted voting to wealthy taxpayers, and (3) gave the king the power to propose new laws. The king's conduct was entirely illegal under the constitution. If the ordinances had been obeyed, France would once more have been at the mercy of an absolute monarch.

The Revolution of July, 1830 · On the day after the appearance of the decrees the newspapers published a protest. They

Louis Philippe Sets Out for the Hotel de Ville · *Louis Philippe begins his famous ride to the republican headquarters of the great Lafayette. The revolutionary tricolor precedes him. Why did he adopt it instead of the Bourbon flag?*

stated that "since the government has violated the law, we are under no obligation to obey it. . . . For our part we shall resist it; it is for France to judge how far her resistance shall extend." The republicans now determined once more to overthrow a despotic king.

On July 27 they began tearing up the paving stones of Paris for barricades, behind which they could defend themselves in the narrow streets against the police and soldiers. Two days later the entire city of Paris was in the hands of the rebels. The king offered to withdraw the hateful ordinances. But it was too late. The insurgents demanded the overthrow of the king himself. When Charles saw that he could no longer keep his crown, he abdicated.

Louis Philippe Becomes King (1830–1848) · Parliament now invited Louis Philippe to the throne as king. He was a member of the house of Orléans, the younger branch of the Bourbon family. Both he and his father had supported the cause of the people during the Revolution.

Louis Philippe had not joined the royalist party, but had sought favor with the people by professing democratic opinions and posing as a plain citizen. He had entertained businessmen and intellectuals at his home, and sent his children to ordinary schools. He therefore seemed a wise choice to those who wished to retain the monarchy and yet keep the middle class in power.

The hopes of the republicans, who had borne the brunt of the revolution, were crushed. They saw that their party was not strong enough to prevent another monarch from reigning over France. Both the republicans and the old aristocracy had been forced to give way before the rising middle class of wealthy businessmen.

The "Bourgeois Monarchy" · The new king announced that his policy would be the golden mean between conservatism and liberalism. He himself appeared to be an excellent *bourgeois*, and his rule was called the "Bourgeois Monarchy." He lived without the luxury which the Bourbon kings had assumed and was fond of going shopping with his green umbrella under his arm. Under his democratic manner, however, Louis Philippe was autocratic at heart and loved power. As time went on, he became more and more conservative and at last highly intolerant.

Parliament did make some improvements in the Charter. Freedom of the press and the responsibility of the ministers to parliament were expressly stated. Hereafter laws were to be proposed not by the king alone but by the king and parliament. The provision making the Roman Catholic religion official in the state was omitted, and the influence of the clergy in politics was greatly reduced.

But the revolution of 1830 had really accomplished little. While one king had been exchanged for another, the government was hardly more democratic than before. The right to vote was still limited to the wealthy. Bankers and merchants now exercised the kind of power formerly enjoyed by the nobility and clergy. France was still a monarchy, and the labors of the republicans appeared to have been spent in vain.

Rise of the Socialists · Among the republican opponents of Louis Philippe were a large number of radical reformers, called *socialists*. They believed that the middle class had no more right to great wealth than had the nobility and clergy. They desired a government organized for the benefit of the working classes.

The industry of France was changing from handicraft in the home and small shop to large-scale production in factories. New laws were needed to meet new conditions and to safeguard the millions of workers

The Chamber of Deputies as seen by Daumier · *This famous cartoonist ridiculed the wealthy legislators of the "Bourgeois Monarchy." His drawings brought him a prison sentence.*

now employed. Most workers were poor and illiterate and unable to protect themselves against the employers. They had to work long hours for pitifully low wages. Yet the government did nothing to improve their lot.

The socialists thought that the government should handle this problem. They carried on propaganda through secret societies and through pamphlets. To curb these activities a law was passed forbidding the formation of any association without the consent of the government. The press was strictly censored, even as to the drawings and cartoons that were published. It was made a crime to question the right of private property, to criticize the government, or to incite the people to riot.

The Second French Republic, 1848 · Although the government was able to put down its enemies by harsh measures, there was widespread discontent. Both the ministry and parliament retained power through political corruption. Finally, public demonstrations calling for the reform of parliament and a widening of the suffrage became so insistent that public meetings were banned. On February 24, 1848, after several days of street riots, the Paris crowds demanded the overthrow of the king.

A mob invaded the Chamber of Deputies, crying, "Down with the Bourbons, old and new! Long live the Republic!" The king was thoroughly frightened and abdicated. A provisional government was set up, and it joined with the radical group to proclaim a republic (February 27, 1848).

The life of the Second Republic was brief and troubled. It had come into existence as the result of an insurrection in Paris. During the months that followed there was great disorder. Business suffered and securities fell in value.

Conservatives vs. Socialists: the Bloody June Days · The provisional government succeeded in putting down a movement to place the working classes in control. But it was forced to grant one of the demands of the radical group, the "right to labor." That meant that the government must see to it that all had work, or pay for their relief while unemployed.

The government therefore unwillingly established "national workshops," an idea of the socialist leader, Louis Blanc. The undertaking was badly organized. Those in power were not eager to have the plan succeed. Much useless work was provided, yet the number on relief mounted steadily. By June, 1848, over 100,000 men were receiving unemployment payments.

When the newly elected National Assembly met to draft the constitution of the Republic, it was firmly in the hands of the middle class. It immediately abolished the unemployment payments which had become a heavy financial burden on the government. The result was a terrific battle in the streets of Paris between the army and the socialist-led unemployed. In the "bloody June days" which followed, over ten thousand persons were killed or wounded. The conservatives were once more in the saddle.

Louis Napoleon Becomes President · The "bloody June days" led the people to believe that a strong man was needed at the head of the government. The constitution provided that the president should be elected, and the choice now fell upon Louis Napoleon Bonaparte. He was the son of the former king of Holland (Louis Bonaparte), and nephew of the Napoleon of legend.

Louis Napoleon firmly believed that the magic name he bore would one day make him ruler of France. Indeed, he had twice tried (1836 and 1840) without success to seize the government. And he had suffered imprisonment and exile as a result. Like his famous uncle, however, he was a man of determination. He returned to France at a moment when the *Bonaparte* name seemed to promise security to a confused people. He offered himself as candidate for president of the Republic and was elected by an overwhelming majority in December, 1848.

By Coup d'état, and Plebiscite, to Emperor · For three years Louis Napoleon prepared the way to gain the throne of France. Republicans were quietly removed from office and republican newspapers were suppressed. Important ministries, such as those of war, interior, and police, and important military positions were filled by his supporters.

On December 2, 1851, Louis Napoleon resorted to a *coup d'état* (a sudden overthrow of a government) and set up a new government. All the leaders who might oppose him were arrested, and printing establishments were brought under his control. He then announced the restoration of universal suffrage and appealed to the people for the power to revise the constitution.

With the approval of the people in a plebiscite (popular vote) he prepared a new constitution. It greatly enlarged his power as president and extended his term of office from four to ten years. Step by step this shrewd politician used loyal newspapers and paid supporters to build up public enthusiasm for his rule.

In 1852, with the approval of another plebiscite, the Second Empire was established. Thus Louis became Napoleon III, "Emperor of France by the grace of God and the will of the people."

Napoleon III and Empress Eugenie · *Unable to marry into the Hohenzollern family, Napoleon III chose a beautiful Spanish countess. She influenced him and the day's fashions.*

CHECK ON YOUR READING

1. *What did the liberals want?*
2. *Why were Louis XVIII's Charter and moderate policy popular?*
3. *Why and how was Charles X overthrown?*
4. *Why was Louis Philippe called the "Citizen King," and his reign the "Bourgeois Monarchy"?*
5. *Account for the (a) rise of the socialists, (b) establishment of the Second French Republic, (c) "bloody June days."*
6. *Explain how Louis Napoleon used (a) security, (b) legend, (c) coup, (d) plebiscite to become Napoleon III.*

5. Revolution Spreads through Europe (1830–1848)

Belgium Becomes Independent · News of the successful French revolts of 1830 and 1848 spread like a chain reaction throughout Europe. Belgium was first to catch fire. The Congress of Vienna, it will be recalled, had awarded the Austrian Netherlands to Holland (p. 340). The southern (Belgian) provinces of the Netherlands differed from the northern, or Dutch, provinces in language and religion. They deeply resented being annexed to a little country whose population was smaller than their own.

When the revolution of 1830 broke out in Paris, the people of Brussels rose to demand self-government and drove the royal Dutch troops out of the city. Riots broke out elsewhere in the country. In October a provisional government declared Belgium independent.

A constitutional monarchy was set up, and Leopold of Saxe-Coburg was chosen as king. Through the influence of England and France the powers finally agreed to recognize the independence of the Belgians and to guarantee the neutrality of the little kingdom.

Poland Becomes a Russian Province (1830) · A less successful revolt was that of Poles against their Russian masters. The Poles feared that their regiments were to be sent to put down the Belgian insurrection. Believing that they would receive help from France, the Poles drove the Russian Grand Duke out of Warsaw and proclaimed their independence.

The Russian armies easily crushed the rebellion. Then Tsar Nicholas I took vengeance on the unhappy country. He abolished the constitution granted by Alexander I in 1815 and made Poland a province of Russia. Hundreds of Poles were executed or exiled, but many managed to escape.

Success and Failure in Bohemia and Hungary, 1848 · All this time the reactionary Metternich had been able to hold the Hapsburg realms in restless subjection. But with news of the Second French Republic in February, 1848, all the pent-up resentment of the liberals against Metternich and his hated system broke loose.

In Hungary a great liberal patriot, Louis Kossuth, publicly denounced the Austrian government for trying to crush the national spirit of its peoples. Kossuth called upon Metternich to give Hungary an independent constitution. Bohemian liberals made a similar demand.

On March 13 the populace of Vienna rose in revolt. Metternich fled to England. Before the end of the month the helpless Hapsburg emperor gave his permission to the kingdoms of Hungary and Bohemia to draw up constitutions for themselves.

The new constitutions granted equality to all classes in the matter of taxation, religious freedom, and liberty of the press. Each country was to have its own parliament, which would meet once a year.

But the success of the liberals was short-lived. It was not long before the Austrian government was able to take advantage of the mutual jealousies of its people to regain control of the situation.

The Germans opposed the plan of making Bohemia independent because they would be outnumbered by their aggressive Czech countrymen. An insurrection broke out in Prague. This gave the commander of the Austrian forces an excuse for bombarding the city. A military government was then established, and the prospect of Bohemian independence vanished.

The revolutionary government of Hungary was composed of Magyars. They tried to dominate all other nationalities in the country—Serbs, Croats, and Slovenes. Austria now sent armies to aid these minorities against the Magyars. And the tsar sent an army of 150,000 Russians to help the Austrians. In August, 1848, the Hungarians were forced to surrender. Thousands were hanged, shot, or imprisoned. Many others, including Kossuth, fled to the United States or elsewhere. The war for the liberation of Hungary had ended in disaster, and Hungary, like Bohemia, again became an Austrian province.

Success and Failure in Italy · The Italians had been quick to take advantage of the revolts in Austria, Bohemia, and Hungary. Immediately on the news of Metternich's fall, the Milanese had expelled the Austrian troops from their city. Soon Austria was forced to give up a great part of Lombardy. The Venetians followed the lead of Milan and set up an independent republic.

By this time a great part of Italy was in revolt. Constitutions were granted to Naples, Rome, Tuscany, and Piedmont by their rulers. Public opinion then forced Charles Albert, the king of Sardinia (1831–1849), to assume the leadership in a war to expel Austria from the peninsula and establish Italian independence.

But for one reason or another, other Italian rulers became alarmed about the war with Austria and withdrew their troops. Charles Albert soon found himself with only a few volunteers. Thus weakened, his forces were no match for those of the emperor. Austria easily recovered Lombardy and re-established her hold on Italy.

Revolutionary Barricades · *Here workers prepare to defend themselves in the narrow streets. Which city set an example for such fighting?*

Success and Failure in Germany (1848) · The news of the February revolution in Paris had caused great excitement in Berlin too. On March 18 royal guards fired into a crowd that was gathered before the palace. Street fighting followed, and barricades were put up in the sections where the working people lived.

The king of Prussia realized his danger and promised to summon an assembly to draft the constitution which the liberals demanded. He also agreed to lead a movement for a united Germany free from the domination of Austria.

The diet of the Confederation arranged that a national assembly of representatives chosen from all the German states should meet to draft a constitution at Frankfurt in May, 1848.

357

But in Germany, as well as in her own realms, Austria was aided by lack of unity among her enemies. (1) It was impossible to exclude Austria altogether from the boundaries of the new German state. The Assembly therefore agreed to include those parts of her realms which had belonged to the Confederation formed in 1815 (p. 341). The new union thus included both Prussia and Austria—two rival European powers.

(2) The new constitution provided for a hereditary emperor, and the position was offered to the king of Prussia. But Frederick William IV, fearing that there would be war with Austria, refused the crown.

This decision made the year's work of the Frankfurt Parliament fruitless. The hope of getting a better constitution for the German Confederation was given up, and the Assembly dispersed. Austria now insisted on the re-establishment of the old diet, and Prussia submitted. Many German republicans came to America during this troubled period.

Results of the Revolution in Prussia and Italy · Disappointing though the revolutions of 1848 were to liberals, they had certain important effects on the future of Germany and Italy. The king of Prussia granted his country a constitution in 1850. With some few modifications, it served Prussia until 1918.

The constitution provided for a ministry, but made it responsible to the king rather than to parliament. The diet, or parliament, was composed of a house of lords and a house of deputies. All men over twenty-five years of age could vote, but the system was so arranged that the rich controlled the selection of deputies.

Piedmont, which was to be the center of a new Italy, also obtained a constitution. And it was not long, as we shall see, before the king of Prussia founded a German Empire and the king of Sardinia became ruler of a united Italy. Poland, Hungary, and Bohemia, however, were destined to wait until 1919 to gain their independence.

CHECK ON YOUR READING

1. *How did (a) Belgium become independent? (b) Poland become a Russian province?*
2. *Why did the revolts at first succeed, and then fail, in (a) Bohemia, (b) Hungary, (c) Italy, (d) Germany?*
3. *What prevented the unification of Germany at Frankfurt?*
4. *What gains were made in Germany and Italy as a result of revolutions in 1848?*

"The Congress makes no progress; it dances."
—CHARLES JOSEPH, Prince de Ligne

"The American continents . . . are henceforth not to be considered as subjects for future colonization by any European power."—JAMES MONROE

"Democracy is the recurrent suspicion that more than half of the people are right more than half of the time."
—E. B. WHITE

Learning Activities

Think about the chapter

1. Explain this statement concerning the allies who met at Vienna: "They had learned nothing and forgotten nothing."

2. Define and diagram the terms *reactionary, conservative, moderate, liberal,* and *radical*. Illustrate each by some event or person in this chapter.

3. Explain how "repression breeds revolt."

4. How did Louis Napoleon's methods compare with those of his uncle?

5. Why was Vienna the center of the conflict in Prussia and Italy, as well as in Austria and Hungary?

6. Why is this period called the "Age of Metternich"?

7. What was there about the make-up of Austria and Hungary that made it difficult to set up a liberal government in either country?

8. Map study: On a large map of Europe (a) show the territorial settlements made in 1815; (b) where revolutions occurred between 1815–1848.

Go beyond the text

9. Give a report on the diplomacy of Talleyrand and what he obtained for France.

10. What did England get at the Congress of Vienna?

11. Prepare a short report on the character and accomplishments of Bolívar, San Martín, O'Higgins, or Iturbide.

12. How do you account for the effectiveness of the Monroe Doctrine?

13. Louis Blanc, a journalist, was a leader of socialist thought in France. Find out what his plan for national workshops really was and why he criticized the plan set up in 1848.

14. Some French, Poles, Hungarians, Italians, and many Germans migrated to the United States during this period. Report on reasons for their coming and show on a map the areas where large numbers settled.

Follow up your special interests

15. Scan the newspapers for several days for items showing that the Metternich system is still in effect in some parts of the world.

16. Write a "You Are There" program covering highlights of the Congress of Vienna.

17. Make a chart headed "Nationalism: Successes and Failures, 1815–1848." List the nationalist movements by countries, dates, leaders, and outcomes by the end of 1848.

18. Play a recording of Chopin's "Revolutionary Etude" (Etude in C Minor). Tell some of the interesting episodes of Chopin's life.

READ FURTHER

Basic readings: (1) BAUER and PEYSER, *How Music Grew*, Chap. 26. (2) BECKER, *Modern History*, Chaps. 10–11. (3) CARR, *Men of Power*. Bolívar. (4) HOFFMAN, *News of the World*, Nos. 45, 46. (5) ROBINSON, *Readings*, Chap. 39. (6) SCOTT, BALTZLY, *Readings*, Chaps. 1, 2, 5. (7) VAN LOON, *Story of Mankind*, pp. 361–401. (8) Year's *Pictorial History*, pp. 416–422, 432–439, 443–445.

Special accounts: (9) G. FOSTER, *George Washington's World*. (10) M. LANSING, *Liberators and Heroes of South America*. (11) A. PECK, *Pageant of Middle American History* and *Pageant of Latin-American Peoples*. (12) J. SCHAPIRO, *Modern European History*. (13) F. SIMPSON, *The Rise of Louis Napoleon*.

Fiction and biography: (14) N. BAKER, *He Wouldn't Be King*. The story of Simón Bolívar. (15) W. CRESSON, *Diplomatic Portraits*. About Alexander I, Castlereagh, Talleyrand, and Metternich. (16) V. HUGO, *Les Miserables*. Jean Valjean was released from prison in 1815; his story reveals social conditions in France. (17) A. WHITRIDGE, *Men in Crisis*. Excellent chapter on Louis Kossuth. (18) T. YBARRA, *Verdi, Miracle Man of Opera*. Tells of the revolutionary struggles in Italy as well as the life of the composer.

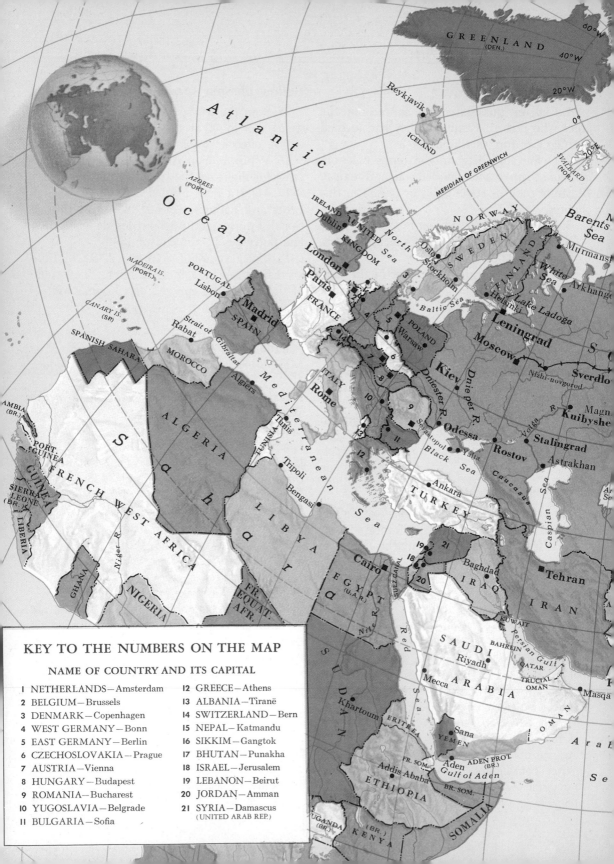

GREENLAND (DEN.)

60°W
40°W
20°W
0°

Atlantic

Ocean

Reykjavik

ICELAND

MERIDIAN OF GREENWICH

20°W

AZORES (PORT.)

SVALBARD (NOR.)

Barents Sea

Murmansk

MADEIRA IS. (PORT.)

PORTUGAL

Lisbon

IRELAND

Dublin

UNITED KINGDOM

London

North Sea

NORWAY

Oslo

SWEDEN

Stockholm

FINLAND

Helsinki

White Sea

Arkhangel

CANARY IS. (SP)

SPANISH SAHARA

Rabat

SPAIN

Madrid

Strait of Gibraltar

PORTUGAL

FRANCE

Paris

Baltic Sea

POLAND

Warsaw

Lake Ladoga

Leningrad

Moscow

Sverdlo

MOROCCO

Algiers

Mediterranean Sea

ITALY

Rome

Kiev

Dnieper R.

Dniester R.

Nizhni-novgorod

AMBIA (BR.)

PORT. GUINEA

GUINEA

SIERRA LEONE (BR.)

LIBERIA

GHANA

SPANISH SAHARA

FRENCH WEST AFRICA

Sahara

ALGERIA

TUNISIA

Tunis

Tripoli

Bengasi

LIBYA

Black Sea

Sevastopol

Yalta

Odessa

Rostov

Stalingrad

Astrakhan

Volga R.

Kuibyshe

Magn

Caucasus

Caspian Sea

Niger R.

NIGERIA

FR. EQUAT. AFR.

EGYPT (U.A.R.)

Cairo

Ankara

TURKEY

Baghdad

IRAQ

Tehran

IRAN

KUWAIT

Persian Gulf

BAHREIN

QATAR

TRUCIAL OMAN

Masqa

SUEZ CANAL

Nile R.

Red Sea

SUDAN

Khartoum

ERITREA

SAUDI ARABIA

Riyadh

Mecca

Sana

YEMEN

OMAN

Arab

FR. SOM.

Aden

ADEN PROT. (BR.)

Gulf of Aden

BR. SOM.

Addis Ababa

ETHIOPIA

SOMALIA

UGANDA (BR.)

KENYA (BR.)

Se

KEY TO THE NUMBERS ON THE MAP

NAME OF COUNTRY AND ITS CAPITAL

1 NETHERLANDS—Amsterdam
2 BELGIUM—Brussels
3 DENMARK—Copenhagen
4 WEST GERMANY—Bonn
5 EAST GERMANY—Berlin
6 CZECHOSLOVAKIA—Prague
7 AUSTRIA—Vienna
8 HUNGARY—Budapest
9 ROMANIA—Bucharest
10 YUGOSLAVIA—Belgrade
11 BULGARIA—Sofia

12 GREECE—Athens
13 ALBANIA—Tiranë
14 SWITZERLAND—Bern
15 NEPAL—Katmandu
16 SIKKIM—Gangtok
17 BHUTAN—Punakha
18 ISRAEL—Jerusalem
19 LEBANON—Beirut
20 JORDAN—Amman
21 SYRIA—Damascus
(UNITED ARAB REP)

EURASIA
POLITICAL-PHYSICAL

0   400   800   1200   1600

AVERAGE SCALE OF MILES

Size of place name indicates relative size of population

Arctic Ocean

Chukchee Sea

Bering Sea

INTERNATIONAL DATE LINE

160°E   180°   160°E   140°E   120°E   100°E

WRANGEL I.

East Siberian Sea

Laptev Sea

Lena R.

Kamchatka

Sea of Okhotsk

SAKHALIN

KURILES

ARCTIC CIRCLE

Yenesei R.

SOVIET UNION

TRANS-SIBERIAN

Irkutsk

Novosibirsk

Lake Baikal

R.R.

Ulan Bator

MONGOLIAN PEOPLE'S REPUBLIC

Mts.   The Gobi

Altai

Amur R.

MANCHURIA

Harbin

Mukden

Port Arthur   Dairen

Peking

Shantung Pen.

Kiaochow Bay

Hwang Ho

Chang-an

Vladivostok

KOREA Sea

Pyongyang

NORTH KOREA   Seoul   Pusan

Japan

Sea of Japan

Tokyo

Kyoto   JAPAN

Hiroshima

Nagasaki

Shanghai

Nanking

East China Sea

RYUKYU IS.

OKINAWA

IWO JIMA

Pacific Ocean

GUAM

Tian Shan

Tarim R.   Tarim Busin

Kunlun Mts.

CHINA

Yangtze Kiang

Chungking

Foochow   Amoy

Canton

Macao (PORT.)   Victoria HONG KONG (BR.)

Taipei   TAIWAN (FORMOSA)

Lake Balkhash

Alma-Ata

TIBET

Lhasa

Himalaya

Mt. Everest   15   17   16

EAST PAKISTAN

New Delhi

Lucknow

HINDUSTAN

TROPIC OF CANCER

Calcutta

INDIA

Hyderabad

Madras

Calicut

CEYLON

Colombo

Ganges R.

BURMA

Rangoon

Hanoi   TONKIN

NORTH VIETNAM

Vientiane   LAOS

ANNAM

Mekong

THAILAND (SIAM)

Bangkok

CAMBODIA

Phnom Penh

SOUTH VIETNAM

Saigon-Cholon

South China Sea

Manila Bay

Quezon City   PHILIPPINES

LEYTE

EQUATOR

Hollandia

MOLUCCAS

Bay of Bengal

ANDAMAN IS.

Kra Peninsula

MALAYA

Kuala Lumpur

Singapore (BR.)

BRUNEI (BR.)   N. BORNEO (BR.)

SARAWAK (BR.)

BORNEO

CELEBES

REP. OF INDONESIA

TIMOR (PORT.)

Indian Ocean

GOA (PORT.)

Yavlovsk

Irtysh R.

Yenesei R.

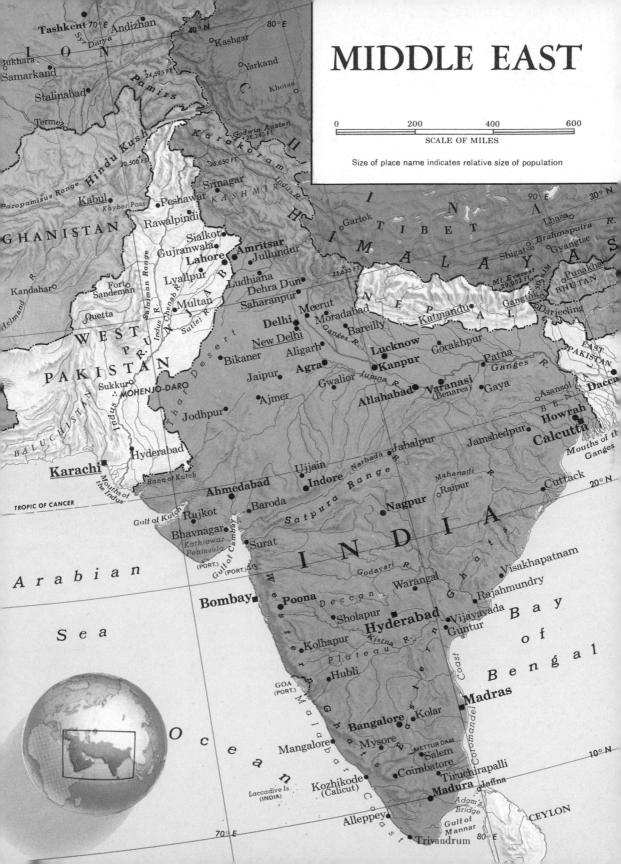

MIDDLE EAST

| 0 | 200 | 400 | 600 |

SCALE OF MILES

Size of place name indicates relative size of population

Tashkent 70°E Andizhan 40°N 80°E
Syr Darya
Bukhara Samarkand Kashgar
Stalinabad Yarkand
Pamirs
Terme Khotan
24,595 FT.
Godwin Austen
28,245 FT.
Karakoram
Paropamisus Range Kabul Srinagar 29,500 FT.
Khyber Pass Peshawar KASHMIR Indus R.
GHANISTAN Rawalpindi
TIBET Gartok Lhasa
HIMALAYAS
Shigatse Brahmaputra R.
Gyangtse
SIKKIM Punakha
Sialkot 25,435 FT. Mt. Everest Gangtok BHUTAN
Gujranwala Amritsar 29,002 FT. Darjeeling
Lahore Jullundur
Lyallpur Ludhiana NEPAL EAST
Multan Dehra Dun PAKISTAN
Saharanpur Katmandu
Delhi Meerut Moradabad
Bikaner New Delhi Bareilly Gorakhpur
Aligarh Lucknow Patna Ganges R.
Jaipur Agra Kanpur Asansol BENGAL Dacca
Gwalior Jumna Varanasi Gaya Howrah
Ajmer Allahabad (Benares) Jamshedpur Calcutta
Jodhpur Mouths of the Ganges
Thar Desert
Ujjain Jabalpur Mahanadi R. Cuttack
Hyderabad Indore Narbada R.
Ahmedabad Satpura Range Nagpur Raipur
TROPIC OF CANCER Baroda 20°N
Rajkot INDIA
Bhavnagar Visakhapatnam
Surat Godavari R. Rajahmundry
Warangal
Arabian Bombay Poona Deccan Bay
Sholapur Hyderabad Vijayavada of
Sea Kolhapur Kistna R. Guntur Bengal
Plateau
Hubli
GOA Madras
(PORT.) Bangalore Kolar
Mangalore Mysore METTUR DAM
Ocean Salem
Coimbatore Tiruchirapalli
Laccadive Is. Kozhikode Madura Jaffna
(INDIA) (Calicut) Adam's CEYLON
Bridge
70°E Alleppey Gulf of 80°E
Trivandrum Mannar 10°N

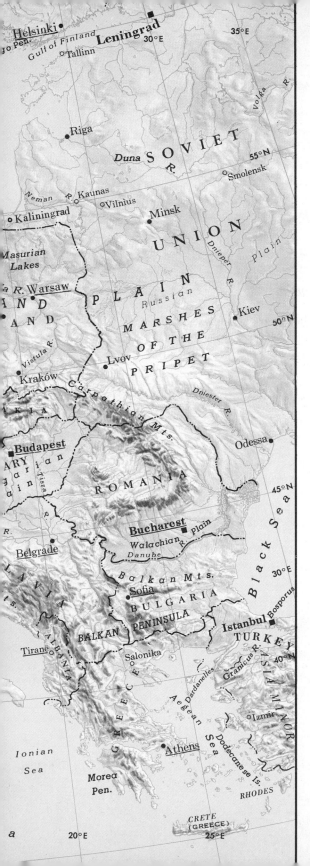

EUROPE
PHYSICAL

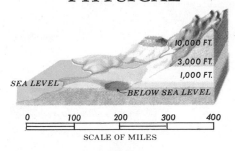

10,000 FT.

3,000 FT.

1,000 FT.

SEA LEVEL

BELOW SEA LEVEL

0   100   200   300   400

SCALE OF MILES

Size of place name indicates relative size of population

Geography Influences History in Many Ways · *Mountains*, such as the Alps and Pyrenees, are natural defenses against invasions. *Plains*, such as those of northern France, Germany, Poland, and Russia, however, are natural routes for invading armies. *Rivers*, such as the Rhine and Danube, may be barriers, or invasion routes, or highways of commerce. Can you see how?

Note the influence of the *seas* and *oceans* upon such seafaring peoples as the Phoenicians, Greeks, Norsemen, Italians, English, Dutch, and Portuguese. Consider too the power which goes to nations which control *strategic corridors*, such as mountain passes (Thermopylae and Brenner), man-made canals (Suez and Kiel), and narrow straits (the Bosporus, the Dardanelles, and Gibraltar).

Possession of *natural resources*, such as iron, copper, precious metals, coal, petroleum, fertile land, and fresh water, has likewise had great influence on the course of human events.

Geography was a key factor in the *growth of cities*. How do you think it influenced Athens? Rome? Istanbul? Venice? Paris? London? Antwerp? Cologne? Vienna? Budapest? Stockholm?

As for *climate*, the great powers of modern history are located in the middle latitudes where more temperate conditions stimulate human endeavor.

10°W 5°W Shetland Islands 60°N 0° MERIDIAN OF GREENWICH 5°E 10°E 15°E

Bergen NORWAY SWED—

Oslo

Stoc—

Hebrides

Orkney Islands

55°N

Moray Firth

Göteborg

SCOTLAND

Skagerrak Kattegat

North

Firth of Forth

Londonderry

Edinburgh

Glasgow

DENMARK

Sea

Copenhagen Malmö

UNITED KINGDOM

ULSTER Belfast

Irish Sea

REPUBLIC OF IRELAND

Dublin

Leeds

HELIGOLAND Kiel Lübeck

B—

Liverpool Manchester

Sz—

Sheffield

Amsterdam

The Wash

Hamburg Bremen

EAST

St. Georges Channel

WALES

Birmingham

The Hague

North

Potsdam Elbe R. Berlin

Cork

Cardiff

London

NETHERLANDS WESTPHALIA Hannover

German Plain Oder

Bristol Channel

Greenwich

Rotterdam Essen THE RUHR Cologne WEST

Leipzig

Bristol

Canterbury

Antwerp Bonn GERMANY

Plymouth Portsmouth

Dover

BELGIUM LUX.

Dresden

Weimar

50°N

Calais Lille

Brussels

Frankfurt

Dunkirk

Channel

English

Le Havre

Rouen

Reims LORRAINE

Nürnberg

CZE—

P—

Cherbourg

Seine

Paris

Verdun Strasbourg

GERMANY

Brest

NORMANDY

Versailles

Chateau Thierry

ALSACE Rhine R.

Stuttgart

BRITTANY

Orleans

Munich

Loire

Belfort

Danu—

45°N

Nantes R.

FRANCE

Zürich SWITZ.

AUSTR—

Bay

Bern Lausanne

of

Geneva Lausanne

Locarno

A L P S

Biscay

Bordeaux

Lyon

Mt. Blanc 15,737 FT.

Trieste

Cape Finisterre

Garonne R.

Rhône R.

Milan

Venice

Vigo

Bilbao

Toulouse

Avignon

Turin

Genoa Bologna

Oporto

Pyrenees AND.

Nice

Rapallo

Florence

A P E N N I—

Ebro R.

Marseille Toulon

CORSICA (FR.)

Zaragoza

Ajaccio

I T A L—

40°N

Madrid

Barcelona

Rome

S P A I N

Lisbon

PORTUGAL

Tagus R.

MAJORCA

MINORCA

SARDINIA (ITALY)

Naples

Valencia

Balearic Islands (SPAIN)

Cagliari

Tyrrhenian Sea

Cordova

Cape St. Vincent

Seville

Granada

Mediterranean

Palermo

Cadiz

Málaga

GIBRALTAR (BR.)

SIC—

Strait of Gibraltar Tangier

MALT— (BR.)

35°N

Algiers

Bizerte

Tunis

Oran

MOROCCO 5°W

0°

ALGERIA

5°E

TUNISIA 10°E

EUROPE
POLITICAL

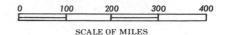

SCALE OF MILES

Size of place name indicates relative size of population

Geography Affects Political Decisions · The lure of *warm water ports* brought Russian invasions of Poland, Lithuania, Latvia, and Finland on the Baltic; of Rumania, Bulgaria, and Turkey on the Black Sea; and constant pressure upon the straits which barred Russia's outlet from the Black Sea to the Mediterranean.

Poland's *lack of defensible frontiers* encouraged partitions by Russia, Prussia, and Austria. The strategic geographic position of Belgium and the Netherlands in the very "cockpit of Europe" led to their neutralization by England, France, and Germany.

The control of the *headwaters* of the Rhine, Rhone, and Danube rivers, and of the *vital passes and tunnels* through the Alps, resulted in the guarantee of Swiss neutrality by France, Germany, and Italy.

After repeated conflict, political control of the Danube River, which is the *vital transportation artery* for Austria, Hungary, Yugoslavia, Rumania, and Bulgaria, has been "internationalized" under a Danubian Commission, representing these nations.

England's *island position* has greatly influenced many of her political decisions regarding the "balance of power" on the continent of Europe, her "lifeline to India" (via Gibraltar, Malta, Suez, and Aden), her basic reliance upon seapower, and her concern with conditions of international trade.

367

ARCTIC OCEAN

GREENLAND

ARCTIC CIR

ALASKA

ALEUTIAN IS.

CANADA

Hudson
Bay

NEWFOUNDLAND

KIN

PACIFIC

UNITED STATES

ATLANTIC

PORT

SPAN
SAHARA

TROPIC OF CANCER

HAWAIIAN
IS.

MEXICO

Gulf of
Mexico

CUBA

DOMINICAN
REP.

PUERTO RICO

HAITI

Caribbean Sea

BR. HON.
HONDURAS

GUATEMALA
EL SALVADOR
NICARAGUA
COSTA RICA
PANAMA

GAMBIA
PORT. GUINEA

SIERRA LEONE

LI

G

OCEAN

VENEZUELA

GUIANAS
BR.
SUR.
FR.

OCEAN

COLOMBIA

ECUADOR

PHOENIX
IS.

LINE IS.

EQUATOR

PERU

BRAZIL

MARQUESAS
IS.

TONGA
IS.

SOCIETY
IS.

BOLIVIA

PARAGUAY

TROPIC OF CAPRICORN

CHILE

ARGENTINA

URUGUAY

COUNTRIES WHICH ARE MEMBERS OF THE
UNITED NATIONS ARE SHOWN IN BLACK

FALKLAND IS.

S. GEORGIA I.

AF

368

10-1-59

TODAY'S

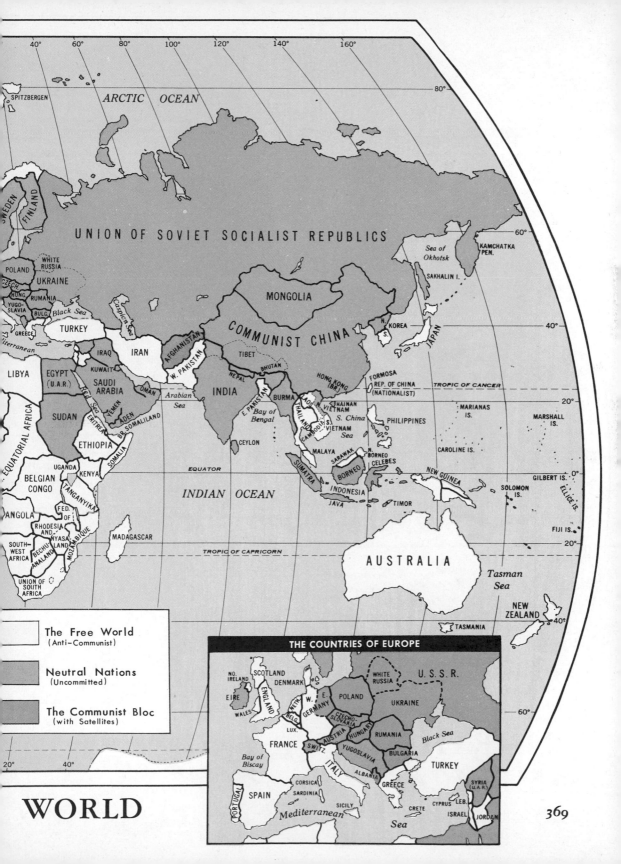

40°   60°   80°   100°   120°   140°   160°

SPITZBERGEN

ARCTIC   OCEAN

80°

SWEDEN

FINLAND

UNION OF SOVIET SOCIALIST REPUBLICS

KAMCHATKA PEN.

60°

Sea of Okhotsk

POLAND

WHITE RUSSIA

SAKHALIN I.

UKRAINE

CZECH.
HUNG.
RUMANIA
YUGO-SLAVIA
BULG.

Black Sea

MONGOLIA

N. KOREA
S. KOREA

JAPAN

40°

GREECE

TURKEY

COMMUNIST CHINA

Mediterranean

IRAQ

IRAN

AFGHANISTAN

Caspian Sea

TIBET

HONG KONG (BR.)

FORMOSA
REP. OF CHINA (NATIONALIST)

TROPIC OF CANCER

LIBYA

EGYPT (U.A.R.)

KUWAIT

W. PAKISTAN

NEPAL

BHUTAN

SAUDI ARABIA

OMAN

Red Sea

YEMEN

ADEN

Arabian Sea

E. PAKISTAN

INDIA

BURMA

LAOS

N. VIETNAM

HAINAN S. China Sea

MARIANAS IS.

20°

MARSHALL IS.

SUDAN

BR. SOMALILAND

THAILAND

CAMBODIA

S. VIETNAM

Bay of Bengal

CEYLON

PHILIPPINES

EQUATORIAL AFRICA

ETHIOPIA

ERITREA

SOMALIA

MALAYA

SARAWAK

N. BORNEO

CELEBES

CAROLINE IS.

ETHIOPIA

UGANDA

KENYA

SUMATRA

BORNEO

NEW GUINEA

GILBERT IS.   0°

EQUATOR

BELGIAN CONGO

TANGANYIKA

INDONESIA

SOLOMON IS.

ELLICE IS.

ANGOLA

FED. OF

INDIAN OCEAN

JAVA

TIMOR

FIJI IS.

RHODESIA AND NYASALAND

MOZAMBIQUE

MADAGASCAR

TROPIC OF CAPRICORN

20°

SOUTH-WEST AFRICA

BECHUANALAND

AUSTRALIA

UNION OF SOUTH AFRICA

Tasman Sea

NEW ZEALAND

40°

TASMANIA

20°   40°

The Free World
(Anti–Communist)

Neutral Nations
(Uncommitted)

The Communist Bloc
(with Satellites)

THE COUNTRIES OF EUROPE

NO. IRELAND

SCOTLAND

DENMARK

WHITE RUSSIA

U.S.S.R.

EIRE

ENGLAND

W. GERMANY

E. GERMANY

POLAND

UKRAINE

WALES

NETH.

BELG.

LUX.

CZECHO-SLOVAKIA

FRANCE

SWITZ.

AUSTRIA

HUNGARY

RUMANIA

Black Sea

YUGOSLAVIA

BULGARIA

Bay of Biscay

ITALY

ALBANIA

GREECE

TURKEY

CORSICA

SYRIA (U.A.R.)

PORTUGAL

SPAIN

SARDINIA

SICILY

CRETE

CYPRUS

LEB.

ISRAEL

JORDAN

Mediterranean   Sea

WORLD

369

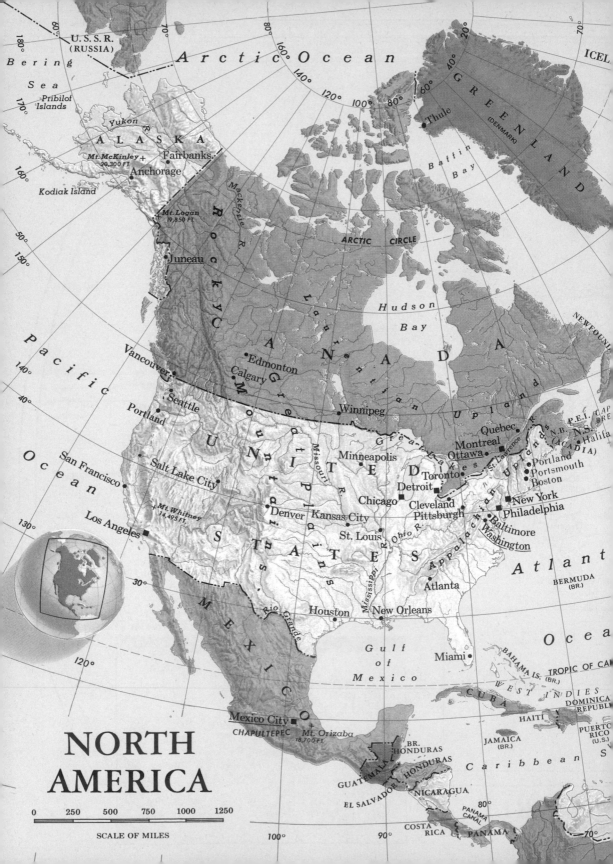

Bering
Sea

*Pribilof
Islands*

U.S.S.R.
(RUSSIA)

180°

170°

160°

150°

Pacific

Ocean

130°

A r c t i c   O c e a n

90°

80°

70°

60°

70°

ICEL

G R E E N L A N D
(DENMARK)

Baffin
Bay

Thule

70°

160°

140°

120°

100°

80°

60°

Yukon R.

A L A S K A

Mt. McKinley +
20,300 FT.

Fairbanks

Anchorage

Kodiak Island

Mackenzie R.

Mt. Logan
19,850 FT.

50°

Juneau

40°

140°

50°

R o c k y

M o u n t a i n s

C A N A D A

Laurentian

ARCTIC   CIRCLE

H u d s o n
B a y

Laurentian   Upland

NEWFOU

Vancouver

Edmonton

Calgary

Winnipeg

Great Lakes

St. Lawrence R.

Quebec

Montreal

Ottawa

P.E.I.
N.B.   N.S.   CA
(ACADIA)   BRE
Halifa

Seattle

Portland

U N I T E D

Minneapolis

Toronto

Detroit

Uplands

Portland
Portsmouth
Boston

40°

San Francisco

Salt Lake City

Missouri R.

Chicago

Cleveland
Pittsburgh

New York

Philadelphia

30°

Los Angeles

Mt. Whitney
14,495 FT.

Denver

Kansas City

St. Louis

Ohio R.

Baltimore
Washington

Appalachian

S T A T E S

Great Plains

A t l a n t

BERMUDA
(BR.)

130°

120°

30°

M E X I C O

Rio Grande

Mississippi R.

Houston

New Orleans

Atlanta

Miami

G u l f
o f
M e x i c o

BAHAMA IS.   TROPIC OF CA
(BR.)

O c e a

W E S T   *I N D I E S*

C U B A

DOMINICA
REPUBL

Mexico City

CHAPULTEPEC

Mt. Orizaba
18,700 FT.

NORTH
AMERICA

BR.
HONDURAS

GUATEMALA

HONDURAS

EL SALVADOR   NICARAGUA

COSTA
RICA   PANAMA

HAITI

JAMAICA
(BR.)

PUERTO
RICO
(U.S.)

C a r i b b e a n

80°

PANAMA
CANAL

70°

100°

90°

0   250   500   750   1000   1250

SCALE OF MILES

SOUTH AMERICA

SCALE OF MILES

| 0 | 250 | 500 | 750 | 1000 | 1250 |

Size of place name indicates relative size of population

Havana 80°

C U B A

W E S T
I N D I E S
70°   60°

JAMAICA
(BR.)

HAITI

DOMINICAN
REPUBLIC

PUERTO
RICO
(U.S.)

BR. HONDURAS

HONDURAS

COSTA
RICA

NICARAGUA

PANAMA

PANAMA CANAL

C a r i b b e a n   S e a

Barranquilla
Cartagena

Maracaibo

Lake
Maracaibo

Caracas

TRINIDAD (BR.)
Port-of-Spain

VENEZUELA

Medellín

Magdalena R.

Bogotá

COLOMBIA

Orinoco R.

Georgetown
BR.
GUIANA

Paramaribo

SURINAM
(NETH.)

FR.
GUIANA

Cayenne

EQUATOR

ÁPAGOS IS.
CUADOR)

0°

Quito

ECUADOR

Guayaquil

Iquitos

Rio   Negro

Manaus

Amazon   R.

Amazon   R.

Belém
(Pará)

Fortaleza

Madeira R.

Tocantins R.

P E R U

Lima

Cuzco

Lake Titicaca

La Paz

B O L I V I A

Sucre

Arequipa

Arica

Iquique

B R A Z I L

Cuiabá

R.

São Francisco R.

Recife

Maceió
10°

Salvador
(Baía)

Belo Horizonte

Antofagasta

PARAGUAY

Asunción

Paraguay R.

São Paulo

Santos

Rio de Janeiro
20°

Tucumán

Paraná R.

Pôrto Alegre

TROPIC OF CAPRICORN

Córdoba

Mendoza

Rosario

URUGUAY

Montevideo

Río de la Plata

30°

Valparaíso

Santiago

Buenos Aires

Concepción

Bahía Blanca

P a c i f i c   O c e a n

A t l a n t i c   O c e a n

40°

Puerto Montt

Andes Mountains

Chilean Mountains

A R G E N T I N A

FALKLAND IS.
(BR.)

Strait of
Magellan

Punta Arenas

TIERRA DEL FUEGO

Cape Horn

100°   90°   80°   50°   60°   50°   40°   30°   20°

50°

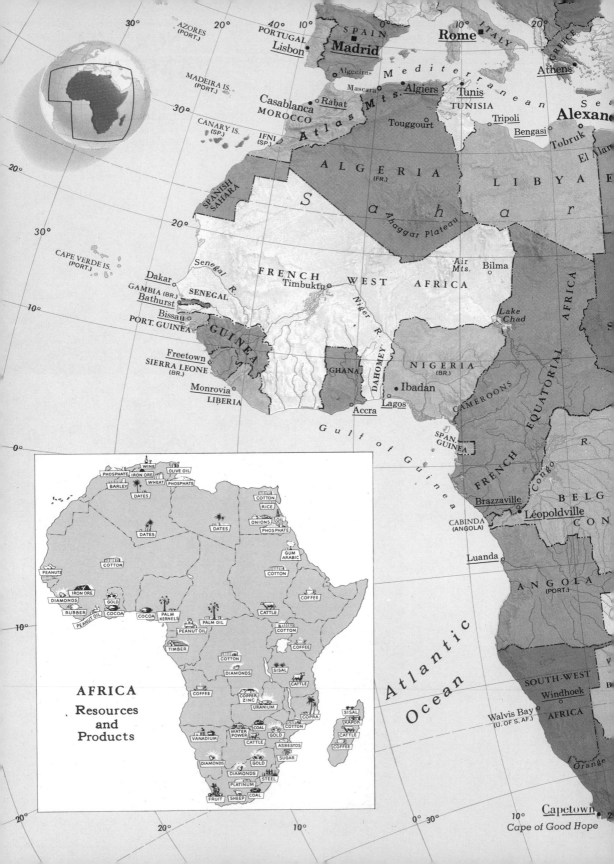

AFRICA

| 0 | 250 | 500 | 750 | 1000 | 1250 |

SCALE OF MILES

Size of place name indicates relative size of population

The Spotlight Is on Africa · "The darkest thing about Africa," someone has said, "has alway been our ignorance of it." For over four hundred years the principal lines of world travel and trade have run east and west—between Europe, America, and Asia. The great land mass of Africa (one-fifth of the world's land area) was only a barrier to be sailed around.

Among the geographical barriers which had to be overcome before the continent could be known were the rugged Atlas mountains in the northwest, the vast Sahara Desert west of the Nile, and the sweltering jungles of the interior. As a consequence, therefore, Europeans tended to settle along Africa's coastal fringe.

In ancient and medieval times, however, the Mediterranean Sea was the principal highway for the exchange of goods and ideas. Along its southern shores were the great north African empires of the Egyptians, Cathaginians, and Moors. These people were in constant contact with the civilizations of Greece, Rome, and medieval Europe.

During the nineteenth century the demands of the Industrial Revolution for raw materials and markets and the desires of the national states for empires led the great powers of Europe to seize portions of Africa. Note the areas taken by England, France, Spain, Portugal, Italy, and Germany. What important products and resources made these holdings especially valuable? (See inset map, page 372.)

Today the fires of nationalism burn brightly among the peoples of Africa. The map on page 644 will help mark the countries which already have won their independence.

373

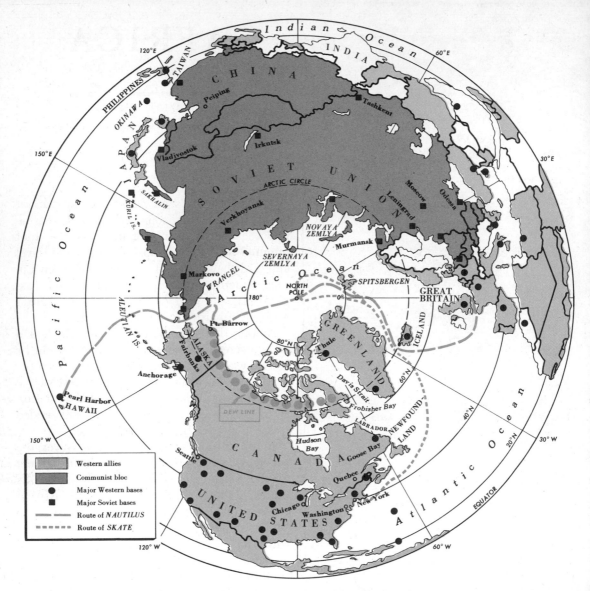

The Arctic · Until modern times the Arctic
was deemed impassable except by dog team
and sled. But today the vast ocean of air over
the north polar region is regularly navigated by
planes following the shortest air routes between North America and Europe. Occasionally ice-breaker ships crush their way through
these frozen waters. And in August, 1958,
the American submarines Nautilus and Skate
made history by traveling under the polar
ice. Trace their routes on the map above.

The polar-projection world map on the flag
of the United Nations bespeaks the vital international importance of the Arctic region. The
United States air base at Thule, Greenland,
and the Distant Early Warning (DEW) line
of radar outposts bear witness to the significance of the area to the defense of Canada
and the United States. And Alaska's admit-
tance to the Union in 1959 focused anew the
attention of Americans upon the Arctic frontier.
Find the DEW line and defense bases.

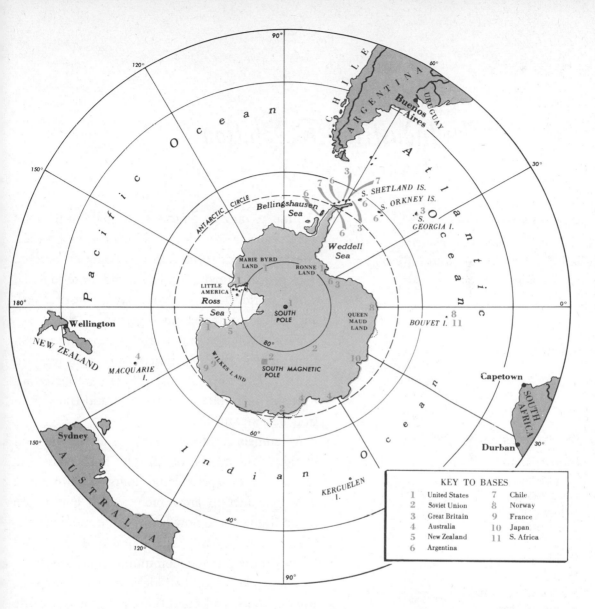

KEY TO BASES

1	United States	7	Chile
2	Soviet Union	8	Norway
3	Great Britain	9	France
4	Australia	10	Japan
5	New Zealand	11	S. Africa
6	Argentina		

Antarctica · Antarctica consists of the land and seas about the South Pole. Most of the continent (two-thirds the size of North America) lies beneath a huge cap of ice several thousand feet thick. Temperatures are far colder than in the Arctic. The presence of coal and fossilized plants, however, indicates that vegetation covered the region millions of years ago.

The first explorer to reach the South Pole was Raold Amundsen of Norway (1911).

American expeditions led by Richard E. Byrd in 1929 and subsequent years added significantly to our knowledge of the area. About a dozen nations now have bases for claims to portions of the continent.

In the International Geophysical Year 1957–1958 scientists of many countries, co-operating in a gigantic world-wide study of the earth, seas, and skies, made special studies here. Their co-operative efforts renew hopes for the eventual internationalization of the region.

CHAPTER 22

The Industrial Revolution

CHAPTER OUTLINE

1. *The Coming of Machinery*
2. *Effects of the Industrial Revolution*
3. *The Rise of Socialism*

KEY WORDS AND DATES

Industrial Revolution
"spinning jenny"
Hargreaves
Arkwright
Crompton
Cartwright
Whitney
Watt
domestic system
factory system
mass production
law of supply and demand
trade unions
capitalists
socialism
Utopians
Marx
means of production
Communist Manifesto
incentives
Fabian Society

WHILE PATRIOTIC LIBERALS throughout Europe were fighting the injustice of the old order, another kind of revolution was going on quietly. This *peaceful* revolution finally did more to make a new world than all the new laws, constitutions, and political reforms put together.

This revolution was the creative work of patient inventors. Machinery was first used in cloth-making operations. Then gradually all forms of manufacturing, mining, and transportation became mechanized.

Machinery revolutionized ways of working and living. Thousands of people flocked to the towns. They spent long hours operating the new machines in great factories for low wages. More things could now be made for more people. Cheap newspapers and books and improved transportation made communication easier.

The workers soon had ideas of their own about wages, hours, and conditions of labor. Because they formed such a large part of the population, they gradually made their demands felt. So it was that machinery not only transformed industry, but gradually broke down the old order.

The loudest critics of the old order were the socialists. Using the arguments of Karl Marx, they demanded revolutionary changes. Socialism grew rapidly in spite of serious flaws in the theories of Marx.

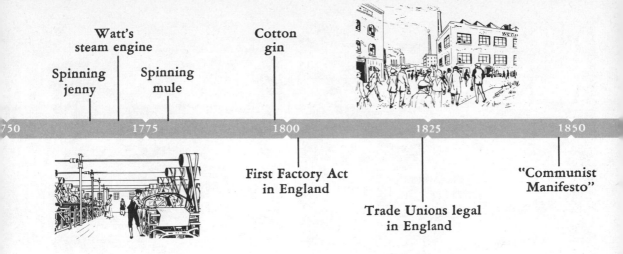

| 750 | 1775 | 1800 | 1825 | 1850 |

Spinning
jenny

Watt's
steam engine

Spinning
mule

Cotton
gin

First Factory Act
in England

Trade Unions legal
in England

"Communist
Manifesto"

1. The Coming of Machinery

The Industrial Revolution · Until about 1800 the people of western Europe continued to till their fields, weave their cloth, and make their living mostly by hand. They had simple machines, such as spinning wheels, but they were operated by hand. They had only the strength of horses or other animals to move their vehicles. And then a great change took place. A series of inventions revolutionized every branch of industry in a few generations and created the Western world as we know it today. This change is known as the Industrial Revolution.

The Industrial Revolution substituted the power and tireless energy of the machine for human and animal power. Machines lessened the time and labor of production and multiplied the output. Engines to pull trains of cars and to propel ships permitted men and goods to be carried from place to place in a fraction of the time formerly required. Machinery on the farm greatly increased agricultural production.

Let us see how this revolution began and some of the ways in which it affected the development of the Western world. We may then be able to understand the tremendous changes which face much of Latin America, the Middle East, Asia, and Africa, where an industrial revolution is barely under way today.

Change in Methods of Spinning · There are, as we know, two processes in the making of fabrics: (1) *spinning* the threads and (2) *weaving* them into cloth. Until well into the eighteenth century both these operations had been carried on by hand. Then, about 1770, a number of devices were introduced into the manufacture of cotton goods which revolutionized this important industry.

By the old method of spinning it was possible for a person to draw out, by hand, only a single thread at a time. This way was, of course, very slow. Then, in the eighteenth century, came a great demand in England for cotton goods similar to the calicoes brought from India. There was need of a device which would spin more rapidly and supply thread as fast as the weavers could use it.

Hargreaves's Improved Spinning Jenny (c. 1770) · *One worker using the above machine could now spin 64 threads. Why was Hargreaves unpopular at first?*

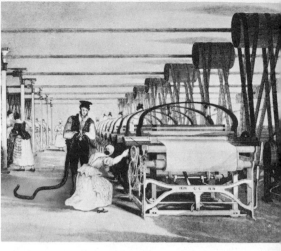

Cotton Weaving by Power Loom (1835) · *What was the source of power? How was it harnessed? How are modern mills powered? Note the costumes of the time.*

About 1764 James Hargreaves, an English weaver, invented a frame with eight spindles. This enabled a workman, by turning a wheel, to spin eight threads at a time. He could thus do the work of eight spinners. Hargreaves named his invention the "spinning jenny," after his wife.

Five years later a barber named Richard Arkwright patented a device which drew out the fibers between rollers and then twisted them into thread by revolving spindles. This machine was soon operated by water power and came to be called the "water frame."

The water frame was too large to be set up in private homes. Therefore Arkwright was soon installing them in factories for manufacturers who wished to produce goods on a large scale. Moving the spinning of thread out of private homes and into factories using power-driven machinery was a real revolution. Arkwright is often called the "father of the factory system."

In 1779 Samuel Crompton invented the spinning "mule." It combined some of the features of the jenny and the water frame. Soon machines spinning two hundred threads at the same time were in use. As they were driven by power and required only one or two watchers, they produced thread so rapidly and cheaply that hand workers could not compete with them.

Changes in Methods of Weaving · The greatly increased supply of thread now called for a much more rapid weaving process than that of the old hand loom. Edmund Cartwright, an English clergyman, set to work to construct a loom run by water power (steam in 1789). This machine was clumsy, and it was some years before it was sufficiently improved to come into general use.

The hand weavers disliked the new methods, which temporarily threw them out of jobs. They were early victims of what is now called "technological unemployment," or loss of work due to the invention of improved machinery. Sometimes they wrecked the factories where the new machines were operated.

By 1830, however, power looms had largely taken the place of hand-weaving, and new workers had been trained to make them and to run them. In our modern factories one machine can do the work done by two hundred weavers in the old days.

One Invention Requires Another · Other inventions required by rapid changes in the cotton industry were machines for cleaning, opening, and combing the fibers before the thread was spun. The time needed for bleaching was reduced from several months to a few days by substituting chemicals for long exposure to sunlight. Chemical dyes were also introduced, and a machine was invented for printing patterns on cloth in place of the use of the old hand blocks.

The new spinning and weaving machines increased the demand for raw cotton. Cotton growers had to find a way to keep up with the mechanized cloth manufacture. In 1793 Eli Whitney, an American, invented the *cotton gin*. This device enabled a person to take the seeds out of three hundred pounds of cotton a day, instead of the five or six pounds formerly cleaned by a hand worker. One result of the tremendous demand for cotton was the great increase in demand for slave labor in the American South.

Need for Iron and Steel · The new mechanical devices greatly increased the demand for iron and steel. It was necessary to have a strong and durable material out of which machinery could be made.

Inventors had been finding new ways of smelting and forging iron. Coal (reduced to coke) began to supplant charcoal for softening the ore. The old-fashioned bellows gave way to great blast furnaces.

Improved processes for removing the foreign elements and making a purer and stronger form of iron and steel were developed. Heavy steam hammers were made which beat the metal into shape, and later these were replaced by great rollers which pressed the metal into sheets and bars. As a result of these and other improvements, better and cheaper iron and steel came on the market. It was used for machinery, boilers, and tools of all kinds.

Watt Harnesses Steam Power · Some more satisfactory form of power had to be found to run heavy machinery. Windmills were common, and waterfalls and streams had long been used to turn water wheels. But the wind was uncertain, and the streams were often low. The growth of industry required a new power which would be dependable and could be made to operate in factories located anywhere.

A simple steam engine was already in use for pumping water out of mines and squeezing the bellows for blast furnaces. But James Watt was the first to make the steam engine a practical device to furnish driving power. As an instrument-maker in Glasgow, he was asked about 1765 to repair the model of a steam engine invented sixty years earlier by an ingenious mechanic, Newcomen. Watt made the steam alternately push the piston back and forth. Thus wheels attached to it were given a *continuous* motion. Soon the steam engine was set to drive spinning machinery, and it was not long before the new engines were becoming commonplace.

Beginning of the Machine Age · The Industrial Revolution was not accomplished all at once. Indeed it did not get fully under way until about 1850. Thus almost

Early Gas Light and Mailbox ·
This street lamp follows the pattern of one designed for a whale-oil lantern by Ben Franklin.

a century passed before steam-powered machinery was widely adopted in all branches of manufacture in England.

Machine methods changed entirely the making of shoes, hats, woolen fabrics, furniture, building materials, and many other articles. Printing was revolutionized, and by 1827 a London newspaper could turn out on its new cylinder presses four thousand copies an hour.

Not only were old industries modernized, but many new ones appeared. Among them were heating and lighting by gas, the making of fine machine tools, canning, and the making of rubber and petroleum products. Improvements were constantly made which raised the quality of goods, lowered costs, and increased the output.

The steam engine made possible the steamboat and the locomotive, which displaced the sailing vessel and the stagecoach. Manufactured goods could then be moved much more rapidly. For a century or more, steam replaced water and wind in running machinery. Later, steam was largely replaced by gasoline and electricity.

Expansion of the Industrial Revolution · England was the first to develop the use of machinery in manufacturing. It thus had the advantage of a good start over other western European countries, which were occupied by the wars of the French Revolution and Napoleon. But after the establishment of peace in 1815, the Industrial Revolution spread to the Continent. It reached Belgium first. Rapid progress was made in modernizing the industry and transportation of that country.

France took hold of the new methods more slowly. She long clung to the making of finer and more luxurious articles by hand. It was not until after 1840 that machinery began to compete seriously with handwork in France. Her mining industry, however, showed great progress. The output of coal increased from 800,000 tons in 1815 to sixteen million tons in 1870.

Germany was even later than France in entering the race. After 1870, however, Germany made enormous strides and became the greatest industrial country on the Continent. In America the demands of the Civil War spurred industrialization.

CHECK ON YOUR READING

1. Define "Industrial Revolution."
2. What inventions and inventors revolutionized the manufacture of cloth?
3. Illustrate how one invention leads to another.
4. Why were iron and steel so important?
5. Explain how Watt harnessed steam power.
6. Define "machine age." When did it reach England? Belgium? France? Germany? the United States?

2. Effects of the Industrial Revolution

The "Domestic System" · Let us now consider some of the ways in which the new inventions changed the conditions under which people worked and lived. Before the Industrial Revolution, *manufacture* still meant literally "to make by hand" (Latin, *manu*, "by hand," *facere*, "to make"). Artisans owned their tools and made articles in their homes or small shops.

With the increase of wealth in England from the sixteenth century on, there had grown up a class of well-to-do businessmen. They had the money (capital) to buy up raw materials in quantity. These they put out to be *manufactured* into various articles by people in their homes. They paid the workers low wages for their monotonous labor, and then sold the finished products for as much profit as they could get. This is called the "domestic system" of industry because the operators still worked at home. Here they could still use part of their time to cultivate a plot of ground and raise food.

New Conditions under the Factory System · The introduction of machinery soon put an end to the domestic system. Hand workers found that they could not compete with the swift and tireless machines.

As markets grew, businessmen began to invest their capital in the newer industries. They put up large factories and in them installed machinery which was too expensive and too cumbersome to be operated in private houses. To have employment, workers now had to leave their homes and operate the new machines in the factories.

In the manufacturing towns the workers lived crowded together in long and unsightly rows of houses which were built around the factories. Thus came into existence the ugly tenement districts and unhealthy slums in our modern cities. Lacking the local government which later developed, cities could not cope with their unruly growth. And Parliament was controlled by country gentlemen unconcerned with city problems.

Division of Labor: Mass Production · The machine method changed the whole process of manufacturing by dividing it up into many separate operations. Formerly a coat, a pair of shoes, or a table might be made entirely by one person. Now it passed through many hands. Special machines were devised for every detail of the work.

As a result, each individual was assigned to some limited task. He might have to spend his entire time at a machine which performed only one small part of the work, such as cutting buttonholes, punching eyelets, or turning the thread of a screw. This endless repetition of the same motions was deadly monotonous for the workers.

In the days of the guilds the artisan had taken pride in the article as a whole. Under the domestic system the piece-work monotony was broken by opportunities to do other home tasks from time to time. But in the factory the worker spent long hours under the eye of an overseer. He was crowded in with other workers, all of them repeating their small tasks over and over again to the point of exhaustion.

Yet for the employer this *division of labor,* as it was called, was most efficient and profitable. The constant repetition of the same motions gave the worker a machine-like efficiency. This resulted in a great saving of time and a large increase of output. Today we speak of the tremendous output of our factories as *mass production* (see Chapter 27).

Capitalists and Workingmen · Another result of the Industrial Revolution was the appearance of capitalists and laborers as distinct social classes. Capitalists owned the factories, lands, and mines. They invested their money, of course, to obtain profits. The workers, on the other hand, had nothing but their labor to sell and were entirely dependent on their employers.

Since machines needed few operators, competition for jobs became so great that an employer could generally force workers to accept any terms he wished. Many could find no work at all, and so the new system at first brought great poverty to many people.

Early London Slums · *The problem of people being ill-fed, ill-housed, ill-clothed is still a glaring one in many crowded cities of the world.*

A middle class of professional people, salaried workers, and skilled craftsmen had not yet grown large enough to exercise the moderating effect which it does today. And ultimately workers won a share in the benefits of increased production. Industrialization brought higher living standards.

Exploitation of Women and Children · The destruction of the domestic system in England had a disastrous effect upon the lives of women and children. Before the invention of the steam engine, when the simple machines were still worked by hand, children could work at only a few tasks. But in the new factories there were jobs like watching machines, piecing broken threads, and pulling and pushing levers. Women and children could be used in place of men and could be hired for lower wages.

Women and children left home early and toiled all day and into the night in crowded factories for miserable wages. The health of the children suffered, and they received little or no education. Their cheap labor increased unemployment among the men. Keep in mind, however, that even before this time few children received an education.

Opposition to Government Regulation · The glaring evils of the factory system led reformers to urge that the government remedy the situation. But businessmen were strongly opposed to any interference on the part of the government. And their stand was supported by a group of economists who held that the government should refrain from any attempt to control business. The most influential of these economists was Adam Smith. His *Wealth of Nations* had a profound effect on economic thinking.

This so-called "classical school" of economic writers held that individual enterprise should be unhampered by laws. Businessmen, they declared, should be allowed perfect freedom in buying and selling and in making contracts. Then certain economic "laws," such as the law of supply and demand, would determine rents, wages, prices, and profits. For example, prices would be kept down by competition. Wages would be fixed by the number of people seeking employment. In short, all issues would be settled in the free competition of the market.

Demands for Reform · Unfortunately, this theory did not seem to work very well in practice. As we have seen, the great manufacturing cities that were growing up were not being filled with happy and prosperous people. Rather they were crowded with poorly fed, ill clothed workers, living under the most miserable conditions. Children under nine were toiling from twelve to fifteen hours a day. Women were forced to neglect their homes for the sake of adding something to the scanty family income.

With the progress of the Industrial Revolution, matters grew worse instead of better, and there was increasing discontent in England. The first English Factory Act, in 1802, limited to twelve hours the working day of children in the cotton and woolen mills. This was followed by other laws and by a general movement to reform the condition of the workers (see Chapter 24)

Workers Organize for Protection · Besides attempting to secure reform through the government, working men formed trade unions. Their aim was to protect themselves by dealing in a body with their employers. At first, unions were forbidden by English law as a "combination in restraint of trade." Men were sentenced to imprisonment or deportation if they joined such "combinations" to raise their wages.

In 1824 Parliament repealed this law, and trade unions increased rapidly. They

Corporal Punishment and Child Labor · *Relations between employers and employees have improved considerably during the past century.*

began to collect dues from their members to provide insurance and to strengthen their organization. The policy of bargaining became the principal method by which workers improved their wages, hours, and conditions of labor. When bargaining failed, the workers would strike.

CHECK ON YOUR READING

1. *Define and illustrate these terms: domestic system, factory system, division of labor, mass production, social classes.*
2. *How were workers' lives changed?*
3. *Why were reforms (a) demanded? (b) opposed?*
4. *Why were trade unions established? Describe their methods.*

3. The Rise of Socialism

The Meaning of Socialism · The *socialists* had no confidence that the conditions in industry would be improved by the law of supply and demand or other economic "laws." Nor did they have any real hope of reform merely through government regulation. They believed in *collective or governmental ownership and management of the essential means for the production and distribution of goods.* This belief, which appeared in the early nineteenth century, is called *socialism.* It continues to play an important role in history today.

By *means of production and distribution* the socialists meant anything which could be used to create goods and distribute them. They desired government ownership and management of the mills, mines, railways, and steamship companies—in short, the great industries which developed as the result of the Industrial Revolution.

The socialist maintained that it was not right for capitalists to own the great business enterprises on which the mass of working-men must depend for their living. Even if trade unions were able to get better wages, this was only a temporary relief. Socialists said that the *capitalistic system* was wrong, for it permitted individuals of great wealth to have control over the lives of the poor. The remedy for this, they said, was to turn all industries over to a government elected by the people. The government would then distribute the profits by means of increased public services.

Utopian Socialists · The early socialists believed that capitalists could be persuaded to turn over their control of industry by oral and written appeals to their humanitarian motives. They dreamed of an ideal society (Utopia) in which all poverty would be wiped out. In this perfect society men would cease to be selfish. They would live by the golden rule and make sacrifices necessary for the common good.

Among such Utopians were the French writers Fourier and Saint-Simon and the humanitarian English manufacturer, Robert Owen. Experimental communities were set up in France and America to try out their ideas. Brook Farm, Massachusetts, and New Harmony, Indiana, were examples. But they soon failed. Economic equality proved easier to preach than to practice.

Karl Marx (1818–1883) and Revolutionary Socialism · These early socialists were looked upon as dreamers. The more practical-minded turned to the workers themselves to bring about reform. They argued that it was labor alone which created wealth and that the wage earners (proletariat) were therefore justified in seizing industry by force if necessary.

The chief teacher of revolutionary socialism, or communism, was a German writer, Karl Marx, who lived most of his life in London. As Marx observed the progress of the Industrial Revolution in England, he developed the *economic-determination* theory of history. He saw history as the story of *class struggle* between different groups in society for control of the *means of production and distribution.* It was a record of how one class gained wealth and power, only to be overthrown by another class. This class struggle, Marx asserted, was *inevitable,* and so was the eventual victory of the working class.

During the French Revolution of 1848, Marx with his friend Friedrich Engels issued a treatise called *The Communist Manifesto.* It called upon the workers of the world to rise and seize the means of production themselves. Marx later wrote a learned work called *Das Kapital (Capital).* In it he explained his theories and sought to show that socialism was certain to prevail.

To Marx the case for socialism was quite simple. (1) Labor produces all wealth. Capital is only the result of past labor. (2) The difference between what labor produces and what it receives is stolen by the capitalists. (3) In the ruthless competition between capitalists a few will eventually win control. (4) As the gap between the capitalists and the wage slaves widens, the injustice of the system will become obvious, as well as insufferable. (5) Then the proletariat will take over both the government and the means of production.

Flaws in Socialist Theory · The overly simplified theories of Marx had tremendous appeal to down-trodden and oppressed peoples, especially in times of economic and social crises. But time has revealed many serious flaws in his theory. (1) By Marxian theory, Russia and China, which were primarily agricultural states at the time the Communists seized control, should have been among the *last,* and the highly capitalistic United States, England, and France, among the first to go socialistic. (2) Marx did not foresee the tremendous growth and influence of the *middle class,* which considers itself as neither "capitalistic" nor "proletariat." According to his theory it would decline.

(3) Marx did not foresee the great many measures of social welfare provided without violence by taxes and by charitable foundations established by men of great wealth. Among these are public schools, scholarships, unemployment insurance, social se-

Karl Heinrich Marx · *He was the father and chief theorist of modern, scientific, or revolutionary socialism.*

curity, and numerous community agencies. (4) Because he believed that communism would bring great political and economic freedom, he would be amazed to find that men are freest today in capitalist nations and most enslaved where communism holds sway.

(5) Marx feared that men were being made slaves to machines. He could not visualize that a time would come when the working man would himself own such machines as automobiles, power mowers, automatic washers, and do-it-yourself tools. (6) Perhaps above all, Marx underestimated the power of personal incentives in

human life. The desire to get ahead in life is a tremendous force. And coupled with it is the pride of personal ownership, summed up in the declaration, "It's mine." Even communist countries have had to supply personal incentives to promote production.

Why Socialism Grew · In spite of the serious loopholes in Marxian theory, socialism grew rapidly through the years. There were several reasons for this. (1) Socialism appealed to the *have-nots*. Millions of hopeless Europeans literally believed "you have nothing to lose but your chains."

(2) Non-socialist humanitarians dramatized man's inhumanity to man. In England, Charles Dickens portrayed the hard lot of the poor and the inhumane treatment of unfortunate people in *Oliver Twist* (1838) and *David Copperfield* (1850). Across the Atlantic, Harriet Beecher Stowe's *Uncle Tom's Cabin* (1852) aroused Americans to the evils of slavery. In France, Victor Hugo's *Les Miserables* (1862) cried out against the injustice of sending men to the galleys for minor crimes. Sympathy for the condition of the poor, the weak, and the oppressed which these writers aroused increased demands for social reform. The socialists were quick to blame all social evils on the "heartless capitalistic system." In the melodrama of misfortune it was easy to paint the wealthy capitalist in the role of the villain. Especially was this true in time of hardship, for "when the stomach is empty, the mind will swallow anything."

(3) Non-socialist political reformers fought for the elimination of property restrictions on the right to vote. The socialists saw the ballot as an instrument for achieving their social and economic programs. When suffrage was extended to the masses (especially in Belgium, France, Germany, and Italy), socialism attracted many.

(4) There were many religious people who welcomed a program which sought to replace competition with co-operation, and profit-seeking with social service. The *Christian Socialists* were among these. Their party gained much support when "the working man's Pope" Leo XIII issued his encyclical letter of 1891 concerning the condition of the working classes.

(5) The Fabian Society of England (1883) exerted an influence far beyond its membership. It favored the waiting policy made famous by the Roman general (Quintas Fabias Maximus) whose small forces avoided formal battle with Hannibal yet wore away his strength. The Fabians opposed the Marxian ideas of class war. They preferred evolution to revolution. Under the leadership of professors Sidney and Beatrice Webb, the historian H. G. Wells, and the playwright George Bernard Shaw, they ridiculed the capitalistic system. The powerful British Labor party grew out of this movement.

Thus socialism came to be a significant force in many countries, even where socialist parties as such were not in control. The *Statesman's Yearbook* for 1958, for example, indicated heavy socialist or labor representation in the legislatures of Austria, Belgium, France, Great Britain, West Germany, Italy, the Netherlands, Norway, Sweden, and Switzerland.

CHECK ON YOUR READING

1. *What does* socialism *mean?*
2. *Who were the Utopians? Why did their experiments fail?*
3. *Summarize Marx's theory.*
4. *What six loopholes or flaws appeared in his theory?*
5. *Why did socialism grow? (Five reasons)*

Learning Activities

Think about the chapter

1. In what ways has the Industrial Revolution benefited, or hurt mankind?

2. Compare the changes produced by the Industrial Revolution and the French Revolution. How did both lead eventually to greater liberty for the common man?

3. What were the ideas of the "classical school" of economists? Do you agree or disagree with their theories? Why?

4. Why are Americans proud of their economic enterprise system?

Go beyond the text

5. Prepare a biographical sketch of one of the important inventors of this period.

6. Why are Socialists and Communists such bitter enemies today?

7. How did the Napoleonic Wars affect the growth of industry in the United States?

8. Report to the class on the socialistic experiments at Jamestown, Virginia; Brook Farm, Massachusetts; New Harmony, Indiana. How do you account for the distaste for socialism in the United States today?

Follow up your special interests

9. Add to your record the inventors and inventions of this period.

10. Indicate on a map the five most and five least industrialized areas in the world today. What problem confronts each group?

READ FURTHER

Basic readings: (1) BECKER, *Modern History*, Chap. 16. (2) CHEYNEY, *Short History of England*, Chap. 18. (3) COTTLER and JAFFE, *Heroes of Civilization*. All the important inventors. (4) HOFFMAN, *News of the World*, Nos. 43, 45. (5) SCOTT, BALTZLY, *Readings*, Chaps. 3, 9. (6) VAN LOON, *Story of Mankind*, pp. 402–426. (7) Year's *Pictorial History*, pp. 428–431.

Special accounts: (8) G. HARTMAN, *Machines and the Men Who Made the World of Industry*. (9) M. and C. H. B. QUENNELL, *Everyday Things in England from 1733–1851*. (10) J. MEYER, *The World Book of Great Inventions*. From the invention of the wheel to the most complex of modern inventions, with clear diagrams. (11) L. LAMPREY, *The Story of Weaving*. The story of the textile industry is useful for an understanding of the Industrial Revolution. (12) E. TUNIS, *Wheels: A Pictorial History*. This story of 5000 years of travel has good material on development of power. (13) *American Heritage*, "When Karl Marx Worked for Horace Greeley," April, 1957.

Fiction and biography: (14) F. BACHMAN, *Great Inventors and their Inventions*. (15) C. DICKENS, *Oliver Twist* and *David Copperfield*. (16) V. HUGO, *Les Miserables*. (17) H. B. STOWE, *Uncle Tom's Cabin*. (18) A. WHITRIDGE, *Men in Crisis*. Excellent Chapter on Karl Marx.

"From each according to his abilities, to each according to his needs."—KARL MARX

"The greatest invention of the nineteenth century was the invention of the method of invention."
—ALFRED NORTH WHITEHEAD

The Growth of Nationalism and Imperialism

1820-1910

B.C. A.D.

4000   2000

SUPPOSE Unit V were a grand-scale motion picture. Notice the time, setting, and cast of characters.

The time is the nineteenth century. The place is not only Europe, but the whole world. Dense smoke from factories rises over growing cities. Railroads stretch into formerly isolated areas. Businessmen and soldiers from England, France, Italy and Germany bring Western control and the Western way of life to far-away peoples. Empires are built. New national states are formed. In the United States the War between the States is fought, huge corporations rise, and the frontier is closed.

The chief characters are not only rulers and statesmen (Queen Victoria, Disraeli, and Gladstone of England, Alexander II of Russia, Bismarck of Germany), but also explorers and scientists (Livingstone, Darwin, Pasteur) and the hundreds of thousands of ordinary men and women (factory workers, soldiers who died for an Empire, colonial people subjected to foreign rule, telegraph operators, and farmers).

In this unit there is much dramatic action. Bismarck, the Iron Chancellor, unites the German states by intrigue and war. Garibaldi's Red Shirts fight to make Italy one nation. The British Empire extends far across the globe. France suffers bitter and humiliating defeat. Ireland struggles against famine and the English. In Russia the serfs are freed, but the people continue to stir restlessly under the cruel government of the tsar. There is an uprising in China to drive out the hated foreigners. Commodore Perry finally persuades the Japanese to open their country to trade. The United States, in a patriotic fever, frees Cuba from Spanish rule. Scientists discover the nature of matter and the existence of bacteria. Huge mechanized equipment revolutionizes farming methods.

As we read and study about this era we can see how the forces of nationalism, imperialism, and industrialism worked together to create the world as it was in 1914.

CHAPTER 23

Germany, France, and Italy (1850-1914)

CHAPTER OUTLINE

1. *Growth of Prussia's Power*
2. *The German Empire (1871–1914)*
3. *The Third French Republic (1871–1914)*
4. *The Making of Modern Italy*

KEY WORDS AND DATES

Zollverein
Junkers
Bismarck
Schleswig-Holstein
North German Confederation
Dual Monarchy
Franco-Prussian War, 1870
Alsace-Lorraine
indemnity
Kaiser
Bundesrat and *Reichstag*
socialism
Social Democrats
social insurance
paternalism
Paris Commune
Third Republic
coalition
clericalism
Mazzini
nationalism
Victor Emmanuel
Piedmont-Sardinia
Cavour
Garibaldi
"Roman Question"

IN THIS CHAPTER we shall follow the fortunes of Germany, France, and Italy between the revolutions of 1848 and World War I. During this period Germany and Italy achieved national unity, and France established her Third Republic. The headlines of the period were dominated by Prince Bismarck of Prussia, Napoleon III of France, and Count Cavour of Piedmont.

Bismarck used cleverness, boldness, and a policy of "blood and iron" to enlarge Prussia, defeat Austria, crush France, and make the king of Prussia head of a German Empire. He mixed cleverness and boldness in dealing with his opponents in Germany as well. He sponsored a program of social insurance to weaken Socialist opposition. When William II came to the throne, Bismarck finally had to step aside.

Napoleon III helped Cavour oust Austria from Italy, but he allowed himself to be tricked into a disastrous war with Prussia. As a result he lost his crown and the rich provinces of Alsace and Lorraine. Under the Third Republic, France made a surprising recovery, built up a colonial empire, and regained her position as a great power.

Cavour built upon the patriotism of the inspired Mazzini and the colorful Garibaldi to make King Victor Emmanuel the ruler of a united Italy.

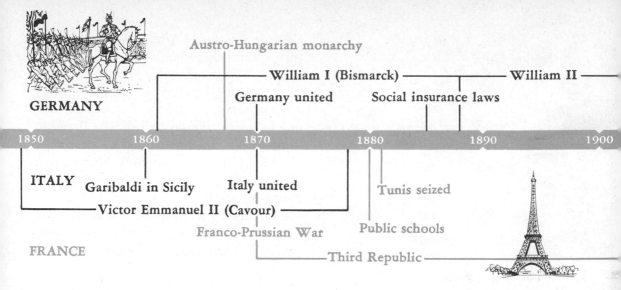

Austro-Hungarian monarchy

———————— William I (Bismarck) ———————— William II ——

GERMANY   Germany united   Social insurance laws

| 1850 | 1860 | 1870 | 1880 | 1890 | 1900 |

ITALY   Garibaldi in Sicily   Italy united   Tunis seized

———— Victor Emmanuel II (Cavour) ————

Franco-Prussian War   Public schools

FRANCE   ———————— Third Republic ————

1. Growth of Prussia's Power

Union through Free Trade · In the years following the formation of the German Confederation in 1815 (p. 341) Prussia made marked advances along economic lines. The country had been greatly enlarged by the addition of part of Saxony and the Rhine provinces, but her territories were divided (see map, p. 340). Rigid economies and tariff reforms helped to make her prosperous.

In 1818 Prussia established a customs union (*Zollverein*). All tariffs within the state were abolished. By 1834 she had persuaded seventeen other German states to come into the group and to permit free trade with one another. Later other states found it to their advantage to join the union. A popular writer of the time said that matches, cows, cheese, paper, ham, and boots had bound German hearts together better than any political ties.

Political Oppression in Prussia (1848–1856) · Prussia had gained a constitution and a parliament from the revolution of 1848, but she was little better off than before. The constitution provided that the propertied classes should have the control of elections. The government was really in the hands of the king and the landed nobility (called *Junkers*). They tried to maintain their old-time feudal privileges and held high offices in the government and army.

A period of serious oppression of the liberals followed 1848. Many hard-working Germans left their fatherland and sought new homes elsewhere. Their influence can be seen in our own country in such cities as Cincinnati, St. Louis, and Milwaukee.

Industrialization Encourages Unity · Germany was to remain for some years longer only a group of allied states. But the Industrial Revolution was unifying the country more successfully than any written constitution. In 1835 the first railway was built, and soon a great system of communications connected the German states.

Germany now began to develop many enterprises which were changing her from an agricultural into a great industrial country. The rich resources of her coal and iron

Bismarck · *Of this Prussian architect of the German state, Gladstone said: "He made Germany great and Germans small." How?*

ally for training. After active service for three years, they should become members of the reserve forces for four years more. This program, however, would require large sums of money. And the Prussian *Landtag* (parliament) refused to vote the necessary funds. William now called to his side as minister Otto von Bismarck, a statesman of experience, well able to put through the king's proposals.

Bismarck's Program and Methods · The new minister belonged to the conservative landed nobility. He hated parliaments and the democratic ideas of the Liberal party. He was convinced that Prussia would become great not through weakening the monarchy, but by increasing its power. His motto was "blood and iron." He put his confidence, therefore, in the mailed fist and the sword.

His program included the following steps: He would (1) build up the army, (2) remove Austrian control from Germany, (3) enlarge Prussia and consolidate her territories, and (4) induce the South German states to join a union under Prussian leadership. Defying the *Landtag*, Bismarck raised money by special taxes. Although the liberals protested, Bismarck continued to build up Prussia's army. Thus, when the moment came, Prussia in three short wars was able to achieve Bismarck's goal.

Prussia owed her success to the cleverness and boldness of her great minister as well. Bismarck planned his moves carefully and struck just at the right moment. He arranged matters so that his enemy always seemed to be the aggressor. And he made sure that no other power would join Prussia's enemy in the midst of the conflict.

The Danish War, 1864 · Bismarck's first war was designed to gain additional territory and to get into war with Austria. Den-

mines were being used, and factories and foundries were springing up.

Enterprising businessmen were now looking about them for wider markets. They were impatient with local restrictions that interfered with the growth of trade. They were eager to have Germany a strong national state which could compete with other powers in international trade.

William I, King of Prussia · The ambitious and forceful William I came to the throne in 1861. His aims were (1) to drive Austria out of the German Confederation, (2) to unite Germany under the domination of Prussia and (3) to make her one of the great powers of Europe.

Believing that Prussia's future greatness depended on her military might, William set to work to strengthen her army. The king and his advisers agreed that a greater number of men should be called up annu-

Richard Wagner · *This great nine-teenth-century composer gave strong expression to German nationalism. His operas glorified legendary German heroes, such as Siegfried. His colossal work,* The Ring of the Nibelung, *is based on an old Germanic epic.* Tristan and Isolde *and* Parsifal *are based on Arthurian legends.*

mark ruled two German duchies, Schleswig and Holstein. In 1863 the Danish ruler decided, in defiance of a treaty, to make the provinces part of his kingdom. Bismarck now induced Austria to join Prussia in a war with Denmark. Together they easily forced the Danish king to give up the two provinces.

Differences arose between the victors, just as Bismarck had foreseen. But a temporary arrangement was made by which Prussia was to govern Schleswig, and Austria would control Holstein.

The Seven Weeks' War (1866) · Bismarck was now planning his second move, which was the defeat of Austria and her exclusion from German affairs. He strengthened his position by an alliance with the king of Italy. This provided that Italy would get Venetia for providing help against Austria. Then by flattering Napoleon III and holding out some vague prospects of "compensations" to him, Bismarck made sure of French neutrality.

Bismarck now managed to renew his quarrel with Austria over Schleswig-Holstein. When Austria brought the matter before the diet of the German Confederation, Prussian forces entered Holstein. The diet then supported Austria and sent federal troops against Prussia. Thereupon Prussia declared the German Confederation of 1815 dissolved. So powerful was the new Prussian army that the whole affair was over in seven weeks.

By the peace treaty (Prague, 1866) Austria ceded Venetia to Italy and Holstein to Prussia. The German Confederation was broken up and with it the domination of Austria over Germany.

Prussia Forms a New Confederation · Prussia now organized the North German Confederation. It included all the states north of the river Main. Bismarck realized that the southern states, which had been hostile to Prussia, were not yet ready to accept her leadership. He therefore left them free for a while to go their own way.

Austria-Hungary and Its Emperor · *Delegates from Austrian and Hungarian parliaments met alternately at their capitals of Vienna and Budapest to discuss common problems.*

Below: Francis Joseph greets William II of Germany at Schönbrunn palace.

On the other hand, Prussia did not hesitate to annex Hanover, Hesse-Cassel, Nassau, and the free city of Frankfurt, along with the duchies of Schleswig and Holstein. The eastern and western possessions of the Hohenzollerns were now united, and Prussia controlled almost the whole seacoast from Russia to Holland. (See map, p. 397.)

The Austro-Hungarian Monarchy (1867) · Austria now settled her relations with Hungary by a compromise. The rebellious Magyars insisted that, as an ancient independent state, Hungary should be permitted to have its own separate constitution.

Finally, Francis Joseph agreed to the formation of a "dual monarchy," composed of the two independent and equal states: (1) Austria, including Bohemia, Moravia, Carinthia, and other provinces, and (2) Hungary, including Transylvania, Croatia, and Slavonia. Each state had its own parliament, but the same monarch ruled as emperor of Austria and king of Hungary. They also had one army and a joint ministry, which managed certain interests.

The compromise suited the Germans of Austria and the Magyars of Hungary. Because the various Slavic peoples deeply resented the power of these two elements, however, there was continued unrest. Yet this federation lasted until 1918.

CHECK ON YOUR READING

1. How was German unity aided by (a) the Zollverein? (b) industrialization?
2. Summarize Bismarck's (a) program and (b) methods.
3. Explain how Prussia (a) gained Schleswig-Holstein, (b) ousted Austria, (c) formed a new federation.
4. Describe the Dual Monarchy's (a) government, (b) major groups, (c) problems.

2. The German Empire (1871-1914)

How the Franco-Prussian War Came About (1870) · Napoleon III was surprised and disturbed by Prussia's speedy victory over Austria. And he was annoyed that France had received nothing in spite of Bismarck's vague promises. French leaders were alarmed at this sudden change in Europe's balance of power. They began to press Napoleon to curb the Prussians before they became too strong.

Bismarck knew that Napoleon would never permit Prussia to add to her growing power by annexing the southern German states. He was therefore eager that France should declare war and thus become the aggressor. He believed that such a war would bring these Germans into alliance with Prussia of their own free will.

He had not long to wait. In 1869 the crown of Spain was offered to Leopold of Hohenzollern, a distant relative of William I. The Paris newspapers excitedly charged that this was only an indirect way of bringing Spain under the influence of Prussia. When Leopold withdrew his acceptance of the Spanish crown, Europe believed the incident to be at an end.

The French ministry was not yet satisfied, however, and wished to humiliate Prussia publicly. The French ambassador was therefore instructed to call on William I to secure a promise that William would not permit the Hohenzollern candidacy for the Spanish throne to be renewed. This, William firmly, but politely, refused to do.

Bismarck's report of the affair to the newspapers made it seem a sharp exchange between William I and the French ambassador and a cause for war. To the Germans it appeared that the French ambassador had insulted their king. To the French it seemed that their ambassador had received an affront. The news, published in Paris on the national holiday, July 14, 1870, stirred up great excitement. The next day the French parliament declared war on Prussia.

Prussia's Victory over France · As Bismarck had hoped, the German states now ranged themselves as a nation against the French. Their superbly trained armies

Victory Parade in Berlin · *Troops carrying captured French flags march before Emperor William I and Bismarck. Some flags commemorate Napoleonic victories. Notice the early "goose step."*

William I Proclaimed Emperor · *Bismarck reads the proclamation in the famous Hall of Mirrors at Versailles. In 1919 the Germans had to sign a humiliating treaty in this hall.*

hastened across the Rhine and in a few days were driving the sadly equipped and poorly commanded French before them. In a series of bloody encounters around Metz one of the French armies was defeated and finally shut up in that town. A second French army was captured along with Emperor Napoleon III himself in the great battle of Sedan, September 1, 1870.

A group of republicans now declared the empire abolished and proclaimed France a republic. A Government of National Defense was set up to continue the war. Meanwhile the Germans laid siege to Paris.

New French armies were raised in the provinces, but they were unable to relieve the capital city. For four months the hungry people of Paris defied the Germans with heroic resistance. But finally an armistice was arranged on January 28, 1871.

Germany Annexes Alsace and Lorraine · In contrast to the easy terms which had been granted to Austria, Bismarck forced France to (1) cede the resource-rich provinces of Alsace and Lorraine, (2) to pay an indemnity of a billion dollars, and (3) to support a German army of occupation until the sum was paid.

Bitter feeling between France and Germany dated from this war. The French never accepted the loss of their provinces, and never forgot their humiliating defeat. The Germans, on the other hand, believed that the French were constantly planning revenge. This mutual distrust was one of the causes of World War I.

Founding of the German Empire (January 18, 1871) · The most striking result of the Franco-Prussian War, however, was the unification of Germany. Bismarck's dream was fulfilled. The South German states—Bavaria, Württemberg, Baden, and South Hesse—had not only fought side by side with the Prussian forces, but they had joined the North German Confederation.

Surrounded by the German princes, William I, king of Prussia, was proclaimed German Emperor in Louis XIV's great palace of Versailles. The triumph of Bismarck was complete. The German Empire was a reality, and Prussia was its leading state.

Government of the German Empire · The German Empire was a federation composed of twenty-five states and the imperial territory of Alsace-Lorraine. Each of the sovereign states belonging to the union retained its own government and control over most of its local affairs.

Prussia, however, played the principal role. She had taken the lead in unifying the empire. She had two-thirds of the land and population. The Prussian king was also the emperor, or *Kaiser*. He was in command of the army and navy and appointed and dismissed the chancellor (chief minister).

The German Parliament · There were two houses of parliament. The upper chamber, called the *Bundesrat*, represented the rulers of the various states. The members of the lower house, the *Reichstag*, were representatives of the people.

The Bundesrat enjoyed more power than any other upper house in Europe. It proposed all the important laws, and no law could be passed without its consent. Prussia controlled this body, and the imperial chancellor presided over its meetings.

The Reichstag consisted of about four hundred representatives. It possessed little power to control the government. It did

The German Empire · *Although the Empire was a federation, what role did Prussia play in it? Locate Berlin and the principal German rivers.*

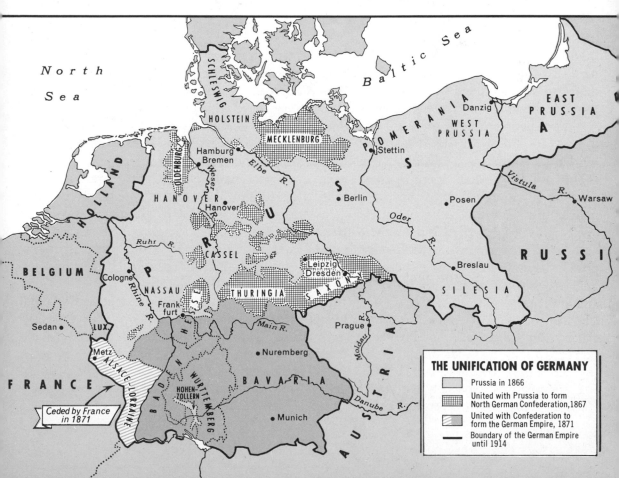

THE UNIFICATION OF GERMANY

Prussia in 1866

United with Prussia to form North German Confederation, 1867

United with Confederation to form the German Empire, 1871

Boundary of the German Empire until 1914

Ceded by France in 1871

not have the right to dismiss ministers, as did the British House of Commons. Moreover, the German chancellor was responsible *not to the Reichstag, but to the emperor*. The emperor could dissolve the body at any time with the consent of the Bundesrat. Hence, while the government appeared democratic in *form*, it proved autocratic in practice. And it was not long before the *state* came to count for more than the *individual*.

Bismarck Establishes Uniformity · For twenty years Bismarck remained chief minister, or imperial chancellor. During this time he established uniform financial, tariff, and military measures.

The German constitution gave the imperial government power to regulate commerce, railways, telegraph, currency, and the criminal and civil law in the interest of the nation. Bismarck used these powers to set up an imperial currency. The mark was made the unit of value. A central *Reichsbank* was founded. A tariff system was designed to encourage home industries and protect them against foreign competition.

Compulsory military service, which had proved so successful in Prussia, was extended to Germany as a whole. The chancellor also saw that appropriations were made large enough to keep the army strong and ready for action.

Bismarck Fights the Church: the *Kulturkampf* · Three groups in the Reichstag opposed Bismarck's autocratic methods. (1) The progressives desired a more democratic and less militaristic state. (2) The Socialists wanted more benefits for the working class. (3) The Catholics favored greater powers for the member states and objected to domination by Protestant Prussia.

Bismarck was especially irritated by the Catholic emphasis on "states' rights" and obedience to the Pope. He feared a revival of the old rivalry between Popes and German emperors. His campaign against the Catholics came to be known as the *Kulturkampf*. A series of harsh laws against Catholics were passed, to bring the clergy under the direct supervision of the government and to give the state control of the Church.

These measures failed. Persecution increased the loyalty of the Catholics to their Church. Their political party (called the *Center*) was strengthened and remained for years the strongest party in the Reichstag. Finally, Bismarck permitted the legislation against the Catholics to lapse. He needed their aid against a new and dangerous enemy—socialism.

Bismarck Fights the Socialists · The rapid changes brought about by the Industrial Revolution in Germany produced much hardship and many abuses. The workers began to feel the need of some defense against the rich factory-owners. Socialistic ideas made a great appeal to the people, but Socialists soon realized that they would never have any power until they obtained a voice in the government.

By 1875 the various socialist groups had joined the Social Democratic party. Its program was based on the teachings of Karl Marx, and it had already gained twelve seats in the Reichstag. Bismarck was now alarmed, for the Socialists denounced the capitalistic system, by which prosperity was being built up in Germany. He determined to crush socialism.

In 1878 a severe law was passed which forbade socialist meetings and the publication of socialist books, newspapers, and pamphlets. Some of the leading agitators were arrested. Despite this law the Socialists continued to carry on their propaganda secretly, and their number increased.

"Dropping the Pilot" · *This* Punch *cartoon shows the aging Bismarck leaving the German ship of state. Who then became pilot?*

Bismarck now changed his tactics. He decided to "steal his opponents' thunder." He had the government enact measures which would remedy some of the evils complained of by the Socialists. Thus he would make the government appear as a public benefactor and take the issue and the votes from the Social Democratic party.

Between 1883 and 1889 the government established a system of state insurance. *It was the earliest social-security system in a modern nation.* Workers were to receive financial help in case of sickness, accident, old age, and disability. Employers were required to furnish part of the funds. These social-insurance laws greatly strengthened the empire.

The Socialists, however, were not satisfied with these paternal, or fatherly, acts of the government. They desired a more revolutionary change, by which industry would be taken out of private ownership and be controlled by the workers themselves.

William II (1888–1918) Dismisses Bismarck and Acquires Colonies · When Kaiser William I died at the age of ninety-one, his grandson, William II, came to the throne. The new ruler was young and vigorous, self-confident and arrogant in his manner. He was a strong believer in the "divine right" of the Hohenzollern dynasty and in the power of German arms. As a prince he had expressed unbounded admiration for Bismarck. But he had not been emperor for two years when he dismissed the Iron Chancellor. He could not tolerate the presence of so powerful a minister or share the duties of government with him. The succeeding chancellors merely acted as deputies to carry out the kaiser's will.

The new emperor soon changed Germany's colonial policy. Bismarck had not been eager to acquire possessions in foreign lands. He had refused to accept colonies as reparations from defeated France, preferring instead to annex Alsace and Lorraine. He believed that Germany should strengthen her position in Europe and avoid conflict with other countries over the question of colonies. He was especially fearful that such conflicts might lead to alliances against Germany. Nevertheless, German businessmen in search of raw materials and markets were soon establishing trading stations in foreign lands. They sought government protection and support for their ventures. Finally, Germany changed her policy not only by helping her citizens in their foreign enterprises, but by embarking on an active colonial program. She expanded her navy and acquired a few possessions in Africa and some islands in the Pacific. But these were insignificant compared to the huge colonial empires of Britain and France.

Growth of Science and Industry · German science and industry continued to advance rapidly in the reign of William II. The rich coal and iron deposits of Alsace-Lorraine provided the necessary materials for building up a great industrial state. In mining and metallurgy Germany made rapid progress until she was the second country in the world in the production of pig iron and steel.

The Germans were greatly interested in scientific research and in the application of their discoveries to the improvement of industry. They excelled in the production of textiles, chemicals, drugs, dyes, electrical equipment, and optical instruments. They had a world monopoly on aniline dyes.

Science and industry provided the sinews for the muscular military machine which came to dominate the state. By 1914 Germany was a great world power. Her population had doubled in sixty years. And her saber-rattling emperor was intent on winning for the fatherland a "place in the sun."

CHECK ON YOUR READING

1. *Summarize (a) the causes, (b) highlights, and (c) results of the Franco-Prussian War.*
2. *Explain how the government was democratic in form and autocratic in practice.*
3. *How and why did Bismarck (a) establish uniformity? (b) fight the Catholics? (c) fight the Socialists?*
4. *Why did William II (a) dismiss Bismarck? (b) change German colonial policy?*
5. *What elements made Germany a great world power?*

---

3. The Third French Republic (1871–1914)

The Revolt of the Paris Commune (1871) · When the French National Assembly met at the end of the Franco-Prussian War, it had a large majority of monarchists. It therefore did not accept the republic which had been proclaimed in Paris (p. 396). Moreover it soon came into violent conflict with the people of Paris, who had borne the brunt of the struggle against Germany.

There was much unemployment in the city as the armies disbanded and war industries ended. To add to the distress, the Assembly decreed immediate payment of all rents and bills which had been allowed to lapse during the war. This meant ruin to many small shopkeepers and much hard-

ship for the poor. Then, too, the Assembly decided to hold its sessions in Versailles instead of in the capital.

The Parisians were now alarmed lest the Assembly restore the monarchy and with it the evils of the old regime. The city government of Paris was now organized as an independent revolutionary commune. It revolted against the authority of the Assembly and prepared to defend itself against the national troops. It called on other large cities to organize communes, as it had done, and to declare themselves independent of the Assembly.

The struggle that followed was terrible. The rebels were guilty of atrocities, such as the murder of the archbishop of Paris and other prisoners. The army that was sent against them was equally brutal. After two months (April and May) the forces of the Commune were completely routed in a series of violent street fights. The victorious government showed no mercy. Hundreds were shot after a hasty trial, and the rebellion was put down in blood.

Tasks of the National Assembly · The National Assembly governed France from 1871 to 1875. Louis Adolphe Thiers, a veteran statesman from the days of Louis Philippe, was made president of the republic. The first task was to restore order and to free France from German garrisons by paying the billion-dollar war indemnity. The French people showed great patriotism and courage in this hour of distress. They willingly lent the government the money to pay off the war debt six months ahead of the required three years.

The government now faced the problem of national security. It reorganized the army, requiring every Frenchman to serve actively for five years and to remain for fifteen years in the reserve forces.

In 1875 the Assembly passed three laws which served as the constitution of the Third Republic. But these laws did not openly proclaim a republic, because there was still much sentiment in France for a king.

Organization of the Republic · According to the laws of 1875 the legislative power was vested in a parliament of two houses. The upper house, or Senate, was composed of three hundred members, elected indirectly. The members of the lower house, or Chamber of Deputies, were elected by direct suffrage. The executive duties were in the hands of a president, elected every seven years by both houses united as a National Assembly.

Goodbye and Good Riddance! · *Interpret this contemporary French cartoon. What is the meaning of the sword, helmet, and banner? the black bag? the grim La Belle France?*

Actually, the real executive power was exercised by the *premier* (prime minister) and his cabinet of departmental ministers. They were responsible, as in England, to parliament. If the measures proposed by the cabinet were not approved by a majority of the deputies, the cabinet had to resign. The president then appointed a new premier, who undertook to form a cabinet which would win the confidence of a majority in the Chamber.

Frequent Change of Ministries · Few cabinets over the years lasted longer than a few months. The reason is that France failed to develop two or three strong parties as in England or America. The members instead belonged to one of a large number

A French Classroom (1890) · *The French system became famous for intellectual discipline. Yet few students reached the university.*

of small parties or groups, each holding some special ideas of its own.

To get a majority several of these "parties" in parliament would have to work together in a *coalition government*. The premier would choose his cabinet from members of each of the co-operating parties. But such a coalition would fall apart as soon as some measure was proposed that members of one or more of the co-operating groups could not support.

It was not until the establishment of the Fifth French Republic under General Charles de Gaulle in 1958 that weaknesses of this system were remedied.

The Clergy, the Schools, and Separation of Church and State · One of the difficult problems which caused cabinets to fall was the relation of Church and state. The Catholic clergy, from the first, were hostile to the Republic. They showed increasing preference for the royalist cause. The republicans therefore came to view *clericalism* as a danger to the state. Republican leaders believed that the best solutions were (1) to take education out of the hands of the Church and (2) to separate Church and state.

A national public-school system was established about 1880. By a series of laws (1) education was made free and compulsory for young children. (2) Only laymen were allowed to give instruction, and no religious teaching was allowed in the schools. (3) High schools and technical schools were provided for advanced students. (4) Training schools for teachers were established. (5) Every religious order in charge of schools, hospitals, or missions had to be specially authorized and regulated by the state. Soon afterward almost all religious orders were dissolved.

The republicans now turned to the problem of the clergy in politics. By the Concordat of 1801, between Napoleon I and the Pope, the bishops were appointed by the government, and the salaries of all the clergy were paid by the state. The French clergy, therefore, were in a sense government officials, as well as priests. Many of the republicans believed that the clergy should not take any part in political matters. Finally, in 1905, a law was passed to separate the Church from the state. The government ceased paying the salaries of the clergy and gave up the right to nominate the bishops.

Public Works and Aids to Industry · The Republic carried on large-scale public improvements. Thousands of miles of new roads were built and old ones repaired. The canal system, so important for inland transportation in France, was extended. Harbors were improved, and new ones were constructed.

Government aid was given to the many small farmers. This encouraged them to improve and increase their production of grapes, flax, hemp, and silk.

Many new factories were built, and the manufacture of French goods for export trade was greatly increased. A tariff act, passed in 1892, was designed to protect the French farmer and manufacturer.

The French people became noted for their thrift and industry. The savings of the peasants, placed in the banks, enabled these institutions to lend money to other nations. In time Paris came to rival London and New York as a money center.

France Rebuilds a Colonial Empire · France had lost most of her overseas possessions in India and North America in unsuccessful wars (pp. 283, 287). During the reign of Louis Philippe, however, she had conquered and annexed Algeria. Under Napoleon III she added the island of New Caledonia in the Pacific and Cochin China and Cambodia in Asia. Some of the republican leaders were opposed to further expansion. But others believed that France should get new markets across the seas.

Under the Third Republic, France built up a great colonial empire. In 1881 she seized Tunis and shortly afterward extended a protectorate over Annam and Tonkin, dependencies of China. The island of Madagascar and a part of Somaliland, on the east coast of Africa, were added later. She also made settlements on the west coast and in the interior, until she ruled most of northwest Africa.

In 1904 France came to an agreement with Britain, by which she was allowed a free hand in Morocco (p. 468). Here she

The French Capture a Tunisian Fort · *France sent troops into Tunisia from Algeria—and thereby antagonized Italy. Why?*

came into conflict with the rising power of Germany. By this time Germany had become concerned over the growth of British and French possessions and was determined to make her influence felt in world affairs.

CHECK ON YOUR READING

1. *Describe the causes, events, and outcome of the revolt of the Paris Commune.*
2. *What three great tasks faced the National Assembly? How were they met?*
3. *Describe the government of the Third Republic. Why did cabinets fall so easily?*
4. *How did the Republic deal with (a) clericalism? (b) education? (c) public works? (d) industry?*
5. *Use a map to show where France rebuilt her empire.*

4. The Making of Modern Italy

Mazzini · *This idealistic poet was imprisoned, exiled, and sentenced to death for revolutionary activities. Yet he never abandoned his dream of a united, democratic Italy. Who achieved it?*

Mazzini Arouses Italian Nationalism · In the years following the Congress of Vienna discontented Italians from time to time had attempted to free their land from foreign rule and to unite the various Italian states. But the early revolutions all failed. They had been largely local insurrections, poorly organized and directed. What was needed before Italy could achieve her independence was a widespread feeling of patriotism which would wipe out jealousies among the various states and bring the people together to work and fight for *national* freedom.

The most famous of the early patriotic leaders was Joseph Mazzini, poet and man of letters. His speeches and writings inspired many with his passionate love of country. His slogan was "Liberty, Equality, Humanity." In 1831 he founded an association called "Young Italy." Its members were dedicated to awaken enthusiasm for the new ideas of unity and independence and stir Italians everywhere to work for its achievement. By 1833 there were 50,000 members of the society.

Mazzini believed that Italy should be a republic, as it was in the glorious days of early Rome. Other leaders preferred to see the country organized as a federation of states under the leadership of the Pope. But all agreed in one thing, that Austria must be driven out of the peninsula. This awakening of nationalism in nineteenth-century Italy is called the *Risorgimento* ("resurrection").

Victor Emmanuel of Piedmont-Sardinia Leads the Way · After 1848 a growing number of liberals began to look to the kingdom of Sardinia (often called Piedmont-Sardinia) as the nucleus around which to build the nation. Although Charles Albert, king of Sardinia, had been severely defeated by the Austrians (p. 357), the people remembered that he had twice led the Italians in a war of liberation. Moreover, he had granted his country a constitution and after his defeat had abdicated in favor of his son, Victor Emmanuel II, in 1849.

Victor Emmanuel proved to be a courageous and patriotic ruler. He refused to take back the constitution granted by his father, in spite of Austrian bribes and threats. The hopes of Italian liberals became more than ever fixed on the House of Savoy (the Sardinian ruling family) as the leader of the national movement.

Cavour's Plans for Strengthening Italy · In 1852 Victor Emmanuel appointed as his prime minister Count Cavour, one of the greatest statesmen of the nineteenth century. Cavour was liberal and progressive. He greatly admired the parliamentary system as he had observed it during a stay in England. A businesslike minister with very practical plans, he increased the size of the army and undertook large public works. He favored the new scientific methods in agriculture and the introduction of machinery into manufacturing.

When Piedmont began to prosper, Cavour looked about for a strong ally to help rid Italy of Austrian control. To win recognition for the kingdom of Sardinia as a European power he entered the Crimean War in 1855 (p. 439). He had no quarrel with Russia, but he joined the war against her in order to ally himself with England and France and thus gain their favor.

Fortunately for Cavour, his allies were victorious. At the peace conference he obtained what he had sought. He was able openly (1) to denounce Austria for her interference in Italy, (2) to awaken sympathy for his cause, and (3) to interest Napoleon III. Piedmont-Sardinia was now established even more solidly as the leader of Italy.

Napoleon III Helps Sardinia · The French emperor promised aid in freeing Italy if Austria could be led to attack Piedmont. France would then appear justified in coming to her defense. With Austria out of the peninsula, Victor Emmanuel would rule over a kingdom of Northern Italy, and Napoleon in return for his help would receive Savoy and Nice. Napoleon persuaded himself that this would bring him great glory and that a war against Austria would be popular with his people.

Cavour · *Although born into the nobility, Cavour championed liberalism. He was unimpressive in appearance, but shrewd, realistic, skilled in diplomacy, and tireless in his efforts.*

Cavour thereupon cleverly managed to get Austria to declare war. Immediately the French came to Victor Emmanuel's assistance. In the fierce battles of Magenta and Solferino (June, 1859) the Austrian armies were defeated. But the losses on both sides were terrible. Lombardy was conquered, and Milan was occupied.

In the midst of these successes, however, Napoleon suddenly stopped fighting. Without consulting at all the wishes of Victor Emmanuel, he arranged an armistice with Austria. According to its terms Lombardy was to go to Italy, but Venetia was to remain an Austrian province. Whether it was because Napoleon was shocked by his heavy casualties, or fearful that a united Italy might become too powerful, he left his work half done.

SWITZERLAND AUSTRIA-HUNGARY

SAVOY

TYROL

LOMBARDY
1859

Novara
Magenta
Milan
Solferino
Turin

(FRANCE)
1860

PIEDMONT

Genoa

NICE

Nice

KINGDOM OF SARDINIA 1859

Rapallo

PARMA

MODENA

ROMAGNA

Florence

TUSCANY

1860

ELBA

PAPAL

STATES

Rome
1870

Naples

VENETIA
(FROM AUSTRIA)
1866

Custozza

Venice

Trieste

Adriatic Sea

CORSICA
(TO FRANCE)
1768

SARDINIA

Tyrrhenian Sea

KINGDOM OF THE TWO SICILIES
1860

THE UNIFICATION OF ITALY
1859-1870

Kingdom of Sardinia, 1859

United with Kingdom of Sardinia to
form Kingdom of Italy, 1859-1860

United with Kingdom of Italy, 1866

United with Kingdom of Italy, 1870

The Unification of Italy · Which kingdom formed the nucleus? Which country was the chief loser? Locate Rome, Naples, Florence, Elba, Nice, Genoa, Turin, Milan, Venice, and Trieste. What part did each play in Italy's history?

This was a great disappointment to Cavour. But the movement for unification was now so well started that it could not be halted, even by Napoleon's withdrawal. Modena, Parma, and Tuscany, which had revolted against their sovereigns, now refused to obey the terms of the armistice and restore their Austrian rulers. They asked to be united with Piedmont (1859). Finally, Cavour and Napoleon made a new agreement (1860). Tuscany, Parma, Modena, and Romagna joined the growing Italian kingdom, and Savoy and Nice passed to France (see map above).

Garibaldi Helps Unite Southern Italy · In 1860 the people of Sicily revolted against their despotic Bourbon king. This offered

an opportunity for Garibaldi, a patriotic hero of earlier revolutions, to come once more to the aid of his country. In May, 1860, he sailed to Sicily with his followers. After a few months of courageous fighting against overwhelming odds, he made himself the master of the island. He then crossed to the mainland and entered Naples just after its king had fled.

Garibaldi next proposed to march on Rome, but Victor Emmanuel knew that this would endanger all that had so far been gained. A French garrison was in the city. Napoleon III, in view of the strong Catholic sentiment in France, could not possibly permit any interference with the Pope. He agreed that Victor Emmanuel might annex the papal possessions to the north, but Rome and its surrounding territory must be left to the Pope. Accordingly, Victor Emmanuel took possession of the Papal States (except Rome). Then he entered Naples in October, 1860, where he rode through the streets in triumph with Garibaldi at his side. The king of Naples surrendered, and all southern Italy became a part of the new kingdom.

Victor Emmanuel II Becomes King of Italy · In February, 1861, the first Italian parliament was opened in Turin, the capital of Piedmont-Sardinia. Victor Emmanuel II was proclaimed King of Italy. But Venetia and Rome were still to be won to complete the unification.

We have already learned that Bismarck in 1866 induced Victor Emmanuel to attack the Austrians in Italy at the same time that Prussia struck from the north. Although the Italians were unsuccessful, the Prussian victory nevertheless brought them Venetia.

Rome with its surrounding district was finally gained as a result of the Franco-Prussian War. In order to strengthen his hard-pressed forces, Napoleon was compelled to call home the French troops that had been stationed in Rome. An Italian army occupied the "eternal city" in September, 1870, and the people of Rome voted to join the kingdom of Italy. Rome was made the capital, and the unification of Italy was complete.

The New Government and Its Relations with the Catholic Church · A limited monarchy was established, modeled after that of England. There was a parliament consisting of two houses—a senate and a house of representatives elected by the people.

Garibaldi as Bootmaker · *This simple-hearted patriot never forgave Cavour for yielding Nice, his birthplace, to France in exchange for aid. This cartoon from Punch is entitled "Right Leg in the Boot at Last." In the caption Garibaldi says, "If it won't go on, sire, try a little more powder." Who is trying on the boot? What did Garibaldi mean?*

The right to vote, however, was restricted. A man had to possess some property and pay taxes in order to vote. The ministry was responsible to parliament.

One of the most delicate problems of the new government was to arrange satisfactory relations with the Catholic Church. Shortly after the occupation of Rome the government passed the Law of Papal Guaranties. This assured the Pope the rank and privileges of a sovereign prince within the Vatican and control of the restricted church property. The Pope was to have his own court and officials and the right to deal freely with foreign governments. He was also to receive an annual payment of over $600,000 for the loss of other possessions.

The Pope, however, condemned the law and refused to recognize the right of the Italian government to occupy Rome. Nor would he accept the money offered by the invader. He regarded himself as a prisoner, and from 1870 until 1929 no Pope set foot outside the Vatican and St. Peter's. Strained relations between the Pope and the government lasted until 1929, when a settlement of the "Roman question" was finally made.

Development of Modern Italy · The new Italian government took an active part in building up the economic strength of the country. It encouraged industry and commerce, built roads and bridges, constructed railroads, made new harbors, and granted subsidies to shipping and commercial undertakings. It reorganized the army and built a navy. It introduced universal military training and spent large sums for modern equipment. The cost of armaments was very heavy. The high taxes fell heavily on the peasants and working people, whose standard of living was already low. Thousands of Italians migrated to the United States and South America.

The country was ruled by the House of Savoy until 1923, when the Fascist party came into power. After that time, although the monarchy remained, Italy for twenty years was governed by a fascist dictatorship under Benito Mussolini. He was overthrown during World War II, and in 1946 Italy became a republic. (A table showing members of the House of Savoy from 1831 to 1946 appears on page 277.)

CHECK ON YOUR READING

1. How did each of the following men contribute to the unification of Italy: Mazzini, Victor Emmanuel II, Cavour, Napoleon III, Garibaldi?
2. What events brought Venice and Rome into the state of Italy?
3. Explain (a) the new government's organization, (b) the Law of Papal Guaranties, (c) the development of modern Italy.

"The great events of our day will not be decided by speeches and resolutions of majorities . . . but by blood and iron."
—OTTO VON BISMARCK, 1886.

"I am free; free because I am a man, made in God's image."
—MAZZINI

Learning Activities

Think about the chapter

1. Compare the methods used by Bismarck and Cavour. How were they similar? different? Why?

2. What part did Napoleon III play in bringing about (a) the German Empire? (b) the French Republic? (c) a united Italy?

3. Account for the church-state problem in Germany, France, and Italy after 1870. How did the remedies differ?

4. Explain how the seeds of World Wars I and II were planted in 1871.

5. Compare the material progress made in France, Germany, and Italy from 1870 to 1914.

6. *Map study:* Show the step-by-step unification of (a) Germany and (b) Italy.

Go beyond the text

7. Investigate and report on one of the following: (a) the Dreyfus case, (b) the Crédit Mobilier, (c) the Crimean War, (d) Young Italy, (e) Garibaldi's *Red Shirts*, (f) the Ems telegram, (g) Gambetta's escape.

8. List the great German, French, and Italian writers of this period. What characterized their works?

Follow up your special interests

9. Draw cartoons to illustrate Bismarck's policies of paternalism and of "blood and iron."

10. Prepare a chart comparing the German, French, and Italian governments in 1871.

11. Write an account of some community in the United States where many Germans settled in the 1850's. Local histories and source books in United States history will help you.

12. How did the musicians Richard Wagner and Giuseppe Verdi reflect the German and Italian national spirit?

13. Read the famous story "The Last Class" by Alphonse Daudet. It will show you how the French felt about Alsace and Lorraine becoming German territory.

READ FURTHER

Basic readings: (1) Bauer and Peyser, *How Music Grew*, Chap. 25. (2) Becker, *Modern History*, Chaps. 12–14, 18. (3) Hoffman, *News of the World*, Nos. 47, 48. (4) Macy, *Story of the World's Literature*, Chaps. 38–41. (5) Robinson, *Readings*, Chap. 40. (6) Scott, Baltzly, *Readings*, Chaps. 5, 7, 9. (7) Taylor, *Fifty Centuries of Art*, pp. 151–171. (8) Year's *Pictorial History*, pp. 448–453, 462–471.

Special accounts: (9) W. Durant, *The Story of Philosophy*. The section on Nietzsche and Wagner will help good readers understand this period in Germany. (10) F. Ogg and H. Zink, *Modern Foreign Governments*. Political developments in France and Germany from 1871 to 1914 clearly presented. (11) F. Winwar, *The Land of the Italian People*. Excellent background materials.

Fiction and biography: (12) N. Baker, *Garibaldi*. A fast-moving narrative which gives good material on Cavour, Mazzini, and others connected with Italian unification. (13) E. Ludwig, *Bismarck*. One of the best biographies—for good readers. (14) G. de Maupassant, *The Odd Number*. A collection of short stories, including "The Necklace." (15) E. Orczy, *A Spy of Napoleon*. Melodramatic novel of political intrigue under Napoleon III.

24

The British Empire in the Nineteenth Century

CHAPTER OUTLINE

1. *Democratic Reform in Britain*
2. *Britain's Unhappy Relations with Ireland*
3. *British Rule in India*
4. *Canada Becomes a Dominion*
5. *Australia and New Zealand*
6. *South Africa*

KEY WORDS AND DATES

boroughs	De Valera
Tories	East India
Whigs	Company
Reform Bill	Mahrattas
1832	Gurkhas
Liberals	sepoys
Conservatives	Dominion
Dissenters	Upper and Lower
Factory Act	Canada
Corn Laws	Loyalists
free trade	Lord Durham
Gladstone	St. Lawrence
Disraeli	Seaway
Victoria	Captain Cook
Lloyd George	Commonwealth
home rule	Australian ballot
landlordism	Maoris
Ulster	Boers
1847	Rhodes
Sinn Fein	mandate

DURING THE NINETEENTH CENTURY Britain made great progress toward becoming a true democracy. An increasing number of people were granted the suffrage. Religious equality was finally established by ending unfair treatment of those who did not belong to the Church of England. Education was provided for the children of the poor. The condition of the workers in factories and mines was improved, and a beginning was made in the crusade against poverty and unemployment.

At the same time that the government was making reforms at home, Britain was building up the greatest empire in the world. India was brought under British rule, and Queen Victoria became empress. Canada, Australia, and New Zealand gained self-government. The British won South Africa in the Boer War, and the Union of South Africa was formed in 1910. The battle for home rule in Ireland was especially bitter.

It was natural that the peoples of the Empire should eventually demand the rights and opportunities and democratic reforms which were won in Britain. Hence our story is in large measure concerned with the struggle for home rule and for dominion and commonwealth status.

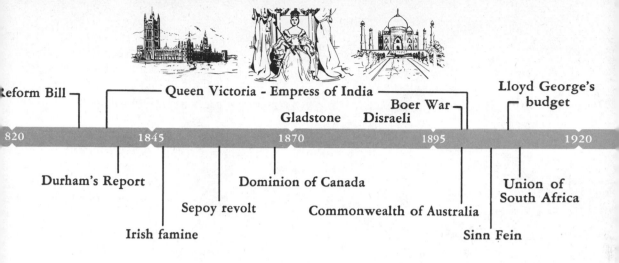

Reform Bill

Queen Victoria - Empress of India

Boer War

Lloyd George's budget

Gladstone   Disraeli

820   1845   1870   1895   1920

Durham's Report

Dominion of Canada

Sepoy revolt

Commonwealth of Australia

Union of South Africa

Irish famine

Sinn Fein

1. Democratic Reforms in the British Government

The Unfair System of Representation · While people on the continent of Europe were fighting for constitutions and representative government in the eighteenth and nineteenth centuries, England was enjoying parliamentary government. The king was a limited monarch. His ministers (the cabinet) could be overthrown by Parliament if their proposals failed to win majority approval. Then new elections might be held to permit the people to express *their* wishes by re-electing or defeating members of the House of Commons. But the system of representation had become unfair.

As late as 1830 there were many survivals of the old aristocratic order in the government. (1) Parliament represented nobles, landowners, and wealthy businessmen, who could run the government for their own benefit. (2) The right to vote was limited to those who had a certain amount of property. Thus the lower middle and working classes had no share in the government. Many of the farmers were merely tenants who rented parcels of ground, and they could not vote.

(3) No new allotment of seats in Parliament had been made in several hundred years. Yet population had increased tremendously in some areas and almost disappeared in others. Old towns (boroughs) which formerly had been permitted to send two representatives continued to do so, even if they had shrunk in size or disappeared. They were known as "rotten boroughs." One of them had actually been covered by the sea.

(4) Many boroughs were under the control of influential nobles or gentry, who could name their candidate for Parliament without fear of opposition. (5) Seats were obtained by bribery, and high prices were often paid by those who could afford it. (6) New and flourishing industrial cities, such as Manchester, Birmingham, and Leeds, had no representatives whatever in Parliament!

The People Demand Reforms · The failure of Parliament to meet some of the problems of the time called public attention to the serious lack of political equality. The period following the Congress of Vienna

411

Parade of the Chartists in London, 1848 · *They demanded universal suffrage, a secret ballot, abolition of property requirements, payment of representatives, equal election districts, and annually elected Parliaments. The movement failed, but all but the last demand was won by 1914.*

was one of hard times in England. The cost of the long wars with France had raised taxes. Manufacturing and trade fell off when the countries on the Continent were at last free to compete with English markets. The Corn Laws, which placed an import duty on foreign foodstuffs to protect the growers of wheat, kept food prices high. The disbanding of the armed forces increased the number of the unemployed.

People began to look about for some remedy for the bad situation, and there arose a general cry for a reform of Parliament as the cure-all for the distress of the day. The Tory party, which was in power, was opposed to any kind of change lest it lead to revolution. This attitude increased the bitter feeling and finally brought about the defeat of the Tories in 1830.

The Whigs, who now came into power, introduced a bill for parliamentary reform. But a majority in the House of Commons opposed it, and the ministry was forced to resign. Parliament then was dissolved, and new elections were held. The result was an overwhelming victory for the reformers.

The Reform Bill of 1832 Extends Suffrage to the Middle Class · After a heated contest the Reform Bill was passed. Under this measure (1) most "rotten boroughs" were abolished and new boroughs created. (2) Representation was, in general, made to correspond more nearly with the distribution of the population. (3) Additional representatives were allowed to Scotland and Ireland. (4) Property requirements were reduced so that a larger number of persons now could vote.

As a result of the Reform Bill, the middle classes, which included the factory-owners and businessmen, now had the vote. Parliament thus represented not only the agricultural interests of the landowners, but the industrial interests of the townsmen. The Whigs, who favored these reforms, came gradually to be called Liberals, and the Tories were called Conservatives.

Later Electoral Reforms · The workers and farmers, however, still clamored for the right to vote. And leaders of both parties realized that the suffrage should be widened to include a larger proportion of the people.

In 1867 a Conservative ministry introduced a bill which gave the vote to townsmen who paid taxes or who rented lodgings costing as much as fifty dollars a year. Similar terms were made for those living in the country. The passage of this measure nearly doubled the number of voters. In 1872 the secret, or Australian, ballot replaced open voting, which had given rise to much disorder at the polls.

In 1884 the suffrage was still further extended to include farm laborers and other classes that had been left out. By 1928 all women too could vote.

In 1885 the country was divided into equal electoral districts. Thus every member of the House of Commons would be chosen by about the same number of voters.

As a result of these reforms Britain became a model for representative government on the Continent and throughout the Commonwealth (the self-governing countries united under the British crown).

British Gain Religious Equality · The Toleration Act of 1689 (p. 256) had granted religious freedom, but this was not the same as religious equality. Only Church of England men could legally obtain offices in the government. Dissenters did succeed in obtaining appointments, but each year Parliament had to pass an act pardoning them for holding their offices illegally.

Members of other congregations had to pay for the support of the Church of England, as well as for that of their own church. Neither a Roman Catholic nor a Dissenter could graduate from the universities of Oxford and Cambridge. Thus the members of the Church of England formed a highly privileged class. After long agitation the laws against Dissenters were repealed in 1828. The next year the Catholic Emanci-pation Act placed Roman Catholics on a political footing with other citizens.

Improvement in Education · Around 1850 there was still a great deal of illiteracy in England. There was no national public-school system. The only education for the children of the working classes was provided by schools maintained by religious denominations. In 1833 Parliament began to grant money to aid these parochial schools, and the amount was gradually increased. Even then, instruction was furnished for only a small proportion of English children. Some districts had no schools at all.

In 1870 a new law aided schools that already existed and established new ones in districts that had none. In 1902 the educational system was reorganized by placing the schools under the direction of local government committees. But denominational schools still had representatives on the governing boards. Both religious and state institutions were supported by taxes and by parliamentary grants.

The Need for Prison Reform · *Gustave Doré's drawing shows prisoners in the exercise yard at Newgate prison in London. How might electoral reforms affect their lives?*

Reform of the Criminal Law · In 1800 the laws against crime were still unnecessarily severe. The death penalty was inflicted for at least two hundred offenses. For example, hanging was the punishment for picking a person's pocket or for stealing an article worth five shillings from a store.

Gradually these harsh laws were removed from the books. By 1861 the death penalty was inflicted for only a very few crimes, including murder and treason. Other severe measures, such as imprisonment for debt and the public whipping of women, had in the meantime been abolished. In 1835 Parliament provided for reform of the horrible conditions in the prisons.

Evils of the Factory System · Parliament for a long time delayed taking any action on the evils of the factory system. This was because statesmen and economists insisted on a *laissez-faire* (hands off) policy. The public consequences were often tragic. (1) Factory buildings, hurriedly put up with no thought of the workers' health, safety, or comfort, were frequently hazardous, unsanitary firetraps. (2) Women worked twelve or more hours a day at dangerous tasks. (3) But it was the wretched plight of the child workers which first attracted the attention of reformers. Poor orphans were sent to work long hours for practically no pay. Many other children were forced by poverty to toil in the mills under unhealthy conditions.

At last reformers were able to have a Factory Act passed (1833) which reduced the working hours of children in spinning and weaving mills. The employment of children under nine was prohibited. Sanitary conditions were to be improved and factory inspectors were to see that the law was obeyed. Other factory acts in the 1840's set a ten-hour limit on the working day of women and children and forbade their employment in mines.

England Adopts Free Trade · The British had long believed in protecting their home products by imposing tariff duties on most articles coming from other countries. With the growth of factories, businessmen began to complain that the system of protection was harmful to manufacture and trade. They argued that other countries would be better able to buy British goods if they could dispose of their own products in England.

The reformers now centered their attack on the Corn Laws (tariff on grain). They protested especially that duties on breadstuffs made food prices high. In 1845 the failure of crops in England and in 1846–1847 the potato famine in Ireland caused widespread distress. In the midst of this crisis the prime minister was able to secure the repeal of the Corn Laws (1846).

Between 1852 and 1867 all navigation laws and protective duties were done away with. England then followed a policy of free trade until after World War I.

Political Parties and Reform · Most of these stirring years of the reform movement came during the reign of Queen Victoria (1837–1901). Two great English statesmen alternated as prime ministers in the years from 1868 to 1894. They were William E. Gladstone, of the Liberal party, and Benjamin Disraeli, leader of the Conservatives.

Both of these leaders sponsored reform measures. Gladstone was particularly interested in political reforms. Disraeli led the way in improving public-health services, aiding labor unions, and improving housing conditions of the poor. He also sponsored additional factory legislation.

Queen Victoria (*above*) *ruled Britain and the Empire sixty-four years. Her greatest prime ministers were* **William E. Gladstone** (*left*), *representing the Liberals, and* **Benjamin Disraeli** (*right*), *leader of the Conservatives. With what great achievement can you associate each?*

The Conservative party's interest in reform, however, began to decline around 1888. For eighteen years their control of the government was almost uninterrupted. But in 1906 a general election took place. The Liberals, strengthened by a new Labor party and the Irish Nationalists, came into control of the House of Commons. A new period of far-reaching improvement then began.

The parties in power agreed that something must be done to relieve the poverty of a large part of the people. Programs of aid were introduced. These provided (1) help to those injured in factories; (2) pensions for aged workmen who could no longer earn a living; (3) improved working conditions in sweatshops where people toiled for miserably low wages; (4) work for the unemployed; (5) meals for poor school children; and (6) proper housing for the poor.

Lloyd George Makes War on Poverty · In 1908 David Lloyd George became Chancellor of the Exchequer, in charge of the nation's finances. Lloyd George and his sympathizers were shocked at the uneven distribution of wealth. They felt it unfair that ten men should own a quarter of London. They were angry over the fact that dukes controlled vast estates, charged high rents for miserable cottages, and drove out tenants at their pleasure.

The new budget submitted by Lloyd George included high taxes on luxuries and a heavy tax on large incomes. Great estates were also heavily taxed at the death of their owners. The most startling novelty was a

415

land tax which distinguished between landowners who farmed their lands and those who reserved vast areas as country estates or held city real estate with a view to selling it later at a great profit. Lloyd George proposed a tax of 20 per cent on "unearned increment" (an increase of land value which was not due to the owner's improvements).

Power of the Lords Reduced (1911) · The House of Commons passed Lloyd George's budget, but it was defeated in the House of Lords. Parliament was dissolved, and a new House of Commons was elected. Finding that the lower house was determined that the bill should pass, the Lords yielded. But the Liberals had been angered by their obstruction. They started a movement to make it impossible for the Lords to interfere again with the will of the people as expressed by their representatives in the Commons.

In 1911 a bill was passed taking from the Lords the power to defeat money bills. Any other bill passed by the Commons at three consecutive sessions, even though rejected by the Lords, might still become law. (In 1949 this period was reduced to one year.) This bill also provided that a new parliamentary election must be held every five years, instead of every seven as was formerly the case. Provision was also made for the payment of salaries to the members of the House of Commons.

CHECK ON YOUR READING

1. *In what six ways was the system of representation unfair?*
2. *What stimulated demands for reform?*
3. *Summarize the Reform Bill of 1832 and later electoral reforms.*
4. *What reforms were made in (a) religion, (b) education, (c) criminal law, (d) factory conditions, (e) trade?*
5. *How was each of the following involved in the reform movement: (a) Gladstone, (b) Disraeli, (c) Lloyd George, (d) House of Lords?*

---

2. Britain's Unhappy Relations with Ireland

Irish Resent Union with Britain · About 1870 the British government made a serious effort to improve its relations with Ireland. There were a number of long-time grievances which needed to be remedied. (1) The Irish continually resented forced union with Britain. They desired "home rule" (self-government). (2) Much Irish land was owned by absentee English landlords. (3) Catholic Ireland wanted religious equality with Protestant England.

After an insurrection in Ireland, Parliament had passed an Act of Union in 1801. It abolished the Irish parliament at Dublin and brought the two governments under one rule to form the United Kingdom of Great Britain and Ireland. The act provided that Ireland should be represented in the British Parliament by one hundred members in the House of Commons and twenty-eight Irish peers in the House of Lords. The British Isles were henceforth to have one sovereign and one Parliament at London, and were to form one state.

The Scots and Welsh tended to merge peacefully with the English. But the Irish resisted a union based upon force. They resented the abolition of their parliament at Dublin and eagerly desired to re-establish their independence.

The English Had Taken Irish Lands · Irish hatred of the English was of long standing. As early as the time of Henry II (1154–1189) Ireland was invaded by English nobles. They would go to the aid of a native king against his enemies, and were then rewarded for their services with large tracts of land. Henry II even took the title "Lord of Ireland." In 1494 the Irish parliament, which was now controlled by the English, provided that no measure should be introduced until it had been approved by the English king.

When Henry VIII broke with Rome, he set up his national church in Ireland as well as in England. Irish monasteries were suppressed, and their property taken. These acts of tyranny were bitterly resented by the Irish, who remained loyal Catholics. They did not hesitate to seize every opportunity to revolt.

Settlement of Ulster · A number of Irish rebellions during the reigns of Elizabeth and James I were cruelly put down. In 1610 a large part of the province of Ulster (Northern Ireland) was declared forfeit to the crown. Within a few years twenty thousand colonists, mostly Scotch Presbyterians, established themselves permanently there. Belfast became the capital of the Protestant Ulstermen, or Scotch-Irish. And Londonderry was one of their chief cities.

Cromwell punished Ireland terribly in the 1650's for its rebellion against the Commonwealth (p. 252). His armies destroyed cities and castles and seized large tracts of land. In 1688 the Irish sided with the Catholic king James II. After the successful Glorious Revolution, William II's army went over to Ireland and reconquered it (1690). At this time many Irish nobles

Landlordism—A Galway Eviction · *Irish tenants sometimes fought eviction by barricading themselves in their homes. But the law was on the side of the absentee landlords, and without "home rule" such resistance was useless. Why?*

and leaders emigrated to France, Spain, and other Catholic countries rather than live under a Protestant regime. Bitter feuds are still fought between the "Orangemen" and the "wearers of the green."

Landlordism, Famine, and Emigration · Almost no industries had been developed in Ireland, so that most of the people were dependent on farming for a living. Yet a large part of the land had come into the hands of absentee landlords who lived in England. They rarely set foot in the country and took no interest in their tenants beyond the money their agents could extort from them.

417

The British Isles before 1920 · *Name the four major parts. In 1920 Ireland was partitioned between Northern Ireland (Ulster) and the Irish Free State.*

If the tenant could not pay, he was promptly evicted. But even a tenant who paid was not secure. He might be put out of his home so that the landlord could get a higher rent from the next occupant. If an evicted tenant had made any improvements, he could not claim payment for them.

The peasants were often on the verge of starvation. In 1847, the "Black Year of Forty Seven," the potato crop failed almost entirely. Thousands died of starvation in spite of the relief given by the government. It was in the midst of this terrible famine that Irish emigrants began to come to America. Within half a century four million Irish left the shores of their native land. Many came to New York and to Boston. They carried with them a bitter hatred of England.

Separation of Church and State in Ireland (1869) · Although the English had succeeded in making Ulster Protestant, nearly all the Irish remained Catholic. Nevertheless the Anglican Church had been established as the official church. The people had to pay for its upkeep out of their scanty incomes even though they did not attend. At the same time, they tried to support their own Catholic priests as best they could.

The Irish parliament consisted only of Protestants, so that four-fifths of the people were excluded from the government. Harsh laws discriminated against the Catholics. Their children had to go to Protestant schools or remain at home. Catholics were not permitted to attend the university, nor could they hold public office.

It was not until 1869 that Catholics were able to break the hold of the established church in Ireland. With strong support from Gladstone, the Liberal prime minister, they succeeded in winning complete separation of church and state. The people were no longer required to pay taxes for the support of the Anglican Church. Henceforth it was to be maintained by voluntary gifts.

Land Reform · The Irish now turned to the great struggle to free themselves of landlordism. Land Acts passed in 1870 and 1881 granted their chief demands ("the three F's"). These were (1) a fair rent based on the value of the property as determined by the land courts, (2) a fixed rent, and (3) freedom of the tenant to sell his own property or the improvements he had made on the land.

These measures were followed by several land-purchase acts (1888–1903). The government set aside sums of money from which tenants wishing to buy their farms might borrow. These loans were to be repaid to the government in installments.

Demand for Home Rule in Ireland
Neither the settlement of the religious question nor the improvement of the land laws satisfied Irish patriots. Many still demanded the repeal of the Act of Union. Agitation for home rule (self-government) had been carried on by prominent leaders for years. Later, groups of violent radicals started a reign of terror in Ireland. They burned houses, maimed cattle belonging to English landlords, and even committed murder. In the meantime the Home Rule party in Parliament increased in number until by 1886 it had eighty-six members.

Gladstone finally proposed a bill establishing once more a separate parliament in Dublin and introducing home rule in the country. But many Liberals feared that this would mean the breakup of the unity of the Empire. They deserted their leader when the vote came, and the bill was defeated. Seven years later Gladstone tried again. This time the bill passed the House of Commons but was defeated in the House of Lords.

The question was a difficult one. The northern province of Ulster, with its large city of Belfast, had a slight majority of Protestants. They did not wish to be controlled by their Catholic countrymen and preferred to remain under British rule.

A Republican Party Arises in Ireland · In the early 1900's a party bent on making Ireland a free and independent republic grew up. These Republicans called themselves *Sinn Fein* (shĭn fān), Irish for "we ourselves." The Republicans gradually grew in strength, and during World War I some of them entered into negotiations with the Germans. The British easily put down the revolt, but their severe treatment

Agitation for Home Rule · *Police found it increasingly difficult to prevent the many "unauthorized" meetings organized to fight for Irish home rule.*

of the rebels greatly increased the ranks of the Republican party. In 1919 it set up a parliament of its own at Dublin and chose Eamon de Valera as its president. For later events in Ireland see Chapter 30.

CHECK ON YOUR READING

1. What long-standing grievances did the Irish have against the English?
2. How did the following influence Irish history: (*a*) English invasions, (*b*) Scotch Presbyterians, (*c*) landlordism, (*d*) famine, (*e*) emigration, (*f*) established church?
3. Describe the events and results of the battles for (*a*) separation of church and state, (*b*) land reform, (*c*) home rule.

3. British Rule in India

India after the Seven Years' War · The victories of Robert Clive during the Seven Years' War (1756–1763) marked the beginning of the British domination of India (p. 283). The empire of the Moguls had fallen apart and the East India Company became involved in many struggles with the native princes, who were constantly at war with one another. But because Clive supported the Mogul emperor, he secured many valuable privileges. The Company increased its territory and derived an immense income from taxes and business monopolies. Its officials gained great fortunes. Clive himself became very rich and frankly admitted that graft was taken by those in charge of the Company.

When this scandalous situation came to the attention of Parliament, it soon passed measures to regulate the affairs of the Company and reserved the right to appoint its officials. The three districts of Calcutta, Madras, and Bombay were placed under one administration. Warren Hastings was made governor of all the British possessions in India (1773).

By 1800 Ceylon and a large part of the Indian peninsula were either governed by the Company or indirectly controlled through influence over the native rulers. The French and Portuguese settlements had dwindled to mere trading posts.

The British Defeat the Mahrattas, the Gurkhas, and the Burmese · In central and western India there still remained a strong military power which threatened the safety of the natives as well as that of the British settlements. This was a union of native princes known as the Mahratta Confederacy. When the Mahrattas rose against the British in 1817, they were defeated in several serious battles. A large part of their land was annexed, but some of the princes were permitted to continue their rule under British sovereignty.

About the same time, the British conquered the Gurkhas, who lived to the north along the great mountain range of the

The British Recapture Delhi · *The city was taken from the mutineers by direct assault on the Kashmir Gate on September 14, 1857.*

Himalayas. These mountain folk were accustomed to sweep down from Nepal and destroy the villages of the peasants in the Ganges plain. When they attacked the British, the Company sent troops against them. After a two years' war (1814–1816) it compelled them to hand over certain recently acquired territory and to accept indirect British control.

The British next came into conflict with the Burmese, who had been moving in from the east. The British defeated the invaders and gained a large strip of territory along the east coast of Bengal. By 1852 the British had made themselves masters of the Irrawaddy valley and a long narrow stretch of land southeast of Rangoon. Finally, in 1884–1885, the whole country of Burma fell into their hands.

Conquest of the Punjab and Sind · On the northwestern frontier of India was a fertile region known as the Sind. It controlled the lower part of the Indus and the commerce which came from northern India by way of the river. The Sind was annexed in 1843.

Two wars (1845, 1849) with the Sikh warriors of the Punjab resulted in the addition of this great region. The British now controlled the river system of the northwest plains and had a natural boundary for India on the borders of Afghanistan. During the next few years the administration of the Punjab region was reformed, the country developed, and roads improved. The Ganges canal was opened and the ground was broken for the first Indian railway.

Gradually other states were added to the British dominions as the native ruling families died out. The chief of these states was Nagpur. Oudh, northwest of Bengal, was annexed in 1856 because of constant misrule in the province.

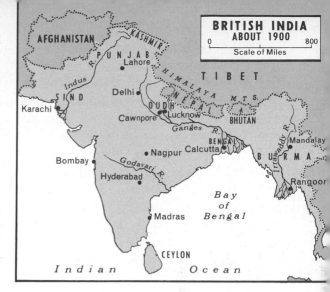

British India · *By 1900 the British controlled what we now call India, Pakistan, and Burma. What great rivers drain these areas? Locate places mentioned in the text.*

The Revolt of the Sepoys (1857) · The annexation of Indian states caused great unrest among the people. They were much disturbed by the interference with some of their native customs and the changes which the Westerners introduced. The Moslems hated the Christian invaders, and the Mahrattas were angry with the British for putting an end to their power.

In addition to the existing grievances of the natives came a new practice. This was the introduction in the army of a new kind of ammunition for the rifles—cartridges greased with the fat of cows and pigs. This shocked the religious ideas of the Indian troops (called sepoys). The cow was sacred to the Hindus, and swine were unclean to the Moslems.

In May, 1857, the sepoys mutinied at Delhi and massacred the English inhabitants of the city. The natives of Lucknow likewise rose against the foreigners. At

421

Cawnpore a thousand British men, women, and children were cruelly murdered. Many of the sepoys remained loyal, however. With their aid the British armies were able gradually to recapture the cities and put down the rebellion.

Direct Rule for India · Parliament now decided to make a complete change in the government. The Better Government for India Act (1858) took the control of the country out of the hands of the East India Company, which had directed it for 250 years. India henceforth was to be governed by the crown.

In England a member of the cabinet—the Secretary of State for India—was to have charge of the country's affairs. The administration in India was to be headed by a viceroy appointed by Parliament and assisted by an executive council. On January 1, 1877, Queen Victoria was proclaimed Empress of India. Her successors had among their titles that of "Emperor of India" until 1947, when India became a self-governing state (p. 629).

CHECK ON YOUR READING

1. *Locate on a map and tell how each of the following was secured: (a) Calcutta, Madras, Bombay, (b) central and western India, (c) Burma, (d) Punjab and Sind.*
2. *Identify: (a) Clive, (b) the Moguls, (c) Hastings, (d) Mahrattas, (e) Gurkhas, (f) Sikhs, (g) sepoys, (h) Victoria.*

---

4. Canada Becomes a Dominion

The French and English in Canada · Canada is the most important member of the British Commonwealth in the Western world today. But the English in 1763 considered trading it for the French sugar island of Guadeloupe. At that time Canada was a vast, unexplored wilderness stretching far into the north. And most of its inhabitants were loyal to the traditions and culture of France. From the first, the difference in religion and national sympathies between the French and the English made the task of governing Canada a difficult one.

In 1774, hoping to win the loyalty of the French population in Canada, Parliament passed the Quebec Act. It granted freedom of worship to Roman Catholics and recognized the rights of the Catholic clergy. It required of these North American subjects only a simple oath of allegiance to the British crown. French civil law was used in the conduct of daily affairs. Thus, at a time when English Catholics still had not gained religious liberty, Britain protected her French colonial subjects by respecting their religion, their language, and their laws.

During and after the American Revolution many Loyalists who preferred to remain under English rule fled from the United States into Canada. Parliament granted them land either in Canada or in Nova Scotia.

So many settled in Nova Scotia that the western part of the province was made separate and given the name New Brunswick. English refugees also settled in the St. Lawrence valley, but the majority pushed farther west.

Canada Divided into Two Provinces · In 1791 Parliament passed a Constitutional Act dividing the country into Upper Canada (now Ontario) and Lower Canada

Canada Today · *In area, Canada is the second largest country in the world. Her population, heavily concentrated along the southeast border, is somewhat larger than that of New York State. Why does the future hold such great promise?*

(Quebec). It established self-government in the two provinces by allowing each to have its own local council and assembly. Anglican and Roman Catholic churches were both permitted.

This generous act, however, did not bring the harmony expected. As newer settlers came to Upper Canada they complained of the power of the Loyalists. In Lower Canada the French resented British rule. Moreover, the division of the country was unwise from the standpoint of efficient government control. In 1837 there were revolts in both provinces. The rebellions were easily put down, but the British gov-

ernment sent over Lord Durham to investigate and report on affairs.

Lord Durham's Report (1839) · Lord Durham remained in America for five months. His *Report* proved to be a noteworthy document in the history of British colonial government. In it he maintained that harmony could best be restored by following the principles of the British constitution which had been found to work so successfully at home.

Lord Durham therefore recommended the introduction of the English cabinet system. This meant that the Canadian Executive Council, which assisted the governor,

The Canadian Parliament, Ottawa · *Inset: Prime Minister Diefenbaker welcomes Elizabeth II of Britain, queen of Canada, on a state visit.*

would carry out the wishes of the elected Assembly. England would continue to control foreign relations, trade, and the disposal of public lands. But in internal matters the colonists would be permitted to manage their own affairs.

Lord Durham urged the rejoining of Upper and Lower Canada into one province. This was done in 1840 in the Act of Union. This act also provided for various administrative reforms.

The Dominion of Canada · In 1867 the British North America Act united Ontario, Quebec, New Brunswick, and Nova Scotia into the Dominion of Canada. Prince Edward Island joined six years later. Newfoundland remained outside until 1949.

Since the passage of this measure, great regions in the west and north have been settled and organized into territories some of which later became provinces. These included Manitoba, 1870; British Columbia, 1871; Saskatchewan and Alberta, 1905.

The federal constitution of Canada provides for a governor-general, appointed by the Crown on the advice of the Canadian government. Although he represents the queen, the governor-general has little real power. The responsibility for governing belongs to the Canadian parliament. It consists of a Senate and a House of Commons, the latter elected by the people. The prime minister and his cabinet are responsible to the House of Commons. Each of the provinces has a lieutenant governor and its own assembly.

People, Resources, and Promise · Canada is larger in area than the United States, although its population is about one-tenth that of its neighbor. Most of the people live in the more temperate areas along the fertile southern border.

In opening up and developing this land of vast distances and resources the railways have played a leading part. On the seacoasts, fisheries are an important business. On the vast prairies of the West millions of bushels of wheat are grown. Canada is rich also in coal, nickel, gold, silver, copper, platinum, iron, oil, uranium, and asbestos. Canadian forests support great lumbering and wood-pulp industries. Cheap hydroelectric power is used to produce aluminum from imported bauxite ores. Manufacturing has been encouraged by protective tariffs and bounties. Today Canadian corporations compete with American companies in nearly every business.

Canada has served as a model to other parts of the Commonwealth. Entirely independent it is still stanchly loyal to the British crown. In both world wars, Canadian forces served with honor and distinction in the cause of the mother country.

Canada has likewise maintained very friendly relations with the United States. Between them is an unfortified 4000-mile border. They have shared in the development of the St. Lawrence Seaway, in vital measures of joint defense, and in the North Atlantic Treaty Organization. The Distant Early Warning (DEW) radar line protects both countries from surprise attack.

The future holds tremendous promise for a people so vigorous, a land so rich in resources, and a nation so responsive to the challenge of greatness.

CHECK ON YOUR READING

1. What difficulties faced the British in Canada?
2. Where did the Loyalists settle?
3. Why was Canada divided?
4. Summarize Lord Durham's Report.
5. How is Canada governed today?
6. Describe Canada's people, resources, and promise.

· 5. Australia and New Zealand

How Australia Was Discovered · In 1642, Tasman, a Dutch navigator from the East Indies, discovered the shores of an island later named Tasmania. Tasman also discovered the islands to the east, which were called New Zealand. On a second voyage he came to the northern coast of Australia, which the Dutch then named New Holland. The Dutch, however, never occupied the islands.

The English did not become interested in the region until after the famous voyages of Captain Cook to the South Seas. On his first expedition (1768–1770) Cook charted the shores of New Zealand. Having surveyed the east coast of Australia, he landed at a point which he called Botany Bay because of its luxuriant foliage. He claimed the country in the name of the British king and called it New South Wales.

British Settlement of Australia · Australia and Tasmania were occupied at this time by a scattered population of savages in an especially low stage of civilization. No European power had made any serious attempt to establish a foothold there. Then the English decided that Botany Bay, near the modern town of Sydney, would be an excellent and remote spot to send criminals and debtors from England.

For many years convicts were landed in Australia and Tasmania. Many, however, were guilty only of political offenses or of being in debt. Around 1850 so many free British colonists also had come to Australia that they induced the government to give up sending convicts to these lands.

Settlements were first made at Hobart (1804), Brisbane (1825), and Melbourne (1835). These towns became the centers respectively of the colonies of Tasmania, Queensland, and Victoria, which separated themselves from the original settlement of New South Wales. South Australia and Western Australia developed independently of the mother colony.

After about 1840 the interior was explored, and routes were sought across the great wilderness. In 1872 an overland telegraph line was carried from Adelaide to the northern port of Darwin, as it is now called. Here it connected with a cable to England.

Australia and New Zealand · *The ANZACS from these great Commonwealths fought against tyranny in two world wars. They are members of the ANZUS and SEATO pacts.*

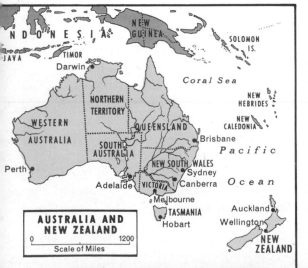

AUSTRALIA AND NEW ZEALAND
0   1200
Scale of Miles

Resources of Australia · Coal deposits were discovered at several places, and Australia has continued to produce large quantities of coal ever since. Sheep were brought to the island, and explorers found that beyond the mountains of the east coast were great, fertile plains suitable for grazing. Sheep-raising developed rapidly, and the production of wool soon became the country's leading industry. Australia today is the world's greatest exporter of wool. Wheat, too, is exported in quantity.

The discovery of gold in New South Wales and Victoria in 1851 brought a rush of adventurers seeking their fortunes. The population almost trebled in the next ten years. Today Australians number over ten million.

Australia Becomes a Commonwealth · In 1900 Parliament passed an act creating the Commonwealth of Australia. It was composed of six states—New South Wales, Tasmania, Victoria, Queensland, South Australia, Western Australia—and the Northern Territory plus several islands.

As in Canada, a governor-general represents the Crown, but executive authority is exercised by the cabinet. The federal parliament has two houses—a Senate with six senators from each state, and a House of Representatives elected by the people.

The system of secret voting which is called the "Australian ballot" was first used in 1855. It has since been adopted in England and the United States. Its purpose is to permit citizens to express their preference freely, without fear or compulsion.

The Islands of New Zealand · Twelve hundred miles to the southeast of Australia lie the islands of New Zealand. About five-sixths the size of Great Britain and Ireland, they stretch from the tropics to the antarctic. In 1840 England made a treaty

Canberra is Named and Made the Capital of Australia, March 12, 1913 · *Foundation stones were laid by the Prime Minister, Governor-General (center), and Home Minister.*

immediately adopted. Railways were built, and generous offers were made to attract settlers from Great Britain to the islands.

Progressive Reforms · New Zealand has attracted much attention on account of its political, economic, and social reforms. (1) The vote was granted to all men in 1879. (2) In 1893 New Zealand became the first country to give women the franchise on equal terms with men. (3) In 1891 a graduated tax was levied on land and incomes. (4) A high property tax discouraged the wealthy from holding vast estates. (5) A Land Settlement Act compelled owners of large tracts of land to sell part of their property for small farms. This was especially important because sheep-raising and dairy farming are the principal sources of income for the two and one-half million people.

with the native Maoris, by which the sovereignty of the islands passed to the British crown. The Maoris were made British subjects and given the right to retain their lands as long as they desired.

In 1852 a Constitutional Act united the six independent settlements in New Zealand into a loose federation. Each province was permitted its own local council. The Maoris were to receive better protection of their rights. As the population increased and the number of provinces grew, the need was felt for a strong central government which would promote the interest of the islands as a whole.

In 1865 the capital was moved from Auckland to Wellington. Eleven years later the provincial system was abolished, and a single government for New Zealand was established. A public-works policy was

The New Zealand Parliament, Wellington · *What important measures have been passed here? What body served as a model for New Zealand's parliament?*

New Zealand also became a pioneer in labor legislation. Laws were enacted (6) to protect factory workers, (7) to provide insurance against accident and old age, and (8) to provide for the arbitration of disputes between employers and employees.

The state has also introduced many socialistic measures. The government owns the telephone and telegraph systems and the railroads. When profits on the railroads exceeded 3 per cent, passenger and freight rates were lowered. New Zealand has a state bank. The government maintains a life and fire insurance department and a Public Trust Office, which settles estates. In order to reduce the level of prices the government has, in some cases, entered the field of private business. It has operated coal mines, sawmills, and other industries when it believed special regulation was needed.

CHECK ON YOUR READING

1. *By whom and when were Australia and New Zealand discovered?*
2. *Describe their (a) resources, (b) government, (c) problems.*
3. *Summarize political, economic, and social reforms.*

---

6. South Africa

The Importance of the Cape · When the Portuguese explorer Dias reached the southern point of the African continent in 1487, he named the land the Cape of Storms. But his monarch is said to have renamed it the Cape of Good Hope because he believed that his sailors could now hope to find their way to India. Ten years later Vasco da Gama did round the Cape and successfully reached the Indies.

After the Dutch took over the Portuguese trade, the Dutch East Indian Company founded a settlement near Cape Town (1652). Soon Dutch farmers ("boers") developed farms and supplied the ships of the company with vegetables and fresh meat on their long journey to India.

During the Napoleonic Wars the British seized the Dutch colony. They feared that the French, who already controlled Holland, would take possession of this important point on the trade route to India.

When the British began to occupy the colony, they changed the system of government and the courts and introduced the English language. In 1822 they abolished slavery. This measure fell heavily on the Dutch, who were dependent on slave labor to work their farms.

The Boers Found the Orange Free State and the Transvaal · Angered by all these changes, the Dutch moved northward into a barren region across the Orange River. There they hoped to have a new home without interference. When the British claimed this district, the Dutch pushed still farther north, this time across the Vaal River. Here they founded the colony of Transvaal. The British apparently thought this wilderness not worth fighting for. They recognized the independence of the Orange Free State and the Transvaal (1852).

In 1886, however, gold was discovered in the southern part of the Transvaal. Land that was formerly judged worthless suddenly seemed of great value. Thousands of foreigners, chiefly English, began to rush

Boer Covered-Wagon on the Great Trek, (1835–1836) · *This ox-drawn vehicle was the means by which the Dutch farmers carried their families and worldly goods in the great migration (trek) northeastward from Cape Town.*

into the Dutch colony. In order to protect their country from the intruders the Dutch made it difficult for them to gain citizenship.

The British claimed that their energy and hard work had changed a poor country into a rich and prosperous one and that that entitled them to a share in making the laws. They tried to have the constitution of the Transvaal altered. When they failed, they planned an attack on the Boers.

The Boer War (1899–1902) · The prime minister of Cape Colony appears to have encouraged the conspiracy. He was Cecil Rhodes, an Englishman who had amassed a great fortune in South Africa. Dr. Jameson, an agent in one of his companies, started into the Transvaal with armed forces to support an uprising of the British in Johannesburg. Jameson's raid failed, and the Boers captured the insurgents.

Under Paul Kruger, the president of the Transvaal Republic, the Boers began to make preparations to defend themselves and entered into an alliance with the Orange Free State. In 1899 they declared war on Great Britain. They proved to be good guerrilla fighters and inflicted heavy losses upon the British.

In the United States and in Britain itself there was much sympathy for the Boers in their struggle to maintain their independence. But British reinforcements were sent to South Africa, and in three years the war was over. The two republics were annexed by Britain in 1902.

The Union of South Africa · *Locate and identify each place mentioned in Section 6 of the text.*

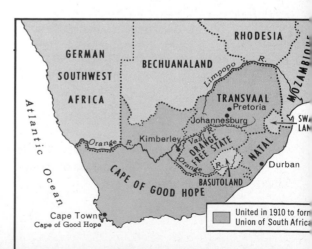

Jan Christian Smuts · *This South African statesman inspired the Commonwealth idea.*

The Union of South Africa (1910) · The British policy toward the defeated people was lenient. The Dutch language was to be used in the schools and courts. A sum of money was set apart to help the Boers rebuild their homes. Britain also gave the colonies self-government.

In 1910 an act of Parliament formed a Union of South Africa on the model of Canada. It included Cape of Good Hope province, Natal, Transvaal, and the Orange Free State. The first premier was General Louis Botha, who had fought against the British in the Boer War. Botha looked after the interests of the Boers, who outnumbered the British. But he was loyal to the Empire. During World War I he took up arms for the cause of Britain. Under his leadership the German colony of South-West Africa was conquered.

Today the Union of South Africa has a population of almost fifteen million, of which about one-fifth are of white European origin. The capital is at Pretoria, but the legislature meets in Cape Town. The country is richest in gold, diamonds, and uranium. Corn, cotton, wool, and wheat are its major farm products.

Other British Possessions in Africa · Britain acquired many other possessions in Africa. Three large colonies were occupied almost entirely by Negroes. These were (1) Bechuanaland, (2) Rhodesia, and (3) British East Africa. This latter region controls the southern approach to the Sudan and Egypt and the great lakes at the source of the Nile.

The British also gained colonies on the west coast of Africa—Gambia, Sierra Leone, the Gold Coast, Lagos, and Nigeria. After World War I, Tanganyika (formerly German East Africa) was placed as a "mandate" under the rule of Great Britain. South-West Africa was mandated to the Union of South Africa. In 1957 the Gold Coast became an independent member of the British Commonwealth under the name of Ghana. (See map, p. 372.)

CHECK ON YOUR READING

1. Show how the Cape was important to three nations.
2. Describe the founding of the Boer republics.
3. What were the (a) causes, (b) highlights, and (c) results of the Boer War?
4. Summarize South Africa's (a) language, (b) leadership, (c) population, (d) resources.
5. Use a map to point out the British possessions in Africa.

Learning Activities

Think about the chapter

1. How did the Industrial Revolution bring about the repeal of the Corn Laws? What is meant by free trade?

2. Summarize the democratic reforms accomplished in the nineteenth century.

3. How do you account for the differences in British relations with the Irish and the Boers compared to the Canadians and Australians?

4. Why has India been so significant in English history?

5. *Map study:* On a world map, label the parts of the British Empire (*c.* 1910) discussed in this chapter. Color the Commonwealth nations.

Go beyond the text

6. Investigate and report on the Peterloo Massacre and Chartist riots. Which demands of the Chartists later became laws?

7. In what countries of the world is religious *freedom* still denied? religious *equality*?

8. Read one of the fine biographies available on Queen Victoria or Cecil Rhodes.

9. Compare and contrast the personalities, policies, and type of leadership of Gladstone and Disraeli.

10. Report on (a) the status of the Irish Republic and Northern Ireland today, on (b) Commonwealth leadership in the United Nations today.

11. What is the relationship today between England and the Commonwealth nations?

Follow up your special interests

12. Dramatize a session in the House of Commons in 1893 when the subject under discussion is home rule for Ireland. Present the points of view of an Irish nationalist, an Englishman who owns land in Ireland, a member from Ulster, a Conservative who opposes home rule, and of Mr. Gladstone.

13. Read some of Kipling's poems and short stories that deal with India.

14. Make a collection of pictures for a bulletin-board display of Australia, Union of South Africa, Canada, Ireland, or India.

15. Prepare a "Who's Who" of Victorian English writers.

READ FURTHER

Basic readings: (1) BECKER, *Modern History*, Chaps. 15, 18. (2) CHEYNEY, *Readings*, Chaps. 19–20. (3) CHEYNEY, *Short History of the English People*, Chaps. 17, 20. (4) HOFFMAN, *News of the World*, Nos. 45–48. (5) MACY, *Story of the World's Literature*, Chaps. 35, 37. (6) SCOTT, BALTZLY, *Readings*, Chaps. 3, 6. (7) TAYLOR, *Fifty Centuries of Art*, pp. 146–150. (8) *Year's Pictorial History*, pp. 380–385, 393–395, 424–427, 440–441, 457–461.

Special accounts: (9) M. MODAK, *The Land and the People of India*. (10) F. ROSS, *The Land and the People of Canada*.

Fiction and biography: (11) T. BONNET, *The Mudlark*. A London waif's adventure with Queen Victoria and Disraeli. (12) E. FORSTER, *A Passage to India*. This novel gives an insight into relations between the Hindus and Moslems and the English rulers —for mature readers. (13) E. GOUDGE, *Green Dolphin Street*. A story of two English girls who are in love with a boy who had sailed to New Zealand. (14) R. KIPLING, *Kim*. The orphan son of an Irish soldier who is brought up among the Hindus is found by members of his father's regiment. (15) R. LLEWELLYN, *How Green Was My Valley*. Scenes of life in a Welsh mining village around 1890. (16) A. MAUROIS, *Disraeli* and *Cecil Rhodes*. Good biographies for mature readers. (17) C. NORDHOFF and J. HALL, *Botany Bay*. Story of the first penal settlement in Australia, but the hero is an American, wrongfully accused of a crime.

CHAPTER

25

The Romanovs, Ottomans, and Revolutions

KEY WORDS AND DATES

oppression	Greece
Alexander I	Crimean War
Romanovs	(1854–1856)
Alexander II	Sevastopol
reforms	Balkans
emancipation	Congress of Berlin
(1861)	(1878)
terrorism	Trans-Siberian
Plehve	Railroad
pogroms	Manchuria
Ottomans	Port Arthur
Constantinople	Korea
Suleiman	Mukden
Crimea	Portsmouth, 1905
Bessarabia	Sakhalin
The Eastern	"Red Sunday"
Question	Duma
Serbia	October Manifesto

WHILE WESTERN EUROPEANS were gaining political rights in the nineteenth century, the peoples dominated by the Romanov tsars and the Ottoman sultans were living under a system of absolute despotism. Hard-won reforms, such as the freeing of the serfs, were grudgingly given to forestall revolt. And many were withdrawn as soon as circumstances permitted. Censorship, secret police, mass imprisonment, exile, and utter absence of civil liberties were as typical then as they are in Communist Russia today.

The Ottoman Empire had expanded throughout the Near East, North Africa, and the Balkans until it posed a threat to Christian Europe. As it weakened, many of its subject peoples revolted. The Serbs and Greeks won their independence. Russian ambitions in the Balkans and Mediterranean led to two wars with Turkey.

During this period the Industrial Revolution was having its impact on Russia. It brought about the rise of political groups, with persistent demands for reform. The building of the great Trans-Siberian Railroad resulted in a conflict of interest between Russia and Japan in Manchuria and Korea. The resulting war ended in Russian defeat, loss of territories, and a revolution.

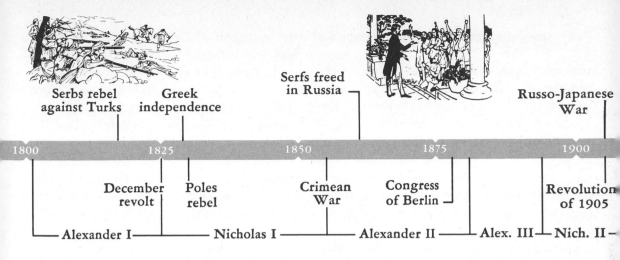

Serbs rebel against Turks	Greek independence		Serfs freed in Russia		Russo-Japanese War
1800	1825	1850	1875	1900	
	December revolt	Poles rebel	Crimean War	Congress of Berlin	Revolution of 1905
Alexander I		Nicholas I	Alexander II	Alex. III	Nich. II –

1. Autocracy, Reform, and Terror (1801-1917)

The Russia of Alexander I (1801–1825) · When Tsar Alexander I returned home from the Congress of Vienna (p. 339), he was one of the most influential rulers of Europe. His armies had started Napoleon on his downfall. At the peace conference the tsar had been able to add Poland and Finland to his dominions.

His vast realm now stretched from the borders of Germany and Austria eastward across Asia to the Pacific. It was made up of many peoples: Finns, Poles, Germans, Lithuanians, Estonians, Ukranians, Georgians, and Mongols. Dominating them all, however, were the Russians, whose tongue was the official language taught in all the schools.

The tsar, as "autocrat of all the Russias," was an absolute monarch ruling by divine right. He held the church and the state in an iron grip. Those who questioned his power were imprisoned, executed, or exiled to Siberia. The great mass of people were serfs, as ignorant and wretched as those of England or France seven hundred years before.

In his early days Alexander had been friendly toward liberal ideas. He had even given the Poles a separate constitution when they were annexed to Russia. His "Holy Alliance" showed his idealism and sense of responsibility toward his subjects.

But as time went on, Alexander fell under the influence of Metternich. Finally he became so alarmed at small revolutionary uprisings that he denounced liberalism as a danger to peace and good order. Liberal newspapers were suppressed, and the universities were watched lest any dangerous ideas be spread. But Alexander could not prevent some of his more intelligent subjects from reading the new books from western Europe which told of scientific discoveries and discussed social reform.

Alexander I died suddenly on December 1, 1825. The revolutionary societies which had grown up as a result of the oppressive measures of the government seized this opportunity to organize a revolt. But this "December revolution" was easily put down with a few rounds of grapeshot, and some of the Decembrist leaders were hanged.

Oppression and Revolt under Nicholas I (1825–1855) · Nicholas I was even more autocratic than his older brother. His ruthless officials sought in every way to prevent the entrance of Western ideas into the country. Books on religion, science, and philosophy were carefully examined by the police. Foreign works containing references to politics were seized, or objectionable pages were blotted out by the censors. Suspicion was so great that even dots indicating some omission in the text were forbidden lest they carry some hidden meaning for the reader. Private letters were opened, even if there was no reason to suspect the writers of disloyalty.

Nicholas also showed his despotism in his treatment of the Poles. Their government offices were filled with Russians. Petitions

The Poles Revolt against Russian Oppression, Warsaw, November 29, 1830. · *The Russians crushed this rebellion, and several others which followed. But their attempts to "Russify" the population failed.*

of the Polish diet were ignored, and freedom was severely restricted.

We have already seen (p. 356) how the revolution against the Bourbons in France (1830) encouraged the Poles to rise against their Russian oppressors. But the tsar's armies crushed the rebellion with great cruelty. The Polish constitution was taken away, the diet abolished, and display of the national flag forbidden. Forty-five thousand Polish families were sent into exile.

The kingdom of Poland henceforth became practically a Russian province, governed from the capital at St. Petersburg. Every effort was made to wipe out the national culture of the subject people and to Russianize the country. Education was discouraged and study abroad was prohibited. Even the works of the great Polish writers were no longer allowed to be printed. The terrible oppression which Poles today associate with communism echoes the time of Nicholas I.

Alexander II (1855–1881) Grants Some Reforms · Before the end of his reign Nicholas I became involved in the Crimean War against Turkey, England, and France. It fell to his son Alexander II to arrange the terms of peace (p. 440). The new tsar also had to face the unhappy results of his father's policies both at home and abroad. The war had wasted the lives of thousands of her young men and brought Russia nothing. It had also dragged into the open (as wars have a way of doing) the dishonesty and incompetence of those in high places.

Alexander was still autocrat of the Russias. But circumstances forced him to grant some reforms to quiet the unrest of the people. (1) Political prisoners were released, and some of the exiles were allowed to return home. (2) Censorship of the press was less strictly applied. (3) A number of local assemblies were created. They could manage primary schools and hospitals. (4) The universities enjoyed greater freedom, and (5) Russians were once more permitted to travel abroad. (6) Above all, Alexander recognized the necessity of improving the lot of the serfs, whose labor was of such importance to the country.

Freeing the Serfs (March, 1861) · The serf was practically the slave of his owner and was regarded as scarcely more than a beast of burden. Some of the serfs were cruelly treated. From time to time driven to desperation by their hard lot, the serfs rose in rebellion. Under Nicholas I over five hundred riots had occurred, and the number seemed to increase, notwithstanding the watchfulness of the police.

Alexander II, fearful of more serious trouble, decided to free forty million of his subjects from serfdom. His emancipation decree abolished all rights of their masters over them. But the serfs still remained bound to the land. They were not permitted to leave their communities without a government order.

Land surrendered by the nobles was handed over to the village community (*mir*) as a whole. The community then allotted land to the peasants for their use. The serfs had no money, and prices set were far greater than real value. The government therefore paid the landlords and then collected the amount from the peasants in installments.

The new freedom brought the peasants mostly hard labor. They lived constantly on the verge of starvation and fell far behind in their land payments. Finally, in 1904, Tsar Nicholas II canceled the debts, which the peasants in any case could never have settled.

Gambling with Human Lives · *Gustave Doré caricatured the heartlessness of landlords who treated their serfs as stacks of poker chips.*

Two years later the tsar issued an order permitting peasants to leave their villages and seek employment elsewhere if they wished. They might become owners of their allotments if they had paid for their land. In this way the old village community holding was abolished, and peasants were permitted to become property-owners. Thus it was not until the twentieth century that Russia did away with the remains of medieval serfdom. Then communism substituted a serfdom of a different type.

Terrorism in Russia · But Alexander had made his reforms merely to prevent disaster. A second revolt in Poland (1863) and an attempt on his life (1866) put an end to any further concessions. Alexander now became as reactionary as the officials who surrounded him.

Despair spread among the members of the educated classes. Young people joined secret societies for the study of history, constitutional government, and socialism. Similar groups were formed in the universities.

Exiles on the Way to Siberia, 1891 · *The prison camps of Siberia have sealed the fate of millions who dared resist autocracy—whether it be Tsarist or Communist.*

The tsar's officials were kept busy tracking down reformers and arresting the more active among them. The prisons were soon crowded, and hundreds were banished to Siberia.

Some of the reformers now became convinced that there was no course left but violence. They began to engage in bombings and assassinations in order to frighten the officials and open the eyes of the world to the injustice of their situation.

But the government fought terrorism with terror. Many revolutionists were hanged, and scores were sent to the dungeons of St. Petersburg or to work in the mines of Siberia. Numerous attacks were made on the life of the tsar and his hated officials.

Finally Alexander agreed to have a commission chosen to discuss possible reforms. But it was too late. On the afternoon that he gave his consent to this move, he was killed by a bomb.

Alexander III (1881–1894) and Nicholas II (1894–1917) Defend Autocracy · Alexander III at once proclaimed his faith in the "right and wisdom of autocracy." The murder of his father convinced him that even greater precautions should be taken to crush out dangerous ideas from the West.

The tsar's ministers worked hard to strengthen the central government. Much of the power which had been allowed the local assemblies was taken away. The independent village communities were again placed under the landowners. Newspapers were strictly censored, and the publication of some of them was prohibited. Education was brought under the control of the Church. The universities, supervised by the state, lost all freedom in their teaching.

Nicholas II carried on the work of his father. But he was lacking in clear and independent judgment and was easily influenced by his superstitious wife and his close associates. One of these was Plehve, head of the police system. Promoted to be minister of the interior, Plehve carried on an active persecution of those outside the official Russian Orthodox Church. Massacres (*pogroms*) of Jews drove thousands to foreign lands, especially to America.

CHECK ON YOUR READING

1. *Describe the Russia of Alexander I.*
2. *Why did the Poles revolt?*
3. *What six reforms were granted by Alexander II? Why?*
4. *Explain: "The government fought terrorism with terror." What were the results?*

2. The Ottomans, the Balkans, and War

Russia Desires Ottoman Territory · While successfully oppressing their peoples at home, the tsars were engaged in disastrous wars abroad. The Romanovs had long wished to take Constantinople from the Turks. For this was the site of ancient Byzantium, and the tsars looked upon themselves as guardians of the Christian-Byzantine culture. What is more, the "Pearl of the Bosporus" controlled the entrance to the Black Sea. It was also the key to the Dardanelles, the outlet to the Mediterranean Sea.

Austria, England, and France strongly opposed Russia's advance on the Turkish realms. England, especially, had no wish to see Russia dominate the eastern Mediterranean lest she interfere with British communication with India. European rivalries over the remains of the once vast empire of the Turks made the Balkan region the great danger spot of the Continent in the nineteenth century. Let us see how this Ottoman Empire had grown through the years.

The Ottoman Threat to Christian Europe · We had occasion to tell earlier how the Ottoman Turks conquered Asia Minor, invaded southeastern Europe, and under Mohammed II finally captured Christian Constantinople in 1453 (p. 205).

The sultan secured the title of Caliph, as head of the orthodox Moslem world, and established his control over the holy cities of Jerusalem, Mecca, and Medina. The Turks built up a strong fleet and acquired the overlordship of the north-African coast westward to Morocco.

Under Suleiman the Magnificent (1520–1566) this great Moslem power in Asia and Africa now threatened the safety of Christian Europe. Suleiman captured Belgrade, defeated the king of Hungary, and then laid siege to Vienna (1529). Although he was unable to take the city, he made Hungary a Turkish province and forced Emperors Charles V and Ferdinand to pay tribute. Suleiman's armies also overran the Caucasus region and made the Black Sea a part of the Turkish Empire.

Turkish pirates continued to rove the Mediterranean and to ravage Sicily, southern Italy, and Cyprus. But an expedition formed by Genoa, Venice, and Spain finally met and destroyed the Turkish fleet in the battle of Lepanto (1571). This victory ended the Moslem danger in the Mediterranean Sea.

Mohammed II, Founder of the Ottoman Empire · *Patron of the arts, the tulip (meaning "turban") was his favorite flower.*

"The Sick Man of Europe" · *This famous cartoon from* Punch *satirizes the attitude of two nations toward a third. Can you identify each? What is the main idea?*

In 1683 the Moslems again laid siege to Vienna. But this time they were defeated through the efforts of John Sobieski, the king of Poland. The Pope then induced a group of Christian leaders to join in a crusade, and after a hard struggle the Moslems were finally driven back. By the Treaty of Karlowitz (1699) they were forced to give up their lands north of the Danube. Hungary was restored to the Hapsburg monarch.

Russia Seizes Crimea and Bessarabia · The sultans who ruled in the eighteenth century allowed the Turkish armies to decline in strength just at the time when Russia was becoming a strong military power.

Catherine the Great took advantage of Turkey's weakness to seize the Crimea and other territory around the Sea of Azov (1774). The tsars also insisted on the right to protect the sultan's Christian subjects in Constantinople. Alexander I forced the sultan to cede him Bessarabia on the Black Sea (1812).

Nationalism and the Eastern Question · Like the Hapsburgs and Romanovs, the Ottoman rulers had many different peoples under their sway. Only in Asia Minor did the Turks form a large part of the population. In the Near East and Africa there were also Jews, Arabs, Egyptians, Berbers, and Moors. In Europe there were Greeks, Bulgarians, Serbs, Albanians, and Rumanians. All these people were stirred by a burning desire for self-government.

Under the oppressive rule of the Turks the Christians had to serve as slaves and were required to pay crushing taxes. As the power of the Ottoman Empire declined, these downtrodden peoples tried to throw off the Moslem yoke. Naturally many quarrels arose among the powers over what was to become of the former Turkish provinces. The breakup of Turkey in Europe and the conflicts over the control of her realms came to be called the Eastern Question.

Serbia Throws off Turkish Rule (1817) · The Serbs had been in revolt against the harsh rule of the Turks for a number of years. Shortly after the Congress of Vienna they started a new rebellion. Finally they were able to establish practical independence under a Serbian leader, with Belgrade as their capital. The new principality of Serbia enjoyed a measure of self-government, though it had to pay tribute to the sultan. This was the first of a series of Balkan states which freed themselves from their Moslem masters during the nineteenth century.

Greece Gains Independence (1829) · The next Balkan country to win its long struggle against oppression was Greece. In two thousand years that country had been invaded by many aliens. Around 1800, however, patriotic leaders who were influenced by the revolutionary movements in the West began to awaken a strong nationalistic spirit in Greece. Gifted writers made the modern spoken Greek into a literary language and used it in stirring appeals to their fellow countrymen. A revolutionary society, founded in 1814, was joined by thousands of liberty-loving Greeks.

The struggle of the Greeks for national independence aroused the sympathy of many Europeans who admired the glories of ancient Greece. The English poet Lord Byron died in Greece while attempting to unify the revolutionists there.

When the sultan launched an especially ferocious attack against his rebellious Christian subjects in 1825, England and France joined with Russia to aid the Greeks. Their combined fleets destroyed that of the sultan in the battle of Navarino in 1827. Russian armies then fought their way almost to Constantinople. The sultan had to sign a treaty (Adrianople, 1829) which granted independence to Greece and local self-government to Serbia and to the provinces of Wallachia and Moldavia (later Rumania) on the Danube. Shortly afterward Prince Otto of Bavaria became the first king of an independent Greece (1832). Russia gained for herself a region in the Caucasus.

The Crimean War (1854–1856) · Some years later the tsar found a new excuse for starting a quarrel with the Turks. In 1853 he learned that the Orthodox Christians were having difficulty in worshiping freely

Lord Byron, Dressed as a Greek Insurgent · *He "dreamed that Greece might still be free," and gave his life to make the dream come true. How was Greek independence achieved?*

at the holy places in Palestine. He immediately seized this opportunity to demand that Russia be granted a protectorate over all the Christians in Turkey.

When news of the tsar's demand reached Paris, Napoleon III declared that France, by virtue of earlier treaties, already had responsibility for the guardianship of Catholic Christians in the Ottoman Empire. The French emperor called on the sultan to oppose Russia's aggression. France now found a ready ally in England, which was unwilling to sit by and see Russia advance to the Mediterranean. When, therefore, the tsar's armies marched into the Turkish dominions, France and England came to the sultan's assistance and declared war on Russia (1854).

439

The Lady with the Lamp · *Florence Nightingale was an angel of mercy in the hospitals she established at Scutari and Balaclava for the Crimean wounded.*

The war was fought in the southern part of the Crimean peninsula and was poorly conducted on both sides. The French, English, and Russians all suffered heavy losses. Casualties were especially heavy in the battle of Balaclava, which witnessed the heroic but futile "charge of the Light Brigade." In spite of the dedicated efforts of Florence Nightingale ("the Lady with the Lamp") there was also much suffering caused by cholera and poor sanitation.

The Russians were especially disheartened by the plight of their ill-fed soldiers and the corruption of the officials who had managed the war so badly. Moreover, after a long siege, they lost their mighty fortress of Sevastopol. In 1856 Alexander II, fearing that Austria might also enter the war against him, consented to peace terms.

By the treaty Russia recognized the independence of the Ottoman Empire and gave up all claim to interfere with its subjects. It also had to restore part of Bessarabia to the sultan. Turkey was thus strengthened by the European powers against a Russian advance in the Balkans. But nothing was done to improve the lot of the Christians within the Ottoman Empire.

Turkish Oppression of the Balkans · After the Crimean War another wave of nationalism swept through the Balkans. Encouraged by the earlier success of the Serbs and Greeks, the oppressed peoples longed to free themselves from the rule of the hated Turks. The sultan permitted his officials to commit any kind of outrage against his Christian subjects, to demand impossible taxes, and to inflict brutal punishment on all offenders.

When a failure of crops increased the misery of the people in 1874, an insurrection broke out in the Serbian provinces of Bosnia and Herzegovina. Aroused by these events, the Bulgarians assassinated some of the Moslem officials. In revenge the Turks murdered thousands of Bulgarians.

Russia Wars on Turkey · While the European powers were exchanging notes and considering what to do, Serbia and Montenegro declared war on the sultan. The Christians in the Balkans made a frantic appeal to the West for immediate help. Gladstone, the leader of the Liberals in England (p. 414), urged his countrymen to break the unholy alliance between England and the "unspeakable Turk." But the Conservative prime minister feared that the Slavic peoples of the Balkans, if they gained their independence, might ally themselves with Russia. England was still fearful of a powerful Russia that might interfere with her communications with the East.

Russia, on the other hand, saw an advantage to herself in defending the cause of the oppressed Slavs, and started a war with Turkey. Although the Turks fought well, Russia was victorious. In 1878 a Russian army moved toward Constantinople. The alarmed sultan now signed a treaty that was very advantageous to Russia.

The Congress of Berlin (1878) · England and Austria had serious objections to this treaty because it increased the influence of Russia in the Balkan peninsula. They accordingly forced the tsar to submit the whole matter to a European congress.

At Berlin it was agreed (1) that Serbia, Montenegro, and Rumania should be independent of Turkey. (2) Bulgaria was to enjoy self-government but to pay tribute to the sultan. (3) Bosnia and Herzegovina were henceforth to be managed by Austria. (4) Russia was given some land east of the Black Sea, and from Rumania she received southern Bessarabia in exchange for the Dobrudja. (5) Cyprus was occupied by Great Britain.

A few years later Bulgaria annexed the neighboring province of Eastern Rumelia. She thus increased her own importance and decreased what little remained of Turkey in Europe.

CHECK ON YOUR READING

1. *Why did Russia desire Constantinople?*
2. *In what sense were the battles of Vienna and Lepanto "turning points"?*
3. *Explain the "Eastern Question" in terms of (a) nationalism, (b) Serbia, (c) Greece, (d) oppression.*
4. *Summarize the causes, highlights, and results of the Crimean War.*
5. *Use the map to point out and explain the terms of the Congress of Berlin.*

Southeast Europe Before and After the Congress of Berlin · *What was gained by Austria? Serbia? Bulgaria? Greece? Russia? Britain? At whose expense?*

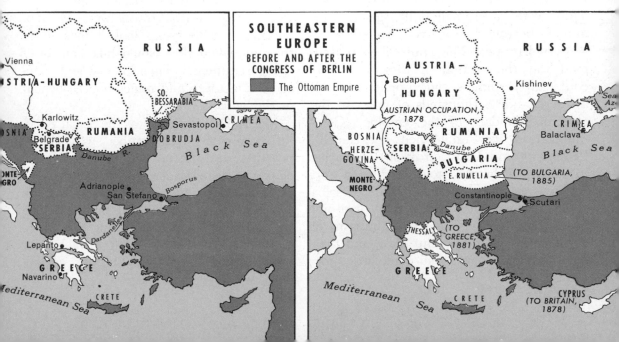

SOUTHEASTERN EUROPE
BEFORE AND AFTER THE CONGRESS OF BERLIN
☐ The Ottoman Empire

3. Industrial Expansion and War with Japan Bring Political Revolution

The Industrial Revolution Comes to Russia · Changes were taking place in Russian economic life which made it ever more difficult to keep the country "frozen" and to stifle by force men's ideas of religion and government. The vast deposits of coal and iron of the Ukraine and the Ural region were mined on a large scale. Machinery was introduced, and factories were speedily built. Moscow became the center of a great textile industry, and Kiev and St. Petersburg grew into important manufacturing cities.

The rapid growth of Russian industry was made possible by foreign capitalists who invested in Russian enterprises. It was also speeded by the cheap labor of the peasants, who now left their villages to seek employment in the towns. Tariffs were set up to protect new businesses, and the volume of trade grew rapidly.

Along with the development of industry went the construction of railway lines. They were government-built, largely with money borrowed from the capitalists of western Europe. The Trans-Siberian Railroad was the greatest of these lines. It could carry soldiers and supplies, as well as merchandise, thousands of miles to the eastern boundary of the empire. Communication was established between St. Petersburg and Vladivostok on the Pacific in 1900. A branch from Harbin to Port Arthur was soon finished. (Map, p. 654.)

The earlier Russian reformers had not been able to arouse much enthusiasm or activity among the peasant class, and their revolutionary schemes had made little progress. But the toiling workers of the crowded cities responded eagerly to talk of reforms. There was much discussion of the people's right to a share in the government.

The Rise of Four Political Groups · Four discontented groups gradually formed in Russia, each with its own ideas as to the most needed reforms. (1) One came to be known as the Constitutional Democrats or Liberals. It was made up of the professional men, university professors, intelligent merchants and manufacturers, and the public-spirited portion of the nobility. All of them detested the cruel and corrupt government of the tsar.

The Constitutional Democrats desired a constitutional government with a parliament made up of the elected representatives of the people. They also sought freedom of religion, speech, press, and assembly. And they demanded the abolition of the secret police system.

(2) The Social Democrats, representing workingmen in the towns were Marxian Socialists. This group looked forward to the time when they would take control of the government. Then they would manage the factories and mines for the benefit of the workers.

(3) The third group was the Social Revolutionary party. Its members were chiefly peasants, and liberals of the intellectual class who were devoted to the cause of the peasants. They too were followers of Marx and believed that the land should belong to those who worked it. But this group maintained that it was right to make war on a dishonest and oppressive govern-

The Longest Railroad in the World · *Construction of the Trans-Siberian Railroad required fourteen years of heavy labor. But it opened a frontier twice the size of the United States.*

ment which denied the people justice and equality. It was responsible, therefore, for many acts of violence, including the assassination of a number of public officials.

(4) To all these critics of the government were added the vast unorganized group of Russia's subject peoples. They yearned for freedom and bitterly resented the tsar's efforts to Russianize them.

None of the groups that we have just listed were real political parties such as we have today. They had neither freedom of speech nor the right to agitate publicly for the reforms that they desired. If they became too active they would be speedily put down by the police. And their leaders often lived in fear of their lives. Yet they found ways to carry on their work among the people. And the more the repressive police under Plehve sought to stamp out protest against the government, the more its enemies increased.

Rivalry of Russia and Japan · In the midst of this internal confusion Russia became involved in another foreign war—this time with Japan. In 1898 Russia had obtained from China the right to build the Trans-Siberian Railroad across Manchuria. Two years later Russia had taken possession of that province. She had also obtained a leasehold on Port Arthur, at the end of the Liaotung peninsula to which a branch line from the main road had been built.

Russia now threatened to take Korea, which lay to the south of her territory (see map). But Japan also had long coveted Korea, and Russia's advance into a country so nearly approaching her home islands appeared to her highly dangerous.

The Russians had far larger armed forces than the Japanese, but they were badly organized and poorly equipped. Japan's smaller army was much more modern, and her fleet was an excellent fighting weapon. Moreover, she could carry on the struggle for Korea near her home bases. Russia had to send her supplies thousands of miles by rail or sea.

Russia Defeated in the Russo-Japanese War · On February 5, 1904, the Japanese suddenly attacked and damaged the Russian warships at Port Arthur and then declared war. By striking without warning, Japan secured a great advantage over her opponent. When the Russian ships later came out to engage the Japanese fleet, they were severely defeated and withdrew. A Russian squadron at Vladivostok was also crippled, so that Japan gained control of the Eastern seas.

A Dangerous Adventure · *This contemporary German cartoon reflects the prevailing belief that Japan was no match for the Russian bear. Was she? What Japanese advantages did the cartoonist overlook?*

In the meantime Japanese forces, advancing in Manchuria and down the Liaotung peninsula, inflicted one blow after another on the Russian armies. Finally, in February, 1905, after a long siege, the great fortress of Port Arthur fell to the Japanese. This was followed by a series of disasters known as the battle of Mukden. The Russians were terribly beaten and lost one-third of their forces. In May, 1905, the Russian fleet from the Baltic arrived in Eastern waters. But in a great sea engagement the Japanese admiral picked off one Russian ship after another until the Russian squadron was practically wiped out.

The Russians finally gave in. The peace treaty was arranged at Portsmouth, New Hampshire, through the mediation of President Theodore Roosevelt. It was signed on September 5, 1905. Russia ceded to Japan Port Arthur and her rights in the peninsula, as well as the southern half of the island of Sakhalin. Korea was to be independent under the "protective influence" of Japan. Manchuria was to be left to China. (See map, p. 462.) Russia was quick to move into these areas again when Japan was defeated in World War II.

The Russian Revolution of 1904–1905 · The Russian people had been heartily against the war. As the bad news from the front kept pouring in, they were more than ever convinced that the plight of the country was caused by the hated government. It became known that officials had been stealing money which should have gone for rifles and ammunition. Even funds of the Red Cross Society for aiding the wounded had been taken.

During the course of the war, opposition to the government became bolder. In July, 1904, Plehve was killed by a bomb. In November some of the liberals in the local councils urged the tsar to remedy matters by granting individual liberty and by establishing a national assembly. The request was disregarded, and a new head of the police was appointed to deal with the growing disorder. Liberals now openly gave support to the demands of the council members. Factory workers went on strike in the cities, and there were uprisings among the peasants in the country.

"Red Sunday" · On January 22, 1905, a group of strikers, led by an Orthodox priest, marched to the Winter Palace in St. Petersburg. They went there to present a petition imploring the tsar to take heed of their sufferings. But the troops that guarded the palace fired on the crowd. Hundreds were killed or wounded in a conflict that gave to the day the name of "Red Sunday." When an official undertook to punish those who had taken part in the procession, a series of strikes broke out all over Russia in every trade and profession. The anger of the people spread to the provinces, where many officials were murdered.

The Tsar's Reforms Fail to Quiet the People · As the situation grew worse, some of the tsar's advisers begged him to make some reforms before it was too late. Unwillingly he granted religious toleration and relaxed the laws against the Jews. And finally, in August, he promised to establish a *Duma,* or assembly, which would assist in making the laws.

The people were not satisfied with these meager reforms, and a general strike soon followed. All railroads stopped running. Gas and electricity were shut off, shops closed in the towns, and the law courts ceased their sessions. The peasants in many places rose against their masters. They burned the manor houses, maimed the livestock, and in some cases drove the owners from the land and took possession themselves.

The situation was now intolerable. On October 29 the tsar issued what came to be called the *October Manifesto.* He promised all people freedom of religion, of speech, of the press, and of public meeting. He announced that no law would be made without the consent of the Duma, and that its members would be elected by almost universal suffrage.

The Government Puts Down the Revolution and Limits the Duma's Powers · In the meantime the Japanese war had ended. The government now turned its homecoming troops against the revolutionists. It was not long before the officials regained control. With the help of armed bands known as "Black Hundreds," they went through the land terrorizing the people into submission and massacring Jews and liberals. The government speedily shot or hanged the revolutionists.

Before the Duma could be called, the powers that it had been promised were gradually taken away, and the tsar announced that it could have no control over the fundamental laws of the country.

When the first Duma met (1906), the government's ministers would not agree to its proposals for reform. The tsar said that he was cruelly disappointed that its members had meddled in affairs that belonged to him. The second Duma had no better success. It demanded such sweeping changes that it too was dissolved.

The Despotism of the Tsars Lasts until 1917 · The electoral laws were then changed so that the third Duma, which met in November, 1907, was a more conservative body. Moderate reforms were granted to improve local government, extend education, and establish a state system of workingmen's insurance. Laws were passed which partially abolished the ownership of land by village communities and permitted the peasants to become property-owners.

Russian Women Demand Reforms, 1905 · *Revolutions occur in minds before they reach the muscles. This was one of many peaceful parades of protest. What followed? Why?*

Tsar Nicholas II Opens the First Duma at the Winter Palace, St. Petersburg, May 10, 1906 · *At the left are members of the Duma to whom he read his "Speech from the throne." Can you find the Tsarina? the Dowager Empress? the clergy?*

Though the Duma continued to be summoned, it now represented the conservative classes of the nation. The tsar's officials did all they could to keep out liberal deputies. The tsar, as "autocrat of all the Russias," retained a despotic power over his realms, and his officials continued to persecute those who opposed the government. We shall see later how the "new despotism" of the Communist party replaced that of the tsar and how it has continued to our own time.

CHECK ON YOUR READING

1. *Cite three effects of the Industrial Revolution in Russia.*
2. *Name the four discontented groups and the principal ideas of each.*
3. *Identify the (a) causes, (b) highlights, (c) results of the Russo-Japanese War.*
4. *How do you account for the Revolution of 1904–1905? Explain (a) "Red Sunday," (b) October Manifesto, (c) Duma, (d) "new despotism."*

Learning Activities

Think about the chapter

1. According to Western standards how was Russia "behind the times" in the 1800's?

2. What were the strengths and weaknesses of the Ottoman Empire? Why did the Balkan peoples revolt?

3. Why was Japan the victor in the Russo-Japanese war?

4. What grievances did the people of Russia have against their government?

5. *Map study:* Draw a map of Russia. Indicate countries and bodies of water on the boundaries. Mark main rivers and cities and label the areas where non-Russians lived. Trace the route of the Trans-Siberian Railroad.

Go beyond the text

6. Read some accounts of the Crimean War. (a) Report on the work of Florence Nightingale. (b) Read "The Charge of the Light Brigade" by Tennyson. Who was responsible for the disastrous order?

7. In spite of the repression of the period, Russia had a kind of literary renaissance in the nineteenth century and some of the great Russian composers lived in this century. Report on these writers and musicians.

8. Building the Trans-Siberian Railroad was a great achievement. Read some details about it. What were the difficulties around Lake Baikal?

9. Many Russian and Polish Jews migrated to America near the end of the nineteenth century. Find out in what ways their life in Russia was especially difficult.

10. Report on the relations between the United States and Russia for this period; for example, the visit of the Russian fleet during our Civil War, purchase of Alaska, President Roosevelt and the Treaty of Portsmouth.

11. What parallels can you see between the autocracy of the tsar and that of the Communist party in Russia today?

Follow up your special interests

12. Count Leo Tolstoi developed a social philosophy that resulted in giving up his property and living like a peasant. Imagine that you visited him (as some foreigners did) and write an article describing your impressions.

13. Select a variety of pictures from the *Picture History of Russia* or other sources. Use an opaque projector to show the pictures to the class. Explain the phases of Russian life they represent.

READ FURTHER

Basic readings: (1) BAUER and PEYSER, *How Music Grew*, Chap. 29. (2) BECKER, *Modern History*, Chap. 15. (3) EVANS, *Costume Throughout the Ages*. (4) HOFFMAN, *News of the World*, Nos. 47–48. (5) MACY, *Story of the World's Literature*, Chap. 42. (6) SCOTT, BALTZLY, *Readings*, Chaps. 8–12. (7) Year's *Pictorial History*, pp. 381, 446–447, 476–481.

Special accounts: (8) S. EKREM, *Turkey, Old and New*. (9) ERIC KELLY, *The Land of the Polish People*. (10) J. MARTIN, (*ed.*) *A Picture History of Russia*. (11) F. OGG and H. ZINK, *Modern Foreign Governments*. (12) B. PARES, *A History of Russia*. By an outstanding authority—for good readers. (13) E. SEEGER, *A Pageant of Russian History*.

Fiction and biography: (14) M. ANTIN, *The Promised Land*. A Russian immigrant's impressions of America. (15) E. CURIE, *Madame Curie*. Read about her youthful days in Poland under Russian rule. (16) *The Education of a Princess* by Marie, Grand Duchess of Russia. (17) C. PURDY, *Stormy Victory*. A life of Tschaikowsky. (18) L. TOLSTOY, *Anna Karenina*. A literary classic of life in Russia—for good readers. (19) C. WOODHAM-SMITH, *Lonely Crusader*. The story of Florence Nightingale. (20) A. YARMOLINSKY, (*ed.*) *A Treasury of Great Russian Short Stories*.

How Europeans Came to Control
Much of the Earth: Imperialism

KEY WORDS AND DATES

imperialism	Livingstone
spheres of influence	Stanley
protectorate	Congo
Manchus	Sudan
Opium War	Adowa
Treaty of Nanking (1842)	Cape-to-Cairo
	Khartoum
extraterritorial	Kitchener
"open door"	Suez
Boxer Rebellion	isolation
Sun Yat-sen	Monroe Doctrine
1912	Maximilian
Xavier	Roosevelt corollary
Shogun	"Good Neighbor"
Bushido	policy
Perry	Pan-Americanism
1853	O.A.S.

A MAP OF THE WORLD in the early twentieth century showed more than half the earth's surface ruled or controlled by European nations. France, for example, claimed an empire twenty times as large as the mother country. Belgium had possessions eighty times her own size. Great Britain had an empire on which, she proudly asserted, "the sun never sets."

European countries, as we know, had long been interested in foreign trade. But in the nineteenth century there were reasons for new ventures overseas. As a result of the Industrial Revolution, Europeans were eagerly looking for new markets and sources of raw materials.

The building-up of empire and control over alien peoples we call *imperialism*. Unhappily, the competition for trade and territory brought the rival powers into serious conflicts. Imperialism became one of the major causes of war.

We recall how military conquests once *Hellenized* and then *Romanized* the Mediterranean world. Modern imperialism *Europeanized* a large part of the globe. European history thus became *world* history, for the fate and fortunes of many European states were bound up with their interests thousands of miles from home.

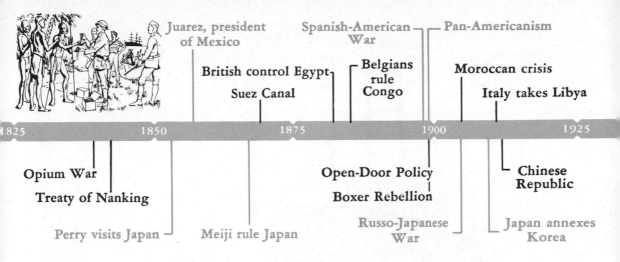

Juarez, president of Mexico   Spanish-American War   Pan-Americanism

British control Egypt   Belgians rule Congo   Moroccan crisis

Suez Canal   Italy takes Libya

1825   1850   1875   1900   1925

Opium War   Open-Door Policy   Chinese Republic

Treaty of Nanking   Boxer Rebellion

Perry visits Japan   Meiji rule Japan   Russo-Japanese War   Japan annexes Korea

1. Empire-Building in the Nineteenth Century

Industrialism Promotes Imperialism · The desire for empire is an old story in history. But reasons for gaining territory and control over other peoples have not always been the same. Around 1850 a new race for colonies was spurred on by the Industrial Revolution. European statesmen could see the importance of securing colonies in undeveloped countries where their merchants could have the exclusive right to sell and the government could control the trade.

Businessmen at this time were seeking (1) new markets, (2) new sources of raw materials, and (3) new opportunities for investment. They were aided in their search by (4) improved transportation and (5) better systems of communication.

Markets, Raw Materials, and Investments · The Industrial Revolution brought a vast increase in production. In industrialized countries surpluses were a problem.

The new machines could handle a greatly increased amount of raw materials. Egypt and India produced a fine quality of cotton,

much in demand to feed the new machines, especially in Britain. The great need for rubber led King Leopold of Belgium to annex the Congo region in Africa. Coal, iron, tin, coffee, tea, and cocoa, as well as the silks and spices so desired in earlier days, also played an important role in the struggle for empire among the European powers.

Businessmen had grown rich from the profits of machine industry and large-scale production. They sought new undertakings in which to employ their wealth to gain even greater returns. In undeveloped countries there were golden opportunities to build railroads, to open mines and oil wells, and to start banks and businesses of every kind.

Improved Transportation and Communication · The great expansion of commerce was made possible by the revolution in transportation and communication.

In 1807 Robert Fulton launched the first successful steamboat, the *Clermont*, in New York. In 1819 steamships began to cross the ocean, and by 1838 the *Great Western*

449

The *Great Eastern* Laying Atlantic Cable · *After the 1858 cable proved defective, the "biggest ship afloat" (with masts, paddle wheel, and screw propeller) was employed to lay new cable between Ireland and Newfoundland in 1866.*

crossed the Atlantic in less than sixteen days. Gradually freight and passenger service was extended all over the world.

At the same time railroads were revolutionizing land transportation. George Stephenson, an Englishman, developed the first successful locomotive. The first short railroad, the Stockton and Darlington, opened in 1825 in northern England. From that time on railway mileage increased in Great Britain until by 1900 there were 22,000 miles of track and over a billion passengers were carried annually.

Similar progress was taking place on the Continent and in the United States, and at a slower pace in Africa and Asia. The Trans-Siberian Railroad across Russia connected Europe overland with the Pacific.

Russia also pushed lines southward toward Persia and Afghanistan, while the British constructed over 41,000 miles of railway in India.

Steamship and railway lines made it possible to reduce the cost of mailing letters, which was very high up to 1839. In 1874 the Universal Postal Union was established, and standard low postal rates were accepted by nearly all countries.

Telegraph cables were laid under the oceans connecting the different continents. In 1907 an Italian inventor, Marconi, established wireless communication across the Atlantic.

Imperialism Has Many Forms · Nineteenth-century imperialism took various forms. (1) Sometimes it meant only the securing of trading privileges or rights to develop enterprises in a foreign country. (2) Sometimes it amounted to creating a sphere of influence in another land. This meant that a favored nation had controlling rights and other nations must not interfere. (3) Sometimes it assumed the form of a protectorate over a backward country. In this case the country's affairs were managed by a foreign power. (4) Finally, imperialism at times took the form of annexation at the desire of the natives or involved the seizure of the territory by conquest.

Missions, Schools, and Hospitals · The sharp edges of imperialism were often smoothed by missionaries, teachers, and doctors. They spread the knowledge of Christianity, education, and public health. They put in written form the languages of people who knew nothing about an alphabet. They also carried with them modern scientific ideas and inventions and taught the people Western ways.

Mission schools and hospitals were especially beneficial. Most of the people of Africa and Asia were illiterate and without medical care. The death rates from controllable diseases were tragically high. Medical missionaries like Gordon Seagrave (*Burma Surgeon*) and Albert Schweitzer (Africa) became world famous because they *practised* the Christianity they preached.

CHECK ON YOUR READING

1. How did industrialism promote imperialism?
2. How did transportation and communication improve?
3. What forms did imperialism take?
4. How did medical missionaries and teachers help the native peoples?

---

2. China and the West

China's Relations with the West · We reviewed early Chinese history in Chapter 10, and saw that at various periods there was some contact with the West. But trade was slight. China remained shut off by natural barriers and unimpressed by what she learned of distant Europe. In 1842, however, after the Opium War with Great Britain, she began unwillingly to open her ports to foreigners, whom she still regarded as barbarians. After that time, trade between China and the West steadily grew.

Coming of the Portuguese, Dutch, and English · It was during the latter half of the Ming period (p. 146) that the European voyages of exploration took place. The Portuguese were the first to reach China (soon after 1500) by following the route of the Arab merchants from India to the southern ports.

The early Portuguese traders treated the Chinese as a conquered people. They made so much trouble that the Chinese government drove them out. Later, in 1557, they were allowed to lease a strip of the seacoast at Macao, which they were able to hold permanently.

The Portuguese merchants who settled there were followed by Christian missionaries. Especially active were the Jesuits, who soon won the respect of Chinese officials and scholars because of their learning. Some of them even were appointed to advisory positions in the government.

In 1622 a Dutch expedition established a post on the Pescadores Islands and later moved to Formosa. It was not until 1762 that they were allowed to trade with Canton. The English did not secure a share of the trade with China until 1699.

Manchus Rule China (1644–1912) · The Manchus, a group of tribes related to the Mongols and Tatars, lived in what is now southern Manchuria. In 1644 a serious rebellion against the weak Ming emperor permitted them to seize the throne.

The Manchus then organized an efficient government. They forced the Chinese to adopt the Manchu headdress—the shaved forehead and long queue—as a mark of submission. But they wisely retained most of the familiar Chinese institutions and supported education, literature, and art. They honored Confucius and tolerated various forms of religion, including Christianity.

China prospered, and the population increased rapidly. Roads and waterways were improved. Better communication increased the trade among the provinces. The Manchus protected the empire from invasion by conquering the outlying regions. They held Mongolia, Tibet, Chinese Turkestan, Burma, and Annam under their direct rule or as tributary states.

Attitude toward Foreigners · The second Manchu emperor, K'ang-hsi, had a friendly attitude toward Europeans. He favored the growth of commerce with the rest of the world. For thirty years Chinese ports were opened to merchants and missionaries. Then in 1717 an imperial edict abolished these privileges, and foreigners were restricted to the use of one port—Canton. The teaching of Christianity was forbidden, but laws against missionaries were not strictly enforced.

Nevertheless the volume of business grew. In 1699 the British East India Company had established a trading station at Canton. By 1750 it dominated the China trade, though the Dutch, Swedes, Danes, and French also had their share. From the

The Thriving Port of Canton, China, in 1804 · *Note the warehouses, docks, and Chinese junks. The five flags represent Denmark, Spain, the United States, Sweden, and Britain. The picture is from the Peabody Museum in Salem, Massachusetts.*

East the Europeans carried home tea, spices, silks, satins, cotton, porcelain, and ginger root. They sold furs and opium to the Chinese and brought in silver and gold. Their pressure on China to open her ports to trade increased with the spread of the Industrial Revolution.

The Opium War (1839–1842) · For some years the profitable sale of opium had been carried on by British merchants. The Chinese government objected to the debasement of its people through this habit-forming drug. It suddenly seized the stocks of the British merchants, and the "Opium War" broke out. The British, with their modern military equipment, were speedily victorious. In the Treaty of Nanking (1842) the Chinese were forced (1) to open four additional ports, including Shanghai; (2) to cede to the British the island of Hong Kong at the mouth of the Canton River; (3) to accept a revised schedule of tariff duties; (4) to pay a large indemnity.

Westerners Secure Privileges in China · Treaties with the United States and France soon followed. The agreements included a provision granting extraterritorial rights to foreign citizens. This meant that foreigners guilty of committing offenses in China were to be tried not in her courts, but by foreign officials. This was very irritating to the Chinese, for it reduced their sovereignty within their own boundaries. It was justified by the Western powers on the basis of the wide differences between Eastern and Western law.

The hostility of local officials created much friction in carrying out the terms of the various treaties. In 1856 England again began a war on China and was soon joined by others. Again the Europeans were victorious, and treaties were signed which

Peking: the Temple of Heaven · *In this majestic sixteenth-century temple the emperor prayed to heaven for an abundant harvest.*

opened ten more Chinese ports. They also permitted foreigners to travel into the interior of the country. Christianity was legally recognized. Tariff rates were further revised, and diplomatic representatives of foreign countries were to be allowed to live in Peking. Britain was granted a strip of coastland opposite Hong Kong. Russia secured a piece of territory on the Pacific, where she built Vladivostok.

Decline of the Manchus · After these unsuccessful wars with the Western nations the Manchus gradually lost their hold on China. There were revolts against the dynasty and against foreigners. Banditry and disorder increased.

453

By this time European nations were attempting to get a permanent foothold within the empire (see map, p. 457). The French acquired Cochin China (1862) and forced China to sign a treaty (1885) recognizing a French protectorate over Annam and Tonkin (later French Indochina). Meanwhile Britain was pushing from India into Burma, where her authority was acknowledged in 1886.

The Sino-Japanese War (1894–1895) · Japan, having become a successful manufacturing nation, now looked at Korea and China as the closest and most desirable fields for economic expansion. War broke out over Korea, the tiny country lying between China and Japan. Each of them claimed to control it.

In 1894 the Japanese defeated the Chinese in a short war, and as a result Korea was declared independent. This really meant that Korea was opened up to Japan. Japan also took Formosa and the Pescadores Islands. Her plan for annexing the Liaotung peninsula was prevented by the European nations, which feared that Japan might bar them from the East.

Western Powers Begin to Divide China · China's inability to defend herself against Japan encouraged the Western powers to try to get more of her territory. As a reward for keeping the Japanese out of the Liaotung peninsula, Russia was permitted to build her Siberian railway across Manchuria to the Pacific (p. 443). This amounted to giving her control of this region. Russia also obtained a lease on Port Arthur.

France obtained mining and railway concessions in southern China and additional territory on her boundary lines in Indochina. Great Britain pushed her Burmese border farther into China. She

The "Open Door" Policy · *This cartoon, by* W. A. Rogers, *appeared in* Harper's Weekly *on November 18, 1899.* What does it mean?

also forced China to lease her the port of Weihaiwei on the coast of Shantung.

The Germans also found an excuse for establishing a foothold in China. When one of their missionaries was murdered in the province of Shantung in 1897, the Germans secured a ninety-nine-year lease on a district bordering Kiaochow Bay. They immediately built up a modern town, Tsingtao, and began building railways and opening up mines in Shantung.

As all these leases were intended to provide naval bases, it became clear that the Western powers meant to remain in the Far East. One of their main purposes was to be able to exert pressure on one another in their contest for trade and profitable enterprises. There followed a scramble among the European nations to secure spheres of influence where they could build railways and develop the country undisturbed.

The "Open Door" · The activity of the European powers alarmed the United States, whose commerce with China had grown to large proportions. Accordingly, in 1899 Secretary of State John Hay addressed a note to the great powers, asking them to pledge themselves not to violate the existing rights of others. They were also asked to respect the "open-door" policy in China. It aimed to give all foreigners equal trading privileges in Chinese ports.

The major powers publicly agreed to the policy—with many private reservations. This was not because of any sudden acceptance of the Golden Rule, but rather because they did not trust one another.

Beginning of Reform in China · China's helplessness finally convinced some of her progressive leaders that she must give up her fight against Western ideas and adapt herself to the new age. In 1898 the young emperor, influenced by the progressive party, issued a number of decrees to reform the government and military service. But most of the officials were still conservative and were horrified by these novelties.

In the fall of 1898 the Empress Dowager seized control of the government, forced the emperor into retirement, and canceled the reform edicts. Then followed a wave of antiforeign feeling, which reached its climax in the so-called Boxer Rebellion.

The Boxer Rebellion · The Boxers (the "Righteous Fists of Harmony") were a party in North China who hated foreigners. They now rose to rid the country of the "foreign devils" whom they believed to be the cause of all China's misfortunes. With the approval of the Empress Dowager, the Boxers were permitted to kill foreigners wherever they might be found.

The chancellor of the Japanese legation and the German minister were murdered in 1900. Europeans in Peking were shut up in the city and besieged for months.

The foreign powers—Japan, Russia, Great Britain, France, Germany, and the United States—now sent a joint expedition to China. It fought its way from the coast to Peking and brought relief to those in danger in the capital. The Europeans looted the imperial city, and China was forced to pay a heavy indemnity. The Boxers were suppressed, and officials who had permitted outrages against the Westerners were put to death. Foreign troops were to be placed in the capital as guards for the legations. The United States later returned much of its indemnity, which the grateful Chinese used for scholarships in American colleges.

The Empress Dowager of China, by Hubert Vos · *She imprisoned the emperor and ordered all reformers, foreigners, and Chinese Christians killed. Why? With what result?*

China Adopts Western Ways · The Manchu government soon realized that China must be modernized in order to keep its independence. Many of the earlier reforms favored by the young emperor were approved, especially those which concerned the armed forces. Government schools were established which taught English and other Western studies, as well as Chinese subjects. Many students went abroad to study in Europe and America. Thousands went to Tokyo because the Chinese were much impressed by Japan's victory over Russia. Foreign works were translated, and newspapers were published.

A more friendly attitude was adopted toward foreigners in China, and concessions were granted to Westerners wishing to invest in enterprises to develop the country's resources. Railways were built, and tele-graph lines connected distant parts of the country. Mines were opened, and factories for the manufacture of silk and cotton goods were established. The government undertook to put an end to opium-smoking. The importation of opium and the planting of the poppy from which the drug is made were forbidden.

The government began to revise the laws and improve the courts to bring them into line with legal procedure in Western countries. The old civil-service examinations, based on the Confucian Classics, were abolished. It was realized that a knowledge of modern government was more useful in the conduct of the state. Finally, in 1906, an imperial decree announced that local and provincial assemblies were to be established and later a national parliament.

Dr. Sun Yat-sen and the Chinese Republic (1912) · While these reforms were being made, a patriotic movement had been growing in the south. Its leader, Dr. Sun Yat-sen, believed that a republic would be the best government for China.

By 1911, the revolutionary movement was so strong that Yuan Shih-kai, the organizer of China's modern army, persuaded the young emperor to abdicate. Thus, after more than 260 years, the rule of the Manchus came to an end.

The southern provinces had already organized a provisional republic, with its capital at Nanking and Dr. Sun as president. Early in 1912 Dr. Sun, who desired above all that the country should be united, resigned his office. Yuan Shih-kai was elected provisional president of the Republic of China.

China's Difficulty with a Republican Government · Yuan was really a conservative, and he soon made himself virtually a dictator. To assist him he appointed mili-

Sun Yat-sen · The "father of the Chinese republic" proclaimed nationalism, socialism, and democracy as the goals of his movement.

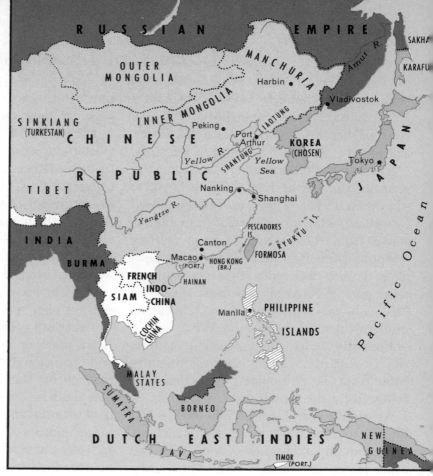

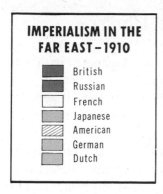

IMPERIALISM IN THE FAR EAST – 1910

- British
- Russian
- French
- Japanese
- American
- German
- Dutch

The Far East in 1910 ·
*Name one important
Asian area held by each
of the major powers in
1910. Who rules these
areas today? (See map,
page 361.)*

tary governors over the provinces. But his
desire to become emperor was opposed by
the foreign powers, as well as by the republicans. Yuan was forced to announce the
restoration of a republican government.

There was much disorder throughout the
country, and China seemed on the point of
falling into anarchy when Yuan Shih-kai
died in 1916. Although Li Yuan-hung, who
succeeded him, was an able and upright
leader, it was difficult to restore unity.
There were many differences between north
and south in language, culture, and sentiment. The provincial governors plundered
their territories and made war on one
another. But World War I had broken
out in 1914, and this catastrophe was to

have an important effect on affairs in China,
as we shall see in Chapter 31.

CHECK ON YOUR READING

1. Use the map to show early European
   settlements in China.
2. Describe (a) the rule of the Manchus,
   (b) early trade with China.
3. Why were the following important: (a)
   Treaty of Nanking, (b) Western privileges, (c) the Sino-Japanese War, (d)
   the "open-door" policy?
4. How did the following influence Chinese
   history: (a) Boxer Rebellion, (b) West-
   ernization, (c) Sun Yat-sen, (d) disorder?

3. Japan Becomes an Imperialist Power

Europeans Come to Japan · In Chapter 10 we traced the history of Japan up to the time of her first contacts with the West. Let us now pick up the thread of the story.

The first Portuguese traders came to Kyushu, the southernmost of the Japanese islands in 1542. They were soon followed by others, who brought silks from China, spices from the East Indies, and military weapons from Europe. The warring Japanese daimio welcomed the merchants at their port of Kagoshima because they were especially eager to obtain possession of the modern firearms used in the West.

For fifty years the Portuguese had no rivals. But in 1592 the Spaniards began to come from the Philippines. Soon they were followed by the Dutch and the English.

Missionaries in Japan (1549–1603) · Not long after the Portuguese merchants appeared in Japan, Francis Xavier, with two other Jesuit missionaries, arrived at Kyushu (1549). They were well received by the local daimio, who wished to keep the good will of the Portuguese traders. Xavier remained in the country for two years and made about a hundred converts to Christianity. Other Jesuit missionaries continued to come, and by the end of the century over a hundred thousand Japanese, including some nobles, had accepted the new religion.

For some time the Christian missionaries were treated quite well in Japan. But then an incident occurred that aroused suspicion against them. A disabled Spanish ship had been beached by the Japanese, who claimed the vessel and cargo as the property of the provincial lord. The Spaniards, hoping to regain possession of their ship, threatened the Japanese with the anger of their monarch.

They told the Japanese that it was the custom to send missionaries into foreign lands, and then, after the people had been converted to Christianity, to send troops. With the aid of the converts, these troops then overthrew the native government. This misleading story so enraged the ruler that a number of priests and Japanese Christians were executed, and all missionaries were ordered to leave the country. Those who did not obey went into hiding.

Tokugawa Shogunate (1603–1867) · After nearly a hundred years of civil war and confusion (p. 150), order was restored throughout the Japanese empire. Three able leaders combined to overthrow the rival daimio and unite the country once more under a strong central government. In 1603 the survivor of the three, who was named Iyeyasu, founded the Tokugawa Shogunate. It lasted for 264 years.

During this period the emperor remained at Kyoto, but the Shogun used the small town of Yedo (later Tokyo) as his government headquarters. The Shoguns held all the real power. They made all appointments to high offices. They weakened the rival nobles by their policy of distributing land, and kept around them only faithful daimio and samurai (fighting men). Their law code, called *Bushido*, established a strict code of morals, education, and behavior for the daimio and samurai.

The Shogun Iyeyasu favored the development of trade with the West. He encouraged foreign merchants to come to Japan and permitted missionaries to enter. Although the Spaniards no longer visited

A Japanese Court · *This painting shows a court of the Tokugawa period. Since class distinctions were rigidly preserved, penalties were determined by the rank of the offender. The poor received the most cruel sentences of all.*

Japan, the Dutch were making regular voyages from the East Indies by 1609.

Iyeyasu also encouraged the daimio to build their own ships, and soon Japanese vessels were trading in the Philippines, Siam, and the ports of the East Indies.

Japan Drives Out the Foreigners · After Iyeyasu's death in 1616, his successors adopted a different policy toward outsiders. The hostility of the government had been aroused when it was found that a large number of Christian daimio belonged to an anti-Tokugawa faction in Osaka. Although the enemies of the Shogun had been overcome, Christians were hunted out and put to death, and missionaries were not tolerated in the country.

The government also changed its policy toward foreign trade. In 1624 the Span-iards were ordered to leave the islands, and Japanese were prohibited from visiting the Philippines. In 1636 all Japanese were forbidden to travel abroad or to build ships. For two hundred years the only contact of Japan with the outside world was through the Dutch in one little settlement in Nagasaki harbor.

What Happened inside Japan · But Japan did not stand still. The country enjoyed a period of relief from civil wars, and domestic trade flourished. Yedo grew to be a rich and prosperous city whose population by 1800 had reached a million. The daimio built handsome residences there, and merchants were attracted by the presence of this wealthy class of nobles.

As Yedo became a rich commercial city, even the laws of the military regime could

A Ceremonial Musket Drill · *In this painting, imperial commissioners at Perry's invitation watch an American military drill. They were amazed at the troops' precision and speed in loading and firing their muskets. Soon Japan copied Western military techniques.*

not prevent the warrior daimio and their samurai from desiring the luxuries and diversions which they saw around them. Many of them fell into debt to merchants and money-lenders.

Opposition to the Tokugawa Shogunate · By 1850 there was much dissatisfaction with the Tokugawa Shogunate. (1) The later Shoguns were not always men of great ability. (2) The nobles grew to resent the restrictions placed on them. (3) The Japanese people remembered that their own emperor, and not the Shogun, was their rightful ruler. This prompted a movement to restore the emperor's authority. (4) Finally, military leaders felt that the policy of isolation was causing Japan to fall behind the rest of the world in military equipment.

Westerners Make Their Way into Japan; Commodore Perry · In the meantime there was an increasing demand from the Western nations that Japan give up her policy of isolation. Foreign ships appeared in Japanese waters, and numerous attempts were made to persuade the Shogun to enter into some treaty arrangements.

In 1853 Commodore Matthew C. Perry of the United States Navy entered the harbor of Yedo with a small squadron. He carried a letter from the President of the United States to the emperor of Japan, requesting that he open his country to trade with the United States. After several days Perry was permitted to leave the letter. Then he withdrew, saying that he would return later for an answer.

Some months later Perry reappeared with a fleet of warships. The Shogun was much impressed by this show of force. He finally concluded a treaty opening two ports to American ships and permitting a consul to reside at one of them.

Through the patient efforts and diplomacy of the first American consul, Townsend Harris, a second and more important commercial treaty was concluded in 1858. This opened to America five ports for trade and residence. It provided a schedule of tariffs, and granted the United States extraterritorial rights over its citizens in Japan. Similar treaties were soon made by the Shogun with England, France, Russia, and Holland.

The End of the Shogunate · But the granting of these concessions, which put an end to Japan's proud isolation, roused the wrath of all the anti-Tokugawa elements against the Shogun. Foreigners were insulted and a number were killed. Some of the daimio took matters into their own hands and began to fire on Western ships. In reply, a British squadron bombarded and destroyed Kagoshima in 1863. The next year an allied fleet demolished a number of coastal forts.

After this proof of the strength of the Western powers, the lords ceased their antiforeign activities. They now turned their hostility against the Shogun. Shortly afterward, both the Shogun and the emperor died within a few months of each other. In 1867 the newly appointed Shogun was forced to resign his office. The new emperor—the first of the Meiji—was given his rightful authority.

Japan Becomes a Modern Nation · Japan now began to be Westernized and modernized very rapidly. Feudalism was broken. Japan adopted a friendly policy toward other powers. Embassies and commissions were sent abroad to study the ways of the Western world. Japanese students flocked to European and American universities.

Japan quickly began to develop an industrial economy. Railroads, telephone and telegraph systems, and modern manufacturing were begun with the help of foreign experts. The government founded and supported many industries, some of which it turned over to private capitalists. Cheap labor aided the growth of industry.

A constitution was granted by the emperor in 1889, but it asserted his divine right to rule. The legislature contained representatives of the people in the House of Representatives, but the House of Peers was made up of nobles, the wealthy, and special appointees of the emperor. The real governing power was in the hands of an advisory body, the Privy Council. One

View of Ueno Railway Station in Tokyo about 1885 · *Perhaps the Japanese artist realized the importance of the scene he painted. What was its importance?*

of the most dangerous features of the constitution was the fact that it gave great independence and power to the military officers of army and navy.

Within fifty years Japan changed from a feudal society into a modern state. She adopted the latest ideas in science, education, and industry, and built up a modern army and navy on Western models. She began to look abroad, as had the Western powers, for wider markets for the products of her industry.

In foreign affairs Japan's first aim was to revise the "unequal treaties" which had been forced upon her. By 1894 she had begun to conclude new treaties. These abolished the extraterritorial rights of outsiders in Japan, and made a beginning in the revision of tariff rates.

Japan Begins to Build an Empire · As a new industrial nation Japan now began to look abroad for wider markets. We have already seen that she easily won a war in 1894 with China (p. 454). As a

result she secured Formosa, the Pescadores, and a free hand in Korea.

In 1899 Japan joined the Western powers in putting down the Boxer Rebellion and collected her share of the indemnity imposed on China.

Japan was now especially anxious to check the expansion of Russian power in Manchuria. In 1902 Japan made an alliance with Great Britain, which promised her British support if any other power should join Russia against Japan. Shortly afterward, in 1904, Japan struck her enemy without warning by attacking Russian warships at Port Arthur.

In this Russo-Japanese War, Japan came out victorious (p. 443). This time she gained a protectorate over Korea, the lease of the Liaotung peninsula (with Port Arthur), and the southern half of the island of Sakhalin. In addition, she obtained important fishing rights in the northern Pacific. In 1910 Japan annexed Korea outright, changing its name to *Chosen.*

In the meantime Japan's trade had multiplied several times, and her shipping had risen to over a million and a half tons per year. Japan now ranked as one of the great powers of the world. We shall see in Chapter 31 how World War I favored her ambitious schemes for dominating the Far East.

Russo-Japanese War, 1904–1905 · What territory did Japan take from Russia? from China? Locate Tsushima Strait and Port Arthur.

RUSSO-JAPANESE WAR

Japan in 1904   Annexed in 1905
Japanese protectorate in 1905 and annexed in 1910

SAKHALIN
MANCHURIA
Amur R.
RUSSIA
Harbin
Vladivostok
KURILE IS.
Mukden
LIAOTUNG
Sea of Japan
Tsientsin
Port Arthur
Pyongyang
KOREA
HONSHU
aiochow
ANTUNG
Weihaiwei
Seoul
Tokyo
Tsingtao
Kyoto
Korea Strait
Tsushima Strait
Osaka
anking
Nagasaki
KYUSHU
JAPAN
Kagoshima

CHECK ON YOUR READING

1. *Why did the Japanese first welcome, then attack foreigners?*
2. *What were the results of Commodore Perry's visit to Japan?*
3. *How did Japan (a) modernize? (b) build an empire?*

4. How Africa Came Under Control of Europeans

Early Settlements in Africa · The last great region to be opened up by Europeans in their search for trade was Africa. This second largest continent in the world has an area three times that of Europe. The northern African countries had, as we know, been in contact with Europe since the days of ancient Greece, Carthage, and Rome.

In the seventh century the Arabs had swept westward across northern Africa, conquering the whole region from the Red Sea to the Atlantic. The native tribes had fused with the Arabs and had adopted the religion of the Moslem invaders. Since that time they have belonged to the Moslem world.

In the fifteenth century the Portuguese pushed their way down the western coast, establishing trading stations and a traffic in slaves, gold, and spices. Spaniards, Dutch, French, and British were soon setting up stations here and there for trade. (See map, p. 465.) Except for the Portuguese colonies of Angola and Mozambique, these footholds were mainly limited to the coasts. The vast stretches of inland Africa were still unknown to white men.

Europeans Open Up Africa · Between 1850 and 1880 European explorers braved the torrid heat and the dangers from fever, savages, and wild beasts in order to trace the course of great rivers to their sources and open up the riches of the vast interior. The best known of this group of pioneers are David Livingstone, a Scottish explorer and missionary (1813–1873), and Henry M. Stanley (1841–1904), an Anglo-American journalist.

For thirty years Livingstone led expeditions for the English into the jungles of south-central Africa. He discovered Lake Nyasa, the course of the Zambezi, its great Victoria Falls, and the region of the upper Congo (see map). When Livingstone was believed to be lost in 1871, Henry Stanley was dispatched on a mission to find him. Stanley was successful, and everyone is familiar with his immortal greeting, "Dr. Livingstone, I presume?" Then Stanley and Livingstone together discovered the northern shores of Lake Tanganyika.

After Livingstone's death in 1873, Stanley headed an expedition which accomplished more than any other single undertaking in Africa. In the face of overwhelming difficulties Stanley started from the east coast, reached the head of the Congo, and followed its course of 2700 miles to the Atlantic.

The discovery of the Congo and Stanley's account of his travels in *Through the Dark Continent* opened the eyes of Europeans

"Doctor Livingston, I presume" · *As reporter for the* New York Herald, *Stanley reached the sick explorer (right) at Ujiji near Lake Tanganyika on November 10, 1871.*

to the possibilities of this great undeveloped area. Within ten years after his triumphant return, Africa had been pretty well divided among the European powers.

How Belgium Created a Congo State · King Leopold of Belgium quickly formed a company which sent out another expedition to the Congo under Stanley's leadership. Its aims were to acquire territory and establish trading stations. Then Leopold declared his right to rule over the vast region (1885).

The Belgian company's treatment of the natives was an example of the inhuman methods which the European invaders sometimes used. Each village was required to produce a certain amount of raw rubber and ivory (elephant tusks) every year. If it failed to do so, its people were cruelly punished.

The atrocities committed in the Congo finally brought protests from other powers. The king was forced to give up his personal control of the company (for a handsome sum). The Belgian Congo was turned over to the management of the government. Thus Belgium acquired an empire eighty times her own size.

The French Build an Empire in Africa · King Leopold's promptness in sending Stanley out to the Congo roused other European powers to activity. A French explorer, striking eastward from Gabon, reached the Congo before Stanley arrived. When Stanley came to what is now Stanley Pool on the Congo in 1881, he found the French flag planted on the north shore of the river. Later this region came to be known as French Equatorial Africa.

The French also built up colonies on the coast at Senegal and Dahomey and on the Ivory Coast, and established themselves in French Guinea. From her coastal colonies France pushed inland, conquering great stretches of territory until she controlled a vast region in the Sahara and the western Sudan. France later combined this with French Equatorial Africa and her holdings in North Africa to form a great colonial empire fourteen times as large as France itself (see map).

German Colonies in Africa · Germany was slow to enter the race for overseas empire. Bismarck's policy, as we have seen (p. 399), was to strengthen the home government and avoid friction with other powers over foreign territory. But German merchants and businessmen were active in various enterprises in Africa and the Far East.

At last they persuaded Bismarck that it was to Germany's interest to protect her commerce. The activity of France and Britain also convinced him that Germany must look for a colonial empire. Between 1884 and 1890 Germany acquired four considerable areas of African territory—Togoland, the Cameroons, South-West Africa, and German East Africa (Tanganyika). Altogether they covered nearly a million square miles.

The Germans spent large sums building railways, bridges, harbors, and many other public works. But the German colonies did not pay. The land was not very productive. Labor was scarce, and there were continual wars with the natives. Few Germans were willing to settle there. Germany was bitterly disappointed with her share in Africa and made various attempts to get part of the Portuguese, Belgian, French, and British possessions there.

British in West Africa · The British colonies in West Africa covered less territory than the French, but they were much more valuable commercially. The most important was Nigeria. The Niger River and its

464

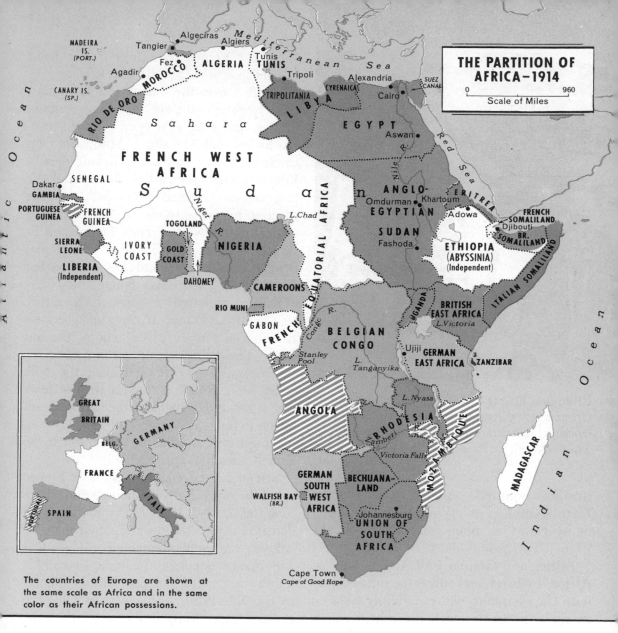

European Possessions in Africa, 1914 · *Which areas were held by Britain? France? Germany? Portugal? Spain? Italy? Belgium? Which were independent? Compare this map with that of Africa today on page 644.*

tributaries furnished a fine waterway to the interior of the continent. French, British, and German trading companies eagerly competed for this prize, but in the end the British won.

Britain's other colonies on the west coast were small (Gold Coast, Sierra Leone, Gambia) but of increasing economic importance. The volume of exports of palm oil, cocoa, rubber, and other products

Ethiopian Priests · *Most Ethiopians are Coptic Christians. Missionaries from Alexandria introduced Christianity in the fourth century. Their church is an offshoot of the Orthodox.*

steadily mounted. At the same time the British colonies in West Africa imported many times as much from Britain as the French possessions did from France.

British and German East Africa · In East Africa, British merchants came into contact with the Germans, who were busily engaged in making treaties with the native rulers. In 1886 England, Germany, and France appointed a commission to determine the right of the sultan of Zanzibar to this region. The decision allowed the sultan to retain a coastal strip a thousand miles long. The northern part of this territory was to become a British sphere of influence, and the southern a German. Behind this strip the British and Germans divided the territory between them as far inland as Lake Victoria. France was given a free hand in Madagascar. (See map, p. 465.)

Conflict over the Sudan and Ethiopia · A triangular struggle between Britain, France, and Italy developed over the eastern Sudan and Abyssinia. Study the map carefully as you read the following details. France wanted the eastern Sudan and the kingdom of Abyssinia (Ethiopia) in order to join her possessions in northern and western Africa with French Somaliland in the east. Italy, a late comer in the colonial field, had decided to add Abyssinia to her single possession, Italian Somaliland.

Britain preferred a weak Italy rather than a strong France in Abyssinia, because Britain could more easily acquire the Sudan. The British wanted the Sudan for two reasons: (1) It controlled the Nile valley. (2) Britain wanted a strip of territory running the length of the continent on which to build a Cape-to-Cairo railway connecting Egypt and South Africa, which the British already dominated.

Britain helped the Italians, but France aided the Abyssinians by training and equipping their army. In 1896 the Italians were defeated completely by the Abyssinians at Adowa. Abyssinia remained independent and France obtained the right to build a railway across the kingdom from Djibouti to the Nile valley. (Forty years later the Italians under Mussolini avenged their defeat at Adowa by conquering Ethiopia—only to lose it again during World War II.)

How the British Gained the Sudan · Soon after the British occupied Egypt in 1882 (p. 469), a revolt against the government was organized in the Sudan by Mohammed Ahmed. This leader claimed to be the Mahdi (guide) divinely appointed to protect the people against the infidel foreigners. General Gordon, who was in charge of the British garrison at Khartoum, was besieged by the fanatical followers (dervishes) of the Mahdi in 1885. After a stubborn defense, he and his men were killed.

Shortly after the Italian defeat at Adowa, the British General Kitchener was ordered to proceed south to occupy the Sudan. It was a long way and the general took two years, building a railway as he advanced. In a memorable battle at Omdurman he killed twenty thousand dervishes and then recaptured Khartoum.

In the meantime the French had already sent an expedition from the French Congo to the Nile valley under the explorer Captain Marchand. It reached the village of Fashoda in July, 1898. Kitchener hastened to Fashoda only to find the French flag flying above the village. He maintained that the Sudan was part of Egypt and under British protection. But Marchand insisted that it now belonged to France. For a while the two countries were on the brink of war over the "Fashoda Affair." But finally the French yielded and Marchand reluctantly withdrew. The British received the Sudan, and the French received privileges in North and West Africa.

The French Gain North Africa · France had long been carving out an empire just across the Mediterranean from the mother country. In 1830 King Charles X, on the pretext of avenging an insult to a French envoy, sent an expedition to Algiers. It captured the city and took possession of the surrounding country. But it was not until 1871 that the rebellious Moslem tribes were crushed.

Next to Algeria lies Tunis, the seat of the ancient Carthaginian empire (p. 81). It was ruled by a Moslem Bey (governor), as part of the Ottoman Empire. In the

Scene in the South Sudan · *Four Sudanese tribesmen approach their village on the bank of the White Nile. The Sudan was proclaimed independent on January 1, 1956.*

1860's Europeans began to flock to Tunis, attracted by the possible profits to be made from the development of this backward country. Here they engaged in various ventures and readily lent money to the Bey, who soon found himself hopelessly in debt.

Finally his foreign creditors stepped in and took charge of his finances. French, British, and Italians competed against one another to get concessions which would enable them to develop the country and thus control the government. In 1881 raids on the Algerian border gave the French a pretext for invading Tunis and taking it as their colony.

The action of the French was strongly resented by Italy, which felt that the ancient Carthaginian territory should belong

Gateway in Fez, Morocco · *Its arch is modeled after a hoof of Mohammed's horse. Through it can be seen two minarets, one topped by a stork's nest.*

to Rome. From this time on, Italy was a colonial rival of France.

What Became of Morocco · Morocco, a land somewhat smaller than France, with a healthful climate and fertile soil, was the last African territory to fall to Europeans. For years France carried on secret negotiations, trying to persuade other nations to support any action she might take there. Italy finally made a bargain with her not to interfere with French plans if France would agree to allow Italy to take Tripolitania and Cyrenaica. The British promised to leave France free in Morocco, provided Britain was permitted to retain Egypt. Spain signed a secret document, dividing Morocco between herself and France (1904).

Germany, which had been overlooked, now rose to interfere with French plans,

and a European war crisis developed in 1905. It was not until 1912 that France obtained control of Morocco.

Italy's Empire in Libya · When Italy lost Tunis to the French, her hopes turned to Tripolitania and Cyrenaica, two Turkish provinces lying to the south of Sicily. Although larger than Tunis, they were mainly desert land. In 1911 Italy notified Turkey of her intention to occupy the provinces. The next year, after a short war, she took possession of her new empire and called it by its ancient Roman name, Libya (see map, p. 465). For this sop to her national pride Italy paid well. The population of Libya was small. And the revenue from the few industries, olive groves, and cotton plantations was never sufficient to meet expenses.

Egypt Long under Moslem Rule · Egypt was conquered by the Arabs in the seventh century (p. 135). Through the Middle Ages she fell under various Moslem rulers and in 1507 became part of the Ottoman Empire. When Napoleon failed to bring Egypt under French rule, a military adventurer from Albania, Mehemet Ali, forced the sultan to acknowledge him as governor of Egypt. His heirs were later recognized as the rightful rulers of the country.

Mehemet's grandson Ismail I (1863–1879) was an admirer of European civilization and was eager to modernize his realm. He built canals, railways, and harbors, and brought in the telegraph. He supported European scholars who were studying the monuments of ancient Egypt, and founded a famous museum at Cairo. In 1869 he celebrated the completion of the Suez Canal, which united the waters of the Mediterranean with the Red Sea. In this enterprise alone he invested eighty million dollars. He also spent large sums on the conquest of the Sudan.

British Gain Control of Egypt · As a result of his extravagance, Ismail soon owed his British and French bankers much more than he could repay. To ward off bankruptcy he sold his shares in the Suez Canal to the British. But even this did not save him. The next year he had to allow foreigners to supervise his finances. When he tried later to rid himself of these advisers, he was deposed.

Foreign intervention aroused such discontent in Egypt that the natives revolted in 1882. The French refused to put down the rebellion, but the British bombarded Alexandria and occupied the country. The government was still headed by a Khedive, but the British were in control.

We Have a Secret · *This* Punch *cartoon depicts Disraeli's glee upon purchasing 177,000 shares of Suez Canal Stock from the extravagant Khedive. What is the secret?*

The British made many reforms. They straightened out the national finances, established a fairer administration of justice, and created a legislative assembly. Their most striking achievement was the construction of a great dam at Aswan, to store up water so that it could be distributed regularly through irrigation canals to the fields and farms. The British also put an end to the practice of flogging laborers to make them work. They introduced the payment of wages for labor.

The beneficial results of British management were seen in the increased production of farm products and the mounting revenues of the country. But the Egyptians resented the rule of foreigners. This was to lead to many further troubles in Egypt, as we shall see later.

One sore spot was foreign control of the Suez Canal. It was operated by the Suez Canal Company on a 99-year concession. The British government's share in the company permitted it to exercise great influence. In 1888 an international convention provided that the canal was to be open to the ships of all nations on equal terms, both in peace and in war.

CHECK ON YOUR READING

1. Point out the early settlements in Africa on a map.
2. Describe and trace the discoveries of Stanley and Livingstone.
3. How and where did each of the following carve up Africa: (a) Belgium, (b) England, (c) France, (d) Germany, (e) Italy, (f) Portugal?
4. Why were the following important: (a) the Congo, (b) the Niger, (c) the Sudan, (d) Adowa, (e) Fashoda, (f) Tunis, (g) Morocco, (h) Suez?

Latin America Today · *Left: The Cathedral of Mexico City symbolizes the important role of the Catholic Church in Mexican civilization. Below: Sheepherding is an important industry of the great ranches of Argentina.*

Left: Bolivian Indians sell their produce in open-air markets. Many of the people of Latin America are Indians. Below: This new building of the University of Panama reflects the desire of the people for more and better education.

5. The United States and Its Latin-American Neighbors

American Isolation · Foreign affairs assumed great importance in the first twenty-five years of American national history. A half-dozen treaties and conventions were concluded in the period. The nation fought a brief naval war with France in 1798, and the Barbary pirates in 1805, and the War of 1812 with England while the latter was busy with Napoleon.

But with the peace of 1815 the independence of the United States was fully achieved. It turned its back on Europe and began in earnest the exploration and development of its own territory. This had been doubled in size by Jefferson's purchase of the Louisiana Territory. Up to the very close of the nineteenth century the United States, following Jefferson's warning against "entangling alliances" and relying on the Monroe Doctrine of 1823 (p. 349), remained in almost complete political isolation from the Old World.

Now and then cases of friction with European powers did arise. But these cases were only exceptions which proved the rule. They were all settled without resort to war. There arose a general feeling of relief among the American people that they could continue unmolested in their industrial development. They felt protected by the oceans which separated them from the Old World and by their own lack of any desire to compete for colonies and dominions.

The Spanish-American War · This course was interrupted by events in the Spanish colony of Cuba. From time to time the Cubans had rebelled against the harsh Spanish rule. Americans were especially disturbed by the cruel treatment of the Cubans by the Spanish governor, General Weyler. Moreover, they wanted protection for their heavy investments in the sugar and tobacco industries of the island.

Protests to Madrid were met by the rebuke that the nation should mind its own business and stop aiding the rebels. Therefore, when the United States battleship *Maine* was blown up in the harbor of Havana (February 15, 1898) with great loss of life, the war fever in the United States reached a high pitch. President McKinley finally yielded to the demands of the people and Congress, and war was declared.

The Spanish-American War (April to August, 1898) resulted in an easy victory for the United States. Commodore George Dewey, in command of the American fleet in the Pacific, destroyed the Spanish fleet in Manila Bay (the Philippines) on May 1. On July 3 Admiral William T. Sampson destroyed every ship of a Spanish squadron off the southern shore of Cuba. Dewey took the city of Manila, and General Shafter received the surrender of the Spanish army in Santiago, Cuba.

Measured in military terms, the war was insignificant. But in its effect upon the nation's foreign policy it was of great importance. By the terms of the peace the United States took possession of the Philippines and Guam in the Pacific and Puerto Rico in the Caribbean. Cuba was given its independence. The Philippines became independent in 1946, and Puerto Rico has been granted commonwealth status.

American Participation in World Affairs · In these same eventful years the United States assumed a share in the responsibility for the fate of China by its "open-door" policy (p. 455).

Theodore Roosevelt, who came to the Presidency upon the assassination of McKinley in 1901, strongly believed that the United States should take a more active role in the affairs of the world. He intervened in the Russo-Japanese war of 1904 to bring the envoys of the two countries to the peace table at Portsmouth, New Hampshire (p. 444). He sent his representative to the Algeciras conference for the settlement of the dispute between France and Germany over Morocco (p. 497). He pushed the building of the Panama Canal without regard for the obstacles put in its way by the state of Colombia.

Let us now look more closely at Latin America and see what kind of neighbors the United States had by 1900. We last discussed the Latin-American countries when they achieved their independence from Europe (pp. 346–349).

Social Classes, the Church, Education, and Government · There were distinct social classes in Latin America. (1) At the top were the government officials and the great landholders of vast estates (*haciendas*). (2) The *creoles*, the people of Spanish ancestry born in America, were the middle class. They were small farmers, tradesmen, artisans, and professional men. (3) Then came the vast mass of illiterate and toiling natives. They included Indians, Negroes, mestizos (of mixed Spanish and Indian blood), and mulattoes (of mixed white and Negro blood).

Roman Catholicism was the religion brought in by the Spaniards and Portuguese. So dedicated was the work of its missionaries that most of the natives were converted to Christianity. Jesuit, Dominican, and Franciscan monks did most of the teaching, for education was dominated by the Church. There were excellent universities at Mexico City, Lima, and Santo Domingo.

The written constitutions of Latin-American countries were patterned largely on that of the United States. But democracy, as we know it, was long delayed. The great landholders controlled the government, and there was no middle class to give it balance. Factions, often dominated by the Church and the army, took the place of orderly political parties. There were many revolutions. Time and again dictators seized the presidency and plundered the treasury.

Threats to the Monroe Doctrine · Although the Monroe Doctrine was generally respected, some countries attempted to encroach on the sovereignty of the Latin-American states from time to time.

The Execution of Maximilian, Emperor of Mexico, 1864–1867 · *Napoleon III forbade Manet to display this painting. Why?*

(1) The most serious threat was the attempt of the French emperor Napoleon III to put Archduke Maximilian of Austria on an imperial throne in Mexico in 1864. But the War between the States was over the following year, and General Sheridan was sent to the Mexican border with 50,000 men. An ultimatum was served on France to withdraw her troops from Mexico. Napoleon then abandoned Maximilian to his fate. He was captured by the Mexican president Juárez and executed by a firing squad on June 19, 1867.

(2) Great Britain had a long quarrel over the boundary between Venezuela and British Guiana. In 1895 President Cleveland insisted that the question be submitted to arbitration, and war was averted.

(3) A few years later Germany persuaded England and Italy to join with her in forcing Venezuela into the payment of debts owed to citizens of the three countries. They bombarded some ports before President Theodore Roosevelt threatened to send Admiral Dewey's fleet to force them to stop.

(4) Theodore Roosevelt also sent troops to occupy the customs ports of Santo Domingo to prevent several European nations from a similar move to collect their debts. On that occasion he announced the Roosevelt corollary to the Monroe Doctrine. He said that "chronic wrongdoing" or political weakness in a Latin-American country justified the United States, "however reluctantly," in exercising "an international police power." In other words, the United States would move in to help a nation meet its international obligations to prevent European powers from sending troops. This led to widespread Latin-American suspicions of the intentions of the "Colossus of the North." Most of

"That's a Live Wire, Gentlemen!" · *Who were involved in the Venezuelan crisis of 1902? How did it end?*

these were not removed until after the inauguration of the "Good Neighbor" policy.

The Growth of Pan-Americanism · As early as 1826 the "Liberator," Simon Bolívar, had planned a congress of the new Latin-American republics at Panama, to which delegates from the United States were invited. But the congress (which the two North American delegates never reached) was a complete failure.

However, the idea was revived in October, 1889. At that time delegates from nineteen of the Latin-American states met at Washington at the invitation of James G. Blaine, the American Secretary of State. They discussed questions of currency, arbitration, and trade agreements. Trade pacts were negotiated by the United States with about a dozen of the countries.

At Mexico City in 1901 an International Bureau of American Republics was established. This was later renamed the Pan-American Union. With headquarters in Washington, it became an agency for the exchange of economic, scientific, and cultural information.

Delegates to the First International Conference of American States, Washington, 1889–1890 · *James G. Blaine, U. S. Secretary of State, called the conference and presided.*

The Inter-American System · Gradually the idea, embodied in the Monroe Doctrine, of the United States as a protecting "big brother" was transformed into a true Pan-Americanism. All the republics began to feel an equal responsibility for the common welfare.

Highlights in the achievement of this objective are these: (1) In 1933 Franklin Roosevelt announced his "Good Neighbor" policy. (2) The next year in Montevideo an agreement was reached that "no state has the right to intervene in the internal or external affairs of another." (3) Trade was stimulated when the United States began to negotiate reciprocal trade agreements. (4) The Act of Chapultepec (Mexico City, 1945) provided that an attack on an American state by *any* state should be considered an attack against *all*. (5) The Rio Treaty of 1947 defined the "region" of the American states with a line enclosing the Western Hemisphere from pole to pole. (6) The Bogotá Conference of 1948 set up an Organization of American States (O.A.S.). An executive council of foreign ministers decides on collective measures of self-defense. The Pan-American Union is the Secretariat for the council.

Economic and Cultural Progress · The Latin-American republics have made remarkable economic and cultural progress through the years. The cattle and wheat of Argentina, the coffee and rubber of Brazil, the copper and nitrates of Chile, the oil and iron of Venezuela, the sugar and tobacco of Cuba, and the silver and sulphur of Mexico have brought increasing wealth.

Populous cities like Buenos Aires and Rio de Janeiro rival the European capitals in broad avenues, magnificent parks, and modern architecture. Schools and universities have multiplied. Many distinguished musicians, artists, poets, historians, and scientists have won world acclaim.

When the resources of the region are developed in such a way as to raise the standard of living of its people, the future of Latin America will appear assured.

CHECK ON YOUR READING

1. *Why did the United States follow a policy of isolation after the War of 1812?*
2. *How was this policy modified by (a) the war with Spain? (b) Theodore Roosevelt?*
3. *Describe social classes, religion, and government in Latin America.*
4. *Explain how four threats to the Monroe Doctrine were met.*
5. *Trace the growth of (a) Pan-Americanism, (b) the Inter-American System.*
6. *Cite evidences of the remarkable economic and cultural progress in Latin America.*

Learning Activities

Think about the chapter

1. Cite events which happened in the nineteenth century in either Africa or Asia to show how imperialism led to war.

2. Discuss the advantages and disadvantages of imperialism from the point of view of (a) the colony, (b) the nation in control. Use specific examples.

3. What European countries were least successful in building an empire? Why?

4. *Map study:* On a map of China mark with different colors the spheres of influence of the major powers around 1900.

5. *Map study:* Draw a map of Africa similar to the one on page 465. Be able to explain the value of each possession to the country that held it.

6. *Map study:* Make a map of Latin America on a scale large enough to show its topographical features and mark by symbols its chief resources. See maps on pages 370–371.

Go beyond the text

7. Report on the building, operation, control, and significance of the Suez Canal. Explain the "Suez crisis" of 1956.

8. Report on one of the following interesting persons touched upon in this chapter: Perry, Livingstone, Stanley, "Chinese" Gordon, and Teddy Roosevelt.

9. Report on recent events in Latin America, such as (a) fall of dictators, (b) the work of the O.A.S., (c) U.S. economic aid.

10. European imperialism brought about many changes in Africa and the changes are continuing. Read about Africa as it is today. Articles in the *National Geographic*, August, 1953, and December, 1954, and those in *Life* in later years will give an over-all picture of life in many sections of Africa. Bradley's *World Geography* will be helpful. Consult the *Readers' Guide* for more recent articles. For an overview see Chapter 34 in this text.

Follow up your special interests

11. Make an illustrated time line that will show the developments in transportation and communication in the nineteenth century.

12. The clipper ship linked the United States to China in the nineteenth century. Make a drawing or model of a clipper.

13. Make a collection of pictures that illustrate various aspects of life in the Latin-American countries for a bulletin-board display.

14. Add to your history-of-art scrapbook examples of the art of Asia, Africa, and Latin America.

READ FURTHER

Basic readings: (1) BECKER, *Modern History*, Chap. 19. (2) CHEYNEY, *Readings*, Chap. 20. (3) CHEYNEY, *Short History of the English People*, Chaps. 20–21. (4) HOFFMAN, *News of the World*, Nos. 46–49. (5) SCOTT, BALTZLY, *Readings*, Chap. 12. (6) Year's *Pictorial History*, pp. 386–392.

Special accounts: (7) M. DILTS, *The Pageant of Japanese History*. Japan's historical development is described in an easy manner, with excellent illustrations. (8) J. GUNTHER, *Inside Africa*. (9) A. PATON, *The Land and People of South Africa*. Excellent account of the geography, history, people, and problems of this area. (10) E. SEEGER, *The Pageant of Chinese History*. (11) *National Geographic*, "Safari through Changing Africa," August, 1953; "Safari from the Congo to Cairo," December, 1954; "Yankee Sailor Who Opened Japan: Commodore Perry and His Black Ships Changed the Course of History," July, 1953.

Fiction and biography: (12) P. BUCK, *The Good Earth*. A family in North China is driven south by a famine, but returns after the revolution. (13) J. EATON, *David Livingstone, Foe of Darkness*. (14) J. GOLLOMB, *Albert Schweitzer: Genius of the Jungle*.

27

The March of Science and Technology

KEY WORDS AND DATES

mass production	cell theory
automation	anesthetics
electronics	antiseptics
Diesel	Lister
Lyell	Pasteur
galaxies	vaccination
Darwin	Salk
Mendel	antibiotics
mutations	public health
historical method	Reed
atoms	Gorgas
nuclear fission	fluoridation
chain reaction	mental health
synthesis	Freud

THE STORY of man's development is one long, continuous tale of change. Very gradually new ways take the place of old. Various forms of government are tried. Men move to distant lands and start new homes. Inventions change the way of raising crops, making and distributing goods, and communicating ideas. With increasing knowledge old ways are slowly abandoned. And though life seems not to alter much day by day, the cumulative result of new things steadily added is great indeed.

With the spread of the Industrial Revolution, however, the rate of progress increased in geometric proportion. More changes came in a hundred years than in the previous eighteen centuries. Discoveries such as the telegraph, the reaper, the vulcanization of rubber, the telephone, the electric light, the electric motor, and the gas engine led to further discoveries. The sciences of geology, physics, chemistry, biology, and psychology underwent great expansion.

Indeed the groundwork was laid for the phenomenal scientific advances which have characterized our own lifetime and which face us in the fabulous future. Standards of living have been raised and death rates reduced. Yet ahead of us lie great challenges to extend further the frontiers of knowledge and to bring the benefits of technology to underdeveloped areas.

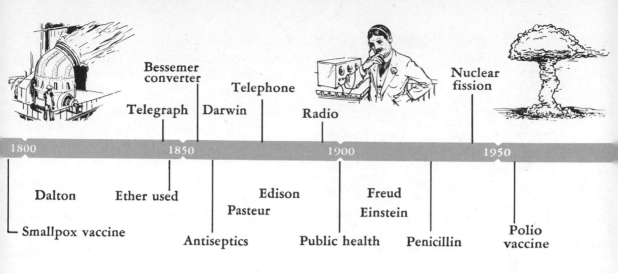

Bessemer converter · Telegraph · Darwin · Telephone · Radio · Nuclear fission

1800 — 1850 — 1900 — 1950

Dalton · Ether used · Edison · Pasteur · Freud · Einstein

Smallpox vaccine · Antiseptics · Public health · Penicillin · Polio vaccine

1. Science and Invention Bring the Machine Age

From Mechanization to Automation · We have seen how the introduction of machinery changed the whole system of manufacturing and transportation beginning in the late eighteenth century. Great as was the achievement of this early Industrial Revolution, the progress which was to follow was even more wonderful.

(1) Power-driven machinery began to take the place of hand labor. Old industries, such as the making of boots, shoes, and hats, expanded as by magic, and new industries developed. (2) "Precision tools," used in various processes of manufacture, were perfected. (3) Turning out duplicate parts in great quantities (standardization) made *mass production* possible.

(4) The belt-conveyor system made possible the assembly line. The product now could move from station to station in the factory as various parts were attached. Or a piece of metal could move from machine to machine to be shaped in steps to its finished form. (5) Specialization of labor increased the efficiency of workers. By 1900 "time and motion" studies of industrial jobs were being made by "efficiency experts" to learn the best way of performing the work. Today scientific management is also concerned with discovering workers' aptitudes and improving employee morale.

(6) In some industries machinery has become increasingly automatic. One man at a control panel may operate an entire production line. The key factor in such *automation* is "feedback." This means that the mechanism feeds back information (through electronic devices) to control its own production. Errors in size or quality are immediately detected and corrected automatically. (7) And mass communication via newspaper, magazine, radio, and television advertising creates mass demands for mass-produced goods.

Electricity and Electronics · Building on the work of earlier investigators, scientists turned their growing knowledge of electricity to practical uses. The electric motor and generator developed by Michael Faraday began to furnish power for railways

477

Henry Ford (1863–1947) **Talking to Thomas Edison** (1847–1931) · *Edison's 1300 inventions won him the title "Wizard of Menlo Park." Ford became the apostle of mass production.*

and machines. In 1879 Thomas A. Edison perfected the incandescent electric lamp. Three years later his system of central station power production began to promote the widespread use of electrical power. Many applications of electrical power for home conveniences quickly followed. The electric kitchen, laundry, and do-it-yourself workshop in our homes today are examples of this trend.

After Samuel F. B. Morse sent the first electrical telegraph message in 1844, the whole system of communication was revolutionized. About twenty years later a transatlantic cable linked America with Europe. In 1876 Alexander Graham Bell invented the telephone, and in another twenty years Marconi was sending messages by wireless telegraphy (radio).

The invention of the electronic tube greatly increased the range of receiving radio signals. A great new entertainment industry developed as a result (p. 490). The electronic tube today is an essential part of radio, television, radar, modern telephone systems, industrial controls, and electronic computers. With the development of the tiny transistor, electrical currents can be amplified with only a fraction of the power required by the smallest electronic tubes. And the end of this trend toward *miniaturization* is nowhere in sight.

A New Kind of Engine · Inventors had long been working to perfect a kind of engine which would get its power from an explosion rather than from the pressure of steam. It was not until 1876, however, that the first practical engine run by the explosion of a mixture of gas and air was devised. This early gas engine was in use for some time before it was discovered that the petroleum product gasoline, which had heretofore been permitted to go to waste in oil wells, was highly suitable for this type of machine.

In 1897 Rudolph Diesel produced a very efficient engine which burned oil instead of gasoline. Diesel engines today are widely

Bell Telephones Long Distance from New York to Chicago, 1892 · *His message was part of the ceremonies opening the Columbian Exhibition at the Chicago World's Fair.*

used in trucks, buses, ships, and railroad locomotives.

Several great industries owe their importance to the internal-combustion engine. In recent years automobile factories in the United States alone have turned out six to nine million motor vehicles a year. A dependable gasoline engine made the airplane possible. The petroleum and steel industries have expanded as well.

The Steel Age · The manufacture of engines, of course, depended upon the production of vast quantities of iron and steel. Neither the hand-hammered methods used by the ancient Egyptians to make their sickles and saws nor the crude blast forges of medieval smithies were sufficient. "Breakthroughs" came with the invention of the crucible process (1740), the Kelly-Bessemer converter (1850), the cold-rolling mill (1860), and the open-hearth furnace (1864).

Today about 40 per cent of all manufacturing jobs in the United States depend upon steel-making or its use. Steel is the backbone of modern industry, and the war potential of a nation is frequently measured by its steel-producing capabilities.

The Rubber Industry · Another great industry, which developed along with motor vehicles and oil, was that of rubber. Charles Goodyear in 1839 discovered that crude rubber, when heated and combined with other substances, can be made tougher and more elastic. This process, called vulcanizing, made rubber useful for many purposes. Rubber was used to make many articles for household use, as well as equipment for railroads and motor vehicles.

Improvements in Methods of Farming · With the gradual development of mechanical devices and the introduction of the gas engine, farming methods were completely

Skyscraper of Steel and Glass · *The 38-story Seagram Building in New York contains twelve acres of office space enclosed by 3676 windows and 12,500 tons of steel.*

transformed. Up to the nineteenth century, farmers' implements had been improved but little since the days of the Roman Empire.

First to be developed was the metal plow. The reaper made it possible to bring vast new areas under cultivation. With other machinery, fertilizer, and scientific methods, the productivity of the farm was increased as human labor decreased. This means that a smaller percentage of men are needed for food production and many farmers have been able to turn to other pursuits.

But most of the people of Asia are still tillers of the soil living under the constant threat of starvation—which is to say that the benefits of the agricultural revolution have yet to reach many areas.

Machinery Has Raised Standards of Living · The mechanical revolution made possible the growth of great industries in certain areas as well as rapid transportation and communication. Men in industrialized states could now build more comfortable homes, have more varied food, produce it in greater quantity with less effort, and enjoy many luxuries from afar. They could have finer clothing, travel about with ease, and save much time.

The introduction of machinery resulted in the making of goods on such a large scale that the prices of many articles were reduced. They became available to any who had the money with which to buy them. Never before in the world's history had so many people enjoyed conveniences and comforts previously restricted to the wealthy few.

The standard of living in industrial nations thus made them the envy of peoples still dominated by feudal, agricultural, and pastoral economies. And one of the great challenges of our own age is the problem of helping less fortunate peoples close the gap between the ox-cart and automation.

CHECK ON YOUR READING

1. *Summarize seven great steps from mechanization to automation.*
2. *What discoveries highlighted the advances in (a) electricity and electronics? (b) internal-combustion engines? (c) the steel industry? (d) the rubber industry? (e) methods of farming?*
3. *How have these great changes affected (a) standards of living? (b) men's hopes?*

---

2. Study of the Earth and Living Things

A New Attitude toward the Earth · The progress made in science meant more than an increase in material comforts. It meant new understandings about the nature of the universe and about man himself. The study of the earth (geology) brought a new idea of its age and structure, and led to the discovery of the vast riches which lay hidden beneath its surface.

In 1830 Sir Charles Lyell published *Principles of Geology*. In this work he showed how natural forces, such as wind, rain, and frost, had, through countless ages, formed the valleys and mountains and laid down thick beds of limestone, clay, and sandstone.

Many of these rocks contain fossils (traces of ancient life), showing that plants and animals have existed on the earth from very remote periods. Today scientists believe that "the most probable age of the earth, the solar system, and perhaps the universe itself is in the neighborhood of five billion years."

Modern astronomers tell us that our planet Earth is only a tiny part of one galaxy of billions of stars. Among 500 million galaxies, our sun is a tiny candle indeed compared to the giant red stars. The distance between galaxies runs as high as five million light-years, or 30 billion billion miles. Measured in terms of time and space, then, recorded history is but the tick of a watch, on a stage much smaller than the point of a pin.

Darwin and Evolution · Even in the eighteenth century, investigators began to suspect that plants and animals had slowly developed through the ages. Charles Darwin, an Englishman, was the first to put forward such convincing arguments for this view that it was accepted by large numbers of people. He published *The Origin of Species by Means of Natural Selection* in 1859.

Darwin held that the various species of animals and plants—all the different kinds of fishes, snakes, birds, mammals, trees, and shrubs—are not descendants of original separate and distinct species, created in a fixed form. Rather, as they exist today, they are the result of many changes which have modified them through the millions of years of their existence.

The theory that higher and more complicated kinds of animals and plants are derived from lower and simpler ancestors is called *evolution*. It proved to be more disturbing to the older ideas of the world even than the discovery of Copernicus that the earth revolves around the sun (p. 202). Nevertheless it made rapid headway, and today most zoologists, geologists, biologists, and others who have received a scientific training accept parts of Darwin's theory.

Mendel, Heredity, and Mutations · At the same time that Darwin published his views, an Austrian monk, Gregor Mendel, was experimenting with plants in his garden. He discovered by cross-pollination that he could predict with great accuracy the hereditary characteristics of new generations of plants.

Around 1900 biologists began to take notice of Mendel's findings in genetics. From their studies we know that changes in species are due mainly to changes (mutations) in their genes. Today our scientists

Charles Darwin (1809–1882) · *"I have steadily endeavored to keep my mind free so as to give up any hypothesis . . . as soon as facts are shown to be opposed to it."*

are using atomic research to speed up the occurrence of mutations in plant, insect, and animal life. They appear to be on the threshold of tremendous discoveries in the field of artificial photosynthesis (using sunlight to manufacture food as in the leaf), in creating disease-resistant hybrid plants, and in producing meatier livestock.

How Darwin's Ideas Influenced Modern Study · Darwin's belief in evolution greatly influenced investigators in all fields. Today students agree that one of the most profitable ways to approach any subject is by the *historical method*—that is, by tracing its origin and early history to the present and thus learning how it came to be as we now find it.

The influence of Darwin's work was soon evident in the publication of many studies on the evolution of language, the evolution of the family, the evolution of institutions and laws, and even the evolution of history. This idea of the emergence of the present from the past and the influence of the past on the present leads historians to seek for the sources of our civilization in far-distant times. When we know more about the past, we have new light on the present, for we understand better how habits, institutions, and ideas have developed.

CHECK ON YOUR READING

1. How did scientists change our ideas about the earth in time and space?
2. Explain (a) Darwin's theory of evolution, (b) Mendel's findings, (c) mutations.
3. How have Darwin's theories influenced modern study?

---

3. Scientists Discover the Nature of Matter

About Atoms, Electrons, and Molecules · Far back in the time of the Greeks we recall that philosophers offered various explanations of how the physical world came about (p. 65). Democritus and his followers held that everything was made up of tiny particles of different kinds—hard and soft, round and jagged. These particles they thought of as flying about or falling through space and constantly forming new bodies. Some of them might make iron. Others might make a vegetable, which would quickly decay. These tiny specks the Greeks called *atoms*, which means "things that cannot be divided." They thought that they had come upon the most tiny and permanent part of nature.

In the early part of the nineteenth century an Englishman by the name of Dalton found that chemical substances combined in certain definite proportions. This led him to believe that all gases, liquids, and even solids were composed of small particles. These he called by the old name—atoms. It was gradually discovered that there are many kinds of atoms: hydrogen, oxygen, nitrogen, carbon, uranium, iron, and many others.

As research continued it was found that each atom has a central nucleus around which revolve electrical charges called *electrons*. The electrons are very small compared to the nucleus. They move at terrific speed around the nucleus in paths relatively far from it. Thus most of the atom is "empty space." Although a piece of steel may look very solid and quiet to us, it is mostly empty space in which its atoms are in constant motion.

We know that all matter is composed of single atoms or combinations of atoms called *molecules* ("little masses"). For example, a molecule of water consists of two hydrogen atoms and one oxygen atom (H_2O). There are some 33 billion billion molecules in a drop of water! In chemical reactions the atoms are not changed but merely rearranged to form new molecules. Thus nylon contains the same atoms that were in the water, coal, and air of which it is made, but now they are rearranged.

Another important discovery was that some heavy atoms, such as that of uranium, tend to fly apart and shoot off portions of themselves into space. This discovery opened the doorway to the Atomic Age.

Atomic Energy: Servant or Enemy? · During World War II President Roosevelt assigned American scientists the task of releasing the energy of the atom. It was known that a neutron, when shot into the nucleus of a uranium atom, splits the atom (nuclear fission) and releases tremendous amounts of energy. The neutrons released from the nucleus hit and split other atoms, releasing further neutrons and energy in a *chain reaction*. The basic problem was to produce a *controlled* chain reaction. With the aid of scientists from several nations, this feat was finally accomplished at the University of Chicago in December, 1942.

The bomb which ushered in the Atomic Age at Hiroshima, Japan, on August 6, 1945, exploded with a force equal to 22,000 tons of TNT. Its terrible destructiveness was produced by shock waves, radioactivity, and heat of unbelievable intensity. While it brought the war to a hasty conclusion, the awful lesson of the hour was obvious. Unlimited atomic war could mean the destruction of life on this planet.

But the peaceful uses of atomic energy hold tremendous possibilities for the benefit of all mankind. Among these are the following:

(1) Nuclear energy is a new source of energy. Nuclear power plants are used to generate electricity. In areas lacking coal, oil, or water power, they may increasingly supplement these fuels.

(2) Nuclear power has tremendous possibilities for propulsion purposes. The atomic submarine *Nautilus*, for example, traveled over 62,000 miles without refueling. Merchant ships and air transports may be next.

(3) Radioisotope "tracers" are used to study the life processes in plants and animals and to diagnose and treat diseases.

Albert Einstein (1879–1955) *set forth a theory of relativity which revolutionized man's ideas of space, time, mass, and motion.* **Niels Bohr** (*Danish physicist, below*) *saw the atom as a miniature solar system, and used the cyclotron* (*particle accelerator*) *to produce radioisotopes.*

Dmitri I. Mendeléyev (1834–1907) · *This Russian chemist stated the Periodic Law classifying the chemical elements. He predicted the properties of three undiscovered elements.*

(4) Radiation is used in industry to locate defects in products and to measure thickness of material.

(5) Research and career opportunities in this new field are multiplying each year. Whether atomic energy will become man's servant or his enemy, however, may well depend upon the statesmanship of those now striving for a system of international control.

Services of Physicists and Chemists · Physicists are concerned with the properties and behavior of matter. They study its hardness, lightness, density, specific gravity, and so on. They have made great progress in the study of light, heat, energy, optics, electricity, electromagnetism, electronics, and X rays. The tremendous advances in radio,

television, electronics, and nuclear energy which we have already discussed are due to the application of their great discoveries.

The chemist is interested in the composition of substances, their elements and compounds. He is concerned with the changes that take place in them as the result of heat, the mixture of substances, the application of an electric current, the action of air, etc.

Chemistry, like physics, has made great progress. For example, an analysis of soils, fertilizers, and the composition of plants has greatly aided agriculture. It has shown what minerals are taken from the earth by certain plants and what fertilizers must be used to replenish the soil and prevent its exhaustion. Such knowledge has enabled farmers to get a much greater yield from their acreage.

Chemistry has given us modern processes for bleaching and dyeing cloth. It has played a leading role in the important study of food and its preservation. It has revealed the changes that take place in the human body from various causes and has revolutionized the study of medicine.

The Rise of Chemical Industries · Armed with modern knowledge, the scientist can combine atoms in their proper proportions and reproduce (synthesize) many familiar substances which had previously been produced only by plants or animals. For example, from such an unattractive substance as coal tar have come beautiful dyes, exquisite perfumes, artificial flavorings, and many drugs and disinfectants.

Moreover, the modern chemist can make substances which do not occur in nature, and so enlarge our resources and replace many which are rapidly being consumed. He can make steel alloys by mixing iron with any number of other metals to get greater durability or beauty. Plastics of all kinds are being produced in ever-increasing amounts and variety.

One of the first plastics was celluloid, first made in 1869. In 1907 Dr. Baekeland successfully combined a liquid and a gas (carbolic acid and formaldehyde) and produced a resinous substance which he called *Bakelite*. When heated, Bakelite can be molded into many shapes and polished.

Later, other beautiful plastics were developed, some of which are transparent. Brushes, combs, fountain pens, telephone receivers, and many, many other useful and decorative articles which were formerly made of rubber, wood, or metal are now made of plastics. Cellophane and other plastics are widely used in packaging, insulating, and waterproofing.

After long experimentation a way of making a substitute for silk (from cellulose) was finally discovered. The enormous rayon industry was followed later by the manufacturing of nylon, Dacron, Orlon, Acrilan, and other synthetic fibers.

Other industries which have developed mainly because of advances in chemistry are those producing glass products, photographic film, antifreeze solutions, synthetic rubber, petroleum products, detergents, fertilizers, and insecticides.

CHECK ON YOUR READING

1. *Explain the nature of matter in terms of atoms and molecules.*
2. *How do physicists and chemists serve mankind?*
3. *Give examples of the development of coal-tar products, plastics, alloys, fibers, and other synthetic products.*

---

4. Study of Man and the Prevention of Disease

The Cell Theory of Biology · While some investigators were occupied with the study of the earth and the properties of matter, others turned their attention to living things. They studied plants and animals and man himself. Early naturalists were much interested in finding out how plants and animals grow from the very beginning, when life starts. About 1838 two German naturalists, one of whom had been studying plants and the other, animals, compared their observations. They reached the conclusion that all living things are composed of minute bodies, which they named *cells*. The cells are composed of a jelly-like substance, to which the name *protoplasm* was given in 1846. Every living organism, whether toadstool or man, springs from a germ consisting of but a single cell.

The cell theory became the foundation of the modern study of biology. It has helped to explain the causes of many diseases and in some cases to suggest remedies.

Anesthetics to Reduce Pain · A revolution in surgery was produced by the successful use of drugs which could keep a patient unconscious during a period of great pain or during an operation. In 1800 Sir Humphry Davy, a famous British chemist, advised the use of nitrous oxide (laughing gas) during surgical operations. In the 1840's Dr. Long of Georgia and Dr. Morton and Dr. Warren of Boston did much to bring ether into use and Dr. Simpson of Edinburgh began to suggest the use of chloroform.

Local anesthetics were developed to make particular parts of the body insensitive. In

Louis Pasteur (1822–1895) · *This famous French chemist disproved the theory of spontaneous generation, developed pasteurization, controlled the silkworm disease, and perfected vaccines against anthrax and hydrophobia.*

1905 chemists introduced novocain, a synthetic narcotic resembling cocaine, but not habit-forming. Before the days of anesthetics few persons could endure the pain and shock of an operation. Nowadays surgeons are able to take as long as several hours for careful work. Even long operations on the human heart can now be performed.

The Use of Antiseptics · Although the introduction of anesthetics resulted in more successful surgery, it was found that many wounds would not heal, but became infected. Poisoning and death often followed. Hospitals seemed to be centers of pestilence rather than of health, because so many of the patients died. The causes of infection were not known, and the simple methods used to provide cleanliness were entirely insufficient.

When Joseph Lister, an English surgeon, became professor at Glasgow in 1860, he was much depressed by the ill effects which he saw following most operations. He had long been interested in the causes of inflammation in wounds, and he now began to experiment. Lister first used carbolic acid to cleanse the instruments and the wound. The results were so successful that his work introduced a new era of aseptic (Greek *a-*, "not," *septikos*, "poisonous") surgery.

The Germ Theory of Disease · Lister was greatly influenced by a discovery made by a French chemist, Louis Pasteur (1822–1895). Pasteur announced that decomposition in organic substances was due to the presence of germs. These are tiny organisms, visible only through a microscope, which multiply rapidly and cause chemical changes in the medium in which they are located.

Pasteur also discovered that a particular disease may be caused by the activity of a distinct microbe, which brings about chemical changes in the blood or tissues. The next step was to identify the germs of different diseases.

It was known that a very mild case of a disease sometimes prevented further attack. Inoculation against smallpox had been practiced since around 1700. But in 1796 Edward Jenner used cowpox vaccine instead of a deliberate dosage of smallpox. This produced an immunity to smallpox and greatly reduced the spread of the disease. Yet no one at the time knew exactly why the vaccination was successful.

Pasteur's greatest discovery was the means of preventing rabies (hydrophobia) in man and animals. Koch of Berlin discovered the germs that cause tuberculosis and Asiatic cholera. Antitoxins (counterpoisons) have since been discovered for diphtheria, tetanus, typhoid fever, and many other deadly diseases.

Bacteriology and the War on Disease · Since the discoveries of Pasteur, bacteriology has developed into one of the most important branches of research. Great laboratories are centers for the study of microorganisms. These are identified, isolated, and observed. Some disease-producing bacteria and viruses are grown under varying conditions and are finally made into vaccines. In recent years one of the notable successes has been the development of a vaccine to prevent paralytic poliomyelitis. Nationwide use of Dr. Jonas E. Salk's vaccine has cut the polio rate drastically in the United States.

Moreover, many diseases have been found to yield to the so-called "miracle drugs." These include the sulfa drugs and antibiotics. Hundreds of specific antibiotics have been isolated from molds and organisms in the soil. The first was penicillin, discovered by Sir Alexander Fleming in 1929, but not used widely until the 1940's. Pneumonia and many other infectious diseases have now been brought under almost miraculous control.

Public-Health Measures · Yellow fever and malaria had long been dreaded by people living in the tropics. Indeed work on the Panama Canal had to be postponed because the workers were dying like flies. Then Major Walter Reed of the United States Army and his assistant, Jesse W. Lazear, discovered the mosquito which carried the yellow-fever virus. When Dr. William Gorgas wiped out the mosquitoes in the Canal Zone, completion of the "big ditch" was assured.

Such dramatic demonstration convinced men that health and sanitation were matters of *public* as well as individual concern.

The knowledge that mosquitoes spread yellow fever, that typhoid was spread through infected water or milk, and that tuberculosis was spread through coughing or spitting—was not enough by itself. Precautions against the spread of disease needed to be taken on a community-wide basis. As a result we now have departments of public health with powers to test the water supply, enforce the pasteurization laws, require mosquito-control measures, regulate rubbish, garbage, and sewage disposal, and quarantine persons with communicable diseases—for the welfare of all.

One of the most worthwhile public-health measures taken in the United States in the twentieth century was designed to protect children's teeth. The breakthrough came with the discovery that wherever water

Conquerors of Yellow Fever · *Doctors Reed, Lazear, and Carroll conducting experiments at Havana, Cuba, which led to the discovery that yellow-fever virus was spread by a mosquito.*

Sigmund Freud, Founder of Psychoanalysis ·
As a psychiatrist he used free associations to encourage his patients to recall and recognize their repressed fears and thus overcome them.

on animals have shown that strong emotions throw the bodily functions out of order and produce chemical changes in the blood.

The study of psychology has opened up a vast field of research. Though scientists believe that there is still much to be learned, there is already a much better understanding of the causes of mental, as well as bodily, ills. Physicians, by beginning with our childhood, can sometimes show that troubles later in life are the result of shocks or fright long since forgotten. When the hidden cause is revealed, the patient often makes a recovery. The man who did the pioneer work in this and who has had the greatest influence on later studies was a Viennese doctor, Sigmund Freud (1856–1939).

Today modern governments spend considerable sums for mental hospitals. Here mentally disturbed patients can be given adequate psychiatric treatment. Unfortunately, the pace of industrial society is so great and the conflicting pressures upon the individual so strong that thousands of persons break under the strain. A strong mental-health program of a preventive nature is necessary if this problem is to be solved.

supplies contained fluoride at the ratio of one part per million, tooth enamel was excellent, tooth decay (dental caries) at a minimum, and tooth retention high. After exhaustive scientific studies, the fluoridation of public water supplies was endorsed by the American Dental Association, the American Medical Association, and dozens of other scientific organizations, and recommended by public-health departments throughout the nation.

Mental Health · In the late nineteenth century a new way of treating some diseases was developed as a result of discoveries in psychology, the study of the mind and its relation to the body. It has become increasingly clear that the body and the mind are not two separate entities, as was formerly believed, but parts of the same organism.

Disturbed mental states are sometimes the real cause of bodily disorders. All of us notice that bad news makes us feel sick, that worry can produce a headache, or that fear takes away our appetite. Experiments

---

CHECK ON YOUR READING

1. *Explain the following terms: (a) cell theory, (b) anesthetics, (c) antiseptics, (d) inoculation, (e) germ theory.*
2. *What is preventive medicine? What diseases can now be almost eliminated or their prevalence greatly reduced?*
3. *What contributions were made by (a) Lister, (b) Pasteur, (c) Koch, (d) Jenner, (e) Salk, (f) Reed and Lazear, (g) Fleming, (h) Freud.*
4. *Describe three important public-health measures.*

5. Knowledge Brought within the Reach of All

The People Learn to Read · This new knowledge about man and his world was at first known by only a few people, and many of these were specialists in their field. Indeed up to the middle of the eighteenth century most of the people of Europe could neither read nor write. And this is still true of most of the people of Africa and Asia today. But during the last two centuries many new ways of spreading information have been developed. Among these are public libraries, public schools, newspapers, motion pictures, radio, television, and the like. In all probability, more people learned to read in modern times than in any similar period of time in the history of the world. The bringing of knowledge within the reach of all—rich and poor alike—is one of the striking features of democratic government.

Religion, Democracy, and Education · It is interesting to note the role played by religion and democracy in teaching people to read. In the Middle Ages the few who could read or write were churchmen, scholars, wealthy townsmen, and a few of the nobility. Theirs were the inquiring minds which produced the Reformation and Counter-Reformation. Protestant churchmen stressed Bible reading by all the people as an absolute essential. And the Jesuits and other teaching orders of the Catholic Church looked upon education as an ideal instrument for spreading the faith.

The groundwork was thus laid for an educated group of ever-increasing proportions. The major breakthrough came when and where members of the growing middle class demanded a greater voice in government. They were quick to see that the strength of democracy lay in an informed citizenry.

Thereafter tax-supported education increased in strength with each extension of the suffrage. Thus it has come to be that today democratic governments and democratic schools go hand in hand.

Industrialization, as well as democracy, depends on education. For this reason countries attempting to become modern in a hurry, whether democratic or dictatorial, make great efforts to wipe out illiteracy. The success of the Soviet school system in producing technologists is very apparent today. No attempt is made, however, to build goodwill and world understanding. Dictatorships attempt to control the mind rather than free it for independent thinking.

Increase of Books, Magazines, Newspapers, and Libraries · The nineteenth century saw a great increase in the publication of books on all subjects—textbooks for schools, descriptions of travels, histories, biographies, novels, and scientific treatises. In more recent years the sale of inexpensive "paperbacks" has been phenomenal. Their low cost now makes it possible for most Americans to have a respectable library of their own. Today we have great public libraries which are vast storehouses of learning and entertainment. Supported by local, state, and national governments, they are open to all. Even small villages are proud of the libraries that they maintain for their people.

There has also been a steady increase in weekly, monthly, and quarterly magazines. Many of these now bring the people and events of the world to us in pictures as well.

Our great source of daily information, however, is the newspaper. At little cost it enables us to keep abreast of what is going on everywhere. The modern newspaper is the product of many inventions. The telephone, telegraph, and cable constantly dispatch news collected by the great press services from all parts of the world. This material is prepared by the editors for the typesetting machines. Then, by the use of great roller presses, millions of copies of our daily journals are turned out in a few hours. Today pictures of all kinds can be flashed even across the ocean, and these add greatly to the vividness of the written story.

Newspapers vary greatly from country to country. In democratic nations the press is open to anyone who can afford to publish. In many European countries newspapers are published by political parties, each of which presents its own point of view. In dictatorships the newspapers all reflect the "party line" of the one party permitted to exist.

The Motion Pictures · Scientists of the nineteenth century began also to perfect the cinema, or motion pictures. By 1906 the motion-picture industry had been organized, and films were being shown in many countries. At first there were only silent films, but in 1928 the sound film was introduced, in which the characters talk as well as act. And with the coming of wider screens, third-dimensional projection, and color film—the possibilities for pleasure as well as instruction have been increased tremendously.

American movies have had a great impact all over the world. Many people in other lands get their main impressions about life in the United States from Hollywood films. Excellent motion pictures are now being made in many countries. Every year the best films from all over the world are exhibited and judged at international film festivals.

The Marvels of the Radio and Television · Radio and television are two of the most powerful agencies for wiping out space and bringing closer together the different parts of the world. Both are the outcome of the scientific research done and discoveries made during the nineteenth century. News, speeches, and music can be sent instantly throughout the world. Radio has assumed a great importance in Asia and Africa as a means of spreading information and ideas to people who don't yet know how to read. The uses of television in industry, education, and the exploration of outer space are only beginning.

CHECK ON YOUR READING

1. *Why is the ability to read so important?*
2. *How are religion, democracy, and education related?*
3. *What ways of spreading information have developed since 1800?*
4. *What inventions made possible the modern newspaper, motion pictures, radio, and television?*

"In the fields of observation, chance favors only the prepared minds." —Louis Pasteur.

Think about the chapter

1. How has science and invention raised our standards of living?

2. What has science done for man besides giving him more material comforts?

3. What are some important advances made in the field of psychology?

4. Why is universal education necessary for democracy?

5. What problems has mechanization created?

Go beyond the text

6. Who were some of the other nineteenth-century scientists not mentioned in this chapter? What did they discover?

7. What recent developments in medicine would you add to those described here?

8. Prepare a report on the latest *peaceful* uses of atomic energy.

Follow up your special interest

9. Make a list of words added to our vocabulary as a result of the developments discussed in this chapter; for example, virus, vaccine.

10. "Knowledge Brought within the Reach of All" is the heading of section 5. Write an editorial on this topic and develop some ideas as to the responsibility this fact puts on each individual.

11. Collect from advertisements enough examples of synthetic products to make a poster. What would make a good title for it?

12. Make a trip to a natural-history museum, or find pictorial material, for a report on fossils. Explain what these fossils prove to the geologist.

13. Diagram and explain to the class the principle of (a) the internal-combustion engine, or (b) jet propulsion, or (c) rocket propulsion.

14. Report to the class on recent developments in the exploration of outer space.

READ FURTHER

Basic readings: (1) F. TAYLOR, *An Illustrated History of Science.* (2) Year's *Pictorial History*, pp. 498–513. Also Year's *Pictorial History of Science and Engineering*.

Special accounts: (3) L. BARNETT, *The World We Live In.* Articles appearing in *Life* magazine during 1953–1954 collected in book form. (4) B. LEYSON, *Marvels of Industrial Science.* Cellulose, nylon, plastics, rayon, telescopes. (5) J. MEYER, *World Book of Great Inventions.* A section at the end of the book discusses "the fifteen greatest inventions of all time." (6) D. TAYLOR, *A Pictorial History of the Movies.*

Fiction and biography: (7) R. BAKER, *The First Woman Doctor.* Elizabeth Blackwell had to fight many prejudices to become a doctor, but many advances were made in medicine due to her influence. (8) J. BEATY, *Luther Burbank.* Tells of America's plant wizard and his contributions to better living. (9) R. BURLINGAME, *Inventors behind the Inventor.* Gives good accounts of how each important invention has depended on preceding ones. (10) D. COE, *Marconi, Pioneer of Radio.* (11) R. FOX, *Great Men of Medicine.* Stories of Harvey, Jenner, Koch, Lister. (12) J. GARLAND, *The Story of Medicine.* A history of medicine from the time of primitive practices to modern drugs and treatments. (13) R. HOLT, *George Washington Carver.* Experiments in agriculture and botany by this scientist make an interesting story. (14) B. JAFFE, *Crucibles.* Story of chemistry from the beginning to nuclear fission; includes stories of Lawrence and Fermi. (15) P. DE KRUIF, *Microbe Hunters.* Pasteur, Koch, Metchnikoff, Walter Reed are some of the heroes of this book. (16) E. LEVINGER, *Albert Einstein.* Life of one of the great geniuses of our time. (17) M. WILSON, *American Science and Invention: A Pictorial History.*

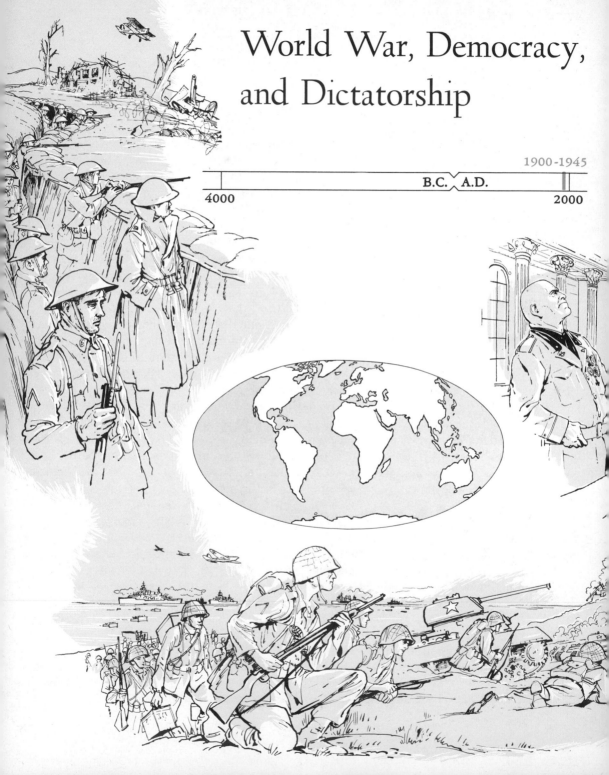

World War, Democracy, and Dictatorship

1900-1945

B.C. A.D.

4000   2000

IN THE SUMMER of 1914 World War I began. It had been years in the making, and before it was over seven-eighths of the world's population was involved. No country fully escaped its disastrous effects. When it was ended both the victors and the vanquished faced a broken world.

The peacemakers had a difficult task. They had to settle the claims of the victors and in some way establish a just and durable peace. As a result of the treaty arrangements a League of Nations, designed to preserve peace, was established. The map of Europe took on a new form. Democratic reforms were attempted in many countries.

Idealists had hoped that the war would "make the world safe for democracy." But their hopes were in vain. There was economic chaos in Germany and Austria, and the whole world in 1929 became involved in a great economic depression. The democracies managed to work out their problems. But in Italy, Germany, Spain, and Russia dictators arose. They promised their peoples economic security and a glorious future. In return the people gave up their freedom.

And in 1939 war came again. Men who had fought in World War I sent their sons to fight in an even more terrible war. The militaristic dictators hoped to conquer the world and it seemed for a time that they would succeed. But they were doomed to failure. World War II ended in disaster for Hitler, Mussolini, and Tojo.

These were dark years. And yet in spite of the clouds of war and depression, hope shone through. Men were trying to build a better world. First the League of Nations and then the United Nations were organized to prevent the scourge of war, to affirm faith in human rights and dignity, and to promote social progress.

28

World War I

KEY WORDS AND DATES

Sarajevo	neutrality
1914	Zimmermann
Balkans	note
ultimatum	1917
Central Powers	Rasputin
Allies	Kerensky
Triple Alliance	Soviet
Triple Entente	Lenin
Morocco	Trotsky
Young Turks	proletariat
Marne	Brest Litovsk
Verdun	Hindenburg line
Lawrence of	Fourteen Points
Arabia	Ludendorff
Balfour	Foch
Declaration	Pershing
contraband	Château-Thierry
U-boats	armistice
Lusitania	November 11,
Wilson	1918

IN 1914 the nations of Europe cried havoc and loosed the dogs of war. It was a new kind of war, eventually involving millions of men from thirty-two nations. The immediate spark (the assassination of the Austrian Archduke) fell upon the Balkans—the powder keg of Europe. But fear, suspicion, economic rivalry, nationalism, militarism, alliances, and imperialism were the underlying causes. Science and industry added new weapons of destruction, such as machine guns, airplanes, tanks, and submarines. The war dragged on for four terrible years with frightful losses of men, money, and material. For over three years neither side could win any decisive advantage.

The deadlock was broken when the eastern front collapsed and Russia withdrew from the war. The Communists had taken over that country and deposed the tsar. But the balance of power was restored and victory assured for the Allies by America's entry into the conflict.

Startling changes in the map of Europe followed the Armistice. Four great monarchies fell (in Germany, Austria-Hungary, Turkey, and Russia) and their empires were broken up. In the treaties which followed, new countries were created and machinery for a League of Nations was established. This chapter will consider the causes and principal events of this world struggle.

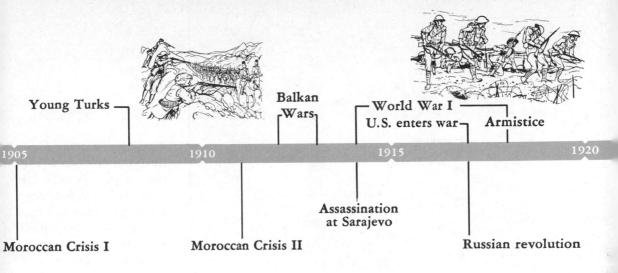

Young Turks

Balkan Wars

World War I
U.S. enters war

Armistice

1905   1910   1915   1920

Assassination
at Sarajevo

Moroccan Crisis I   Moroccan Crisis II   Russian revolution

1. Causes of the War

World War I Breaks Out · On June 28, 1914, members of a Serbian secret society lighted the match which set off a great world war. They assassinated the heir to the throne of Austria-Hungary, Archduke Francis Ferdinand, and his wife at Sarajevo in the Austrian province of Bosnia.

A few weeks later the major powers of Europe were at war. Let us see how this happened. (1) The Hapsburgs were now determined to put an end to the anti-Austrian movement promoted by Slavic secret societies in the Balkans. (2) But Austria first made certain that she would have German support in case Russia should intervene on the side of Serbia.

(3) On July 23 Austria sent Serbia a severe ultimatum. It demanded strict measures to suppress the anti-Austrian movement and to punish the assassins. (4) The Serbian reply accepted most of the terms and offered to submit the rest for arbitration. But Austria refused and broke off diplomatic relations.

(5) Austria declared war on Serbia on July 28. (6) Russia, France, and Germany mobilized for war, and Britain promised to support France. (7) On August 1 Germany declared war on Russia. Two days later she declared war on France, and began the invasion of Belgium. (8) Great Britain then declared war on Germany.

Soon Germany, Austria-Hungary, Turkey, and Bulgaria (the *Central Powers*) were facing Serbia, Russia, France, Belgium, Great Britain, Montenegro, Japan, Rumania, and Italy (the *Allies*). Before the struggle was over four years later, thirty-two nations were taking part.

Underlying Causes · The assassination in Sarajevo merely set off a fire which was a long time in preparation. Two basic causes are revealed in the events of June-August, 1914. (1) The subject peoples of Europe wanted national independence (*nationalism*). (2) Two powerful blocs of European nations, each joined by *alliances* and secret understandings, faced each other.

495

WORLD WAR I
- Central Powers
- Allied Powers
- Neutral countries
(1914 Boundaries used)

The Allies vs. the Central Powers · *Name the four major powers on each side. What happened to Serbia and Rumania? Which non-European power upset the balance and turned the tide? Find six neutrals in World War I.*

Furthermore, we have already noticed that (3) imperialistic rivalries led the great powers to try to preserve and extend their possessions and trade advantages. And, finally, (4) great armies and navies had been created by nations which saw war as the only practicable way of settling international disputes. Let us look for a moment at the rival camps.

The Rivals: Triple Alliance versus Triple Entente · With the defeat of France in 1870, Germany became the strongest military power in Europe. But fearful that France would rise again to seek revenge, Bismarck resolved to isolate her and to win the friendship of his other neighbors. In 1879 Germany and Austria formed a per-

manent alliance. In 1881 they were joined by Italy in a *Triple Alliance*.

France and Russia were drawn together by their distrust of Germany. They formed an alliance in 1894. Ten years later England and France announced that they had come to a cordial understanding (*entente cordiale*) on all their differences.

Three years later this became the *Triple Entente* when England came to terms with France's ally Russia over their conflicting interests in Persia. The two powers divided Persia into three zones with the Russian sphere of influence in the north, the English in the south, and a buffer zone between.

War Scares in Morocco · There was friction between members of these opposing alliances in two geographic areas. One was the Balkans, where Russian and Austrian interests conflicted. The other was Morocco, where France and Germany clashed.

In 1905 the French decided to absorb all of Morocco without regard for German commercial interests there. But the Kaiser openly encouraged the sultan of Morocco to resist. Fearing war, the French agreed to a conference of the powers at Algeciras. The French were granted "police powers" in Morocco but an "open door" to other nations there for trade was also guaranteed. Germany appeared the victor in this case, but her sabre rattling had resulted in bringing England and France closer together.

Six years later the French took over several towns in putting down a Moroccan revolt. Germany saw this as a breach of the Algeciras agreement and demanded an indemnity. War was averted by a compromise agreement in which France won a free hand in Morocco, and Germany was given a tract of 100,000 square miles in the French Congo. But the second Moroccan crisis only resulted in angry dissatisfaction on all sides. The nations increased their preparations for the showdown which they felt was sure to come.

The Balkan Powder Keg · It is not surprising that the trouble started in the Balkans. We have noticed before the restlessness of these people under Austrian (p. 394) and Turkish (p. 438) rule. Russia complicated the situation by insisting that she was the natural protector of her brother Slavs.

A Balkan crisis occurred in 1908 when Austria annexed the Turkish provinces of Bosnia and Herzegovina, which she had been administering since 1878. Serbia especially was enraged. She wanted to add these provinces to an enlarged Slavic nation of her own. But Russia, unprepared for war, persuaded Serbia to wait.

In Italy all the old fears of the Hapsburgs were renewed. Austria's advance to the Adriatic Sea threatened her control there. Thus, in spite of an alliance she had with Austria, Italy now made a secret treaty with Russia. Under it each would grab other parts of Turkish territory.

Carving Up Turkey · Bulgaria took advantage of the Bosnian crisis to proclaim her complete independence of Turkey. (She had been enjoying self-government within the Ottoman Empire since 1878.) Then a group of reformers, the Young Turks, deposed the sultan and established what was practically a military dictatorship. But the attempts of these inexperienced patriots to Turkify all their subject nationalities stirred up revolts both in Asia and in the Balkans.

"Turkey Gobblers after Their Rations" · What was each of the following powers planning to gobble: Britain? Austria? Russia?

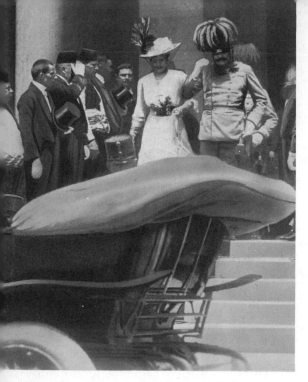

Their Last Ride · *Archduke Ferdinand and his wife were assassinated a few minutes after this picture was taken at Sarajevo on June 28, 1914. What chain-reaction followed?*

In September, 1911, Italy took advantage of this confusion to declare war on Turkey and force her to give up Tripoli. Then the Balkan states of Montenegro, Serbia, Bulgaria, and Greece (under Russian guidance) formed a league and declared war to free their Slavic brothers from Moslem rule. The Young Turks were forced to sign a treaty (May, 1913) surrendering all Turkish territory in Europe except Constantinople and a strip of land protecting the Bosporus, the Sea of Marmara, and the Dardanelles.

The Second Balkan War · The victors, however, immediately began to quarrel over the booty. The territory Serbia had seized for an outlet to the Adriatic was denied her by Austria and Italy. They created instead an independent state of Albania. Serbia

therefore demanded some part of the Macedonian territory which Bulgaria had received. Greece also had a quarrel with Bulgaria over the division of Thrace. When Bulgaria suddenly attacked Serbia (June, 1913), Greece, Rumania and even Turkey joined with Serbia. After a month of conflict the Bulgarians sued for peace.

A European war now loomed larger than ever. (1) Bulgaria was eager for revenge on Serbia. (2) Serbia had doubled her territory and now was determined to pull away the Slavic provinces from Austria-Hungary. (3) Russia strongly supported a union of the Slavs because she wished to dominate southeastern Europe and gain the Straits. (4) But this would interfere with Germany's economic plans for a railroad from Berlin to Baghdad. (5) Austria-Hungary looked upon the rising tide of Slavic nationalism as a threat to her existence. (6) Germany, France, and Britain, in turn, felt that their own security required them to support to the point of war the demands of their allies.

Each side assumed that in a final test of strength the other would back down. But when the fatal shot was fired at Sarajevo, neither side gave in. And so the war came.

CHECK ON YOUR READING

1. *Summarize the chain of events following Sarajevo.*
2. *What were the underlying causes of the war?*
3. *How were the rival alliances formed? Why?*
4. *Describe the Moroccan crisis.*
5. *Why were the Balkans called the "powder keg of Europe"?*
6. *Why did a European war loom larger than ever after the second Balkan War?*

2. Two Years of Deadlock (1914–1916)

The German Drive to the Marne · The military leaders on both sides had carefully prepared plans for an early victory. The Russians and French intended to strike Germany from the east and west at the same time and thus crush her in the vise of a two-front war.

The German plan was to avoid the French fortifications by striking across neutral Belgium. After a lightning victory in France, the Germans would be free to handle the Russians.

So it was that on August 2 the German armies poured across the Belgian border. The forts at Liége and Namur soon fell before their powerful attacks, and Brussels was taken on August 20. All the opening battles went against the French and the British, who had been speedily rushed across the Channel to aid them. The Allies retreated farther and farther south until they stood fast on the line of the Marne River within twenty-five miles of Paris.

Here they launched a counteroffensive which forced the over-extended Germans back to entrenched lines. At the end of three months the Germans were in possession of Luxembourg, most of Belgium, and the northeastern part of France. The loss of this area with its rich farm lands, manufacturing towns, railways, and iron and coal greatly crippled the French war effort. But German inability to achieve a quick victory was to prove her eventual undoing.

Trench Warfare · The opposing armies were now deadlocked behind lines which did not change significantly for three and a half years. Here the soldiers settled down in rows of trenches or ditches. These were connected with others to the rear and with dugouts, or rooms, where supplies could be kept and soldiers could find fitful "rest." Men stood long hours in water-soaked, rat-infested trenches, ate cold rations, and slept in their clothes.

The stretch between opposing lines was called "no man's land." It was filled with mines and barbed-wire entanglements and was torn by exploding shells. Surprise advances were impossible. But the men went "over the top" at command and fought with bayonets in bitter combat.

Until the last year of the war neither side was able to gain more than ten miles in the various battles. Yet tons of ammunition were used and millions of lives sacrificed.

The Western Front, 1914–1918 · *Note the forests and forts south of Verdun. Can you see why the Germans drove through Belgium? With which places are you most familiar?*

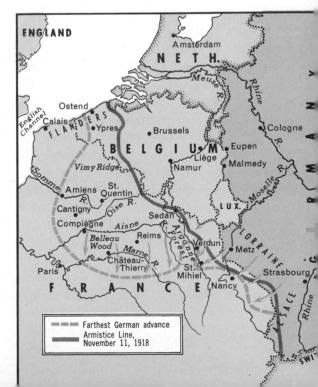

Farthest German advance

Armistice Line,
November 11, 1918

An Incident in the Battle of the Somme · *This photograph shows the second wave of "doughboys" and "Tommies" going "over the top" across the shell-pocked "no-man's land." Why was trench warfare so costly in human lives?*

Verdun and the Somme (1915–1916) · Throughout 1915 the Allies hurled themselves again and again at the entrenched Germans, with frightful losses.

In February of 1916 the Germans likewise strove to break the stalemate on the western front. They attacked the historic and seemingly impregnable stronghold of Verdun. The battle raged for five months, but the French held on heroically with the resolve "They shall not pass." Just as the Germans with the aid of poison gas seemed about to break through, the Austrian front gave way under the blows of the Russians (p. 502). A heavy British bombardment also began on the Somme. No more reinforcements could be spared for Verdun and the attack was given up. Each side lost 350,000 men, but the battle of Verdun, like the first battle of the Marne, was a blow to German morale.

Now the Allies pinned their hopes upon a gigantic offensive of their own which they launched along the river Somme (July-November, 1916). They too introduced a new military device—the tank. This heavy armored car could crawl over trenches, shell-torn ground, and barbed-wire entanglements. But by November the autumn rains had turned the battlefield into an ocean of mud and the attack bogged down. The Germans had lost 400,000 men, and the Allies had sacrificed 600,000—for a few square miles of mud.

The Eastern Front · Death stalked the eastern front as well. In August, 1914, the southern wing of one huge Russian army surprised the Austrians, drove them back

150 miles with losses of 350,000 men, and seized the entire province of Galicia. In the north, however, two other Russian armies, sweeping into East Prussia, met with disaster. Here the German forces under the command of General von Hindenburg won a decisive victory at Tannenberg (August 29). When winter came the two sides settled down in long trenches.

Turkey joined the Central Powers in November. This closed the Dardanelles, the only route by which much-needed munitions could be sent to Russia. Moreover, the Turkish armies were now a threat to the Suez Canal and other British interests in the Near East. Britain thereupon declared Egypt independent of Turkey (December, 1914), set up a new ruler, and established a protectorate.

Disasters at Gallipoli and Gorlice · Some Allied strategists (chief among whom was Winston Churchill, First Lord of the Admiralty) now urged that Germany could be beaten speedily and at less cost by striking first at her weaker partners. They favored a campaign to (1) conquer Turkey, (2) open the Dardanelles and Bosporus in order to make contact with Russia through the Black Sea, (3) gain support of the Balkan states, and (4) knock Austria out of the war. But the leading French and British commanders on the western front absolutely opposed weakening their forces for such purposes.

A compromise was finally reached by sending a small expedition to attempt to seize the Gallipoli peninsula and force the Dardanelles (February-November, 1915). Failure to send sufficient men and ships, however, ended in disaster. It was a tragic case of "too little, too late" in what might otherwise have been an easy victory. What is more, Bulgaria, influenced by this Allied defeat and tempted by promises of territory, now joined the Central Powers.

Affairs went badly for the Allies on the Russian front as well. Fighting through blizzards in February of 1915 the Germans under von Hindenburg broke the Russian lines near the Masurian Lakes and captured 90,000 prisoners. Then German reinforcements were rushed to the hard-pressed Austrians, who now were able to pierce the Russian line at Gorlice and take 400,000 prisoners. By September the Central Powers had established a new eastern front in Russian territory—occupying Poland, Lithuania, Kurland (Latvia), and Estonia.

Austrian, German, and Bulgarian forces conquered Serbia in October. By January, 1916, Albania and Montenegro had also fallen.

The Eastern Front · *How did the Russian advance affect the fate of France and Italy? What resulted from the collapse of the eastern front? Locate Gorlice, Tannenberg.*

Italy and Rumania Join the Allies · Early Russian victories against Austria and secret promises of territories to be taken from Austria, Germany, and Turkey persuaded Italy to join the Allies (May, 1916). Her entrance opened another front which the Central Powers had to defend. But her large untrained army was no match for the Austrians, and her losses in men and material were heavy. Only a second Russian breakthrough in Galicia prevented Austria from knocking Italy out of the war.

Rumania, like Italy, had bargained with both sides and chose the Allies in hope of greater rewards. In August, 1916, she declared war on Austria-Hungary and invaded the province of Transylvania, which she had long coveted. Here she was defeated by strong Austro-German forces, and two-thirds of Rumania was soon in enemy hands. Except for neutral Greece, the entire Balkan peninsula was now under control of the Central Powers.

The Fight for the Fertile Crescent · In the Near East the Allies met with greater success. With the aid of Indian troops the British conquered the Tigris-Euphrates valley. By March, 1917, they had captured the ancient city of Baghdad. Turkish forces threatening the Suez Canal were defeated by British, Australian, and New Zealand troops. Then the Arabs, under Husein ibn-Ali, the Grand Sherif of Mecca, revolted against Turkish rule. In return Britain promised, at the end of the war, to support Arab independence.

T. E. Lawrence, a daring young British archaeologist at Cairo, now entered the picture. Well acquainted with the Arabic language and customs, and well supplied with funds, he visited the Sherif and his sons as an agent of the British government. With them he planned revolts which spread like wildfire among the tribes of Arabia. Clad in native costume, Lawrence time and again led his Arab forces in brilliant raids against Turkish garrisons and the vulnerable Hejaz railway, which was their sole means of supply.

By October, 1917, British forces under General Allenby were in Palestine. Jewish support was won with the declaration by Lord Balfour (November 2, 1917) that the British government favored "the establishment in Palestine of a national home for the Jewish people . . ." A month later the British armies occupied Jerusalem.

Thus the end of over two years of bloody war on land saw a stalemate in the west, success for the Central Powers in the Balkans, and important gains for the Allies in the Near East.

Lawrence of Arabia · *A real scholar, he was also a born leader. His ability to inspire the Arabs was remarkable. The peace settlement bitterly disappointed him.*

The U-Boats' Deadly Sting · *What did Germany hope to gain from torpedoing merchant ships? What did she risk by engaging in unrestricted submarine warfare? (See pp. 504–505.)*

The Naval War · But the war on the sea took a different course. In 1914 the British navy laid a blockade across the Kiel Canal and the outlet of the Baltic Sea. Except for the inconclusive battles of Heligoland (1914) and Jutland (1916) the German fleet was bottled up in its harbors.

Germany's merchant fleet fled to neutral ports. Her commerce, colonies, and naval bases were cut off, and the Allies ruled the seas. They claimed the right to stop all neutral ships bound for Holland, Norway, and Sweden to make sure that no militarily useful material could get to Germany.

In February, 1915, the Germans sent out U-boats to slip under the blockade and torpedo Allied vessels. The waters around England were declared a war zone. All merchant ships (including those of neutrals) were warned to stay clear on penalty of destruction. German submarines struck without warning and took a heavy toll of ships.

Britain replied by bringing into her ports all ships carrying articles which might be destined for Germany. Such disregard for the rights of neutrals brought her close to war with the United States. But the Germans threw away their advantage here by an act which aroused the anger of the American people. On May 7, 1915, the great British liner *Lusitania* was torpedoed—with the loss of nearly 1200 passengers, including over a hundred Americans. Only the strong desire of President Wilson to keep the United States neutral and the promise of the German government to avoid such acts in the future postponed American entrance in the war.

CHECK ON YOUR READING

1. *What is trench warfare? Why did it cause a deadlock on the western front?*
2. *What was the result of two years of war in the Balkans? in the Near East?*
3. *What happened in the war at sea between 1914 and 1916?*
4. *Locate on the map and tell why important: (a) Belgium, (b) the Marne, (c) Verdun, (d) Tannenberg, (e) Gallipoli, (f) Hejaz.*

3. The U. S. Enters, Russia Withdraws, and Germany Surrenders

American Neutrality · From the start of the conflict President Wilson had urged strict neutrality "in thought and deed." In January, 1916, he proposed a "peace without victory" and sent his close friend and adviser, Colonel Edward M. House, to Europe to attempt to mediate the dispute. But both sides wanted a peace *with victory*. Each was willing to negotiate only when ahead, at which time the other would scorn such a conference. Time, however, was on the side of the Allies if they could keep the sea lanes open to draw upon the vast economic resources of the United States.

Unrestricted Submarine Warfare · The Germans finally concluded (January, 1917) that unrestricted submarine warfare was their only means of bringing England to her knees. They reasoned that sinking 600,000 tons of shipping a month would result in starvation for Britain within six months. War with the United States was probable, but the knockout blow would be delivered before American help could be decisive.

To exploit the ill-will then existing between the United States and Mexico, the German foreign minister sent secret instructions (the Zimmermann note) to his minister in Mexico to arrange for an alliance with Mexico and Japan. For her help Mexico was promised return of the territories she had lost to the United States in 1848.

The United States was notified that unrestricted submarine warfare would begin on February 1, 1917. Two days later Wilson severed diplomatic relations with the German government. Bolivia, Chile, Peru,

American Troops "Over There" · *The first American troops, under General Pershing, reached France in June, 1917, and reinforcements kept coming "like an avalanche." Europeans were amazed at American speed in mobilization.*

and other Latin-American states did like-wise. During the month of March, five American ships were sunk and feeling rose to a high pitch. It was at this point that the British exposed the Zimmermann note which their secret service had intercepted and deciphered. The die was now cast.

The U. S. Enters the War · On April 2, 1917, President Wilson appeared before a joint session of Congress. He proposed that the nation should fight side by side with the free and self-governing peoples of the earth "to make the world safe for democracy." The Congress approved the President's resolution by a large majority and on April 6, 1917, the United States entered the war against Germany.

Gigantic preparations were soon under way. Loans were made to the Allies for the purchase of war materials. In May conscription (the draft) was introduced. Before long the United States, for the first time in its history, began to send troops to fight on European soil.

The war was now widened. Soon Cuba, Panama, Greece, Siam, Liberia, China, and Brazil likewise entered the contest and seven-eighths of the population of the world was finally involved. Holland, Switzerland, the Scandinavian countries, Spain, and several Latin-American states remained neutral. But as we shall see, no country fully escaped the disastrous effects of the world at war. In the troubled years which followed it was difficult to distinguish victor from vanquished.

The Russians Overthrow the Tsar (March, 1917) · Just before the United States entered the war, revolutions in Russia put an end to the autocratic rule of the Romanovs and later resulted in Russian withdrawal from the war. The causes were many. Food was scarce in the cities.

The Last of the Romanovs · *In this family portrait are Grand Duchesses Anastasia, Tatiana, Olga, and Marie, Empress Alexandra, Tsar Nicholas II, and his son Alexis.*

Workers clamored for a living wage, and peasants angrily demanded land. Defeated and hopeless, the millions of civilians who had been drafted to swell the ill-led armies were on the point of desertion and mutiny.

Meanwhile the court and imperial officials seemed utterly irresponsible. The tsarina and her circle were under the influence of a "mad monk" named Rasputin, who was reputed to possess hypnotic powers. This sinister figure haunted the court and was able to block attempts at reform. When finally Rasputin was murdered by a group of noblemen, the angry tsar dismissed all liberals from office and appointed vengeful men to do his bidding. Warnings by the Duma and foreign ministers of coming disaster were of no avail.

Leon Trotsky (*left*) *addresses the Red Army which won the Civil War.* **V. I. Lenin** *overthrew Kerensky and became father of the U.S.S.R.* **Joseph Stalin** *succeeded Lenin in 1924, exiled Trotsky, and liquidated many of the "old Bolsheviks."*

Strikes increased, and the streets were filled with angry mobs. The Duma begged Nicholas II to save the monarchy by forming a responsible government. Instead he sent orders that his troops were to put down all disorder and clear the streets. But it was too late. On March 12, 1917, when bread riots broke out in Petrograd (St. Petersburg), the garrison refused to fire on the crowds and deserted to the side of the people.

The Duma hastily formed a provisional government, whose representatives secured the tsar's complete abdication. The liberal government thereupon decreed many reforms, freed thousands of political prisoners, and prepared to establish a permanent organization. But as it had no dependable army, it lacked the power to carry out its policies. Moreover, it did not go far enough in reform to please some. In May, Prince Lvov resigned and Alexander Kerensky became head of the government.

Communists Seize Control (November, 1917) · In the meantime a group of revolutionary socialists, called Bolsheviki, had organized a *Soviet* (Council) of Workers' and Soldiers' Deputies and installed themselves in one of the palaces of the capital. They refused to co-operate with the middle-class ("bourgeois") provisional government. And their executive committee began to assume wide powers in the name of the Russian people. They took over the railroads and telegraph and began to get control of the army. They did not choose to co-operate with the capitalistic countries or to continue with the war.

They were greatly strengthened by the early reappearance of a number of revolutionary exiles, chief among whom were Vladimir Lenin, Leon Trotsky, and Joseph

Stalin. Lenin's return from Switzerland was aided by the Germans, who were glad to encourage revolution in Russia.

Lenin became the acknowledged leader of the Bolshevik party, for which he preferred the name *Communist*. He openly denounced the provisional government and called for a *class* revolution to place the power in the hands of the wage workers (proletariat). He declared the world war a "capitalistic" conflict and demanded an immediate peace on the basis of "no annexations and no indemnities."

In July, 1917, Kerensky was urged by the sorely pressed Allies to undertake an offensive against the Austrians. The drive ended in a terrible failure. Crying "peace, bread, land" the troops then mutinied against their officers. The peasants rose up to seize the lands of the wealthy, and the workers in the towns took possession of the factories.

Soviets of workers and soldiers were set up throughout the country. Leon Trotsky organized the Red army to carry out the party policy. In the bloody revolution of November, 1917, the Communists overthrew the provisional government of the moderates and established a "dictatorship of the proletariat." Lenin decreed the abolition of private property and canceled all the secret treaties and obligations of the tsarist regime. He called upon the Allies to make peace, and immediately began negotiations with the Central Powers.

Russia Withdraws from the War · On March 3, 1918, at Brest Litovsk, the Communists concluded a separate treaty with Germany. They agreed to permit self-government in the Ukraine, Finland, Poland, Lithuania, Kurland (Latvia), Livonia, and districts in the Caucasus. These districts, however, were really under the control of Germany.

The harsh terms of the treaty had taken from Russia large portions of her territory, including her rich grain fields in the Ukraine and the largest part of her iron, steel, and sugar production. The Communists had put an end to the foreign conflict, but had let loose a terrible civil war at home. For several years Red (Communist) and White (anti-Communist) armies ravaged the land in a class conflict in which defeat meant death.

Talk of Peace · The Allies had rejoiced when the Russians overthrew the autocratic tsar. It was now possible to talk about making the world "safe for democracy" without too much hypocrisy. But joy turned to dismay when the Russians withdrew from the war. For huge German armies in the east were now free to turn their full fury against the western front. What is more, the French and British drives to break the Hindenburg line had failed with such frightful costs in casualties as to lead to mutiny. To make matters worse the German and Austrian armies (in October, 1917) had broken through the Italian front at Caporetto and captured 250,000 men.

Civilians on both sides were heartily sick of the war. Defeatist sentiment was strong. Emperor Charles of Austria had for some time been engaged in secret negotiations for a separate peace. In late summer the Pope appealed to both sides to end the conflict. The time appeared ripe for a negotiated peace. All that seemed to be needed was some dramatic pronouncement which might provide a just basis for settlement.

Wilson's Fourteen Points · President Wilson fulfilled this need in a ringing message to Congress on January 8, 1918. He outlined "the world's peace program" in what came to be known as the "Fourteen

Points." These may be summarized as follows: (1) Open treaties openly arrived at without secrecy of any kind. (2) Absolute freedom of the seas in war and peace. (3) The removal of economic barriers to trade, such as tariffs. (4) Reduction of armaments. (5) Fair adjustment of colonial claims. (6) Evacuation of Russian territory and self-determination for her peoples. (7) Evacuation and restoration of Belgium. (8) Evacuation of France and restoration of Alsace-Lorraine. (9) Readjustment of Italian frontiers along lines of nationality. (10) Self-government (autonomy) for the peoples of Austria-Hungary. (11) Evacuation of Rumania, Serbia, and Montenegro, with Serbia given free access to the Adriatic Sea. (12) Assurance of eventual self-government for the nationalities now under Turkish rule. (13) Creation of an independent Poland with free and secure access to the Baltic. (14) A General Association (League) of Nations "to guarantee political independence and territorial integrity to great and small nations alike."

This statement of principles proved to be a powerful piece of propaganda. It greatly heartened the Allies and drove a wedge between the exhausted German people, who craved peace, and their military leaders, who saw victory just around the corner. Because of the Allied blockade the German people were facing starvation. Submarines were taking a deadly toll of Allied ships, it is true, but the use of the convoy system and the vast American production of "Liberty Ships" was turning the tide. Troops from the United States were arriving safely in France in ever-increasing numbers.

The German Offensives of 1918 · To the German General Staff, therefore, it was now or never. The situation at home was becoming so grave that General Ludendorff determined to risk all in a last supreme effort to win victory. With huge forces free from the Russian front he launched a gigantic offensive (March, 1918) designed to smash the separate Allied armies and end the war. Advancing in heavy fog from St. Quentin, the Germans broke through the British lines near Vimy, advanced forty miles in six days, and cut one of the railways between Amiens and Paris before they were stopped.

In grave danger, the Allies finally agreed to put their separate national armies under the direction of a single commander in chief, the French General Ferdinand Foch. In April the British halted German attempts to drive through to the Channel west of Ypres. Ludendorff then turned

President Wilson Reading His War Message to Congress, April 2, 1917 · *"We shall fight . . . for democracy . . . for the rights and liberties of small nations . . . [to] make the world itself at last free."*

World-War Generals ·
*Left: von Hindenburg
and Ludendorff of Germany. Center: Supreme
Allied Commander Foch
of France. Right: Haig
of Britain, and Pershing
of the United States.*

southward and pushed to within forty miles of Paris. Here he was stopped in the famous second battle of the Marne (July 15–August 7).

The Tide Turns · In the meantime things were going badly for Germany elsewhere. An Austrian offensive against the Italians had failed. Czechs, Poles, and Yugoslavs by the thousands fled Austria-Hungary and fought in the Allied armies. In Germany some of the chief statesmen had already given up hope. Discontent was spreading among the people. Socialists were demanding an early peace. Even the discipline of the army was now giving way. Desertions increased rapidly at the rear while sickness and fighting took their toll at the front. The "victory" offensive had failed.

While the Germans had been exhausting their reserves, each day marked the arrival of thousands of fresh United States troops. By mid-July a million American soldiers were available for a great counteroffensive. Under General John Pershing they struck the exposed German salient (bulge) at Château-Thierry and forced a retreat. The Allied attacks now grew in strength and never ceased until the Germans asked for peace. By early September the Germans had been driven back to the Hindenburg line, and by late October they had lost most of northeastern France.

Bulgaria, Turkey, and Austria-Hungary Surrender · The fortunes of war were turning against the Central Powers on all fronts. The Allied forces moved up from Salonika to strike the war-weary Bulgarians, who quickly signed an armistice (September 29, 1918).

In October the British and French troops overran Syria, occupied Damascus, and captured the Turkish army in Mesopotamia (Iraq). Turkey surrendered on October 31, and Allied troops immediately opened the Dardanelles and occupied Constantinople.

Austria-Hungary was also in desperate shape. The rickety old empire, no longer held together by a firm hand (Francis

Joseph had died in 1916) or supported by a strong army, was falling apart. The Czechs and Yugoslavs were making ready to assert their independence. Hungary also was ready to withdraw from the Dual Monarchy. Hence, when the British and Italians crossed the Piave and attacked the Austrian line, the troops, half starved and weakened by sickness, retreated in confusion. Austria now asked for an armistice, which was granted on November 4.

Downfall of the Hohenzollerns · Fearing the collapse of the western front under the terrific blows of the Allies, Ludendorff urged his government to make an immediate offer of peace. On October 3 the German government appealed to President Wilson to arrange an armistice and expressed its willingness to make peace on the basis of the Fourteen Points. But the President replied that the Allies could not consider any settlement unless it was made with a *new and responsible* government which represented the German people.

In vain the German leaders tried to save the old system, but a revolution against the monarchy soon began. The navy mutinied, and 40,000 men from Kiel began marching across northern Germany, setting up soldiers' and sailors' councils in the large industrial towns. Emperor William II fled to Holland, where he lived in exile until his death in 1941. The proud empire of the Hohenzollerns was at an end, and Germany was declared a republic.

The Armistice (November 11, 1918) · At five o'clock on the morning of November 11, in a railway car in the forest of Compiègne, the German delegates signed the armistice. At eleven o'clock all firing ceased, and World War I was at an end.

The armistice required the Germans to (1) evacuate Belgium, Luxembourg, and northeastern France and (2) give up Alsace-Lorraine. (3) Their disarmed troops were to return beyond the Rhine River. (4) The west bank of the Rhine and certain key bridgeheads were to be occupied by Allied forces, and the east bank demilitarized. (5) Germany was to surrender most of her war equipment. (6) The treaties of Brest Litovsk (with Russia) and Bucharest (with Rumania) were canceled.

Stupendous Cost of the War · Although the war was over, both victors and vanquished now faced a broken and desolated world. It is estimated that over ten million men in service lost their lives. Many more were wounded, and some faced life as cripples. The losses among the civilian population from disease, famine, and massacre were enormous.

The national debts of the Central Powers were immense. The governments now had long pension lists, to be paid for by taxes levied on the peoples for years to come. Property damage was staggering. Years were to pass before the stricken European continent recovered.

CHECK ON YOUR READING

1. *Why did (a) neither side want Wilson's "peace"? (b) Germany resort to unrestricted submarine warfare? (c) the United States enter the war?*
2. *Describe (a) the March and November revolutions in Russia and (b) their effect on the Allied cause.*
3. *Summarize Wilson's Fourteen Points.*
4. *Identify (a) Liberty ships, (b) Ludendorff, (c) Brest Litovsk, (d) Foch, (e) Pershing, (f) Château-Thierry, (g) Nicholas II, (h) William II, (i) November 11, 1918.*
5. *What were the terms of the armistice?*

Learning Activities

Think about the chapter

1. What were the (a) immediate and (b) underlying causes of the war?
2. Why was it called a world war?
3. What were the advantages and disadvantages of each side?
4. Summarize the highlights of the war (a) on the western front, (b) on the eastern front, (c) in the Near East, (d) on the sea.
5. List the Fourteen Points. What was Wilson's purpose in stating them?
6. Why did the "tide turn"?
7. Why were there no real "victors"?
8. *Map study:* On a map of Europe, the Near East, and North Africa show the nations that made up the Triple Alliance and the Triple Entente. Locate the following: Marne, Piave, Verdun, Caporetto, Gallipoli, Brest Litovsk, Tannenberg, Dardanelles, Château-Thierry, Jerusalem, Damascus, Compiègne, Kiel.

Go beyond the text

9. Make a list of the military and civilian leaders of the period. Choose one for a report.
10. Why and how did the United States remain neutral until 1917?
11. Find examples of how the war influenced one or more of the following: (a) poetry, (b) art, (c) music, (d) attitudes, (e) science.

Follow up your special interests

12. Look through picture histories of World War I to find pictures typical of the times.
13. Plan a music program based upon the songs of World War I. "Over There" and "Tipperary" are two.

READ FURTHER

Basic readings: (1) Becker, *Modern History*, Chaps. 20–21; pp. 691–696 on the Russian Revolution. (2) Cheyney, *Readings*, Chap. 21. (3) Cheyney, *Short History of the English People*, Chap. 22. (4) Hoffman, *News of the World*, No. 49. (5) Scott, Baltzly, *Readings*, Chaps. 13, 14. (6) Year's *Pictorial History*, pp. 514–521.

Special accounts: (7) S. Fay, *Origins of the World War*. (8) F. Ogg and H. Zink, *Modern Foreign Governments*. Good treatment of the political situation in France, Germany, and Britain, 1914–1919. (9) C. Seymour, *Woodrow Wilson and the First World War*. One of the *Chronicles of America* series. (10) P. Slosson, *The Great Crusade and After, 1914–1928*. Chapter 1 on the outbreak of the war is excellent. (11) L. Stallings (*ed.*), *The First World War: a Photographic History*. Text and pictures help to recreate the period. (12) M. Sullivan, *Our Times*, Vol. 5, "The War, 1914–1918." An excellent supplementary account with emphasis on the effect of the war on the United States. (13) Year's *Your Lifetime in Pictures: the Story of the Twentieth Century*. Many pages deal with World War I.

Fiction and biography: (14) N. Baker, *Lenin*. This man was the one who turned the Russian revolution into a Communist revolution. (15) W. Cather, *One of Ours*. Experiences of a young American farmer at the front in France. (16) E. Ellsberg, *Pigboats*. Submarine warfare. (17) C. Nordhoff and J. Hall, *Falcons of France*. Experiences of two Americans in the Lafayette Flying Corps. (18) E. Remarque, *All Quiet on the Western Front*. A young German soldier writes a gruesome and realistic account of war as he saw it. (19) E. Robinson, *Lawrence, the Rebel*. An authoritative biography of one of the colorful figures of World War I. (20) L. Thomas, *Count Luckner, the Sea Devil*. A surface raider, commanded by a former German sea captain, caused millions of dollars of losses to Allied shipping.

The Peace Settlements
and Their Aftermath

KEY WORDS AND DATES

Treaty of Versailles	Weimar republic
dictated peace	*Anschluss*
Wilson	Dollfuss
Lloyd George	Horthy
Clemenceau	Masaryk
"war guilt" clause	Bohemia
reparations	Serbs
Saar Valley	Croats
Covenant	Polish Corridor
League of Nations	Pilsudski
Geneva	Paderewski
Article X	Baltic states
mandates	Venizelos
sanctions	Mustapha Kemal
self-determination	Zionist movement
coalition	Husein
Ebert	Ibn-Saud

THE PARIS PEACE CONFERENCE was the largest body that had ever met to write a peace treaty. To satisfy the claims of the thirty-two nations represented was an almost impossible task.

A novel feature was the prominent part played by the American President, who was the first to attend a peace conference abroad. Having outlined the basis of the settlement in his Fourteen Points, Wilson now journeyed to Europe in the hope of seeing these ideals embodied in a "just and durable peace." But he soon found himself involved in a bitter struggle to keep his principles from being brushed aside as vague and impractical.

Serious clashes among the Allied leaders led to compromises and disappointments. But the President did realize one cherished hope. There was established an association of nations which he believed would promote international understanding and prevent future wars.

The map of Europe and the Near East took on a new form. The emphasis on "self-determination" in the peace settlements encouraged the growth of nationalism. Faith in democracy led to the setting up of new republics and to the introduction of reforms.

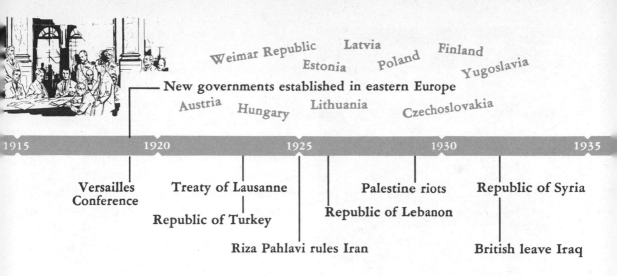

New governments established in eastern Europe

Weimar Republic · Latvia · Estonia · Poland · Finland · Yugoslavia · Austria · Hungary · Lithuania · Czechoslovakia

1915	1920	1925	1930	1935

Versailles Conference

Treaty of Lausanne

Republic of Turkey

Riza Pahlavi rules Iran

Palestine riots

Republic of Lebanon

Republic of Syria

British leave Iraq

1. The Treaty of Versailles and the League of Nations

Task of the Peace Conference · On January 18, 1919, delegates of the victorious powers met at the opening of the Paris Peace Conference to settle their accounts with a crushed and defeated Germany. The Central Powers were not permitted to attend. It was to be a dictated, not a negotiated peace.

The task awaiting this conference was a tremendous one. In the two months which had passed since the armistice was signed, many changes had already taken place in Europe. Germany, Austria, and Hungary had declared themselves republics. Italy, Serbia, and Rumania, acting on the secret treaties made with them during the war, had annexed territory belonging to their neighbors. Poland had appeared as a republic. The new state of Czechoslovakia had been recognized by the Allies.

The sessions of the full assembly were few because it proved too difficult to handle rapidly the many questions which came before it. The responsibility eventually fell to the chief delegate of each of the five great powers. Later Japan's representative

and then Italy's dropped out temporarily, leaving finally the "Big Three." They were Prime Minister David Lloyd George of Britain, Premier Clemenceau of France, and President Woodrow Wilson of the United States. They assumed authority and made all the important decisions.

Germany Accepts the Treaty (June 28, 1919) · After months of work the great document, which would fill an ordinary book, was completed. On May 6 the final draft was submitted to a full session of the Conference and was approved.

When the Germans learned the terms of the treaty, they denounced it as unjust and ruinous to their country. They protested that it violated Wilson's Fourteen Points, which they had accepted as the basis for peace. They declared that even if they signed the treaty, its requirements could never be fulfilled.

A few modifications were made by the Allies. Finally, on June 28, the representatives of the German republic appeared before the Conference. Under protest, they signed the Treaty of Versailles in the great

513

The Big Three of 1919 · *Left to right: Lloyd George, Clemenceau, and Woodrow Wilson. What nation did each represent? Who would qualify for today's "Big Three"?*

Hall of Mirrors, where in 1871 Bismarck had proclaimed the German Empire.

Separate treaties were signed with Austria, Hungary, Bulgaria, and Turkey in the following months. They provided for extensive territorial changes in eastern Europe and the Near East (pp. 515, 523).

Territory Lost by Germany · Study the map on the next page to see territorial changes in the treaties. Germany gave up Alsace-Lorraine to France and some border towns to Belgium. Most of the province of Posen and a strip of West Prussia went to Poland. The port of Memel was handed over to the Allies. Plebiscites, or a vote of the people, were to be held to decide whether certain other districts would be granted to Poland or Denmark.

Danzig was to be a free city under the control of the League of Nations. Germany surrendered all her colonies in Africa and the Pacific. These were to be turned over to the guardianship of Great Britain, France, and Japan as mandates under the supervision of the League of Nations.

Disarmament and Reparations · Germany was almost entirely disarmed. Her navy was reduced to a few ships. She was to have no submarines and no military air force. The army was limited to 100,000 men, and compulsory military service was forbidden. Fortifications on the east bank of the Rhine were to be destroyed.

A "war guilt" clause in the treaty forced Germany to accept full responsibility for the war. This was designed to establish the *right* of the Allies to make claims for reparations, even if they were not able to collect them. This clause was bitterly resented by the Germans, who later used it to build up the opinion that the entire Versailles Treaty was unjust.

A Reparations Commission was established to determine the amount that was to be demanded of Germany. An initial payment of five billion dollars was required. In the meantime, she had to replace the shipping she had destroyed, and for a period of years send coal to France, Belgium, and Italy. She was forced to cede the rich coal mines of the Saar valley to France for fifteen years. Allied troops were to be stationed on the west bank of the Rhine to see that the provisions of the treaty were carried out.

Provision for a League of Nations · President Wilson believed that the most important part of the peace settlement should be an association of nations pledged to prevent future wars. Despite much opposition a committee headed by President Wilson

Europe after World War I · *Which countries appear on this map which do not appear on the map on page 496? Why was the boundary between Germany and Poland a potential source of trouble?*

Map legend:

TREATIES 1919-1926
TERRITORY LOST BY:
- Austria-Hungary
- Russia
- Germany
- Bulgaria
- Boundaries in 1926

was appointed to draft a Covenant for the League of Nations. On April 28 the Covenant was finally adopted by the conference and became part of the peace treaties.

When Wilson was forced to consent to certain objectionable provisions in the treaties, he justified his actions on the ground that the League would be able to make adjustments later.

Organization and Duties of the League · The League was at first open to the victorious powers and most neutral countries. Membership was also offered to all self-governing states. There was a Council, an Assembly, and a Secretariat. The headquarters of the League were established at Geneva, Switzerland.

Two other bodies closely associated with the League, but independent of it, were organized. These were the Permanent Court of International Justice and the International Labor Organization.

The chief duties of the League were to promote international understanding and peace and to handle some responsibilities left to it by the treaties. Members were pledged to submit serious disputes to arbitration, judicial settlement, or inquiry by the Council. Article X stated that if any member should disregard these provisions and resort to war it would be held to have committed an act of war against all other members of the League. In such a case, *sanctions*, or penalties, would be applied.

The Home of the League of Nations · *Overlooking beautiful Lake Geneva, the League headquarters represented man's hope for peace. Known today as the Palace of Nations, it houses various UN agencies.*

Among the responsibilities assigned to the League were the protection of minority groups and the administration of the Free City of Danzig and of the Saar district. Former German colonies and parts of the Turkish Empire were placed under the guardianship (*mandate*) of member nations.

The United States Rejects the Treaty and the League and Signs a Separate Peace · Although President Wilson had been the chief promoter of the League, there was a division of opinion in the United States as to the wisdom of joining that body. The chief objections centered on Article X of the League Covenant. Some argued that it would pledge America to go to war to defend any country that might be attacked. Finally, the Senate refused to ratify the treaty, and the United States remained outside the League.

The adoption of the Treaty of Versailles was made an issue of the presidential election of 1920. The Republican party, which

opposed ratification, was victorious and its candidate, Warren G. Harding, became President. On July 2, 1921, President Harding signed a joint resolution of Congress declaring the war with Germany at an end, and six weeks later a separate treaty was agreed upon.

CHECK ON YOUR READING

1. *Why was the task confronting the Peace Conference a tremendous one?*
2. *What were the major provisions of the Treaty of Versailles as to (a) territories, (b) disarmament, (c) reparations?*
3. *(a) What were the aims of the League of Nations? (b) How were they to be enforced? (c) Why did the U.S. not join?*
4. *How were the following important: (a) Big Three, (b) dictated peace, (c) "war guilt" clause, (d) Saar valley, (e) sanctions, (f) mandates, (g) Article X, (h) election of 1920?*

2. New Governments in Europe

Democracy and Self-determination · In striking contrast to the Congress of Vienna a century earlier (p. 339), the delegates to the Paris Peace Conference did not talk about the hereditary claims of kings and emperors. Rather they discussed the right of the peoples to have *democratic governments* and to have their own national states (*self-determination*). These two revolutionary ideas account for most of the changes which were made in the map of Europe after 1918.

Large empires ruling over heterogeneous peoples were broken up. A number of small, independent states took their place. In central and eastern Europe the proud dynasties of the Hohenzollerns, Hapsburgs, and Romanovs were toppled off their thrones. Hardly less astonishing was the overthrow of the sultan and the creation of a republic in Turkey.

Parts of Germany and Russia and most of Austria-Hungary and Turkey, went into the making of new national states. Four republics—Finland, Estonia, Latvia, and Lithuania—were formed from the northwestern fringe of the tsar's dominions. Two independent countries, Austria and Hungary, succeeded the Dual Monarchy. The rest of the Hapsburg territory helped to restore Poland; enlarged Rumania, Yugoslavia, and Italy; and made the new republic of Czechoslovakia. In most cases the boundaries were adjusted with some attention to the wishes of the peoples concerned, but in some instances these wishes were ignored.

Republican Governments and Democratic Constitutions · Though a few countries, such as Rumania and Yugoslavia, retained their monarchs, the large majority became republics. There was everywhere a growing feeling that if the people were in control, peace somehow could be maintained. It had been the kings in earlier years who had dragged their people into terrible wars.

Even the presidents of the republics were given no great power over the governments set up by the new constitutions. The upper houses of parliaments, which formerly had been composed of nobles or appointees of the sovereign, now tended to become less important. Greater authority was vested in the lower houses, composed of elected representatives of the people.

Other democratic features of the new constitutions were the widening of the suffrage to permit women to vote and the provision for freedom of religion and of the press. Everywhere there was a tendency to give the working classes more influence and to extend education among the masses.

Unfortunately, some of the new republics were weakened by the fact that they had no experience with the methods and traditions of democratic government. Furthermore, there were many political parties instead of just two. To gain enough support to form a government, the largest party was forced to rely on a *coalition* of these groups. Such a coalition was unstable and the result was frequent changes of government.

Germany Becomes a Republic · Two days before the armistice was signed Germany was proclaimed a republic. Friedrich Ebert, a Socialist, became chancellor. The provisional government of Ebert arranged at once for the election of a Constituent Assembly, which met at Weimar on February 6, 1919. The Assembly had before it two important tasks: to make a peace settlement with the Allies and to draft a permanent constitution for the Reich.

Constitution of the Weimar Republic · The Weimar constitution vested supreme power in the people and described Germany as a federation of republican states. The right to vote was granted to all men and women over twenty years of age, and women were given civil equality with men. The president was to be elected by universal suffrage for a term of seven years. The chancellor (prime minister) was to be appointed and dismissed by the president.

Parliament was to consist of two houses. The *Reichsrat,* or upper house, was to be composed of the delegates of the states of the realm. The *Reichstag,* or lower house, representing the people, was to be the chief legislative body. Its members were to be chosen by popular vote for terms of four years.

Struggle of the Republic · The moderate Socialists, led by Ebert, failed to win a majority in the Reichstag. They therefore had to win the support of other political parties to form a coalition strong enough to carry on the government. During the early years the republic was threatened by extremists of both left and right. Radical Socialists and Communists demanded drastic changes, but conservatives feared even mild socialistic reforms and desired a restoration of the monarchy. Several unsuccessful attempts were made to seize the government. Germany's economic problems will be discussed in the next chapter.

The Republic of Austria · Austria, which had been the center of the great Hapsburg empire, was now a tiny state. About one-third of its population was concentrated in its capital, Vienna. Most Austrians thought this state could not survive and favored union with Germany (*Anschluss*). But such a union was forbidden by the peace settlement. The Constitution of 1920 established a federal republic with a parliament of two houses.

The new democracy faced many difficulties. (1) The break-up of the empire deprived Austria of much of her farm land, coal and iron deposits, seaports, and railway system. (2) There was much unemployment and poverty. (3) Her money was almost worthless.

(4) Not everyone had faith in the new republic. Some people favored recalling the Hapsburgs from exile. (5) There was serious hostility between the socialist workers of industrial Vienna on the one hand and anti-socialist business interests and conservative peasants on the other. Both groups built up private armed forces which frequently clashed.

Facing bankruptcy, the government appealed to the Allies for aid. In September, 1922, the League of Nations arranged a loan of 135 million dollars. This loan provided temporary relief, but Austria's financial condition grew steadily worse.

The world-wide depression brought collapse. In 1931 Austria's principal bank crashed, starting a train of financial ruin in Europe. Again the League came to the rescue, on condition that Austria would consider no union of any kind with Germany for twenty years.

In 1933 Chancellor Dollfuss suspended the democratic constitution and, crushing the Socialist Workers' party, established a dictatorship the next year.

Republic, Revolt, and Regency in Hungary · In November, 1918, a republic was established in Hungary. But it experienced

The Austrian Parliament on Vienna's Famous Ringstrasse · *During the twenties heated disputes between the Conservatives and the Socialists took place within this building. Outside, the struggle continued as party troops marched around the Ring demonstrating their strength.*

immediate difficulty because the peace conference assigned parts of its territory to Rumania, Czechoslovakia, and Yugoslavia. The people revolted, and for five months in 1919 the government was a Communist dictatorship.

When the Communists tried to regain some lost territory, Rumanian troops invaded the country. A counter-revolution put Admiral Horthy in control. He proclaimed Hungary a monarchy with a vacant throne and was appointed regent.

During the years which followed, Hungary retained its semi-feudal organization. The wealthy aristocracy and the Church continued to hold most of the land. There were constant efforts by the government to have the peace treaties revised.

Czechoslovakia · The most prosperous of the states carved from the Dual Monarchy was Czechoslovakia. It was composed of the Austrian provinces of Bohemia, Moravia, and Silesia (whose Slavic peoples were known as *Czechs*), and the Hungarian territories of Slovakia and Ruthenia. Two-thirds of its population were Slavs. The remaining third consisted of about three million Germans in the Sudeten area, about a million Hungarians, and other smaller nationality groups.

The young republic faced a serious problem in trying to satisfy its minority groups. Before the war the Germans and the Magyars had held the bulk of the land in large estates. This wealthy class resented the land reforms which broke up their large

Thomas G. Masaryk (1850–1937) · He was father and first president of the Republic of Czechoslovakia. Scholar, writer, and statesman, he was noted for his moderate policies.

holdings and provided farms at low cost to the peasants. As great tracts were owned by the Church, the government also came into conflict with the Catholics.

President Thomas G. Masaryk handled most of these difficulties with great tact. In 1929 the government at Prague passed a law which granted the provinces greater independence in the management of their local affairs.

Czechoslovakia made great economic progress, for the republic had received a rich inheritance from Austria. She secured good railways and four-fifths of the monarchy's industries. These included the famous Bohemian glassworks, textile and pottery plants, coal and iron mines, and the great Skoda armament works. Her people were industrious and soon built up a flourishing export trade.

Yugoslavia · The southern Slavs combined to form the kingdom of Yugoslavia, with its capital at Belgrade. But King Alexander (of Serbia) had a difficult time trying to establish harmony among his many different subjects. They included Serbs, Croats, Slovenes, Bosnians, Herzegovinians, Dalmatians, and Montenegrins. Although they were all Slavs, these people had long lived apart, and they held strongly to their own customs. They were divided on religious questions. The Serbs were Orthodox, the Croats and Slovenes were Roman Catholics, and in the south there were many Moslems.

The Croats objected strongly to the dominant position given to the Serbs. They wished a *federal* form of government within which each state would have the right to make its own laws and manage its own provinces. The strong Croatian party kept up an active agitation against the government.

Constant dissension led finally to the assassination of King Alexander in 1934. His son Peter was still a boy, and a Council of Regents governed until Peter came to the throne in March, 1941.

Restoration of Poland · Poland again became an independent nation. In January, 1919, General Josef Pilsudski became chief of state. The famous pianist Ignace Jan Paderewski became premier and foreign minister.

The boundaries drawn by the peace conference had given the new state a region unquestionably Polish and had also awarded it a strip of German territory to give it an outlet to the sea. The Germans deeply resented this "Polish Corridor" through their country.

But the Poles were not satisfied. They quickly claimed additional territory, and waged war with the Ukraine, Russia, and Lithuania to seize it. As a result the new Poland was soon faced with the problem of

German, Lithuanian, White Russian, Ukranian, and Jewish minorities.

The constitution (1921) made Poland a republic with the capital at Warsaw. But the government was inefficient, and the country fell more and more into the hands of General Pilsudski. His power finally became so great that Poland was virtually a constitutional dictatorship.

Rumania · Rumania emerged from the war with a kingdom more than double its former size. But it now had the problem of discontented minorities also. To provide a living for its varied peoples the government undertook to divide up large estates. Soon most of the farm lands had come into the hands of the peasants despite violent protests from the Magyars of Transylvania, who were the chief sufferers.

After King Ferdinand died in 1927, the National Peasant party came into power. The new government stabilized the currency, built railways and other public works, and floated a foreign loan. Carol II became king in 1930, and Rumania soon became a dictatorship, ruled by the king and his premier, Jorga.

The financial condition of the country was so serious that in 1933 the League of Nations had to take charge of its finances. After this date the government was much occupied in suppressing Fascist organizations, such as the Iron Guard, which plotted the overthrow of the monarchy.

The Four Baltic Republics · Four former provinces of the Russian Empire appeared on the map as new states—Finland, Estonia, Latvia, and Lithuania.

Finland, the largest of the Baltic states, had been, since 1809, an autonomous duchy under the rule of the tsar. The Finns showed great ability in governing their new state. They were progressive, industrious,

Ignace Jan Paderewski (1860–1941) · *This famous Polish pianist, composer (Minuet in G for Piano), and statesman devoted his life to the cause of Polish freedom.*

and thrifty. They balanced their budget and paid their debts. They established a good educational system, wiped out illiteracy, and maintained a high standard of living for their people.

In spite of the difficulties of organizing their new governments, the other three Baltic states soon balanced their budgets. They broke up the large estates, which had been held by German and Russian landowners, and created thousands of small farms, which could be bought or rented by the peasants. All the states had minority groups, but the only complaints came from the Poles in Lithuania.

The Baltic republics feared lest one day the powerful Soviet government should decide to regain her coast line along the Baltic. Latvia, Estonia, and Lithuania therefore signed a ten-year pact of friendship as a protection against Russia (1934).

Greece · During and after the war, Greece was divided between supporters of the king and followers of Premier Venizelos. And when the Greeks tried to take territory from Turkey (1919–1922) they were badly defeated. In 1924 the country became a republic, but internal divisions continued to cause difficulties.

Four years later Venizelos became premier again and tried to improve economic conditions. He also made treaties of friendship with Italy and Yugoslavia, ending Greece's isolation from its former friends. Greece settled its old differences with Turkey over property claims and refugees. In 1934 Greece signed the Balkan Pact, designed to maintain peace in southeastern Europe.

In 1935 the Greeks overthrew their republic and restored King George II to the throne. He appointed General Metaxas premier. Metaxas persuaded the king to dissolve parliament, suspend the constitution, and abolish all political parties. Metaxas then set up a military dictatorship, and in 1938 declared himself dictator for life.

CHECK ON YOUR READING

1. *What two ideas account for most of the new governments after the war? Locate these nations and their capitals on the map.*
2. *Identify the principal leaders and postwar problems of (a) Germany, (b) Austria, (c) Hungary, (d) Czechoslovakia, (e) Yugoslavia, (f) Poland, (g) Rumania, (h) the Baltic republics, (i) Greece.*

---

3. *Changes in the Near East*

Turkish Nationalism and the Treaty of Lausanne · At the close of the war the Allies demanded that Turkey give up its chief seaport, Smyrna, and eastern Thrace to the Greeks. This so aroused the Turks that a strong Nationalist group under General Mustapha Kemal was organized in opposition to the demand.

The Nationalists refused to recognize the treaty which the sultan had been forced to make with the Allies. A Greek army attempting to seize the territory was routed in 1922. And a million Greek residents were expelled from Turkey with great suffering.

The Nationalists now signed a new treaty with the Allies at Lausanne (1923). By its terms (1) the Allied forces were to leave Constantinople. (2) The Dardanelles, though open to ships of all nations, would be under Turkish control. (3) Turkey kept Anatolia, eastern Thrace, and some of the islands of the Aegean Sea. (4) Italy kept the Dodecanese, including Rhodes, and Britain kept Cyprus. Most of the remaining islands went to Greece. (5) Syria, Mesopotamia, and Palestine became mandates of Britain and France under the League of Nations.

The Nationalists then forced the sultan to leave Constantinople. In October, 1923, Turkey was declared a republic with Mustapha Kemal as president.

Mustapha Kemal Modernizes Turkey · Mustapha Kemal was actually a dictator who transformed Turkey into a modern state. He ended the special status of Islam as the state religion. Old legal codes were discarded and new ones drawn up modeled on those of Europe. Education was made compulsory, and the Roman alphabet was substituted for the Arabic in all Turkish books and newspapers.

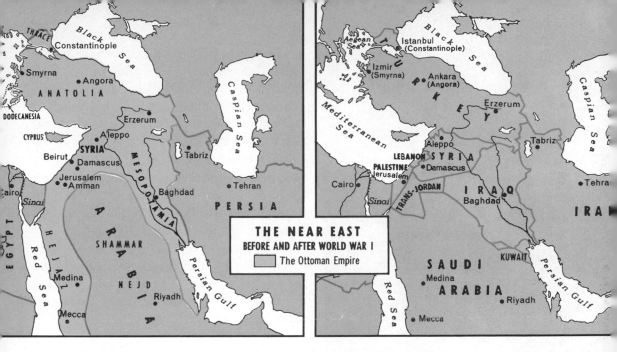

The Partition of the Ottoman Empire · *Which new states appeared in the Near East after World War I? Which old state took a new name? Which Near Eastern states were independent? mandates? What sources of trouble remained?*

The position of women was greatly improved when the veil was abolished and polygamy prohibited. Western clothing was adopted, and women could attend schools and colleges. They could vote and enter such professions as teaching, writing, the law, and politics.

Finally, Mustapha Kemal improved Turkey's economic position by developing agriculture, commerce, and industry. He won the friendship of both Great Britain and France, and made nonaggression treaties with his neighbors.

The Arab Awakening · For nearly four hundred years Arab civilization had been submerged under oppressive Turkish rule. Divided into tribes often hostile to one another, the Arab peoples of desert and town remained in a backward condition and had no solidarity to make them a political force within the empire.

After 1850, however, there was a gradual awakening of a sense of nationalism among the Arabs. Religious reformers, patriotic leaders, and native poets began to arouse their people to a consciousness of their kinship and their common language and traditions, and to promote religious unity within Islam. Western missionaries and teachers established schools in Syria and set up printing presses which supplied books, periodicals, and newspapers in Arabic. Thus, interest in Arabic literature and culture among the educated class was stimulated.

After the revolution of the Young Turks in 1908 (p. 497), the Arabs had high hopes that the new constitution would promote their welfare and grant them equal rights within the empire. But they were soon bitterly disappointed. They then began to form a number of societies to serve as centers for the exchange of ideas and to

523

The ABC's of the New Turkey · *School children parade the Latin alphabet. What advantages did this alphabet have for the Turkish people? How did this alphabet originate?*

promote enthusiasm for the nationalistic movement.

The Arabs Revolt in Return for a Promise of Independence · Shortly after Turkey had joined the Central Powers, the sultan issued a call to all Moslems throughout the world to join in a Holy War against the enemies of Islam. But his appeal was ignored by most of the Arab rulers. The most important figure in the Moslem world, Husein ibn-Ali, Grand Sherif of Mecca, pretended to weigh the proposal. But he secretly arranged with the British to organize a revolt of the Arab tribes against Turkey (p. 502). In return the British were to recognize and support the independence of the Arab countries after the war.

The peace settlement, however, was a bitter disappointment for the Arabs. The Hejaz (western Arabia) became an independent state under Husein ibn-Ali, it is true. But Syria and Iraq were made mandates of Western powers. Syria was divided into separate zones. Northern Syria was placed under the control of France, while Palestine and the new state of Transjordan came under British administration. Iraq also became a British mandate.

The Arabs were angry and bewildered. They felt that they had been betrayed by their former allies. Therefore disorder and rebellion broke out as the Arabs continued their revolt against domination by foreign powers.

Syria and Lebanon under French Mandate · The French established their control in Syria in 1920. They divided the country into two districts. Lebanon, the region around Beirut, was inhabited chiefly by Christians long friendly to France. The district of Syria was mainly Moslem. This division of the country increased Arab suspicions that the French meant to destroy Arab unity and oppose Syrian independence.

During the 1920's and 1930's, the French tried in various ways to repress Arab nationalism in Syria. They had to contend with armed rebellion, a general strike, riots, and refusal to obey laws. The French finally permitted the establishment of a republic in Lebanon in 1926 and in Syria in 1932. But opposition to continued French interference led to unstable governments and suspensions of the constitutions.

The British Recognize Iraq · The announcement of the British mandate for Mesopotamia (Iraq) was followed by a rebellion of the native tribes. In 1921 the British permitted Faisal, son of the Arab leader Husein, to become king.

King Faisal's chief tasks were to satisfy the demands of the minority groups in the country and to persuade the tribal chieftains to co-operate with the new government. In 1932 Iraq joined the League, the mandate came to an end, and British troops were withdrawn. Britain's agreement with the country, however, permitted her to have air bases in Iraq, the use of means of communication, and other privileges in time of war. Britain also retained large oil and other concessions. Faisal was succeeded in turn by his son and then his grandson, Faisal II.

Conflict of Jews and Arabs in Palestine · Britain's most difficult problem as a mandatory power was Palestine. Here the Arabs had a double grievance: (1) Palestine had been separated from Syria. (2) The British had begun to set up a national homeland for the Jews within the country.

That part of Palestine lying east of the Jordan, called Transjordan, Britain entrusted to Emir Abdullah, another son of Husein. Abdullah was to have charge of local affairs, under British supervision.

A national home for Jews in Palestine, the land of their ancestors, had been promised in 1917 by Lord Balfour (p. 502). This was not to interfere, however, with the civil and religious rights of the non-Jewish peoples living there. France, Italy, and the United States expressed their approval of the idea. The League Council in its mandate to Great Britain, therefore, instructed the British to proceed with the plan.

Jews began to settle in Palestine in large numbers. This was bitterly opposed by the Arabs, who formed nearly 90 per cent of the population—and had occupied this land for centuries. They also pointed to violations of their rights guaranteed in the Balfour Declaration. While the Arab leaders were willing to receive a fair number of immigrants, they objected to the creation of a Jewish home within their country. They claimed it would dispossess their own people of the land, and deprive them of their living.

Serious riots in 1929 led the British to announce a change of policy which would restrict immigration and land purchases.

Members of the Transjordan Frontier Troops with Bedouins · *For centuries most of the Arabs of this region have been nomadic herdsmen. Some are farmers, but farming is poor. Why?*

This brought loud protests from the World Zionist Organization and other Jewish sympathizers. The *Zionists* were Jews who believed that their religion and culture were threatened unless they were re-established as a nation. Many of them insisted that this nation must be in the ancient homeland of Palestine.

Those who favored the Jews claimed that they improved the country by transforming barren lands into farms, bringing in modern equipment, and raising the standards of public health. But the prosperous condition of the Jews only increased the bitterness of the Arabs, who claimed to have benefited little from their presence.

By 1936 the Jewish population had risen to 28 per cent of the total, and Arab resentment showed itself by a general strike and violence. A British commission of investigation now decided that the mandate was unworkable. It proposed a division of the country into (1) a Jewish state, (2) an Arab state, and (3) a neutral zone around Jerusalem and the sacred places which was to be administered by the British. This plan was strongly opposed by both sides.

But after World War II Palestine was partitioned (p. 635).

The Arabian Peninsula · The Western powers showed little interest in the principalities of the Arabian peninsula. Native rulers were permitted to run their seemingly barren lands.

Husein, as king of the Hejaz, ruler of the holy cities, and champion of Arab independence, occupied a very special position in the Near East. Two of his sons had been set up as rulers in Iraq and Transjordan. Yet he was faced with many difficulties. The chiefs of the independent states were irritated that he called himself "King of the Arabs." His prestige was damaged by his close association with Great Britain, for her promises of Arab independence were not being kept.

Husein aroused the hostility of the whole Moslem world in 1924, when he took the title of Caliph (successor of Mohammed). He especially antagonized the Wahhabi sect, whose leader was Sultan Abdul-Aziz ibn-Saud, his chief rival. Ibn-Saud invaded the Hejaz, and Husein was easily defeated and forced to abdicate.

Jewish Colony of Nahalal in Palestine · *This was on the plain of Esdraelon, of Biblical renown. The plan was typical of more than three hundred immigrant settlements in Palestine before World War II.*

Ibn-Saud Honored at Feast · *Seated at center (checkered headdress), ibn-Saud dines on roast sheep, chickens, eggs, and camel. The occasion was the king's inspection of a refinery of the Arabian-American Oil Company.*

The Kingdom of Saudi Arabia · Ibn-Saud now emerged as the leading figure in the Arab world of the Near East. As absolute monarch of the kingdom of Hejaz and Nejd (later called Saudi Arabia), he proved to be an able statesman, as well as warrior. He gained control over some nearby areas and also made treaties with Great Britain and other European powers.

Ibn-Saud's first difficult task was to control the fanatical zeal of his followers. The Wahhabis wished to force other Moslem sects, at the point of the sword, to adopt their puritanical views. With great patience he was able to reduce the outbreaks between the various sects under his rule. To establish order and security, he forbade tribal raids and attacks on caravans and pilgrims. Offenders were severely punished.

Some social and economic reforms were begun. Lands were assigned to tribal groups, and the wandering tribes were encouraged to settle down and take up farming and cattle-raising. Communication was improved, and projects for the discovery of water and minerals were undertaken. Concessions to develop the rich oil resources of his kingdom were granted to foreign countries. At his death in 1953 he was succeeded by his son, King Saud.

Modernizing of Iran · In Persia, as in Turkey, a national leader arose after the war. Riza Shah Pahlavi became ruler of Persia in 1925. He was determined to modernize his country and reclaim it for its own people. He substituted modern codes for the law of the Koran and restricted the Moslem clergy to religious activities.

Riza Shah Pahlavi · *This self-made Shah, a former army leader, set an example of energy, decisiveness, and enthusiasm for progress to his people.*

The new Shah began a campaign against illiteracy, placed education under the control of the state, and made it compulsory. He founded a university at Tehran, and the state was henceforth called by its Persian name, *Iran*. Towns were modernized, factories built, roads improved, and a railway started. In 1937 Iran signed a nonaggression pact with Turkey and Iraq to maintain peace in the Near East. Riza Shah Pahlavi abdicated in 1941 and was succeeded by his son Mohammed Riza Pahlavi.

Afghanistan · Before World War I, Afghanistan was fearful of Russia and had permitted Britain to control its foreign policy. But after the overthrow of the tsar the government declared itself independent of all foreign powers.

Attempts to Westernize the country met the armed opposition of the Moslem tribes, which followed the laws laid down in the Koran. In 1929 the Amir was forced to abdicate. The new ruler abolished some of the hated decrees. Islam was acknowledged as the religion and law of the state.

Egypt · Early in the war Britain had declared Egypt independent of Turkey (December, 1914). A protectorate was established over the country, but then in 1923 the Egyptians adopted a constitutional monarchy with Sultan Fuad as king. The British, however, continued to station troops there. In 1936 the British agreed to limit their troops to the Suez Canal zone only. They were not withdrawn entirely until 1956 (p. 638).

CHECK ON YOUR READING

1. How was Turkey affected by (a) its war with Greece? (b) the Treaty of Lausanne? (c) Kemal's modernization policies?
2. What factors contributed to the growth of Arab nationalism before and after World War I?
3. Identify the important postwar leaders and problems in (a) Lebanon, (b) Syria, (c) Iraq, (d) Palestine, (e) Arabia, (f) Iran, (g) Afghanistan, (h) Egypt.

"There is only one way to assure the world of peace; that is by making it so dangerous to break the peace that no other nation will have the audacity to attempt it."
—WOODROW WILSON, 1920

Learning Activities

Think about the chapter

1. What is the difference between a negotiated and a dictated peace? Which term applies to the Treaty of Versailles?

2. How was the peace settlement received in the United States? Germany? Hungary? Poland? the Near East?

3. Compare the nationality problem of the Hapsburg monarchy with the problem in the new countries of eastern Europe. How do you account for the lack of serious conflict among nationality groups in the United States?

4. In what countries did the governments become dictatorships? What conditions brought this about?

5. What problems in the Near East today have their roots in the events of the 1920's and 1930's? Explain.

6. *Map study:* Draw on a map of Europe and the Near East the boundaries of the various countries as set up after World War I. Shade the countries that had not existed as separate countries before the war. Locate the boundaries of the mandates in the Near East and write in the names given to the new countries with the mandatory power in parentheses.

Go beyond the text

7. Report on why the United States refused to join the League of Nations but took the lead in establishing the United Nations.

8. Explain why many European countries have coalition governments. (See a civics text on multi-party systems.)

9. The Zionist movement is often discussed in news items about Arab-Israeli affairs. Learn what it is and report. A biography of Chaim Weizmann is an excellent source for the historical development of Zionism.

10. Find out the importance of the oil resources of the Near East (a) to the countries there, (b) to the West, (c) to international affairs.

Follow up your special interests

11. Prepare a bulletin-board display of one of the Near Eastern nations showing progress since 1920. "Persia—Old and New" is a possible caption.

12. Make a chart for the nations sometimes called the "Buffer States," including Finland right through to Greece, with the headings: Area, Population, Type of Government, Minority Groups, Religions, Foreign Policy after World War I. Use your text and BRADLEY, *World Geography*, for information.

READ FURTHER

Basic readings: (1) BECKER, *Modern History*, Chap. 22. (2) HOFFMAN, *News of the World*, No. 49. (3) SCOTT, BALTZLY, *Readings*, Chaps. 15–16. (4) Year's *Pictorial History*, pp. 521, 527, 541–543.

Special accounts: (5) J. BRADLEY, *World Geography*. (6) S. EKREM, *Turkey, Old and New*. (7) E. KELLY, *The Land of the Polish People*. (8) W. LANGSAM, *The World since 1919*. This is an invaluable text to supplement all topics in the remaining chapters. (9) S. NEVIL, *The Picture Story of the Middle East*. (10) A. NEVINS, *The United States in a Chaotic World*. A chronicle of international affairs, 1918–1933. One of the *Chronicles of America* series. (11) R. WOHLRABE and W. KRUSCH, *The Land and People of Austria*. (12) Year's *Your Lifetime in Pictures*. See section on "The Gay Twenties."

Fiction and biography: (13) R. BAKER, *Chaim Weizmann: Builder of a Nation*. (14) A. BRIDGE, *Dark Moment*. Two young couples follow Mustapha Kemal in the postwar revolution in Turkey. (15) M. BUSHAKRA, *I Married an Arab*. An American girl marries and goes to live in Lebanon. (16) A. HATCH, *Woodrow Wilson: A Biography for Young People*. (17) C. KELLOGG, *Paderewski*. (18) N. NAJAFI, *Persia Is My Heart*.

30

Problems Left by World War I

KEY WORDS AND DATES

war debts	Baldwin
reparations	Statute of
Ruhr	Westminster
Dawes Plan	Commonwealth
Young Plan	Eire
moratorium	De Valera
depression	Cosgrove
Weimar Republic	Gandhi
inflation	civil disobedience
von Hindenburg	Government of
National Socialists	India Act
Stresemann	Little Entente
Briand	World Court
Popular Front	disarmament
dole	Locarno treaties
Labor party	Pact of Paris
MacDonald	Kellogg

THE ARMISTICE IN 1918 ended only the fighting. Europe still faced many difficult problems. Not only the losers of the struggle had to pay. The tremendous costs of the conflict had made victory an empty one. Millions of young men had been killed or disabled. Starvation and disease stalked the Continent. The prewar economy had been shattered.

All the countries were burdened with debt. The French policy of occupation of the Ruhr and the Rhineland proved a failure. Internal political disputes left her government weak in a period which required dynamic leadership. Financial disaster threatened everywhere, and a world depression in 1929 added to the difficulties. Besides trying to restore business prosperity and a sound financial system, the problem of reparations and war debts had to be worked out.

Britain likewise faced difficulties at home and great unrest within her empire. Ireland and India were demanding complete independence, and a solution had to be found.

The need for national security caused each country to seek safety through treaties and alliances. But these only awakened further fears and suspicions. In spite of the League of Nations, World Court, disarmament conferences, nonaggression pacts, and treaties renouncing war, peace was more a hope than a reality.

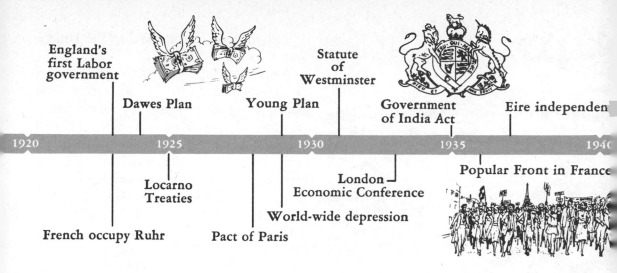

England's first Labor government

Dawes Plan

Young Plan

Statute of Westminster

Government of India Act

Eire independen[]

1920   1925   1930   1935   194(

Locarno Treaties

London Economic Conference

Popular Front in France

French occupy Ruhr

Pact of Paris

World-wide depression

1. Reparations and War Debts

Heavy Burdens Left by the War · The victors as well as the vanquished had to pay the terrible cost of the war. They were forced to borrow from their citizens and from foreign powers as well. The Allies borrowed heavily from the United States and as much as they could from one another. This created the difficult problem of international debts, which required interest payments annually. With the economic depression that soon developed, these charges became an increasing burden.

During the war many countries resorted to issuing paper money. Great Britain managed to maintain the value of its paper money, but France finally fixed the franc at about one-fifth its former worth. The Italian lira sank to one-fourth of its earlier rate. In Germany the mark became worthless and the government bankrupt.

The Reparations Question · In February, 1921, the Reparations Commission announced that Germany's debt to the Allies was 56.5 billion dollars. When the Germans protested that it was absolutely impossible to pay such a sum, the amount

was reduced to 33 billions. But Germany soon fell behind in her payments and asked for a moratorium (delay of payments).

Britain favored a moderate policy toward Germany. But France insisted that Germany *must* pay, to help rebuild French farms and industries. When Germany fell behind in deliveries of coal and wood, France occupied the Ruhr Valley (1923). The result was that France received much less coal than formerly because the Germans quit work. The Ruhr was the heart of German industry, and its occupation greatly speeded the decline in value of the German mark (p. 533).

The Dawes, Young, and Hoover Plans · Three American efforts were made to settle the reparations question. (1) In 1924 the Dawes Plan geared German payments to her prosperity over a five-year period, and granted her a large loan. But when the loan was used up, payments again ceased. (2) In 1929 the Young Plan cut down Germany's bill to about 8 billion dollars and set up a long-term schedule of payments. But this failed also. Germany was caught

531

Another Parade of Figures · *French war debts to the United States were a subject of repeated proposals. France wanted to tie repayments with German reparations.*

up in the world-wide depression, which had started in 1929.

(3) In 1931 President Hoover suggested a moratorium postponing all payments on reparations and inter-Allied debts for one year. Germany thereupon stopped payment to the Allies, and the Allies paid nothing to the United States during the period.

Depression Leads to Default · Early in 1932 the chancellor of Germany announced that his country would not be able to resume payments at the end of the moratorium. The European powers then held a conference at Lausanne which scaled down the German debt to less than one billion dollars. But this depended on the willingness of the United States to forgive the Allied governments their debts. Congress, however, insisted that reparations were a European problem and should not be con-

nected with war debts owed to the United States.

But the terrible economic depression led to defaults in payments of interest and principal on these debts by nearly every government concerned. And in the end the billions borrowed by the American government from the people to aid the European governments during the war and the postwar periods had to be paid by the American taxpayers.

Failure of the London Conference (1933) · A World Economic Conference was held at London in 1933 to discuss the best methods to be taken to restore world prosperity. Such topics as money, trade, and tariffs were to be considered.

The first question to come up was that of currency. A demand was made that the United States stabilize the dollar. President Franklin D. Roosevelt refused because his program of national recovery was not far enough advanced to permit fixing the value of the dollar. The conference adjourned without making any contribution to the settlement of the world crisis. Each nation thereafter tried to solve its own economic problems without much thought about the consequences abroad. This was unfortunate, as we shall see.

CHECK ON YOUR READING

1. *How did the governments meet their financial problems?*
2. *What were the provisions of the Dawes, Young, and Hoover plans? How successful were they?*
3. *How did the powers relate reparations to war debts? With what results?*
4. *How did the following affect the world situation: (a) depression? (b) default? (c) London Conference?*

2. Germany Under the Weimar Republic

Economic Chaos in Germany · Defeated Germany was faced with economic ruin. The country's business and finances were in a desperate state, owing to the tremendous cost and dislocation of the war plus the reparations claims of the Allies. Moreover, Germany was having to import more than she could export. Her raw materials were nearly exhausted and her colonies gone. And on all sides countries were setting up high tariffs against foreign goods.

Unable to meet its debts, the government turned to making paper money. As the inflated currency flooded the market, prices skyrocketed and the purchasing value of the mark plunged downward. In 1923, after the French occupied the Ruhr, the decline was especially severe. A postage stamp cost two and a half billion marks. Under these conditions, contracts and loans were impossible to make. Money was spent immediately, for fear that it would buy even less the next day. Debts were paid off in the worthless currency, and thus creditors lost all their savings. Thousands who depended on fixed incomes were impoverished by this inflation.

Attempts to Save the German Economy · It was beginning to dawn on economists, however, that economic collapse for Germany might spread to all Europe. For Germany stood in the very center of the complex European industrial system. Could she fall further without dragging her neighbors with her? The great English economist John M. Keynes in his book *The Economic Consequences of the Peace* said, "No!"

Great efforts were now made to save Germany from collapse. With the aid of foreign loans and the regulations of the Dawes Plan (p. 531), the government started on the slow road to recovery. All internal debts were canceled, and a new mark of prewar value was created. Better management methods in German business increased output and lowered costs. Coal production mounted, the great chemical industry expanded, and shipping was built.

Depression Dooms the Republic · In 1925 President Ebert died and Field Marshal von Hindenburg, the war hero, was elected to succeed him. Though a conservative and a member of the Prussian

Getting the Payroll · *A cartload of German marks was worth little more than the paper on which they were printed. Whom does inflation rob? How?*

landed gentry, the veteran soldier supported the republican government. His name gave the republic a certain prestige, but its problems were too great and its enemies too many.

In 1929 Germany was caught in the great world depression. Foreign loans ceased, banks closed, businesses failed, and unemployment spread. The general distress gave the enemies of the republic their chance to undermine the confidence of the people in the government.

The idea was spread that the republic was responsible for all the ills which Germany now suffered. The Socialists were accused of having caused the downfall of the empire by "stabbing it in the back" through propaganda for revolution and peace. In the elections of 1930 the Communists gained at the expense of the Socialists. And a new *National Socialist* party for the first time showed surprising strength. It was led by a fanatical Austrian corporal named Adolph Hitler.

Germany's Foreign Relations (1919–1929) · After 1918 Germany stood almost alone. Her former enemies were still very bitter against her, and her friends were defeated and helpless. On foreign policy her leaders were divided. In a treaty with Russia (1922) the two countries canceled all their claims and prewar debts against each other and came to a trade agreement.

Gustav Stresemann, who was foreign minister from 1923 to 1929, believed that co-operation with the Allied powers was the best hope for Germany's future. He managed to secure substantial loans from the United States, and new commercial treaties were negotiated. In 1926 Germany was admitted to the League and given a permanent seat on the Council. Beginning in 1928, other plans for the reduction of Germany's indebtedness were set in motion, and in 1932 reparations were practically canceled.

By this time Hitler's National Socialist party was coming to power. We shall see in the next chapter that these Nazis, as they were called, had a very different idea of how to restore German power.

CHECK ON YOUR READING

1. Describe and explain the economic chaos in Germany.
2. What attempts were made to save her from collapse? Why?
3. Summarize German foreign relations (1919–1929).

---

3. Postwar Problems in France

Why the French Were Bitter and Fearful · France had suffered terribly from the four years of combat on her soil. Her northern provinces had been turned into battlegrounds, her farms and vineyards plowed with shells and trenches. Her towns were battered, her mines and industries destroyed, her wells polluted, and her livestock carried off to Germany. The ruin of her homeland stiffened her attitude toward the peace terms to be made with her enemy and made her fearful as to her security in the future.

France had to spend hundreds of millions of francs in reconstruction work. She had to re-establish economic and financial order, for her business was depressed and the franc had fallen to a fourth of its former value. She expected that reparations from Germany would help her solve these tremendous problems. But these questions, together with foreign policy, soon became matters of party politics, and cabinet after cabinet fell when its measures failed to win confidence. The French became increasingly bitter as the fruits of victory proved more imaginary than real.

Difficulties of the First Decade (1919–1929) · Immediately after the war the conservative parties joined to form a National Bloc, under the leadership of the "Tiger," Clemenceau. His policy was one of reparations and revenge. But at his retirement, in 1920, a wise and conciliatory statesman, Aristide Briand, became premier. Briand wished to co-operate with Great Britain in the management of the reparations question. But when Germany failed to meet her payments in 1923, he was accused of being under British influence and was forced to resign. He was succeeded by Raymond Poincaré, an able financier but an extreme nationalist, who favored putting pressure on Germany by invading the Ruhr (p. 531).

The failure of the occupation and the continued fall of the franc caused a reaction which brought the Radical Socialists to power under the premiership of Édouard Herriot (June, 1924–April, 1925). This party followed a more lenient policy toward Germany. Foreign troops were withdrawn from the Ruhr, the Dawes Plan was adopted, and the Locarno treaties were signed with Germany (p. 544). But the government was unable to balance the budget and in the next fourteen months there were six ministries.

Finally, in July, 1926, Poincaré was recalled to save France from a financial crisis. Radical reforms were now introduced. New

Inhabitants of Amiens Return Seeking Their Homes · *Why was Amiens badly destroyed? (See map, p. 499.) Were the people of Amiens victors or vanquished?*

taxes were levied, and government expenses were sharply reduced. Business improved with the possession of the Saar mines and the reconstruction of industries in the north. France's export trade had increased and her farm production had grown, so that for the moment it seemed as if France had recovered some of her prosperity.

Effects of the World Depression · In 1930 the effects of the great depression were being felt in France. Industry and trade slowed down, unemployment increased, the national debt rose, and the budget showed a deficit.

By 1935 the situation was critical. Cabinet after cabinet was overthrown as its measures were voted down in the Chamber of Deputies, and premiers who asked for greater powers to cope with the situation were refused. Finally, Pierre Laval, who had formed a new ministry, succeeded in balancing the budget (1936).

The Popular Front · One reason why parliament had refused to grant special powers to the premiers was the activity of certain right-wing organizations. These, it feared, might try to establish a fascist dictatorship, such as that in Italy or Germany. In the elections of 1936 several left-wing groups united to form a Popular Front against the right-wing extremists.

This Popular Front won the election, and a Socialist leader, Léon Blum, became premier. To settle the numerous strikes and meet the demands of the workers, the government passed laws providing for a forty-hour work week, increased wages, holidays with pay, and collective bargaining. The country's armament works were to be nationalized (taken over by the government).

In September the franc was devalued, but foreign trade did not improve, as had been hoped. When Blum asked for dictatorial powers over finance, he was refused, and the government fell. Shortly afterward France went off the gold standard, and the value of the franc dropped to 3.75 cents. Another period of political conflict among the parties followed. Then in April, 1938, Edouard Daladier formed a cabinet of Radical Socialists (actually they were less radical than the Socialists). This group remained in office until the outbreak of World War II in 1939.

CHECK ON YOUR READING

1. *Why were the French bitter and fearful?*
2. *Trace the course of the French government policies between 1919 and 1929.*
3. *Why was the Popular Front formed in 1936? How did it deal with internal problems?*

---

4. *Postwar Problems of Great Britain*

Effect of the War on Great Britain · Great Britain had escaped invasion, but the cost of the struggle had been stupendous. Her debts were ten times what they had been in 1914. Over two thousand of her ships had been sunk. Now that peace had come, many of her factories and manufacturing methods seemed old-fashioned. Germany and Russia, which once had bought heavily from Britain, were no longer able to do so, and other countries had found new markets.

Tariff barriers were being raised everywhere, and these increased the difficulties of export business. As Britain's trade and shipping services declined, the output of her factories grew less. Unemployment rose from one million to two million in 1921. Government relief, called the dole, together with interest charges on her debt, caused ever-increasing taxes.

The Labor Party Takes Office · During the war the Liberal and Conservative parties formed a coalition government under the Liberal prime minister Lloyd George. It was re-elected in 1918 on campaign promises (1) to "make Germany pay," (2) to aid industry and labor, and (3) to settle the Irish question (p. 416). But in 1922 the Conservatives withdrew their support, and in the elections which followed won a large majority. The Labor party, whose

Labor Demonstrations in Britain · *Following World War I the unemployed of London held almost daily mass rallies to demand public assistance. The inset shows miners from Wales protesting their plight during the depression.*

platform called for gradual socialism, gained the second largest number of seats and became the Opposition in Parliament.

The next year the Conservative prime minister, Stanley Baldwin, proposed a protective tariff on certain articles to aid British industry. But the desertion of Britain's free-trade policy was so unpopular that new elections were necessary. The Liberals now joined with the Laborites, and Ramsay MacDonald, leader of the Labor party, was asked to form a ministry.

Although the Labor party was in *office*, it was not really in *power*, however, since it needed the support of the Liberals. It therefore decided not to press such socialistic measures as a tax on large fortunes and the nationalizing of mines and railways. Instead, the Labor government won the confidence of the people by its wise handling of financial matters and its firm action in settling strikes.

In foreign affairs MacDonald followed a policy of co-operation with other powers. In 1924 the government recognized the Soviet Union. But when this was followed by new commercial treaties, the Conservatives and Liberals became suspicious of radicalism. The Labor ministry, after eight months in office, was forced to resign.

Conservatives in Power (1924–1929) · The Conservatives now returned to power, with Stanley Baldwin again as prime minister. They were faced with a serious situation owing to the growing use of oil and hydroelectric power, which decreased the market for coal. As prices fell, the government spent millions of pounds to aid the mine operators.

When a fact-finding commission recommended the end of government aid and a reduction of wages, a strike was called. It soon spread and threatened to tie up all the railways and other essential services in

537

the kingdom (1926). This was prevented only by volunteers who took the place of the strikers. The strike failed, and in 1927 Parliament passed the Trade Disputes Act, which made a general strike illegal.

A pension bill was passed (1925) which provided more extensive insurance for widows, orphans, and the aged. Women were given the right to vote. The Conservative government co-operated with the League in its efforts for peace, but broke off diplomatic relations with Russia when communist activities against the Empire were discovered (1927).

A Second Labor Government (1929–1931) · In the regular general elections in 1929 the Labor party again secured control of the government, with Ramsay MacDonald as prime minister for the second time.

Although MacDonald was successful in his foreign policy, the world depression was too great for any government. The national income was falling and the deficit in the budget increasing. Foreign countries began to draw gold from the Bank of England as soon as Britain's financial troubles became known. To save the nation's credit, MacDonald proposed to cut the dole and reduce pensions and social services. But a storm of protest arose from the Labor party, which maintained that the burden would fall on the poorer classes. It urged increased taxation, although businessmen declared that this would ruin British industry. The cabinet divided on this issue, and the Labor government resigned (August, 1931).

How a "National" Government Met the Crisis · The king immediately invited MacDonald to form a new government. Placing national above party interest, MacDonald accepted and organized a government composed of representatives of all parties which would work together to save the country. The Labor party now denounced him as a traitor and expelled him and other Labor ministers from the party.

In September, Britain went off the gold standard in the hope that this would reduce the cost of production and thus enable Britain to compete more favorably with other countries. In the national elections which were held to obtain the views of the people on the government's policy the Conservatives won a large majority. The "National government" was therefore practically Conservative, although MacDonald was retained as prime minister.

By making only a "token payment" on its war debt to the United States, the government was able to balance the budget. Then, as prosperity returned, taxes were reduced and government salaries and unemployment-insurance payments restored. In 1937, however, Britain found it necessary to undertake a great rearmament program, and this called again for rising taxes.

Abdication of Edward VIII · In January, 1936, King George V died and was succeeded by the Prince of Wales as Edward VIII. After a reign of less than a year, and before his coronation, Edward abdicated because of the government's opposition to his proposed marriage to an American divorcée. His brother the Duke of York came to the throne as George VI and with his queen, Elizabeth, was crowned on May 12, 1937.

The British Commonwealth of Nations (1931) · There was a good deal of unrest in various parts of the Empire during these years. Ireland clamored for separation and the Indian Nationalists demanded self-rule. But a strong sentiment still bound all parts of the Empire together.

Since 1911, imperial conferences had been held at which the premiers of the

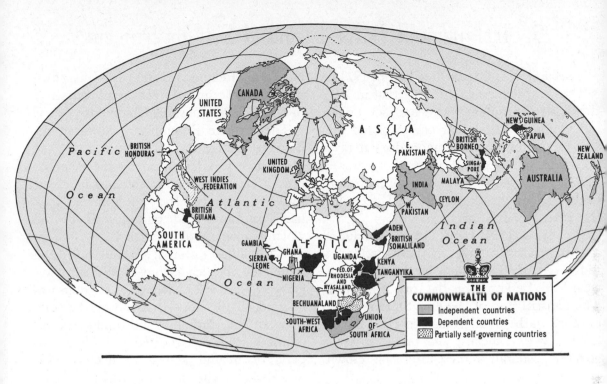

The British Empire Becomes the Commonwealth · *The term* Commonwealth, *sometimes used to designate only former colonies which have won independence, now is often used to include British dependencies as well.*

dominions discussed their varied problems in their relation to the mother country and worked out a more satisfactory basis of co-operation. After the war the dominions signed treaties with foreign countries, joined the League, and exercised many of the powers of sovereign states.

Parliament, in 1931, respected the growing desire for more independent action by passing a momentous act affecting the whole constitutional structure of the British Empire. *The Statute of Westminster declared that Great Britain and the dominions were henceforth to be self-governing communities within the British Empire "equal in status . . . though united by a common allegiance to the crown and freely associated as members of the British Commonwealth of Nations."* No future law passed by a dominion could be declared void as being against the law of Great Britain, and no British law could affect any dominion unless the latter consented to its application within its own domain.

CHECK ON YOUR READING

1. *What were Britain's postwar problems?*
2. *How did the successive governments attempt to solve these problems?*
3. *What was the Statute of Westminster?*
4. *Identify each of the following: (a) dole, (b) Labor party, (c) MacDonald, (d) Baldwin, (e) British Commonwealth.*

5. Ireland and India Demand Self-government

Creation of the Irish Free State (1921) ·
We have already seen (p. 419) that in 1919
the Irish Sinn Fein party had set up an
independent parliament and declared Ireland a republic, with Eamon de Valera as
president. For several years there was a
bloody struggle between English troops,
supported by the Protestants of Ulster, and
the Irish Republicans.

Finally, in 1921, Lloyd George concluded
a treaty which made southern Ireland a
self-governing Dominion in the Commonwealth, to be known as the Irish Free State.
The constitution of the Free State required
that an oath of allegiance to the king be
taken by its officials, and provided for a
governor-general, representing the crown.

Irish Parliamentarians · *De Valera, seated far
left, once narrowly missed execution possibly because of his American birth. Chance
brought Cosgrave, seated far right, to power.*

Northern Ireland (Ulster) had its own
separate government, with representatives
in the British House of Commons.

The extreme Republicans, however, denounced the treaty, and for over a year the
Free State was terrorized by the Republicans. They assassinated some of its ablest
leaders. Finally, the government took
harsh measures and put an end to the
violent activities of the rebels.

With order restored, Ireland prospered
under the able leadership of William Cosgrave (1922–1932). Religious freedom was
granted, in the hope that the old hostility
between the Catholic south and the Protestant north would be reduced. The two
parts of Ireland agreed to live as good
neighbors. The ancient Irish speech—
Gaelic—was revived and substituted for
English. A national flag—green, white, and
gold—was adopted. The Free State was
admitted to the League of Nations and
sent its diplomatic representatives to foreign countries.

Eire Becomes Independent (1937) · By
1932, however, the demand for absolute independence had spread more widely
through the country, and De Valera was
made president. He was determined to
gain complete separation from Britain.
The British government, however, feared
that an independent Ireland might be used
by a foreign power in time of war as a base
from which to attack England.

In 1933 Ireland abolished the oath of
allegiance. Four years later a new constitution was drawn up, which declared Ireland a "sovereign, independent, democratic
state," to be henceforth known by its Gaelic
name, *Eire*. · This constitution did not ap-

ply to Northern Ireland, which still remained loyal to Britain.

India Demands Self-government · India had come to the assistance of Great Britain during World War I with money and troops. At the same time, her patriotic leaders continued to demand self-government. In 1919 Parliament passed a new Government of India Act. This was intended as a beginning in the gradual development of home rule for India. The army, police, and administration of justice remained under British control. Such other matters as the regulation of agriculture, education, and public health were handed over to provincial councils most of whose members were elected by the people. Further reforms in ten years were promised.

Mahatma Gandhi · The moderates accepted this program as a step in the right direction. But the Nationalists, under the leadership of Mahatma Gandhi, were wholly dissatisfied with anything less than immediate self-government.

The Indians were divided among themselves. The native princes were friendly toward the British, for they were left comparatively free. Gandhi, on the other hand, was regarded as a "holy" man (*Mahatma*, or Great Soul). He had millions of disciples, who joined him in resistance to British rule.

Gandhi was one of the most remarkable men of modern times. He was opposed to all forms of violence. His way of protest was that of civil disobedience, or passive resistance to the government. His followers were taught to refuse any position in the government service, to withdraw their children from British schools, to boycott British goods, to wear homespun clothing, and to refuse to appear in British courts. Gandhi tried to make his crusade nationwide by

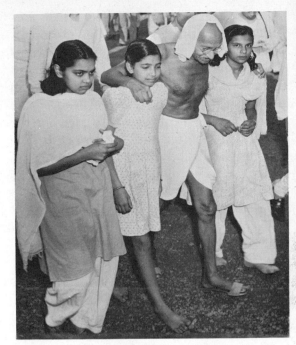

Gandhi and His Granddaughters · *Accompanied by his granddaughters (left) and their friend, Gandhi walks to a prayer meeting. Gandhi lived a simple and devout life.*

including Moslems, as well as Hindus, in the movement. In carrying out their leader's plans, however, his followers created disorder and rebellion and in some cases suffered heavy penalties. Gandhi himself was imprisoned several times. But there were not enough jails in India to hold the millions who followed him.

Government of India Act of 1935 · Three conferences to find a new solution to the problem were held in London in the early 1930's. Gandhi himself was present at one of them. These meetings revealed one of the chief difficulties of the Indian question to be the fear of the Moslem minority that it would not secure equal rights with the Hindus.

In 1935 Parliament enacted a new constitution for India. It was put into operation in 1937. This Government of India Act declared India to be a federation of Indian states (ruled by their princes) and governors' provinces. At the head of the federal government was the governor, or viceroy, appointed by the crown. The viceroy was to be assisted by a council of ministers, heads of the various departments of the government.

The federal legislature was composed of two chambers, a Council of State and a Federal Assembly. Each had representatives of the provinces and of the princely states. The local affairs of the latter states were left to their rulers. The governors' provinces had legislatures, part of whose members were elected by the people.

The extreme nationalists still demanded absolute independence, although the moderates were willing to accept dominion status. The Indians insisted that they had a right to govern their own country. The British held that by reason of the differences in race, religion, language, and caste, and the general illiteracy of the people, India was not yet able to manage its own affairs. India, if left to herself, they said, would fall into anarchy and become a prey to a stronger power. The British policy, they declared, was to educate the Indians and gradually prepare them to take over the government themselves.

CHECK ON YOUR READING

1. *Outline the steps by which the Irish won self-government.*
2. *Identify the part played by (a) Lloyd George, (b) De Valera, (c) Cosgrave, (d) Ulster, (e) Republicans.*
3. *Describe Mahatma Gandhi's policies.*
4. *How was India governed under the Act of 1935? Why wasn't independence granted at once?*

---

6. The Search for Security and Peace

Need for National Safety Leads to Many New Alliances · All the countries of Europe felt a need to achieve a sense of security. The horrors of war had made such a deep impression that most countries felt that they must protect themselves against future attack. They were willing to join the League of Nations to promote peace. But the League had no armies to enforce its will, and there was a growing belief that in case of emergency it would be able to offer little help.

The nations therefore entered into a great number of pacts to supplement the League and to keep the peace. (1) France took the lead in this respect. As a substitute for the old Russian alliance she formed alliances with Poland, Czechoslovakia, Yugoslavia, and Rumania (1921–1927). In this way France hoped to encircle Germany and maintain the peace settlement without change.

(2) In the meantime the states which had acquired Hungarian territory (Czechoslovakia, Yugoslavia, and Rumania) formed an alliance known as the *Little Entente*. Its purpose was to maintain the settlement with Hungary intact and oppose any move to restore the Hapsburgs. France supported the Little Entente with huge loans and extensions of credit for the purchase of munitions in France.

(3) The two "outcasts" of international society, Germany and Russia, surprised the world by signing the Treaty of Rapallo (1922). When the German Republic moved closer to the West, Russia made nonaggression pacts with her neighbors.

(4) Italy, too, negotiated a number of treaties. Some were with the defeated states, such as Hungary, Turkey, and Austria. They, like Italy, were dissatisfied with the peace settlement and hoped to have revisions made.

Tragically enough, instead of giving a greater sense of safety, these new alliances only awakened old fears and suspicions. Europe seemed to be falling back into the system of armed camps that had led to World War I.

Achievements of the League of Nations · Even while diplomats were arranging alliances, there remained a strong hope that the League of Nations would become an effective instrument for peace. The League's task was not easy, but in spite of many discouragements it performed a number of useful services. (1) It settled numerous disputes between its members and in some cases prevented war. (2) It carried on relief work among the refugees of war-stricken countries, notably Russia, Greece, and Armenia. (3) It aided in the repatriation of Greek and Turkish people. (4) It arranged financial aid to Austria and Hungary when they were in desperate need. (5) The League fulfilled various duties assigned to it by the peace treaties, such as the supervision of mandates and minority groups and the administration of the Saar region and Danzig. (6) It organized commissions for the study of important problems of finance and economics, health, transit and communications, the opium industry, and traffic in women and children.

But in the last analysis it was only a loose *league* of independent nations. It could do no more than the majority of the big powers were willing for it to do. In the next chapter we shall see why and how it failed to prevent aggression by military dictators.

The World Court · One of the most notable achievements of the League was the founding of the Permanent Court of International Justice. The World Court, as it came to be called, was a tribunal of eminent judges, selected from different countries. Their task was to hear and give opinions on disputes arising between nations. It also acted as an advisory body to the League. Acceptance of the Court's decisions was to be voluntary. Most of the nations joined the Court.

The World Court · *The court was composed of distinguished jurists of many nations. Yet states were unwilling to submit for judgment disputes involving national interest.*

The International Labor Organization · Another independent body, but one associated with the League, was the International Labor Organization. At least sixty states joined this body, including the United States (1934). Its headquarters at Geneva became the center for information on world labor problems. Representatives of employers, workers, and governments met in annual conferences. Recommendations for improving labor conditions were submitted to the proper authority in each country for further action.

Difficult Question of Disarmament · At the Peace Conference it was believed that one of the surest ways to secure a lasting peace would be to reduce the great armies and navies of the world. One of the duties of the League was to present plans for a general disarmament. But it soon became clear that no scheme would be accepted by the powers which did not include some mutual guarantee of security. Nations will not give up their means of protection unless they have some assurance that it is safe to do so. Beginning in 1923 various proposals for mutual agreements were drawn up but were rejected by one or another of the powers.

In spite of these setbacks an International Disarmament Conference was held in Geneva in 1932 with delegates from sixty countries. But this great congress also ended in failure because the powers were not ready to give up their military defense. Germany demanded that either the other nations disarm or that she be allowed to rearm on an equal basis with them. France was strongly against this proposal.

Germany in protest then withdrew from the conference, the League, and the World Court. The disarmament conference dragged on for two years longer but accomplished nothing. Soon the military machines of Germany, Italy, and Russia were greater than they had been in 1914.

Reduction of Navies · Discussions held by the great naval powers were more successful. Representatives of nine powers met in Washington in 1921. (1) Here Great Britain, France, Italy, Japan, and the United States agreed upon ratios which set for a time the relative sizes of their capital fleets. (2) Great Britain, France, Japan, and the United States pledged themselves to respect one another's island possessions in the Pacific. (3) A nine-power treaty was signed guaranteeing the independence of China. (4) But destroyers and submarines were not limited. And soon a race developed along these lines.

The London Naval Conference (1930) extended for six years the period of time during which the number of capital ships would not be increased. But in 1934, Japan gave notice that at the expiration of her agreements she would follow an independent policy. The other nations were beginning to build up their fleets. By 1936 the great powers were entering a more costly naval race than ever before.

The Locarno Treaties (1925) · Great Britain, France, Belgium, Germany, Poland, and Czechoslovakia sent delegates to Locarno, Switzerland, in October, 1925, to discuss the great question of security. Seven treaties were signed as the result of this conference.

Germany made agreements with France and Belgium to keep the western boundaries fixed by the Treaty of Versailles (including the demilitarized Rhineland zone). But no specific guarantee was made regarding Germany's eastern frontier. And for this reason France renewed her ties with Czechoslovakia and Poland.

The nations pledged themselves not to attack, invade, or go to war with one another, but to settle their future difficulties by arbitration. This was the first time since the war that Germany had become a party to an international move for peace and had joined in a common enterprise with the Allied powers. In case of a treaty violation, the parties agreed to go to the aid of the country attacked.

The Briand-Kellogg Treaty, or Pact of Paris (1928) · Realizing that there was strong support for peace measures in the United States, the French Foreign Minister, Briand, proposed that a perpetual treaty of friendship between France and the United States be made, outlawing war between the two countries.

The American Secretary of State, Frank B. Kellogg, replied that the two governments might make an important contribution to world peace by securing, if possible, the agreement of all the principal world powers to a declaration renouncing war.

As a result, on August 27, 1928, the representatives of fifteen nations met at Paris and pledged their governments (1) "to renounce war as an instrument of national policy" and (2) to seek the settlement of future quarrels with one another only by peaceful means. Within a short time thirty other nations had signed, including Russia.

The Four-Power Pact (1933) · In June, 1933, an "Agreement of Understanding and Co-operation," was signed at Rome by Great Britain, France, Germany, and Italy. The four powers pledged themselves to support the League of Nations, the Locarno treaties, and the Pact of Paris, and to collaborate on all economic questions.

War: Lucky for me they didn't do that in 1914 · *A European conference was proposed in 1914 but was not held. This cartoon reflects the general feeling that the Locarno Conference would prevent war. But the world-wide depression ended the "spirit of Locarno."*

Seven years later, however, they were engaged in the bloody struggle which came to be known as World War II.

CHECK ON YOUR READING

1. *How and why did the following attempt to gain security? (a) France, (b) Little Entente, (c) Germany, (d) Russia, (e) Italy?*
2. *What was accomplished by the (a) League, (b) World Court, (c) I.L.O.?*
3. *Why did military and naval disarmament end in failure?*
4. *Why was great hope held for (a) the Locarno treaties, (b) the Kellogg-Briand Pact, (c) the Four-Power Pact?*

The Postwar Decade: the Twenties · *Above: Charles A. Lindbergh receives a hero's welcome in Paris after his historic nonstop flight from New York in 1927. Right: Comedian Charlie Chaplin and the German movie star Pola Negri. Below: French women campaign for voting rights, which were not won until 1945.*

Learning Activities

Think about the chapter

1. Compare the effects of the world depression on the victors and the vanquished.

2. Why did the reparations and debt settlements fail?

3. Why was the League of Nations unable to guarantee security?

4. What accomplishments can be credited to the League?

5. In what respects were the causes of the troubles between England and Ireland, and England and India similar? Contrast the methods used in Ireland and India to achieve independence.

6. *Map study:* On a world map mark with different symbols the parts of the British Empire as it is today. Include (a) members of the Commonwealth, (b) dependent areas with some self-government, (c) colonies. A *World Almanac* will give the classification.

Go beyond the text

7. What is the status of Eire, Ulster, and India today in relation to the British Commonwealth?

8. The International Labor Office was an important body associated with the League of Nations and continues to be one of the important specialized agencies connected with the UN. Make a report on its work.

9. What was happening in the United States in 1929 and the 1930's?

10. Read about Mahatma Gandhi's fascinating life. How effective were his techniques?

11. Contrast (a) the treatment of Germany after World Wars I and II; (b) European economic recovery in both periods.

Follow up your special interests

12. Find some pictures to illustrate the charms of the "Emerald Isle" for tourists. Add some material to show the occupations and economic situation in Eire today.

13. What were some of the things happening between 1920 and 1935 that are not mentioned in this chapter? Draw sketches of them for a bulletin-board display. For example, when did Lindbergh fly solo across the Atlantic? What were the styles in dress of that period? in automobiles?

14. Paris in the 1920's was thought of as the world center for art and literature. Describe the paintings of that period and add examples of them to your history-of-art scrapbook. What famous American writers were in Paris in the 1920's?

READ FURTHER

Basic readings: (1) BECKER, *Modern History*, Chap. 23. (2) CHEYNEY, *Short History of England*, Chap. 23. (3) HAGEDORN, *Book of Courage.* (4) Year's *Pictorial History*, pp. 532–538, 544–551.

Special accounts: (5) F. ALLEN, *Only Yesterday.* Social history of the 1920's in the U. S. (6) W. CHURCHILL, *The Gathering Storm.* Chapter 5 on British politics. (7) K. GOULD, *Windows on the World*, Chaps. 8–9. (8) W. LANGSAM, *The World since 1919.* (9) E. O'BRIEN, *The Land and People of Ireland.* (10) Year's *Your Lifetime in Pictures: the Twentieth Century.* See section "The Troubled Years, 1930–1938."

Fiction and biography: (11) J. EATON, *Gandhi, Fighter without a Sword.* (12) A. HALL, *Nansen.* This famous Arctic explorer is equally famous for his work in the League of Nations. (13) C. LINDBERGH, *The Spirit of St. Louis.* The planning and execution of the famous flight to Paris. (14) S. RAMA RAU, *Home to India.* The daughter of an Indian ambassador to Western countries returns home and sees her country almost as a stranger. (15) N. SAHGAL, *Prison and Chocolate Cake.* The author is the daughter of Madame Pandit and niece of Nehru.

31

The Rise of Totalitarian Governments

KEY WORDS AND DATES

totalitarianism	fifth column
Bolsheviks	Falange
soviets	Nazis
Politbureau	Hitler
NEP	*Mein Kampf*
Lenin	1933
Trotsky	swastika
Stalin	Goebbels
Five-Year Plans	*Gestapo*
collective farms	Dollfuss
Comintern	Sudetenland
Cominform	appeasement
Mussolini	Rome-Berlin-Tokyo
fascism	Axis
Black Shirts	Sun Yat-sen
1922	Kuomintang
Roman question	Chiang Kai-shek
Franco	Nanking
Loyalists	Manchukuo

THE MOST VIOLENT REVOLUTION of the era following World War I took place in Russia. The Communists' disregard of the right of private property, the brutal character of their uprising, and their doctrine of world revolution greatly alarmed other countries. Tragically enough, fear of communism in such countries as Italy, Spain, and Germany opened the way for fascist dictatorships. Mussolini set the pattern in Italy, General Franco in Spain, Hitler in Germany, and the militarists in Japan.

These new governments, communist and fascist alike, were *totalitarian* in nature. In a totalitarian country not only the government but the total life of the citizen is under the absolute power of the one party permitted to exist. The leader is a *dictator*. Resistance to the party is crushed by use of secret police and terror.

The dictators waged aggression against their neighbors in the 1930's. And members of the League of Nations were unwilling to run the risk of war to stop them. For a while leaders of the democracies thought they could *appease* the hungry appetites of the dictators by yielding the territory of weaker states, but they failed.

Italy, Germany, and Japan joined forces in the so-called "Rome-Berlin-Tokyo Axis." And when Russia joined Germany for the dismemberment of Poland all hope for peace faded.

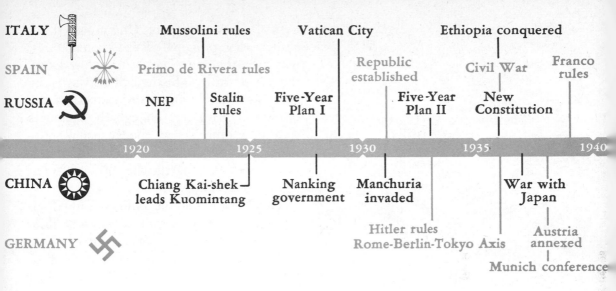

ITALY		Mussolini rules		Vatican City		Ethiopia conquered	
SPAIN		Primo de Rivera rules		Republic established		Civil War	Franco rules
RUSSIA	NEP	Stalin rules	Five-Year Plan I		Five-Year Plan II	New Constitution	

1920　　　　　1925　　　　　1930　　　　　1935　　　　　1940

CHINA	Chiang Kai-shek leads Kuomintang	Nanking government	Manchuria invaded		War with Japan	
GERMANY			Hitler rules Rome-Berlin-Tokyo Axis		Austria annexed	
					Munich conference	

1. Communism in Soviet Russia

The Bolsheviks Establish Communism · Following the revolution in November, 1917 (p. 506), three important tasks faced Lenin and the other Bolshevik leaders. (1) They had to come to terms with Germany, and they did so in the Treaty of Brest Litovsk. (2) The government and economic system had to be reorganized. (3) Their enemies had to be suppressed.

Within four months the Bolsheviks instituted communism by several sweeping decrees. (1) All land was proclaimed the property of the state. (2) Banks were nationalized and private accounts seized. (3) Workers' Councils (Soviets) took over the factories and all workers were required to join government-controlled unions. (4) All church property was seized and religious instruction in the schools was abolished. (5) Private trade was gradually suppressed and rationing was started.

In July, 1918, the government announced a constitution for the Russian Federated Socialist Republic. It proclaimed, "He shall not eat who does not work." Those who hired labor for their own profit, those who lived on an income, and the clergy might not vote or have any part in the government. Workers in the cities and peasants in the country were organized in local councils called *soviets*. They elected delegates to provincial congresses, which in turn elected delegates to an All-Russian Congress of Soviets.

This congress, however, could not make laws as ours does. A Central Executive Committee, chosen by it, made the laws, and the congress could only vote its approval. Administration of government affairs was in the hands of a Council of People's Commissars.

These two small governing groups were composed only of members of the Communist party, the only party permitted in the country. A small group of Communists, called the Political Bureau or *Politbureau*, exercised complete control over the party and the government.

549

Threshing Grain in the Shevshenko Commune in the Ukraine (1920) · *Note the crude equipment and the high proportion of women workers. Why were peasants resentful?*

The Anti-Communists Are Defeated in a Terrible Civil War · Such sweeping changes aroused great opposition from former landlords, liberals, moderate socialists, nobles, priests, and many peasants. Counterrevolutionary movements were led by Russian generals of the old regime. Their armies were called the Whites because they flew a white flag in contrast to the red banner of the Communists.

The Allies refused to recognize the Bolshevik government and sent troops to aid the White armies. The Communists now resorted to a reign of terror. The secret police arrested and executed thousands of suspects. Finally, the Allies began to withdraw their forces, and by the end of 1920 the Communists had forcibly established peace in Russia.

In 1923 a Treaty of Union joined together the principal Russian territories, which by that time had come under Communist control. This federation was to be known as the *Union of Soviet Socialist Republics* (U.S.S.R.). Though the members were proclaimed equal, the Russian Republic embraced nine-tenths of the Soviet territory and dominated the Soviet Union from the capital at Moscow.

The New Economic Policy · The Communist leaders were soon faced with difficulties that they had not expected. They had killed, imprisoned, or exiled most of the capitalist and professional class. And the management of industries, railways, and mines required knowledge and experience that the workers did not have. Consequently, production declined and costs rose.

The peasants were resentful when they found that they could keep only a small portion of their crops and must turn the rest over to the state. Many slaughtered their livestock rather than give it to the government. They determined to raise less, and in 1921 the harvest was particularly poor. Starvation stalked the land. Millions died in spite of tremendous shipments of relief supplies from the United States. With a shortage of goods and food, opposition to the government grew.

Lenin and his associates found that they would have to restore some of the features of the capitalistic system which they had discarded. They now adopted a New Economic Policy (NEP). This permitted a limited amount of private business as an incentive to larger production. Under government regulation, small shops and factories with not more than twenty workers were allowed. Peasants could sell some of their surplus crops in the market. The government, however, still retained control over all large-scale business and trade.

Stalin Becomes Dictator (1924) · For nearly seven years Lenin was the outstanding leader of Communist Russia. As Chairman of the Politbureau he was chief of the party and dictator of the Soviet Union. At his death in 1924, however, there was a bitter contest for his high position.

Among the chief rival candidates were Leon Trotsky and Joseph Stalin. Trotsky had organized and led the Red army. But he was an arrogant little man with a fiery temper. He wanted Russia to lead a world-wide revolution to overthrow capitalism. His insistence on having his own way made him unpopular in the party.

Stalin, an ardent admirer of Lenin, had been a revolutionary in tsarist days and an able military leader during the revolution. He believed that communism must first be firmly established in Russia. He used his position as secretary-general of the Communist party to win complete control of this all-important organization. Only his candidates won party positions.

Stalin was finally chosen to succeed Lenin as Chairman of the Politbureau. Trotsky was accused of a counterrevolutionary conspiracy and was permanently exiled. He was later murdered in Mexico. Stalin became dictator of the party and of the state.

The Five-Year Plans · A Five-Year Plan was set up in 1928 to increase production along all lines. Its purpose was to make Russia self-sufficient and independent of the capitalistic countries. The plan called for making industrial and farm machinery; building steel mills and hydroelectric plants; increasing coal, iron, and oil output; and constructing railways.

Foreign engineers were invited to Russia, and technical and engineering schools were

The Dnieper Dam · *This huge dam and hydroelectric power station on the Dnieper River was built in 1927–1932 to supply power for heavy industry.*

established to teach the Russians the necessary know-how of modern industry. It was hoped to finance the plan, in part, by saving in the cost of production.

Two methods of raising agricultural production were tried. (1) Vast areas were put under cultivation as state farms, the products of which would belong to the government. (2) Peasant holdings were now combined into "collective farms." Their lands, machinery, and working animals were to be part of the collective. A portion of the income was to be set aside for new machinery and other expenses, and part went to the government. The remainder would be divided among the peasants according to their contribution to the enterprise.

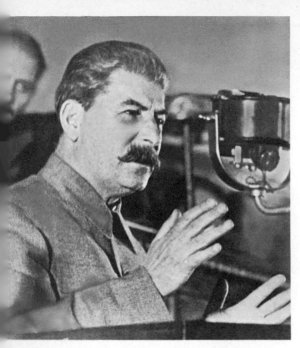

Joseph (Djugashvili) Stalin, 1879–1953 · *Son of a Georgian shoemaker, he studied for the priesthood, succeeded Lenin, purged all opponents, aided and later helped destroy Hitler.*

Success of the Plan · In the building of modern plants, machinery, and railways, the goals set were reached ahead of time. But the shortage of skilled workers resulted in slow output, poor quality goods, and injury to the equipment. The cost of production was not reduced as had been expected.

The yield from the farms was increased, but not enough. The property-owning peasants (*kulaks*) objected to joining the collectives. In 1930 this class was liquidated. The government seized their lands, houses, tools, and livestock, and arrested or banished thousands to hard labor in distant places. Many died of hunger and disease. A terrible famine in 1932–1933 caused many deaths.

The government, however, undertook a second Five-Year Plan (1933–1937), and proposed others to follow. Under the second plan, Russia advanced considerably in the production of iron and steel. Yet it was still far behind the United States and western Europe.

Stalin Purges the Party · Stalin's costly program and brutal methods aroused discontent even among some of his associates. They felt he had departed from the principles of Marx and Lenin. Instead of a "temporary" suppression of free discussion, it became more and more dangerous to criticize government policy. Instead of a "classless society," a new ruling class of privileged bureaucrats was rising.

In 1933 about a million Communists (one-third of the membership) were expelled from the party. In the next five years a great number of "old Bolsheviks" were tried for conspiracy and "Trotskyism." Some were imprisoned and others put to death.

After Stalin's death in 1953 his methods were denounced by the new leaders, who had co-operated with him during his long dictatorship. But publication of this criticism was suppressed within the country.

The Constitution of 1936 · In the 1930's the Soviet government was making non-aggression treaties with her neighbors and seeking world-wide recognition. Perhaps to impress foreign powers and to reduce domestic ill-will, Stalin in 1936 granted a new constitution.

On its face it seemed to be more democratic than the old one. Universal suffrage was adopted and certain fundamental rights were specified though never practiced. The government was reorganized. But the Communist party was still supreme, and Stalin kept it in a firm grasp.

Under this constitution, which still exists on paper, there is a two-house "legislature," the Supreme Soviet. It consists of the Soviet of the Union and the Soviet of Nationalities. The Supreme Soviet meets in joint session twice a year to ratify decisions of the Communist party. The Council of Ministers, formerly the Council of People's Commissars, has broad powers between sessions. This body, whose chairman is the premier, consists of the heads of the various state departments.

The Communist party, whose membership is limited to a few million people, controls all important state activities. Its members occupy all important political positions. The Central Committee of the party elects various groups to carry out its wishes. Most powerful of these is the Presidium, or executive body, concerned with political matters. Since 1952 this body has replaced the Politbureau as the party's executive. The most important Communist leaders are members of this group. Voting in the Soviet Union means endorsing candidates already chosen by the Communist party.

The Comintern · In 1919 the Communist International (*Comintern*) was formed to promote world revolution. This body soon had branches in foreign countries. They received their orders and funds from Moscow. The activities of the Comintern's secret agents included propaganda, espionage, sabotage, and the stirring up of discontent and strikes among workers.

The Comintern aided revolutions in Germany, Hungary, Poland, and Italy after World War I. Later, the policy of the Comintern was to act as a political agent. Its members tried to spread communist ideas in foreign labor unions, banks, the press, and even in government offices.

Because of its revolutionary and subversive methods, foreign countries distrusted the Soviet Union. But after Russia had signed nonaggression and neutrality treaties with her neighbors, she was recognized by the United States (1933). This was done on condition that Communist propaganda should cease in that country and that Americans in Russia should be allowed religious liberty. The Comintern was dissolved in 1943, and later replaced by the *Cominform*, the Communist Information Bureau. Its methods, however, were no less subversive.

Education and Religion · The Soviet government began to introduce compulsory education for all children between the ages of eight and sixteen. It extended elementary training and established additional high schools, technical and vocational

Teaching Adults to Read and Write · *One of the great tasks of the Soviet government was to wipe out illiteracy, which in places ran as high as 95 per cent.*

schools, and universities. Students were promoted by competitive examinations and went to school six days a week the year around. On graduation they were assigned to occupations according to the needs of the state.

The Communists took a hostile attitude toward religion, maintaining that it had too long made the people subservient. (The Russian Orthodox Church had for centuries been closely identified with the tsarist government.) All church lands and buildings were seized. The government actively propagandized against religion and sought to substitute communist philosophy for religious beliefs.

In 1929, however, churches were again permitted to hold public worship. But they could not engage in educational work or try to win new converts.

Intolerance of the Government · Although the Communist government claimed to be organized for the benefit of the masses, many people from the first were antagonized by its measures. After the brutalities of the revolution itself, thousands of intellectuals—professors, scientists, artists, musicians—who could not survive the methods of the regime were driven into exile. The government robbed the citizens of their property, liquidated the *kulaks*, and took harsh and relentless measures against any who criticized it.

Thousands were put to death and millions to slave labor. In spite of the freedoms set down in the constitution, a body of secret police (the OGPU) exercised unlimited power in seeking out and arresting anyone suspected of opposing the regime. A strict censorship was observed. Newspapers and magazines published "the party line," repeating over and over the official view which everyone must follow. During the years many Communists themselves have been accused of disloyalty and treason and have been executed.

CHECK ON YOUR READING

1. *Name five measures instituting communism in Russia.*
2. *Describe government and party organization before and after the 1936 constitution.*
3. *Who were the anti-Communists? What happened to them?*
4. *Identify: NEP, Lenin, Trotsky, Stalin, Five-Year Plans, collective farms, kulaks, Comintern, Cominform, OGPU.*

---

2. Fascism in Italy

Fascism a Reaction against Communism · There was great discontent in Italy after World War I. Agriculture and industry had suffered greatly, and the country was deep in debt. Italy's claims for territories had been brushed aside by the Paris Peace Conference. As the soldiers came home from the front, they could find no work. The Communists, encouraged by the revolution in Russia, began to commit lawless acts. There were strikes and sabotage in the factories, and in some towns workers took possession of the plants. As street fighting and rioting spread, the government failed to act.

These conditions favored the success of a new nationalist group, called Fascists (from *fasces*, the bundle of rods and ax which symbolizes the authority of government). Their energetic leader, Benito

Mussolini, was a former corporal, Socialist, and newspaperman. After the war he organized a group of war veterans to push his demands for a more efficient government. Armed bands of these young Fascists, wearing black shirts, began to attack the Italian Communists. Businessmen and property-holders welcomed and supported this rightist organization which promised to protect them against the "Reds."

By 1921 the Fascists had secured thirty-five seats in parliament and set up the National Fascist party. Mussolini called for the overthrow of the weak liberal ministry. In October, 1922, at a party gathering in Naples, he threatened that unless the government resigned, his army would march on Rome. Shortly afterward, as Fascist troops moved towards the capital, the king sent for Mussolini and asked him to form a cabinet.

Mussolini's Fascist Dictatorship · The new premier began immediately to remodel the government. In 1923 he secured from parliament dictatorial powers, which he used to place Fascists in every department of state. A new electoral law soon gave them control of parliament.

By a series of measures (1925–1928) Mussolini brought the government into his own hands. He could issue decrees with the force of law. Local officials were made responsible to him directly. Newspapers which criticized his policies were suppressed and secret societies were forbidden. While Italy retained its monarchy, it had nevertheless become a Fascist dictatorship.

All political parties were abolished except the Fascist. In 1928 popular voting for members of parliament was taken away. Instead, the people were permitted to vote only for or against a list of candidates prepared by the Fascist Grand Council.

For Fascism and the Fatherland · *Mussolini, with arm extended in the Fascist salute, emotionally addresses a crowd. Below: Fascist training for militarism began early.*

In order to secure government control over the working classes the old Italian labor unions were abolished. A very complicated system of unions of employers and employees was established to deal with labor questions. Later even representation in the parliament was based on these labor-management syndicates (called *corporations*).

The Roman Question Is Settled (1929) · One of Mussolini's most important achievements was the settlement of the so-called

Roman question. Ever since Italian troops had taken Rome in 1870 (p. 408), the Popes had considered themselves "prisoners." They had refused compensation for their lost territories.

Mussolini's agreement with the Church recognized the Pope as sovereign over the "independent state of the Vatican City." This tiny area includes St. Peter's and the Vatican. The Pope gave up his former claim to Rome, and the papacy was compensated for its losses. The Roman Catholic religion was recognized as the official religion of Italy. Compulsory religious instruction was to be provided in the schools.

"Believe! Obey! Fight!" · Mussolini accomplished much in the material improvement of Italy. Railways were improved,

Haile Selassie in Exile · *This enlightened ruler (center) was modernizing Ethiopia when the Italians invaded. He fled to England.*

roads were laid out, shipping was built up, and foreign trade was increased. Automobile and aircraft industries were developed. To make up for the lack of coal, great hydroelectric plants were built.

The price of these achievements to the Italian people, however, was the loss of democratic institutions and personal liberty. The Fascists tolerated no criticism. "Believe, obey, fight" was the slogan, and regimentation was the order of the day.

Foreign Policy of Fascist Italy · Fascism emphasized militarism. Mussolini spent large sums of money to build up the armed forces. Universal military service was required, and boys from the age of eight were put through drills. Mussolini was fond of martial parades. He loved to appear on balconies to give the Fascist salute while frenzied mobs shouted, *"Il Duce!"* (Leader). He made many arrogant speeches in which he praised war as a sign of vitality in a nation. And he looked eagerly about for opportunities to use his military power.

In 1923, after Italian members of a boundary commission were killed in Greece, Mussolini ordered the occupation of the Greek island of Corfu. Here the League intervened and successfully solved the dispute. In 1924 the troublesome question of Fiume was settled. The "Pact of Rome" gave Fiume to Italy but the suburb and the port of Susak to Yugoslavia.

Italy Conquers Ethiopia (1936) and Annexes Albania (1939) · Italians had long smarted under the memory of their defeat by the Ethiopians at Adowa (p. 466). In 1935, on the pretext of border clashes between the soldiers in Italian Somaliland and Ethiopia, Mussolini sent a large army to invade Ethiopia. When Italy refused all offers of arbitration, the League of Nations ruled that she was the aggressor and voted to apply economic sanctions. This was a peaceful form of pressure including the refusal to sell to or buy from an aggressor nation.

Mussolini, however, defied the League, and effective sanctions, such as the closing of the Suez Canal or refusal to sell him oil, were never applied. By April, 1936, his modern tanks, guns, and airplanes had driven Haile Selassie, the Ethiopian ruler, from his capital of Addis Ababa. The king of Italy was hailed as Emperor of Ethiopia. Shortly afterward Eritrea, Ethiopia, and Italian Somaliland were organized as Italian East Africa.

In 1939 Mussolini annexed Albania, which had been practically an Italian protectorate since 1927. This gave Italy control of the Adriatic and assured protection to her eastern coast.

CHECK ON YOUR READING

1. List (a) the causes of, and (b) the steps in, Mussolini's rise to power.
2. How was the Roman question settled?
3. Identify these terms in relation to Italy: (a) fascism, (b) slogan, (c) Il Duce, (d) sanctions, (e) Selassie.
4. Show on a map territory gained by Mussolini.

3. Civil War and Fascism in Spain

Unrest in Spain after World War I · Spain had remained neutral during World War I and had profited by selling supplies to both sides. But when the war boom was over, trade fell off, unemployment grew, and hard times followed.

The Spanish government, an old-fashioned monarchy, was under the control of conservatives and of army cliques. These groups opposed every liberal reform. There were many strikes and riots, especially in the industrial city of Barcelona. The province of Catalonia demanded independence. Besides, the government was carrying on a disastrous war against the tribesmen in Morocco.

Dictatorship of Primo de Rivera · Unrest reached a peak in 1923. The king therefore gave his secret approval for General Primo de Rivera to establish a military dictatorship. The dictator took severe measures to restore order. He suspended the constitution, dissolved the Cortes (parliament), established strict censorship, and sent liberal leaders into exile. However, he failed to solve Spain's fundamental problems, and in 1930 he suddenly resigned.

Spain Becomes a Republic (1931) · The king agreed to restore certain liberties, but this was not enough. People demanded a republic. In April, 1931, King Alfonso fled to France, and Spain was declared a republic. A democratic constitution was adopted.

The reform program of the new government aimed at reducing the great power of wealthy landlords, the army, and the Church. Large estates were divided among the poverty-stricken peasants. The Catholic Church was no longer to be the state church. The Jesuit order was dissolved and church schools closed.

Civil War in Spain (1936–1939) · These changes aroused the bitter opposition of those who had lost their property and ancient rights. The radicals, on the other

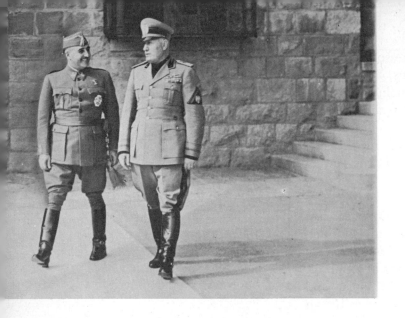

El Caudillo and Il Duce · *Franco (left) chats with his friend Mussolini (right). The two dictators held many views in common. Later, when the tide turned against Mussolini, Franco became less friendly.*

hand, complained that the reforms did not go far enough.

Fearing the power of conservative army officers, the government dismissed some and transferred others to commands overseas. General Francisco Franco was sent to the Canary Islands, but he soon returned to lead a revolt organized by the army. By July, 1936, civil war had broken out between Franco's "insurgent" forces and the government's "loyalists."

As the war progressed, great fear arose in other countries lest the conflict should spread outside Spain. Hitler and Mussolini both openly helped Franco, who declared that he was fighting communism. Techniques developed in Spain were later used by the Germans in Poland. Russia sent aid to the Loyalists. But Britain and France refused to intervene for fear that the war might become general.

The struggle lasted through 1937–1938, with heavy losses on both sides. But with Hitler's air force and Mussolini's tanks against them, the Loyalists were doomed. As they retreated, thousands of refugees poured into France. In March, 1939, Franco entered Madrid and a few days later proclaimed the war at an end.

During the last days of the war, one of the rebel generals declared that four columns were marching on Madrid and that a "fifth column" would meet them there. Since that time subversive forces within an area have been called *fifth-columnists*.

Fascist Dictatorship in Spain · Franco now established a nationalist government on fascist lines with himself as dictator (*El Caudillo*). Only one party, the *Falange*, was permitted to exist. The government returned the land to its former owners and restored the authority of the Church. Catholicism was once again declared the religion of the state.

CHECK ON YOUR READING

1. *Describe postwar conditions in Spain.*
2. *Identify: De Rivera, Alfonso, insurgents, Loyalists, fifth-columnists, Falange.*
3. *What were the (a) causes, (b) key events, (c) results of the civil war in Spain?*

4. The Nazi Revolution and German Expansion

Beginnings of the National Socialist Party · In the early 1920's a large number of unemployed veterans were wandering about Germany. There was no future for them in the army, since the Versailles Treaty limited their country's forces to 100,000 men. And jobs were hard to find. Armed with weapons which had not been handed over to the Allies, some began to loot and plunder. Many of them joined the new National Socialist German Workers' party (called *Nazi* for short). The Nazis held their first meetings in a Munich tavern. Their leader was an obscure young Austrian house-painter named Adolph Hitler. As in Italy, they represented the rightist reaction against communism.

Early Career of Hitler · Although an Austrian by birth, Hitler had been a corporal in the German army. An ardent German nationalist, he believed that the tall, blond, blue-eyed Aryan Germans were supermen, a "master race." Under the symbol of the swastika they should rightfully dominate the inferior peoples of the rest of Europe. Hitler himself was short, brunette, and brown-eyed, but was made an "honorary Aryan."

Hitler turned out to be a spell-binding orator. He won devoted followers by denouncing the Versailles Treaty, the leaders of the republic, the Jews, and the Communists. He appealed to all the discontented. He made his first bid for power in 1923, the year of the Ruhr occupation and the disastrous inflation. With General Ludendorff and others, Hitler tried to seize the government at Munich. This plot, known as the Beer-Hall *Putsch*, failed. Hitler was arrested and sent to jail.

Here Hitler wrote the first volume of *Mein Kampf* ("My Battle"). This book became the Nazi bible. In it Hitler outlined his program for exterminating the Jews, wiping out France, and establishing German supremacy. Such a program seemed too insane to be taken seriously, yet millions were to die because of it.

Rise of the Nazis to Power · Once out of jail, Hitler with his Nazi followers worked tirelessly to build up a strong party and to spread its influence. They borrowed the techniques of the Italian Fascists, including shirts, songs, salutes, and brutal terror. Meetings, torchlight parades, pamphlets, and street fights constantly spread Nazi propaganda. Hitler promised a new and glorious Germany whose people would fulfill their destiny as leaders of Europe.

The first Nazis appeared in the German Reichstag in 1928, when they won twelve seats. The great depression, however, brought economic disaster once more to Germany, and Nazi strength took a sudden spurt. By 1932 their 230 representatives constituted the largest party in that body. The program of this aggressive and militant group appealed to patriotic youths, middle-class businessmen whose savings had been wiped out, and industrialists and land owners who feared communism.

In January, 1933, President von Hindenburg appointed Hitler chancellor. By April he was granted dictatorial powers for four years by the Reichstag. The Weimar republic had come to an end. In its place emerged the *Third Reich*, as Hitler called his dictatorship. (The *First Reich* was the Holy Roman Empire, the *Second Reich* was the German Empire, 1871–1918.)

Nazi Pageantry and Book-burning · *The Nazis used dramatic rallies to cast a spell over the masses. Above: Hitler addresses a May Day rally. Note the soldiers, flags, and swastikas. Hitler loved to speak from balconies. Below: The Nazis burn "subversive" books. What books did they consider subversive?*

A Totalitarian State · By means of the Nazi party, Hitler created a centralized state which dominated every aspect of the public and private life of the German people. Other political groups were abolished or absorbed. The Nazi emblem, the swastika, was to be seen everywhere.

The old German states were brought under the control of the central government, and the Reichsrat, whose members represented the German states, was abolished.

When President von Hindenburg died in 1934, Hitler took over the presidential powers as well. He chose as his title *Reichsführer* (leader of the realm), but he was usually called *Der Führer*. In his hands was concentrated greater power than Bismarck or the German emperors had ever known.

Thought Control and Persecutions · One of the characteristics of a totalitarian state is that the government tries to make people think the way it wants them to. The Nazis were ruthlessly efficient in this respect. The Department of Propaganda and Enlightenment under Joseph Goebbels exercised a strict censorship, and publicly burned books considered contrary to Nazi beliefs. It spread Nazi influence through speeches, broadcasts, and publications.

The whole educational system was revised to conform to Nazi beliefs. Biology instruction in schools and colleges attempted to prove that the Germans were a superior race. History textbooks glorified war and nationalism. Hitler youth organizations for boys and girls were formed in order to develop good Nazis at an early age. Religious organizations were subject to government control. Trade unions were abolished, and strikes prohibited. Business groups were subject to state control.

To insure strict loyalty to the Nazi regime, a well-organized secret police, the *Gestapo*, spied into the lives of the people and seized suspects without notice. Jews were among the chief victims. They were driven out of businesses and schools, and were deprived of their citizenship. Thousands were herded into the concentration camps, where they suffered cruel torture and death in gas chambers. Many Germans ignored the horrors of the regime, noticing only the increasing prosperity, power, and prestige of the Third Reich.

The Nazis Rearm Germany and Take Over the Saar and Rhineland · After Hitler became Führer, he tried to soften the effects of his earlier warlike speeches by insisting that Germany would seek to win her rights only by peaceful means. In January, 1934, he made a nonaggression pact with Poland, accepting the boundary lines as drawn in the Versailles Treaty. The next year 90 per cent of the inhabitants of the Saar district voted to return to Germany, and the League of Nations transferred the region to the Reich.

In March, 1935, Hitler made the startling announcement that universal military training was to be introduced. This was an open defiance of the Treaty of Versailles, but Hitler justified this act on the ground of Germany's insecurity in a world where all other nations were armed. Britain and France failed to act on this treaty violation, and Hitler had won his first victory over his former enemies.

A year later, Hitler announced to a wildly cheering Reichstag that German troops had marched into the unfortified Rhineland. This act violated not only the Versailles Treaty but the Locarno treaties, which Germany had willingly signed. For a second time Hitler had rightly judged

Nazi Atrocities · *Nazi cruelty seems unbelievable to people accustomed to strong democratic traditions. Yet it was horribly real to the thousands of Nazi victims.*

the reaction of the Allies, for no troops opposed him.

Creation of the Rome-Berlin-Tokyo Axis (1936) · Hitler now began to establish closer relations with those governments whose aims were similar to his own. Germany and Italy acted together to support Franco in the Spanish civil war, and Germany recognized Italy's new Ethiopian empire. Thus was formed the much-advertised "Rome-Berlin Axis."

In November, 1936, Japan signed an Anti-Comintern Pact with Germany, and a year later Italy joined, thus creating the Rome-Berlin-Tokyo Axis. The announcement that these three powers would resist the spread of communism served as a cloak to cover up their own aggressions.

Hitler Prepares for War · Hitler now prepared for total war. The building of armaments, highways, bridges, and fortifications took care of all unemployment. Hitler encouraged people to raise large families (future soldiers) and at the same time loudly demanded more living space (*lebensraum*).

Hitler began to talk ominously about the sufferings of Germans outside the Reich and their need for "liberation." It became his policy to absorb territories in which German-speaking people were living. German Austria was first on his list. Countries with German minorities, such as Czechoslovakia and Poland, were to come next. The destruction of "inferior" peoples would follow.

Hitler Annexes Austria (1938) · Ever since the Nazis had come to power in Germany, secret encouragement had been given their supporters in Austria. How many Austrian Nazis there were we shall never know, since Chancellor Dollfuss had closed the parliament. But in 1934 they were a small minority. Dollfuss himself was murdered by the Nazis. His successor, Kurt Schuschnigg, continued the struggle to resist Nazi pressure.

Hitler had promised to respect Austria's independence, but by 1938 he felt ready to disregard his promise. Germany's historic "drive to the East" was to be resumed.

Pressure was put on Schuschnigg to include Nazis in his cabinet. When the Austrian chancellor announced a plebiscite to determine how many people favored union with Germany (*Anschluss*), Hitler replied with an ultimatum. To avoid bloodshed, Schuschnigg resigned. German troops promptly marched in, and on March 13 the union of Austria and Germany was proclaimed. German power now extended to the borders of Yugoslavia and Hungary.

The Sudetenland Crisis · Czechoslovakia, within whose Sudeten area lived three million Germans, was the next victim. Hitler used the demands of the Sudeten Nazis for local self-government to create a crisis. Eager to keep the peace, the British prime minister, Neville Chamberlain, flew to Germany to consult with Hitler. Hitler now demanded the cession of the Sudetenland to Germany.

Britain and France, an ally of Czechoslovakia, notified the Czech government that it would have to yield. They were not prepared to help her if she refused. Russia agreed to support Czechoslovakia, but was refused transit rights across Polish territory to join her. Deserted by the West, Czechoslovakia gave in.

Munich, September 28, 1938 · *From left to right are Chamberlain, Daladier, Hitler, Mussolini. Was it "peace in our time," or "appeasement"?*

GERMAN AGGRESSION TO 1939

SWEDEN · LATVIA · LITH. · E. PRUSSIA · TO RUSSIA, 1939 (4th. partition of Poland) · DENMARK · Baltic Sea · NETH. · Berlin · GERMANY · Weimar · Oder R. · Warsaw · POLAND · BELG. · Rhine R. · RUHR · LUX. · SAAR TO GERMANY, 1935 · Danube R. · BOHEMIA · CZECHOSLOVAKIA · MORAVIA · SLOVAKIA · TESCHEN TO POLAND 1938 · TO HUNGARY 1938, 1939 · Munich · Vienna · SWITZ. · AUSTRIA · HUNGARY · RUMANIA · ITALY · YUGOSLAVIA · Danube R.

Hitler Scraps Versailles · *Explain how Hitler violated the Versailles Treaty in: (1) the Rhineland, 1936; (2) Austria and (3) Sudetenland, 1938; (4) rest of Czechoslovakia, (5) Danzig, Memel, and (6) Poland in 1939. Was occupying the Saar (1935) a violation?*

Yet the crisis continued. Hitler made further demands, and war seemed certain. The world breathed a sigh of relief when it was announced that a four-power conference would be held to deal with the crisis.

Munich and the Dismemberment of Czechoslovakia · Prime Minister Chamberlain, Premier Daladier of France, Mussolini, and Hitler met at Munich, Germany, on September 29, 1938. Czechoslovakia and Russia were not represented. With Hitler and Mussolini dominating the conference, the dismemberment of Czechoslovakia was agreed upon. Germany took over her mountain barrier, with its line of fortifications, and most of her industrial resources.

Within six months Czechoslovakia disappeared. Poland seized the Teschen area. Hitler then annexed Bohemia and Moravia. Slovakia became a German protectorate, and Hungary gobbled up the easternmost Czech province.

Up to now a policy of *appeasement* had been followed by the Western democracies. "Munich" became a byword of this policy. Peace had been kept, but for how long? Actually a war was already in progress—in the Far East.

CHECK ON YOUR READING

1. Describe (*a*) *the beginnings of the Nazi party, and* (*b*) *the Nazi rise to power.*
2. Identify: (*a*) *Mein Kampf,* (*b*) *Third Reich,* (*c*) *totalitarian state,* (*d*) *swastika,* (*e*) *Der Führer,* (*f*) *thought control,* (*g*) *Gestapo,* (*h*) *concentration camps.*
3. Use the map to locate and explain Hitler's moves relative to (*a*) *the Rhineland,* (*b*) *Poland,* (*c*) *the Rome-Berlin-Tokyo Axis,* (*d*) *Austria,* (*e*) *Sudetenland,* (*f*) *Czechoslovakia.*
4. How are the following terms related to Hitler's foreign policy: (*a*) *Lebensraum?* (*b*) *Anschluss?* (*c*) *Appeasement?*

5. China and Japan after World War I

Japan's Gains from World War I · The fact that the Western powers were busy with their war in Europe had afforded Japan a golden opportunity. Soon after she entered the war on the side of the Allies, she seized China's Shantung region, which had been a German sphere of influence. The Japanese government then pressed upon Yuan Shih-kai, the president of China, demands which would have made the country practically a protectorate of Japan. In May, 1915, Japan was able to force China to give her most of what she wanted in spite of protests by the Western powers.

In return for her naval aid in the Mediterranean, Japan received British assurance of support of Japanese claims to Shantung and the German islands in the North Pacific at the Peace Conference. The Conference duly awarded these territories to Japan, although the islands were given as mandates. China objected to Japan's possession of Shantung and refused to sign the Treaty of Versailles. In 1922 Japan returned Shantung to China as a result of the Washington Naval Conference.

China under Two Governments · China's internal divisions caused grave problems for the young republic. In 1917 President Li Yuan-hung had illegally dissolved the Chinese parliament because of political difficulties arising over China's entry into the war. Thereupon the Nationalist party (called the *Kuomintang*) set up a rival government at Canton. Until 1928 the country had two governments, one at Peking and another at Canton. To add to the confusion governors of the provinces were plundering the country.

For many years Dr. Sun Yat-sen, leader of the Kuomintang, worked to unite north and south. His attempts to reach an agreement with Peking failed because there was no stable government to deal with.

Influence of Communism on the Kuomintang · Soviet leaders pretended to be very sympathetic with the efforts of the Nationalist party to unite China. Soviet advisers assisted Dr. Sun in preparing a more definite program of party action against the war lords, who were destroying China. A military academy was established at Canton, where Soviet officers assisted in training Nationalist forces. At the head of this academy was General Chiang Kai-shek.

As a young military officer, Chiang had come under the influence of Dr. Sun and had become his trusted assistant. Dr. Sun sent him to Moscow to study Russian military organization. But when he returned to China, Chiang became suspicious of the Communists.

Communism spread rapidly among the people, and in 1924 Chinese Communists were permitted to join the Kuomintang. But they soon stirred up strikes and incited antiforeign feeling, which brought the party into clashes with the foreign police. By the following year a split had occurred in the Kuomintang. The moderates strongly opposed the violent communistic methods and wanted to end the close ties with the Soviet Union.

After Dr. Sun's death in 1925, General Chiang Kai-shek became leader of the Kuomintang party. While he was faithful to the principles of Dr. Sun, he suppressed the Communists as being harmful to the cause of a peaceful and united China.

A New Nationalist Government at Nanking (1928) · In the meantime rival war lords kept Peking in a state of anarchy. General Chiang then marched northward with his Nationalist troops and captured Peking. The government of the reunited republic was established at Nanking (1928).

The name of the former capital was changed from Peking ("northern capital") to Peiping ("northern peace"). In October, Chiang Kai-shek was made chairman of the new Council of State, which was to rule China. By the end of the year the Nanking government was recognized by Japan, as well as by most of the Western powers.

China under Chiang Kai-shek · China now had a leader who was at once chief of the government, commander of the army, and chairman of the Nationalist party. General Chiang undertook to carry forward the program outlined by the great republican hero Sun Yat-sen. This program aimed at educating the people for self-government and setting up a constitutional democracy.

The new leader had a difficult task. Constant communist uprisings had to be suppressed. The war lords, long accustomed to having their own way in the provinces, stirred up many revolts. Within the Kuomintang itself there were rebellious factions which charged Chiang with trying to become a dictator.

Yet China under Chiang Kai-shek's leadership made great progress. Projects for controlling floods, improving agriculture, developing harbors, and constructing highways were undertaken. Great opportunities for education were offered by providing more schools and textbooks. By 1929 the Nanking government had persuaded most of the foreign powers to give up their rights to fix the rate of Chinese

General and Madame Chiang Kai-shek · *In 1927 General Chiang married Meiling Soong, sister of Madame Sun Yat-sen. He was much influenced by his wife. Madame Chiang is an alumna of Wellesley College.*

tariffs. It then set up a tariff schedule of its own.

The Rising Power of Japan · During World War I Japan had been kept busy supplying materials to the Allies. As a result she built up her gold reserves and increased her investments abroad. During the 1920's Japan was able to keep up a high level of industry and trade, even though a gradual slump set in. Her population increased from 56 million in 1920 to 65 million in 1930. Her great business houses (like the Mitsui), which were combines of manufacturing, trade, shipping, and banking services, exercised great influence over the government.

On the whole, Japanese capitalists favored a liberal party government and a friendly policy toward foreign powers in the interest of business. On the other hand, the military party, supported by certain businessmen and bankers, advocated a program of expansion by force to secure raw materials, markets, and "living space" for the country's growing population.

In the depression of 1929 the extremists in the army party saw their opportunity to get control of the government. Their solution of Japan's problem was to take possession of Manchuria and Mongolia, invade China, and dominate the Far East.

Japanese Invade Manchuria (1931) · Manchuria had long tempted Japan. Its fertile land produced abundant crops. It was rich in coal, iron, gold, silver, copper, and lead. The Japanese had already invested millions of dollars in business projects in the region and controlled the South Manchurian Railway. The population, however, was almost entirely Chinese.

In September, 1931, an excuse for interference occurred when a portion of the South Manchurian Railway was blown up. Without warning, Japanese troops occupied a large area in Manchuria. China appealed to the League of Nations and the United States, but received no help.

The Chinese now made use of their only weapon of defense against their enemy, the

Scraps of Paper? · *Nations which relied too much upon treaty promises found themselves helpless to resist aggression. Why?*

boycott. As China usually took about one-fourth of Japan's exports, this was a serious blow to Japanese industry. In reply, the Japanese now landed troops in Shanghai. The Chinese stubbornly resisted the invaders, and finally an agreement was reached. China put an end to the boycott, and the Japanese withdrew their forces from Shanghai.

Manchukuo Becomes a Japanese Puppet State · In the meantime the Japanese had supported a revolution in Manchuria. In March, 1932, the country declared itself an independent state under the name of Manchukuo. The former Manchu boy-emperor of China, known as Pu-yi, was made head of the government, but the country was really a protectorate of Japan.

Two years later Pu-yi was recognized as ruler of Manchukuo by the Japanese, with the title Emperor Kang Teh. The Soviet Union accepted Japan's occupation of northern Manchuria and in March, 1935, sold its rights in the Chinese Eastern Railway to Manchukuo.

Japan Defies the League · The Western powers refused to recognize Japan's conquest. In reply to China's appeal, League committees studied the situation and made various proposals. Japan disregarded these, and gave notice that she would resign from the League. This caused many nations to lose faith in the power of the League and encouraged Italy and Germany to proceed with their military plans.

From this time on, Japan made it increasingly plain that she was determined to follow her own course in Asia. She ignored protests of the Western powers, which were alarmed at the threats to their business interests. The Western nations, as a result, suffered a loss of prestige in the East.

After the invasion of Manchuria moderate Japanese statesmen who opposed the policy of the extreme militarists tried unsuccessfully to regain control of the government. The program of the militarists was the further penetration of China, the expansion of the empire, and a fascist government at Tokyo. In 1936 Japan started on a large-scale rearmament program and signed the Anti-Comintern Pact with Germany.

Japan Makes War on China (1937–1945) · During 1935–1936 Japan brought increasing pressure to bear on China, with the purpose of securing control of her northern provinces. Some of these provinces were encouraged to break with Nanking and set up semi-independent governments under officials sympathetic to the Japanese.

The Growing Japanese Empire · Trace the steps by which Japan expanded beyond her home islands. How was each territory acquired? What does Japan control today?

THE EXPANSION OF JAPAN

Before December 7, 1941

Added after December 7, 1941 (With year of Japanese occupation)

A War Victim · *This now classic photograph shows a tiny baby, helpless in the ruins of Shanghai's South Station, which was bombed by the Japanese in September, 1937. Thousands of children were to suffer before peace came.*

Chiang Kai-shek, feeling unable to match his powerful enemy, yielded to Japan's demands. This stirred up a strong protest, especially among the student groups of China, which resented the general's policy of appeasement. In 1937, however, Japan began a determined drive on China, and the Chinese united under General Chiang's leadership to resist with all their strength.

There was heavy and stubborn fighting in Tientsin and Peiping. In August the Japanese blockaded the China coast. In December they took possession of Nanking, but the Chinese had already moved the government farther inland, to Chungking. In the same month the Japanese sank the United States gunboat *Panay* and tankers belonging to the Standard Oil Company. Several Americans were killed. The Japanese were forced to apologize and pay damages to the American government.

The Japanese captured one important Chinese city after another, and finally controlled the entire coastal region. Yet they were unable to break Chinese morale. Deep inland the Chinese continued to resist stubbornly. Only a few years later this conflict became part of a great world struggle.

CHECK ON YOUR READING

1. Describe the unsettled conditions in China following World War I. How did communism get a start there?
2. What progress was made under the leadership of Chiang Kai-shek?
3. What policies did the Japanese militarists follow from 1931 to 1937?
4. Identify the following: (a) Shantung, (b) Kuomintang, (c) Dr. Sun, (d) Chiang Kai-shek, (e) Nanking, (f) puppet state.

Think about the chapter

1. Is the Soviet government democratic? Explain your answer.

2. How were the Fascist and Nazi systems similar to Russian Communism? In what respects were they different?

3. Would it ever be possible for the United States to have a totalitarian system? Explain.

4. Winston Churchill called one of his books about this period *The Gathering Storm.* Show by listing the actions of Hitler, Mussolini, Stalin, Franco, and the Japanese militarists from 1931–1939 how the clouds of war were gathering.

5. *Map study:* On a map of Europe and North Africa shade the totalitarian countries. Shade or indicate by a symbol the areas taken over by Germany up to 1939; the territories gained by Mussolini.

6. *Map study:* On a map of Asia and the Pacific show the Japanese empire gained by treaty and conquest.

Go beyond the text

7. How does the U.S.S.R. stand today in industrial production compared with the United States, Britain, and West Germany?

8. How does education in totalitarian states differ from education in the United States?

9. Read about the Nazi book burnings. Why must every totalitarian state have a controlled (a) press? (b) church? (c) party system?

10. Spain was not admitted to the UN until 1956. Why was there such delay? Report on the relations between the democracies and Spain after World War II and today.

Follow up your special interests

11. Play the record "I Can Hear It Now," edited by Edward R. Murrow, which includes some of the speeches and events of the 1930's.

12. Life in the U.S.S.R. is illustrated in *A Picture History of Russia.* Study these pictures and, using an opaque projector, show them to the class.

13. Try to write a short story describing an episode in a totalitarian state.

READ FURTHER

Basic readings: (1) BECKER, *Modern History,* Chap. 23. (2) CARR, *Men of Power.* Mussolini, Stalin, Hitler, Franco. (3) CHEYNEY, *Short History of England,* Chap. 24. (4) HOFFMAN, *News of the World,* No. 50. (5) *Year's Pictorial History,* pp. 522–531, 552–555.

Special accounts: (6) W. CHURCHILL, *The Gathering Storm.* Chaps. 4, 6, and 8 describe the rise of Nazism and crises of the 1930's. (7) K. GOULD, *Windows on the World.* Chap. 16 is on communism; Chap. 17 on fascism. (8) J. GUNTHER, *Inside Europe.* Realistic treatment of Nazi methods and personalities. (9) R. KETCHUM, W. ANDERSON, R. TRAURIG (eds.), *What is Communism?* (10) W. LANGSAM, *The World since 1919,* Chap. 21. (11) J. MARTIN (ed.), *A Picture History of Russia.* Excellent material on affairs since 1917. (12) A. NEVINS, *The United States in a Chaotic World.* Chapter 6, "Japan Defies the World." (13) R. and E. PACKARD, *The Balcony Empire.* Fascist Italy from 1934 to World War II as seen by two American news correspondents. (14) W. SHIRER, *Berlin Diary.* A personalized account of events in Germany and Austria from 1934 to 1939 by a CBS man. (15) E. SEEGER, *The Pageant of Russian History.*

Fiction and biography: (16) I. COOK, *We Followed Our Stars.* Two English girls help many famous musicians escape from Nazi-dominated Austria and Germany. (17) G. ORWELL, *Animal Farm.* A satire on communism. (18) *1984* by the same author is a forecast of a totalitarian state. (19) N. WALN, *Reaching for the Stars.* Germany in the 1930's. (20) *The House of Exile* by the same author tells of life in China.

32

World War II

KEY WORDS AND DATES

Danzig	Lend-Lease
Polish Corridor	Roosevelt
Nazi-Soviet Pact	Atlantic Charter
1939	Pearl Harbor
blitzkrieg	United Nations
buffer zone	Montgomery
Maginot line	Eisenhower
"phony war"	D-Day
"Quislings"	Battle of the Bulge
Churchill	V-E Day
Dunkirk	MacArthur
Vichy	Potsdam
De Gaulle	Declaration
Battle of Britain	Hiroshima
arsenal of	V-J Day
democracy	1945

THE YEARS following the war "to make the world safe for democracy" found democracy in graver danger than before. The new crop of dictators openly defied the League of Nations by aggressive action. And the depression-weary democracies, craving peace and unprepared to take a firm stand, drifted along from crisis to crisis in a sea of indecision which led to the final appeasement at Munich.

Then came Hitler's annexation of Czechoslovakia, his pact with Stalin, and their invasion and partition of Poland. War had come. Denmark, Norway, the Netherlands, Belgium, and France fell in rapid succession. In less than a year Britain stood alone to meet and defeat the full fury of the German air power. Having lost the "Battle of Britain," Hitler suddenly turned on Russia (June, 1941). Six months later the Japanese struck at Pearl Harbor and brought the might of America into the conflict.

In the Declaration of the United Nations (January, 1942) twenty-six countries pledged their unity in a global war against the Axis powers. Within a year they turned the tide of battle with victories at Midway, Guadalcanal, North Africa, and Stalingrad. How the Allies, with the decisive advantage of the American "arsenal of democracy," finally crushed the Axis forces is the story of this chapter.

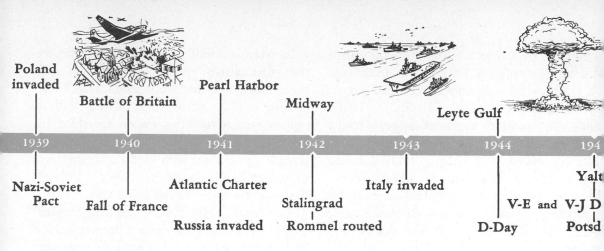

Poland invaded

Battle of Britain

Pearl Harbor

Midway

Leyte Gulf

| 1939 | 1940 | 1941 | 1942 | 1943 | 1944 | 194 |

Nazi-Soviet Pact

Fall of France

Atlantic Charter

Russia invaded

Stalingrad

Rommel routed

Italy invaded

D-Day

V-E and V-J D

Yalt

Potsd

1. The Failure of Appeasement

Some Causes of the War · We have already seen that after 1919 many forces were working to bring Europe again to the brink of war. (1) The former Allies continually quarreled among themselves. (2) The League of Nations, lacking powers to enforce what little authority it possessed, proved unable to fulfill the hopes of its founders. (3) A wave of disillusionment and pacifism weakened the democracies. They generally allowed their armed forces to become obsolete, and put their faith in conferences, anti-war pledges, arbitration, and nonaggression pacts to preserve the peace. (4) Aggressive militarists gained control of Germany, Italy, and Japan. They denounced the Treaty of Versailles and scorned the League of Nations as a device by which the "have" nations maintained their hold on the territory and resources of the world and excluded the "have nots." They brushed aside whatever treaties stood in their way and strove to establish a New Order which would create a Greater Germany, a Modern Roman Empire, and a "Greater East Asia Co-prosperity Sphere."

(5) Economic and financial breakdown followed World War I and led to worldwide depression. Instead of co-operating to find some general solution to the problem, each country went its own way.

(6) The dictators fought the depression by mobilizing their economies for total war. Their industries hummed as they accumulated the vast stockpiles of armaments essential to victory. Unemployment disappeared—and so did freedom of choice for their peoples.

(7) Propaganda strengthened the totalitarian powers and undermined the democracies. By clever use of such psychological devices as the big lie, rumors, and "scapegoating" they turned the hopes, fears, and prejudices of the masses into effective weapons for support of their tyranny.

Hitler's denunciation of the Versailles Treaty found a certain response with public opinion in the democracies. Many people felt that the peace treaty had in fact been an injustice, so they were not prepared to resist when Hitler started tearing it up.

(8) Aggressive moves by the dictators were aided by a policy of appeasement.

Effects of Hitler's War Preparations · We have seen that Hitler soon mobilized his country for war and created the Rome-Berlin-Tokyo Axis (pp. 561–562). Hitler made his warlike measures appear to be directed solely against communism. He thus deceived the Allies, whose ruling classes feared Marxism in all its forms. They overlooked the simple fact that his new planes, tanks, and mobile guns, while aimed at Russia, might eventually roll westward.

As a result of Hitler's warlike alliances, France found herself faced with unfriendly governments along the Rhine, the Alps, and the Pyrenees. England now had to worry about Axis fleets in the North Sea, the Mediterranean, and the Pacific. The rising tide of fascism had caused the Russians to join the League of Nations, make an alliance with France, and support the Spanish Loyalists. But they were suspicious of their allies and fearful of attack from both east and west.

Hitler Creates a Polish Crisis after Dismembering Czechoslovakia (1939) · The sacrifice of helpless Czechoslovakia at Munich (p. 563) was a "defeat without a war," as Churchill bitterly described it. Yet the desire for peace was so strong that Chamberlain was met with cheers as he returned to London declaring that he had brought "peace with honor" in agreements which would mean "peace for our time."

But in reality this tragic appeasement spelled disaster for the Allies. France stood isolated. Her security pacts with eastern European nations and Russia were now worthless. Italy even became bold enough to demand Savoy, Nice, Corsica, and Tunis. Hitler's bloodless victory had completely upset the balance of power in Europe.

In March, 1939, the Germans annexed the Lithuanian port of Memel and launched a furious propaganda attack on Poland. They demanded Danzig and a right-of-way across the Polish Corridor to German East Prussia. Greatly alarmed, Britain and France now pledged themselves to preserve Polish independence. Poland thereupon refused Hitler's demands.

The Nazi-Soviet Pact · The drift toward a general war was now unmistakable. Britain and France attempted to persuade Russia to join them. But the message of *Mein Kampf*, the open aim of the Anti-Comintern Pact, and above all the memory of Munich now conspired to convince Stalin that time must be bought to prepare for the inevitable conflict with Germany.

On August 23, 1939, the Soviets signed a nonaggression pact with Germany. Each pledged not to attack the other and to remain neutral in the event of a war with a third power. Attached to this pact was a secret agreement for partitions of Poland and eastern Europe into German and Soviet spheres of influence. This diplomatic revolution not only came as a shock to Britain and France but upset their entire strategy. They hated communism and all it stood for, yet they had counted upon the huge Russian armies to keep the Nazis busy in the east. Now freed from worry over possible Russian action, Hitler pressed his demands on Poland with renewed force.

The War Breaks · There was little hope of saving Poland. But Britain and France announced their full intention of aiding their ally in case of German aggression. Appeals to Hitler by Chamberlain, Daladier, Roosevelt, and others were of no avail. The Führer was determined to enlarge the Reich. He knew he had the advantage of trained manpower, a vast stockpile of modern arms,

and industry fully mobilized for war. These would insure quick victory. The democracies might bluster and bluff, but he was convinced that in the end they would recognize that he was the master of Europe.

And so on the morning of September 1, 1939, motorized Nazi troops supported by thousands of tanks and Stuka bombers swept without warning into Poland. The British and French kept their pledges to Poland by declaring war, and World War II was under way.

A Surprise Act · *Hitler, the boasted anti-Communist champion, and Stalin, the proclaimed foe of Nazism, reach agreement. Why? Why was the West stunned?*

CHECK ON YOUR READING

1. *Identify some of the underlying causes for the war.*
2. *How did each of the following contribute to the outbreak of World War II: (a) Munich? (b) the Polish crisis? (c) the Nazi-Soviet Pact?*
3. *What were Hitler's advantages when the war started?*

---

2. *Europe Falls under the Terror*

Blitzkrieg and Total War · The storm of fire which consumed the Polish republic was a lightning war, or *blitzkrieg*. There was no "front" as such. The battle raged everywhere. Armored tanks raced through open country, flowed around areas of resistance, and enveloped and destroyed the Polish armies in huge pincer movements. Nazi troopers parachuted from planes to seize strategic points, disrupt communications, and paralyze transportation. Pro-Nazi Poles sabotaged key facilities and spread panic from within. Clearly the Germans had developed new military tactics, for which their enemies were unprepared.

Meanwhile the German *Luftwaffe* rained ceaseless death and destruction from the Polish skies. Bombers blasted bridges and schools, factories and hospitals, rail centers and churches, troop concentrations, and roads choked with fleeing women and children. In Hitler's concept of total war such mechanized terror was calculated to break the people's will to resist.

Hitler and Stalin Partition Poland · On September 17, the Russians drove in from the east to occupy the portion of eastern Poland promised by the secret agreement with Hitler. Crushed between the mechanized might of two totalitarian powers, the Polish forces laid down their

The Meaning of the Blitzkrieg · *Right: This new warfare brought sudden terror from the skies as wave after wave of invaders dropped to earth in undefended areas. Above: A Nazi motorcycle unit followed by trucks and tanks races grimly into a Polish village. Hitler counted on speed and unconventional tactics to carry all before him. Was he correct?*

arms. Warsaw alone continued its heroic resistance until September 27. Hitler and Stalin then divided the country between them. Thousands of Poles were driven from their homes and robbed of their property. Many were sent to concentration camps or gas chambers in Germany or deported to forced-labor camps in Russia. And to forestall future anti-communist revolts, Stalin ordered the execution of thousands of captured Polish officers.

Stalin Invades the Baltic States, Finland, and Bessarabia · While Hitler consolidated his gains in western Poland, Stalin forced Lithuania, Latvia, and Estonia to grant him strategic air, land, and naval bases and to accept Russian "protection." In less than a year the three states became part of the Soviet Union.

Having moved his defense lines to the Baltic, Stalin now determined to protect the approaches to Leningrad. From Finland he demanded parts of the Karelian Isthmus, where the frontier in places was only about twenty miles from Leningrad. He also demanded territory in the Arctic and a lease of the Hangö peninsula, which commanded the Gulf of Finland. The Finns were ready to make some concessions but not those deemed vital by Russia. On November 30, Russian troops invaded Finland.

The spectacle of a tiny nation of four million people attacked by a great country of 190 millions aroused the anger of the world. The League of Nations condemned Russia as an aggressor and expelled her from membership. Money, medical aid, and supplies were sent to Finland, but no military help could reach her across neutral Norway and Sweden. For three months the little republic carried on her unequal fight alone, but in the end had to yield. On March 12, 1940, a treaty was signed by which Finland lost vital strategic areas.

Four months later (June 26, 1940) Stalin took advantage of Hitler's concentration on the western front to seize the strategic Rumanian provinces of Bessarabia and northern Bukovina. In nine months he had seized most of the territory taken from Russia after World War I. He now had a protective buffer zone reaching from Finland, through the Baltic states, eastern Poland, and Bessarabia, to the Black Sea. It would cushion the shock of the Nazi attack should one come.

There still remained the question of how to prevent invasion from the east. Russia solved this in April, 1941, by signing a non-aggression pact with Japan. In the short space of less than two years three dictators had insured themselves against the danger of two-front wars by nonaggression pacts. Such pacts proved to be very temporary, as we shall see. But, for the moment, Japan was given a free hand in Asia, Russia was free to prepare for the Nazis, and Germany was free to turn against the West.

The "War of Nerves" on Land and Sea · It had been expected that Hitler, after his victory in Poland, would at once launch a great assault in the west. But the blow did not come. The French waited behind their fortified Maginot line. The British moved their army into France. London sent its children to rural areas. The capitals of both countries were blacked out for safety. But no bombs fell.

This curious period of inactivity came to be known as the "war of nerves." It was part of Hitler's strategy to keep his opponents wondering where he would strike next. On the sea the terror came from the prowling submarines which struck without warning at any ship afloat. In addition Nazi planes dropped magnetic mines by the thousands in and around Allied rivers, harbors, and channels. Hitler thus hoped to cut Britain's supply lines and to convince neutrals of the hopelessness of the Allied cause.

But this lull, which journalists labeled the "phony war," was as deceptive as it was temporary. For during these six months Hitler was marshalling his forces for the surprise blows which were calculated to bring total victory.

Hitler Conquers Denmark and Norway · On April 9, 1940, the gigantic German offensive began. Fifty thousand troops moved into Denmark, announcing that they had come to "protect" the people from the Allies. To avoid useless bloodshed, King Christian accepted the Nazi occupation under protest.

At the same time German warships steamed into six Norwegian ports. Nazi troops, concealed in merchant ships lying in the harbors, were already awaiting them. Their task was made easy by a subversive group of Norwegian Nazis who betrayed their country. They came to be called "Quislings" after the name of their leader, Vidkun Quisling, who later made himself dictator.

After a brief and bitter struggle the Norwegian armies surrendered (June 9, 1940). King Haakon and his ministry fled to London, where they established a government-in-exile.

The conquest of Norway and Denmark gave Germany a thousand-mile seacoast. She now had harbors and bases for her

V for Victory · *When Britain stood alone with her back to the wall, Prime Minister Winston Churchill symbolized the British will to victory. His victory greeting became famous throughout the world. Churchill proved to be a great orator and one of the inspired leaders of modern times.*

submarines and airplanes within easy striking distance of England. She had gained fresh stocks of food and supplies and at the same time deprived Britain of Danish butter, eggs, and bacon. Fortunately for the Allies, most of the Norwegian and Danish merchant ships escaped capture and played an important role in helping win the "battle of supply."

Churchill Becomes Prime Minister · On May 10, 1940, Winston Churchill became prime minister of England. He was a man of insight, action, and magnificent courage. For years he had been urging Britain to arm herself for the struggle against Nazi Germany. As he took up his heavy task Churchill said:

I have nothing to offer but blood, tears, toil and sweat. . . . You ask what is our policy? I will say: It is to wage war . . . with all the strength that God can give us . . . against a monstrous tyranny never surpassed in the dark, lamentable catalogue of human crime . . . You

ask what is our aim? I can say one word. Victory—victory at all costs, victory in spite of terror, victory however long and hard the road may be, for without victory there is no survival.

Britain needed Churchill's strength, bulldog tenacity, and dynamic leadership. For on the day that he became prime minister, Hitler invaded the Low Countries.

Rapid Conquest of Holland and Belgium · The lightning techniques employed against Poland and Norway were just as successful in Holland. The overwhelming weight of tanks, planes, heavy guns, motorized infantry, and paratroops crushed the country. Queen Wilhelmina and the royal family escaped to England, and on May 17 Holland came under the Nazi heel.

In the meantime the Germans had overrun Luxembourg and had swept through Belgium. Paratroopers took the "impregnable" fortress of Eben Emael by landing on its vast roof. This enabled them to encircle Liége and outflank the defenses along the Albert Canal.

King Leopold appealed to the Allies for aid, and French troops were shifted from a crucial sector of their line to help the hard-pressed Belgians. This move proved fatal, for the Germans thereupon drove through the weakened line and separated the armies in eastern France from the Allied forces in Belgium. As one vast wing swept northward to seize the Channel ports, other Nazi divisions pressed the Belgians back toward Ostend. Fearing that his armies faced destruction, King Leopold suddenly, and against the advice of his ministers, surrendered unconditionally to the Germans (May 28, 1940).

The Miracle of Dunkirk · The collapse of the Belgians appeared to seal the fate of the Allied armies. It exposed their whole left flank and line of retreat. The port of Dunkirk remained the only way of escape. If it could not be reached in time, the entire British army would be lost.

With unbelievable courage the Allies worked their way toward this port. A terrible struggle followed as the Royal Air Force wrested control of the skies over Dunkirk and the army fought a desperate rear guard action. Meanwhile the British navy, supplemented by private craft of all sorts, undertook a dramatic rescue by ferrying the troops across the channel. That 335,000 British and French soldiers were snatched from the flaming beaches was, as Churchill said, "a miracle of deliverance."

The Fall of France · The Nazis now began a gigantic drive against the French. Within five days they were threatening Paris. Mussolini, wishing to share the spoils of victory, struck at France and occupied a few square miles on her southeastern border (June 10, 1940). As the Germans swung eastward to outflank the Maginot line, the disorganized French armies fell back toward the Loire River.

Encouraged by Churchill's offer of British-French union with a common citizenship, Premier Reynaud favored carrying on the struggle with the aid of the French fleet and the Empire, even if it meant retreat to North Africa. But Marshal Pétain, Pierre Laval, and others favored surrender. Pétain became premier and immediately sued for peace. An armistice was signed on June 25 in the same railway car in which the German armistice had been signed in 1918.

De Gaulle versus Hitler · *Hitler danced for glee when France surrendered. Swastikas appeared beside the Eiffel Tower, landmark of Paris. Yet General de Gaulle never lost hope of ultimate victory. His resistance abroad encouraged resistance at home. He symbolized French liberty.*

The fall of France marked the end of the Third Republic (1870–1940). Northern and western France was occupied by the Nazis. At Vichy, Pétain set up an authoritarian government for unoccupied France. It was, however, only a puppet state.

The Free French versus Vichy · But thousands of patriots within France refused to surrender. They formed a secret underground resistance movement. Armed with weapons stolen from the Nazis or later dropped by Allied planes, the French Forces of the Interior (F.F.I.) sabotaged German supplies, helped Allied prisoners and fliers to escape, gave information to Allied agents, and prepared for the day of liberation.

From abroad French patriots also continued the resistance. Leader of the National Committee of Free French was General Charles de Gaulle. From headquarters in London he called upon Frenchmen throughout the Empire to continue to fight. He thus provided a cause around which the forces of freedom might rally. French Equatorial Africa supported General de Gaulle, units of the fleet came over, and thousands of men joined the army in exile. Great Britain backed de Gaulle's government-in-exile and broke off relations with Pétain's régime.

Britain Stands Alone · With the French surrender, Britain stood alone. Churchill stated the vital issue in his speech to the House of Commons:

The whole fury and might of the enemy must very soon be turned on us. Hitler knows that he will have to break us in this island or lose the war. If we can stand up to him, all Europe may be free. . . . But if we fail, then the whole world . . . will sink into the abyss of a new Dark Age.

Always Britain had been saved by her protecting waters. King Philip of Spain and later Napoleon had learned this to their sorrow. Were the Channel and the fleet sufficient to save her now? Bombers could destroy her cities. Airborne troops could drop on her shores. Submarines could cripple her navy. Her army had lost most of its equipment at Dunkirk. The prospect was dark indeed.

Yet in the face of this mortal danger Churchill expressed the firm resolution of the British people with a defiant growl:

We shall defend our Island, whatever the cost may be. We shall fight on the beaches, we shall fight on the landing grounds, we shall fight in the fields and in the streets, we shall fight in the hills; we shall never surrender . . .

"Operation Sea Lion" · But Hitler was not prepared to cross the Channel. He had not thought invasion necessary. With the fall of France he had expected the British to quit. Their stubborn defense enraged him. Now he lacked a plan, the necessary landing craft, control of the Channel, and command of the skies.

Precious days of June and July slipped by as Hitler consolidated his gains and prepared plans for "Operation Sea Lion." Under it (1) the German navy proposed to lay two huge mine fields across the Channel with a narrow invasion corridor between. (2) Giant batteries of long-range coastal artillery and big guns taken from the Maginot line would bombard the British fleet as well as defenses on the opposite shore. (3) The *Luftwaffe* would destroy the British fleet in the narrow waters of the Channel and provide the air cover essential to the crossing. (4) Thousands of small landing craft would then transport the German troops and tanks to certain victory.

It was obvious to the Nazi High Command, however, that the success of this great operation depended upon the *Luftwaffe's* destroying the Royal Air Force. Otherwise the British fleet under fighter cover would wipe out the entire invasion force. Air Marshal Göring assured Hitler that complete control of the skies would be his within a month, and the day of attack was tentatively set for late August.

The Battle of Britain · On August 8, 1940, the *Luftwaffe* launched its great air offensive with mass raids on British airfields and vital aircraft industries. Wave after wave of bombers came over daily. With the aid of secret radar, however, the British outmaneuvered and outfought them. Though small in number, the R.A.F. pilots used their local bases, speedier planes, su-

perior tactics, and inspired courage to full advantage. Pausing only for refueling and fresh ammunition, they frequently flew four sorties a day. Many an ace who parachuted to safety rose to fight again. "Never in the field of human endeavor," said Churchill, "was so much owed by so many to so few."

Enraged by his losses in pilots and planes, and infuriated by a defiant air raid on his own capital, Hitler made a strategic error. He turned from the destruction of the R.A.F. to the destruction of British cities. All major English cities were soon subjected to the terror of fire bombs and "blockbusters" with delayed fuses. Thousands of civilians were killed or wounded, and large areas were laid waste. Throughout this two-month ordeal the people were under a constant strain from lack of sleep and from the interruption of their work,

The Dictators Dominate Europe · Locate places mentioned in text (use inset map). Note how close the Axis came to victory. What stood between them and complete success at this period? How did Russia advance her interests?

Albert Canal
Fortress of Eben Emael

WAR IN EUROPE TO JUNE, 1941
Axis-controlled lands before June, 1941
Main Nazi drives, 1939-1941
Main Russian drives before June, 1941
(Pre-war boundaries are used)

London Withstands the Blitz · *Blocks of London were reduced to rubble by bombardment. Yet the Dome of St. Paul's stood firm while fire raged—a symbol of the unconquerable spirit of Britain.*

but their morale remained high. By the end of the year the R.A.F. was stronger than when the Battle of Britain began, and hope of successful invasion was gone forever.

A New Order and a New Strategy · The three Axis powers were so certain of final victory that in the midst of the Battle of Britain (September 27, 1940) they concluded a ten-year military and economic alliance known as the *Pact of Berlin*. They pledged themselves to establish a New Order in Europe under the leadership of Germany and Italy, and a New Order in Asia under Japan. And they openly speculated over how they would divide the riches of the British Empire.

But Britain's refusal to accept defeat destroyed Hitler's hopes for a speedy victory and forced a shift in strategy. He was still confident that his air-sea blockade would eventually starve the British into submission. (Indeed, Churchill later admitted, ". . . the only thing that ever really frightened me during the war was the U-boat peril.")

An economic war would take time, however, and meanwhile Axis Europe itself was in the vise of a British blockade. For the long pull ahead Germany would need greater supplies of food, raw materials, and above all oil. And should the United States come to the aid of Britain, the wealth of all Europe would not be too much.

Rich sources of supply were available in three places: (1) the Balkans, (2) European Russia, and (3) the British Empire. The seizure of the first would speed conquest of the second and both would provide stepping stones to the third. On December 18, 1940, Hitler issued his Secret Directive Number 21, *Operation Barbarossa*, a plan to crush Russia in a lightning campaign the following summer. Meanwhile he turned southward to bring the Balkans under his control, smash British power in the eastern Mediterranean, and cut Stalin's lifeline to the west.

The Nazis Overrun the Balkans · We have seen (p. 575) how Stalin took advantage of Hitler's concentration on France and Britain in June, 1940, to seize the former Russian provinces of Bessarabia and Bukovina from Rumania in the east. Berlin and Rome responded by pressing Rumania to make similar territorial transfers to Hungary and to Bulgaria. Then, to secure the vital Rumanian oil fields and to forestall further Russian moves, German troops took over the rest of Rumania (October, 1940). In November Hungary joined the Axis.

Hoping to gain his share of the Balkan spoils, Mussolini thereupon launched an invasion of Greece from Albania. But he failed dismally. In December the Greeks broke through the Italian lines and were only prevented from overrunning Albania by the prompt dispatch of German troops.

Mussolini's invasion of Egypt also failed. British forces in Africa drove back the Italian armies. Ethiopia was recovered, and Haile Selassie returned to the throne. Again Hitler found it necessary to save his Italian partner. Nazi troops under General Rommel were rushed to North Africa to hold Libya and to threaten Egypt and the Suez Canal.

Bulgaria joined the Axis in March, 1941, and Nazi troops occupied Sofia. In April the Germans invaded and occupied Yugoslavia. Athens was occupied on April 27 and Crete was taken from the British in a tremendous paratroop invasion in late May.

The conquest of the Balkans was complete. British power in the eastern Mediterranean was crippled. Russia's outlet to the Aegean was sealed. The German armies were poised to strike eastward in a vast arc from Finland in the north to Bulgaria on the Black Sea. The time for "Operation Barbarossa" was at hand.

The Nazis Invade Russia · On June 22, 1941 (the 129th anniversary of Napoleon's invasion of Russia) the Nazis launched a surprise offensive along the whole Russian front. The plan was to crush the Communist armies in a quick campaign, seize the bases of the Baltic and Black Sea fleets, and establish a line reaching from the White Sea to the Caspian. With the wheat and sugar of the Ukraine, the oil of the Caucasus, and the removal of any threat from the east, Hitler might with greater confidence survive the British blockade or turn to the destruction of Britain.

Initial Nazi successes were staggering. The Baltic provinces were overrun within a week, and Leningrad came under siege. By late October the industries and agricultural resources of the Ukraine were in Nazi hands. By early December the mechanized Nazi columns in the center had reached the outskirts of Moscow. Hitler announced that the doom of the Soviet Union was at hand.

But he spoke too soon. Four tremendous forces soon combined to destroy him. They were (1) the Russian winter, (2) Russian reserves, (3) American aid, and (4) his own weaknesses.

The Russian winter of 1941-42 came unusually early and was the coldest in twenty years. Temperatures fell as low as 60°

General Winter Aids the Russians · *Sinking into the snow on the fields near Moscow, German troops begin to retreat. What other invasion did the Russian winter check?*

below zero, freezing the unprepared Nazis in their tracks. Meanwhile hordes of hardy Siberian troops descended upon the blizzard-bound invaders. An amazing weight of men and equipment poured westward from the new industrial cities of the Trans-Ural region. The Germans were forced to retreat.

With the coming of spring the Nazis struck again. For a while they were victorious (p. 587). But when they attempted to gain control of Stalingrad, a vital industrial and railroad center, they began to lose in the struggle. By this time America had entered the war. American supplies helped the Russian armies to stop the German drive at Stalingrad (p. 588). The legend

that the German armies were invincible began to crumble.

Hitler's own weaknesses contributed greatly to his downfall. He misjudged the British after Dunkirk. He likewise failed to understand the peoples he conquered in Russia. Indeed, millions of Ukrainians hailed the German soldiers as liberators. Had Hitler recognized their aspirations for independence, he might well have destroyed the Soviet Union. Instead the conquered peoples were treated so brutally that they resorted to guerrilla warfare and sabotage on a huge scale.

The Führer's early military successes gave him delusions of grandeur. Advice and criticism enraged him. He dismissed or overruled generals who advised caution. Nazi armies were sacrificed in consequence.

Far from being a prelude to victory then, the attack on Russia sealed the fate of the Axis powers. Meanwhile the Japanese at Pearl Harbor were arousing the industrial giant whose strength ensured eventual victory for the Allies.

CHECK ON YOUR READING

1. *How did Stalin aid Hitler?*
2. *Which countries fell under the Soviet terror before June, 1941?*
3. *Outline Hitler's conquests: (a) order of occurrence, (b) location, (c) why undertaken, (d) why successful.*
4. *Explain these terms: (a) blitzkrieg, (b) total war, (c) buffer zone, (d) "Quislings," (e) miracle of Dunkirk, (f) Vichy French, (g) Free French, (h) Operation Sea Lion, (i) R.A.F., (j) Pact of Berlin, (k) Operation Barbarossa.*
5. *Why did Hitler fail (a) at Dunkirk? (b) in the Battle of Britain? (c) to conquer Russia?.*

3. The Global War

The Arsenal of Democracy · When the war opened in 1939 American sentiment favored strict neutrality. Many people believed that Britain and France could hold their own against Germany and that America was in no danger. At first an embargo was placed on the sale of arms to all belligerants. But in November, 1939, Congress set up a "cash and carry" plan which permitted purchases of war materials for cash, if they were carried in the ships of the country which bought them. Since Nazi vessels could not pass the British blockade, this amounted to exclusive aid to the Allies.

It was not until France had fallen that the American public realized what it would mean if Britain went under and the Nazis won control of the Atlantic. The program of the United States, therefore, was to build up its military resources, secure the co-operation of the other American republics in a plan of hemisphere defense, and give all possible help to Britain.

When the British army lost most of its equipment at Dunkirk, President Roosevelt rushed emergency arms from American reserve supplies. A few months later he transferred fifty reconditioned American destroyers to the British navy. In return, Britain gave the United States a ninety-nine-year lease on seven bases in the Caribbean to protect approaches to the Panama Canal, and an eighth base in Newfoundland.

"We must be the great arsenal of democracy," President Roosevelt warned the American people. On March 7, 1941, Congress passed the historic Lend-Lease Act. It empowered the President to lend, lease, or transfer war materials to any country whose security was vital to that of the United States. It threw the entire weight of American economic resources on the side of the Allies and thus insured eventual victory.

The Atlantic Charter · But it was one thing to vote Lend-Lease and quite another to deliver the goods. Allied and neutral shipping losses from German submarine action were heavy.

To ensure even closer harmony of policy, Winston Churchill secretly conferred with President Roosevelt on a warship off the coast of Newfoundland. On August 14, 1941, they issued a joint statement setting forth the ideals for which they strove. The Atlantic Charter, as it came to be called,

The President and the Prime Minister Meet in the North Atlantic · *Roosevelt and Churchill attend a religious service during their Atlantic Charter meeting.*

declared (1) that Great Britain and the United States sought no territorial gains. (2) They would try to secure for all nations equal access to the trade and raw materials of the world. (3) They respected the right of all people to choose their own form of government. (4) They sought a peace with justice and relief from the crushing burden of armaments. (5) They would strive for a world in which "all the men in all the lands may live out their lives in freedom from fear and want."

These sentiments lifted the hopes of oppressed peoples everywhere and encouraged those desperately fighting for freedom.

Japanese Aggression in Asia · While attention was focused upon the Nazi danger in Europe, however, another storm was brewing in the Far East.

We have seen that ever since World War I Japan had been steadily advancing in the Pacific (p. 566). She had been given mandates on the former German islands and had secretly proceeded to build up formidable air and sea bases throughout the Pacific area. In 1931 she occupied Manchuria and since 1937 had been busy carving up China.

Hitler's victories had been hailed with delight by his Axis partner in Asia. The plight of France, the Netherlands, Britain, and Russia made it possible for Japan to have a freer hand in the Far East. Her leaders openly proclaimed a New Order in Greater East Asia. This was to include Japan, Manchuria, China, Indochina, Thailand, Burma, and the East Indies.

When France fell, Japan pressed the Vichy government to grant her the right to station troops in Indochina. She blockaded the British and French possessions in Tientsin, occupied the mainland opposite Hong Kong, and demanded that Britain cease shipments to China through Hong Kong and Burma. Hitler's conquest of the Netherlands left the vast resources of the Dutch East Indies open to invasion. And Britain's battle for survival prevented defense of the English rubber plantations and tin mines of Malaya. By 1941 only the United States stood in Japan's way, and she was heavily committed to defense of her Atlantic frontier.

Japan's Relations with the United States · The United States refused to accept any of Japan's conquests as legal. But American public opinion would not approve of war with Japan, and the government was forced to resort to verbal protests, "moral embargoes," and economic pressures. When Japanese planes bombed Chinese civilians, the State Department advised aviation companies not to sell planes and parts to Japan. And when the destruction of lives and property continued, the government canceled its trade treaty. Finally it placed an embargo on the sale of aviation oil, machine tools, and steel scrap to Japan.

The Japanese insisted that the United States stop all aid to Chiang Kai-shek. They then sent troops into Indochina and established new air bases there. This was a direct threat to the Indies, the Philippines, and Malaya. When Japan refused to withdraw, an embargo was placed on exports of petroleum (July 26, 1941).

Each side now recognized that war between them was inevitable unless the other backed down. Oil was essential to the Japanese war machine. Denied by the West, it could be obtained only by seizure of the Netherlands East Indies, which the West was pledged to protect. According to the new Japanese foreign minister, Shigenori Togo: "The growth of a spirit of bravado, of seizing this 'opportunity of a thousand years' for the glorification of Japan, without shrinking from a war against Britain and America, could be observed throughout the country." The Japanese army was proud of its mechanized strength and the Japanese navy "believed itself invincible."

Hence on September 6, 1941, the Emperor and his advisers secretly decided to (1) go ahead with preparations to carry out the action against the East Indies "with the determination not to decline war" with the United States, Britain, and the Netherlands. (2) In the meantime Japan should "endeavor to exhaust diplomatic measures to attain her demands." (3) "Diplomacy was to have primary emphasis . . . during the month of September, with war preparations foremost . . . after early October."

The United States welcomed new negotiations, which would likewise give it time to prepare. But the American people were in no mood to tolerate further appeasement. Indeed the Gallup Poll of September, 1941, revealed that 70 per cent of the people favored stopping further Japanese expansion even at the risk of war. Japan's military and naval power was grossly underestimated, however. The feeling was widespread that "they won't *dare* attack us."

"Day of Infamy" (December 7, 1941) · In late November negotiations with Tokyo reached a deadlock. Intelligence reports

Destruction at Pearl Harbor · *In the Japanese surprise attack of December 7, 1941, nineteen ships were sunk or disabled including the battleships* Arizona, California, *and* Utah. *One hundred and twenty planes were destroyed on the ground. Over 2400 men and officers were lost. This was the most terrible military disaster the United States ever suffered.*

indicated Japanese intentions to attack "the Philippines, Thai or Kra peninsula, or possibly Borneo," and American commanders in Hawaii, the Philippines, and other Pacific outposts were warned to be on the alert. A huge American battle fleet of 96 ships was gathered at the great naval base at Pearl Harbor, Hawaii.

The point proclaimed on the cover of the Army-Navy football game program of November 29, 1941, was obvious: ". . . despite the claims of air enthusiasts no battleship has yet been sunk by bombs." The chances of a surprise attack, said the naval operations officer at Pearl Harbor, were exactly "None."

The Japanese thought differently. Ten months before, Admiral Yamamoto had remarked to an associate, "If we are to have war with America, we will have no hope of winning unless the U.S. fleet in Hawaiian waters can be destroyed." In deepest secrecy plans were drawn for a surprise raid on Pearl Harbor. Sunday, December 7, was chosen as the date providing "the best

chance to catch the ships in port and the men off duty."

While Oahu lay under the "hypnosis of peace," waves of torpedo, dive, and high-level bombers from six Japanese aircraft carriers swooped down upon Pearl Harbor with devastating effect. Surprise was complete. It was a "major military disaster" for the United States.

Paralyzing surprise attacks were likewise made on American bases in the Philippines, Wake, and Guam, and on British forces in Hong Kong and Malaya. Thus, within a matter of hours, Japan had achieved air and naval supremacy in the Pacific.

The United Nations · The United States and Britain responded with declarations of war on Japan, December 8, 1941. Germany and Italy declared war on the United States three days later. By January 1, 1942, twenty-six nations were at war with the Axis powers. Meeting in Washington their representatives pledged support of the Atlantic Charter. The members of the United Nations, as they called themselves, promised full military aid against the Axis and agreed never to make a separate peace.

The Axis powers now faced a mighty coalition. One of its strengths lay in the policy of joint planning in the conduct of the war. Even before the United States entered the war, Roosevelt had been consulting with Churchill. Now the heads of the principal powers in the United Nations met in conferences from time to time to iron out difficulties and decide strategy.

At Casablanca, in January, 1943, Roosevelt and Churchill, with General de Gaulle representing the Free French, made plans for the invasion of Europe. Towards the end of the year Churchill and Roosevelt met with Chiang Kai-shek in Cairo and with Stalin at Tehran. The Big Three

Stalin, Roosevelt, and Churchill at Tehran, Iran (1943) · *The Big Three discussed war strategy. Stalin was informed of the decision to invade France in the spring.*

conferences at Yalta and Potsdam in 1945 were particularly important (pp. 595, 607).

As we shall see, such conferences continued into the postwar period. The Axis powers, on the other hand, never developed such a system of co-operation.

Japan's Rapid Conquests · In the six months following Pearl Harbor, the Japanese piled victory upon victory. There were several reasons for such success. (1) Japan controlled the air and seas in the far Pacific. (2) As the aggressor she had the advantages of surprise and concentration of forces. (3) She had stockpiled the equipment and mastered the special techniques required for amphibious and jungle warfare. (4) Her network of island bases cut the American lines of communication to the Far East. (5) Most important of all, the United Nations were busy elsewhere. They decided to concentrate their major effort against Nazi Germany, the greater danger, first.

Despite heroic defense against insuperable odds, therefore, Wake, Guam, Hong Kong, Singapore, Bataan, Corregidor, the Philippines, Malaya, Thailand, Burma, and the Dutch East Indies fell in rapid succession (see map, p. 594). By late April, 1942, the Japanese had established bases on New Guinea and the Solomons and were threatening Australia. The outlook for the Allies in the Pacific was dark indeed.

New Nazi Offensives · The dark cloud of defeat and retreat also hung over North Africa, southern Russia, and the western Atlantic. (1) In June, 1942, General Rommel (the "Desert Fox") recaptured Tobruk from the British in a victorious drive across Libya. His forces swept on to El Alamein, only 70 miles from Alexandria. Control of Egypt and the Suez appeared within his grasp. (See map, p. 591.)

(2) In July the Russian strongholds of Sevastopol (in the Crimea) and Rostov (on the Don) fell to the Nazis. And by September they had overrun the area north of the Caucasus and were fighting from house to house for control of the vital city of Stalingrad on the Volga.

(3) Meanwhile the U-boat wolf-packs were sinking millions of tons of Allied shipping in the western Atlantic.

The End of the Beginning · But the Axis position was not so strong as it seemed. The Axis powers had paid heavily in men and material and seriously over-extended their lines. Now the Allied armies, reinforced with superior weapons from the "arsenal of democracy," struck back with deadly effect. Five examples well illustrate the dramatic turn of the tide.

(1) In early May, 1942, Japanese drives toward Australia were turned back in the naval and air battles of the Coral Sea. Between June 3 and 6, a huge Japanese naval squadron attempted an invasion of Midway Island. American carrier planes intercepted the attack, sank four carriers, and destroyed the best units in Japanese naval aviation. The balance of naval power was now restored in the Pacific and the threat to Hawaii and the West Coast of the United States was removed. In August, 1942, American marines captured the Japanese airfield on Guadalcanal in the Solomons, and after six months of very bitter fighting in the area built a base for a great counteroffensive in the Pacific.

(2) In early November the British Eighth Army under General Montgomery drove Rommel's *Afrika Korps* out of Egypt and chased it across North Africa. Meanwhile Anglo-American forces under General Dwight D. Eisenhower captured French Morocco and Algiers. When the Germans

The Tide Turns · *Above left: In the battle for Midway American pilots shoot down most of the attacking Japanese planes. Below: Allied tanks drive against the enemy in North Africa. Above: Russian assault troops, fighting through the rubble of Stalingrad tighten the ring about the Nazis.*

responded by taking over unoccupied France, the crews of the French fleet at Toulon scuttled their ships.

(3) On November 19, 1942, powerful Russian reserves swept down from the hills to forge an iron ring around the German Sixth Army besieging Stalingrad. Twenty-two Nazi divisions were caught in the trap. Further west the Russians forced the Germans to retreat and recaptured Leningrad.

(4) By the end of 1942 production of shipping in British and American yards was exceeding the tonnage lost to submarines. Moreover, the use of radar and sonar and an improved convoy system were thwarting the submarine strategy. The Allies were prepared to win command of the Atlantic.

(5) Increased control of the air by the Allies made ultimate victory certain. Al-

lied bombers were systematically destroying German war industries, railways, power plants, and refineries. Thus the year 1942, which had started with bitter defeats, closed with brighter prospects everywhere.

CHECK ON YOUR READING

1. *What were the provisions of the (a) Lend-Lease Act, (b) Atlantic Charter?*
2. *Explain these terms: (a) global war, (b) arsenal of democracy, (c) Day of Infamy, (d) United Nations, (e) war conferences.*
3. *Summarize (a) Japanese aggression in Asia, (b) Japanese-American relations before Pearl Harbor.*
4. *How do you account for the (a) early Japanese successes? (b) three new Nazi offensives? (c) "end of the beginning"?*

4. The Liberation of Europe

The Invasion of Italy · The hard-pressed Russians were calling now for a second front in Europe. The Allies responded with the invasion of Italy.

Such an invasion, however, depended on control of North Africa and the Mediterranean. In early 1943 Rommel's forces, pressed from the east by Montgomery and from the west by Eisenhower, were driven out of Tunisia. By May, North Africa was in the hands of the Allies.

From North Africa the victorious Allies launched a successful invasion of Sicily. As a result Mussolini was blamed for Italy's losses and removed from office by the Fascist Grand Council. His successor, Marshal Badoglio, surrendered unconditionally on September 8, and Allied forces landed in the South. Some months later the new Italian government was accepted as a co-belligerent in the war with Germany.

But the Germans in Italy were not ready to surrender. They rescued Mussolini and seized all major Italian cities. For the next year and a half they fiercely contested every inch of Italian soil.

It was not until late April, 1945, after a bitter struggle in which many lives were lost, that the Germans were driven out. Mussolini was captured and shot by anti-fascist guerrillas while attempting to escape to Switzerland.

Prelude to Invasion · Essential to the opening of a second front in France was the destruction of the German air force. To accomplish this the Allies launched a tremendous air offensive in the early spring of 1944. Day and night the vital German centers of aircraft production were bombed into rubble.

Special attention was paid to the Nazi chain of defenses, airports, hangars, and

Supplies Pour Ashore for the Invasion of France · *After D-Day (p. 590)* the *Normandy coast was crowded with reinforcements and supplies. Note the balloon barrages floating overhead to protect the ships from enemy strafers.*

ammunition dumps on the channel coast of France. In addition, the highways, bridges, and railroads within a hundred miles of the coast from Cologne to Spain were put out of commission.

In a last desperate attempt to stave off defeat, Hitler hurled at Britain the "secret weapon" which he had been promising the German people. The jet-propelled V-1 flying bombs and the V-2 rockets which began to drop from the skies over England did much damage, but they did not save Germany.

The time had now come for the invasion of France. Allied forces in England had been preparing for this moment for several months. Over-all command of the operation was in the hands of General Eisenhower. During the night of June 5, 1944, a large paratroop division dropped silently behind the Atlantic Wall to surprise sentries, capture vital points, and be ready to aid assault troops who would land at dawn.

"D-Day" and After · As dawn broke on the sixth of June, 1944 (D-Day), American, British, and Canadian forces under cover of thousands of planes landed on the beaches of Normandy. No other expedition in history equaled it in the difficulty of the task, the size of the forces involved, or the importance of the object at stake.

Within a week the Allies had established a beachhead sixty miles long and ten miles deep between Cherbourg and Le Havre. The Americans under General Bradley were on the right, with the British and Canadians under General Montgomery anchoring the left of the line. Capture of Cherbourg provided a major port of entry and the seizure of Caen gave the Allies a vital railway junction.

The Liberation of France and Belgium · By mid-July Allied armored units had broken through the German lines and were racing forward. As the shattered divisions of the *Wehrmacht* retreated across northern France, a new invasion army landed in southern France (August 16, 1944). The French underground now rose against the retreating Nazis. Paris was liberated on August 28, with General de Gaulle receiving great acclaim. By the end of September France and Belgium were free.

Germany Loses Her Satellites · Meanwhile the Allied successes in the West were matched by equally great gains in the East. While the Battle of Normandy was in progress, the Red armies were driving the Nazis out of Russia and pursuing them in full retreat along the old route taken by Napoleon. By August their columns were invading East Prussia, Poland, and Rumania. King Michael of Rumania asked for an armistice and then joined the war against his former ally. Now Finland sued for peace, and Bulgaria was occupied by the Russians.

Some Soviet divisions then pressed into Yugoslavia to join Marshal Tito's guerrillas in the capture of Belgrade (September 11), and to threaten Hungary from the south. Others drove toward Budapest from the east. On October 15, Hungary, the last of the Nazi satellites, dropped out of the war. Germany stood alone.

The Battle of the Bulge · Hitler's Reich was now caught in a gigantic vise, with the Red armies pressing from the east and south and the Americans, British, and French from the west. In mid-December Hitler ordered a last desperate counterattack to throw the Allies back before they reached the Rhine. The Nazis struck a thinly held sector in the Ardennes forest ("the Bulge") and succeeded in driving a wedge of some fifty miles in the Allied lines.

THE LIBERATION OF EUROPE

- Axis conquests at greatest extent.
- Allied powers
- Neutral
- Main allied drives with year of advance.
- Maginot Line   Westwall

Allied Offensives · *What were the advantages and disadvantages of a central position to the Axis? Trace the steps by which Europe was liberated. Note particularly the countries which Russian troops entered.*

An American airborne regiment which had been surrounded at the important highway junction of Bastogne fought off attacks for nine days until relieved by Patton's tanks. When the skies cleared, 6500 planes roared into the air to blast the Nazi columns and communication lines. By mid-January the Germans were in full retreat. The

The Allied Generals Chat · *Marshal Zhukov, General Eisenhower, and General Montgomery meet socially after signing an historic document by which supreme authority over Germany was assumed by their governments and France.*

"Battle of the Bulge" had cost them 120,000 men and vast quantities of equipment.

The Battle for Germany and V-E Day · The Allies now launched drives which became a series of military disasters for the German armies. In the east Russian tanks poured across Poland and rolled on to the gates of Berlin. Equally overwhelming Allied armies crossed the Rhine and overran the great industrial centers of the Ruhr and the Saar. In the north, Montgomery's troops liberated the Netherlands and drove to the German Baltic ports. In the center, Bradley's men struck through Saxony to the Elbe. General Devers's divisions in the south crossed the Bavarian plains to Nuremberg and Munich. Meanwhile, over a million German and Italian troops surrendered to General Clark in Italy. As Marshal Zhukov's tanks rumbled through the blazing ruins of the German capital,

Adolph Hitler named Admiral Doenitz his successor and then committed suicide.

Germany surrendered unconditionally at General Eisenhower's headquarters at Rheims, France, on May 7, 1945. The next day President Truman announced the news, proclaiming May 8 a holiday for the celebration of Victory-in-Europe. Nazi tyranny and terror were at an end.

CHECK ON YOUR READING

1. Describe (*a*) *Rommel's defeat in Tunisia*, (*b*) *the invasion of Italy*, (*c*) "*D-Day.*"
2. What Allied gains made possible the great vise which threatened the Reich?
3. Describe the Battle of Germany which ended with V-E Day.
4. Identify (*a*) *Eisenhower*, (*b*) *Montgomery*, (*c*) *Bradley*, (*d*) *Bastogne*, (*e*) *De Gaulle*, (*f*) *Clark*, (*g*) *Zhukov*.

5. The Defeat of Japan

Allied Strategy in the Pacific · Initial Allied strategy had wisely concentrated upon Europe as the major theater of war while fighting a holding action against Japan. But the amazing American production of ships, planes, and munitions and the rapid training of fighting men made it possible to mount powerful offensives in the Pacific much sooner than anticipated.

While General Eisenhower's forces were sweeping through France, General MacArthur's troops were taking Hollandia in New Guinea and Leyte in the Philippines. The forward sweep of over 3500 miles from Australia and Hawaii to Tokyo was made possible by increasing American naval and air supremacy and superiority in amphibious tactics (that is, combining naval and land forces to seize various islands).

The Japanese forces were distributed among hundreds of islands scattered over thousands of miles in the Pacific. To keep these many garrisons supplied required long lines of communication which were highly vulnerable to submarine, plane, and torpedo-boat attack. This burden taxed the facilities of the Japanese armed services to the utmost.

The American plan, as drawn up by Generals Marshall and MacArthur and Admirals King and Nimitz, was to take certain key islands, on which the Allies could establish bases and landing strips. The others, with their Japanese garrisons cut off from supplies, were to be bypassed until "mopping-up operations" later.

The Japanese defenders of such islands as Tarawa, Kwajalein, Saipan, and Peleliu, fought with fanatical courage, and casualties were usually high. But the ultimate decision was never in doubt, and each new island base became a stepping stone on the road to victory. The many islands bypassed by the leap-frog technique were teeming with Japanese soldiers (140,000 in the Solomons alone). But these troops were cut off from home support and were incapable of harming the Allies.

On the Offensive in the Pacific · *Left: The battleship* Missouri *blasts the enemy and paves the way for troops to invade a Japanese-held island. The Japanese surrender was signed on board this ship. Below: American troops crowd together on their beachhead on Wake Island to protect themselves against Japanese machine gunning.*

The War in the Pacific · *Which important territories controlled by Western powers were overrun by the Japanese? Locate the places mentioned in the text. Why were many islands "by-passed" in the drive on Japan? Why were the Coral Sea, Midway, Guadalcanal, Leyte, and Okinawa especially important? Explain the symbols placed at Hiroshima and Nagasaki.*

Return to the Philippines · In March, 1942, when the Japanese had overrun the Philippines, General MacArthur had been ordered to leave Corregidor for Australia by submarine, leaving most of his forces behind under General Jonathan Wainwright. "I shall return," was the message of hope he sent back to the conquered peoples and to the American troops in Japanese prison camps. Now, two and one-half years later, he had the military resources to fulfill this promise.

On October 20, 1944, American amphibious forces made successful landings on the island of Leyte in the Philippines. Almost immediately three Japanese naval squadrons bore down upon the island. In the furious three-day Battle for Leyte Gulf which followed, the Japanese navy was completely routed.

Landings on the island of Luzon in January, 1945, resulted in recapture of Bataan, Corregidor, and Manila. By the end of February the Filipinos were again free.

Closing the Ring · The ring around Japan now began to tighten. (1) Tokyo was blasted by bombers. (2) The island fortress of Iwo Jima was taken after a month of fierce struggle and at the cost of 20,000 American lives. But it gave the Americans an air base 570 miles south of Yokohama. Thenceforth no enemy military objective was safe from air attack.

(3) Meanwhile Allied land forces had driven the Japanese from India and linked up the Stilwell (Ledo) Road with the Burma Road (January 28, 1945). Now aided by increasing supplies and the help of General Chennault's "Flying Tigers," the Chinese under Chiang Kai-shek regained the offensive.

(4) On April 1, 1945, a landing was made on Okinawa, the largest island in the Ryuk-yus group, only 362 miles from Japan. This bold invasion, supported by an armada of 1400 ships, required eighty-two days of the bloodiest fighting in the Pacific. Swarms of suicide (*Kamikaze*) pilots hurled their bomb-laden *Zeros* directly at American ships, sacrificing their lives and their planes in one supreme effort. American losses in ships and men were heavy indeed. But the army and the fleet had come to stay.

The Potsdam Declaration · On July 27, 1945, President Truman and British Prime Minister Attlee (then meeting with Marshal Stalin at Potsdam near Berlin) sent an ultimatum to Japan. The Potsdam Declaration called upon the Japanese government to "proclaim now the unconditional surrender of all Japanese armed forces" or face "prompt and utter destruction." The Japanese ignored the declaration. President Truman thereupon decided to use a new scientific weapon, the development of which has been called "the best-kept secret of the war." Its destructive power was calculated to shorten the conflict, prevent huge Allied casualties, and dramatize the sheer hopelessness of further Japanese resistance.

The Atom Bomb Brings V-J Day · On August 6, 1945, an atomic bomb was dropped on the city of Hiroshima. The blast, equivalent to 20,000 tons of TNT, churned the earth into a mushroom cloud of smoke and dust which rose to a height of seven miles. Only a desolate heap of rubble remained where once had stood a teeming city. Three days later a second bomb was dropped on Nagasaki. Meanwhile, the Soviet Union (in fulfillment of its pledge given at Yalta and anxious to have a say in the peace settlement) declared war on Japan and sent its armies into Manchuria and northern Korea.

The End of the War in the Pacific · *Left:* *The mushroom cloud of the atomic bomb rises over ruined Nagasaki. What did the atomic bomb mean for Japan? for the world? Above: General MacArthur witnesses the signing of the document of surrender on board the flagship* Missouri.

At 7 o'clock in the evening of August 14, 1945 (V-J Day), President Truman announced that Japan had accepted the terms of the Allies. By these terms the Japanese Empire was to be shorn of all its conquests and reduced to the home islands. The military forces were to be disarmed, war criminals punished, and a new order of peace established. Occupation forces under the command of General MacArthur were to insure enforcement of these terms until a treaty of peace could be ratified. Formal documents of surrender to the United Nations were signed aboard Admiral Halsey's flagship, the *Missouri,* in Tokyo Bay on September 2, 1945.

Thus ended six years of the most destructive war in history. Three of the four dictatorships responsible for the tragic suffering of this period had gone down in defeat. But the fourth, Communist Russia, whose support was deemed essential to the Allied victory over Hitler, now emerged more powerful than ever. As the great waves of joy and thanksgiving which came with the news of V-E Day and V-J Day passed away, two vital questions arose. How co-operative would the Soviet Union be in meeting the problems of peace? Would the mighty power of the atom be used to *serve* or *destroy* mankind?

CHECK ON YOUR READING

1. *Explain the Allied strategy in the Pacific.*
2. *Use the map to show how the ring was closed on Japan.*
3. *Identify (a) MacArthur, (b) Battle for Leyte Gulf, (c) Iwo Jima, (d) "Flying Tigers," (e) Kamikaze, (f) Potsdam Declaration.*
4. *How is Hiroshima related to V-J Day?*

596

Learning Activities

Think about the chapter

1. What is appeasement? Is appeasement a sound basis for foreign policy?

2. Why was Operation Sea Lion a failure?

3. Contrast the leadership qualities of Churchill and Roosevelt with those of Hitler and Mussolini.

4. Why did the Allies finally win the war?

5. How was World War II different from any previous war?

6. *Map study:* On a map of the world shade in the countries that were involved in World War II. Indicate which were Axis countries and which were Allied countries.

Go beyond the text

7. Investigate various propaganda techniques. Where do we meet propaganda in our daily life? How can we detect it?

8. How was daily life in the United States affected by World War II?

9. Find out about German treatment of the Jews. *The Diary of Anne Frank* and *The Wall* are excellent sources.

10. Prepare a series of thumbnail biographies of notable people connected with World War II. Give the facts of their lives briefly and explain why they were important.

Follow up your special interests

11. The story of Dunkirk, the plight of civilian refugees, the resistance of the Free French, and many other such topics provide excellent material for those who enjoy writing short stories or poems.

12. Those interested in science can report on how atomic energy is released and how it can be used to benefit mankind.

13. Report on medical advances made during the war.

14. Interview someone who fought in World War II for a personal account of the war.

READ FURTHER

Basic readings: (1) BECKER, *Modern History*, Chap. 24. (2) CHEYNEY, *Short History of England*, Chaps. 25–26. (3) HOFFMAN, *News of the World*, No. 51. (4) Year's *Pictorial History*, pp. 558–565.

Special accounts: (5) W. CHURCHILL, *The Second World War*, Vols. 2–6. To supplement knowledge of a given campaign or battle. (6) D. EISENHOWER, *Crusade in Europe*. A one-volume account by the commander-in-chief of the Allied forces. (7) E. ELLSBERG, *No Banners, No Bugles*. Submarine warfare in the Mediterranean and the Atlantic, written in adventure-story style. (8) W. LANGSAM, *The World since 1919*. (9) A. NEVINS, *The New Deal and World Affairs: A Chronicle of International Affairs, 1933–1945*. Very helpful for understanding the part played by the U. S. in this critical period. (10) Year's *Your Lifetime in Pictures: the Twentieth Century*, pp. 156–201.

Fiction and biography: (11) A. FRANK, *The Diary of a Young Girl*. Genuine diary of a young Jewish girl in hiding in Nazi-occupied Amsterdam. (12) P. GALLICO, *The Snow Goose*. A beautiful story about the miracle of Dunkirk. (13) A. HATCH, *General Ike*. An easy to read biography that covers all phases of Eisenhower's life, including the Presidency. (14) J. HERSEY, *Hiroshima*. (15) J. HERSEY, *The Wall*. A gripping story of the Warsaw ghetto after the German occupation of Poland. (16) W. LORD, *Day of Infamy*. Best account of the attack on Pearl Harbor. (17) E. PYLE, *Brave Men* and *Here Is Your War*. True-life stories of the G.I. (18) N. SHUTE, *Most Secret*. An absorbing tale of a naval expedition against German patrols on the coast of France. (19) W. THOMPSON, *Assignment: Churchill*. The Prime Minister's bodyguard writes an amusing description of Churchill. (20) W. L. WHITE, *They Were Expendable*. About the brave men on PT boats.

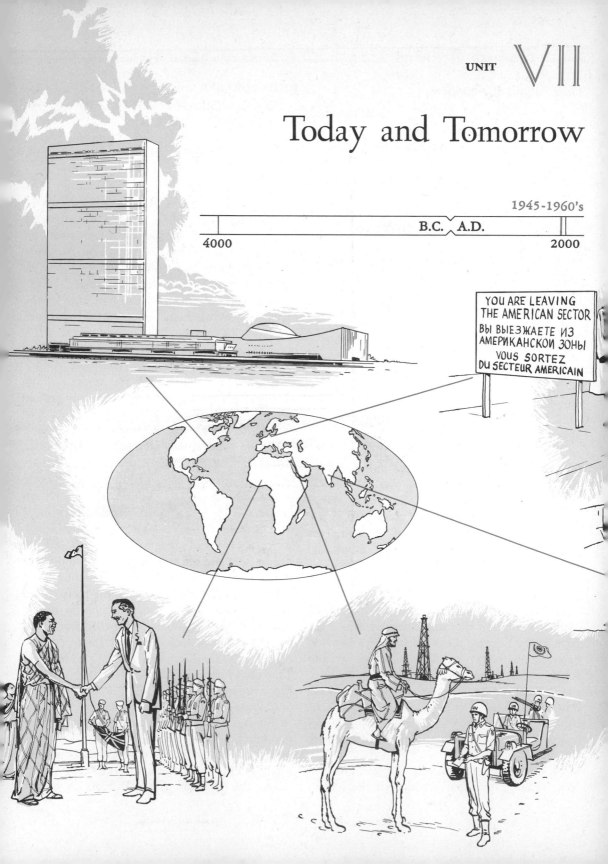

UNIT VII

Today and Tomorrow

1945-1960's

B.C.   A.D.

4000   2000

YOU ARE LEAVING
THE AMERICAN SECTOR
ВЫ ВЫЕЗЖАЕТЕ ИЗ
АМЕРИКАНСКОЙ ЗОНЫ
VOUS SORTEZ
DU SECTEUR AMERICAIN

WORLD WAR II left the world torn and exhausted. The cloud of the atomic bomb cast a dark shadow. Men, realizing that another world war would be suicidal, once more founded an organization to keep the peace—the United Nations.

It was hoped that through the UN the wartime allies would continue to work together, that peace treaties would be signed, and that better economic and social conditions would be achieved through joint efforts. But it soon became clear that the Soviet Union and the Western democracies were in bitter disagreement on many issues. No agreement could be reached on a German treaty, and the country remained divided.

The Soviet Union established Communist control in all the eastern European countries its armies had occupied, and dropped an Iron Curtain between these countries and the West. Communists worked ceaselessly to spread their influence beyond it.

The United States countered this threat of Communist expansion with the Truman Doctrine. This was followed by the Marshall Plan for European recovery. Later the United States promoted regional defense arrangements such as NATO and SEATO. The conflict had become a "cold war."

In Asia and Africa the postwar period was marked by momentous upheavals. Nationalism was exploding the old colonial order. Communism, too, was on the march, sometimes allied with nationalism, sometimes thwarted by it. Civil war in China led to a Communist state on the mainland and a Nationalist government on Formosa. In Japan ancient traditions were cast aside and democratic institutions established. The United Nations intervened to check Communist aggression in Korea.

India, Pakistan, Burma, Ceylon, and Indonesia were granted independence. The Middle East, aflame with nationalistic feeling, was shaken by warfare and revolution. This crucial area remains one of the acute danger spots in the world. Africa, too, began to stir with demands for independence. Self-government has been achieved peacefully in some cases; in others there has been violence.

As we look at the world in mid-century we see over eighty nations working together through the UN toward the solutions of world problems. How shall peace be preserved? What shall be done about atomic energy? How shall the conflict between the West and the Soviet Union be resolved? How can nationalism in Asia and the Near East develop for the good of all? How will man's conquest of outer space affect world conditions? How can all nations make the social and economic progress to which their teeming millions aspire?

33

The Search for Peace

CHAPTER OUTLINE

KEY WORDS AND DATES

Truman

Attlee

Molotov

UNRRA

October 24, 1945

General Assembly

Security Council

veto

specialized
    agencies

Trusteeship
    Council

Secretariat

Hammarskjold

neutral nations

Yalta

Potsdam

free elections

Iron Curtain

occupation zones

cold war

Truman Doctrine

Marshall Plan

ERP

Berlin blockade

West Germany

Adenauer

Western European
    Union

Council of Europe

NATO

Schuman Plan

common market

Warsaw Pact

THE BOMBS which brought the war in Japan to dramatic close marked the opening of a new era in human history—the Age of Atomic Power. The joy of victory was tempered by the realization that man now possessed the means utterly to destroy his world.

Countries in all parts of the world now joined in establishing the United Nations, pledging themselves to renounce war and to maintain peace. The four victorious powers on whom rested the responsibility of restoring order created a Council of Foreign Ministers to settle the accounts of war and prepare peace treaties.

But the tragedy of the postwar years soon started to unfold. The Soviet Union proved unco-operative in the Council of Foreign Ministers and used its veto to prevent achievement of the major purposes of the United Nations. Peace treaties were delayed. Finally, the Western powers decided to go their own way to restore peace and prosperity in Europe.

Communist threats to Greece and Turkey were answered by the Truman Doctrine. European economic recovery was stimulated by the Marshall Plan. The Soviet threat in Germany was met by a Berlin airlift. European efforts to achieve unity made some halting first steps, and a Western defense network was set up in the North Atlantic Treaty Organization.

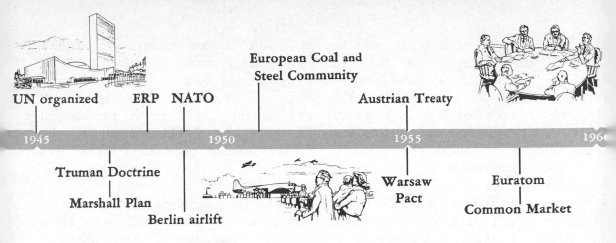

UN organized   ERP NATO

European Coal and
Steel Community

Austrian Treaty

1945   1950   1955   196(

Truman Doctrine

Marshall Plan

Berlin airlift

Warsaw
Pact

Euratom

Common Market

1. Founding the United Nations

Rebuilding a Broken World · During the last six months of World War II new men had replaced two of those who had carried the major burden of world leadership. President Truman now acted for the United States. In Great Britain, general elections had installed a Labor government, and Prime Minister Clement Attlee replaced the great Winston Churchill. Premier Stalin and Foreign Secretary Molotov still represented the Soviet Union.

The ruin and the cost of the war were appalling. Fourteen million men had been killed, and there were fifty-six million other casualties. A fantastic sum approaching five hundred billion dollars had been required to finance the great struggle. The vast destruction of wealth in the form of buildings, farms, railroads, ships, and other property was immeasurable.

The task of the Allies was to change a world geared for total war back to a peacetime basis. In the defeated countries this meant a period of military occupation by the victors. In countries which had been overrun by the Axis forces, there were millions of starving, homeless people to be fed.

For the Allies, there was the demobilizing of their armed forces, reconverting vast war plants to peacetime production, and devising means to pay the interest on the gigantic debts piled up during the war years.

In international affairs, there were peace treaties to be made before business and world trade could be revived. Above all, there was the need of establishing an international association to guard the peace bought at so great a price.

Relief and Reconstruction (UNRRA) · The immediate tasks of relief and reconstruction were entrusted to an international body. In 1943 the United Nations Relief and Reconstruction Agency (UNRRA) was set up. Although international in theory, the United States contributed 90 per cent of its supplies and paid 72 per cent of its bills. It preceded by two years the actual formation of the United Nations organization.

Between 1943 and 1947 UNRRA distributed almost four billion dollars worth of supplies to thousands of suffering people. In 1946 the United States withdrew from UNRRA when it became apparent

601

that relief supplies were being used for political purposes in certain countries. Later the United States sponsored its own program for economic recovery (p. 612).

Plans for a United Nations Organization · Allied war leaders, realizing the need to guard the peace, had laid plans for an international organization long before victory had been gained. The principles on which the organization should rest found expression as early as 1941 in the Atlantic Charter, and to this charter twenty-six nations had pledged their support in January, 1942.

In creating a new international organization the Allied leaders were able to draw on the experience of the ill-fated League of Nations. They were resolved to avoid some of the mistakes which they felt had been made in 1919.

The peacemakers in 1919 had made the League Covenant (charter) a part of the Treaty of Versailles. The League was therefore associated with a treaty which many people felt was unjust. It was now decided that the charter of the new organization should be kept separate from the peace treaties to be made with the Axis powers.

It was also felt that the League had not devoted sufficient attention to economic problems. Economic councils and specialized agencies which the League had lacked should now be created.

In 1944 proposals for the new organization were drafted at Dumbarton Oaks in Washington, D.C. At Bretton Woods, New Hampshire, plans were worked out for an International Monetary Fund and an International Bank for Reconstruction.

How the United Nations Is Organized · On April 25, 1945, at the invitation of Great Britain, the United States, Russia, and China, a great conference of nations met at San Francisco to prepare a charter for the United Nations. Two months later fifty powers signed the completed charter and also the Statute of the International Court of Justice. On October 24, 1945, the United Nations organization came into being when the required number of countries had ratified the documents.

It must be remembered that the United Nations is not a world government, but a *voluntary association* of states—each retaining its own sovereignty. It is only as strong as the *will to peace* of its members. Any member-nation may, by obstruction or defiance, injure the effective working of its machinery.

The Charter provides for six principal agencies to carry on the work of the United Nations. These are (1) the General Assembly, (2) the Security Council, (3) the Economic and Social Council, (4) the International Court of Justice, (5) the Trusteeship Council, and (6) the Secretariat.

The General Assembly · The General Assembly has been called "the official voice" of the United Nations. It is composed of representatives of all the member nations (over eighty by 1960). As it continues to grow, its resolutions represent ever more nearly the will of the majority of the earth's governments. The ability which it thus has publicly to express world opinion is in itself a power for peace. Few nations can stand out indefinitely against the sentiments of a united world.

The General Assembly may *discuss* any subject of world interest within the scope of the Charter and *make recommendations* to the Security Council. If the Council fails to act when peace is threatened, the Assembly may be called to handle the matter. It also admits new members on the

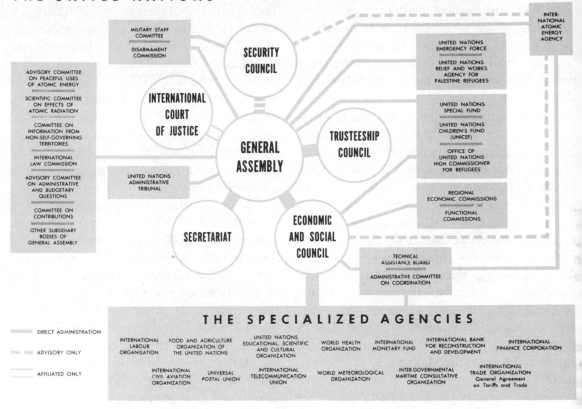

ADVISORY COMMITTEE
ON PEACEFUL USES
OF ATOMIC ENERGY

SCIENTIFIC COMMITTEE
ON EFFECTS OF
ATOMIC RADIATION

COMMITTEE ON
INFORMATION FROM
NON-SELF-GOVERNING
TERRITORIES

INTERNATIONAL
LAW COMMISSION

ADVISORY COMMITTEE
ON ADMINISTRATIVE
AND BUDGETARY
QUESTIONS

COMMITTEE ON
CONTRIBUTIONS

OTHER SUBSIDIARY
BODIES OF
GENERAL ASSEMBLY

MILITARY STAFF
COMMITTEE

DISARMAMENT
COMMISSION

SECURITY
COUNCIL

INTERNATIONAL
COURT
OF JUSTICE

GENERAL
ASSEMBLY

TRUSTEESHIP
COUNCIL

UNITED NATIONS
ADMINISTRATIVE
TRIBUNAL

SECRETARIAT

ECONOMIC
AND SOCIAL
COUNCIL

INTER-
NATIONAL
ATOMIC
ENERGY
AGENCY

UNITED NATIONS
EMERGENCY FORCE

UNITED NATIONS
RELIEF AND WORKS
AGENCY FOR
PALESTINE REFUGEES

UNITED NATIONS
SPECIAL FUND

UNITED NATIONS
CHILDREN'S FUND
(UNICEF)

OFFICE OF
UNITED NATIONS
HIGH COMMISSIONER
FOR REFUGEES

REGIONAL
ECONOMIC COMMISSIONS

FUNCTIONAL
COMMISSIONS

TECHNICAL
ASSISTANCE BOARD

ADMINISTRATIVE COMMITTEE
ON COORDINATION

THE SPECIALIZED AGENCIES

DIRECT ADMINISTRATION

ADVISORY ONLY

AFFILIATED ONLY

INTERNATIONAL
LABOUR
ORGANISATION

FOOD AND AGRICULTURE
ORGANIZATION OF
THE UNITED NATIONS

UNITED NATIONS
EDUCATIONAL, SCIENTIFIC
AND CULTURAL
ORGANIZATION

WORLD HEALTH
ORGANIZATION

INTERNATIONAL
MONETARY FUND

INTERNATIONAL BANK
FOR RECONSTRUCTION
AND DEVELOPMENT

INTERNATIONAL
FINANCE CORPORATION

INTERNATIONAL
CIVIL AVIATION
ORGANIZATION

UNIVERSAL
POSTAL UNION

INTERNATIONAL
TELECOMMUNICATION
UNION

WORLD METEOROLOGICAL
ORGANIZATION

INTER-GOVERNMENTAL
MARITIME CONSULTATIVE
ORGANIZATION

INTERNATIONAL
TRADE ORGANIZATION
General Agreement
on Tariffs and Trade

recommendation of the Security Council and elects members to various UN agencies and committees. In addition, it prepares and approves the budget. It meets annually, oftener if necessary. Each member has one vote, and on important questions a *two-thirds majority* of those present and voting is required for a decision.

The Security Council · The Security Council has the primary responsibility for maintaining peace. This important body of eleven members is in permanent session and meets generally once every two weeks. Five powers (Great Britain, the United States, the Soviet Union, France, and Nationalist China) have permanent seats.

Six non-permanent members are elected for a period of two years each by the General Assembly.

The duties of the Council include determining the existence of any threat to peace and investigating any dangerous dispute. The Council must decide what measures are to be taken. It may call upon parties to settle their differences by peaceful means, and it may ask members to take action (such as breaking economic and diplomatic relations) against those who fail to heed its advice. All members of the United Nations are pledged by the Charter to make available to the Council certain military forces and assistance.

Each member of the Council has one vote. For important matters seven votes, *including those of all permanent members,* are required. Since the veto of any one of the five will defeat a measure, the veto power has become a matter of the greatest importance.

Other Agencies · In non-political fields the United Nations through its many agencies and affiliated organizations has been able to promote the well-being of peoples all over the world. This is a very positive factor in maintaining peace.

The Economic and Social Council, of eighteen members, has as its chief concern the creation of those world conditions which promote peaceful and friendly relations among nations. It studies standards of living, employment, and other economic, social, cultural, educational, and health problems. It also supervises the work of a number of specialized agencies (see chart, p. 603).

One of these is the Food and Agriculture Organization (FAO). It helps governments to increase food production to ward off mass starvation. The World Health Organization (WHO) has carried on active campaigns against contagious diseases in Egypt, Greece, India, and other areas. The Office of the High Commissioner for Refugees has cared for thousands of homeless persons until they could be resettled. The United Nations Educational, Scientific, and Cultural Organization, called UNESCO, sponsors international study programs and conferences on social and educational problems. These are examples of the undertakings which form a long-term program whose achievements can be measured only after the passage of years.

The Trusteeship Council is composed of an equal number of countries administering trust territories and those who do not. The United Nations trust territories are former mandates of the League of Nations as well as territories, taken from the defeated Axis powers, which have not yet become independent. The Council receives reports on conditions in the trust territories and may receive petitions from the dependent peoples themselves. Some trust territories have already been granted independence and many are on the way to self-government.

The Secretariat · The Secretariat, or permanent staff of 4000 technical experts, is headed by the Secretary-General, who is the chief administrative officer of the UN. The Secretary-General is elected for a term of five years by the General Assembly on the recommendation of the Security Council. His staff is drawn from all the member states. However, the Secretary-General and his staff neither represent nor take orders from their own states. They are truly international civil servants responsible to the United Nations alone.

Dag Hammarskjold, who succeeded Trygve Lie as Secretary-General in 1953, has assumed an important role as international trouble-shooter. On different occasions he has flown to the danger spots of the world to try to ease tensions. In this work he has had outstanding success.

United Nations Headquarters · The permanent home of the United Nations is in the United States, the country whose leadership is deemed most essential to its success. John D. Rockefeller, Jr., gave the property on the East River in New York City upon which the principal buildings have been erected.

Certain of the UN agencies, however, are located in other countries. The headquarters of UNESCO is in Paris. The

The United Nations Works for Peace · *Left: Trygve Lie, the first Secretary-General, welcomes his successor, Dag Hammarskjold. Right: This view of the UN headquarters shows the General Assembly building and the Secretariat.*

Permanent Court meets in The Hague. The Office of the High Commissioner for Refugees is in Geneva. In this way many countries share the responsibility for acting as host to various UN bodies.

Problems of the United Nations · The great hope in 1945 was that the five great Allied powers would continue to work together in peacetime. We shall see in the next section of this chapter that this hope has not been realized.

The growing conflict between the Soviet Union with its satellites and the nations of the free world has dominated the discussions and actions of these powers within the UN. For several years the use of the veto by the Soviet Union prevented the admission of a number of countries to membership in the United Nations. Soviet ob-

jections have also made it impossible to set up regular armed forces as called for in the Charter (Art. 43). Special volunteer forces have been used, however, to police certain specific areas. The Disarmament Commission of the Security Council has also been unable to find common ground among the powers for the reduction of arms.

Because the Soviet veto has blocked action by the Security Council on many occasions, the General Assembly has assumed increasing importance. It was called into emergency session to deal with threats to the peace in Egypt (p. 639), in Hungary (p. 663), and in the Middle East (p. 640).

For the first ten years the Western powers won substantial majorities for their

A Security Council Session · *Delegates are wearing earphones. Translators in booths give instant translations of the speeches in the five official languages.*

proposals in the General Assembly. Thereafter an increasing number of the newly independent states of Asia and Africa have taken an independent position. The support of these neutral nations has been eagerly sought by both the democracies and the Communist nations. World opinion is thus becoming an increasingly important factor in settling disputes.

UN Accomplishments · The Economic and Social Council and its affiliated specialized agencies have done much to promote human dignity and welfare. The Trusteeship Council has done notable work in checking on the government of colonial areas. The Secretary-General has often proved to be a skillful mediator.

Considering the great unrest and opportunities for war in the world today, it is remarkable that so many disputes have been settled with such little shooting.

In the remaining pages of this book are a number of accounts of UN action, but a few cases deserve special mention here. (1) The withdrawal of British, French, and Russian troops from the Middle East was hastened in 1946. (2) A Balkan Commission (1947–1952) helped to stop the flow of Communist aid to Greek rebels and to prevent the destruction of Greek independence. (3) "Cease fire" arrangements halted fighting in Indonesia, Kashmir, and Palestine in 1947–1948 and in Suez in 1956. (4) Communist aggression in Korea was halted. (5) The problem of what to do with the former Italian colonies in Africa was settled peacefully.

When the General Assembly began its twelfth annual session in 1957, Secretary-General Dag Hammarskjold was asked, "If there were no UN, what would, in your opinion, be the state of the world today?" He replied, "The world would be in a state where everybody would agree that such an organization had to be created." In the words of President Eisenhower, "It still represents man's best organized hope to substitute the conference table for the battlefield."

CHECK ON YOUR READING

1. *Name three leaders of the postwar world. What tasks confronted them?*
2. *List the steps leading up to the birthday of the UN on October 24, 1945.*
3. *Name and tell the main purpose of each of the six main UN agencies.*
4. *Identify each of the following in relation to the UN: (a) Five Powers, (b) UNESCO, (c) WHO, (d) FAO, (e) veto, (f) Rockefeller, (g) Hammarskjold.*
5. *Summarize (a) the problems confronting the UN, (b) some of its accomplishments.*

2. The Peace Treaties

Peace Plans of the Western Allies · The United States and Great Britain represented the ideals and strength of the Western democracies during the war. Only after their liberation were France and the smaller states of western Europe able gradually to assume their proper role.

American and British leaders were in essential agreement as to the terms of the peace. (1) They wished to see all the countries that had been overrun by the Axis free to decide their own forms of government. (2) They also assumed that the former enemy states would be required to compensate, so far as possible, for the damage they had done.

(3) They nevertheless realized that even the wartime enemies would have to be accepted as members of the international community sometime soon. (4) They also believed that every effort should be made to avoid dividing the world into rival alliance systems. President Roosevelt was especially eager to put into effect the declaration of President Wilson that "There must be, not a balance of power, but a community of power—not organized rivalries, but an organized peace."

The Soviet Viewpoint · The Russians were especially concerned with the problem of security. Their homeland had been invaded twice since Napoleon's time. And they were resolved to control this historic invasion route for all time. They believed that Communist dictatorships should be established in countries bordering on Russia. And they did not hesitate to use their armed forces to achieve this aim. As the various peoples of Europe were liberated from the Axis, the organized Communist underground movements seized control wherever possible. The Communists expected the democracies to collapse under the staggering political and economic problems following the war. They used every subversive method possible to hasten the process.

Yalta and Potsdam · The differences between the Western allies and the Soviet Union in their approach to peace became apparent at two major wartime conferences in 1945. The first of these was held in the Russian town of Yalta on the Black Sea in February. The second was at Potsdam, a suburb of conquered Berlin, in July and August. While these discussions were taking place, the war in Europe came to an

Prime Minister Attlee, President Truman, and Generalissimo Stalin at Potsdam · *German aggression had united the Big Three. What later happened to Allied unity?*

end. By the time of the Potsdam conference, the Western allies had overrun all of western Europe and a good part of Germany. The Russians, for their part, had overrun eastern Europe and were also in occupation of the eastern portion of Germany. At the same time, plans were afoot for a final offensive against Japan.

The expected need of men and supplies for the war in the Pacific led to a rapid withdrawal of American forces from Europe. Demobilization was spurred by the cry, "Bring the boys home." The result was a serious weakening of the bargaining power of the Western allies at the very time that the most important decisions regarding the peace of Europe were being made. The Soviet government, on the other hand, could ignore public opinion and keep its armed forces on a war footing during this decisive period of negotiations.

Areas of Agreement · At the major allied conferences at Yalta and Potsdam, and in other negotiations during the year of victory, apparent agreement was reached on several important principles of a peace settlement. (1) Each great power would have primary responsibility for political developments in the countries occupied by its armies. Under this principle, Great Britain was to be predominant in the eastern Mediterranean region, including Greece. The United States and the United Kingdom together would play the leading role in establishing new governments in Italy, France, and the rest of western Europe. And the Soviet Union would take the initiative in eastern Europe. (2) It was agreed that Germany and Austria should be occupied jointly by France, the Soviet Union, Great Britain, and the United States. (3) The most important of the frontier changes were agreed to. These included

the cession of eastern Poland and part of East Prussia to the U.S.S.R., and the rest of East Prussia and the German territories east of the Oder and Neisse rivers to Poland (see map on p. 609). Less important cessions of territory were made by Czechoslovakia, Finland, Italy, and Rumania.

(4) It was also agreed that the foreign ministers of the Big Four (France was now included) should meet to draft peace treaties for the countries associated with Nazi Germany: Italy, Hungary, Bulgaria, Rumania, and Finland.

Areas of Controversy · There were, however, other issues of equal or greater importance on which the wartime allies failed to reach agreement. (1) Should Europe be divided into a Soviet and a Western sphere of influence? The Soviet government excluded all Western influences from the areas of Europe where its armies were in occupation. The Western allies, on the other hand, permitted Communist parties to operate freely in western Europe.

(2) This controversy led to disagreement on the administration of the joint occupation of Germany. Russia refused to admit Western influence into its zone of occupation. The three Western powers, on the other hand, worked for a plan of occupation which would democratize all parts of Germany.

(3) Also closely related to this general issue was the question of free elections. At the end of the Yalta conference, the Big Three promised "free elections" for all the liberated peoples of Europe. But the Communists never fulfilled this promise in areas under their control.

Peace Treaties with the Axis Satellites · After several stormy meetings of the Council of Foreign Ministers, as well as extensive negotiations outside that body, peace treaties were finally agreed upon for Italy, Hungary, Bulgaria, Rumania, and Finland. The peace treaties were signed in Paris on February 10, 1947. The map on this page shows the territorial changes in Europe. Notice that Russian territory now reached the mouth of the Danube River.

Italy lost her overseas territories. Ethiopia was given immediate independence. Libya, Eritrea, and Italian Somaliland became United Nations trust territories until they could be established as independent states. Modest reparations were required from each of the former enemies, but they were not severely punished.

The Iron Curtain · More important than the terms of the peace treaties was the fact that they recognized the establishment of a Soviet zone of control in eastern Europe (see map on p. 613). This zone included seven important countries in addition to the Soviet zone of Germany. They had a combined population and wealth equal to about one-half that of the Soviet Union.

From the Soviet point of view, this zone served two purposes. (1) It was a defensive zone, designed to prevent Western ideas, institutions, and political influence from entering Russia. (2) It provided a strategic position which gave Soviet armies ready access to western Europe.

In March, 1946, Winston Churchill startled many of his listeners when he asserted, in a speech at Fulton, Missouri, that the Soviet leaders had drawn an "iron curtain" between their zone and the rest of Europe. Events soon proved that Churchill was right, and the term Iron Curtain came to be accepted as a vivid and accurate description of the way in which the Soviet Union isolated areas under its control.

Soviet pressure on the countries within its sphere of influence was exerted through

Postwar Territorial Changes · Italy *ceded strategic Alpine areas* (1) *to France; lost Triest* (2), *which became a free territory; ceded most of Venezia Giulia* (3) *to Yugoslavia; and Dodecanesia* (4) *to Greece.* **Rumania** *ceded southern Dobrudja* (5) *to Bulgaria, and northern Bukovina and Bessarabia* (6) *to Russia.* **Hungary** *ceded parts of Slovakia* (7) *to Czechoslovakia; Ruthenia* (8) *to Russia; and Transylvania* (9) *to Rumania.* **Finland** *ceded Petsamo* (10), *and leased Porkkala Peninsula* (11) *to Russia for fifty years.*

armies of occupation, police and diplomatic agents, and ties with the local Communist parties. In no case did the Communists come to power as a result of a free election.

The importance of occupation forces can be seen in the case of Yugoslavia. Here a Communist government had been established by Marshal Tito without Soviet troops. By 1948, however, the nationalistic Yugoslavs had had enough of Soviet domination, and Marshal Tito made a dramatic break with the Soviet Union.

The Problem of Germany · The key to the German problem lies in her great potentiality for political and economic strength in the heart of Europe. United under Hitler, Germany had come close to conquering all of Europe and Russia. Although Germany lay helpless in 1945, great fear of her persisted, particularly in the countries which she had occupied. The problem was that of rebuilding Germany along peaceful lines. To the West this meant a prosperous democratic state; to the Russians, another Communist satellite.

Since the disagreement between Russia and the West was so basic, it proved impossible to draft a peace treaty for Germany. Instead, the Soviet occupation zone (East Germany), with about one-third of Germany's territory and one-quarter of its population, remained under Soviet control. The rest of Germany (West Germany) continued under the joint control of American, British, and French occupation forces. The four powers agreed to establish a joint government over Berlin and to divide the city into four sectors.

The Austrian Treaty · The Allies agreed that Austria should again be an independent country. But when it came to drawing up the terms, Russia and the Western allies were confronted by the same problem that they had faced with Germany. Would an independent Austria come within the Soviet or the Western zone of influence? Unable to agree, they divided Austria into separate zones, with a four-power occupation of Vienna.

It took ten years of negotiation to reach a compromise regarding Austria. The Soviet Union finally agreed to sign the treaty on condition that Austria would remain neutral in international relations. Austria and the Western allies accepted this condition, and Austria again became an independent state (May, 1955).

Occupation Zones in Germany and Austria · *Why were these zones drawn up? How does this map help to explain the Berlin problem? Do these zones still exist?*

ZONES OF OCCUPATION

CHECK ON YOUR READING

1. *Summarize the viewpoint of (a) the Western powers and (b) the Soviet Union toward the peace. (c) Why did they differ so greatly?*
2. *What were the areas of agreement and controversy at Yalta and Potsdam?*
3. *Explain (a) the Iron Curtain, (b) the German problem, (c) occupation arrangements in Germany and Austria, (d) the Austrian treaty.*

3. From Peace to Cold War

Obstruction, Propaganda, and Subversion · The Communist leaders of the Soviet Union did not wish to see a stable peace established. Instead, they took advantage of the postwar unrest to extend the influence of communism and of Soviet power. Their conflict with the Western powers came to be called a "cold war." Their methods were obstruction, propaganda, and subversion.

As early as February, 1946, when the armed forces of the United States and Great Britain were being rapidly demobilized, Soviet leaders began accusing these countries of being "imperialist aggressors." The Soviets did what they could to obstruct the agencies of the United Nations designed to foster international co-operation. Moreover, they used the United Nations as a platform for Communist propaganda. Throughout the world, Communist parties were instructed in methods of subversion. Like termites they worked from within to undermine existing governments wherever there seemed to be a chance of success.

In Iran, Soviet troops had been stationed during the war by agreement with the Western allies to protect lines of supply. Now the Soviet government refused to withdraw its forces, as it had agreed to do. Only after the Western allies had mobilized world opinion by raising this issue forcefully in the United Nations were the Russian troops withdrawn from Iran.

Threats to Greece and Turkey · During the Nazi occupation of Greece, Communists had succeeded in dominating the underground guerrilla movement. They rose against the Greek government-in-exile, which returned at the end of the war. With the aid of British troops they were driven into the territory of the Soviet satellite states of Albania, Yugoslavia, and Bulgaria. But during the winter of 1946–1947 the Greek Communists launched new guerrilla attacks on the Greek government. They were supported by the Soviet Union and its satellites.

Turkey was also subjected to Communist pressures after the war. The Soviet Union made demands on Turkey which would, if accepted, have resulted in its becoming a Communist satellite. But the Turks resisted these pressures firmly. By 1947 it was clear that the Soviet Union was trying to expand its sphere of influence into the eastern Mediterranean region. And Britain, once an obstacle to Russian expansion, was now powerless to stop it.

The Truman Doctrine (1947) · The Soviet challenge in Greece and Turkey marked a turning point in the American attitude. Until this time the United States had acted as though its wartime ally were essentially a friendly, though suspicious, state. But the threat of Communist aggression was now clear.

In March, 1947, President Truman issued the historic statement that came to be known as the Truman Doctrine. He proclaimed that it was a national interest of the United States to prevent Soviet domination of Greece and Turkey. President Truman also asked Congress for authority to give 400 million dollars in aid to these two countries. General Van Fleet was sent to build up the Greek forces, and the Communist guerrillas were beaten.

In the meantime Greece had sought the assistance of the United Nations. After

In Defense of Liberty · *How does the cartoon illustrate the idea behind the Truman Doctrine? Below: Secretary of State Marshall visits Athens. Which nations were invited to participate in his recovery program? Which refused?*

investigating the nature of the Communist aggression against Greece, the General Assembly established a special Balkan Commission. It stationed observation groups along the Greek frontier, and this helped stabilize the situation.

Europe's Economic and Political Weakness · Europe had been devastated by almost six years of war. Its many governments had been seriously disorganized. Requirements for food and essential products were much greater than the ability of the people to produce or buy them. If Europe did not receive assistance, it was in grave danger of falling into the hands of the Communists, for communism thrives on misery and despair.

Europe's weakness was also political. The different governments had in the past been unable to co-operate closely in economic matters. Many of Europe's problems, which could have been solved by joint effort, continued to worsen because of political disunity.

The Marshall Plan (1947) · The countries of western Europe were important allies of the United States in meeting the Soviet challenge. Indeed, Europe's economic health was essential to American security. In June, 1947, Secretary of State George C. Marshall announced a new United States approach to the problem of European recovery. American aid was offered on condition that the European countries themselves take the initiative in working out a common recovery program. This offer, which embraced the U.S.S.R. and its satellites as well as the rest of Europe, was called the Marshall Plan.

The plan was greeted eagerly by the leading statesmen of western Europe. Sixteen European countries, including Turkey, co-operated in preparing an aid plan

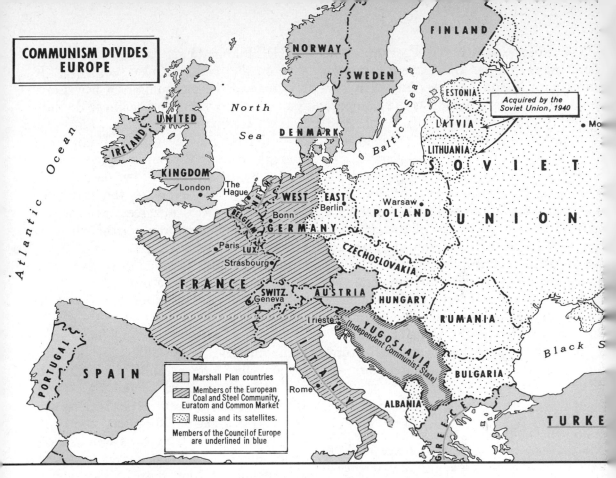

Acquired by the
Soviet Union, 1940

Marshall Plan countries

Members of the European
Coal and Steel Community,
Euratom and Common Market

Russia and its satellites.

Members of the Council of Europe
are underlined in blue

A Divided Europe · *How did the Marshall Plan promote western European unification? Which country bordering on Russia is not a satellite? Which satellite does not border on Russia? What is Yugoslavia's position?*

which was presented to the United States in September, 1947.

Communists Reject the Plan and Seize Control in Czechoslovakia · The Soviet Union itself took part in the early discussions of this plan, and several of the eastern European countries, especially Czechoslovakia and Poland, were also eager to participate. But Russia feared that the plan might undermine its hold upon the satellite states. It therefore decided not to join and refused to allow any of its satellites to do so. The danger that Czechoslovakia would turn to the West appeared so serious to Soviet leaders that they took steps to bring that country wholly under their control. In February, 1948, they sponsored a revolution which overthrew the democratic government of Czechoslovakia and placed the Communist party in power.

This act greatly shocked the West. Of all the states within the Soviet sphere Czechoslovakia had enjoyed the most stable prewar democracy. But it served to warn the democracies that the dangers from Communist subversion were grave indeed.

The European Recovery Program · The plan submitted by the sixteen European states and accepted by the American government came to be known as the European Recovery Program (ERP). In April, 1948, Congress agreed to start the program with a grant of about five billion dollars.

In Europe the participating governments formed an Organization for European Economic Co-operation (OEEC), with Paris as headquarters. The task of this organization was to prepare economic-aid plans for the different countries and to work out a long-term program for European economic co-operation and recovery. By 1950 some 18 billion dollars worth of aid had been supplied to Europe by the United States.

Many regard this aid program as the turning point in postwar European history. It

Rotterdam, a Postwar Miracle · *German fire bombs destroyed Holland's great city in hours. Today, where once were ashes, stands a remarkable modern city.*

enabled Europe to get back on its feet and start on the road to a new prosperity. It also marked the beginning of a new European effort to overcome political disunity through economic co-operation. Finally, it gave the peoples of western Europe the strength to resist Communist pressures.

The Berlin Blockade · The Western allies made a last effort in the spring of 1948 to obtain Russian agreement to much-needed economic reforms for the whole of Germany. But the Russians once again refused to agree on a joint policy. The Western allies therefore proceeded to carry out reforms in their three zones and to unify their activities.

The Russians responded by blockading Berlin in June, 1948. This city of three million, the former capital of Germany, was under four-power administration but was located in the heart of the Soviet zone. The Russians cut off all railroad and highway approaches to the city as well as electricity supplied to West Berlin by power stations under Soviet control. They hoped thereby to drive the Allies out.

President Truman accepted the challenge by ordering the Berlin airlift. A remarkable "air bridge" of American, British, and French transport planes was organized to supply the city with food and coal. The success of the West in making this tremendous effort convinced the Russians that the blockade was a failure (May, 1949).

The German Federal Republic (West Germany) · In September, 1949, military occupation was terminated in the three Western zones, and a new German Federal Republic was established. Its capital was at Bonn. The constitution of this new government provided for a lower chamber elected for four years by universal suffrage. An upper chamber represented the eleven

The New Germany · Left: West Berliners watch as Western planes overcome the Soviet blockade. Above: Chancellor Adenauer, a firm champion of co-operation with the West.

federated provinces into which the three zones were divided. Konrad Adenauer became chancellor.

The German Federal Republic had two-thirds of the area of postwar Germany, and three-fourths of its population. It was about equal in size and population to Great Britain and Northern Ireland. The strength of the new state was a great tribute to the industry of the German people, and its democratic spirit was regarded as a hopeful sign for the future of Europe.

East Germany · The Soviet authorities created a "German Democratic Republic" out of their zone in October, 1949. "Democratic" in name, but "Communist" in fact, the new state was closely modeled on the other puppet regimes under Soviet control. Its political and economic institutions were tightly controlled by the Russians through the local Communist party.

East Germany did not have as much natural wealth as West Germany, and the policies of its government did not permit it to develop properly the resources which it had. If you visit Berlin today you can see the difference between the two systems. West Berlin has heavy traffic in the streets, gay crowds, and shops full of things to sell. East Berlin is shabby, regimented, and dull. Millions of East Germans fled to West Berlin during the postwar years. We shall see that the Berlin problem became critical again in 1959 (p. 668).

CHECK ON YOUR READING

1. *Explain the Communist threats to (a) Iran, (b) Greece, (c) Turkey, (d) disunited Europe. What methods did they use? How was each crisis met?*
2. *What were the purposes and results of (a) the Truman Doctrine? (b) the Marshall Plan?*
3. *Why did the Soviets blockade Berlin? With what results?*
4. *Contrast West and East Germany as to (a) government, (b) living conditions.*

4. Towards European Unity

Western European Union and the Council of Europe · We have seen how the aggressive tactics of the Soviet Union awakened the West to the need for greater European unity. The Truman Doctrine and the Marshall Plan marked the turning point in American policy. Thereafter the United States led the movement to "contain" communism and to promote European co-operation.

The idea of a United Europe was not new. Thoughtful citizens in many countries had worked toward achieving a closer relation between European nations. Billions of American aid now provided the means, and the statesmen of western Europe responded with vigor.

Already in 1947 Belgium, the Netherlands, and Luxembourg had formed a customs union known as Benelux. Then in March, 1948, five western European nations—Britain, France, and the Benelux countries—signed at Brussels a fifty-year treaty. The aims of this alliance were to strengthen the economic, social, and cultural ties of its members and to provide mutual assistance in resisting aggression. They called themselves the Western European Union.

In January, 1949, the members of this union resolved that a Council of Europe should be formed. A Council of Ministers and an Assembly would represent the parliaments of its members. Five months later ten nations signed the statute which brought the Council of Europe into being. The other members were Norway, Denmark, Sweden, Italy, and Ireland.

The first meeting was held at the Council's permanent headquarters in Strasbourg.

Winston Churchill, who had long wished to see a closer relationship of peoples on the Continent, declared in his opening speech, "We are met in this ancient and war-scarred city to set up an assembly which, we hope, will one day become the Parliament of Europe."

North Atlantic Defense Treaty · Two World Wars had demonstrated that the security of the United States was linked with that of western Europe. Soviet vetoes prevented the United Nations from insuring the peace. But the UN Charter (Arts. 51–52) permitted regional arrangements for self-defense. It therefore seemed advisable for the United States to unite with western Europe in a plan for the protection of the whole North Atlantic area.

In April, 1949, twelve nations signed the North Atlantic Defense Treaty in Washington. They were the United States, Great Britain, France, Italy, Portugal, Belgium, the Netherlands, Luxembourg, Norway, Denmark, Iceland, and Canada. Later Turkey, Greece and West Germany were included.

The purposes of the treaty included (1) the promotion of the principles of democracy and the rule of law, and (2) the support of peaceful methods in international relations. (3) It aimed at protecting its signatories and their friends from armed Soviet aggression. Each member agreed *"that an armed attack against one or more of them in Europe or North America shall be considered an attack against them all."*

The administrative body set up by this treaty was the North Atlantic Treaty Organization, popularly known as NATO. It included a Council of Foreign Ministers

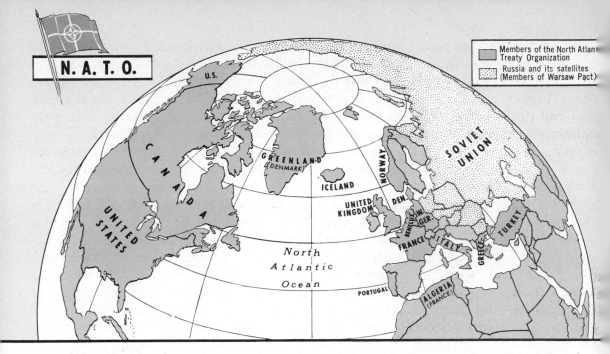

N.A.T.O.

NATO Defends the West · *Notice how the New World helps to maintain a balance of power in Europe. How may polar routes affect NATO's defense lines? What is the basic difference between NATO and the Warsaw Pact (p. 618)?*

and various subsidiary bodies. Supreme Headquarters of the Atlantic Powers in Europe (SHAPE) was established in Paris. General Eisenhower became Supreme Commander.

Apart from its military aspect, NATO provided invaluable experience in peacetime political and economic co-operation. It also provided the framework within which West Germany was brought back into the community of nations.

The French Defeat EDC · The armed forces of NATO are formed from parts of the national armies of the member states, and they remain essentially under their control. An attempt to create a European Defense Community (EDC), independent of the member states, failed for two main reasons. (1) The nations involved would need to yield some sovereignty. (2) The

French in particular were fearful of a European army in which many of the officers and men would be Germans. A treaty providing for an EDC was drafted in the spring of 1952, but after a long debate it was finally defeated by the French National Assembly in the summer of 1954.

Toward European Economic Union · Experience with the European Recovery Program and with NATO had convinced Western statesmen of the need for greater economic unity in Europe. They began to argue for the creation of a single, vast, free-trading market in Europe. Her industry could then take advantage of large-scale, low-cost production. But this would require (1) removing all restrictions on the movement of goods between countries, (2) abolishing currency difficulties, and (3) lowering tariffs.

617

The *Schuman Plan* was a significant step toward these goals. Robert Schuman, the French foreign minister, proposed that the entire French and German production of coal and steel be placed under a joint high authority within an organization open to others. It would provide common economic development, and make war between France and Germany impossible. Moreover, the binding decisions of a high authority on all who participated would form a foundation for a European federation. In April, 1951, a treaty was signed which placed the coal and steel production of France, Italy, Belgium, the Netherlands, Luxembourg, and West Germany under the European Coal and Steel Community for fifty years.

The European Economic Community, or *Common Market*, grew out of the outstanding success of the Schuman Plan. The six member states of the Schuman Plan agreed to a carefully planned reduction of the tariff barriers between them. At the end of a fifteen-year transition period, which began on January 1, 1958, all economic barriers were to be ended. Goods would then flow as freely from Rome to Rotterdam as they do now from San Francisco to New York. A concrete step forward was taken on January 1, 1959, when the member states cut their tariffs toward each other by 10 per cent.

A separate but vital part of the unification trend is called *Euratom*, which came into being on January 1, 1958. It is the six-nation co-operative project for the peaceful development of atomic energy as a fuel.

Soviet Regional Arrangements · Movements for European unity did not take place for Europe as a whole. This was due to the fact that the Iron Curtain divided the Continent. In eastern Europe the Soviet Union developed its own system of political and economic co-operation. In some technical respects this Soviet regional system was similar to that in the West, although its spirit and purposes were quite different.

(1) A series of treaties between the U.S.S.R. and its satellites provided for mutual assistance in case of an attack by Germany or a power associated with Germany. (2) To co-ordinate Communist political and propaganda aims, a Communist Information Bureau, known as *Cominform*, was formed in September, 1947. Its membership included the Communist parties of France and Italy, as well as those of eastern Europe. Tito's Yugoslavia was expelled in 1948 for refusing to follow Soviet dictates. (3) A Russian-sponsored Council for Economic Mutual Assistance was formed. But it failed to give real economic aid, for Russia tended to treat the satellites as colonies and drained them of their economic resources. (4) As an answer to NATO, however, the Soviet Union concluded the Warsaw Pact in 1955. This was a twenty-year mutual defense treaty with Albania, Bulgaria, Czechoslovakia, East Germany, Hungary, Poland, and Rumania. It merely formalized the military control which the Soviet Union had already established over these countries.

CHECK ON YOUR READING

1. How did each of the following contribute to western European unity: (a) Benelux, (b) Brussels Treaty, (c) Council of Europe, (d) NATO, (e) Schuman Plan, (f) Common Market?
2. Explain the four Soviet regional agreements.

Learning Activities

Think about the chapter

1. Why is the search for world peace more vital now than ever before?

2. Why did the United States do so much to promote economic unity in Europe?

3. Why is the Marshall Plan considered to be the turning point in postwar European history?

4. Why did the Soviets institute the Berlin blockade? Why did it fail?

5. Contrast the policies of the Western powers toward Germany with Soviet Russia's policies in East Germany. What have been the results for the German Federal Republic and the German Democratic Republic?

6. *Map study:* (a) Draw a map showing East and West Germany. Locate Berlin and Bonn. (b) Use a map to show the countries in Benelux, Western European Union, NATO, the Schuman Plan, the Common Market.

Go beyond the text

7. When the Senate voted approval of U. S. membership in NATO it approved the biggest change in foreign policy in our history. Why is this true? Read some accounts of the debates in the Senate on the ratification of the treaty.

8. Report on the results of the European Economic Community after several years of operation.

9. Compare the organization of the UN with the League of Nations. What strengths does the UN have that the League lacked? What great handicap to co-operative action has developed in the UN?

Follow up your special interests

10. One of the class may have visited the UN in New York. Describe your trip. Make a bulletin-board display of postcards of the UN buildings. You can get a collection from the UN Information Service.

11. Use the *Readers' Guide* of 1948 to locate comment and then draw a cartoon or write an editorial on the fate of Czechoslovakia.

12. Many excellent illustrated articles in such magazines as *Life* and *Look* show life in postwar Europe. Use the *Readers' Guide* to locate such articles, and show the pictures to the class.

READ FURTHER

Basic readings: (1) Becker, *Modern History*, Chap. XXV. (2) Hoffman, *News of the World*, No. 52 (1947–1952). (3) *Year's Pictorial History*, p. 582.

Special accounts: (4) S. Arne, *The United Nations Primer*. This has chapters on the Atlantic Charter and all the conferences leading up to the formation of the UN, with texts of the various declarations. (5) B. Bolles, *The Armed Road to Peace*. Foreign Policy Association Headline book; an analysis of NATO up to 1952. (6) *Everyman's United Nations*, frequently revised and brought up to date. (7) W. Langsam, *The World since 1919*. Chaps. 23–26 give postwar history of all the countries of Europe and Asia, the UN, and European integration. (8) E. Stevens, *This is Russia–Uncensored*. This account by a correspondent of the *Christian Science Monitor* covers postwar Russia up to 1950. (9) T. White, *Fire in the Ashes: Europe in Midcentury*. The relations of the U.S.S.R. to its former allies and the impact of the Marshall Plan and NATO are analyzed. (10) W. Willkie, *One World*. (11) *Year's Your Lifetime in Pictures*, pp. 202–272. (12) *National Geographic*, "Turkey Paves the Path of Progress," August, 1951.

Fiction and biography: (13) A. Compton, *Atomic Quest: a Personal Narrative*. An important scientist's viewpoint on the implications of the use of atomic energy. (14) Watch for current biographies and other personal accounts of important men and women who have helped to make postwar history.

34

Asia and Africa in Transition

KEY WORDS AND DATES

Chiang Kai-shek	Colombo Plan
Marshall	Malaya
Formosa (Taiwan)	Sukarno
Mao Tse-tung	Ho Chi Minh
two Chinas	Vietnam
recognition	Middle East
Dalai Lama	Arab League
MacArthur	Israel (1948)
Shintoism	refugees
Dulles	Mossadegh
mutual defense	royalties
38th parallel	*colons*
June, 1950	De Gaulle
two Koreas	Nasser
SEATO	Aswan Dam
Magsaysay	Suez (1956)
Jinnah	UAR
Gandhi	Lebanon (1958)
Nehru	Ghana
Pakistan	*apartheid*
Kashmir	Bandung (1955)

THE WAR left a burden of responsibility on the victorious powers in Asia as well as in Europe. First they had to receive the surrender of Japan's widely-scattered armies and administer the Japanese homeland, pending a peace settlement.

The great upheaval marked the passing of the long era of colonialism in the Far East. Throughout Asia the political ideals of the West had taken root, and there was a growing demand for freedom from foreign control. India, Burma, Ceylon, Malaya, and Indonesia gained self-government.

The issues between the West and East were further confused by activities of the Communists, who stirred up discontent and denounced Western "imperialism," while at the same time extending Communist imperialism in Asia. The danger that in the confusion following the war all Asia would fall into anarchy and then into their hands was very grave. China was plunged into civil war. The victorious Communists then aided the North Korean invaders of the Republic of Korea. They also sent men and supplies to conquer Indochina.

The flames of nationalism were spreading through North Africa and the Middle East as well. Grave dangers of war arose between the Arab states and Israel. Africa south of the Sahara was likewise in a state of ferment.

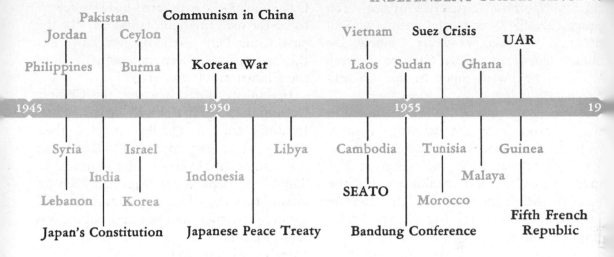

Pakistan · Communism in China · Vietnam · Suez Crisis · UAR

Jordan · Ceylon

Philippines · Burma · Korean War · Laos · Sudan · Ghana

1945 · 1950 · 1955 · 19

Syria · Israel · Libya · Cambodia · Tunisia · Guinea

India · Indonesia · Malaya

Lebanon · Korea · SEATO · Morocco

Japan's Constitution · Japanese Peace Treaty · Bandung Conference · Fifth French Republic

1. Communism Sweeps over China

Bitter Struggle between Chinese Nationalists and Communists · The surrender of Japan did not bring peace to China, for the country continued to be torn by civil strife. During the war the Communists had fought well against the enemy, but they had troubled Chiang Kai-shek by their independent action in seizing large areas in the north. After V-J Day Russia aided them with vast quantities of military supplies captured from the Japanese. They then proceeded to turn against the Nationalists.

The Kuomintang party was accused of corruption and poor administration of the government. Chiang promised to see that reforms were made, but nothing important was accomplished. As the party in power seemed to ignore criticism, it began to lose its authority while the strength of the Communists increased.

President Truman sent General George C. Marshall to China as special envoy in the hope that he could bring the warring factions together. After his arrival a truce was signed (January, 1946). A reorganization of the government and the army on a broader basis to include Communists was agreed upon.

A National Assembly was formed, and a constitution adopted which provided parliamentary government, universal suffrage, and the secret ballot. But efforts to put the reforms into effect were blocked by extremists on both sides. The Communists would have nothing to do with these moves for reform and peace. Instead they rushed troops into Manchuria, took over the province, and barred the Nationalists from landing at its ports. Moscow-trained, their tactics in the Far East were as aggressive, obstructive, and subversive as those of the Soviets in eastern Europe.

The Communist Victory in China (1947–1949) · From their well-equipped base in Manchuria the Communists launched a full-scale war on Nationalist China. One by one, the Nationalists lost

621

their important cities. Province after province went over to the enemy without fighting. To the war-weary Chinese, the choice lay between two Chinese dictatorships. They were quick to line up with the winning side.

Towards the end of 1949 the Nationalists were driven from the mainland entirely. With the remnants of his forces Chiang Kai-shek retreated to the island of Formosa (Taiwan) and established his government headquarters at Taipeh. Here he provided a refuge for free Chinese and a thorn in the flesh for the Communists.

On October 1, 1949, the victorious Communists proclaimed at Peiping the Central People's Government of China, with Mao Tse-tung as president. The next day the Soviet Union recognized the new government and severed all relations with the Nationalist regime. In 1950 Russia concluded a treaty of friendship and mutual aid with the new government.

The victory of the Communists in China had important consequences for the world as a whole. It greatly increased the prestige of communism in Asia. China was an agricultural country with one of the lowest standards of living in the world. The Communists were pledged to a program of land reform and development of industry. Other poverty-stricken countries in Asia and Africa watched to see the results. Would the Communists on the mainland or the Nationalists on Formosa best serve the people they ruled? Could communism in Asia be "contained"?

Chinese Communists Seize Tibet · The pattern of Chinese aggression under its new leaders was quickly revealed by the seizure of the remote country of Tibet in the Himalaya mountains. At the head of this community of three million people is the Dalai Lama, who is believed by his followers to be the reincarnation of Buddha. In the past, China held suzerainty over Tibet, but the country had been autonomous since the Chinese revolution of 1911.

In January, 1950, however, the Chinese Communists again claimed Tibet as their territory, and in October ordered their armies to take possession. The Dalai Lama fled temporarily to India, later returning to Tibet. Premier Nehru, who had been asserting that the Chinese Communists were agrarian reformers and not imperialists, was now disturbed to find the Chinese on India's northeast border. On May 27, 1951, the Chinese government announced that it had completed the "peaceful liberation" of Tibet, which now became virtually a Communist Chinese province. During an unsuccessful revolt in 1959 the Dalai Lama again fled Lhasa, his capital.

American Policy in China · The loss of the Chinese mainland to the Communists shocked the American people. The administration therefore issued a White Paper defending its policy. This statement declared that since V-J Day the United States had given aid and supplies to Chiang worth three billion dollars. A large part of this had fallen into the hands of the Communists, through the surrender of the Nationalists. Only the full-scale support of American troops might possibly have prevented the disaster. And the rapid demobilization of those troops had made such support impossible.

The Problem of Two Chinas · The United States refused to recognize the Communist government at Peiping, which it looked upon as a Soviet puppet state. It continued to recognize and support the Nationalist government of Chiang Kai-shek on Formosa. Its policy thus differed from that of Britain, France, India, and others who recognized Peiping as a matter of routine.

This made the question of China's representation in the United Nations a very touchy one. Which China should occupy the permanent seat in the Security Council? Russia maintained that the Communist government, which controlled the mainland, obviously should. The United States held (1) that Chiang Kai-shek's Chinese Nationalist government was the wartime ally for whom the seat was established and (2) that the representative thereby held the seat legally and should continue to do so as long as Free China existed.

Proposals have been made that both governments might be represented in the UN Assembly as separate states. But the Communists as well as the Nationalists have vigorously rejected this solution.

In 1957 and 1958 trouble flared between the two Chinas as the Communists shelled the Nationalist-held islands of Quemoy and Matsu. The Formosa Strait remains one of the tension spots of the world.

CHECK ON YOUR READING

1. Describe the struggle between the Nationalists and the Communists in China.
2. How do you account for the Communist victory?
3. Explain the (a) American policy in China, (b) the problem of two Chinas.
4. Identify the following as they relate to China: (a) Kuomintang, (b) Marshall, (c) land reform, (d) Taiwan, (e) recognition, (f) UN seat, (g) Tibet.

COMMUNISM DIVIDES ASIA

- Communist-controlled areas outside of the Soviet Union
- Asian members of SEATO

Communism Divides Asia · *Locate and explain the importance of Manchuria, Peiping, Formosa, Tibet. Which countries has communism split in two? Why might India, Nepal, Burma, and Laos be worried? Which countries are in SEATO?*

2. The Rehabilitation of Japan

Japan after V-J Day · One of the striking postwar developments in the Far East was Japan's great change from enemy to trusted ally of the United States. This change was hastened by American generosity, the threat of communism, and the amazing adaptability of the Japanese people.

General MacArthur was appointed Supreme Commander of the Allied occupation (p. 596), and the occupation troops were American. The principal objectives of the Allied occupation were to demilitarize and to democratize Japan.

General MacArthur followed the *policy of working through Japanese authorities* to put his orders into effect. Since the Japanese people were accustomed to taking orders, results were swift indeed. But the difference between the old and the new lay in the nature of the orders. For the latter involved setting up democratic institutions based upon freedom of choice. These proved remarkably successful.

MacArthur's Reforms · General MacArthur's reforms made sweeping changes in Japanese society. (1) The country was disarmed. (2) The old military class was broken up, and all active advocates of aggression were removed from office. (3) Women were given the right to vote. (4) Shintoism, which had taught that the emperor was descended from a god, ceased to be the state religion. It was no longer included in school instruction. And the Emperor himself publicly renounced all claims to divinity.

(5) The grip which a few powerful families had exercised over the Japanese economy was broken. Giant monopolies, like the Mitsui and Mitsubishi corporations, began to take steps to dissolve their interests. (6) Estates were divided to provide plots of land for the landless. These measures did much to lessen the appeal of communism.

Japan's New Constitution (1947) · A new constitution came into force in May, 1947. It changed the ancient aristocratic society into a modern democratic state. It stated that *the sovereignty rests in the people,* and *from them* the emperor derives his position. He performs only ceremonial duties.

Like most modern parliamentary states, Japan has a two-house legislature (the Diet). The executive power is vested in a cabinet, headed by the prime minister, who is chosen by the Diet.

Fundamental rights including "life, liberty, and the pursuit of happiness" are guaranteed to the people. All persons are equal before the law, regardless of race, creed, sex, or social status. Freedom of speech, press, and association is established, and persons are protected from arbitrary arrest. One of the most striking provisions of Japan's new constitution is the nation's renunciation of war and the use of force as a means of settling disputes.

Amazing Japanese Recovery · In spite of the collapse of the economy resulting from defeat and the loss of their colonies, the Japanese worked with amazing skill and energy to revive their country. They were helped by reasonable occupation regulations and by extensive American assistance. Foreign trade quadrupled between 1946 and 1950. Shipbuilding, textile, and other industries were revived. Foreign capital began once more to flow into Japan.

Crown Prince Akihito of Japan and His Princess, Michiko Shoda · *Breaking all royal tradition, Prince Akihito chose for his bride a beautiful commoner. Monarchy, formerly considered a divine institution, now moved closer to the people.*

Part of the explanation for her rapid recovery may lie in the fact that Japan had earlier taken steps to modernize and copy the West (p. 461). In terms of literacy rate Japan equaled the countries of western Europe. She was close to them also in economic development. And the billions of dollars which other nations spent on armaments could be devoted to reconstruction. But the release of the boundless energies of a free people enjoying democratic institutions had much to do with her postwar recovery.

Peace Treaty with Japan (September, 1951) · The United States in 1947 recommended an early treaty with Japan. As in the case with Germany, however, differences with the Soviet Union regarding procedure and policy led to a stalemate. To get results the United States decided to negotiate directly with the countries which had been at war with Japan. John Foster Dulles led the consultations which brought agreement. Representatives of forty-eight nations then met in San Fran-

cisco on September 8, 1951. Here they signed a treaty of peace which recognized Japan as an independent power. The terms were unusually generous.

(1) Japan renounced all right to areas she had taken from other nations so that her territory was reduced to her home islands. (2) She recognized her obligations to make reasonable reparations in services for the damages she had caused. (3) She accepted the principles of the United Nations Charter. (4) Occupation was ended, and foreign defense forces were to remain only with her consent.

The Japanese premier hailed the treaty as a "pact of reconciliation" and as "unparalleled in history for its fairness and magnanimity." Russia, Czechoslovakia, and Poland refused to sign the treaty.

It was not until 1956 that the Soviet Union officially ended the state of war with Japan. Russia then agreed to return Japanese war prisoners and to support the admission of Japan to the United Nations. A final peace treaty could not be signed, however, because of continued disagreement over the territorial settlement involving Russian-held islands north of Japan.

Japan, an Ally of the United States · Japan granted American air, naval, and army forces the right to maintain bases in Japan for her defense (1952). And Communist threats to the security of Southeast Asia led to a Mutual Defense Assistance Treaty (March, 1954). Japan was given economic and military aid to meet the growing menace from Communist China and the Soviet Union.

3. The Korean War

The Control and Partition of Korea · Lying between the three powerful states of Japan, Russia, and China, little Korea had long been of strategic importance. As we have seen, her powerful neighbors fought for possession of her territory (p. 462).

Japan annexed Korea in 1910, abolishing its ancient dynasty and installing a Japanese governor. During World War II the United States, Britain, and China promised the Koreans their independence. This promise was reaffirmed in the Potsdam Declaration. When the war came to an end, Russian troops received the surrender of the Japanese north of the 38th parallel while American troops moved in from the south.

In spite of the Potsdam agreement the Soviet Union resisted all efforts to unify the country. Even when the Foreign Ministers (1945) agreed that plans should be made for a government of all Korea, every move was blocked by the Russians. Finally, the United States brought the matter before the United Nations in September, 1947.

The General Assembly ordered elections to be held in Korea in preparation for a national government. But the Russians refused to allow the United Nations Commission to enter North Korea. Elections were held in South Korea, however, and the Republic of Korea was established by the UN (1948). In the meantime the Russians made North Korea a puppet state in defiance of the United Nations.

Communists Invade Republic of Korea (June, 1950) · On the morning of June 25, 1950, without warning, the Russian-trained armies of North Korea swept across the 38th parallel in a full-fledged invasion of South Korea. The South Korean defenses, utterly unprepared to withstand a major assault, collapsed.

The United States immediately requested an emergency meeting of the Security Council. By a twist of fate the Russian seat was empty, for the Russian representative had walked out earlier to protest Communist China's exclusion from the UN. Unhindered by a Russian veto, the Council called for an immediate end to hostilities and the withdrawal of North Koreans beyond the 38th parallel.

Security Council Calls for Military Aid · When the North Koreans did not withdraw, the Security Council called on the members of the United Nations to furnish such assistance to the Republic of Korea as would be necessary to repel the armed attack and restore peace. This was the first time the Security Council had resorted to the use of military force. Fifty-two nations responded.

President Truman announced that, in accordance with the Council's resolution, he had ordered General MacArthur to aid the Republic of Korea with American air and sea forces. The Seventh Fleet was directed to stand by, to prevent Communist attack on Formosa.

The United States appealed to Moscow to use its influence to halt the invasion, but the Kremlin blamed the South Koreans and called the war an "internal affair."

On July 7 the Security Council placed all United Nations forces in the area under the command of General MacArthur. The commander was authorized to use the flag of the United Nations along with the emblems of the participating countries.

Pusan, Inchon, and a New War · For six weeks the token United Nations forces, outnumbered and ill-equipped, fought a delaying action against overwhelming odds until, by August, they held only a small beachhead at Pusan (see map).

Then on the morning of September 15, an armada of 262 ships carrying 40,000 men made an "end run" to strike behind the Communist lines at the port of Inchon. Six North Korean divisions were trapped as the retreat became a rout.

With the approval of the United Nations (October 7), MacArthur then ordered his forces to cross the 38th parallel, seized the North Korean capital of Pyongyang, and pushed the remnants of the North Korean armies towards the Yalu River boundary of Manchuria.

There was every prospect for a united Korea at last, and the UN was making plans for relief and reconstruction. But this bright picture soon changed. A flood of Chinese "volunteers" poured across the Manchurian border to engulf the UN

Prisoner Round-Up in Korea · *Scores of Chinese Communists were finally captured. When the armistice was signed, many refused to return home. Note the padded jackets some are wearing.*

forces. It required several weeks of desperate fighting before the UN troops could stabilize a defense line along the 38th parallel. Thereafter Communist offensives were beaten back with terrible losses.

The United Nations condemned Communist China as an aggressor. But it decided to make every effort to confine the war to Korea. Successive commanders were ordered to avoid any action which might spread the war in Asia and let loose the tremendous Soviet armies upon western Europe. In the meantime American forces were rushed to General Eisenhower in newly formed NATO. For it was feared that the Soviets were using Korea as a diversion from their main objective in Europe.

The policy of limiting the war to Korea brought strong objections from General MacArthur. He wanted to break up the enemy's "sanctuary" behind the Yalu River. His opposition to United States and UN policy led to his dismissal by President Truman (April, 1951).

The Truce and Two Koreas · In the spring of 1951 the Chinese launched several major offensives against these UN lines along the 38th parallel. But they were hurled back with such frightful losses that they decided to ask for a truce.

For two years truce negotiations continued. The terms finally agreed upon in July, 1953, were these: (1) Neither side should strengthen its existing military forces. (2) A neutral commission should supervise this agreement. (3) Prisoners of war could return home if they wished. But over half of the men captured by the UN forces chose freedom instead.

UN attempts to unify Korea by free elections were rejected by the Communists. Two Koreas resulted. The northern state under Communist domination was called the Democratic People's Republic of Korea. This puppet state is surrounded by a high wall of secrecy, the "bamboo curtain." Members of the neutral commission have not been free to fulfill their duties of inspection there. The Republic of Korea, while smaller in area, has three times the population of the North. It has benefited greatly from extensive American aid and support. And its defense is guaranteed by a treaty of mutual aid.

A Defense Policy in the Far East · The war in Korea and events in Indochina (p. 632) made the United States more determined than ever to build up defenses

Korea · Locate and explain the importance of the 38th parallel, Pusan, Inchon, Pyongyang, Seoul, and the Yalu River.

against communism in the Pacific. By 1954 the United States had signed mutual aid pacts with the Philippines, Australia, New Zealand, and Japan. And a Southeast Asia Defense Treaty was agreed upon at Manila (map p. 623).

Under its terms a Southeast Asia Treaty Organization (SEATO) was established at Bangkok, the capital of Thailand. The strength of SEATO lay in the agreement of the United States, Great Britain, France, Australia, and New Zealand to stand together in the Pacific area. Its weakness, however, was reflected in the fact that only three Asian states joined the organization: Pakistan, the Philippines, and Thailand.

Nor had it any official armed forces such as those of NATO in Europe.

CHECK ON YOUR READING

1. How was Korea (a) of strategic importance? (b) ruled before the war? (c) mentioned in the Potsdam Declaration? (d) divided in 1945? (e) made a republic?
2. Describe (a) the Communist invasion of Korea, (b) the UN response, (c) Pusan, Inchon, and the new war.
3. Summarize (a) the terms of the truce, (b) the two Koreas which resulted, (c) the defense policy in the Far East.

---

4. New Nations in the East

The Republic of the Philippines (1946) · Since 1945 one colonial territory after another has achieved independence. The Philippines set the pace.

In accordance with her promise made in 1934, the United States launched the Republic of the Philippines on July 4, 1946. The constitution and government of the new republic were modeled on that of the United States. Generous amounts of American economic aid helped the Filipinos overcome problems of postwar reconstruction. And a mutual aid pact and membership in SEATO guarantee its safety.

With political independence, however, came serious political, economic, and social problems which previously had been met with American aid. Success in meeting some of these problems appeared to be very promising under the republic's fifth president, Ramon Magsaysay. Important land reform measures were passed, and dis-

honest officials were swept out of office. Magsaysay was killed in an airplane accident in 1957, however, just as his program was getting under way.

The Republic of India and the Islamic Republic of Pakistan · Even before World War II the British had been preparing the Indians for self-government (p. 541). But plans for independence had foundered on the rock of Hindu-Moslem distrust.

During the war the Moslem League, under the leadership of Mohammed Ali Jinnah, demanded a separate Moslem state. It should consist of the districts in northeastern and northwestern India in which Moslems were in a majority. The Hindus, under the leadership of Gandhi, Nehru, and the Congress party, stood for a *united* India. No possible solution seemed in sight, and the British finally adopted the Moslem plan for partition.

On August 15, 1947, the Indian Independence Act ended British sovereignty over the country and set up two dominions, India and Pakistan. Both of the new states became members of the British Commonwealth and were admitted to the United Nations. India voted to become a republic in 1950 and Pakistan in 1956.

Quarrels between India and Pakistan · The boundaries of the two states were drawn on the basis of religious groupings rather than on considerations of geography or economics. One thousand miles of Indian territory lay between East and West Pakistan. The economic well-being of Pakistan and India depended to a large extent on good relations between them, but hatreds ran too deep. Millions fled to escape persecution. Mass migrations took place as Hindus moved into India, and Moslems into Pakistan. Gandhi appealed in vain for peace. But on January 30, 1948, he was assassinated by a Hindu fanatic.

The most pressing problem facing the dominions was unifying their many divisions. Most of the princes of the 562 princely states chose one dominion or the other. Only Kashmir remained a source of trouble. Both India and Pakistan wished to include this large border province in its territory, for it controlled the headwaters of the Indus River system.

What complicated the problem was the fact that the Maharajah who ruled Kashmir was a Hindu. According to the Hindus, his choice decided the matter. Yet 85 per cent of Kashmir's people were Moslems who wanted to join Pakistan. The Pak-

A Vital Area · *This region has much oil, tin, rubber, gold, iron. Which states became independent after 1945? Which powers gave them independence?*

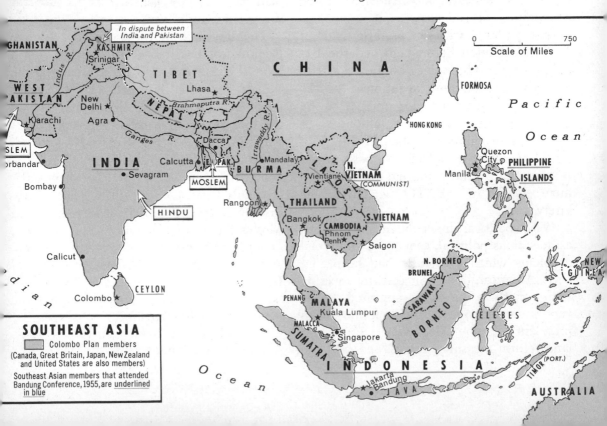

istanis insisted upon self-determination by way of a plebiscite.

When the Maharajah joined the Indian union, Moslem tribesmen entered the country to aid the resistance movement. Then Indian troops were dispatched to Kashmir. The United Nations finally persuaded the two states to accept an armed truce. But Kashmir remains a potential powder keg.

Language and Caste in India · The people of the Republic of India are divided by languages and caste distinctions. Five or six major languages, and hundreds of dialects are spoken. Attempts to draw political boundaries which do not coincide with linguistic areas have led to serious riots. Widespread illiteracy handicaps efforts to solve the problem.

Social divisions are still a problem in India. The former untouchables have been granted legal equality under the constitution and are represented in the parliament. Yet many inequalities of the caste system still exist.

Burma and Ceylon Gain Independence (1948) · The next member of the British Empire to become a free state was Burma. In 1937 Burma was separated from British India and became self-governing. On January 4, 1948, the Union of Burma was granted full independence and became a member of the UN the same year. After ten years of independence Burma was still struggling with the problem of a lagging economy and political instability (p. 664).

Ceylon, formerly a Crown Colony, became a fully self-governing dominion within the Commonwealth on February 4, 1948. Under its constitution, it has a parliamentary government. Its capital, Colombo, was the meeting place for representatives of British Commonwealth nations in 1950. The Colombo Plan, which grew out of this meeting, is designed to help the underprivileged peoples of Asia better their living conditions (see p. 660).

The Federation of Malaya (1957) · The suppression of native Communists occupied the British in Malaya in the postwar years. The Communists claimed to be fighting for Malayan independence, but when independence was offered they refused to lay down their arms. By 1957, however, the Communist danger had subsided sufficiently for the colony to become an independent dominion in the British Commonwealth (August 31). In the same year it was admitted to the United Nations.

The Federation of Malaya was formed from nine Moslem princedoms and the colonies of Penang and Malacca. Political power is concentrated in the hands of the three million Malayans, while the two and one-third million Chinese have economic superiority. The land is rich in tin and rubber. Its prospects for successful self-government depend a great deal on cooperation between the Malayan and Chinese people.

The Republic of Indonesia · The spirit of nationalism was likewise strong among the peoples of the Dutch East Indies. Even before Japanese troops had been completely withdrawn in 1945, a "republic," headed by Achmed Sukarno, gained control of parts of Java and Sumatra. The Netherlands government had announced that the people of Indonesia would eventually be permitted to determine their own future. But the nationalist group demanded immediate recognition of the "republic" as a sovereign state.

In 1947 an agreement was reached by Dutch and Indonesian leaders for the formation of a Netherlands-Indonesian Union.

Gathering Tea Leaves in Indonesia · *Plucking tea leaves is women's work. The hats serve more as umbrellas than as sunshades. Mineral-rich Indonesia may become industrialized, but most people are still farmers.*

Serious differences arose, however, between the Dutch and Indonesians over the plans for carrying out the agreement.

Bitter fighting broke out as the Dutch attempted to restore their control over the islands. The United Nations Security Council intervened on two occasions to stop the fighting. Finally, in 1949, the terms of the Union were settled, and the two nations agreed to join under the guardianship of the Queen.

On December 27, 1949, at a ceremony in Amsterdam, Queen Juliana transferred the sovereignty of the islands to the Indonesian peoples, thereby ending four hundred and fifty years of Dutch rule. Sukarno was elected president. Batavia, renamed Jakarta, became the capital of the new state.

The union did not last long, however. Disagreement with Dutch policies persisted, and on August 15, 1950, Indonesia proclaimed itself the Republic of Indonesia. It was admitted as the sixtieth member of the United Nations.

The French Lose Indochina · The French colony of Indochina was composed of the states of Laos, Cambodia, and what came to be known as Vietnam. Like the Dutch East Indies, it had been occupied by the Japanese during the war. And here too a movement for postwar independence developed.

The French failed to recognize the strength of national feeling and anti-colonialism in their colony, and the result was a bloody war. The principal leader in the independence movement was a Moscow-trained Communist, Ho Chi Minh. During the war he had formed a nationalist society on Chinese territory. As soon as the Japanese began to withdraw, his organization set up committees in Vietnam and declared its independence.

Ho Chi Minh was offered limited self-government within the *French Union*, but he demanded outright independence. In 1946 a bloody guerrilla war began in Vietnam and lasted over seven years. The forces of Ho Chi Minh received considerable help from the Chinese Communists, while the French were aided financially by the United States. But the political situation in France was unstable. The war was a drain on her economy, and the cost in casualties was high. By 1954 Ho's position in northern Vietnam was so strong that the French were forced to negotiate.

A conference at Geneva in 1954 arranged a settlement. Under its terms (1) Cambodia, Laos, and Vietnam were declared independent. (2) Vietnam was partitioned between a Republic of Vietnam in the south and a Communist-controlled state in the north. (3) Provision was made for a general election in the whole of Vietnam in 1956, but this election never took place. As a result, the Western powers recognized South Vietnam; and China, Soviet Russia, and their allies recognized North Vietnam. Both governments claim to represent the whole country.

CHECK ON YOUR READING

1. (*a*) How did the Filipinos get their independence? (*b*) How are they governed? (*c*) protected?
2. (*a*) What great problem confronted the British in India? (*b*) How was it finally settled? (*c*) Why is Kashmir a problem?
3. Summarize the highlights of the struggle for independence in (*a*) Malaya, (*b*) Indonesia, (*c*) Indochina.
4. Identify (*a*) Gandhi, (*b*) Jinnah, (*c*) Colombo Plan, (*d*) Sukarno, (*e*) Ho Chi Minh, (*f*) Geneva settlement.
5. Use the map to locate each of the new nations in the Far East discussed in this section.

---

5. Nationalism in the Middle East and North Africa

Spotlight on the Middle East · The Middle East includes Turkey, Lebanon, Syria, Jordan, Iran, Iraq, Israel, Saudi Arabia, Yemen, and Egypt. Portions of this area are sometimes called the Near East. The peoples of this region are largely Arab and Moslem. (Turkey and Iran are Moslem, but not Arab.) North Africa is often associated with the Middle East since its peoples are also predominantly Arab and Moslem. They share many of the problems and attitudes of their neighbors in the Middle East proper.

We remember the area as the birthplace of early civilizations and the meeting place of three continents. Here many empires have risen and fallen as men and nations fought to control its resources and trade routes. Conflicting religious claims and interests have contributed to the strife of this area, for it is the home of the Jewish, the Christian, and the Moslem religions.

The Middle East possesses the richest known oil reserves in the world. And oil is one of the basic fuels of industralized nations. The Western powers have invested

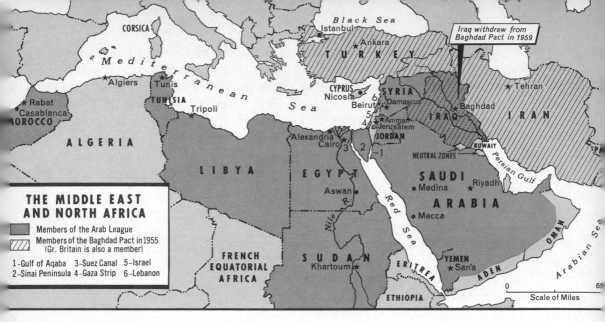

THE MIDDLE EAST
AND NORTH AFRICA

■ Members of the Arab League
▨ Members of the Baghdad Pact in 1955
(Gr. Britain is also a member)

1—Gulf of Aqaba 3—Suez Canal 5—Israel
2—Sinai Peninsula 4—Gaza Strip 6—Lebanon

Iraq withdrew from
Baghdad Pact in 1959

A Region of Crises · *Explain why this region is one of the world's recurrent trouble spots. Locate the countries in which specific crises have occurred. Why did the name "Baghdad Pact" become out of date (see p. 641)?*

(see p. 641)

billions of dollars in finding, refining, and shipping the oil to markets. Other billions are paid in royalties to the rulers of the economically retarded states involved. But the benefits have not reached the masses of half-starved, illiterate people inhabiting the area.

Here, as in the Far East, nationalism today is on the march. "Colonialism," and anything remotely resembling it, is bitterly resented. The majority of the people of this area live in extreme poverty under semi-feudal governments. Demands for a social revolution combine with blind · nationalism to produce a very unstable situation. Communists have found this fertile soil for their new imperialism under the cloak of "anti-colonialism."

The Rise and Rivalries of New Arab States · As in Asia, the postwar period has been marked by the appearance of newly independent states in the Middle East and North Africa. In 1946 Syria and Lebanon won their independence from France, and Jordan was freed from British control. The former Italian colony of Libya became independent in 1952. And Tunisia and Morocco finally freed themselves from French control in 1956.

The driving force behind the creation of these new states was Arab nationalism.

> "NATIONALISM IN OUR DAY is an impatient, irrational, burning demand for freedom from outside control at all costs—and immediately. The result is often material suffering for all concerned, internal ferment and a weakness that offers opportunities to totalitarianism, and hence to a possible loss of freedom once more."
>
> From an editorial in
> *The New York Times*, March 27, 1959

Although the peoples of the Arab world varied greatly in their political and economic development, they were united by ties of language and religion and by their antagonism to Israel.

The Arabs remembered the time when the Arab empire had stretched from the Pyrenees to the Indus River. They began to preach Arab unity. In 1945 the Arab League was formed by Egypt, Iraq, Lebanon, Syria, Jordan, Saudi Arabia, and Yemen. It was later joined by Libya, Tunisia, Morocco, and the Sudan. The purpose of the League was to consult on common Arab problems and to formulate joint policies.

Yet it would be a mistake to consider the Arabs more united than they actually are. As you remember, the former Arab empire split into rival regions based on Baghdad and Cairo. Likewise today, political, dynastic, and economic rivalries of long-standing divide the Arab world. Not all the Arab states possess oil. There is friction between the "have" states and the "have-not" states. Some leaders see their future best secured by friendship with the United States. Others look to the Soviet Union. Still others bargain with both. These rivalries have weakened the Arab League, and have left the region in constant ferment.

The Partition of Palestine (1947–1948) · The mandate for Palestine, given to Great Britain at the end of World War I, proved to be a major headache. The British had made conflicting promises to the Arabs and the Jews. We have seen (p. 525) that bad relations between the three peoples existed throughout the inter-war period. These relations became more troubled as large numbers of Jews sought refuge from Nazi persecution.

The British finally announced their decision to end their mandate, and handed the problem over to the United Nations. In November, 1947, the General Assembly voted to partition Palestine into an Arab state and a Jewish state.

The Arabs Refuse to Accept the New State of Israel · The Jews welcomed the partition and proclaimed the Republic of Israel (May, 1948). Chaim Weizmann was its first president, and David Ben-Gurion its most famous premier. The Arabs, on the other hand, regarded the creation of Israel as an act of aggression against Arab territory. The armies of Egypt, Lebanon, Transjordan, and Syria now attacked Israel. Only after the Arabs had suffered

Prime Minister Ben-Gurion with an American Rabbi · *Under Ben-Gurion's strong leadership Israel absorbed immigrants from many lands and became a true "melting pot."*

defeat by Israel was the United Nations able to arrange a truce. Israel held most of Palestine. But the territories occupied by the British-trained Arab Legion in the vicinity of Jerusalem were joined with Transjordan to form the new state of Jordan under young King Hussein, cousin of the king of Iraq. The Gaza strip in the southwest was annexed by Egypt.

Almost a million Arab refugees from Palestine had to be supported by a United Nations relief agency in camps established for the purpose. They served as a constant reminder to the Arabs of the defeat that they had suffered. The Israelis did not wish to resettle the Arab refugees, as they doubted their loyalty. Although an armistice was signed in 1949 it brought no real

Nationalism on the Rampage · *How does the Iranian crisis demonstrate that violent nationalism may sometimes work against the best interests of a country? How does its solution demonstrate that some compromise with nationalism may be necessary?*

peace to the area. The Arab states exerted constant political and economic pressure against Israel. Egypt refused to let Israeli ships or products use the Suez Canal. A constant source of trouble was the frequent exchange of raids by armed bands between Israel and her Arab neighbors.

Both sides therefore found it necessary to spend money on armaments which might better have been used for purposes of reconstruction. With such mutual hate and distrust existing, a dangerous explosion was possible at any time. Such an explosion occurred in 1956, as we shall see.

The Iranian Crisis (1951–1953) · Trouble erupted next in the weak and unstable kingdom of Iran. The discovery and development of rich oil fields there meant the introduction of modern techniques into an area whose social structure was largely feudal. Yet it also meant the possibility of a better life for the Iranian people.

Iran's oil was being produced and distributed by the Anglo-Iranian Oil Company, the largest stockholder of which was the British government. Although the company paid the Iranian government millions of dollars in royalties, the nationalists looked upon it as a symbol of Western imperialism. Since the poverty-stricken people could see little improvement in their lot, it was easy for the nationalists to blame all their ills upon the "foreign imperialists."

When the prime minister was shot in 1951, Mohammed Mossadegh came into power. He gave expression to the mood of anti-Western nationalism which was sweeping Iran. Mossadegh seized the oil wells and refineries and ordered the British out. When they left, however, Mossadegh was faced with an unforeseen problem. He had won the oil, but lost his customers.

For the very same "imperialists" he attacked, stopped buying oil and paying the royalties upon which his government depended. Finally, Mossadegh plotted against the Shah (king) and was overthrown. An army leader became prime minister.

After this a compromise was reached in which an international association of oil companies agreed to buy the oil for twenty-five years, paying royalties of 50 per cent. The economic facts of life were now plain to see. Modern industrial states would be expected to share more generously the profits made in developing the natural resources of underdeveloped states. But the latter would remain underdeveloped without the capital, the know-how, and the markets which more industrialized nations alone can supply.

Crisis in French North Africa · The hopes of the nationalists in French North Africa (Tunisia, Algeria, and Morocco) were stirred by successes in the Arab states. After a series of disturbances, France granted independence to Tunisia and Morocco (1956).

But the French were determined to keep Algeria, three departments of which had been represented in the French Assembly since 1881. For nearly eighty years French colonists (*colons*) had settled in Algeria and raised their families there. Although vastly outnumbered by the Moslem population, they administered Algeria as a part of France itself.

In 1954 the Algerian nationalists started guerilla attacks which the French were unable to crush. These became a constant drain on French manpower and resources. As in Indochina, the war became a major source of economic and political difficulties for the French government. The flames of

General de Gaulle with Moslem Algerians · *De Gaulle aimed at restoring peace. In 1959 he offered Algeria self-determination after four years of peace.*

rebellion were fed by agents, arms, and supplies from Egypt and Tunisia.

In 1958, units of the French army, supported by *colons*, staged a coup d'etat in Algeria and Corsica. They then called on General Charles de Gaulle, the hero of Free France, to come out of retirement and take control of France.

The French Assembly chose de Gaulle as premier and gave him a free hand to make necessary reforms. A new constitution was drafted for the Fifth French Republic. The powers of the president were greatly strengthened, and de Gaulle was elected to that office by an overwhelming vote.

Egypt's President Nasser · *Riding the crest of Arab nationalism, Nasser appeals to the masses. Although accepting Russian aid, he suppressed Egyptian Communists.*

President de Gaulle thereupon offered the Moslem people of Algeria real political equality with the French. But the Algerian nationalists refused to consider anything less than outright independence.

Nasser and Egyptian Nationalism · One of the poorest of the Arab countries was overpopulated Egypt. Its government under the luxury-loving King Farouk was corrupt and inefficient. But a group of young army officers deposed Farouk in 1952, and shortly thereafter Colonel Gamal Abdel Nasser emerged as the new leader of Egypt. Although he was first elected premier and later president, he was in fact a military dictator.

Nasser proved to be a fiery nationalist of great energy, determination, and ambition.

His popularity rose when he persuaded the British to agree to withdraw their troops from the Suez Canal zone (1954). Setting out first with a reform program for Egypt, he gradually came to assume the role of spokesman for all Arab peoples. Violent propaganda broadcasts from Radio Cairo constantly played upon their hopes and hatreds.

In foreign policy Nasser announced that Egypt would steer an independent course between East and West. This enabled him to bargain with both sides to his own advantage. But to achieve his ends he needed modern arms and equipment. When the Western powers refused to provide him with armaments, he traded Egyptian cotton for planes, tanks, and artillery from Czechoslovakia and Russia (1955).

This "arms deal" greatly contributed to tension in the area. Israel saw itself threatened. The West was alarmed at the spread of Communist influence. The United States therefore changed its mind about financing Nasser in his most spectacular project for developing Egypt, the building of a second great dam at Aswan.

Nasser Seizes the Suez Canal · Nasser had pinned great hopes on this project. For the Aswan Dam would provide water for the irrigation of two million more acres of rich soil and enough electricity to make industrialization possible. The reaction in Egypt to the withdrawal of the offer of American aid was swift and violent. To provide revenue for the dam, Nasser seized the Suez Canal (1956).

Permission to operate the Suez Canal had been granted to the Suez Canal Company, whose stockholders were largely French and British. The agreement was due to expire in 1968, and then operation of the canal would have been entirely in

Egyptian hands. Nasser's hasty act now set off a major crisis.

The Invasion of Egypt · Reaction in Britain, France, and Israel was sharp. The British and French saw Nasser as an inciter of trouble in their colonial territories. Now they were alarmed lest he cut off the oil supplies which they imported through the Suez Canal. Israel was especially concerned by Nasser's insistence that a state of war still existed and that the modernized Egyptian army would drive the Israelis into the sea.

The Israelis decided not to wait for extermination. In October, 1956, they launched what they regarded as a "preventive war." To the Arabs it was aggression. Israeli forces overran the Sinai peninsula in a matter of days and forced Nasser's army into headlong retreat. Under the pretext of keeping the canal open, the British and French landed troops in the Canal Zone. But Nasser responded by sinking ships in the canal and blocking all passage. The result was a severe oil shortage in western Europe.

An emergency session of the United Nations General Assembly was now called. In a startling reversal of the usual pattern, the United States joined with the Soviet Union to demand that Great Britain, France, and Israel withdraw from Egyptian territory. After some delays this was done. Then a United Nations Emergency Force was sent into the troubled area to patrol the borders between Israel and Egypt. Its presence has greatly reduced border incidents, but danger of war still exists.

The United Arab Republic · The fact that three powers invaded Egypt allowed Nasser to appear as an innocent victim of aggression. In spite of his disastrous military defeat, therefore, he emerged more of

Salvage Operations in the Suez Canal · *This work was organized by the UN. It cost over 8 million dollars and took several months to remove the sunken ships.*

a nationalist hero than ever. But the weakness of the Arab League was exposed, for members had not sent troops to aid him.

In 1958, however, Egypt and Syria merged to form the United Arab Republic. President Nasser of Egypt became president of the new state, and Egyptians provided the leadership of its combined armies. Shortly afterward the tiny state of Yemen joined the federation, but it retained its monarchy.

A rival Arab Union was then proclaimed by King Faisal of Iraq and his cousin, King Hussein of Jordan. But an army uprising in Iraq led to the assassination of Faisal and his pro-Western prime minister (July, 1958). The Arab Union was no more.

Crisis in Lebanon · *Left: President Nasser's photo hangs in this rebel stronghold. Many rebels favored Nasser's brand of nationalism. What was Nasser's attitude toward the revolt? Right: American marines land at Beirut. Why did they come? What role did the United Nations play? How was the crisis settled? American forces were promptly withdrawn.*

Crisis in Lebanon (1958) · The government of tiny Lebanon was pro-Western in its foreign policy. The Christian Arabs looked to the West for support, while the Moslems sympathized with Nasser.

In May, 1958, when President Chamoun proposed changing the constitution so that he could be elected to a second term, a revolt broke out. President Chamoun's supporters were largely Christians and the rebels predominantly Moslems. Radio Cairo was not slow in broadcasting its enthusiasm for the rebellion. Agents and weapons were smuggled across the Syrian border.

President Chamoun charged that the UAR was guilty of "massive interference" and appealed to the United Nations for aid. A United Nations observation team was sent but had great difficulties at first in carrying out its mission, since the rebels controlled most of the border regions. At last it did report that it found no evidence of "massive interference."

When the July army revolt broke out in Iraq, however, it was thought to be part of a nationalist conspiracy to overthrow the pro-Western governments of Jordan and Lebanon as well. President Chamoun therefore appealed to the United States for immediate aid. Marines landed in Beirut on July 14, 1958, and British troops were flown to Jordan at the request of King Hussein.

Once again the United Nations proved to be an effective agency for smoothing troubled waters. In a conciliatory resolution introduced in the General Assembly, the Arab nations pledged themselves not to interfere in each other's affairs. The Secretary-General was authorized to take practical steps to ease the situation.

In August an orderly election took place in Lebanon. A new president was elected who won the support of the Moslems and Christians as well. The American forces were then withdrawn from Lebanon and the British forces from Jordan.

Continued Trouble in Iraq · As a result of the army coup d'etat in July, 1958, Abdul Karim Kassem became the new dictator of Iraq. He promised a new deal for the Iraqi people. He also promised that Iraq's oil would continue to flow to the West. But Communist influences upon the new government were increasingly evident. In 1959 an unsuccessful revolt against Kassem's government broke out in northern Iraq. The rebels charged that Kassem had opened the door to communism. Survivors of the revolt fled into Syria (UAR). Nasser denied playing any role in the situation but denounced Kassem for allowing the "cancer of communism" to grow in the Arab world.

The Baghdad Pact and the Eisenhower Doctrine · It was inevitable that the strategic Middle East should become a theater of the cold war. All the great powers had interests in this vital area, and Russia was in the best geographic position from which to exploit Arab discontent. Indeed the invasion of Egypt gave the Communists an excuse to pose as friends of the Arabs against "Western imperialism." It thus opened the door to greater Communist penetration of the Middle East.

American policy sought to prevent further Communist advance into this vital area. An alliance formed in 1955 by Britain, Turkey, Iran, Iraq, and Pakistan was created to serve this purpose. It came to be known as the Baghdad Pact. I[ts] members agreed to consult on defense po[l]icies and to co-operate in the econom[ic] field. Iraq was the only Arab state to joi[n] although four of the powers were Moslem[.] While pledging the security of each member of the pact and giving generous mili tary and economic aid, the United State[s] did not formally join. It did, howeve[r] send observers to all meetings. In March 1959, Iraq officially withdrew from th[e] Baghdad Pact, which then became know[n] as the Central Treaty Organization.

As a further move against communis[m] in the Middle East, President Eisenhowe[r] proposed in 1957 that American militar[y] forces should be made available to an[y] Middle Eastern country which requeste[d] assistance against Communist aggression[.] Congress authorized the President to gran[t] such aid. This proposal became known a[s] the Eisenhower Doctrine.

CHECK ON YOUR READING

1. Why is the spotlight on the Middle East and North Africa?
2. How do you account for the rise and rivalries of new Arab states?
3. Explain the causes for and results of (a) the partition of Palestine, (b) the Iranian crisis, (c) the crisis in North Africa.
4. Why did Nasser (a) make the "arms deal"? (b) seize the canal? (c) emerge as a hero?
5. Summarize the highlights of (a) the invasion of Egypt, (b) the crisis in Lebanon, (c) the trouble in Iraq.
6. Locate the following places on the map and tell why each is important: (a) Middle East, (b) Arab League States, (c) Israel, (d) UAR, (e) Suez Canal, (f) Baghdad Powers.

Arab peoples of the Moslem faith predominate in North Africa. They are represented on this page by the Egyptian (upper left) and the veiled Moroccan (lower left).

Africa south of the Sahara has a predominantly Negro population. The young man in the Belgian Congo biochemistry laboratory presents a striking contrast to the proud Tanganyika warrior and the women of Kenya.

Below: A woman of Hong Kong carries water in the traditional manner. Right: With UN technical assistance these Burmese people have developed a thriving pottery industry.

Africans and Asians, Bound by Tradition, Seek Progress

Ancient customs affect the rate of change in Africa and Asia. But while keeping many colorful traditions, the people are demanding a more abundant life.

Right: The dance in Bali, Indonesia, is a religious ritual. Bottom right: Tibetans worshipping before Buddha. Bottom left: Wedding in India.

6. Africa South of the Sahara

New States South of the Sahara · Africa south of the Sahara desert barrier is geographically and culturally very different from North Africa. We have seen that its tropical lands were unexplored until about a hundred years ago (p. 463). But improved means of transportation and communication have enabled the revolutionary idea of nationalism to sweep the interior of the continent. Liberia, Ethiopia, and the Union of South Africa were the only independent states in the area before World War II. But an increasing number have since achieved self-government.

In 1955 the (Anglo-Egyptian) Sudan became the Republic of Sudan. Two years later the British Gold Coast voted to become the independent state of Ghana within the British Commonwealth. And in 1958 the French colony of Guinea voted for immediate independence. The British colony of Nigeria and the trust territories of the Cameroons, Togoland, and Somalia were slated to become independent in 1960. The United Nations, through the Trusteeship Council, has played a key role in guiding these and other trust territories towards independence.

Other lands are in various stages along the road to self-government. Almost all of the French colonies in this area voted for autonomy within the French community created by General de Gaulle. And the king of Belgium has promised eventual independence to the Belgian Congo. Spain and Portugal, however, have resisted any talk of independence for Spanish West Africa, Angola, and Mozambique. How long they can hold back the tide of nationalism, however, is a question.

Racial Tensions in East and South Africa · The new nations of West Africa are largely Negro states. But many Europeans settled in East and South Africa because of the more favorable climate. These white minorities fear that they will be submerged by the African majority if the latter gains control. Anti-white revolts have broken out in Kenya (led by the *Mau Mau*, a tribal secret society), in Nyasaland, and in Rhodesia.

The ruling white group in the Union of South Africa insists that self-preservation depends on complete racial segregation (*apartheid*). Members of the non-white majority are required to live apart and are

Africa Awakes · *Compare this map with the map on page 465. What are the most striking differences? What further changes have occurred or may be predicted?*

AFRICA
TODAY

■ Independent

▨ Under U.N.
Trusteeship

1-60

severely limited in their political, social, and economic opportunities. This restrictive policy has led to widespread racial tension. The problem of balancing the rights and responsibilities of majorities and minorities is not a simple one. It will require all the statesmanship which leaders on both sides possess.

The Bandung Conference (1955) · As a means of asserting their common aims and aspirations, representatives of twenty-three Asian and six African countries held a conference at Bandung, Indonesia, in April, 1955. Speeches and discussions stressed the desire of the underdeveloped Afro-Asian nations for equality, economic progress, and an end to the spirit of colonialism.

The West was made aware (1) that the Afro-Asian nations were on the march. (2) They represented a majority of the world population. (3) They would no longer tolerate an inferior status. (4) They held the balance of power in the United Nations. But the leaders at Bandung were realistic enough to see that the fate of the East as well as the West lay in a co-operative approach to common problems.

African Unity · Many African nationali[st] leaders dream of federation for Afric[a] They realize that the political boundarie[s] south of the Sahara were drawn by coloni[al] powers without regard to geography or eve[n] to tribal groupings.

An African federation is still only [a] dream. The immediate goal of the Africa[n] nationalists is independence for all [of] Africa. In 1958 at Accra, the capital o[f] Ghana, the first conference of independen[t] African states took place. It was followe[d] by an all-African conference, which set up [a] permanent body for consultations. Apri[l] 15 was proclaimed Freedom Day.

CHECK ON YOUR READING

1. (a) *Locate each of the new states sout*[h] *of the Sahara.* (b) *What power last con*[-] *trolled each?*
2. (a) *How do you account for the racia*[l] *tensions in East and South Africa?* (b) *What is the basic problem?*
3. (a) *Locate Bandung and Accra.* (b) *How have these conferences challenge*[d] *the West?*

Egypt: "Its people are playthings, its soil is gold, and it belongs to those strong enough to take it."
—Amr Ibn Al Aas, 640 A.D. (From *Nasser of Egypt* by MILTON WYNN.)

We definitely accept the democratic process because . . . . we attach great value to individual freedom."
—NEHRU

"Asia is not going to be civilized after the methods of the West. There is too much of Asia and she is too old." —KIPLING

"When the stomach is empty, the mind will swallow anything." —DOROTHY RICE SIMS, 1949

645

Think about the chapter

1. Why did communism sweep Asia?

2. How did the postwar occupation arrangements in Japan differ from those in Germany and Austria?

3. Why was the UN intervention in Korea a history-making step in international relations?

4. Explain how (a) nationalism and (b) the United Nations influenced the rise of new states in Asia and Africa.

5. In what sense are the underdeveloped areas of the world (a) *in ferment?* (b) *uncommitted?* (c) *in transition?*

6. *Map study:* Show on a world map the new nations which arose in the postwar era.

Go beyond the text

7. Prepare a report on one or more of the following Afro-Asian leaders: Romulo, Nehru, Ho Chi Minh, Chiang Kai-shek, Mao Tse-tung, Sukarno, Nasser, Nkrumah.

8. Should Communist China be admitted to the UN? Why or why not?

9. Tibet was long a land of mystery. Find what you can about it.

10. Report on (a) any recent developments to unite any Asian or African states; (b) the UN Emergency Force in Egypt; (c) the Eisenhower Doctrine.

Follow up your special interests

11. A committee of students might present a panel discussion on Asia. Each panel member could represent one Asian country and be prepared to discuss and answer questions concerning its government, economy, geography, culture, and history.

12. Why not hear about history at first hand? Invite as a guest speaker someone who served in the Korean War or in the occupation forces in Japan or in Lebanon.

READ FURTHER

Basic readings: (1) BECKER, *Modern History,* Chap. 25. (2) CARR, *Men of Power.* Mao Tse-tung. (3) HOFFMAN, *News of the World,* No. 52. (4) Year's *Pictorial History,* pp. 586–593.

Special accounts: (5) W. DOUGLAS, *Strange Lands and Friendly People* and *Behind the High Himalayas.* Travel books on Asia by a Supreme Court justice. (6) H. B. ELLIS, *Heritage of the Desert: The Arabs and the Middle East.* (7) J. GUNTHER, *Inside Africa.* (8) W. HENDERSON, *New Nations of Southeast Asia.* (9) W. LANGSAM, *The World since 1919.* Excellent chapters on the Far East. (10) K. LATOURETTE, *A Short History of the Far East.* (11) J. McDONALD, *My Mission in Israel.* By a U.S. ambassador. (12) W. MAULDIN, *Bill Mauldin in Korea.* In letter form, this is a down-to-earth commentary on experiences in Korea. (13) J. MICHENER, *The Voice of Asia.* Based on interviews with Asians from many walks of life. (14) E. ROOSEVELT, *India and the Awakening East.*

Fiction and biography: (15) C. BOWLES, *At Home in India.* By the fifteen-year-old daughter of the American ambassador to India. (16) M. BROWN, *Over a Bamboo Fence.* Life in postwar Japan. (17) A. KEITH, *Bare Feet in the Palace.* Life in the independent republic of the Philippines. (18) J. KUGELMASS, *Ralph J. Bunche, Fighter for Peace.* (19) J. NEHRU, *Toward Freedom.* Helps you understand Nehru's ideals. (20) A. PATON, *Cry, the Beloved Country.* A novel about South Africa. (21) C. ROMULO and M. GRAY, *The Magsaysay Story.* (22) C. SPENCER, *Romulo: Voice of Freedom.* Romulo is probably the best known Filipino in the West. (23) E. VINING, *Windows for the Crown Prince.* By a tutor of Japan's crown prince. (24) S. WATSON, *To Build a Land.* Two orphans become immigrants to Israel.

MAJOR RELIGIONS OF THE WORLD

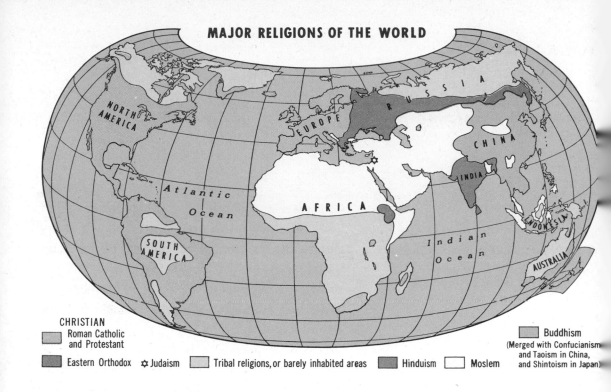

CHRISTIAN
| | Roman Catholic and Protestant

| | Eastern Orthodox   ✿ Judaism | | Tribal religions, or barely inhabited areas | | Hinduism | | Moslem

| | Buddhism
(Merged with Confucianism and Taoism in China, and Shintoism in Japan)

World Religions Today · Religion is one of the powerful forces affecting the lives of most of the inhabitants of the earth. We have seen how the five major religions of the world originated. Yet many people today—in the underdeveloped regions of the earth—belong to none of these religions. They worship nature gods and spirits as early man did. Locate these regions on the map.

Note the geographical distributions of the world's religions. Which is the principal religion or religions of the West? of the Middle East? of Central Asia? of the Far East? Missionaries of which religions would be likely to work in Africa and Australia?

Religion is very much a factor in international politics. How did religion help to create new states in the postwar period? Locate these states.

In the past we have seen that bloody wars were fought in the name of religion. While the principle of religious toleration is firmly established in democratic countries, freedom of worship is denied in dictatorial countries. Religion faces a challenge in Communist countries, where the government attempts to substitute a materialistic ideology. Which is the dominant church in Russia? What religions are the Chinese Communists attempting to suppress? It should be pointed out that Christians bear the brunt of Communist persecution in China because they follow a Western religion.

647

35

Problems of Our Own Age

KEY WORDS AND DATES

"open skies"	Bhave
all-out	technical assistance
test ban	Point Four
Geneva	World Bank
atoms-for-peace	population explo-
Vienna	sion
IGY, 1957–1958	Titoism
Antarctica	new imperialism
October, 1957	neutralism
earth satellites	Sukarno
Sputniks	Nkrumah
Explorer I	Peron
ballistic missiles	Castro
welfare state	single-crop country
nationalize	IADB
Khrushchev	Operation Pan-
Mao Tse-tung	America
communes	refugees
Nehru	Berlin crisis
community devel-	summit meeting
opment	German unification

OUR OWN AGE is one of great contrasts. Man hurls satellites into outer space, and yet struggles to lift the weight of hunger, disease, and warfare on the earth. It is an age of rapid change, giving rise to such urgent problems as harnessing atomic energy and finding peace for a troubled and divided world.

It is a troubled age, to be sure, but it is also one that offers great challenges. Soviet objection to international inspection has prevented agreement on the control of atomic weapons. Co-operation has been achieved, however, in an atoms-for-peace program and the International Geophysical Year.

All over the world nations are trying to meet the demands for rising standards of living. Both democratic and totalitarian methods are being used. The underdeveloped countries are trying desperately to keep production ahead of their exploding populations. They are being aided by a growing number of technical-assistance programs.

Political problems concern the growing unrest in satellite states, the rise of new dictatorships, the need of new homes for millions of refugees, and the crisis arising out of the cold war. They can be solved when men become aware that they are all fellow passengers on the same planet.

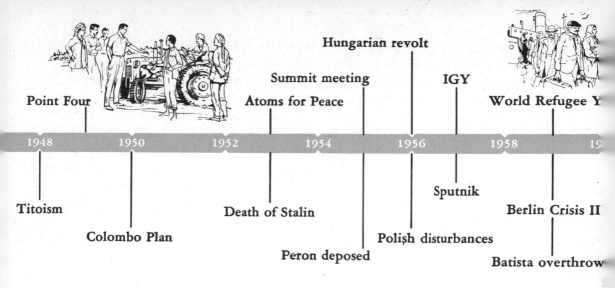

Point Four · 1948 · Titoism · 1950 · Colombo Plan · 1952 · Atoms for Peace · Summit meeting · Death of Stalin · 1954 · Peron deposed · Hungarian revolt · 1956 · Polish disturbances · IGY · Sputnik · 1958 · World Refugee Y · Berlin Crisis II · Batista overthrow

1948 · 1950 · 1952 · 1954 · 1956 · 1958 · 19

1. Atomic Energy and Outer Space

From Rocks to Rockets · The ladder of progress has taken us from the Old Stone Age to the Atomic Age. But peoples in various parts of the world are on different rungs of that ladder. Many Afro-Asian peoples, for example, are still living under conditions comparable to those in Europe in the Middle Ages. Their leaders wish to bridge the gap of six hundred years by means of "five-year plans." And in their headlong rush to catch up with modern industrialized states, they tend to forget that social changes take much more time than technological ones.

Even in nations which like to think of themselves as "advanced," however, there are great gaps between preachment and practice. The "Golden Rule," for example, is several thousand years old. Yet men still resort to suicidal war to settle their disputes. With nuclear science it is now possible for man to destroy civilization itself or build a better world. To achieve the latter requires self-control as well as the control of atomic energy.

Control of Atomic Energy · Since the Atomic Age was ushered in by an act of violence, the first world reaction was one of fear. No one recognized the bomb's destructive power more clearly than those who had dropped it. The United States immediately drafted a far-reaching plan for the international inspection and control of nuclear energy. This plan was submitted to the United Nations and accepted by all members except the Soviet bloc. The Communists feared that international inspection would undermine their totalitarian political system.

In the absence of any agreement, therefore, a deadly atomic arms race began. Within a few years both the United States and the Soviet Union had developed the much more destructive hydrogen bomb. Great Britain became the third power to possess A-bombs and H-bombs.

649

Despite the critical urgency of the problem, the deadlock over the issue of international inspection continued. In 1955 President Eisenhower proposed that mutual inspection be made by aerial photography. By preventing a surprise attack, it was hoped that international tensions might be relaxed. But his "open skies" proposal for mutual aerial inspection has yet to be fully agreed upon.

The Problem of Testing · Meanwhile the atomic powers continued to test their latest nuclear weapons. Fears arose as the radioactive debris (fall-out) which accompanied each test poisoned the atmosphere. As particles of strontium were absorbed in the soil and water they found their way into

"Swimming Pool" Reactor · *This was a U. S. exhibit at the First Atoms-for-Peace Conference. Speeding atomic particles in the water cause the blue glow.*

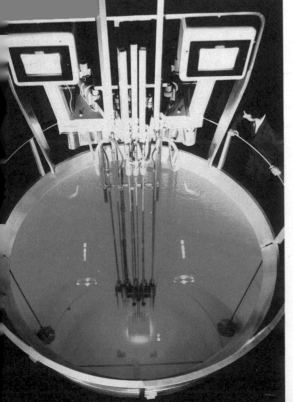

man's food and thence into his body with possible serious effects. The safe limits of radiation were a matter of dispute in the postwar years.

Capitalizing on the fears raised by many scientists and religious leaders in the West, the Soviets took the lead in calling for an immediate test ban. And the United States and Great Britain agreed to do so as soon as a reliable system for detecting violations could be set up.

In 1958 scientists of the East and West met in Geneva to consider how a foolproof detection system might be established. They were able to reach agreement on a detection system, but the political experts could not agree on how to put the system into operation. Russia maintained that inspection within each country should be carried on primarily by nationals of that country and that the veto should apply to decisions of the control agency. The United States and Great Britain held out for international inspection without a veto.

Atoms for Peace · President Eisenhower dramatized the world's longing for peace by proposing an "atoms-for-peace" program to the United Nations General Assembly in December, 1953. He offered to donate enough uranium to establish an international pool of atomic materials which could be administered by an international agency.

His proposal was enthusiastically endorsed by the General Assembly, which then voted to hold an International Conference on the Peaceful Uses of Atomic Energy. The conference met in Geneva in August, 1955. As a result, vast amounts of hitherto secret scientific data were exchanged. Two years later the newly created International Atomic Energy Agency opened its headquarters in Vienna.

IGY Projects Probe the Earth, Sky, and Sea
*Above left: A scientist uncovers the protectiv[e]
dome of an all-sky camera at Fritz Peak, Col[-]
orado. Below: An oceanographer prepares t[o]
photograph the ocean bottom with a deep-se[a]
camera. Above: A crevasse detector leads [a]
march through Antarctica.*

In 1958 the second such international conference met in Geneva. Once again it was demonstrated that science cuts across political boundaries.

The International Geophysical Year (IGY) · The twentieth century, like the sixteenth century, may well be regarded as one of the great ages of exploration. Not since the 1500's has there been such an outpouring of energy on the part of so many nations to explore unknown regions.

One of the most dramatic experiments in world-wide co-operation began on July 1, 1957. This eighteen-month study of man's environment was known as the International Geophysical Year. Scientists from some sixty-six nations engaged in studies of the earth's structure, its heat and water supplies, and the vastness of outer space.

In setting up the program, the participating countries agreed to exclude politics.

One of the major projects was centered in Antarctica. Here international cooperation and good will among scientists was effectively demonstrated. Expeditions sent out by eleven countries established forty-eight scientific bases in the area. Information gained was freely exchanged. An American meteorologist was stationed at Mirny, the main Russian base, while a Soviet scientist worked at Little America.

The Race for Outer Space · Yet Russian-American relations, excellent in frozen Antarctica, were bitterly competitive in the race to conquer outer space. On October 4, 1957, the world was startled to learn that Russia had successfully launched Sputnik I (literally, fellow-traveler), the first man-

651

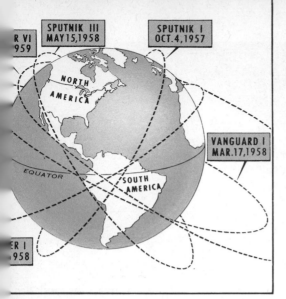

SPUTNIK III MAY 15, 1958

R VI 959

SPUTNIK I OCT. 4, 1957

NORTH AMERICA

VANGUARD I MAR. 17, 1958

EQUATOR

SOUTH AMERICA

ER I 958

A Growing Number of Earth Satellites

Name	Weight (lbs.)	Height (mi.)	Expected Life
Sputnik I	184	588	Fell Jan. '58
Explorer I	30.8	1,573	5 years
Vanguard I	3.25	2,465	200 years
Sputnik III	2,925	1,167	6 months
Explorer VI	142	26,400	1 year

made earth satellite. Soon afterward they launched a second and heavier satellite carrying a small dog.

Many people felt that this breakthrough to outer space would have as great consequences for the future as had Columbus's discovery of America. The immediate importance was obvious. Satellites carrying scientific equipment could radio back to earth important information about the stratosphere. Such information was necessary before man could fulfill his dreams of flight into outer space.

But the satellites had great military importance as well. Hence the American reaction to Sputnik was not that of pure admiration for an important scientific accomplishment. Rather there was bewilderment that the Russians should have scored such an impressive "first."

On January 31, 1958, the United States succeeded in launching its own satellite, Explorer I. This was followed by other American and Russian satellites. In December the United States sent up the first "talking" satellite, which broadcast President Eisenhower's message of good will.

Soon afterward a Russian-launched rocket missed the moon and went into orbit around the sun, thus creating the first man-made planet. This was joined in March, 1959, by Pioneer IV.

International Problems of the Space Race · From the beginning the penetration of outer space raised complex political and military questions. Who controlled outer space? Could a nation object to a passing satellite taking photographs of its installations? Could the moon be claimed by the first nation to plant a flag upon it? Suppose several satellites were mistaken for intercontinental ballistic missiles (ICBM's). Would they set off an atomic war?

Such questions concerned too many nations to be settled by any one of them. In December, 1958, the General Assembly therefore established a special committee to study what programs the United Nations might undertake to promote the exploration of outer space for peaceful purposes.

CHECK ON YOUR READING

1. *Explain the lag between technological and social change.*
2. *Why is control of atomic energy (a) a serious problem? (b) difficult to establish?*
3. *Identify these terms: (a) "open skies" proposal, (b) fall-out, (c) atoms-for-peace, (d) IGY, (e) Sputnik, (f) Explorer I, (g) space race.*

2. The Search for Economic Progress

Different Paths to Common Goals · The peoples of the world wish to improve their cultural, social, and economic well-being as they see it. They want better opportunities for their children. They wish higher returns for their labor. They seek a greater voice in government. They try to prevent starvation, disease, unemployment, and war. They hope for greater security for themselves and their nation. But while human goals have much in common, different peoples achieve them in different ways. There is perhaps no single best way for all peoples. So much depends on the traditions and resources of the individual countries.

In general, however, people have increased their demands upon government as an instrument of progress. Mature democracies (such as Britain, the United States, and Canada) have been able to secure economic benefits for all without sacrificing basic individual liberties. This is especially true where a large middle class has provided a balance against dictatorship.

Younger states, however, find this balan[ce] difficult to achieve. Let us examine son[e] attempts to secure economic progress.

The British Welfare State · Brita[in] emerged from World War II determined [to] rebuild its prosperity, and to do this in [a] manner which would assure greater soci[al] and economic opportunity for its people.

The Labor party with its call for a pr[o-] gram of nationalization (public owne[r-] ship) had won the elections in 1945 by [a] landslide. Under Prime Minister Cleme[nt] Attlee it boldly set out to create what cam[e] to be known as the "welfare state." [It] nationalized the Bank of England, th[e] railroads and long-distance trucking, th[e] coal and steel industries, civil aviation, ga[s] and electric supply, and telecommunica[-] tions. It established a broad system [of] free secondary education and extended th[e] social-security laws.

The benefits of the welfare state prob[-] ably reached the average Englishman mos[t] directly through the National Health Ac[t.] This provided him with free medical car[e]

The British Parliament and Clock Tower · *Over the centuries Parliament has moulded British democracy. Big Ben, the great bell of the clock tower, has faithfully struck the hour for over 100 years.*

m the cradle to the grave. The government financed these social services by vast increases in income and inheritance taxes. Substantial American and Canadian aid helped finance the postwar reconstruction. The Conservative party was returned to power in 1951 under Winston Churchill, and later Anthony Eden (1955–1956), and Harold Macmillan. The Conservatives made only small attempts to undo the changes brought about by the Labor party. They did denationalize the long-distance trucking business and the iron and steel industry. And they sought to make the welfare state more efficient. The responsibility of the government to promote the welfare of its citizens and still remain their servant was accepted by both parties. Thus the British welfare state combined socialism and democracy.

Russia after Stalin · We have seen how the Communists in a period of forty years transformed a rural, backward state into a modern industrial giant, but at a terrible price in life and liberty. As long as Stalin ruled, there was little hope for a better life for the Russian people. Heavy machinery and armaments came before shoes, washing machines, and radios. Stalin used terror to stay in power and to compel his people to make the great sacrifices which his program of industrialization required.

In 1953, however, Stalin died, and a struggle to succeed him took place. Gradually the new secretary of the Communist party, Nikita Khrushchev, demoted his rivals and emerged as the real leader of the Soviet Union. He became premier in 1958.

Khrushchev launched a program to expand agriculture in Siberia. By ploughing new lands he aimed at achieving agricultural self-sufficiency. This program involved risks because of the poor climate.

But Khrushchev was prepared to take risks. He had publicly promised to overtake the United States in the production of meat, milk, and butter.

In the interests of efficiency, Khrushchev radically reorganized industry. By giving greater power to local factory managers to plan production, he cut through party red tape. Many old-time Stalinists opposed him.

The Russian people are now impatient for a better life. The "new class" of Communist scientists, technicians, and engineers wants better housing, better clothing, and more leisure time. The workers want shorter hours and higher pay. Peasants want decent housing, more electricity, and better roads. In 1958 a "seven-year plan" was launched to achieve higher economic goals.

In the late fifties cautious steps were being taken to increase civil liberties. The rights of accused persons were increased slightly. Some protection against the terror of the secret police was given. Opportunities to travel abroad were enlarged. Party members who dared to disagree with the leaders were demoted rather than liquidated. Only time can tell how permanent such concessions will be.

SPITSBERGEN
(NORW.)

AREA COMPARISON

AL
(U

Baltic Sea

Murmansk

4 · Riga · 2
Leningrad · L. Ladoga
Minsk · L. Onega
7 · 5 · 3 · Archangel
6 · Kiev
Odessa
Krivoi Rog · Kharkov
RIMEA · Dnepropetrovsk
Rostov
Stalingrad · Volga
8 · Astrakhan
9 · Tiflis
Erivan
10 · Baku

NOVAYA ZEMLYA
NEW SIBERIAN IS.
Arctic Ocean
ARCTIC CIRCLE

Moscow
Gorki
Saratov · Kazan · Perm
Kuibyshev · Sverdlovsk
Chelya-binsk
Magnitogorsk
Kustanay

Vorkuta
Salekhard
Dudinka · Norilsk
Nordvik
Tiksi
Nordvik

R U S S I A N   S O V I E T   F E D E R A T E D

Ob R. · Yenisei R. · S I B E R I A · Lena R. · Okhotsk · Petrop

S O C I A L I S T   R E P U B L I C

Yakutsk · Sea of Okhot
Aldan R. · Ayan
SAK

1

Caspian Sea
Aral Sea
13
Karaganda

Omsk · S I B E R I A N · Angara R.
Tobol R. · Irtysh R. · TRANS-
Tomsk
Novosibirsk · R. R.
Krasnoyarsk · Bratsk

Komsomolsk
Birobidzhan
Khabarovsk

L. Balkhash

11 · 12
Tashkent · Alma-Ata
Samarkand · 15
14

Irkutsk · L. Baikal
Chita

Vladivosto
Sea of Japan

0 ___ 800
Scale of Miles

THE SOVIET UNION
THE FIFTEEN SOVIET SOCIALIST
· REPUBLICS ·

1 · RUSSIAN (includes small area north of Poland)	2. ESTONIAN	5. BYELORUSSIAN	8. GEORGIAN	11. TURKMEN	14. TADZHIK
	3. LATVIAN	6. MOLDAVIAN	9. ARMENIAN	12. UZBEK	15. KIRGHIZ
	4. LITHUANIAN	7. UKRAINIAN	10. AZERBAIJAN	13. KAZAKH	

The Soviet Union Today · *Note the vast extent of the Russian Republic. Locate cities which have grown up wherever the Trans-Siberian railroad crosses a river. They are becoming key industrial centers. Compare the areas of the Soviet Union and the United States. Below: The Kremlin, Moscow's great fortified enclosure, faces Red Square and St. Basil's Cathedral (right).*

Life in Communist China · *Lacking modern equipment the Communists exploit China's huge labor force to achieve progress in agriculture and in construction projects. Parades glorify communism and eliminate free time.*

Character of Chinese Communism · Mao Tse-tung, the leader and philosopher of the Communist party, was of peasant background. He relied, therefore, more on the peasants to build a socialist state than did the Russians. Although taking Russian experience and methods for his guide, Mao managed to give a distinctly Chinese flavor to his communism.

Mao's great object was to hasten the industrialization of China, which the Japanese invasion had interrupted. In five-year plans which were adopted, great emphasis was placed on heavy industry—steel, electricity, coal, railroads. To meet their goals the workers were driven to produce as never before. Yet they did not receive any of the benefits of their increased productivity.

At the same time private business was gradually crushed by forced loans, threats, and confiscation. Impressive results in terms of industrialization were achieved under the first five-year plan, but the cost lay in several million lives.

Collectives and Conformity · Immediately on coming to power, the Communists seized the large estates belonging to the more fortunate Chinese and redistributed them in small plots among the peasants. But a few years later the peasants were "persuaded" to merge their small holdings with those of their neighbors to form large state-owned collective farms. Heavy machinery could then be used to increase productivity. But party control of the farm machinery enabled the Communists to keep a tight grip on the peasants.

In 1957 Mao appeared to welcome criticism of his program by declaring, "Let a hundred flowers bloom; let a hundred schools of thought contend." But so many people seized the opportunity to point out injustices that he changed his mind. Gardener Mao not only uprooted the flowers but lost no time in "re-educating" any critics who remained.

The Communes · In 1958 a new and drastic organization of Chinese society was begun with the establishment of the first *communes.* Each commune has about 5000 families, living army style. Its members have few personal possessions, live in barracks, and eat in large mess halls. Children are raised in community nurseries. Battalions of women thus "liberated" from "degrading" housework march like the men to work in the fields and factories on the basis of "complete equality." Workers receive pocket money instead of wages, since the commune provides for all their needs.

Privacy, quiet, and free time necessary for thinking have been abolished. To the long working day, an hour of political instruction is added three times a week. Committees have been set up to spy on people's behavior. Opposition in thought or deed is ruthlessly suppressed.

Refugees report that the communes are extremely unpopular. But the Communists count upon this massive program of regimentation (1) to break down the traditional Chinese family system and (2) to achieve a "great leap forward" in farm and factory production. Like the Russians under Stalin, they appear prepared to sacrifice an entire generation, if necessary, to attain their end.

Democracy in India · Like China, India is a poor, overpopulated country which has embarked on an ambitious program of modernization. Unlike China, however, India under Prime Minister Nehru is attempting to achieve her goals through democratic methods.

In 1952 Indians went to the polls to vote for the first time in independent India. The Congress party, under Nehru's leadership, won a sizeable majority in the Federal government and in all but one of the state governments. In 1957 it again scored a great success. But in the state of Kerala the Communists came into power by promising that they would hasten the reforms pledged by the Congress party.

Benares, the Holy City of India · *Here thousands of devout Hindu pilgrims bathe in the sacred waters of the Ganges in a ceremony of purification.*

The Old and the New in India · *Women transport goods in the time-honored way. But modern machinery has introduced change. Why is an improvement in agricultural methods essential for Indian progress?*

Plans for Community Development · The Indian government inaugurated a series of five-year plans to raise standards of living through rural community development and industrialization. Before a rural country can be transformed into a modern industrial state, there must be an improvement in the agricultural production. Only in this way can peasants get money to buy goods, and workers in new factories be fed.

The community development program was launched in 1952. Under it, agricultural workers are trained in animal husbandry, gardening, crafts, social education, and public health. These experts are then sent into the villages to demonstrate new farming methods, such as the use of hybrid seed, improved tools, and natural fertilizer. They achieve amazing results in contrast to the primitive methods of Indian agriculture.

The peasants then volunteer their services in building roads, simple irrigation systems, schools, or local craft industries.

By 1957 more than 155 million people living in 260,000 villages had been reached by the community development program. Under the second five-year plan this program is to be extended to include 500,000 villages.

Land Reform and Industrialization · India's agricultural problem is complicated by the fact that the bulk of the land is owned by a very small number of people. The influence of landlords in the state legislatures has blocked any widespread land reform.

For a number of years Vinoba Bhave, a disciple of Gandhi, has been walking across India from village to village, persuading landlords to redistribute some of their land. Since 1948 "India's walking saint" has thus secured over five million acres of land. This may pave the way for action by the state legislatures.

A major goal of India's planning is to promote the growth of industry, both public and private. The central government has assumed responsibility for new heavy industry as well as the development of transportation and communications.

New public projects include the construction of steel mills and factories to produce heavy machinery, and the development of massive river-basin projects somewhat similar to the TVA. The Bhakra-Nangal dam, India's largest valley project, will irrigate nearly ten million acres and generate a vast amount of electricity. However, it is recognized that private initiative may be more effective than public enterprise in many areas. To this end foreign capital is invited to make investments in Indian industry.

Already the results of the first five-year plan can be noted. Increases in grain production, industrial production, and the national income averaged 20 per cent. Sixteen million acres of new land were irrigated. Over 100,000 schools were opened. The second five-year plan, ending in 1961, promised further increases.

Technical Assistance to Underdeveloped Areas · One of the striking features of the postwar world is the extension of Western technology to underdeveloped countries not yet able to make full use of the discoveries of modern science.

If we think back to the ancient civilizations of the Near East, we can recall their amazing accomplishments in irrigation and engineering at a time when our stone-age ancestors were roaming over "underdeveloped" Europe. Now, after many centuries in which the center of material progress shifted to the West, the peoples of the non-Western world have revived their interest in science and technology. They call upon us for the capital and know-how essential to modernize their lands.

The United Nations sends many food and health experts to work in underdeveloped countries and in turn grants scholarships to specialists in those countries for further study abroad. Through the International Bank for Reconstruction and Development (World Bank) it provides capital for industrialization projects. A United Nations Technical Assistance Administration, organized within the Secretariat, co-ordinates the programs of the various UN agencies.

The United States was a pioneer in the field of international aid. We have already mentioned the billions spent under the Marshall Plan to aid devastated Europe. The United States had much to do with the establishing of the World Bank and contributed most of the money used by the United Nations agencies working in the technical-assistance field. "Point Four" in President Truman's 1949 inaugural address called for the sending of technical experts to underdeveloped areas.

Between 1945 and 1960 the United States spent over $75 billion for foreign aid. About one-fifth of this went for economic assistance to underdeveloped countries. The balance was essentially military.

United Nations Technical Assistance in Burma · *Above: An anti-malaria team examines children. Below: FAO experts teach the use of modern machinery.*

ince 1956 greater emphasis has been placed on economic development projects because of the growing challenge of the Soviet program in this field.

The Colombo Plan · The success of the Marshall Plan in Europe inspired members of the Commonwealth of Nations to plan for economic development in Southeast Asia. The Colombo Plan was drawn up by the foreign ministers of the Commonwealth countries at Colombo, Ceylon, in 1950. These countries were later joined by the United States, Japan, Burma, Thailand, Indonesia, and other countries of Southeast Asia.

The Colombo Plan aimed to provide its members with capital and expert help in carrying out their individual projects. Assistance is extended by means of separate agreements reached between donors and recipients rather than through a joint pooling of funds.

The Soviet Technical-Assistance Program · The Soviet Union was a relative latecomer in the field of economic assistance. This was because it needed all of its resources to build up its major industries and feed its huge war machine. After Stalin's death the Russians began to see the possibilities of Communist expansion through peaceful economic penetration. In 1953 Moscow launched an economic offensive, a major part of which was directed toward the underdeveloped countries.

Although her total aid is still many billions less than that given by the United States, the program is rapidly expanding. It is especially effective by concentrating its aid in such key areas as Afghanistan, the United Arab Republic, Yemen, Iraq, and Nepal. Instead of using gifts (which imply charity), Communist aid takes the form of long-term, low-interest loans. It concentrates on large projects which will have psychological as well as economic importance. The projects are supervised by local experts who have been trained in Moscow, assisted by Russians who speak the language of the country concerned. The propaganda advantages of this approach are tremendous.

The Population Explosion · One of the most serious problems facing the future is the amazing expansion of the world's population. A United Nations study shows that it is increasing most rapidly in the underdeveloped countries of Asia, the Middle East, and Latin America—the very areas which can least afford it. If the present population trend continues, the earth in 1975 will contain a billion more people than in 1960.

The world's population used to be checked by starvation and disease. As the benefits of science have spread to the underdeveloped countries, however, death-dealing epidemics have been nearly wiped out. The effects of floods and droughts have been modified by the building of huge dams and irrigation systems.

But while death rates, especially among infants, have been drastically cut, the high birth rates continue. The result is a mushrooming population which threatens to wipe out the economic gains made by the underdeveloped countries. For production of the necessities of life barely keeps pace with the number of new persons to be fed, clothed, and housed.

We have already seen how population pressures in Germany, Italy, and Japan tempted their rulers to seek living space by force of arms. In like manner China's huge population may well be of concern to the world. For it is already triple that of Russia and is growing at a fantastic rate.

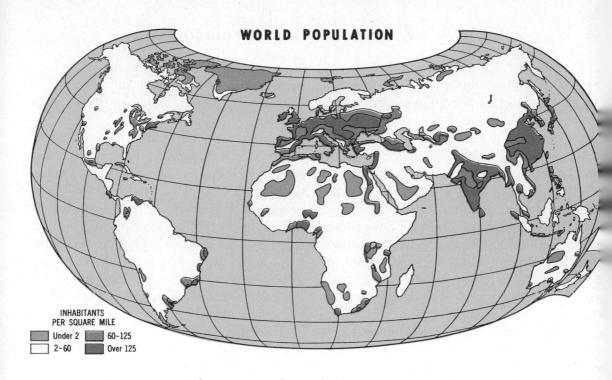

INHABITANTS
PER SQUARE MILE

▨	Under 2	▨	60-125
☐	2-60	▨	Over 125

The Distribution of the World's Population • *Can you explain why certain areas have relatively few people? Why is the rising population a great problem?*

Some scientists believe that the answer to the population problem lies in the discovery of new food sources. The culture of algae (seaweeds), which is high in protein, is one promising source. But the initial costs of production are high. Other scientists see the answer to the population problem in new drugs which will bring about a reduction in birth rates. But economists point out that greater industrialization and higher standards of living normally take care of the problem. Birth rates tend to fall as people adjust to an industrialized society. A great challenge faces the world to achieve industrialization with speed and yet without totalitarian methods.

CHECK ON YOUR READING

1. What goals do the peoples of the world have in common?
2. Briefly describe the economic programs of (a) Britain, (b) Russia, (c) India, and (d) Communist China.
3. Identify the following persons and terms: (a) Attlee, (b) Khrushchev, (c) Mao, (d) Nehru, (e) Bhave, (f) nationalization, (g) new class, (h) Communes, (i) land reform, (j) five-year plans.
4. Explain how the underdeveloped areas are affected by each of the following: (a) UN Technical Assistance, (b) U.S. foreign aid, (c) the Colombo Plan, (d) Soviet assistance, (e) the population explosion.

3. Recent Political Problems

Communist Satellites and the New Imperialism · Two events in the postwar decade threatened the tight control which the Soviet Union and Communist China held over their satellites. One was Marshal Tito's break with Moscow in 1948 and his proclamation that there were independent roads to socialism. The other was the death of Joseph Stalin.

Tito's successful defiance of Soviet leadership led to much unrest in the various satellite states. However, the spread of "Titoism" was halted by a wave of trials and the execution of satellite leaders charged with "deviation."

Stalin's death in 1953 led many Communists to believe that greater freedom would follow. The workers in East Germany rioted to demonstrate their dislike of their puppet regime. Russian troops quickly suppressed this revolt. But rumblings of discontent continued. East Germans continued to pour into the West through the Berlin loophole in the Iron Curtain.

Trouble broke out next in Poland (1956) when the nationalistic Poles demanded greater freedom to pursue their own national policies. Wladislaw Gomulka, a Communist who had been imprisoned earlier on charges of Titoism, became the secretary of the Polish Communist party and head of the puppet government. While still under Soviet domination, he was granted more independence than Stalin had ever allowed.

Soon afterward a full-fledged revolt took place in Hungary. Imre Nagy, a national Communist leader, came to office. He announced that Hungary would withdraw from the Warsaw Pact and be neutral in the cold war. He promised free elections.

Russians Go Home! · *Hungarians gather around a toppled statue of Stalin in downtown Budapest. An overturned street car bears inscriptions "Russians Go Home" and "Free Elections." Were these wishes realized?*

A neutral, democratic Hungary was intolerable to the Russians, and Russian troops, which had earlier withdrawn from Budapest, returned to crush the revolt.

The Hungarian rebels—mostly students and young workers — fought heroically against overwhelming odds. They were savagely suppressed. Thousands of refugees poured across the Austrian border. Tiny Austria accepted this flood of oppressed humanity until homes could be found for them in other freedom-loving states as well.

The suppression of the Hungarian revolt shocked the world. The United Nations condemned the brutal Soviet action, but had no power to remedy the situation. Nevertheless, the exposure of the Kremlin's ruthless disregard for the patriotic aspirations of its satellite peoples cost it dearly. Many Communists in the West quit the party. Many who had hitherto excused Communist actions now changed their minds.

But the Suez crisis, which occurred at the same time, clouded the issue and gave the Soviets an opportunity to turn the spotlight upon Western imperialism (p. 639). It was not until the equally brutal Chinese suppression of a revolt in Tibet that the eyes of the Asian and Arab leaders were fully opened to the ruthlessness and brutality of communism. Many of these anticolonial "neutralists" now recognized the danger of a *new* imperialism.

Neutralism · Washington's advice to the young United States to avoid alliances has found a ready echo in many of the new Asian, African, and Arab countries of today. Their leaders have feared that involvement in the great struggle between communism and democracy might lead to loss of their new-found freedom. They

The Three Leading Neutralists · *Prime Minister Nehru (left) and President Nas*(right) discuss world problems with their ho*Marshal Tito (center) in 1956. What cou*try does each represent? What attitudes they share in common?*

believe that it is dangerous for the wor to be divided into hostile military blo They have therefore followed a policy neutralism, not identifying themselves wi either side. Such a policy makes them t object of intense economic courtship the big powers, who seek to win their fav with generous gifts, loans, technical assi ance and surplus products. Their princi spokesmen, Nehru, Tito, and Nasser, ha come under increasing pressure to comm their nations to one side or the other the world struggle.

Independence No Guarantee of Dem **racy** · Most of the leaders of the new independent states of Asia and Africa we inspired by Western ideals of liberty a freedom. They attempted to model th governments on the democracies of t West. And their constitutions reflect

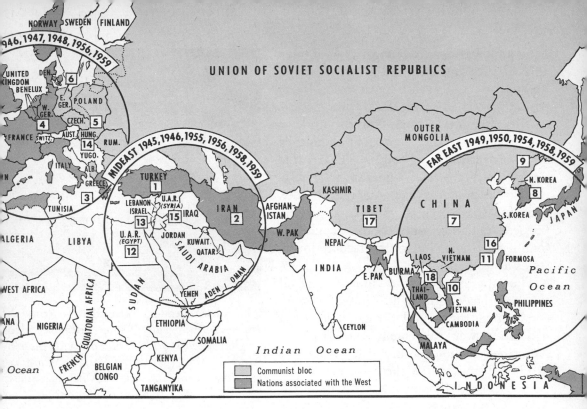

UNION OF SOVIET SOCIALIST REPUBLICS

Communist bloc
Nations associated with the West

Major Communist Moves in the Cold War · *Where did these moves succeed?
fail? Why?* (1) *1945—Demand Turkish bases.* (2) *1946—Refuse to withdraw
troops from Iran.* (3) *1946—Aid guerrillas in Greece.* (4) *1947—Strikes fail to
sabotage Marshall Plan.* (5) *1948—Seize Czechoslovakia.* (6) *1948—Blockade
Berlin.* (7) *1949—Complete conquest of Chinese mainland.* (8) *1950—Invade
South Korea.* (9) *1950—Chinese enter Korean War.* (10) *1954—Force division
of Indochina.* (11) *1954—Shell offshore islands.* (12) *1955—Supply arms to
Egypt.* (13) *1956—Threaten England and France on Suez.* (14) *1956—Crush
revolt in Hungary.* (15) *1958—Threaten to intervene in Middle East.* (16) *1958
—Renew shelling of Quemoy.* (17) *1959—Tibet.* (18) *1959—Laos.*

eir hopes. But independence is no guar-
tee of democracy. Indeed, democracy is
very complex form of government. It
quires literacy, self-control, initiative, and
lf-sacrifice.

In most new states the conditions neces-
ry for real self-government, as we know
simply did not exist. Hence it was not
ng before an army leader stepped in to
ovide more efficient government. Such
as the case, for example, in Pakistan,

Burma, and the Sudan. In other places
the political leader tried to exercise more
power. In Indonesia, Sukarno proclaimed
the necessity of a "guided democracy."
In Ghana the leader for independence,
Nkrumah, has shown increasing impatience
with his opposition in parliament.

Military Dictatorship in Burma · The
case of Burma illustrates the difficulties met
by a new parliamentary government. Politicians took advantage of their positions to

secure benefits for themselves. Graft-ridden city councils allowed their cities to degenerate into slums. Private companies borrowed from the government with no intention of paying back their loans. Bribery and political patronage flourished. The ruling party finally split into hostile factions.

To maintain order and to prevent a possible Communist seizure of power, the army stepped in. General Ne Win immediately restored order with a firm hand. A great clean-up campaign began. There was a sharp crackdown on government corruption. The people were awakened to a new sense of responsibility and responded with enthusiasm.

Although the army was in fact the government, parliamentary machinery did not disappear. The Burmese people felt the need for a strong man, and General Ne Win was named premier with the overwhelming approval of the assembly.

Corruption is something which also occurs in well-established democracies such as the United States. But older democracies have developed such institutions as free speech, a free press, and free elections with which they can expose and control it.

Even in countries where there has been considerable experience in democracy, however, people may turn in time of crisis to a strong man. We have seen, for example, how the unstable Fourth Republic of France was replaced by the Fifth Republic dominated by General Charles de Gaulle.

Problems Facing Latin America · Strong men have been especially numerous in the countries south of the Rio Grande. Even though the peoples of Latin America freed themselves from Spanish and Portuguese rule over a century ago, their countries have experienced many revolutions. The costs of such instability have been high. It h been common practice for those in pow to drain the public treasury.

In Argentina, Juan Peron governed dictator from 1943 to 1955. He left t nation close to bankruptcy. Civil strife Guatemala almost resulted in a Comm nist take-over. Bolivia, Paraguay, and t Dominican Republic suffered the exploit tion of dictatorial regimes. So great we political disturbances in Colombia that 1957 the nation voted for a sixteen-ye truce between the Conservative and Liber parties, with the presidency alternati between them.

In 1958 the dictator of Venezuela w forced to flee. And in 1959 the brut government of Batista was overthrown

Fidel Castro, Cuban Revolutionary · *Aft leading his bearded guerrillas to victory, spent hours explaining his goals.*

Cuba. The victorious young rebel leader, Fidel Castro, promised his people liberty and social justice. But oratory would not fill an empty treasury.

These political difficulties reflect the economic ups and downs of "single-crop" agricultural and mining countries. Prosperity depends upon the prices which their sugar, or coffee, or wheat, or meat, or nitrate, or tin, or oil may bring in the world market. To decrease their dependence upon a single major source of income a variety of economic enterprises is necessary. But this requires more capital than these nations at present possess.

In recent years the United States has loaned over three billions to Latin-American governments and industries through its Export-Import Bank. And it agreed to provide 45 per cent of the funds for a

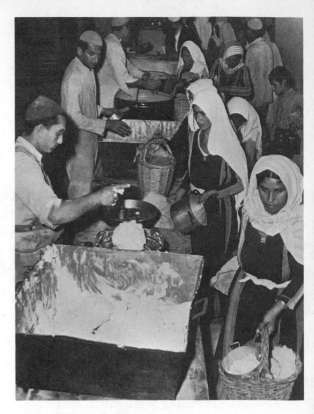

Drying Coffee Beans in Brazil · *Brazil produces two-thirds of the world's coffee crop. Overproduction brings hardship.*

A Food Distribution for Arab Refugees · *Most refugees have spent over ten years in camps, where life is depressing.*

new Inter-American Development Bank set up in 1959 to provide further help. With funds provided in "Operation Pan-America," great projects such as steel mills, airports, highways, power dams, and the like are now possible.

Latin America has a rising population, great mineral resources, plenty of room for growth, and a desire to modernize. At the same time her transportation system is primitive, her industries are scattered, her currencies are weak, her governments are disunited, and half her adults are illiterate. Much remains to be done in this area—but the people are on the march and the promise of the future is great indeed.

Algerian Refugees · *Desperately poor, these homeless people are cared for by the League of Red Cross Societies.*

The Refugee Problem · Thousands of people still remain in refugee camps as living evidence of man's inhumanity to man. Many others remain unsettled, seeking permanent homes and employment. Many of the refugees from Hungary remain in Austria, some because they hope to return to their homeland, others because they can find no place else to go.

There are a million Arab refugees in camps in the Gaza strip. Hong Kong is choked with refugees from Communist China. Algerian refugees wait in Tunisia and Morocco. Thousands of displaced persons resulting from the partition of India still remain to be settled. And there are

Tibetan refugees in India, waiting fo the liberation of Tibet from China.

To call world attention to the plight o these forgotten millions, the United Na tions proclaimed a World Refugee Yea beginning in July, 1959. Patterned afte the highly successful International Geo physical Year, it stimulated internationa co-operative efforts to find new homes fo these homeless people.

Conferences and Summit Meetings
After World War II the Security Counc was supposed to provide the forum fo postwar great-power consultations. Ye the Soviet veto frequently prevented this Certain of the most troublesome questions such as the peace treaty for Germany, ha been left as the responsibility of the majo allies. We have seen that the foreig ministers met frequently to try to reac

"First Fitting" · *The 1959 Foreign Ministers Conference was to pave the way for a summi meeting. Find out what happened.*

WHAT COMES AFTER BERLIN?

SCHEDULE OF CRISES

MIKOYAN

ECONOMIC WAR

EXPANSION

The Kremlin Looks Ahead? · *How does this cartoon interpret Russian foreign policy? What crises occurred before the 1959 threat to Berlin? Where might future crises occur? Russian policy has traditionally had several lines of action.*

agreement (p. 608). When they failed to make progress, elder statesman Churchill began to urge a meeting "at the summit," that is, by the heads of government of the major powers. The Russians favored this kind of diplomacy, and used the suggestion to launch a gigantic "peace offensive." The United States was skeptical of the value of such meetings, maintaining that failure to reach agreement at the summit would increase world tensions.

By 1955, however, the after-Stalin thaw seemed to promise hope for success, and the United States agreed to participate. President Eisenhower, and Prime Ministers Nikolai Bulganin of the U.S.S.R., Anthony Eden of Great Britain, and Edgar Faure of France therefore met in Geneva in July,

1955. The meetings lasted for six days and were carried on in a spirit of great cordiality. But they resulted only in the repetition of the policies and points of view which had already been expressed many times by the four governments. Another and longer conference was held at Geneva in October and November, 1955, by the foreign ministers of the four powers. While no great progress was made, the way was paved for some cultural exchanges between Russia and the West.

The Second Berlin Crisis, 1959 · Possibly to force the allies into meeting him at the summit, Nikita Khrushchev suddenly demanded that the Western powers withdraw from West Berlin leaving it a "free city." He threatened to sign a separate peace treaty with East Germany and to give it control over Western access to the city.

President Eisenhower reaffirmed Western rights to be in West Berlin and warned Khrushchev of the danger of nuclear war. He was supported by President de Gaulle, Chancellor Adenauer, and Prime Minister Macmillan. The United States took the position that a foreign-ministers' conference should precede any summit meeting, and the Russians finally agreed. The foreign ministers, with Christian A. Herter now representing the United States, spent most of the summer at Geneva without coming to any agreement on Berlin or Germany.

At the root of much of the East-West tug of war is the question of German unification. We have seen that over the years two German states have developed. The economy of East Germany has been closely tied to the Eastern bloc, and West Germany is an integral part of the six-nation European Economic Community. Neither side wishes to see a united Germany *con-*

trolled by the opposing camp. Countries which experienced German rule during World War II, and the Soviets as well, still fear a reunited and rearmed Germany in which a new and violent nationalism might arise once more.

Thaw in the Cold War? · In an endeavor to bring about a thaw in the cold war, President Eisenhower invited Premier Khrushchev to visit the United States and accepted an invitation to return the visit. Before the meeting, however, the President went to Europe to confer with MacMillan, Adenauer, and de Gaulle. He gave them assurances that he would only explore current problems with the Communist chief and not negotiate solutions.

On September 13, 1959, a Soviet rocket hit the moon. Two days later Khrushchev arrived in Washington. In a two-week tour he visited New York City, Los Angeles, San Francisco, Des Moines, and Pittsburgh. Addressing the United Nations General Assembly he proposed a four-year total disarmament plan, but provisions for inspection and control were still vague. In the private talks the two leaders agreed to continue to negotiate troublesome issues.

While Khrushchev was talking peace Communists in Asia were practicing aggression. The government of Laos charged Communist North Vietnam with aiding Laotian rebels. The UN Security Council responded to the appeal by sending a team of observers to make an on-the-spot study of the charges. India also protested violations of its northern frontier by Communist China.

CHECK ON YOUR READING

1. What were the (a) causes, (b) leaders and (c) results of the revolts in the Soviet satellites?
2. State the case for "neutralism."
3. How does Burma illustrate the difficulties met by a new parliamentary government?
4. What was done about (a) the problems facing Latin America? (b) the refugee problem? (c) the second Berlin crisis?

"The world is moving so fast these days that the man who says it can't be done is generally interrupted by someone doing it." —ELBERT HUBBARD

"The future is for men who dare to have great expectations; who have the courage, the persistence, the wisdom, and the patience to transform these expectations into realities." —G. K. CHESTERTON

"The grim fact is that we prepare for war like precocious giants and for peace like retarded pygmies." —LESTER PEARSON, 1957

"The twentieth century will be chiefly remembered . . . as an age in which human society dared to think of the welfare of the whole human race as a practical objective." —ARNOLD TOYNBEE

Learning Activities

Think about the chapter

1. What is the risk (a) in one nation's stopping nuclear testing? (b) in continued testing?

2. Summarize (a) the progress made and (b) the problems involved in the space race.

3. Contrast the methods used by India and China to promote economic progress. What role do you think the government should play in promoting economic welfare?

4. What benefits do the contributing nations receive from their foreign-aid programs?

5. Explain (a) the reasons for and (b) the results of the crises in the satellite states.

6. Explain the meaning of this statement: "The world is divided into three blocs." What is the reason for the attitude of the neutral bloc?

7. What problems confront (a) the newly independent states? (b) Latin America? (c) statesmen at the summit?

8. *Map study:* Be sure you can locate on a world map *all* the countries mentioned in this chapter.

Go beyond the text

9. Prepare a program on *The World Today.* Select a committee to look up current articles in the *Readers' Guide,* each person choosing one country. Mention the leaders of the country, its chief problems, its state of prosperity, and whether you would like to visit that country. You may have some pictures to show to illustrate some of your points.

10. Report on some of the achievements of (a) the IGY or (b) the International Refugee Year.

11. Prepare a bulletin-board display of pictures of key leaders of our time.

12. Preview a film or filmstrip dealing with some problem discussed in this chapter. Prepare a commentary to precede or accompany the showing of the film in class.

Follow up your special interests

13. Make a collection of cartoons from newspapers showing aspects of current affairs discussed in this chapter.

14. Bring your history-of-art scrapbook and record of scientific discoveries and inventions up to date.

15. Use the "You Are There" technique to dramatize any one of the revolts or crisis situations of recent times.

READ FURTHER

Basic readings: (1) BECKER, *Modern History,* Chap. 25. (2) CARR, *Men of Power.* Peron. (3) Year's *Pictorial History,* pp. 583–586, 592–595.

Special accounts: (4) C. BOWLES, *Ambassador's Report.* Chester Bowles traveled to every part of India and talked to all kinds of men. (5) W. DOUGLAS, *Russian Journey.* By a Supreme Court Justice. (6) Headline series of the Foreign Policy Association. No. 119, *Underdeveloped Lands: Revolution of Rising Expectations.* No. 120, *The Population Explosion.* (7) M. HIGGINS, *Red Plush and Black Bread.* Descriptions of some of the less-well-known parts of the U.S.S.R. (8) W. LANGSAM, *The World since 1919.* (9) F. ROUNDS, *Window on Red Square.* A cultural attaché in the U.S. Embassy writes of some aspects of Russian life not usually described. (10) W. SULLIVAN, *Quest for a Continent.* The story of Antarctic exploration.

Fiction and biography: (11) E. CHANG, *The Rice-Sprout Song.* A beautifully written novel about life in Communist China by a woman who escaped to Hong Kong in 1952. (12) H. TENNYSON, *India's Walking Saint.* The story of Vinoba Bhave by the grandson of the great English poet. (13) M. YEN, *The Umbrella Garden.* A true story of what Marie Yen saw and heard as a student in a Communist-controlled country.

History Makers of Our Own Age

How Many Can You Identify?

1. 2. 3. 4. 5.

6. 7. 8. 9. 10.

11. 12. 13. 14. 15.

16. 17. 18. 19. 20.

21. 22. 23. 24. 25.

Identifications are on page 678.

The above pictures are reproduced by special permission of *Time, the Weekly Newsmagazine*, whose colorful covers feature the history makers of our own age.

"Whether we like it or not."

'WHAT A PLIGHT THE WORLD IS IN!'

'MAKING WAY FOR A NEW SUPERMARKET'

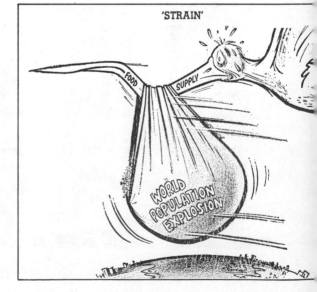

'STRAIN'

Problems of Our Day

Interpret These Cartoons · (1) What is the principal idea of each? (2) How are the "Plight" and the "Nationalism" cartoons related? (3) In the missile race, who is now ahead? Why? (4) Identify (a) the sidewalk superintendent, (b) the man with the saw, (c) the bird with the bent beak. How does each feel? Why? (5) What obstacles stand in the way of a United States of Western Europe?

"Re-unification is a matter for the German people itse[...]

"Who's ahead?"

"Increasing the Tempo."

673

Table of Key Dates

.41 B.C.   Egyptian solar calendar

00–2900 B.C.   Early civilization in Egypt

;15–2294 B.C.   Pyramid Age in Egypt

*00–2350 B.C.   Sumerian city-states

;50 B.C.   Sargon of Akkad

)00 B.C.   Movements of peoples from the Caspian Sea (a) into Asia (Medes, Persians); (b) into Greece; (c) into Italy

1700 B.C.   A code of laws given to Babylonia by Hammurapi

;600–1200 B.C.   Egyptian Empire

400–1200 B.C.   Hittite Empire

. 1000 B.C.   Beginning of Hebrew kingdom in Palestine

'53 B.C.   Traditional date for the founding of Rome

50–500 B.C.   Greece: Intellectual and industrial revolution and extensive colonization
Rome: a city kingdom

;12 B.C.   Fall of Nineveh

;th cent. B.C.   China: Classical Age
India: Buddhism

:. 550–330 B.C.   Persian Empire

;00–31 B.C.   Rome, a republic

490 B.C.   Battle of Marathon

5th century B.C.   Age of Pericles

334–323 B.C.   Alexander's empire

323–31 B.C.   Hellenistic Age

264–31 B.C.   Mediterranean world conquered by Rome

146 B.C.   Destruction of Carthage and Corinth

44 B.C.   Death of Caesar

31 B.C.–14 A.D.   Augustan Age

31 B.C.–180 A.D.   Pax Romana

c. 4 B.C.   Birth of Christ

∧∧∧∧∧∧∧THE REMAINING DATES ARE A.D.∧∧∧∧∧∧∧

284–305   Roman Empire reorganized by Diocletian

311   Edict of Galerius

325   Council of Nicaea, called by Constantine

410   Rome sacked by Alaric, the Visigoth

476   Last of the Western Roman emperors

6th century   Justinian Code of Roman law

622   The Hegira

732   Moslems stopped in Europe at the battle of Tours

800   Charlemagne crowned Emperor by the Pope

843   Treaty of Verdun

871–901   Alfred the Great in England

962   Holy Roman Empire established

987   Beginning of the Capetian dynasty in France

1066   Norman conquest of England

1077   Henry IV of Germany humbled by Pope Gregory VII at Canossa

900–1200   Height of feudalism in Europe

1096–1290   The Crusades

12th–13th centuries   Beginning of several universities

1206–1227   Empire of Genghis Khan

1215   English Magna Carta signed by John

1273   Beginning of the Hapsburgs as Holy Roman emperors

1295   Model Parliament in England

1309–1377   "Babylonian Captivity" of the papacy

1337–1453   The Hundred Years' War between France and England

1378–1415   The Great Schism

15th–16th centuries   Italian Renaissance in art and literature

c. 1453   Invention of printing

1453   Fall of Constantinople to Turks

1485–1603   Tudor dynasty in England

1492   America discovered by Columbus

16th century   Beginning of the scientific revolution

1517   Luther's Ninety-five Theses

1519   Charles V elected Emperor of Holy Roman Empire

1519–1522 Circumnavigation of the globe (Magellan)
1534 Copernican theory stated
1540 Jesuit order founded
1555 Peace of Augsburg
1588 Spanish Armada destroyed
1598 Edict of Nantes issued by Henry IV of France
1603–1714 Stuart dynasty in England
The Commonwealth 1649–1660
1607–1733 Settlement of the 13 English colonies in America
1628 Petition of Right (England)
1643–1715 Louis XIV (France)
1648 Treaties of Westphalia
1685 Revocation of Edict of Nantes
1689 Bill of Rights (England)
1689–1725 Peter the Great (Russia)
1713 Treaty of Utrecht
1763 Peace of Paris
18th century Industrial Revolution begins
Steam engine 1769
First railway 1825
1772, 1793, 1795 Partitions of Poland by Russia, Austria, and Prussia
1789 U.S. Constitutional government begins
French Revolution
1799–1815 Period of Napoleon's power
1815 Congress of Vienna
1823 Monroe Doctrine stated
1829 Greece independent
1830 Revolutions in France and Belgium
1832, 1867, 1884, 1911, 1928 Political democracy in England by Reform Bills
1842 Treaty of Nanking (Opium War)
1848 Revolutions in France, Austria, Hungary, Italy, Germany
19th century Imperialism in Africa and Pacific areas
1854–1856 Crimean War
1853–1858 Japan opened to Western influence
1861 Emancipation of Russian serfs
1870–1871 Franco-Prussian War
1878 Congress of Berlin

1898 Spanish-American War
1899, 1907 Hague Peace Conferences
1900 Boxer Rebellion
1904–1905 Russo-Japanese War
1912 China, a republic
1914–1918 First World War
1917 Russian Revolution
1919 Treaty of Versailles
1921 Washington Disarmament Conference
1922 World Court established
Fascist revolution in Italy
Irish Free State established
1925 Locarno Treaties
1928 Pact of Paris
1931 Statute of Westminster
Revolution in Spain
Japan in Manchukuo
1933 Nazism in Germany
New Deal in the United States
1936–1939 Civil War in Spain
1939–1945 Second World War
1941 Pearl Harbor
1945 United Nations established
Atomic Age begins
1946–1954 War in Indochina
1946 Philippine independence
1947 India and Pakistan independent
Marshall Plan drawn up
1948 Israel, a republic
1950–1953 War in Korea
1951 European Coal and Steel Community
1952 NATO permanently established
1954 Southeast Asia Defense Pact
1955 Bandung Conference
Summit Conference
1956 Suez crisis, Hungarian revolt
1957 Sputnik—Space Age begins
1957–1958 International Geophysical Year
1958 European Common Market
Euratom
1959 Geneva Conferences
Soviet rocket hits moon
Eisenhower-Khrushchev talks
1960 More African states win independence

Basic Reference Library

Atlases
Any good up-to-date atlas.
SHEPHERD, WILLIAM R. *Historical Atlas*. Barnes & Noble, Inc.

Collected Biographies
CARR, ALBERT. *Men of Power: a Book of Dictators*. The Viking Press, Inc.
COTTLER, JOSEPH, and JAFFE, HAYM. *Heroes of Civilization*. Little, Brown and Company.

Pictorial Histories
Life's *Picture History of Western Man*. Simon and Schuster, Inc. Based on *Life's* magazine articles on Western culture.
Editors of *Year*. *Pictorial History of the World*. Simon and Schuster, Inc.

Social and Cultural Histories
BAUER, MARION, and PEYSER, ETHEL. *How Music Grew*. G. P. Putnam's Sons.
CHEYNEY, SHELDON. *A New World History of Art*. The Viking Press, Inc.
EVANS, MARY. *Costume Throughout the Ages*. J. B. Lippincott Company.
MACY, JOHN. *The Story of the World's Literature*. Liveright Publishing Corporation.
TAYLOR, FRANCIS H. *Fifty Centuries of Art*. Harper & Brothers.
TAYLOR, F. SHERWOOD. *An Illustrated History of Science*. Frederick A. Praeger, Inc.

Source Books
DAVIS, W. S. *Readings in Ancient History* (2 volumes). Allyn and Bacon, Inc.
ROBINSON, JAMES H. *Readings in European History*. Ginn and Company.
SCOTT, J., and BALTZLY, A. *Readings in European History since 1814*. Appleton-Century-Crofts, Inc.
SCOTT, J., HYMA, A., and NOYES, A. *Readings in Medieval History*. Appleton-Century-Crofts, Inc.
BECKER, CARL. *Modern History*. Silver Burdett Company.
BREASTED, JAMES H. *Ancient Times*. Ginn and Company.
CHEYNEY, EDWARD. *A Short History of England*. Ginn and Company.
HOFFMAN, SYLVAN, and GRATTAN, C. HARTLEY. *News of the World: A History of the World in Newspaper Form*. Prentice-Hall, Inc.

General Works
VAN LOON, HENDRIK W. *The Story of Mankind*. Liveright Publishing Corporation.
World Almanac and Book of Facts. The New York World-Telegram. Published yearly.

Illustration Acknowledgments

Historical maps by Norman C. Adams. Drawings in the book and on the cover by Nathan Goldstein. Time lines by Hagstrom Company.

The illustrations on the pages indicated were gathered from the following sources:

4 (top) J. Covello from Black Star; (bottom) Paul Hufner from Shostal
5 (top) Copyright, J-Y Cousteau; (bottom) Humble Oil & Refining Co.
7 Wall Street Journal
8 American Museum of Natural History
9 From *Die Malerei der Eiszeit* by Herbert Kuhn, Delphin-Verlag
10 American Museum of Natural History
11 Photo Researchers, Inc.
16 (top) Metropolitan Museum of Art; (bottom) Bradford from Shostal
18 Metropolitan Museum of Art
19 (right) Metropolitan Museum of Art
20 Photo by R. Paul Larkin, courtesy, Museum of Science, Boston
21 Metropolitan Museum of Art
22 Krainin from Photo Researchers, Inc.
24 Metropolitan Museum of Art
25 Metropolitan Museum of Art
26 British Museum
31 The Oriental Institute, University of Chicago
32 The Oriental Institute, University of Chicago
33 British Museum
35 The Oriental Institute, University of Chicago
40 Bettmann Archive
42 The Oriental Institute, University of Chicago
44 Metropolitan Museum of Art
50 Agora Museum, Athens
56 Alinari
58 Staatliche Museen zu Berlin
59 Alinari
64 Royal Greek Embassy Information Service
65 Bettmann Archive
66 Brown Brothers
68 (top) British Museum; (bottom) Davis Pratt from Rapho-Guillumette
69 British Museum
70 Alinari
73 (bottom) Bettmann Archive
78 Metropolitan Museum of Art
80 Brown Brothers
82 Brown Brothers
85 Bettmann Archive
86 Brown Brothers
89 Vatican Museum
90 Alinari
94 Alinari
95 Dr. Paul Wolff & Tritschler from Black Star
97 Alinari
98 Alinari
99 Alinari
101 Pan American World Airways
102 Alinari
103 Bettmann Archive
116 Bettmann Archive
118 Aéro-Photo from Black Star
122 Brown Brothers

125 Bettmann Archive
126 Bettmann Archive
128 (top) Josef Muench
129 (both photos) Giraudon
134 Arab Information Center
136 Copyright 1953, Parke, Davis & Co.
137 (left) Barnell from Shostal; (right) Omnia from Three Lions, Inc.
138 Marc Riboud from Magnum
139 Metropolitan Museum of Art
140 Ewing Krainin
142 Boston Museum of Fine Arts
143 Paul Hufner from Shostal
144 Boston Museum of Fine Arts
146 Bettmann Archive
147 D. Winbray from Shostal
149 Boston Museum of Fine Arts
150 Horace Bristol from Photo Researchers, Inc.
159 Giraudon
160 New York Public Library Picture Collection
164 Bettmann Archive
166 Archives Photographiques d'Art et d'Histoire, Paris
167 British Crown Copyright reproduced by permission of the Controller of Her Britannic Majesty's Stationery Office
172 (top) Bettmann Archive; (bottom) Pickow from Three Lions, Inc.
174 Bettmann Archive
177 Bruxelles, Bibliothèque royale de Belgique, MS 9066, f. 11r
178 British Museum
182 Alinari
183 Alinari
186 Henricks Hodge
193 Alinari
194 Bettmann Archive
196 Bettmann Archive
201 (all photos) Alinari
203 Brown Brothers
207 Bayerische Staatsgemäldesammlungen, Munich
213 Alinari
214 Alinari
216 Alinari
218 Brown Brothers
219 Bettmann Archive
221 Brown Brothers
224 Alinari
225 Photo from Royal Academy of Arts, London, by permission of Simon Wingfield Digby, M. P.
226 National Maritime Museum, Greenwich
228 Brown Brothers
233 Rijksmuseum, Amsterdam
235 Brown Brothers
237 Brown Brothers
241 Reproduced by permission of the Trustees of the Wallace Collection, London
248 The Folger Shakespeare Library, Washington
249 Alinari
251 National Portrait Gallery, London
253 British Museum
254 British Museum
257 British Museum
258 British Information Service
265 Sovfoto
266 Brown Brothers
268 Bettmann Archive

270 Reproduced by permission of Trustees of the Wallace Collect London
272 (left) Bettmann Archive; (rig British Museum
274 Giraudon
280 Rijksmuseum, Amsterdam
282 National Portrait Gallery, Londo
286 Parker Gallery, London
289 Franklin Technical Institute, ton; mural by Charles E. Mills
296 Bettmann Archive
297 The Rockefeller Institute
298 Alinari
300 Giraudon
301 Photo Bulloz
302 Giraudon
303 The Prado, Madrid
304 New York Public Library Pict Collection
307 Les Archives Photographiques d' et d'Histoire
309 Photo Bulloz
311 Photo Bulloz
313 Brown Brothers
314 Photo Bulloz
316 New York Public Library Pict Collection
322 Alinari
325 National Gallery of Art, Washiton, D. C., Samuel H. Kress Colletion, Loan
326 Alinari
329 Brown Brothers
331 The Prado, Madrid
334 Giraudon
341 Österreichische Nationalbiblioth Vienna
344 Österreichische Nationalbiblioth Vienna
347 Bettmann Archive
348 Pan American Union
349 Library of Congress
351 Alinari-Giraudon
352 Giraudon
353 Weyhe Gallery, New York
355 Bettmann Archive
357 Bettmann Archive
378 (both photos) Bettmann Archive
380 Consolidated Edison Co. of Ne York, Inc.
382 From *London, a Pilgrimage* Gustave Doré and Blanchard Je rold, London, 1872
383 Frontispiece from *The White Slav of England* by John C. Cobde Auburn, New York, 1853
385 Brown Brothers
392 Brown Brothers
394 Library of Congress
395 Library of Congress
396 Brown Brothers
401 *Punch*
402 Culver Service
403 Culver Service
404 Alinari
405 Alinari
412 *The Illustrated London News*
413 From *London, a Pilgrimage* b Gustave Doré and Blanchard Je rold, London, 1872
415 (left and center) Brown Brothers (right) Culver Service
417 Bettmann Archive
419 Culver Service

677

The persons pictured on page 671 are (1) Ben-Gurion of Israel, (2) President Truman, (3) Nehru of India,
(4) Winston Churchill, (5) Eleanor Roosevelt, (6) Adenauer of West Germany, (7) John Foster Dulles, (8)
Chiang Kai-shek, (9) Tito of Yugoslavia, (10) UN Secretary-General Hammarskjold, (11) President Eisenhower, (12) Kubitschek of Brazil, (13) Nasser of Egypt, (14) MacMillan of Great Britain, (15) Diefenbaker
of Canada, (16) Khrushchev, (17) Sukarno of Indonesia, (18) Charles de Gaulle, (19) Pope John XXIII,
(20) Mao Tse-tung of Communist China, (21) Castro of Cuba, (22) Crown Princess Michiko of Japan, (23)
Kassim of Iraq, (24) the Dalai Lama of Tibet, (25) Queen Elizabeth II.

Index

687

688

Smallpox, 486
Smith, Adam, 382
Smuts, Jan Christian, *illus.*, 430
Smyrna (smûr′nà), 522
Sobieski (sò byĕs′kê), John, King of Poland, 438
Social classes: in China, 142; in Egypt, 22; in eighteenth-century Europe, 296; in England, 162–163; in Greece, 49–50, 57–58; in India, 138; Industrial Revolution and, 382; in Latin America, 472; Marxian theory of, 384–385; in Middle Ages, 127, 181; suffrage in Great Britain, 411–413; Sumerian, 31. See also Middle Class, Nobles
Social Contract, The (Rousseau), 299
Social Democratic party (Germany), 398–399
Social Democrats, in Russia, 442
Social Revolutionary party (Russia), 442–443
Social security: in Germany under Bismarck, 399; in Great Britain, 538
Social welfare: in ancient China, 146; legislation in Great Britain, 414–415; legislation in New Zealand, 427–428; and socialist theory, 385; welfare state, 653–654
Socialism: in China, 656–657; in Great Britain, 536–537, 653–654; instituted by Communists in Russia, 549–552; in New Zealand, 428; rise of, 384–386. See also Socialists
Socialist Workers′ party (Austria), 518
Socialists: Bismarck fights the, 398–399; in France, 353–354, 535–536; in Germany, 398–399, 509, 518, 534; in postwar Austria, 518; in Russia, 442–443. See also Socialism
Society of Jesus, *see* Jesuits
Socrates (sŏk′rà tēz), 64, 66–67
Socratic method, 66
Sofia (sō′fĭ à), 581
Solferino (sŏl′fĕ rē′nō), battle of, 405
Solomon, Hebrew king, 38
Solomon Islands, 587, 593
Solon (sō′lŏn), 49–50
Somalia (sò mä′lê à), 644
Somaliland (sò mä′lê lănd), 403, 466
Somme (sôm) River, battle along, 500
Sonar, 588

Song of Roland, 192
Sophists (sŏf′ĭsts), 59
Sophocles (sŏf′ò klēz), 64
South Africa: British rule in, 428–429; *map,* 429; racial problems in, 644–645; Union of, 430
South America, 186
South Australia, 426
South Hesse, 396
South Korea, 626–628
South Manchurian Railway, 566
South Vietnam (vê ĕt′năm′), 633
Southeast Asia Treaty Organization (SEATO), 629
South-West Africa, 430, 464
Soviet of Nationalities, 553
Soviet of the Union, 553
Soviet Union: aids Chinese Communists, 621–623; atomic-energy control, 649–650; communism in, 549–554; differs with West on peace treaties, 607–610; economic progress in, 654; education and, 489; established, 549–550; influence in Middle East, 639, 640, 641; Japan and, 566; Japan peace treaty and, 625–626; Korean War and, 626–628; launches earth satellites, 651–652; *map,* 655; regional alliances of, 618; relations with Great Britain, 537, 538; relations with satellites, 662–663; at summit meeting, 668; technical assistance program, 660; United Nations and, 605–606; wages cold war, 611–615. See also Russia
Soviets, 506, 507, 549
Spain: African colonies of, 644; American territory of, 290; art in, 202; becomes a great power, 204–205; Carthage and, 81, 82; Charlemagne in, 122; defeats Turks, 437; expeditions, 186; before 1492, *map,* 204; Franco-Prussian War and, 395; in French Revolution, 313; Goths in, 110; loses American colonies, 346–348; Louis XIV′s wars against, 239, 242, 243–244; Moors driven out, 204; Morocco and, 468; Moslems in, 136, 137; in Napoleonic wars, 330–331; neutral in World War I, 505; and Peace of Paris, 287; Philip II rules, 231; revolution of 1820, 345; rise and fall as leader of trade, 279–280; serfdom in, 295; Spanish-American War, 471; Stuarts and, 248, 249; in Thirty Years′ War, 236–238; trade with Japan, 458–459; after World War I, 557–558

Spanish-American War, 471
Spanish Armada, 226–227, 2?
illus., 226
Spanish colonies, gain indepen
ence, 346–348. See also La?
America
"Spanish Fury," 233
Spanish Hapsburgs, France defea
239
Spanish Main, 186
Spanish March, 122
Spanish Netherlands, 233; Fran?
and, 238, 239, 242, 243
Spanish Succession, War of, 24?
285
Spanish West Africa, 644
Sparta, 49; education in, 60; fig??
Persia, 52; resists Alexander, 6?
rivalry with Athens, 54
Spartan League, 55
Spears, 7
Specific gravity, discovered, 72
Spectacles, 197
Speyer (shpī′ẽr), 220
Spheres of influence, 451; in Afric?
466; in China, 454
Sphinx (sfĭngks), 22, 24
Spice Islands, 255, 279, 280, 281
Spices, exploration for, 185–186
Spies, used against liberals, 344
Spinning, change in methods o?
377–378
Sputniks (spōōt′nĭks), 651–652
map and *chart,* 652
Squire, 127; becomes a knight, *illus*
125
Stained-glass window, 118
Stalin, Joseph, 506–507, 551, 552?
death of, 654, 662; *illus.*, 552?
586, 607; in World War II, 572?
573–575, 586, 595, 601
Stalingrad (stä′lĭn grăd), 582, 587?
588; battle for, *illus.*, 588
Stamp Act, 288
Standard Oil Company, 568
Standards of living, raised by ma?
chinery, 480
Stanley, Henry M., 463–464
Star Chamber, Court of, 250
State farms, in Soviet Union, 551
Statute of Westminster, 539
Steam engine, 379, 380
Steamships, 449–450
Steel, *see* Iron and steel industry
Stein, Baron vom, 334
Stephenson, George, 450
Steuben (stū′bĕn), Baron von, 290
Stilwell Road, 595
Stockton and Darlington Railroad, 450
Stoics (stō′ĭks), 74, 90, 103
Stone Ages, 6–12